Game Theory
with Economic Applications

The Addison-Wesley Series in Economics

Game Theory with Economic Applications

SECOND EDITION

H. SCOTT BIERMAN
Carleton College

LUIS FERNANDEZ
Oberlin College

ADDISON-WESLEY

An imprint of Addison Wesley Longman

Reading, Massachusetts • Menlo Park, California • New York • Harlow, England
Don Mills, Ontario • Sydney • Mexico City • Madrid • Amsterdam

Sponsoring Editor: Denise Clinton
Senior Development Manager: Sylvia Mallory
Project Editor: Lena Buonanno
Assistant Editor: Rebecca Ferris
Production Supervisor: Heather Garrison
Marketing Manager: Quinn Perkson
Production Services: Ruttle, Shaw & Wetherill, Inc.
Cover Design: Jeannet Leendertse

Reprinted with corrections July 1998.

Library of Congress Cataloging-in-Publication Data

Bierman, H. Scott.
   Game theory with economic applications / H. Scott Bierman, Louis
Fernandez. — 2nd ed.
      p.   cm.
   Includes bibliographical references and index.
   ISBN 0-201-84758-2
   1. Game theory.   2. Decision-making.   I. Fernandez, Luis
Florentin.   II. Title.
HB144.B54   1998
330'.01'5193—dc21   97–37181
                                                                      CIP

Printed in the United States of America.

   3 4 5 6 7 8 9 10—MA—02 01 00

Brief Contents

Contents

---

*These sections appear at the end of each chapter.

Preface

Sophisticated use of game theory has become an integral part of economic graduate education. Yet, most undergraduate economics majors currently leave college with little knowledge of game theory beyond the Prisoner's Dilemma. *Game Theory with Economic Applications*, Second Edition, is designed to introduce undergraduates to the power of this new tool of economic analysis and can be read by any student who is comfortable with basic economic concepts and has taken a semester of differential calculus.

The book has five parts, each of which examines games that have a common informational structure. Each part begins with a core chapter in which equilibrium concepts and solution techniques are developed. The core chapters are followed by from one to five chapters of economic applications.

We have learned much since the publication of the first edition, not the least of which is how to better organize a game theory text. Although we have aimed this book at undergraduate economics majors, the book can be useful for anyone who wants to learn the language and ideas of game theory at an introductory level. Those readers familiar with the first edition will see major structural changes in the second. Yet, the emphasis remains on applying a relatively small set of game-theoretic tools to understand important economic phenomena.

In writing this book we have tried to avoid trivializing either the economics or the game theory. When the economics is made too trivial, an application often looks contrived and applicable to only a narrow set of circumstances. When the game theory is made too trivial, on the other hand, it is easy to lose sight of its role in the analysis. In each of the applications in this book both the game-theoretic and the economic foundations have been laid out in detail. Although we have provided fewer examples than other game theory texts, we have tried to be more detailed.

We have chosen examples from a wide range of fields so that students can see the power of game theory for studying economics. Applications can be found from labor economics, the economics of the public sector, international trade, natural resource economics, macroeconomics, corporate finance, banking, and, of course, industrial organization, to name a few. A student who makes it through the book will not only learn a great deal of game theory but also will see a lot of modern economic modeling.

Instructors can use the book as a supplement for an Industrial Organization class by assigning Chapter 1 (Nash Equilibrium), Chapter 2 (Oligopoly), Chapter 6 (Subgame Perfect Equilibrium), and Chapter 9 (Repeated Games and Dynamic Competition). A more ambitious plan would also include Chapter 13 (Bayesian Nash Equilibrium), Chapter 15 (Perfect Bayesian Equilibrium), Chapter 19 (Limit Pricing and Entry Deterrence), and Chapter 20 (Cartel Enforcement).

Instructors who want to use the book as a supplement for a course in intermediate price theory will find this edition of the book far more congenial. After covering Chapter 1 (Nash Equilibrium), the instructor can choose up to four applications or move directly to Chapter 6 (Subgame Perfect Equilibrium).

Prerequisites

Most of the economics in the book can be understood by students who have taken only a Principles of Economics class. There are, however, a few applications where a previous course in Intermediate Microeconomics is very useful. Drafts of the second edition have been used at both Oberlin College and Carleton College to teach courses that did not have an Intermediate Microeconomics prerequisite, but the lack of that common background slowed down the pace of the class. Faculty teaching a course on game theory and economics for the first time will probably want to make Intermediate Microeconomics a prerequisite for the course.

When we began writing this text, we hoped that calculus would not be necessary. Alas, we were unable to write a book in which the economics was not horribly unrealistic without using differential calculus. There are simply too many examples in which the important decision variables are continuous and not discrete. Students are expected to know how to take derivatives of simple functions (i.e., polynomials and exponential functions) and to be able to use the chain rule.

Probabilistic and statistical concepts of expected value and variance are not used until Part III (Games with Uncertain Outcomes). Conditional probability is not used until Part IV, and Bayes' theorem is not used until Part V. We believe it is relatively easy to give students who have no previous exposure to probability or statistics the background they need so that they will not be at a disadvantage.

Changes to the Second Edition

NEW ORGANIZATION

In response to reviewers and adopters of the first edition, the structure of the book has changed significantly from that of the first edition. The book now begins with static games with complete information. This allows the instructor to start right away with the Prisoner's Dilemma and Battle of the Sexes without having to first cover decision theory and expected utility. The elimination of dominated strategies and Nash equilibrium are introduced in the first chapter along with best response functions. Instructors interested in using subsets of the book as a supplement for either an Industrial Organization class or a Microeconomics class should find this new organization much better than the first edition.

Dynamic games with complete information now appears in Part II (Dynamic Games with Complete Information). The emphasis is on the extensive form and the concept of subgame perfection. An extensively revised chapter on repeated games is the capstone of this portion of the book.

Part III introduces static and dynamic games with complete information but random outcomes. The expected utility hypothesis and mixed strategies are presented for the first time in the core chapter. Two application chapters involve moral hazard.

Games in which the players have incomplete information are examined in the last two parts of the book. Part IV looks at static games, and Part V looks at dynamic ones. The Harsanyi transformation and Bayesian updating are the principal theoretical concepts introduced here. Among the application chapters is a new one on the popular topic of auctions.

NEW CHAPTER CONTENT

Besides completely revamping the core chapters, all of the applications have been revised in the second edition with an eye toward emphasizing the power of game-theoretic analysis. For example, Chapter 2 (Oligopoly) has a new section on Bertrand games with capacity constraints, and Chapter 15 (Perfect Bayesian Equilibrium) presents Spence's model of education signaling. Users of the second edition will note two completely new chapters, Chapter 13 (Bayesian Nash Equilibrium) and Chapter 14 (Auctions).

To streamline the book, some of the application chapters in the first edition were removed based on feedback from adopters and reviewers. These chapters include Chapter 9 (Patents and Product Variety), Chapter 22 (Public Goods and Preference Revelation), and Chapter 25 (Durable Goods and Monopoly Power) from the first edition. Chapter 12 (The Coase Theorem) and Chapter 15 (The Use of Common Resources) in the first edition have been combined into Chapter 4 (Property Rights and Efficiency) in the second edition.

Nearly all of the application chapters have a new feature entitled Game Theory in Action, which discusses empirical evidence that either confirms or disconfirms the theoretical models. New exercises have also been added to most of the chapters.

An Overview

The book is divided into five parts corresponding to five different informational structures. Each part begins with a core chapter identifying the general characteristics of games that will be analyzed in that part. This chapter carefully describes the equilibrium concepts that will be used in the application chapters that follow. The core chapters also introduce analytical methods (such as backward induction or the elimination of dominated strategies) that can be used to help solve the games in that part of the book. Concepts learned in the core are applied to carefully developed economic models. The applications have been designed both to reinforce the concepts and methods used in the core chapters and to show how game theory has modified the way we think about important economic issues and phenomena.

Part I (Static Games with Complete Information) introduces students to strategic form games and the fundamental solution concept of Nash equilibrium. In Chapter 1 (Nash Equilibrium) games are defined and Nash equilibrium and payoff matrices are introduced and then used to analyze a series of well-known games including the Prisoner's Dilemma and the Battle of the Sexes. Other concepts introduced include dominance, iterated dominance, and best response functions. Chapter 2 (Oligopoly) presents the historically important oligopoly models of Cournot and Bertrand. Chapter 3 (Strategic Trade Policy) explains the puzzling phenomenon of cross-hauling. This chapter also explains why a country might rationally enact an export subsidy and simultaneously engage in multilateral negotiations with other countries to make such subsidies illegal. Chapter 4 (Property Rights and Efficiency) looks at two ways in which property rights could affect economic behavior. The first model is the common resources model of an overfished fishery. The second is a model of pollution with high transaction costs in which the Coase theorem does not hold. A conclusion of that chapter is that tort law can be expected to have important efficiency implications even in a laissez-faire market economy. Part I concludes with a look at Voting Games (Chapter 5). The chapter begins with Arrow's impossibility theorem and concludes with a look at some so-called voting paradoxes.

Dynamic games with complete information are examined in Part II. Chapter 6 (Subgame Perfect Equilibrium) introduces the concepts of the extensive form and subgame perfection along with the solution procedure of backward induction. Chapter 7 (Bargaining) presents Ariel Rubinstein's model of alternating-offer bargaining over a trading surplus, starting from bargaining situations in which there is symmetric discounting and a fixed number of rounds. Chapter 8 (Time-Consistent Macroeconomic Policy) examines a highly stylized macroeconomic model with rational expectations in which in equilibrium the Federal Reserve Bank reaches neither its low inflation nor its high employment goals. Chapter 9 (Repeated Games and Dynamic Competition) reexamines the Cournot and Bertrand models of oligopoly in a world of repeated interactions. We show how cooperation can emerge in equilibrium in a strategic situation in which there are strong incentives for noncooperation.

Part III (Games with Uncertain Outcomes) extends Parts I and II by adding uncertainty. Chapter 10 (Uncertainty and Expected Utility) introduces the state-of-the-world approach to uncertainty. Utility maximization on the part of the players is replaced by expected utility maximization, and risk neutrality and risk aversion are discussed. The two applications that follow are both moral hazard problems. Chapter 11 (Moral Hazard and Incomplete Insurance) shows how the inability to monitor risk avoidance by the policyholder can lead to underinsurance. Chapter 12 (Moral Hazard and Involuntary Unemployment) shows how the inability to monitor employee work effort can lead to involuntary unemployment.

Some of the most interesting theoretical work done by economists in the last twenty years has involved games in which players have private information. Such games are the subject of Parts IV and V. Part IV (Static Games with Incomplete Information) is completely new to the second edition. Chapter 13 (Bayesian Nash Equilibrium) shows how static games with incomplete information can be converted into games with complete but imperfect information, which then can be solved using the tools of Parts I to III. Chapter 14 (Auctions) begins with an extensive discussion of auction rules and the games they generate. It goes on to demonstrate the revenue equivalence theorem, the truth revelation property of Vickrey auctions when there are independent private values, and the phenomenon of the winner's curse when there are common values.

Although Part V (Dynamic Games with Incomplete Information) is the most challenging part of the book, we have structured it so that the most difficult material appears in the last two application chapters. Chapter 15 (Perfect Bayesian Equilibrium) takes the concept of Bayesian Nash equilibrium developed in Part IV and refines it. The refinement amounts to assuming that rational players use Bayes' theorem to update their beliefs whenever this is possible. These ideas are used to study Spence's seminal model of education signaling. Chapter 16 (Bargaining with Private Information) revisits the problem of bargaining using three examples. The chapter concludes by showing how costly strikes can reveal to the employer the worker's reservation wages. Chapter 17 (Corporate Takeovers and Greenmail) shows how management efforts to fight off a hostile takeover, such as by paying "greenmail," may be in the best interest of shareholders. Chapter 18 (Adverse Selection and Credit Rationing) examines the conditions under which a competitive market equilibrium can exist in which there are borrowers who cannot borrow "at any price." Chapter 19 (Limit Pricing and Entry Deterrence) provides a greatly simplified version of Milgrom and Roberts' model of entry deterrence and predatory pricing. We show how an incumbent firm may try to signal that it has a cost advantage over a potential entrant by charging a low price. Chapter 20 (Cartel Enforcement) concludes the book with Porter and Green's model of self-enforcing cartels and the necessity of occasional price wars to keep the members of the cartel honest.

It is our experience that getting through the entire book in a quarter or semester, even with well-trained and highly motivated students, is difficult, if not impossible. This provides the instructor with scope for choosing among the application chapters. Some application chapters, however, present material that is referred to later in the book and, hence, should not be cut. These include Chapter 2 (Oligopoly), Chapter 7 (Bargaining), and Chapter 9 (Repeated Games and Dynamic Competition). The other applications are independent of each other.

Instructor's Manual

An Instructor's Manual, including answers to the end-of-chapter problems, is available free of charge to instructors adopting the text.

Acknowledgments

The first edition of this book benefited from the advice and help of many people. The list has more than doubled with the second edition. We have been helped tremendously from adoptors who have freely offered useful advice and criticism. And we are indebted to reviewers of the second edition for hundreds of improvements, both large and small.

The initial impetus for the first edition of the book came from a summer workshop on game theory in the social sciences sponsored by the Alfred P. Sloan Foundation and directed by Professor Alan Taylor of Union College and Professor Steven Brams of New York University. Steven Brams, Samuel Goldberg at the Sloan Foundation, and our colleagues at Carleton College and Oberlin College encouraged us to develop and teach an undergraduate game theory course. The lecture notes from these courses provided the first draft of the book. A grant from the Dana Foundation to Professor Fernandez allowed him to spend a year visiting the Cowles Foundation at Yale University. We wish to thank William Brainard, William Nordhaus, and Peter Cramton for their many helpful suggestions and ideas.

The first edition of the book was greatly improved as a result of reviewer comments solicited by Addison-Wesley. We wish, once again, to thank Kyle Bagwell, Northwestern University; Jeff Baldani, Colgate University; Jonathan Hamilton, University of Florida; Ignatius Horstmann, The University of Western Ontario; Dan Kovenock, Purdue University; David Levine, University of California at Los Angeles; Jeffrey Weiss, The City University of New York; and Kay Widdows, Wabash College.

If possible, an even greater debt is owed to a helpful group of reviewers of the second edition. These include Daniel Arce, University of Alabama; Steven Beckman, University of Colorado at Denver; Peter Coughlin, University of Maryland at College Park; Tyler Cowen, George Mason University; James Dearden, Lehigh University; John Hamilton, University of Florida; Charles Noussair, Purdue University; Ingrid Peters-Fransen, Wilfred Laurier University; Craig Stroup, Clemson University; S. Abu Turab Rizvi, The University of Vermont; Xinghe Wang, University of Missouri at Columbia; and Keith Weigelt, University of Pennsylvania.

A special thanks goes to James Dearden for providing very helpful content and accuracy checking of the entire book.

Our colleagues at Carleton and Oberlin have provided us with a great deal of support and help. We thank David Cleeton, Barbara Craig, Donna Gibbons, Michael Hemesath, Mark Kanazawa, Hirschel Kasper, George Lamson, Martha Paas, William Perlik, Robert Piron, Stephen Sheppard, Steven Strand, Douglass

Williams, Steven Yamarik, and James Zinser. Secretarial assistance has come from Che Gonzalez, Sandra Kolek, Janice Sanborn, Betty Kendall, and Susan Quay. We also want to thank Rebecca Bloomfield and Jaafar El Harouchi for their help in proofreading.

Our students at Carleton and Oberlin who have used earlier drafts of this edition have been generous and insightful with their comments. Many of their suggestions have been incorporated into this edition of the book. We wish to thank Alex Barchenkov, David Bender, Frank Boley, Alejandro Borja, Eric Carr, Charles Carre, Josh Cohen, Alex Diaz-Matos, Yoko Endo, Alex Freuman, Andrew Kim, Kwang Kim, Lionel Marion-Landais, Alex McCarthy, Cori McNair, Bryan Melmed, Chandrika Rai, Noah Samuels, Abbey Scott, and Gregory Shalov for their help in shaking down the early drafts of this edition.

A small army of people at Addison-Wesley has been very patient and supportive of this effort. These include Denise Clinton, Senior Editor; Heather Garrison, Production Supervisor; and Quinn Perkson, Marketing Manager. Very special thanks goes to Lena Buonanno, Project Editor, for the many hours she spent helping us bring this project to completion. The improvements in the second edition owe much to her tenacity in finding good reviewers and sifting their advice through her good judgment.

Our final thanks is to our wives and children, Barbara, Melody, Danielle, Emily, Lauren, and Rachel. Scarce time was reallocated away from them to complete this effort. They were unfailingly patient and understanding.

About the Authors

Luis Fernandez is Professor of Economics at Oberlin College in Oberlin. Ohio. He received a B.S. from Cornell University and an M.A. in Mathematics and a Ph.D. in Economics from the University of California at Berkeley. He has been on the faculty at Oberlin since 1980. He has published articles on signaling, nonparametric estimating, and altruism. More recently he has begun to use experimental techniques to test various game-theoretic hypotheses, such as expected utility. Dr. Fernandez has received grants and fellowships from the Dana Foundation, the Sloan Foundation, the National Science Foundation, and the Culpepper Foundation. In 1994–95 he served as an Economics Program Director at the National Science Foundation, and in 1989–90 he was a Dana Teaching Fellow at Yale University.

H. Scott Bierman is Professor of Economics and President of the Faculty at Carleton College in Northfield, Minnesota. He has been on the faculty there since 1982. He received a B.A. from Bates College and a Ph.D. in Economics from the University of Virginia at Charlottesville. He is the author of several software tutorials and has received grants from the Alfred P. Sloan Foundation and the Ford Foundation. He was selected as a Mondale Fellow for the Mondale Public Policy Forum of the Hubert H. Humphrey Institute of Public Policy. He has published and presented papers on such topics as Housing Policy, Corporate Tax Reform, and Contestable Markets.

PART I

Static Games with Complete Information

CHAPTER 1

Nash Equilibrium

1.1   Introduction

From the time we were children all of us played games; hide-and-seek, Monopoly, chess, and tennis are all examples. When economists talk about games, however, they have a much larger class of activities in mind. For an economist, all of the social and economic interactions listed in Table 1.1 would be considered games.

What the games listed in Table 1.1 have in common with the garden-variety games children play is that they are all situations in which a decision maker must take into account the actions of others. A chess player who made a move without taking into account the past and expected future moves of her opponent would be foolish. Similarly, a television affiliate in Minneapolis would be foolish not to consider the advertising rates that other Minneapolis TV stations are likely to charge when it sets its own rates. This interdependency among decision makers is the essence of a game.

Table 1.1 **Examples of Market Games**

1. Two television stations in a small city are setting their advertising rates for the coming year.
2. An airline and its pilots' union are negotiating a new labor contract.
3. A cellular phone company is deciding what to bid in an auction of new radio frequencies.
4. A physician is making an out-of-court settlement offer to a patient who is suing her for malpractice.
5. The members of the House Ways and Means Committee are deciding whether to send a bill to the full House.

Game theory is concerned with how individuals make decisions when they are aware that their actions affect each other and when each individual takes this into account. It is the interaction among individual decision makers, all of whom are behaving purposefully, and whose decisions have implications for other people that makes **strategic decisions** different from other decisions. For example, suppose Mary and Sue are submitting sealed bids for a contract to provide mess kits for the U.S. Army. Each wants to submit a high bid in order to earn a high profit; but submitting a high bid is risky since the opponent may submit a smaller bid and win the contract. Both bidders are confronted with a trade-off: the lower the bid submitted, the greater the probability of winning the contract, but the lower the profit earned from the contract. Clearly, Mary's bid will depend on the bid she expects Sue to submit. Similarly, Sue's bid depends on what she thinks Mary will bid. Less obviously, this means that Mary's bid depends on what she thinks Sue thinks she will bid and Sue's bid depends on what she thinks Mary thinks that she will bid, and so forth. This is a problem for game theory.

Many common decision problems can be thought of as games. For example, consider the textbook case of a consumer deciding how much milk to buy at the grocery store. Since the consumer knows her purchase decision will have a negligible effect on the store's profits, she probably ignores the interaction and takes the price of milk as a "given," like the weather. As you know, this is called "price-taking behavior." But when aggregated with other consumers, her behavior is an important component of the milk pricing game played between area grocery stores. While it often makes sense to think of the individual consumer as a price-taker, it is unlikely that the grocery store she is shopping at is a complete price-taker. Small towns often have only one or two grocery stores from which residents can choose. Even in larger cities, the cost of searching for lower prices gives grocery stores some local monopoly power. If we are only interested in understanding the consumer's behavior and preferences, the game-theoretic aspects can be ignored. But if we are interested in understanding the behavior of the grocery stores, we need to take the interaction into account.

Games are sometimes being played where you might not expect them. Consider the pricing decision of the publisher of a new mystery thriller written by a popular author. Since each individual reader's purchase has no effect on the publisher, it would at first appear that potential readers can be treated as simple nonstrategic "price-takers" and that the publisher can be modeled as a classical

GAME THEORY IN ACTION: Game Theory in the News

"Shopping for a PC? Open up almost any computer magazine and you'll find an ad touting Intel Inside. Feel the speed. Experience the power. It's the mighty Pentium, king of the chips. Well . . . for now. If we've learned anything these days, it's how quickly today's mainframe becomes tomorrow's pocket calculator. And so it will be for the vaunted Pentium. Already a successor looms on the horizon: a new-generation microprocessor from Intel Corp., code-named the P6. Intel insists the wondrous chip is still in "testing." In fact, knowledgeable sources report it's almost ready to go—and that Intel is waiting to get more life out of its older sister chip, the hugely popular Pentium. . . . No one expects the new chip to quickly displace the Pentium, chiefly because Intel won't let it. Every P6 that is sold represents a Pentium that isn't, says John Wharton, a Silicon Valley consultant. For that reason, Intel will hold off producing the chip in large volumes until competitors start selling cut-price Pentium clones. Most analysts figure that won't happen for another year or more. . . . Does that mean PC buyers should ignore those glossy ads and wait for the P6? No. For one, Intel probably won't cut prices (and start shipping in bulk) until the Pentium falters. Buyers will get more bang for their buck by not waiting." (Source: From Newsweek, September 18, 1995. ©1995, Newsweek, Inc. All rights reserved. Reprinted by permission.)

What game do you think is being played here? Who are the players? What moves can they make? *Newsweek* has made strong predictions about Intel's future pricing on the basis of slim evidence. Usually it is not possible to solve a game as complicated as this one without much more information than given here and without much more careful analysis. By the time you have completed this book, you will be in a far better position to evaluate news stories such as this.

profit-maximizing monopolist. But if the public believes the publisher will lower the price of the book in the future, then buyers can opt to hold off buying the book until the price drops. Because book buyers know the publisher can change the price of the book at any time, the quantity of books the publisher will sell today at the current price will depend on the price the public expects the publisher to charge in the future. As a result, the publisher can't determine the best price to charge today without taking into account how it will price the book in the future. Another way of describing this situation is that the publisher is *playing a game against itself in the future.* This strategic interaction is crucial to understanding not only the publisher's pricing behavior, but also the consumers' demand behavior.

1.2 An Example: The Oil Drilling Game

Game theorists have developed a large body of concepts and methods for analyzing games. When analyzing a strategic situation, a game theorist first must distill from its ordinary description the essential game-theoretic facts. We will illustrate how this is done using the following hypothetical situation.

Table 1.2 **Costs and Revenues of Drilling a Well and Pumping Oil from the Clampett Deposit**

	Narrow Pipe	Wide Pipe
Drilling cost	$16 million	$29 million
Pumping cost	$20 million	$20 million
Total cost	$36 million	$49 million
Revenue	$80 million	$80 million
Profit	$44 million	$31 million

The Clampett Oil Company has a two-year lease on land that lies above a 4 million barrel crude oil deposit worth $80 million at the current oil price of $20/bl. This price is not expected to change over the next two years and Clampett's drilling decision will have no effect on the price. Clampett has to decide what size well to drill. A wide well costs $29 million to drill and can extract the oil at the rate of 6 million barrels a year, thereby extracting all the oil in a year. A narrow well costs only $16 million to drill but can extract the oil at the rate of 2 million barrels a year, thereby extracting all the oil in two years. It costs $5/bl to extract the oil once the well is drilled. To simplify matters, we will assume that Clampett only has the resources to drill one well. Since the marginal revenue in going from a narrow to a wide well ($0) is less than the marginal cost ($13 million), the most profitable decision is to drill a narrow well, as is confirmed in Table 1.2.

Our conclusion is premature, however, because it ignores the effects of entry by competitors. Suppose that a second company, Texas Exploration Corporation (TEXplor), has a lease on land that is adjacent to Clampett's, which lies above the same oil deposit, and has the same drilling and extraction costs. If both companies drill wells, they will pump from the same reservoir of oil. As a result, the amount that each gets will depend on the *relative* size of their wells. If their wells are the same size, then they each get the same amount of oil, 2 million barrels. If one drills a wide well and the other drills a narrow one, though, then the first firm will extract 3 million barrels of oil while the second will extract only 1 million barrels.

Because of the interdependency between the two companies, Clampett and TEXplor are playing a game. We will assume that each firm must make its drilling decision ignorant of its rival's decision and both are interested only in the immediate consequences of their joint decisions. These two features—the absence of any information about the opponent's choice, and the lack of interest in future interactions—make this a **static game.**[1]

---

[1]As we will see later in this book, repeated interaction can make it possible for the two firms to collude. Collusion is an important issue that will be studied in Chapters 9 and 20.

A static game can be described using its **strategic form.** The strategic form of a game consists of a series of lists. The first is the list of **players.** The players in a game are simply the decision-making entities whose intertwined fortunes we want to study. Although we will often refer to players as individual people, players can also be families, firms, clubs, and governments. The players in the Oil Drilling Game are Clampett and TEXplor.

Next we have the list of **pure strategies** available to each player. A pure strategy for a player is a complete and nonrandom plan for playing a game. By "complete" we mean that the plan allows for every possible contingency, however unlikely. In a static game, a strategy consists simply of the choice of an action. This one-to-one correspondence between strategies and actions is what makes static games relatively easy to study. Later on in this book we will see that if players move sequentially rather than simultaneously, strategies are not the same thing as actions. In the Oil Drilling Game, both players have the same two strategies: *Narrow* (drill a narrow well) and *Wide* (drill a wide well). To emphasize the subtle distinction between strategy and action, we will always display strategies in *italics* and capitalized and will italicize but not capitalize moves. A list of strategies, one for each player, is a **strategy profile** and will be enclosed within curly brackets {}. The Oil Drilling Game has four distinct strategy profiles: {*Narrow, Narrow*}, {*Narrow, Wide*}, {*Wide, Narrow*}, and {*Wide, Wide*}, where the first strategy listed in each pair is Clampett's strategy and the second is TEXplor's strategy.

Finally, every strategy profile leads to an outcome for the game and list of **payoffs,** one payoff for each player. The payoffs represent the change in welfare of the players at the end of the game and are the basis on which the players choose their strategies. The list of payoffs is called the **payoff vector** and is enclosed in parentheses ( ). In the Oil Drilling Game, the payoffs are the total profits earned over the two-year life of each firm's lease. For example, if both players choose the *Narrow* strategy, then they both drill narrow wells at a cost of $16 million, pump out half of the oil at a cost of $10 million, and sell it for $40 million, making a net profit of $14 million. So the strategy profile {*Narrow, Narrow*} results in the payoffs ($14 million, $14 million). The payoffs for the other three strategy profiles can be derived in the same way. A convenient way of presenting the payoff vectors for a two-player, static game is with a **payoff table.** Each column corresponds to a strategy of one player, called the **column player,** and each row corresponds to a strategy of the other player, called the **row player.** Each entry, T_{ij}, in the table contains the payoff vector attained when the row player chooses strategy i and the column player chooses strategy j. The payoff table for the Oil Drilling Game is shown in Table 1.3. Clampett is the column player and TEXplor is the row player. Our convention will be to list the payoffs as follows: (payoff of row player, payoff of column player). There are four cells in this table, each corresponding to one of the four possible strategy profiles.

As you can see, the payoff from a strategy can change dramatically depending on the opponent's strategy. Since neither player has advance information on the opponent's move, each must form some **belief** about what the opponent will do. Not all beliefs are consistent with the assumption that the opponent is rational.

Table 1.3 *The Payoff Table for the Oil Drilling Game*

		Clampett	
		Narrow	Wide
TEXplor	Narrow	(14, 14)	(−1, 16)
	Wide	(16, −1)	(1, 1)

Payoffs (in millions): (TEXplor, Clampett)

What beliefs do you think "rational" players will have about their opponent if they think their opponent is "rational" as well? The rest of this chapter presents a number of powerful ideas about what constitutes a "rational belief" about an opponent's choice of strategy when it is common knowledge that both players are rational.

1.3 Chronological Time and Game Time

When we talk of players moving "simultaneously" in a game, we have in mind something like the following. Two kids are out on a sidewalk playing "rock, paper, scissors." As you probably know, the players in this game recite the words "rock, paper, scissors" in unison. When they come to the word "scissors" each player simultaneously makes a hand signal indicating the choice of rock (a fist), paper (an open hand), or scissors (index and middle fingers extended). The winner of the game depends on the signals chosen by the two players. A rock "smashes" scissors, scissors "cut" paper, and paper "covers" rock. Therefore, a player who chooses the hand signal for rock will beat a player who chooses the hand signal for scissors, but lose to a player who chooses the hand signal for paper, and so on. The important aspect of this game is that neither player learns what the other has chosen until after both have moved.

Now consider a slightly different version of this game. Suppose a third child is present and plays the role of "referee." Instead of counting to three in unison and then simultaneously flashing a hand signal, the referee takes one child out of sight of the other and asks him to reveal the hand signal to her. The referee then goes back to the second child and, without revealing what hand signal the first child selected, asks the second child to reveal the hand signal to her as well. Once this is done, the referee announces the winner. Although the hand signals were chosen in *chronological* sequence, the difference between the two versions of the game is inconsequential. In both versions, the players have exactly the same information at the time they make their decision. There is no reason to think that either child will play differently with or without a referee (although this ignores the possibility of cheating). In this chapter, *chronological* time is important only insofar as it affects when information becomes available to the players of the game.[2]

Interesting economic games are seldom characterized by perfect chronological simultaneity. But there are many important games in which the players move "simultaneously" in our extended sense of the term. For example, consider the two oil drilling companies, TEXplor and Clampett. The two firms are virtual twins: they have the same drilling and pumping costs and sell their oil at the same world price. More important, neither is able to get a "jump" on the other and drill a well before the other has committed itself. So, from a strategic perspective, they move "simultaneously."

1.4 Dominant Strategy Equilibrium

We are interested in answering the following question: Given a set of exogenous constraints *and* a set of players in a game who are rational *and* all the information about these decision makers' objectives, which strategy is the best for each of them to adopt?

We will begin by examining Clampett's decision. Since the outcome of its drilling decision is not entirely in its own hands, but depends on what TEXplor does, and it has no way to know in advance what TEXplor will do, it makes sense to begin by asking some relatively simple questions. Suppose Clampett believes TEXplor will adopt the *Narrow* strategy. What is Clampett's best response to this belief? The answer from Table 1.3 is clear: adopt the *Wide* strategy. But, since we cannot be certain TEXplor will adopt the *Narrow* strategy, we ask a second question: What is Clampett's best response if it believes TEXplor will adopt the *Wide* strategy? The answer is again clear: adopt the *Wide* strategy. Putting these two answers together gives us an interesting result. No matter what Clampett believes TEXplor will do, Clampett does better by adopting the *Wide* strategy rather than the *Narrow* strategy. More succinctly, *Wide* **strictly dominates** *Narrow* or, equivalently, *Narrow* is **strictly dominated** by *Wide*. Whatever a player thinks his or her opponents will do in a game, it is never rational to adopt a strictly dominated strategy. This is such an important idea that we will define the term formally.

The strategy S_1 **strictly dominates** *the strategy S_2 for a player if, given any collection of strategies that could be played by the other players, playing S_1 results in a strictly higher payoff for that player than does playing S_2. The strategy S_2 is also said to be* **strictly dominated** *by S_1. A rational player will never adopt a strictly dominated strategy nor expect a rational opponent to adopt one.*

---

[2]Chronological time does become important in dynamic games where future payoffs must be taken into account. This will be examined in more detail in Part II.

This gives us the first step in solving any static game: find and eliminate from further consideration all the strictly dominated strategies of every player. The only strategy left when we eliminate the dominated strategies in the Oil Drilling Game is the *Wide* strategy. Such a strategy is called **strictly dominant.** Therefore, even without knowing in advance what TEXplor will do, in this simple game we can predict the strategy Clampett will adopt: *Wide.*

---

*A **strictly dominant strategy** for a player is one that strictly dominates every other strategy of that player. A rational player will adopt a strictly dominant strategy whenever it exists.*

Note that if Clampett has a dominant strategy, then so does TEXplor. The reason is the symmetry of the payoff schedules in Table 1.3. We now know what both firms will do: they will both drill wide wells. This is our solution for this game. This solution is known as a **strictly dominant strategy equilibrium.**

---

*The strategy profile $\{S_1, S_2, \ldots, S_N\}$ is a **strictly dominant strategy equilibrium** if for every player i, S_i is a strictly dominant strategy.*

When the equilibrium strategies are chosen, both firms drill wide wells, split the oil, and earn profits of $1 million each. However, were they to both drill cheaper narrow wells, they would also end up splitting the oil but would earn profits of $14 million each, or 1300% more! That is, there is an outcome of this game in which both players are (much!) better off than they are at the equilibrium outcome. The shorthand way of describing this state of affairs is to say that the equilibrium outcome is **Pareto dominated.**

---

*The outcome O of a game is **Pareto dominated** if there is some other outcome O' such that (1) every player either strictly prefers O' to O or is indifferent between O' and O, and (2) some player strictly prefers O' to O. An outcome is **Pareto optimal** if it is not Pareto dominated by any other outcome of the game.*

If, somehow, both parties could agree to adopt the *Narrow* strategy and bind themselves to carrying out the agreement, then it is conceivable that the strategy profile $S^* = \{Narrow, Narrow\}$ might be adopted. Economists have considered strategic situations in which these sorts of binding agreements and commitments can take place. Such games are the province of **cooperative game theory.** In this book, we will deal only with **noncooperative games** and assume that these sorts of agreements and commitments cannot be enforced.

The Oil Drilling Game is an example of a class of games called **Prisoner's Dilemmas.** These are games with strictly dominant strategy equilibria that are also Pareto dominated. When the Prisoner's Dilemma was first studied in the early

Table 1.4 **A Nuclear Arms Race Modeled As a Prisoner's Dilemma**

		The U.S.S.R.	
		Disarm	**Re-arm**
The U.S.A.	Disarm	(10, 10)	(−10, 50)
	Re-arm	(50, −10)	**(0, 0)**

Payoffs: (U.S.A., U.S.S.R.)

Table 1.5 **A TV Advertising War Modeled as a Prisoner's Dilemma**

		Schlitz	
		Don't advertise on TV	**Advertise on TV**
Budweiser	Don't advertise on TV	($5 billion, $5 billion)	($10 billion, $0)
	Advertise on TV	($0, $10 billion)	**($1 billion, $1 billion)**

Payoffs: (Budweiser profits, Schlitz profits)

1950s, it generated a great deal of attention and was used to explain things as serious as the nuclear arms race, and as frivolous as TV beer commercials. You will find simple models of both phenomena in Tables 1.4 and 1.5 (strictly dominant strategies and payoffs are displayed in **boldface**). You be the judge of whether these two models are insightful.

The original Prisoner's Dilemma story goes something like this: Two thieves are caught by the police with incriminating tools of the trade but with no other evidence. The police take each man into a separate room and make him the following offer: If he confesses to his criminal activity (the *Confess* strategy) and his partner does not, he will go free and the other man will get the maximum sentence of 20 years in prison. If he refuses to cooperate with the police (the *Hang tough* strategy) and his partner confesses, then he will get the 20-year jail sentence and the partner will get off free. If both men *Confess*, then the police do not need their further cooperation and will convict them on the basis of their confessions. In this case, both face a prison sentence of 10 years. Though the police don't mention it, the thieves both know that if they both *Hang tough*, the physical evidence is sufficient to convict them only of conspiracy to commit burglary, which carries a sentence of only one year in jail. The police conclude by telling each man that his partner is being made the same offer. Because they cannot communicate with each other, the thieves are forced to play the static game whose payoff table can be found in Table 1.6. You should verify that *Confess* is a strictly dominant strategy for each thief.

Table 1.6 *The Strategic Form of the Original Prisoner's Dilemma*

		Thief #2	
		Hang tough	**Confess**
Thief #1	**Hang tough**	(1 year, 1 year)	(20 years, freedom)
	Confess	(freedom, 20 years)	**(10 years, 10 years)**

Payoffs: (Thief #1, Thief #2)

One reason that the Prisoner's Dilemma has generated so much discussion and analysis is the existence of substantial anecdotal as well as experimental evidence that people often try to cooperate when they play Prisoner's Dilemmas. We will discuss this further in Chapter 9, where we examine the "repeated Prisoner's Dilemma."

When a strictly dominant strategy equilibrium exists, we can confidently predict that this will be the outcome of the game. However, what if a strategy is "almost" but not quite strictly dominant? An example is given in Table 1.7. *Narrow* is no longer strictly dominated by *Wide*. Now both strategies earn zero profits if the opposition adopts a *Wide* strategy. *Wide* **weakly dominates** *Narrow*. As a result, *Wide* is no longer a strictly dominant strategy. It is instead called a **weakly dominant strategy**.

---

*The strategy S_1 **weakly dominates** the strategy S_2 for a player if, given any collection of strategies that could be played by the other players, playing S_1 never results in a lower payoff to that player than does playing S_2 and, in at least one instance, S_1 gives the player a strictly higher payoff than does S_2. The strategy S_2 is said to be **weakly dominated** by S_1. A rational player will seldom play a weakly dominated strategy.*

*A **weakly dominant strategy** for a player is one that weakly dominates every other strategy of that player. A rational player will usually play a weakly dominant strategy.*

*The strategy profile $(S_1, S_2, \ldots, S_N)$ is a **weakly dominant strategy equilibrium** if for every player i, S_i is a weakly dominant strategy.*

Note that these definitions differ from the earlier definitions of strict domination in replacing the phrase "results in a strictly higher payoff" with "never results in a lower payoff." Weak dominance allows for ties. Logically, a strictly dominant strategy is also weakly dominant. To distinguish the two cases more clearly, we will reserve the terms *weakly dominates, weakly dominated,* and *weakly dominant* for those cases in which there is *at least one tie*. When we want to allow for the possibility of either weak or strict dominance, we will drop the words "weak" and "strict" and use *dominates, dominated,* or *dominant*.

Table 1.7 **Another Hypothetical Payoff Table for the Oil Drilling Game**

		Clampett	
		Narrow	*Wide*
TEXplor	*Narrow*	(14, 14)	(0, 16)
	Wide	(16, 0)	(0, 0)

Payoffs (in millions): (TEXplor, Clampett)

1.5 Iterated Dominant Strategy Equilibrium

The assumption that rational players will choose dominant strategies is quite powerful and is not terribly controversial. In many instances, however, the players do not have dominant strategies. An example is provided in Table 1.8. This payoff matrix differs from Table 1.3 in having an additional strategy, *Don't drill*.

Wide strictly dominates *Don't drill*, but it no longer dominates *Narrow*. And *Narrow* dominates neither *Don't drill* nor *Wide*. So no strategy is clearly best. But *Don't drill* is clearly a bad strategy, since a firm can guarantee itself a profit of at least $1 million by adopting the *Wide* strategy. Since the payoffs are common knowledge, it is rational for each firm to believe the other will drill a well, although it is not yet clear what size. This means that both players can simplify the game by eliminating from consideration the dominated strategy *Don't drill*. The new game is the two-strategy game whose payoff matrix is given in Table 1.3. We already know that this game has a strictly dominant strategy equilibrium: (*Wide, Wide*). We propose this as the solution for this game. *Wide* is called an **iterated strictly dominant strategy** because it is selected by iteratively eliminating both players' strictly dominated strategies. In the three-strategy version of the Oil Drilling Game, two iterations are needed before we are left with one strategy for each player: In the first iteration, we eliminate *Don't drill*. In the second iteration, we eliminate *Narrow*. Not surprisingly, when it exists, the strategy profile con-

Table 1.8 **The Payoff Matrix of the Oil Drilling Game with a New Strategy**

		Clampett		
		Don't drill	*Narrow*	*Wide*
	Don't drill	(0, 0)	(0, 44)	(0, 31)
TEXplor	*Narrow*	(44, 0)	(14, 14)	(−1, 16)
	Wide	(31, 0)	(16, −1)	(1, 1)

Payoffs (in millions): (TEXplor, Clampett)

sisting of each player's iterated strictly dominant strategy is called an **iterated strictly dominant strategy equilibrium.** Although, logically, a strictly dominant strategy equilibrium is also an iterated strictly dominant strategy equilibrium, we will reserve the term *iterated* for equilibria in which more than one round of eliminations are needed.

---

*A strategy is **iterated strictly dominant** for player i if and only if it is the only strategy in $\overline{S}_i$, where $\overline{S}_i$ is the intersection of the following sequence of nested sets of strategies: (1) S_i^1 consists of all of player i's strategies that are not strictly dominated; (2) for $n > 1$, S_i^n consists of the strategies in S_i^{n-1} that are not strictly dominated when we restrict the other players $j \neq i$ to the strategies in S_j^{n-1}.*

*The strategy profile $(S_1, S_2, \ldots, S_N)$ is an **iterated strictly dominant strategy equilibrium** if for every player i, S_i is an iterated strictly dominant strategy.*

In games with a large number of strategies and players, it may require many iterations to find the iterated dominant strategies for each player—assuming they exist. As a result, iterated dominant strategies are more difficult to find than are dominant strategies. There is experimental evidence that players may have a hard time finding iterated dominant strategies if doing so involves more than a few iterations.

In the above definition we assumed that, at every iteration, all dominated strategies were deleted simultaneously. But we could have deleted strategies in a different order. For example, we could have deleted player 1's strictly dominated strategies first, then deleted player 2's strictly dominated strategies—restricting player 1 now to her undominated strategies—and so forth. If we had proceeded in this way would we end up with the same limiting set $\overline{S}_i$? Fortunately, the answer is *yes*. Regardless of the order in which strictly dominated strategies are eliminated, we always end up with the same limiting set $\overline{S}_i$. Unfortunately, this is not true if we replace strict dominance by weak dominance. Now the limiting set can be different depending on the order in which weakly dominant strategies are deleted. You are asked to show this by example in the exercises at the end of the chapter. For this reason, we have deliberately not defined *iterated weak dominance*, as any unambiguous definition would have to impose an ordering on the deletions, and any such ordering would be arbitrary.

1.6 Nash Equilibrium

Unfortunately, in most games there are no strictly dominant or strictly iterated dominant strategy equilibria. That is, the sequential elimination of dominated strategies stops before all the players' strategies have been reduced to one. An example of such a game is shown in Table 1.9. These payoffs differ from those in Table 1.3 in only one entry: the profit of a firm that drills a narrow well when its competitor drills a wide well. Instead of taking a $1 million loss, we now assume that the firm makes a modest $2 million profit.

Table 1.9 **Another Payoff Matrix for the Oil Drilling Game**

		Clampett		
		Don't drill	Narrow	Wide
TEXplor	Don't drill	(0, 0)	(0, 44)	(0, 31)
	Narrow	(44, 0)	(14, 14)	(2, 16)
	Wide	(31, 0)	(16, 2)	(1, 1)

Payoffs (in millions): (TEXplor, Clampett)

Table 1.10 **The Payoff Matrix of the Oil Drilling Game after Deleting Dominated Strategies**

		Clampett	
		Narrow	Wide
TEXplor	Narrow	(14, 14)	(2, 16)
	Wide	(16, 2)	(1, 1)

Payoffs (in millions): (TEXplor, Clampett)

We can verify that *Don't drill* is a strictly dominated strategy for both firms, so we can simplify the game by eliminating this strategy. This results in the simpler game displayed in Table 1.10.

This is as far as we can go. There are no more dominated strategies to delete. Both players are left with two undominated strategies. The optimal strategy for each player now depends critically on the strategy that player believes its opponent will adopt. What belief(s) can we identify as "rational," given that it is common knowledge that both players are intelligent payoff maximizers?

Since Clampett is rational, the firm will choose the strategy that is best given its belief as to the strategy TEXplor will choose. Suppose Clampett believes that TEXplor will adopt *Wide.* Then its **best response** is *Narrow.* Now suppose that TEXplor believes that Clampett will adopt *Narrow.* Then its best response is *Wide.* The belief that TEXplor and Clampett will adopt the strategy profile (*Wide, Narrow*) is **self-confirming.** If both firms believe that this strategy profile will be adopted, then it is in their interests to adopt it. Reread this paragraph because it gets at the heart of how to find a "rational strategy." The strategy profile {*Wide, Narrow*} is called a **Nash equilibrium** after Professor John C. Nash, the originator of the concept. For this innovation Professor Nash was awarded the Nobel Prize in Economics. A formal definition of his concept is given below.

---

*Suppose there are N players in a game, X_i is the set of possible strategies for player i, and $v_i(s_1, \ldots, s_N)$ is player i's payoff when the players choose the strategy profile $\{s_i, \ldots, s_N\}$. A **Nash equilibrium** is a strategy profile $\{s_1^*, \ldots, s_N^*\}$ such that each strategy s_i^* is an element of X_i and maximizes the function $f_i(x) = v_i(s_1^* \ldots s_{i-1}^*, x, s_{i+1}^*, \ldots, s_N^*)$ among the elements of X_i. That is, at a Nash equilibrium, each player's equilibrium strategy is a **best response** to the belief that the other players will adopt their Nash equilibrium strategies.*

You may be bothered by how complicated this definition is. Indeed, finding Nash equilibria in even simple games with more than a few players can be difficult. The presumption that players will adopt Nash equilibrium strategies is, not surprisingly, much more controversial than the assumption that they will adopt strictly dominant or iterated strictly dominant strategies. Nevertheless, it carries a virtual monopoly position as a solution concept for noncooperative games.[3]

Let us see why, after more than 40 years, Nash equilibrium has not been superseded by another concept. Imagine for a minute that a CD-ROM existed that contained the "correct" way to play any known game. Suppose a group of players were playing a game and all had access to the CD-ROM. If the solution proposed on the CD-ROM for this game were *not* a Nash equilibrium, then at least one player would do better by *not* following the "correct" play given on the CD-ROM, assuming she believed that all the other players would do what they "should." Hence, to the extent that game theory is normative—meaning it seeks to determine how we "should" play games—it is hard to justify "good play" that is inconsistent with either Nash equilibrium or the rationality of one's opponents. Nash equilibrium is harder to justify as a positive theory of how players actually behave in the real world. Experiments have shown many instances in which players consistently played strategies that are not Nash equilibria.

Nash equilibrium is related in a number of ways to the three previously introduced equilibrium concepts. We leave it as an exercise for you to show:

1. If a strategy profile is a strictly dominant strategy equilibrium or an iterated strictly dominant strategy equilibrium of a game, then it is the only Nash equilibrium as well.

2. If a strategy profile is a weakly dominant strategy equilibrium of a game, then it is a Nash equilibrium of the game, but not necessarily the only Nash equilibrium.

3. The elimination of weakly dominated strategies sometimes eliminates Nash equilibrium strategies as well.

---

[3]You should be aware that there is some dissent among game theorists about the centrality of the Nash equilibrium concept. Alternative equilibrium concepts are B. D. Bernheim and D. G. Pearce's notion of *rationalizability* and R. Aumann's *correlated equilibrium.*

One reason that Nash equilibrium is a controversial solution concept for games is that it is often not unique. For example, you may already have figured out that {Wide, Narrow} is not the only Nash equilibrium of the game in Table 1.9. Another Nash equilibrium (are there more?) is {Narrow, Wide}. This follows from the symmetry of the payoffs in this game. We urge you to verify it directly, though, before going on. When there is more than one Nash equilibrium, it is difficult to predict what strategies will be chosen without more information about the context in which the game is being played and the type of communication possible between the players. That is, Nash equilibrium does not always provide a "solution" to a game. One proposed solution to the problem of multiplicity of equilibrium is the notion of a *focal point equilibrium*, which we will examine in Section 1.7.

A second problem with Nash equilibrium is that games may not always have a Nash equilibrium if the players are confined to pure strategies. The solution to this nonexistence problem is to expand the strategies available to the players. We will discuss this in Chapter 10. For the moment, dominance and Nash equilibrium are sufficient to allow us to study many interesting economic games.

1.7   Focal Point Equilibrium

As you have just seen, one reason game theory can be so frustrating is that many interesting games have more than one Nash equilibrium. Consider the following famous game called the **Battle of the Sexes Game.** In this game, it is assumed that a couple, Rhett and Scarlett, are making a decision about how to spend an evening. Let us suppose that Rhett would prefer to spend an evening in a low-life saloon. Scarlett would prefer to spend the evening at a posh dinner club. Obviously, they could go their separate ways, but this is not as appealing to either of them as being together. A possible payoff matrix is shown in Table 1.11.

This game has two pure strategy Nash equilibria. In Table 1.11 we have printed the payoffs associated with these two Nash equilibrium strategies in **boldface.** You should confirm this before going further. Since there are two Nash equilibria, how are the players to choose between them? Thomas Schelling suggested that in **coordination games** such as this, one of the many Nash equilibria might "stand out" from the others due to some asymmetry that is common knowledge to the players. He called such a Nash equilibrium a **focal point equilibrium.**

Table 1.11   *The Battle of the Sexes Game*

		Rhett	
		Saloon	Dinner club
Scarlett	Saloon	**(5, 10)**	(−30, −20)
	Dinner club	(−2, −5)	**(12, 2)**

Payoffs: (Scarlett, Rhett)

Although Schelling did not provide a formal theory of such equilibria—indeed, the concept of a "focal point" has eluded formalization—he convincingly showed the pervasiveness of such equilibria, usually in the guise of "social conventions." For example, consider the following six two-person coordination games devised by Schelling:

1. Name "heads" or "tails." If you and your partner name the same, you both win a prize; otherwise, you win nothing.

2. Circle one of the following numbers: 7, 100, 13, 261, 99, 555. You win if both you and your partner circle the same number.

3. You are to meet someone in New York City. You have not been instructed where to meet; you have no prior understanding with the other person of where to meet; and you cannot communicate with each other. You are simply told that you will have to guess where to meet, that the other person is being told the same thing, and that you will have to try to make your guesses coincide.

4. You are told the date but not the hour of the meeting in number (3); the two of you must guess the exact minute of the day for the meeting.

5. Write some positive number. You win if your number matches that of your partner.

6. On the first ballot, candidates polled as follows:
   Smith 19%
   Jones 28%
   Brown 15%
   Robinson 29%
   White 9%

The second ballot is about to be taken. You have no interest in the outcome except that you will be rewarded if someone gets a majority on the second ballot and you voted for him. The same is true for every other voter, and this is common knowledge. For whom do you vote on the second ballot?

In all of these coordination games, there are many Nash equilibria. Yet, Schelling found that people zeroed in on a few of these equilibria in every case. For example, 86% of his sample chose "heads" in (1); 87% chose one of the first three numbers in (2); more than half proposed meeting at the information booth in Grand Central Station at 12 noon in (3) and (4); 40% guessed "1" in (5); and over 80% voted for Robinson in (6).

Furthermore, Schelling found that people chose focal points even when such an equilibrium selection process discriminated against them. For example, consider the following variation of (1) above:

1. A and B are to choose "heads" and "tails" without communicating. If both choose "heads," A gets $3 and B gets $2; if both choose "tails," A gets $2 and B gets $3. If they choose differently, neither gets anything. You are A (or B). What do you choose? Notice that if you both chose at random there

is only a 50-50 chance of successful coordination and an expected value of $1.25 each, which is less than either $2 or $3.

Schelling found that 73% of those given the role of player A and 68% of those given the role of player B chose "heads"—substantially better coordination than would occur by chance—despite the bias against B. Note that if both A and B try to get the $3, they end up with nothing. Schelling's solution is troubling because it suggests that there are aspects of games that are important determinants of how people play them, but are outside the currently accepted formalization of the theory.

1.8   Evolutionary Equilibrium

Human beings are not the only animals whose behavior can be understood using game theory. Many animals find themselves in strategic situations in which they must adopt some strategy. For example, when a lion comes across another lion who is eating a fresh kill, the intruder must decide whether to walk away and leave the other alone or fight for the right to eat the carcass. Sociobiologists have found game theory to be a powerful tool for understanding how the animals "solve" these games, although the meanings they give to the terms "strategy," "payoff," and "equilibrium" differs from those we have been developing.

In **evolutionary game theory,** a pure strategy is a behavior by an animal that is "programmed" by a gene. Genes "compete" against each other by being passed on to the next generation in varying proportions. Suppose a strategy encoded by some gene makes the animals who play that strategy have more offspring than those who play a second strategy. Then the proportion of animals who have the gene for the genetically superior strategy will grow until they greatly outnumber the animals that play the inferior strategy. In evolutionary game theory, the "payoff" to playing the strategy S against animals playing the strategy S', denoted $U(S, S')$, equals the expected number of offspring in the next generation that are endowed with the gene for that strategy. A strategy is an **evolutionary stable strategy (ESS)** if a population that adopts it is resistant to the introduction of an initially rare mutant alternative strategy. A more formal definition is given below.

A strategy S^* is an **evolutionary stable strategy (ESS)** *if for every alternative strategy S', $S' \neq S^*$, (1) $U(S^*, S^*) \geq U(S', S^*)$, and (2) if $U(S', S^*) = U(S', S^*)$, then $U(S^*, S') > U(S', S')$.*

The first part of the definition of an ESS should look familiar. It is nothing other than the definition of a Nash equilibrium! But the second part of the definition we have not encountered before. It is required in order to handle the spontaneous generation of mutants. To see the complication that mutants introduce, suppose S' is a mutant strategy that appears within a population where every other animal plays the strategy S^*. If $U(S^*, S^*) = U(S', S^*)$, then, initially, the mutant subpopulation will not be selected out, but will instead grow by genetic drift until the mutants become a significant proportion of the population. Let the proportion of the population that are mutants be π and let the proportion of the population that are not be $1 - \pi$. The *expected payoff* to playing the strategy S, which we will denote by $EU(S)$, is given by

$$EU(S) = \pi \cdot U(S, S') + (1 - \pi) \cdot U(S, S^*) \qquad [1.1]$$

If S^* is an ESS, then $EU(S^*) = \pi \cdot U(S^*, S') + (1 - \pi) \cdot U(S^*, S^*), > \pi \cdot U(S', S') + (1 - \pi) \cdot U(S', S^*) = EU(S')$. As a result, the mutant subpopulation will cease to grow and begin to decline.

An example of the success of this new approach to understanding animal behavior concerns the strange behavior of a species of birds called *bowerbirds*. Male bowerbirds build elaborate nests or bowers to attract female bowerbirds with whom they can mate. That in itself is not unusual, as many animals engage in activity designed to attract mates. What is unusual is that once they have built their bowers, many male bowerbirds attempt to maraud and destroy the bowers of neighboring males and/or steal their "decorations." Among Macgregor bowerbirds, for example, visitations of a bower by neighboring males can be as frequent as once a day. If a male leaves his bower unattended (or is experimentally removed), the bower will be destroyed in the space of a few hours! This behavior seems to be extremely wasteful since the bowerbirds who maraud also end up being marauded and must rebuild their destroyed bowers. During the time spent marauding and repairing their damaged bowers they are unable to forage for food or to mate. Why do they do this?

In order to answer this question, ornithologists Stephen and Melinda Pruett-Jones developed a game-theoretic evolutionary model of bowerbird behavior.[4] In this admittedly simple model there are only two strategies (corresponding to two sets of competing genes): *Marauding* and *Guarding*. *Marauding* bowerbirds visit unattended neighboring bowers and destroy them. *Guarding* bowerbirds spend all their free time at their bower and never visit their neighbors. The benefit to marauding is that it puts the neighboring males "out of commission," thereby increasing the chances of attracting and mating with a female. The cost of marauding is the mating time lost as well as the increased risk of having one's own bower destroyed. The reproductive fitness of each bowerbird—meaning the number of females with which it mates—depends on both the strategy it pursues and the strategy followed by its neighbors. So the birds are playing an evolutionary "game" in which the payoff is reproductive fitness. The Pruett-Joneses show that under a wide range of environments, this game has a payoff table similar to Table 1.12, which resembles the Prisoner's Dilemma: *Marauding* yields a higher payoff than *Guarding* regardless of the strategy followed by the neighboring

---

[4]"Sexual competition and courtship disruptions: Why do male bowerbirds destroy each other's bowers?" *Animal Behavior* 47 (1994), pp. 607–20.

Table 1.12 **The Bowerbird Game**

		Bowerbird #2	
		Guarding	*Marauding*
Bowerbird #1	*Guarding*	(5, 5)	(1, 10)
	Marauding	(10, 1)	(2, 2)

Payoffs: (Bowerbird #1, Bowerbird #2)

bowerbirds, yet *Guarding* bowerbirds who have *Guarding* bowerbirds as neighbors do better than *Marauding* bowerbirds whose neighbors are also *Marauders*. As a result, *Marauding* is a Nash equilibrium of the game played between *Marauding* and *Guarding* gene pools. More important to biologists, *Marauding* is an evolutionary stable strategy.

The success of evolutionary game theory in biology has not been lost on game theorists. Its ideas and methods are being applied to understanding how people learn to play games through trial and error, rather than logical introspection. This work is still in its infancy.

1.9   Games with Continuous Strategies

In the Oil Drilling Game, we assumed the two players could only take one of three moves: don't drill a well, drill a narrow well, or drill a wide well. This probably did not sit well with some of you. It probably seemed more realistic to assume that the firm could choose to drill a well of any diameter it wished. Instead of three strategies, there would be a strategy corresponding to every nonnegative real number. Indeed, many economic games are more naturally cast as games with continuous strategies than as games with finite and discrete strategies: pricing games, location games, investment games, monetary policy games, to name some of those we will examine later in this book. In this section, we will show how to work with such mathematically complex, yet often more realistic, sets of strategies.

In order to keep the mathematics straightforward, we will illustrate our methods using the following simple example. There are two players, labeled A and B. The strategies for both can be represented by real numbers. We will denote their strategies as S_A and S_B. Their payoff functions, U_A and U_B, are given by

$$U_A(S_A, S_B) = -S_A^2 + 4S_A + 2S_A S_B + 3S_B - S_B^2 \qquad [1.2]$$

$$U_B(S_A, S_B) = -S_B^2 + 2S_B + S_A S_B + S_A - S_A^2 \qquad [1.3]$$

For each player we now ask: What strategy maximizes that player's payoff given *any* possible strategy chosen by the opponent? The answer to this question is the player's **best response function**.[5] We will denote these two best response functions as $R_A(S_B)$ and $R_B(S_A)$. We will show how to find the best response function using two techniques. The first method uses only algebra and a few special facts about quadratic equations. The second method uses calculus.

The two payoff functions have a special algebraic form: they are **second-order polynomials** of the two strategy variables. That is, the expressions consist of a sum of terms and each term consists of a constant times either S_A, S_B, S_A^2, S_B^2, or $S_A \cdot S_B$. We will make use of the algebraic fact that $(x - y)^2 = x^2 - 2xy + y^2$ to rewrite the expression for U_A in the form

$$U_A(S_A, S_B) = -(S_A - f(S_B))^2 + g(S_B) \qquad [1.4]$$

where f and g are two expressions in which only the variable S_B appears. Since the first term is nonpositive, the expression is minimized by setting S_A equal to $f(S_B)$ so that this term equals zero. But by definition, this means that $f(S_B)$ is player A's best response function. We begin by collecting together terms in which S_A appears with the same power.

$$U_A(S_A, S_B) = -S_A^2 + (4 + 2S_B)S_A + (3S_B - S_B^2) \qquad [1.5]$$

Next, we factor out a -1 from the two terms in which the variable S_A appears, and then factor out a 2 from the term in which S_A appears with the power of 1.

$$\begin{aligned} U_A(S_A, S_B) &= -(S_A^2 - (4 + 2S_B)S_A) + (3S_B - S_B^2) \\ &= -(S_A^2 - 2(2 + S_B)S_A) + (3S_B - S_B^2) \end{aligned} \qquad [1.6]$$

We now add and subtract the term $(2 + S_B)^2$ to "complete the square" and then manipulate the right-hand terms until we get an expression that looks like Eq. [1.4].

$$\begin{aligned} U_A(S_A, S_B) &= -(S_A^2 - 2(2 + S_B)S_A) - (S_B + 2)^2 + (S_B + 2)^2 + (3S_B - S_B^2) \\ &= -(S_A^2 - 2(2 + S_B)S_A + (S_B + 2)^2) + (S_B + 2)^2 + (3S_B - S_B^2) \\ &= -(S_A - (2 + S_B))^2 + (S_B + 2)^2 + (3S_B - S_B^2) \end{aligned} \qquad [1.7]$$

As we pointed out above, the last expression is maximized by setting S_A equal to $2 + S_B$. So

$$R_A(S_B) = 2 + S_B. \qquad [1.8]$$

---

[5]Some authors call these *reaction functions*. This terminology is now considered dated. It is also somewhat misleading since it suggests a dynamic process of action and reaction instead of a static balance of forces.

We leave it as an exercise for you to show that the expression for U_B can be rewritten as

$$U_B(S_A, S_B) = -(S_B^2 - 2(1 + \tfrac{1}{2}S_A)S_B)^2 + (1 + \tfrac{1}{2}S_A)^2 + (S_A - S_A^2), \qquad [1.9]$$

which is minimized by setting S_B equal to

$$R_B(S_A) = 1 + \frac{S_A}{2}. \qquad [1.10]$$

For those familiar with calculus, a second way to derive the best response functions is to use the following theorem:

> **THEOREM 1.1:** If $f(x, y)$ is twice continuously differentiable and $\dfrac{\partial^2 f}{\partial x^2}(x, y) < 0$ for all values in its domain, then x^* is a global maximum of f if and only if it satisfies the **first-order condition** for a maximum $\dfrac{\partial f}{\partial x}(x^*, y) = 0$.

Since each payoff function satisfies the requirements of the theorem, the two best response functions satisfy the following first-order conditions:

$$\frac{\partial}{\partial S_A} U_A(S_A^*, S_B) = -2S_A^* + 4 + 2S_B = 0 \qquad [1.11]$$

$$\frac{\partial}{\partial S_B} U_B(S_A, S_B^*) = -2S_B^* + 2 + S_A = 0 \qquad [1.12]$$

Solving each equation for one player's optimal strategy, say S_B^*, in terms of the other player's strategy, S_A, results in the expressions

$$S_A^* = \tfrac{1}{2}(4 + 2S_B) = 2 + S_B \qquad [1.13]$$

$$S_B^* = \tfrac{1}{2}(2 + S_A) = 1 + \tfrac{1}{2}S_A, \qquad [1.14]$$

which imply that the best responses are given by Eqs. [1.8] and [1.10].

The graphs of these two functions are displayed in Figure 1.1. The strategy of player A is represented on the x-axis and the strategy of player B is represented on the y-axis. Both graphs are straight lines with a unique intersection point $(S_A^*, S_B^*) = (6, 4)$. We claim that this strategy profile is the unique Nash pure-strategy equilibrium of this static game. The reason is simple. By definition, when player B chooses the strategy $S_B = 4$, then the strategy $R_A(4) = 6$ maximizes player A's payoff function. Likewise, when player A chooses the strategy $S_A = 6$, then the

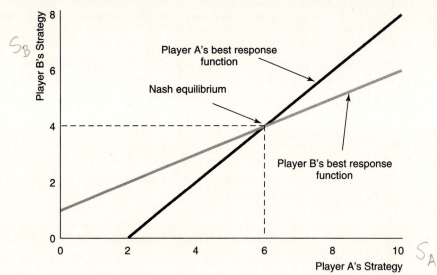

FIGURE 1.1   The best response functions of players A and B, along with their intersection point.

strategy $R_B(6) = 4$ maximizes player B's payoff function. But this means the strategy profile $(6,4)$ is a Nash equilibrium. The extension of the definition of a best response function to games with more than two players is left as an exercise.

> **THEOREM 1.2:** Suppose two players are playing a static game where the set of strategies for both players is represented by points on the real line, each payoff function is a strictly concave and twice continuously differentiable function of the player's own strategy, and $R_A(S_B)$ and $R_B(S_A)$ are the players' best response functions. Then (S_A^*, S_B^*) is a Nash equilibrium of this game if and only if $R_A(S_B^*) = S_A^*$ and $R_B(S_A^*) = S_B^*$.

Theorem 1.2 implies that for two-player games, Nash equilibrium strategies are the "fixed points" of the composite functions $R_A(R_B(.))$ and $R_B(R_A(.))$. For example, if we compose Eqs. [1.8] and [1.10], we get $R_A(R_B(S_A)) = 2 + \left(1 + \dfrac{S_A}{2}\right)$, whose only fixed point is the equilibrium strategy $S_A^* = 6$, as you can easily verify numerically.

1.10   Summary

We have examined games in which every player is ignorant of the actions its opponents have taken. In such games, the player's optimal strategy depends on what it thinks its opponents will do. These beliefs, in turn, depend on what it believes all of its opponents believe the other players, including itself, will do. The infinite regress makes it difficult to determine the players' optimal strategies.

Fortunately, sometimes players can determine that some strategies are inferior regardless of what the other players do. The sequential elimination of such dominated strategies sometimes leads to a single optimal strategy for each player. Such a collection of strategies constitutes a prediction of how players will behave. When such an equilibrium fails to exist, as is often the case, then we must be content with collections of strategies that are "best" in a much weaker sense: each player's assigned strategy is optimal as long as he believes that the other players will adopt the strategy assigned to them in the equilibrium. Put another way, if it is common knowledge that every player expects the other players to play the strategy assigned to them, then it is in fact optimal to play the assigned strategy. Such a collection of strategies constitutes a Nash equilibrium.

Unfortunately, static games will generally have many Nash equilibria. How rational players choose among these Nash equilibria remains an important unresolved problem. In some cases, one equilibrium may be naturally compelling, say because of some social convention. Such an equilibrium is a focal point equilibrium.

We concluded by examining games in which the natural strategies of the players are not finite and discrete, but infinite and continuous. We showed how to use calculus to calculate the player's best response functions and how to use these best response functions to find all the pure-strategy Nash equilibria that exist.

1.11   Further Reading

The original source for the concept of Nash equilibrium is John Nash's seminal paper "Non-Cooperative Games" (*Annals of Mathematics* 51 (1951), pp. 286–95). This paper also contains the first Nash equilibrium existence theorem. The paper can be understood by any reader who has taken an undergraduate course in real analysis. Our formal definition of a Nash equilibrium is taken from Binmore and Dasgupta, *Economic Organizations as Games* (Oxford: Basil Blackwell, 1986, pp. 4-5).

Douglas Bernheim has criticized Nash equilibrium as *the* solution concept for noncooperative games ("Rationalizable Strategic Behavior," *Econometrica*, July 1984, 52(4), pp. 1007-28.). The more technical parts of this paper are very difficult mathematically, but the introductory material can be understood by an advanced undergraduate. Robert Aumann has argued that the fundamental solution concept for noncooperative games is correlated equilibrium, not Nash equilibrium. ("Correlated equilibrium as an extention of Bayesian rationality," *Econometrica* 55 (1987), pp. 1–18.)

The notion of a focal point equilibrium was introduced by Thomas Schelling in his extremely readable and influential book, *The Strategy of Conflict* (London: Oxford University Press, 1960). This book is packed with ideas and shows the benefit of a strategic perspective in social and political analysis. It is remarkably free of technical jargon and highly recommended.

More general Nash equilibrium existence theorems exist for games in which the players have an infinite number of pure strategies (Irving Glicksburg, "A Further Generalization of the Kakutani Fixed Point Theorem with Application to Nash Equilibrium Points," *Proceedings of the American Mathematical Society*, February 1952, 3(1), pp. 170–74) and for games where the payoff function is discontinuous (Partha Dasgupta and Eric Maskin, "The Existence of Equilibrium in Discontinuous Economic Games I: Theory," *Review of Economic Studies*, January 1986, 53(1), pp. 1–26). Both the Glicksburg and the Dasgupta and Maskin results are considerably more difficult to apply than Nash's theorem and their proofs use very advanced mathematics.

Static games have become common in the field of political science, particularly in the subfield of international relations. An example of the better work in this area is Steven Brams and Mark Kilgour, *Game Theory and National Security* (Oxford: Basil Blackwell, 1988).

For a good nontechnical modern introduction to game theory, see *Thinking Strategically* by Avinash Dixit and Barry Nalebuff (New York: Norton, 1991).

Finally, one of the best introductions to evolutionary game theory is Maynard Smith's classic *Evolution and the Theory of Games* (Cambridge University Press, 1982).

1.12 Discussion Questions

1. Below are some of the games discussed in this chapter. Which are good descriptions of strategic situations that you have been involved with?
   a. Prisoner's Dilemma Game
   b. Coordination Game
   c. Battle of the Sexes Game

   In each case, how did you and the other players in this game act? Were your actions "rational"?

1.13 New Terms

Battle of the Sexes game
belief
best response
best response function
column player
cooperative and noncooperative game
  theory
coordination game

evolutionary game theory
evolutionary stable strategy (ESS)
focal point equilibrium
game theory
iterated strictly dominant strategy
iterated strictly dominant strategy
  equilibrium
iterated weakly dominant strategy

Nash equilibrium	static game
Pareto dominated	strategic decisions
Pareto optimal	strategic form
payoff table	strategy profile
payoff vector	strictly dominant strategy
payoffs	strictly dominant strategy equilibrium
players	strictly dominated
Prisoner's Dilemma	strictly dominates
pure strategies	weakly dominant strategy
row player	weakly dominant strategy equilibrium
second-order polynomials	weakly dominated
self-confirming	weakly dominates

1.14   Exercises

EXERCISE 1.1

Consider the Battle of the Sexes Game between Rhett and Scarlett in Section 1.7. Suppose the two players agree to abide by the toss of a coin: if the coin turns up heads, then they go to the saloon; if it turns up tails, they will go to the dinner club. Using a single coin toss to resolve a conflict such as this is an example of what Robert Aumann calls a *correlated equilibrium*.

Suppose their agreement to resolve their conflict with a coin toss *is not enforceable.* But they go ahead and toss the coin, which comes up heads. What do you predict will happen now, and why?

EXERCISE 1.2

The 31 members of the board of the Bid-a-Wee Corp. are about to take a secret ballot on whether to accept the merger proposal of Mammoth Inc. Each member can vote to *accept* the proposal, to *reject* the proposal, or to *abstain.* For the proposal to be accepted, 16 board members must vote to accept it. All the 31 board members care about is being on the winning side. That is, if the proposal is accepted, each member would prefer to have voted to accept it; and if the proposal is rejected, each member would prefer to have voted to reject it. Find the two Nash equilibria of this game. What do you predict the outcome will be, and why?

EXERCISE 1.3

The Guess the Mean Game is played as follows. Each of the N players writes on a piece of paper an integer between 1 and 10 without showing it to any other players. The players then reveal the numbers they have written down. The winner is that person whose number comes the closest to equaling *half the average of the number submitted by the other players.* For example, if there are four players and they write down the numbers 1, 3, 5, and 6, then the score for the first player is $|1 - \frac{1}{2} \cdot \frac{3+5+6}{3}| = 1.33$; the score for the second player is $|3 - \frac{1}{2} \cdot \frac{1+5+6}{3}| = 1$; the score for the third player is $|5 - \frac{1}{2} \cdot \frac{1+3+6}{3}| = 3.33$; and the score for the fourth player is $|6 - \frac{1}{2} \cdot \frac{1+3+5}{3}| = 4.5$. The winner is the second player. What is the unique Nash equilibrium of this game?

EXERCISE 1.4

There are three television stations in a city, each affiliated with one of the three major networks, ABC, CBS, and NBC. All three stations have the option of running the evening network news program at either 6:30 P.M. (a "live feed") or at 7:00 P.M. (a "taped-delayed broadcast"). Among network news viewers, 60% prefer to watch the news at 6:30 P.M. and 40% prefer to watch it at 7:00 P.M. due to competition at 6:30 P.M. with "Wheel of Fortune" on an independent station. In addition, head-to-head, ABC's news program is the most popular, CBS's is the second most popular, and NBC's is the least popular. The share of evening news viewers captured by each station as a function of when they show the news is given in Table 1.13. The stations' objective is to maximize their shares, since that determines the stations' ad revenue.

(a) Find all the dominated strategies.

(b) Eliminate the dominated strategies found in part (a) and find all the Nash equilibria of the simplified game.

EXERCISE 1.5

In 1943, Japanese Admiral Imamura was ordered to transport Japanese troops across the Bismark Sea to New Guinea. U.S. Admiral Kenney was ordered to

Table 1.13 **The Evening News Game**

ABC News: 6:30 P.M.		CBS News	
		6:30 P.M.	7:00 P.M.
NBC News 6:30 P.M.		(24%, 34%, 42%)	(23%, 40%, 37%)
7:00 P.M.		(40%, 26%, 34%)	(18%, 22%, 60%)

Payoffs: (NBC, CBS, ABC)

ABC News: 7:00 P.M.		CBS News	
		6:30 P.M.	7:00 P.M.
NBC News 6:30 P.M.		(26%, 34%, 40%)	(40%, 26%, 34%)
7:00 P.M.		(16%, 60%, 24%)	(24%, 34%, 42%)

Payoffs: (NBC, CBS, ABC)

Table 1.14 **The Battle of the Bismark Sea**

		Imamura		
		Short	Long	50/50
Kenney	Short	2, −2	2, −2	2.5, −2.5
	Long	1, −1	3, −3	2.5, −2.5
	50/50	2, −2	2, −2	2.5, −2.5

Payoffs: (Kenney, Imamura)

intercept Imamura's fleet and bomb the troop transports with his carrier-based bombers. Imamura had to choose among taking a two-day route to New Guinea ("short"), taking a longer three-day route ("long"), or sending half his ships on one route and half on the other ("50/50"). Kenney had to decide whether to send all of his planes to look for Imamura along the short route ("short"), to send all his planes to look for Imamura along the long route ("long"), or to split them ("50/50") and search both routes simultaneously. Once Imamura set out, he could not recall his ships. On the other hand, Kenney's planes returned to their carriers at the end of the day and could be reassigned on the following day. Use the game payoff matrix given in Table 1.14. This matrix assumes that Kenney's objective was to maximize the number of days his planes could bomb Imamura's ships, and Imamura's objective was to minimize the number of days of bombing.

(a) For each player, determine which strategies are: (1) strictly dominant, (2) strictly dominated, (3) weakly dominant, or (4) weakly dominated.

(b) Find all the Nash equilibria.

EXERCISE 1.6

The San Francisco 49ers and the New York Jets are in the Super Bowl. It is fourth down with 10 seconds left in the game. The score is New York 10, San Francisco 7, and San Francisco has possession of the ball 8 yards from the goal line. Neither team has any time-outs left, so this will be the last play of the game. San Francisco has two options: (1) kick a field goal (worth 3 points) and tie the game; or (2) go for the touchdown (worth 6 points) and either win or lose the game. Should San Francisco go for the touchdown, they will end up playing a static "Touchdown Game" with New York. The objective of each team is to maximize the probability of winning the game. The resulting payoff matrix is given in Table 1.15. Notice that New York wants to match its defense against San Francisco's offense, while San Francisco wants to avoid such a match.

Determine whether this game has Nash equilibrium in pure strategies. If you were the coach for San Francisco, what would you have the team do, and why? If you were the coach for New York, what would you have the team do, and why?

Table 1.15 **The Touchdown Game**

		San Francisco	
		Pass	Run
New York	Defend against the pass	50, 50	60, 40
	Defend against the run	90, 10	20, 80

Payoffs: (San Francisco, New York)

EXERCISE 1.7*

Prove that if a static game has an iterated strictly dominant strategy equilibrium, then this is the only Nash equilibrium for the game.

EXERCISE 1.8*

Show by counterexample that a static game with a *weakly* dominant strategy equilibrium may have other Nash equilibria.

EXERCISE 1.9*

An $m \times n$ game is a two-person static game in which the row player has exactly m pure strategies and the column player has exactly n pure strategies. When the row player chooses strategy i and the column player chooses strategy j, row player's payoff is denoted by $R(i, j)$ and column player's payoff is denoted $C(i, j)$. Prove that if a 2×2 game has a unique Nash equilibrium in pure strategies, then the equilibrium is also an iterated dominant strategy equilibrium. Show by counterexample that this proposition is false for 3×3 games.

EXERCISE 1.10*

Extend the definition of a best response function to continuous-strategy games that have more than two players. How can you characterize pure-strategy equilibria in this case?

EXERCISE 1.11

Two players are playing a static game in which the players' moves can be any positive real number. Find the best response function corresponding to each of the following two continuous payoff functions. Use the best response functions to find a pure-strategy Nash equilibrium.

$$U_A(Q_A, Q_B) = (10 - 2(Q_A + Q_B)) \cdot Q_A - (3Q_A + Q_A^2)$$
$$U_B(Q_A, Q_B) = (10 - 2(Q_A + Q_B)) \cdot Q_B - (3Q_B + Q_B^2)$$

*Indicates a difficult exercise.

EXERCISE 1.12

A law is passed requiring a monopolistic soft-drink producer to separate the production department and the marketing department. The marketing department chooses the price P to charge for a bottle of the firm's soft drink and the production department chooses the level of output, Q. The two departments are forbidden to discuss their decisions with each other and, therefore, move simultaneously. Employees in both departments own shares in the firm and want to maximize its profits, which equals $P \cdot S - \frac{1}{2}Q^2$, where S denotes the firm's sales. Sales cannot exceed the firm's output, nor can they exceed the market demand. Unsold output is thrown away. This means $S = \min\{Q, D(P)\}$, where

$$D(P) = \begin{cases} 6 - P & \text{if } P < 6 \\ 0 & \text{if } P \geq 6 \end{cases}$$

is the market demand.

(a) Show that one of the Nash equilibria of this Price/Output Coordination Game is for the production department to choose the monopoly output of $Q = 2$ and for the marketing department to choose the monopoly price of $P = 4$.

(b) Show that the following is also a Nash equilibrium: $P = 3 = Q = MC(Q)$, where $MC(Q)$ is the firm's marginal cost of production at the output level Q. Notice that at this equilibrium, the firm is behaving like a perfect competitor!

EXERCISE 1.13

Jenny and Jim are playing the static game whose payoff matrix is given in Table 1.16. Find each player's strictly and weakly dominated strategies. Show by example that the order in which the weakly dominated strategies are deleted alters the limiting set of iterated weakly dominant strategies.

Table 1.16 **Payoff Matrix for Exercise 1.13**

		Jenny	
		Left	Right
Jim	Top	(3, 2)	(2, 2)
	Middle	(1, 1)	(0, 0)
	Bottom	(0, 0)	(1, 1)

Payoffs: (Jim, Jenny)

CHAPTER 2

Oligopoly

2.1   Introduction

Economics is distinguished among the social sciences in having a unifying core of hypotheses: *greed, rationality,* and *equilibrium.* Economists assume that all decision makers, whether they be farmers, college students, business executives, or politicians, strive to maximize something. The goal may be to maximize crop yields, or grade point averages, profits, or votes. This is the sense in which they are "greedy." Economists assume decision makers are "rational" in the sense that they act so as to do the best they can given these constraints. This maximizing bent is constrained by resources. Decision makers interact through institutions that are assumed to be constantly moving the decision makers toward some sort of balance or equilibrium.

Economics students are first exposed to these ideas in most principles of economics courses in the study of perfectly competitive markets. There they learn how price-taking consumers form their consumption plans by maximizing utility subject to a budget constraint; how price-taking producers form their production decisions by maximizing profits subject to technological constraints; and how market prices adjust so as to equilibrate supply and demand. They are usually then shown how constrained optimization can also be used to study the joint price and output decisions of the monopolist.

Many important markets are neither perfectly competitive nor perfectly monopolized. Examples are automobiles, network television broadcasting, long-distance telephone service, high-performance military aircraft, and electric generating equipment, to name a few. These markets are usually called **oligopolistic** or **imperfectly competitive.** In oligopolistic markets, the pricing and production decisions of every firm in the industry have a significant effect on the profitability of its competitors. These firms are neither competitive price-takers nor monopolistic price-setters. Their prices and outputs are strategic choices in an **oligopoly game.** Unfortunately, when most principles textbooks cover this material, they are forced to skirt around it because of the need to use game-theoretic tools.

This is unfortunate not only because so many of these markets are very interesting, but also because their successful analysis has been one of the important achievements of game theory. Not surprisingly, the subfield of industrial organization, devoted to examining oligopolies, has been in the vanguard of the movement to rebuild economics on game-theoretic foundations. We will consider in this chapter three models of oligopolistic competition. The first is due to Augustin Cournot and assumes that firms choose their outputs simultaneously. This joint output is dumped onto a market and price adjusts so as to clear the market. The second model is due to Joseph Bertrand and assumes the firms choose their prices simultaneously and produce what is demanded. The third model is very recent and is credited to William Baumol, Robert Willig, and John Panzar; it focuses on the potential entry and exit of competitors and the constraints this places on apparent "monopolies."

2.2   The Cournot Game

In 1838, Augustin Cournot, one of the first mathematical economists, developed a model designed to explain how firms in industry structures ranging from duopoly to perfect competition would choose their output in an attempt to maximize profits. Two aspects of Cournot's model set it apart from much of the work in economics that was going on at that time. First, he presented his ideas in the form of a rigorous model in which assumptions were clearly laid out and explicit functional relations were specified. Second, each firm's profits depended on what the other firms chose to do. While Cournot's model preceded the invention of game theory per se, it was an important predecessor to the later work of von Neumann, Morgenstern, Nash, *et al.* In this section, we will present a game-theoretic reformulation of Cournot's original model.

In Cournot's model, the market price is determined by the total output produced by all the firms in an industry. No individual firm directly controls the market price, and all firms receive for their products exactly the same market price. In short (although Cournot would not have put it this way), price is not a strategic variable. Cournot also assumed that the products produced by all the firms are identical, and all outputs appear on the market simultaneously. The price for the product always equals the market clearing price. The Cournot model also assumes that the market price per unit of output, P, received by all firms is a decreasing function of the total output produced by all firms, Q_T, so that $Q_T = \sum_{i=1}^{n} Q_i$, where Q_i is the output of firm i. That is,

$$P = P(Q_T) \ and \ \frac{dP(Q_T)}{dQ_T} < 0 \qquad\qquad [2.1]$$

One implication of this model of price determination is that as one firm increases its output, it not only reduces the price it receives for its own output, but simultaneously reduces the price all other firms receive as well.

In order to see how Cournot's model works, we will consider the following hypothetical shrimping **duopoly.** A duopoly is a market with exactly two producers, in this case, Ms. Ky and Mr. Gump. Both sell their weekly shrimp catch, denoted Q_{Gump} and Q_{Ky}, every Friday at a dockside auction. Ky and Gump are the only two shrimpers who sell at this auction. The shrimp price set at this auction, denoted P, is given by:

$$P = \begin{cases} 1.90 - 0.10 \cdot Q_T & if \ 0 \leq Q_T \leq 19 \\ 0 & if \ Q_T > 19 \end{cases} \qquad\qquad [2.2]$$

where $Q_T = Q_{Gump} + Q_{Ky}$. The price of shrimp will be quoted in dollars per pound ($/lb.), output in thousands of pounds (1,000 lbs.), and firm revenue, cost, and profit in thousands of dollars ($1,000).

At the beginning of each week, the two shrimpers must decide how many shrimp to catch. The two shrimpers are concerned only with that period's profits. While they are at sea, the two shrimpers cannot monitor each other. As a result, when each decides how much shrimp to bring to market, they do so with no knowledge of each other's decision. This means the two players move simultaneously in game time. The capital they have invested in their boats and equipment is a **sunk cost,** that is, unrecoverable, and thus of no import in their subsequent decision making. The cost of catching and bringing shrimp to market is $1.00/lb. Therefore, the total cost (in thousands of dollars) to each shrimper is given by

$$TC_i = Q_i \quad for \ i = Gump, Ky \qquad\qquad [2.3]$$

Since production is costly, we can ignore output levels that are so high that the price is driven below $1, since such output levels are strictly dominated by producing nothing. It follows that profits for each shrimper can be written:

$$\pi_i(Q_{Gump}, Q_{Ky}) = (1.90 - 0.10 \cdot (Q_{Gump} + Q_{Ky})) \cdot Q_i - Q_i \quad for \ i = Gump, Ky$$
$$[2.4]$$

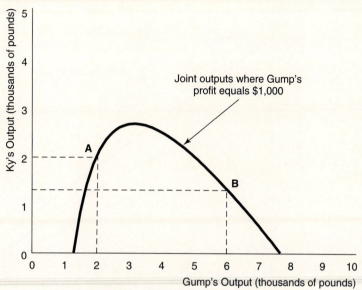

FIGURE 2.1   An isoprofit curve for Gump.

Putting it all together, Ky and Gump play a static game. A pure strategy in this game for each firm consists of a (nonnegative) output level and the payoffs are the profits determined by Eq. [2.4].

2.2.1 ISOPROFIT CURVES AND BEST RESPONSE FUNCTIONS

One way to visualize the two shrimpers' problem is to use isoprofit curves. Equation [2.4] makes it clear that the profit for one shrimper depends on the output of both. There are likely to be many output combinations for Ky and Gump that result in a given feasible level of profit for Gump. The same is true for Ky. Such combinations form an **isoprofit curve.**

Consider Gump. For a fixed level of profit $\overline{\pi}_{Gump}$, Equation [2.4] can be re-written as:

$$Q_{Ky} = 9 - \frac{10 \cdot \overline{\pi}_{Gump}}{Q_{Gump}} - Q_{Gump} \qquad [2.5]$$

For example, suppose we consider $\overline{\pi}_{Gump} = 1$ (which corresponds to profits of $1,000). One way Gump can earn $1,000 in profits is to catch and deliver 2,000 lbs. of shrimp (remember that this corresponds to $Q_{Gump} = 2$) and for Ky to deliver 2,000 lbs. ($Q_{Ky} = 2$). Another way is for Gump to deliver 6,000 lbs. of shrimp while Ky delivers 1,333 lbs. These two points on Gump's isoprofit curve are labeled A and B in Figure 2.1.

There is an isoprofit curve associated with every feasible level of profits for Gump. Four of them are shown in Figure 2.2.

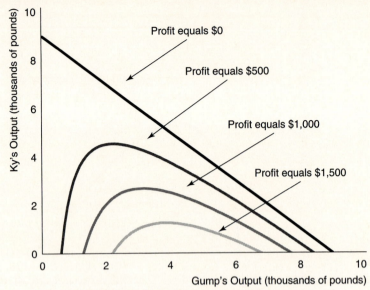

FIGURE 2.2 A set of isoprofit curves for Gump.

Notice that the $0-profit isoprofit curve lies above the $500-profit isoprofit curve, which lies above the $1,000-profit isoprofit curve, which lies above the $1,500-profit isoprofit curve. From this we deduce that isoprofit curves closer to the horizontal axis correspond to higher profits for Gump. We also see that, except for the $0-profit isoprofit curve, the curves are concave to the horizontal axis.

Suppose that Ky brought in 5,000 lbs. of shrimp last time and Gump believes she will do the same this time. What is Gump's best response? Consider Figure 2.3. Gump believes that he and Ky will end up at a point on the horizontal line $Q_{Ky} = 5$. The isoprofit curve that is associated with the highest level of profit Gump believes he can attain will be the curve that is tangent to this horizontal line. The tangency point is at $Q_{Gump} = 2$. At this point, Gump earns a profit of $400.

Of course, we can calculate Ky's isoprofit curves in a completely analogous manner. Because of the symmetry between the two shrimpers, Ky's isoprofit curves will be a reflection of Gump's curves around the 45° line through the origin. The $1,000-profit isoprofit curves for both Gump and Ky are drawn in Figure 2.4.

As we just saw, for any given value of Q_{Ky} the profit-maximizing output level for Gump will be found at the point where Gump's isoprofit curve is tangent to the horizontal line at the height Q_{Ky}. As you saw in Chapter 1, the collection of best responses by Gump to any given strategy by Ky is called Gump's *best response function*. Because Gump's profit function is a quadratic function of his own output, we know from Theorem 1.1 that we can find his best response function by taking

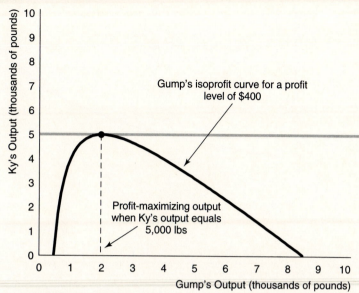

FIGURE 2.3 Gump's best response to his belief about Ky's output.

the partial derivative of Eq. [2.4] with respect to Q_{Gump} and finding the output level at which this derivative equals zero. This is shown in Eq. [2.6].

$$\frac{\partial \pi_{Gump}(Q_{Gump}, Q_{Ky})}{\partial Q_{Gump}} = 0.90 - 0.10 \cdot Q_{Ky} - 0.20 \cdot Q_{Gump} = 0. \qquad [2.6]$$

Solving for Gump's optimal output in terms of Ky's output gives us Gump's best response function:

$$Q_{Gump}^{BR}(Q_{Ky}) = 4.5 - 0.5 \cdot Q_{Ky}. \qquad [2.7]$$

Since the two firms have symmetric profit functions, Ky's best response function is identical.

$$Q_{Ky}^{BR}(Q_{Gump}) = 4.5 - 0.5 \cdot Q_{Gump}. \qquad [2.8]$$

The best response functions of both firms are graphed in Figure 2.5. Notice that both best response functions are bounded above by 4.5 (4,500 lbs.). That is, the best response by Gump to any output by Ky is to catch no more than 4,500 lbs. of shrimp and vice versa. In addition, holding Ky's output fixed at the level Q_{Ky}, Gump's profit is a strictly increasing function of his own output on the interval $[0, Q_{Gump}^{BR}(Q_{Ky})]$ and is a strictly decreasing function of his own output over the interval $[Q_{Gump}^{BR}(Q_{Ky}), +\infty]$.

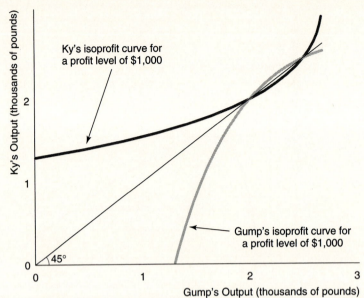

FIGURE 2.4 The $1,000-profit isoprofit curves for Ky and Gump.

2.2.2 COURNOT-NASH EQUILIBRIUM

What quantities will the two shrimpers choose? Cournot argued the two would choose the pair of outputs that correspond to the intersection of the two best response curves graphed in Figure 2.5. Such a pair of outputs is commonly called a **Cournot duopoly equilibrium** and is labeled A in the figure. At this point, both firms are catching and delivering to the shrimp market 3,000 lbs. of shrimp each week. There they are auctioned off for $1.30 per pound, earning each shrimper a pretax profit of $900. This pair of outputs is the unique Nash equilibrium of this game. The proof of this assertion is simple. The strategy profile $\{Q_{Gump}, Q_{Ky}\}$ is a Nash equilibrium if and only if each firm's strategy is profit maximizing *given* the strategy of the other. But this is possible if and only if the point (Q_{Gump}, Q_{Ky}) lies on both shrimpers' best response curves. The only such intersection point is (3, 3). So this is the unique pure-strategy Nash equilibrium. Since this is the Nash equilibrium of a Cournot game, we will refer to it hereafter as the **Cournot-Nash equilibrium.** This is not a new equilibrium concept. It is simply shorthand for the "Nash equilibrium of the Cournot Quantity-Setting Game."

2.2.3 STRONGER PROPERTIES OF THE COURNOT-NASH EQUILIBRIUM

To many people, choosing the Cournot equilibrium output seems risky. After all, this output level is optimal only if the opponent chooses to play his or her corresponding equilibrium strategy as well. Might it not be possible for the two players to rationalize other choices? Suppose neither player will ever choose a strictly dominated strategy, and each believes that his opponent will never choose a strictly dominated strategy as well. Then the game can be simplified by deleting

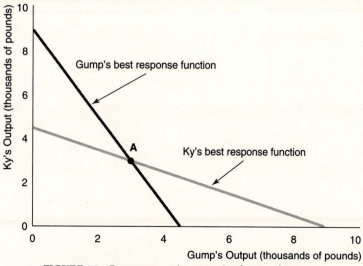

FIGURE 2.5 Best response functions for the two shrimpers.

these strictly dominated strategies. Suppose further that neither player will ever choose a strictly dominated strategy in the simplified game, and each believes the same of his opponent. Then the game can be simplified still further by deleting these strictly dominated strategies. Now suppose further . . . , and so forth. You get the idea. Neither player will ever choose any strategy that is deleted by this process of iterated deletion of strictly dominated strategies. We claim that such hyperrational players will be left with only one strategy: the Cournot-Nash output level. More technically, the Cournot-Nash output levels are iterated strictly dominant, and the Cournot game is solvable by iterated strict dominance.

We begin by searching for dominated strategies. Since both players can guarantee themselves zero profits by choosing zero output, any output level that guarantees a loss is strictly dominated by zero output. An output level above 19,000 lbs. is a case in point since it drives the price down to zero regardless of what the other shrimper does. But output levels far below 19,000 lbs. are strictly dominated as well. Recall from Section 2.2.2, there is no output Ky can choose that should induce Gump to choose an output greater than 4,500 lbs. Gump's profits at an output of 4,500 lbs. are strictly greater than his profits at any output higher than that, regardless of Ky's choice of output. This means that 4,500 lbs. of output strictly dominates any larger output. So the undominated strategies for both players lie in the interval [0, 4.5]. As long as both players are rational, they will never choose an output above 4.5. The two players' strictly dominated strategies are displayed in Figure 2.6.

If Gump is rational and believes that Ky is rational, then he will never expect Ky to produce more than 4,500 lbs. We now search for output levels that are strictly dominated *if we restrict Ky to playing an undominated strategy.* Figure 2.7 shows that if Ky's output is less than 4.5, then Gump's optimal response is always to produce *more* than 2.25. That is $Q^{BR}_{Gump}(Q_{Ky}) \geq 2.25$ if $Q_{Ky} \leq 4.5$.

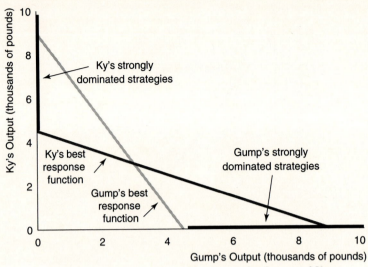

FIGURE 2.6 Strictly dominated strategies for Gump and Ky.

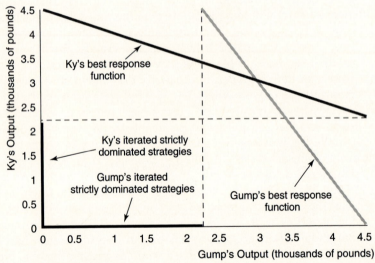

FIGURE 2.7 Strictly dominated strategies for Gump and Ky when each is constrained to playing undominated strategies.

So a rational conjecture for each player to have about the other is that he or she will never choose an output above 4.5 or below 2.25. We are now led to ask whether any strategies are now dominated when the opponent is restricted to choosing an output between 2.25 and 4.5. Compare Figure 2.8 with Figure 2.6. The identical reasoning that helped us find the first group of strictly dominated

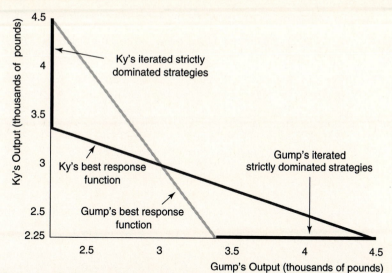

FIGURE 2.8 Strictly dominated strategies for Gump and Ky when each is constrained to playing a larger set of undominated strategies.

strategies leads to the conclusion that every output between 3.375 and 4.5 is now dominated by an output between 2.25 and 3.375.

Clearly we can continue doing this forever. What we end up with is the *iterated strictly dominant strategy* equilibrium for this game. Recall the definition from Chapter 1.

---

*A strategy is **iterated strictly dominant** for player* i *if and only if it is the only strategy in* $\overline{S}_i$, *where* $\overline{S}_i$ *is the intersection of the following sequence of nested sets of strategies: (1)* S_i^1 *consists of all of player* i*'s strategies that are not strictly dominated; (2) for* $n > 1$, S_i^n *consists of the strategies in* S_i^{n-1} *that are not strictly dominated when we restrict the other players* j $\neq$ i *to the strategies in* S_j^{n-1}.

We have shown that $S_{Gump}^1 = S_{Ky}^1 = [0, 4.5]$, $S_{Gump}^2 = S_{Ky}^2 = [2.25, 4.5]$, and $S_{Gump}^3 = S_{Ky}^3 = [2.25, 3.375]$. We assert (and you are asked in Exercise 2.4 to verify) that, in general, $S_{Ky} = S_{Gump}^n = [a_n, b_n]$, and that this sequence of intervals eventually shrinks to the single point (3, 3) the Nash equilibrium output level. This means the Nash equilibrium strategy profile {3,3} is the unique iterated strictly dominated strategy equilibrium of the Cournot Game.

2.2.4 EXPERIMENTAL EVIDENCE

0In 1990, three professors at Indiana University, Roy Gardner, Elinor Ostrom, and James Walker, conducted an experiment that sheds some empirical light on the

GAME THEORY IN ACTION: Avoiding the Prisoner's Dilemma

The Cournot-Nash equilibrium is similar to the equilibrium of the Prisoner's Dilemma introduced in Chapter 1—in both games the Nash equilibrium is Pareto dominated by another strategy profile. One way out of the Prisoner's Dilemma is to change the payoffs. Paradoxically a player may be able to improve the game outcome by *unilaterally reducing its own payoffs.* An instance in which this appears to have been done is reported by Sherer and Ross in their classic industrial organization textbook, *Industrial Market Structure and Economic Performance,* third edition (Boston: Houghton Mifflin, 1990, Chapter 6). The industry was that for large turbogenerators, in which there were only a few manufacturers, the two largest being General Electric Corporation (GE) and Westinghouse Corporation. This industy was convicted in the early 1960s of price-fixing in violation of federal antitrust laws. In 1963 General Electric announced that it would begin offering a "price protection" (sometimes also known as a "most favored customer" plan) to all buyers of its turbogenerators. This plan worked as follows: If GE gave a discount from its list price to any buyer of its turbogenerators, it would retroactively grant the same discount to all buyers who had taken delivery within the previous six months. In effect, GE made it very expensive to lower its prices from its publicly posted ones! Let us call charging the list price *cooperation* and giving a discount from the list price *defection.* By instituting the "price protection" plan GE unilaterally reduced the payoff from defection. As a result, it made the cooperative solution more likely. Although doing this unilaterally appears to be a very risky strategy—if GE's rivals cut their prices, it will be very costly to follow them—in fact it wasn't risky at all. GE and the other turbogenerator manufacturers were not actually playing a one-shot static game, but a *repeated* game in which future profits mattered. In the face of price-cutting by rival firms, GE always had the option of dropping its "price protection plan" and converting the payoffs back to their earlier values. In fact, its main rival, Westinghouse, adopted a similar "price protection" plan of its own the following year. Of course, this reduced its payoff from defection. The strategy appears to have worked because both GE and Westinghouse maintained these plans until they were forced to abandon them by the government in 1976.

behavior of people in a Cournot-type setting. They gathered groups of eight participants and gave each individual within the group ten tokens. Each token could be redeemed for 5 cents or it could be sold on a market. The value of each token sold on the market—that is, its price—was determined by how many tokens all eight participants chose to put up for sale. Specifically,

$$P = 23 - 0.25 \cdot \sum_{i=1}^{8} Q_i$$

where Q_i is the quantity put up by the ith participant, and P is the value of every token put up for sale (in cents per token).

Since the participants were required to choose between selling their tokens on this market and just cashing them in for 5 cents, there is an opportunity cost of 5 cents for each token put up for sale. Hence, the profit for any participant, j, for selling tokens in this market equals:

$$\pi_j = \left(23 - 0.25 \cdot \sum_{i=1}^{8} Q_i\right) \cdot Q_j - 5 \cdot Q_j.$$

It is left as an exercise for you to show that the unique Nash equilibrium of the resulting Cournot Game is for each participant to sell eight tokens on this market (and cash in the other two for 5 cents). The result is a price per token sold on the market of 7 cents. If all eight had colluded, they could have maximized their collective earnings by selling only 36 of their collective tokens for 14 cents apiece.

The surplus the participants earn over their original endowment is given by:

$$\text{Total surplus} = (P - 5) \cdot \overline{Q} = (18 - 0.25 \cdot \overline{Q}) \cdot \overline{Q}$$

where $\overline{Q} = \sum_{i=1}^{8} Q_i$. The maximum possible surplus from colluding is 324 cents. If the participants behave as Cournot-Nash competitors, they earn a surplus of 128 cents, which is about 40% of the maximum. In 18 trials of this experiment, each trial having eight participants, the average surplus attained was 36% of the maximum possible, which is very close to the Cournot-Nash prediction.

2.2.5 PERFECT COMPETITION AS THE LIMITING CASE OF THE COURNOT GAME

We began this chapter by claiming that oligopoly is a market structure that lies between the two extreme poles of monopoly and perfect competition. We can now show something stronger—that monopoly and perfect competition can be viewed as special cases of the more general Cournot Game. It is easy to see that if the industry consists of exactly one firm, then the Cournot Game simply collapses to the standard model of a profit-maximizing monopolist. Less obviously, as the number of firms in the industry grows and the market share of each shrinks to zero, the Cournot-Nash equilibrium converges to that predicted by the standard model of perfect competition. The perfectly competitive equilibrium is displayed in Figure 2.9.

Suppose that instead of only two shrimpers, there are N, with the same costs as Ky and Gump and facing the same industry demand curve. We will number the shrimpers from 1 to N and refer to the output of the ith shrimper by Q_i. Total industry output is Q_T and $Q_{-i} = Q_T - Q_i$ is the output produced by all the shrimpers *except* i. The profit of the ith shrimper is now given by:

$$\pi_i(Q_1, \ldots, Q_N) = P(Q_T) \cdot Q_i - Q_i$$

$$= \begin{cases} (1.90 - 0.10 \cdot Q_T) \cdot Q_i - Q_i & \text{if } Q_T < 19 \\ -Q_i & \text{if } Q_T \geq 19 \end{cases}$$

$$= \begin{cases} (0.9 - 0.1 \cdot (Q_i + Q_{-i})) \cdot Q_i & \text{if } Q_i < 19 - Q_{-i} \\ -Q_i & \text{if } Q_i \geq 19 - Q_i. \end{cases} \qquad [2.9]$$

The last two lines of the expression in Eq. [2.9] show that the ith shrimper cannot make a positive profit whenever the output of the rest of the industry, Q_{-i}, is greater than 9. So

$$Q_i^{BR}(Q_1, \ldots, Q_N) = \begin{cases} 0 & \text{if } Q_{-i} \geq 9 \\ ? & \text{if } Q_{-i} < 9. \end{cases} \qquad [2.10]$$

Since $Q_{-i} < 9$ implies $10 < 19 - Q_{-i}$, the optimal response when $Q_{-i} < 9$ and $Q_i < 9$ is found by solving for the first-order condition for a maximum of π_i with respect to Q_i. That is,

$$\frac{\partial \pi_i(Q_i^*, Q_{-i})}{\partial Q_i} = 0.90 - 0.10 \cdot Q_{-i} - 0.20 \cdot Q_i^* = 0 \qquad [2.11]$$

or

$$Q_i^{BR}(Q_1, \ldots, Q_N) = \begin{cases} 0 & \text{if } Q_{-i} \geq 9 \\ \dfrac{9 - Q_{-i}}{2} & \text{if } Q_{-i} < 9. \end{cases} \qquad [2.12]$$

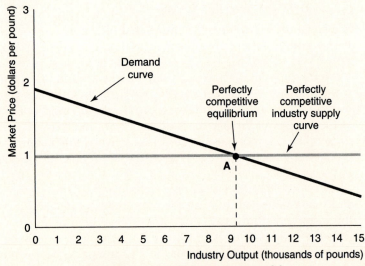

FIGURE 2.9 Perfectly competitive model.

A Nash equilibrium is the strategy profile, $\{Q_1^*, \ldots, Q_N^*\}$ such that $Q_i^* = Q_i^{BR}(Q_1^*, \ldots, Q_N^*)$ is satisfied for each of the N shrimpers. Since the shrimpers are identical, a natural equilibrium to search for is the **symmetric Nash equilibrium,** at which $Q_i^* \equiv Q^*$. At this equilibrium, $Q_{-i}^* = (N - 1) \cdot Q^*$, $Q_T^* = N \cdot Q^*$, and

$$Q^* = \frac{9 - (N - 1) \cdot Q^*}{2}$$

or $Q^* = \dfrac{9}{1 + N}$. As the number of firms increases, the market share of each goes to zero. Equilibrium industry output is $\dfrac{9N}{1 + N}$, which increases to the perfectly competitive output of 9,000 lbs. of shrimp per week as the number of firms becomes arbitrarily large. Since the Cournot Game assumes that market price always clears the market, it immediately follows that the market price falls to the perfectly competitive market price as the number of firms increases without limit.

2.3   The Bertrand Game

As you might suspect, there have been many criticisms levied at the Cournot model. One of the most serious is that firms in the real world usually choose their own *prices* and the consumers determine the firms' sales. This assumption forms the basis of the oligopoly model developed by Joseph Bertrand. Since the Cournot model assumes that the quantity each firm produces affects the market price, you might think price competition is already built into the Cournot model. So you might think that adding explicit price competition does not alter the outcome much. We will now show this is far from true.

In order to illustrate the difference between Bertrand and Cournot competition, consider a duopoly in the bleach industry. We will suppose that both firms in this market, Snow White Inc. (SW) and The Milky Way Inc. (MW), announce prices without knowing what price the other firm will announce. Once announced, however, the firm must sell bleach to whoever wants to buy it at that price. Any positive real number can be chosen. Costs for either firm are common knowledge. Since all bleach is identical, it is reasonable to suppose that consumers will want to buy their bleach from the firm charging the lowest price. If both firms announce the same price, then they split the market equally. The resulting static game is called the **Bertrand Game.**

In order to simplify the analysis, we will assume that both firms have constant marginal costs of 25 cents ($0.25) per quart of bleach, neither firm has any fixed costs, and there is a positive demand for bleach at a price of $0.25.

Imagine the thought process for the manager of Snow White. If she thinks Milky Way will choose a price that is above their common marginal cost, then it is in her best interest to charge a price just slightly below the price of her rival. That way, she will capture the entire market. Since price exceeds marginal cost (which is constant), she will earn additional profits on each quart of bleach sold. Had she chosen a price higher than the price of her rival, she would not have sold any bleach and would have earned no profits. Charging a price identical to her rival means that she will only sell bleach to half the market. Since each firm knows the other firm will be best served by charging a price slightly below their rival's, the only Nash equilibrium price is $0.25. Notice that we needed to know virtually nothing about the demand function for bleach to get this result.

Contrast the outcome of the Bertrand equilibrium with the Cournot equilibrium presented earlier. Is it any wonder firms dislike price competition and prefer to compete against each other in terms of product characteristics, advertising, and market share?

2.3.1 THE BERTRAND GAME WITH CAPACITY CONSTRAINTS

As with the Cournot Game, the unrealistic static nature of the Bertrand Game can only be relaxed once we have the tools needed to analyze such dynamic games. One assumption, however, that can be relaxed is the notion that firms have unlimited productive capacity.

Suppose that the two firms have a constant marginal cost up to a capacity of 500 quarts of bleach per minute. Obviously, the choice of capacity level is itself an interesting strategic choice, but not one with which we will concern ourselves here. The firms are completely incapable of producing beyond this level of capacity. Since we are not interested here in the choice of capacity level, we will ignore the costs of acquiring this capacity. We will treat it as a sunk cost. The total cost for either firm is given by:

$$C_i = \begin{cases} 0.25 \cdot Q_i & \text{for } 0 \le Q_i \le 0.5 \\ +\infty & \text{for } Q_i > 0.5 \end{cases} \quad \text{for } i = SW, MW \qquad [2.13]$$

where Q_i is measured in thousands of quarts of bleach produced per minute and cost is measured in thousands of dollars per minute. If both firms were constrained to charge the same price, the market demand for bleach would be given (in its inverse form) by:

$$P = \begin{cases} 2.00 - (Q_{SW} + Q_{MW}) & \text{if } Q_{SW} + Q_{MW} \le 2 \\ 0 & \text{if } Q_{SW} + Q_{MW} > 2 \end{cases} \qquad [2.14]$$

where P is measured in dollars per quart. We leave it as an exercise for you to show that a profit-maximizing monopolist with no capacity constraints would produce an output of 0.875 units and charge a price of $1.125. In the absence of any capacity constraints, a Bertrand duopoly will charge a price exactly equal to the marginal cost of $0.25.

The existence of capacity constraints makes it necessary to model how goods are allocated among consumers when there is excess demand. While there are many plausible models, we will choose one that is both widely used by economists and easy to work with. When there is an excess demand for a firm's product at the price the firm has chosen to charge, those consumers with the highest willing-

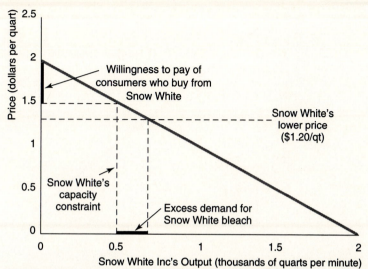

FIGURE 2.10 The rationing of consumers when there is excess demand for Snow White's cheaper bleach.

ness to pay for that product are the ones who end up with it. For example, if Snow White were to charge a price of $1.20 and Milky Way were to charge a price of $1.30, then *initially* consumers would demand 0.8 units of bleach from Snow White. But Snow White can only supply 0.5 units, so there will be an excess demand for bleach. We will assume the 0.5 units supplied by Snow White will go to the consumers willing to pay the most for it. As Figure 2.10 shows, these consumers are those willing to pay at least $1.50. They will end up buying it from Snow White for $1.20.[1] The rest of the consumers will have to buy the bleach from Milky Way at its higher price of $1.30.

Now consider Milky Way's perspective. Maintaining our assumption from above, that Milky Way's price is above Snow White's price, the demand facing Milky Way left over after Snow White has satisfied the customers lucky enough to purchase bleach at the lower price equals

$$P^R = \begin{cases} 1.50 - Q_{MW} & \text{if } Q_{MW} \le 1.50 \\ 0 & \text{if } Q_{MW} > 1.50. \end{cases} \qquad [2.15]$$

Milky Way can't sell anything at a price above $1.50 and its sales go up by 0.1 units with every $0.10 reduction in its price. For example, at a price of $1.30 Milky Way could expect to sell 0.2 units. Equation [2.15], which summarizes algebraically what we have just said, is called the **residual demand curve** for Milky Way.

_____

[1] What is likely to happen, of course, is that these consumers will end up spending something to move themselves to the front of the queue. This will take the form of outright bribes to suppliers, time spent locating supplies in stores, and so on.

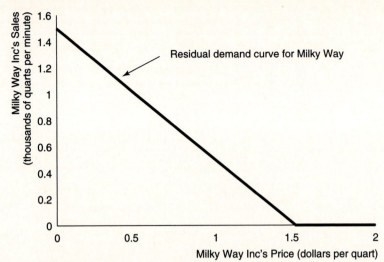

FIGURE 2.11 The residual demand curve for Milky Way when there is an excess demand for Snow White's cheaper bleach.

Eq. [2.15] is graphed in Figure 2.11. If Milky Way were to charge a price lower than that of Snow White, then Milky Way would sell to the consumers with the highest willingness to pay and Snow White would face the residual demand curve. We will find it convenient to express the residual demand curve as

$$Q_{MW}^R = \begin{cases} 1.5 - P_{MW} & \text{if } P_{SW} < P_{MW} \le \$1.50 \\ 0 & \text{if } P_{SW} < P_{MW} > \$1.50. \end{cases} \qquad [2.16]$$

Equation [2.17] displays Milky Way's sales as a function of the price both firms choose. Equation [2.18] is its profit function. This profit function is plotted in Figure 2.12.

$$Q_{MW}(P_{MW}, P_{SW}) = \begin{cases} \min\{1.5 - P_{MW}, 0.5\} & \text{if } P_{SW} < P_{MW} \le \$1.50 \\ \frac{1}{2} \min\{2 - P_{MW}, 0.5\} & \text{if } P_{MW} = P_{SW} \le \$2.00 \\ \min\{2 - P_{MW}, 0.5\} & P_{MW} < P_{SW} \text{ and } P_{MW} \le \$2.00 \\ 0 & \text{otherwise.} \end{cases}$$

$$[2.17]$$

This equation reads that, when Milky Way sets its price above that of Snow White, its sales are constrained by the lesser of the residual demand and the capacity constraint. If both firms choose the same price, sales are constrained by the lesser of half of the market demand at the price chosen or the capacity constraint. And, if Milky Way sets its price below that of Snow White, its sales will be constrained by the lesser of market demand and capacity.

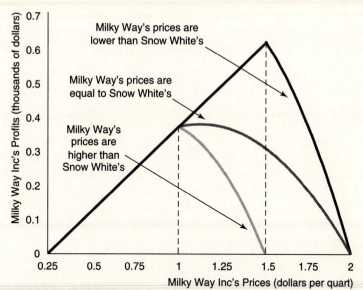

FIGURE 2.12 Milky Way's profit function depending on whether its price is above, equal to, or below Snow White's price.

$$\pi_{MW}(P_{MW}, P_{SW}) = \begin{cases} (P_{MW} - 0.25) \cdot \min\{1.50 - P_{MW}, 0.50\} \\ \qquad\qquad \text{if } P_{SW} < P_{MW} \leq \$1.50 \\ \frac{1}{2}(P_{MW} - 0.25) \cdot \min\{2.00 - P_{MW}, 0.50\} \\ \qquad\qquad \textit{if } P_{MW} = P_{SW} \leq \$2.00 \\ (P_{MW} - 0.25) \cdot \min\{2.00 - P_{MW}, 0.50\} \\ \qquad\qquad \textit{if } P_{MW} < P_{SW} \textit{ and } P_{MW} \leq \$2.00 \\ 0 \qquad\qquad \textit{otherwise.} \end{cases} \quad [2.18]$$

This profit function follows directly from Eq. [2.17] and the fact that profits equal the difference between price and average cost multiplied by the quantity sold.

We begin by searching for dominated strategies. Two sets of strategies are immediately apparent: charging a price below marginal cost (which guarantees losses) and charging a price above the highest consumer willingness to pay (which guarantees no sales). The undominated strategies, therefore, lie in the interval [$0.25, $2.00]. We will hereafter confine ourselves to prices in this interval.

We will now construct Milky Way's best response function. As Figure 2.12 suggests, there are three cases to consider: (1) $0.25 \leq P_{SW} \leq \$1.00$, (2) $\$1.00 < P_{SW} \leq \$1.50$, and (3) $\$1.50 < P_{SW}$.

If Milky Way believes Snow White will choose a price within the closed interval [$0.25, $1.00], what is Milky Way's best response? At least 1.0 units are demanded at any price in this range, which is greater than or equal to the combined capacity of the two firms. As a result, if Milky Way chooses a price in this

Table 2.1 *The Beginnings of Milky Way's Best Response Function*

Snow White's Price	Milky Way's Best Response
$\$0.25 \leq P_{SW} \leq \$1.00$	$P_{MW} = \$1.00$

range, it will sell its capacity output of 0.5 units whether its price is above, below, or equal to Snow White's. So it maximizes its profit among the prices in this interval by charging a price of \$1.00. When Milky Way charges a price above \$1.00, it begins to move along its residual demand curve. Although profit per unit is increasing, the firm is selling fewer units. As Figure 2.12 shows, the effect of the decline in sales more than offsets the increase in the profit margin, and profits fall. So \$1.00 is the optimal price to charge. We have recorded this part of Milky Way's best response function in Table 2.1.

If Milky Way believes Snow White will choose a price within the half-open interval [\$1.00, \$1.50], what is Milky Way's best response? Figure 2.13 displays Milky Way's profit function in this case. The optimal strategy is to charge a price just below Snow White's price, $P_{SW} - \varepsilon$, and sell its capacity output of 0.5 units. The reason is simple. If Milky Way charges a price below $P_{SW} - \varepsilon$, it reduces its profit margin without increasing its sales, since it is already at capacity. If Milky Way increases its price to P_{SW}, then the two firms split the market and its sales fall to $\frac{1}{2}(2 - P_{SW})$. This is less than Milky Way's capacity of 0.5 since we are assuming

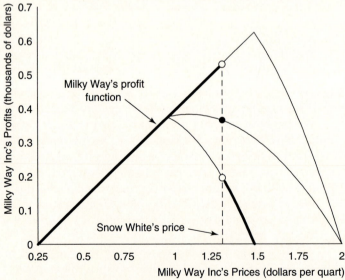

FIGURE 2.13 Milky Way's profit function when Snow White charges a price between \$1.00 and \$1.50.

Table 2.2   **More of Milky Way's Best Response Function**

Snow White's Price	Milky Way's Best Response
$0.25 \leq P_{SW} \leq \$1.00$	$P_{MW} = \$1.00$
$\$1.00 < P_{SW} \leq \$1.50$	$P_{MW} = P_{SW} - \varepsilon$ (where ε is arbitrarily small)

that $\$1.00 < P_{SW}$. If Milky Way charges a price slightly above Snow White's, say to $P_{SW} + \varepsilon$, its sales fall even more to $1.5 - (P_{SW} + \varepsilon))$, which is again strictly less than 0.5 if ε is small enough. By choosing ε small enough, we can ensure that

$$0.5 \cdot (P_{SW} - \varepsilon - 0.25) > (1.50 - (P_{SW} + \varepsilon))(P_{SW} + \varepsilon - 0.25) \qquad [2.19]$$

$$0.5 \cdot (P_{SW} - \varepsilon - 0.25) > \tfrac{1}{2}(2.00 - P_{SW})(P_{SW} - 0.25),$$

which shows that the optimal strategy is to charge the price $P_{SW} - \varepsilon$. Table 2.2 records what we know so far about Milky Way's best response function.

Finally, suppose Snow White charges a price above $1.50. At this price, if Snow White's price is below Milky Way's then Snow White captures the whole market and Milky Way's sales are zero. Figure 2.14 shows that the profit-maximizing strategy is to charge a price of $1.50, thereby capturing the whole market, and selling its capacity output of 0.5 units.

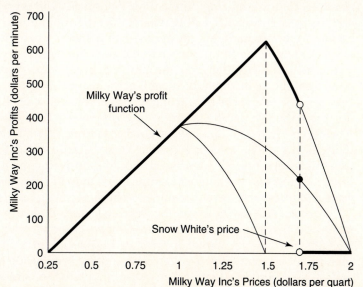

FIGURE 2.14   Milky Way's profit function when Snow White charges a price above $1.50.

*Table 2.3   **All of Milky Way's Best Response Functions***

Snow White's Price	Milky Way's Best Response
$\$0.25 \leq P_{SW} \leq \$1.00$	$P_{MW} = \$1.00$
$\$1.00 < P_{SW} \leq \$1.50$	$P_{MW} = P_{SW} - \varepsilon$ (where ε is arbitrarily small)
$\$1.50 < P_{SW}$	$P_{MW} = \$1.50$

Milky Way's best response function is recorded in Table 2.3 and plotted in Figure 2.15. Since the two firms are identical, Snow White's best response is simply the mirror image of Milky Way's flipped around the 45° line through the origin. The only intersection point is at the price $1.00. So this is the Nash equilibrium price. At this price, both firms sell their capacity output of 0.5 units and earn profits of $500 (per minute). The existence of capacity constraints allows duopolists engaged in Bertrand competition to earn profits after all! Furthermore, it brings the Bertrand and Cournot results into greater accord. We leave it as an exercise for you to show that the same equilibrium outcome would result if both firms behaved as capacity-constrained Cournot competitors.

2.4   Contestable Monopoly

Until recently, there was near unanimity that monopolized markets were inefficient. A profit-maximizing, single-price monopolist will set price above marginal cost. As a result, the price will be greater than the minimum required to induce the monopoly to voluntarily supply the good. In economic jargon, the monopolist earns *economic rents*. At the output chosen by the monopolist, the marginal social benefit of an additional unit (the height of the demand curve) will exceed the marginal social cost of producing that unit (the height of the marginal cost curve). The divergence between marginal social benefit and marginal social cost results in the inefficiency.

Over the last decade, a group of economists led by William Baumol, John Panzar, and Robert Willig have argued that firms in what they call **contestable markets** are unable to earn economic rents because of the threat of entry from **potential competitors.** Furthermore, should the government institute policies that artificially increase the number of firms in the industry, the result would be higher costs and prices and lower consumer welfare.

A *contestable market* is one for which: (1) an unlimited number of potential firms exist that can produce the (homogeneous) product with a common technology; (2) entry into the market does not involve a sunk cost, that is, an expenditure that cannot be completely recovered should the firm decide to leave the market; and (3) firms are price-setting Bertrand competitors. A **contestable monopoly** is a contestable market with a Nash equilibrium in which exactly one firm supplies

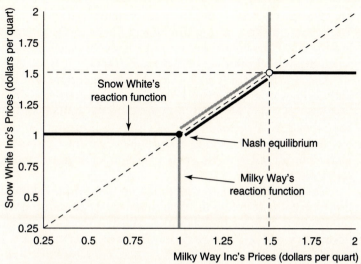

FIGURE 2.15 Milky Way's and Snow White's best response functions.

the entire market. In a contestable monopoly, since the threat of entry drives monopoly rents to zero, the firm will produce the greatest output at which it remains financially viable. This is referred to as a *second-best* output. This means that although marginal benefit does not equal marginal cost, it is as close as is possible without government subsidies to the monopoly.

For an example of a contestable market, consider the provision of scheduled passenger airline service between Cleveland and Kansas City. The inputs for providing this service are gates at both the Cleveland and Kansas City airports, a flight crew, fuel, and an airplane. Although the capital rental cost of the plane is a fixed cost to the firm, it is not a sunk cost. Should an airline decide to leave this market, it can either use its planes on other routes or it can lease the planes to other airlines through a large, international airplane leasing market.

We will suppose there are two firms currently capable of providing regular service on this route, Midwest Airlines and Air Express. Q_M will denote the number of passengers carried on Midwest's planes (in thousands per month) and P_M will be Midwest's ticket price (in dollars per person); Q_X will denote the number of passengers carried on Air Express's planes and P_X will be the airline's ticket price. The cost of carrying Q passengers (in thousands per month) is the same on both airlines and equals (in thousands of dollars per month)

$$C(Q) = \begin{cases} 25 + 100 \cdot Q & \text{for } Q > 0 \\ 0 & \text{for } Q = 0. \end{cases}$$

The market demand curve is given by:

$$P(Q) = 155 - 10 \cdot Q.$$

The average cost curve and the market demand curve are plotted in Figure 2.16. The average cost curve is declining and intersects the demand curve at an output level of 5,000 passengers per month. This volume of airline service is demanded when the market price equals $105 per ticket.

Consumers want to buy a ticket from the airline offering the lowest price. If both airlines offer the same price, then consumers initially choose between the two airlines randomly. Both airlines have the option of limiting the number of seats they sell. A customer turned away from one airline can immediately try to buy a ticket from the other. Should either airline choose to withdraw from the market, it can sell or sublease its planes to another airline and eliminate its fixed operating costs.

The two airlines play a modified Bertrand price-setting game. The modification is that after the two firms simultaneously announce their prices, which they cannot then change, they simultaneously announce the maximum number of tickets they will sell. A strategy for firm i consists of a price, P_i, and a ticket sales limit, T_i. The latter depends on the prices announced by both firms.

We claim this game has exactly two Nash equilibria. In both equilibria, both firms quote a price of $105 per ticket. In one equilibrium, Midwest Airline's ticket limit policy is: sell no tickets if Air Express also announces a $105 price; otherwise, sell to all customers. Air Express's ticket policy is to sell to all customers no matter what price Midwest Airlines announces. In the second equilibrium, the ticket limit policies are exactly the reverse. Both outcomes are examples of a contestable monopoly in which service is provided by only one firm, but the monopolist earns zero profit.

We will now prove these two strategy profiles are Nash equilibria. Because of the symmetry between the two airlines, if one of the strategy profiles is a Nash

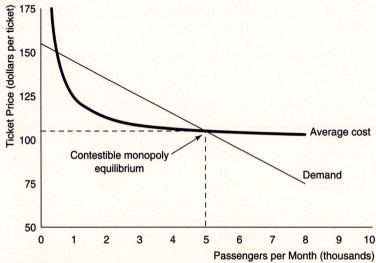

FIGURE 2.16 Hypothetical average cost and market demand for passenger airline travel between Cleveland and Kansas City.

equilibrium, then so is the other. So we can limit ourselves to showing that the first strategy profile—in which Midwest withdraws from the market and Air Express stays in—is a Nash equilibrium. In equilibrium, both firms earn zero profits. So we must show that neither firm can make positive profits given the strategy of the other.

Consider Midwest Airlines first. Given Air Express's strategy, if Midwest announces a price above $105, it will sell no tickets and (after subleasing its planes) make no profits, either. If Midwest announces a price of $105, then it will sell fewer than 5,000 tickets. Since its average costs are declining, $AC(Q_M) > AC(5000)$ = $105 per passenger, where AC is the average cost function of the two firms. Midwest will take losses unless it refuses to sell any tickets. Finally, if Midwest announces a price below $105 then, as Figure 2.16 shows, the firm will also take a loss unless it refuses to sell any tickets. So Midwest's strategy is an optimal response to that of Air Express. The proof that Air Express cannot improve on its equilibrium strategy is similar and is left as an exercise.

2.5 Summary

This chapter presented two of the most widely used models for market structures that fall between the extremes of perfect competition and perfect monopoly—so-called "oligopolistic markets." The Cournot Game assumes that firms simultaneously set their level of output and then sell all of it at the market-clearing price. In a Cournot oligopoly, the firms will earn positive profits in equilibrium and the price will be above both marginal and average cost. When there is only one firm, the Cournot Game collapses to the classical model of monopoly. At the other extreme, as the number of Cournot competitors increases without bound, the Cournot-Nash equilibrium converges to that predicted by the classical model of perfect competition. So the Cournot Game provides a bridge between the extremes of monopoly and perfect competition.

One problem with the Cournot Game is its assumption that the oligopolists are price-takers rather than price-makers. An alternative model of oligopoly, the Bertrand Game, assumes that firms simultaneously set their prices and produce whatever consumers demand, constrained perhaps by capacity. In a Bertrand duopoly with no capacity constraints, both firms will break even in equilibrium. This is in stark contrast to the prediction of the Cournot model that the equilibrium price will be above both marginal and average cost. When we add capacity constraints to the Bertrand game, however, its predictions about output and price are similar to those of the Cournot game.

We concluded by looking at a special form of Bertrand competition, called a contestable monopoly. A contestable monopoly is characterized by many *potential* firms, free entry and exit, Bertrand competition, and declining average cost. In equilibrium, the good is produced by only one firm, but this firm supplies it at its average cost and earns no economic profit.

Both the Cournot and Bertrand models have been criticized for their lack of realism—in particular, their assumption that the products are homogeneous and the firms meet only once. Predictions about the prices rational firms will choose turn out to be sensitive to whether or not these two assumptions hold. But relaxing the assumption that the interaction is static (or that the firms are extremely myopic) and allowing for repeated interactions requires the new techniques introduced in Part II.

2.6   Further Reading

The first translation of Cournot's original work was completed by Nathaniel T. Bacon and is entitled *Researches into the Mathematical Principles of the Theory of Wealth* (1st French ed., 1838; English trans. by Nathaniel T. Bacon, 1897, New York, 1927). Cournot's model has been extended in a wide variety of directions, one of which you will see in Chapter 3. An extremely good, although fairly advanced, treatment of the Cournot model can be found in Jean Tirole's *The Theory of Industrial Organization* (Cambridge, MA: MIT Press, 1988, Chapter 5).

With a good course or two in French, as well as a fairly heavy dose of mathematical training, you can try Joseph Bertrand's major contribution to the economics profession, "Théorie Mathématique de la Richesse Sociale" (*Journal des Savants*, 1883, pp. 499–508).

Much of the early work of contestable markets has been summarized in W. Baumol, J. Panzar, and R. Willig, *Contestable Markets and the Theory of Industry Structure* (New York: Harcourt Brace Jovanovich, 1982). Aside from Tirole's text cited earlier, another excellent treatment of the strategic nature of oligopolistic behavior is contained in James Friedman's *Oligopoly Theory* (Cambridge University Press, 1983).

2.7   Discussion Questions

1. Give examples of real products or services for which the Cournot model might be a good approximation.

2. Give examples of real products or services for which the Bertrand model might be a good approximation.

3. If you were to relax the assumptions of the Cournot model one by one, which would you begin with?

4. If you were to relax the assumptions of the Bertrand model one by one, which would you begin with?

5. Are most passenger airline routes good examples of contestable markets? Why or why not? What might serve as barriers to entry? What might serve as barriers to exit?

6. Can you think of a real-world contestable monopoly?

2.8   New Terms

Bertrand Game
contestable markets
contestable monopoly
Cournot duopoly equilibrium
Cournot Game
Cournot-Nash equilibrium
duopoly
imperfectly competitive

isoprofit curve
oligopolistic
oligopoly game
potential competitors
residual demand curve
sunk costs
symmetric Nash equilibrium

2.9   Exercises

EXERCISE 2.1

Two airlines, Airgo and Flyme, compete against each other on the route between Cleveland and Minneapolis. Each day they must decide on the number of discount seats to offer on this route. The number of seats offered by Airgo is S_A and the number offered by Flyme is S_F. The market-determined discount price, P, depends on the total number of seats offered by both airlines, $S_A + S_F$ according to the equation: $P = \$200 - \$0.10 \cdot (S_A + S_F)$. The marginal cost of flying a passenger on this route equals \$100 for Airgo and \$50 for Flyme. Determine: (a) The profit function of each airline, (b) the best response function of each airline, and (c) the Nash equilibrium.

EXERCISE 2.2

Two stores selling bottled water, Sweetwater and Goodwater, are located at the ends of a mile-long road. Customers are uniformly distributed along this road. This means that D equals the proportion of customers who live within D miles of Sweetwater and $1 - D$ equals the proportion who live within $1 - D$ miles of Goodwater. Sweetwater charges P_S per bottle and Goodwater charges P_G per bottle. Every customer buys one bottle of water per month regardless of the price charged. But because traveling to either store is costly, the prices charged do affect *where* the customer buys water. A customer located a distance D from Sweetwater and $1 - D$ from Goodwater will buy from Sweetwater if and only if $P_S + D < P_G + (1 - D)$; otherwise, the customer buys from Goodwater. Since customers provide their own bottles, the marginal cost of providing water is zero.

(a) Determine the location of the customer who is exactly indifferent between buying at either store as a function of the prices charged by the stores.

(b) Assuming Bertrand competition between the two stores, calculate the payoff functions of each store, their best response functions, and the Nash equilibrium prices charged.

EXERCISE 2.3

This problem concerns the experiment conducted by Professors Gardner, Nostrum, and Walker reported in Section 2.2.4. Eight participants are each given ten tokens. Each token can be redeemed for 5 cents, or it can be sold on a market. The value of each token sold on the market—that is, its price—is determined by how many tokens all eight participants choose to put up for sale. Specifically,

$$P = 23 - 0.25 \cdot \sum_{i=1}^{8} Q_i = 23 - 0.25 \cdot (Q_i + \overline{Q}_{-i}) \qquad [2.20]$$

where Q_i is the quantity put up by the ith participant, $\overline{Q}_{-i}$ is the total quantity put up by everyone other than the ith participant, and P is the value of every token put up for sale (in cents per token). The participants must choose between selling their tokens on this market and cashing them in for 5 cents. Hence, the profit for any participant, i, for selling tokens in this market equals:

$$\pi_i = (23 - 0.25 \cdot (Q_i + \overline{Q}_{-i})) \cdot Q_i - 5 \cdot Q_i$$
$$= (18 - 0.25 \cdot \overline{Q}_{-i}) \cdot Q_i - 0.25 \cdot Q_i^2. \quad [2.21]$$

(a) Show that the unique symmetric Nash equilibrium of the resulting Cournot Game is for each participant to sell eight tokens on this market (and cash in the other two for 5 cents). An equilibrium is symmetric if every player is playing the same strategy, say Q^*. Notice that this means $\overline{Q}_{-i} = 7Q^*$.

(b) Show that if all eight collude, they can maximize their collective earnings, $\sum_{i=1}^{8} \pi_i$, by selling only 36 of their collective tokens for 14 cents apiece. (Hint: Show that $\sum_{i=1}^{8} \pi_i$ depends only on $\sum_{i=1}^{8} Q_i = \overline{Q}$.)

EXERCISE 2.4*

This problem concerns the Cournot Game played between Mr. Gump and Ms. Ky in Section 2.2. In Section 2.2.3 it was claimed that an output of 3 units was an iterated strictly dominant strategy for each player. Recall the definition of an iterated strictly dominant strategy:

---

*A strategy is **iterated strictly dominant** for player i if and only if it is the only strategy in $\overline{S}_i$, where $\overline{S}_i$ is the intersection of the following sequence of nested sets of strategies: (1) S_i^1 consists of all of player i's strategies that are not strictly dominated; (2) for $n > 1$, S_i^n consists of the strategies in S_i^{n-1} that are not strictly dominated when we restrict the other players $j \neq i$ to the strategies in S_j^{n-1}.*

*The strategy profile $(S_1, S_2 \ldots, S_N)$ is an **iterated strictly dominant strategy equilibrium** if for every player i S_i is an iterated strictly dominant strategy.*

---

*Indicates a difficult exercise

In Section 2.2.3 we showed that $S_i^1 = [0, 4.5]$, $S_i^2 = [2.25, 4.5]$, and $S_i^3 = [2.25, 3.375]$. Assume that $S_i^n = [a_n, b_n]$. Find an algebraic formula for the interval endpoints a_n and b_n in terms of n. (Hint: The formulas will be different for even and odd integers.) Use your formulas to show (a) $a_n < 3 < b_n$ and (b) the interval length, $b_n - a_n$, shrinks to zero as n goes to infinity. Together, these imply that $\overline{S}_i = \{3\}$.

EXERCISE 2.5

This question concerns the Contestable Monopoly Game between Midwest Airlines and Air Express from Section 2.4. Suppose Midwest's strategy is to announce a ticket price of $105, and to sell as many tickets as consumers demand unless Air Express matches its price, in which case it does not sell any tickets. Prove that a best response for Air Express is to match Midwest's price of $105 and to always sell as many tickets as consumers demand.

CHAPTER 3

Strategic Trade Policy

OVERVIEW OF CHAPTER 3

3.1 Introduction

Subsidization of firms that engage in international trade is a common practice throughout the world. Yet in the standard, competitive, two-good, two-country model of international trade (often called the **Hecksher-Ohlin-Samuelson model** after the economists who first studied it), such subsidies do not appear to make economic sense. The standard model predicts that an export subsidy will shift the terms of trade against the country imposing it, thereby hurting itself and benefiting overseas consumers. In the standard model, we should readily welcome the exports of any country that is foolish enough to actually subsidize our consumption of its goods. Why would so many countries in the world adopt policies that appear not to be in their best interests? Before we simply conclude that governments are irrational (or captives of certain industries), we would do well to note that the standard trade theory makes other predictions that are also inconsistent with the evidence.

One of these predictions is that a country will specialize in the production of those goods in which it has a **comparative advantage.** The theory also predicts that most trade will take place between countries that have very different endowments, technologies, or preferences; there will be little intraindustry trade between nations (trade in the same category of goods). Instead, countries will export those goods in which they have a comparative advantage and will import those in which they have a comparative disadvantage. The data refute these predictions. International trade statistics reveal that most world trade is carried out by a relatively small number of highly industrialized nations. These countries have similar endowments of factors (particularly human and physical capital), technologies, and consumer preferences, and ship similar goods to each other.

Fortunately, neoclassical trade theory can be brought into alignment with the data by relaxing either of the two main assumptions on which it is based: (1) all markets are perfectly competitive, and (2) there are no increasing returns to scale in the production of any good. In this chapter, we will examine the consequences of introducing imperfect competition. In particular, we will construct a simple two-good, two-country model of international trade in which the two countries have the same consumer preferences, the same production technology, and the same endowments. The neoclassical trade model would predict that there will be no trade. However, we will assume here that one good is produced in each country by one firm. We will show that the domestic monopolist in each country will find it profitable to sell in the foreign market in competition with the foreign monopolist. Entry is profitable even though prices in both countries are initially the same and the production costs of both firms are the same. The result is wasteful **crosshauling** of the good between the two countries. We then show that either government can improve its overall welfare by unilaterally subsidizing the exports of the domestic firm. The subsidy alters the equilibrium price and market shares in the foreign market. This results in a transfer of monopoly profits from the foreign firm to the domestic one. In our example, the profits transferred exceed the subsidy paid. Because of this, the producers and consumers in the country giving the subsidy can, *in principle,* all be better off. If both countries can subsidize exports, though, they play a game with each other that resembles the Prisoner's Dilemma. That is, there is a strictly dominant strategy equilibrium in which both countries enact an export subsidy, yet both countries end up worse off than if they had not intervened in the market. As a result, bilateral and multilateral negotiated reductions in export subsidies—such as the North American Free Trade Agreement (NAFTA), the "Uruguay round" of the General Agreement on Tariffs and Trade (GATT), and the current negotiations within the World Trade Organization (WTO)—will make both countries better off.

3.2   Imperfect Competition and Intraindustry Trade

Suppose two countries, the United States (US) and Great Britain (GB), both produce coal. There is only one coal producer in each country: Amcoal (A) and Britcoal (B). For simplicity of exposition, we will assume that both firms produce with the same constant returns to scale technology. We will consider the case of increasing returns to scale later. Our units are selected so the marginal cost of production in both countries equals $1 billion per unit. For example, if the cost is $100 per ton, then 1 unit = 10 million tons. Unless stated otherwise, the price of coal will be quoted in $ billions per unit and firm revenue, cost, and profits will be quoted in billions of dollars.

Again for simplicity, we will assume that the domestic demand for coal in the two countries is the same and can be represented by the following linear inverse demand functions:

$$P_{US}(Q_{US}) = 6 - \tfrac{1}{8}Q_{US} \qquad\qquad\qquad [3.1a]$$

$$P_{GB}(Q_{GB}) = 6 - \tfrac{1}{8}Q_{GB} \qquad\qquad\qquad [3.1b]$$

where P_{US} and P_{GB} are the prices of coal in the United States and Great Britain, measured in dollars per unit, and Q_{US} and Q_{GB} are the quantities consumed in the United States and Great Britain.

Suppose there is no trade in coal—say, because of extremely high tariffs or transportation costs. Such a situation is referred to as **autarky.** Then each firm will choose its output so as to maximize the following "autarkic profit functions":

$$\pi^{A}(Q_{US}) = (6 - \tfrac{1}{8}Q_{US}) \cdot Q_{US} - Q_{US} \qquad\qquad [3.2a]$$

$$\pi^{B}(Q_{GB}) = (6 - \tfrac{1}{8}Q_{GB}) \cdot Q_{GB} - Q_{GB}. \qquad\qquad [3.2b]$$

We leave it as an exercise for you to show that the profit-maximizing output level and price in each country is the same: 20 units and $3.5 billion per unit. Both Amcoal and Britcoal earn a profit of $50 billion. These monopoly rents are shared by the firms' shareholders, the two governments (through taxes), and the coal miners and other coal industry suppliers.

Now suppose that free trade opens up between Great Britain and the United States. Transportation costs are $1 billion per unit in either direction. Since the pretrade price in each country is the same, yet transportation costs are so high, it would appear that neither firm would want to export coal to the other. But this is misleading. The marginal cost of producing a unit of coal and shipping it to the other country is $2 billion ($1 billion in mining costs and $1 billion in shipping costs), but the marginal revenue earned from exporting this coal to the other country is $3.5 billion. As a result, the firm will earn additional profits from entering the foreign market.

Marginal revenue in the foreign market is initially greater than the marginal revenue in the domestic market. The reason is that the monopolist has to cut the price to *all* its current domestic customers in order to sell additional coal; no such cost is incurred in the foreign market since initially it has no foreign customers. Most of the cost of entry is, instead, borne by the foreign monopolist. As a result, there is a strong incentive for each domestic monopolist to enter the other monopolist's market. Of course, if they both do this, they will drive down the prices in both markets.

Before we go further, we will formalize our trade model as a game. For the sake of simplicity, we will assume that the two firms cannot enter into binding agreements with each other. We will examine the behavior of the firms in a cartel in Chapter 20. In addition, they choose their domestic sales and exports simultaneously, and the price is determined so as to clear the market. This means they play a static, quantity-setting ("Cournot") duopoly game. This game is more complicated than the duopoly games studied in Chapter 2. There are now two markets to consider, and each firm has two quantity decisions. Amcoal must choose the amount of coal to sell in the domestic American market, Q_{US}^A, and the amount to export to Great Britain, Q_{GB}^A. Likewise, Britcoal must choose the amount of coal to sell domestically, Q_{GB}^B, and the amount to export to the United States, Q_{US}^B. The profit functions of the two firms are shown in Eqs. [3.3a] and [3.3b]:

$$\pi^A(Q_{US}^A, Q_{GB}^A, Q_{US}^B, Q_{GB}^B) = P_{US}(Q_{US}^A + Q_{US}^B) \cdot Q_{US}^A$$
$$+ P_{GB}(Q_{GB}^B + Q_{GB}^A) \cdot Q_{GB}^A - Q_{US}^A - 2Q_{GB}^A \quad [3.3a]$$

$$\pi^B(Q_{US}^A, Q_{GB}^A, Q_{US}^B, Q_{GB}^B) = P_{GB}(Q_{GB}^B + Q_{GB}^A) \cdot Q_{GB}^B$$
$$+ P_{US}(Q_{US}^A + Q_{US}^B) \cdot Q_{US}^B - 2Q_{US}^B - Q_{GB}^B. \quad [3.3b]$$

Inspection of these profit functions reveals that, because marginal costs are constant, the profit Amcoal earns from its U.S. operations, $P_{US}(Q_{US}^A + Q_{US}^B) \cdot Q_{US}^A - Q_{US}^A$, depends only on its domestic sales, Q_{US}^A, and Britcoal's exports, Q_{US}^B. Similarly, the profit Amcoal earns from its British operations, $P_{GB}(Q_{GB}^B + Q_{GB}^A) \cdot Q_{GB}^A - 2Q_{GB}^A$, depends only on its foreign sales, Q_{GB}^A, and Britcoal's domestic sales, Q_{GB}^B. The same holds true for Britcoal. This implies that our trade game can be modeled as two separate Cournot games. One game is played in the American market and the other is played in the British market. We know how to find the Nash equilibria of two-player Cournot games: we calculate each firm's best response function and find where the graphs of the two functions intersect. This intersection point represents a pure-strategy Nash equilibrium of the game.

We leave it as an exercise for you to derive the best response functions for each firm in each market from the profit functions (3.3a) and (3.3b). These best response functions are graphed in Figures 3.1 and 3.2.

Since market demand is the same in each country and both firms have the same marginal costs, these two games are essentially identical. In equilibrium, in each country, the domestic firm produces 24 units of coal, 16 units for domestic consumption and 8 units for export, and the price equals $3 billion per unit. The resulting cross-hauling of coal between the United States and Great Britain seems inefficient. After all, it costs Amcoal twice as much as Britcoal to provide coal to British consumers, and vice versa. Since 16 units of coal are being shipped by the two firms at a cost of $1 billion per unit, there is a waste of $16 billion.

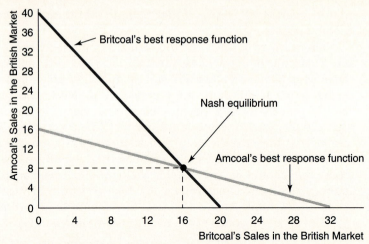

FIGURE 3.1   Best response functions for Amcoal and Britcoal in the British coal market.

Although it appears that free trade results in a reduction of welfare, this conclusion ignores the pro-competitive effects of trade within each country. Under free trade, 24 units of coal are consumed in each country (16 units provided by the domestic producer and 8 units provided by the foreign producer) at a market price of $3 billion per unit. This is more than the 20 units consumed under autarky at a price of $3.5 billion per unit. So more coal is consumed in each country under free trade than under autarky and this coal is sold for less. Each firm earns a profit of $8 billion from its foreign sales and $32 billion from its domestic sales, or $40 billion overall. This is $10 billion less than under autarky.

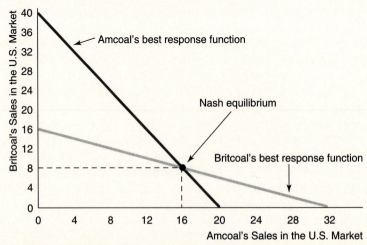

FIGURE 3.2   Best response functions for Amcoal and Britcoal in the American coal market.

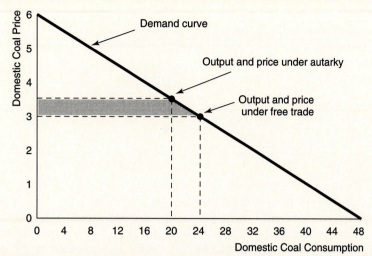

FIGURE 3.3 Consumer surplus increases by $11 billion when free trade is introduced.

Clearly, the coal consumers gain from trade and the coal company owners and coal miners lose. In order to determine the net effect, we need to adopt a method for measuring the joint welfare of producers and consumers. We will use the sum of consumer and producer surplus as our welfare measure. This places equal weight on consumers and owners of firms. Recall that **consumer surplus** equals the difference between each consumer's actual expenditure on coal and the maximum amount of money each coal consumer would pay for the coal it consumes. This is approximately equal to the area under the demand curve minus total expenditures on coal.[1] If Q is total coal consumption in a country, then the consumer surplus equals

$$
\begin{aligned}
Consumer\ surplus &= \int_0^Q P(x)dx - P(Q) \cdot Q \\
&= \int_0^Q (6 - \tfrac{1}{8}x)dx - (6 - \tfrac{1}{8}Q) \cdot Q \qquad [3.4] \\
&= \tfrac{1}{16}Q^2.
\end{aligned}
$$

The gain in consumer surplus in each country generated by the introduction of free trade equals the area of the shaded region in Figure 3.3. This area equals $11 billion, as the reader can easily confirm using geometry. **Producer surplus** equals the difference between the revenue the firm receives for the coal it produces and

---

[1]If coal demand is income neutral, then the market demand curve is identical to the *income compensated demand curve*, which is the appropriate tool to use to derive the change in consumer surplus.

Table 3.1 *Market Equilibrium in Great Britain before and After Trade Is Allowed with the United States*

	Q^A_{GB} (units)	Q^B_{GB} (units)	P_{GB} ($ billions/unit)	π^B_{US} ($ billions)	π^B_{GB} ($ billions)	Consumer Surplus ($ billions)
Autarky	0	20	3.5	0	50	25
Free trade	8	16	3	8	32	36
Change	+8	−4	−0.5	+8	−18	+11

the minimum it must be paid to willingly produce it. Since we are assuming no fixed costs, producer surplus equals firm profits. We have already seen that the domestic monopoly's profits decline by $10 billion when bilateral trade is allowed. Net welfare (the sum of consumer and producer surplus) has improved by $11 billion − $10 billion = $1 billion. This is summarized in Table 3.1.

3.3 Export Subsidies

Suppose the U.S. government gives Amcoal a subsidy of $0.75 billion for every unit of coal it exports. This is known as an **export subsidy.** Consumers must be taxed in order to pay this subsidy. We will assume that this reduction in income has no effect on the domestic demand for coal and reduces consumer welfare by the amount taxed. Since this subsidy will have no effect on Amcoal's or Britcoal's profits from their U.S. operations, it will have no effect on the U.S. market equilibrium. But it will have a big effect on the British market and on Amcoal's profits

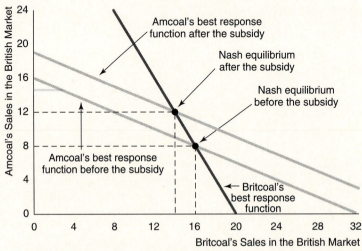

FIGURE 3.4 An export subsidy shifts Amcoal's best response curve right, resulting in an increase in exports to Britain and a decrease in domestic sales by Britcoal.

Table 3.2 *Market Equilibrium in Britain before and after the United States Adopts an Export Subsidy*

S_{US}	Q_{GB}^{A} (units)	Q_{GB}^{B} (units)	P_{GB} ($ billions/unit)	π_{GB}^{A} ($ billions)	π_{GB}^{B} ($ billions)	π_{GB}^{A} − Subsidy ($ billions)	Consumer Surplus in GB ($ billions)
No subsidy	8	16	3	8	32	8	36
$0.75 billion/unit	12	14	2.75	18	24.5	9	42.25
Change	+4	−2	−0.25	+10	−7.5	+1	+6.25

on its exports. The subsidy is equivalent to a 75% reduction in Amcoal's transportation cost from $1 billion to $0.25 billion. Amcoal's new profit function (from sales to Great Britain) is given in Eq. [3.5].

$$\pi_{GB}^{A}(Q_{GB}^{A}, Q_{GB}^{B}) = P_{GB}(Q_{GB}^{B} + Q_{GB}^{A}) \cdot Q_{GB}^{A} - 1.25Q_{GB}^{A} \qquad [3.5]$$

As Figure 3.4 shows, Amcoal's best response curve shifts right. Amcoal's equilibrium exports increase by 50% (from 8 to 12 units) and Britcoal's domestic sales fall by 2 units or 12.5% (from 16 to 14 units). The price in Great Britain falls, but by only 8.3% (from $3 billion/unit to $2.75 billion/unit). As a result, Amcoal's British profits go up from $8 billion to $18 billion (inclusive of the subsidy) and Britcoal's profits go down from $32 billion to $24.5 billion. The fall in prices and the expansion of output results in a $6.25 billion increase in British consumer surplus. Since the subsidy leaves U.S. coal prices unchanged, there is no change in the U.S. market. Since Amcoal's profits increase by $10 billion, yet the subsidy costs American consumers $9 billion in the form of higher taxes, the U.S. is better off by $1 billion.[2] This is summarized in Table 3.2.

3.4 Optimal Export Subsidies

Suppose the U.S. government wants to set the export subsidy so as to maximize Amcoal's profits net of the subsidy; that is, to maximize $\pi^{A} - S_{US} \cdot Q_{GB}^{A}$. Such an objective implicitly ignores the distributional effects of the subsidy, since those citizens who are taxed to pay the subsidy are usually not those who benefit from it. We will refer to this subsidy rate as the "optimal" subsidy. The subsidy will be denoted by S_{US} and is paid on each unit of coal shipped. Amcoal's profit from its British sales (domestic sales can be ignored since they are unaffected by the size of the subsidy) equals

---

[2]This conclusion assumes that the subsidy is financed by a lump-sum tax on the American coal industry. If the subsidy is financed in any other way, then it may reduce allocative efficiency within the United States and redistribute income. In this case, some Americans could be made worse off by the subsidy. We are also ignoring the possibility of retaliation by Britain, since we will examine this in the next section.

$$\pi_{GB}^A(Q_{GB}^A, Q_{GB}^B, S_{US}) = P_{GB}(Q_{GB}^B + Q_{GB}^A) \cdot Q_{GB}^A + (S_{US} \cdot Q_{GB}^A) - 2Q_{GB}^A \qquad [3.6a]$$

and Britcoal's profits from its domestic sales equals

$$\pi_{GB}^B(Q_{GB}^A, Q_{GB}^B, S_{US}) = P_{GB}(Q_{GB}^B + Q_{GB}^A) \cdot Q_{GB}^B - Q_{GB}^B. \qquad [3.6b]$$

If we maximize π_{GB}^A with respect to Q_{GB}^A, we obtain Amcoal's best response function:

$$Q_{GB}^{A*}(Q_{GB}^B, S_{US}) = 16 - \tfrac{1}{2}Q_{GB}^B + 4S_{US}; \qquad [3.7a]$$

and if we maximize π_{GB}^B with respect to Q_{GB}^B we obtain Britcoal's best response function:

$$Q_{GB}^{B*}(Q_{GB}^A, S_{US}) = 20 - \tfrac{1}{2}Q_{GB}^A. \qquad [3.7b]$$

Solving Eq. [3.6a] and [3.6b] simultaneously for Q_{GB}^{A*} and Q_{GB}^{B*} results in the two expressions

$$Q_{GB}^{A*}(S_{US}) = 8 + \tfrac{16}{3}S_{US} \qquad [3.8a]$$

$$Q_{GB}^{B*}(S_{US}) = 16 - \tfrac{8}{3}S_{US}, \qquad [3.8b]$$

which implies an equilibrium price of

$$P_{GB}^*(S_{US}) = P_{GB}(Q_{GB}^{B*}(S_{US}) + Q_{GB}^{A*}(S_{US})) = 3 - \tfrac{1}{3}S_{US}. \qquad [3.9]$$

The government's objective is to maximize Amcoal's profits net of the subsidy paid:

$$V_{US}(S_{US}) = \pi_{GB}^A(Q_{GB}^{A*}(S_{US}), Q_{GB}^{B*}(S_{US}), S_{US}) - S_{US} \cdot Q_{GB}^{A*}(S_{US}) = 8 + \tfrac{8}{3} \cdot S_{US} - \tfrac{16}{9} \cdot S_{US}^2.$$
$$[3.10]$$

V_{US} is maximized at $S_{US} = \$0.75$ billion per unit. So the subsidy level assumed in Section 3.3 turns out to be optimal.

3.5   Subsidy Wars

If both countries are free to subsidize their coal industries, then the U.S. and British governments, Amcoal, and Britcoal will find themselves playing a four-player Subsidy Game. In this game, the two governments move first and simultaneously decide whether to grant export subsidies to their domestic coal manufacturers and, if so, at what rate. Amcoal and Britcoal observe the subsidy rates granted by the two governments and then play a Cournot game in each market.

If neither country imposes a subsidy, then we know from Section 3.2 that

Table 3.3 **Profits of Both Firms (Net of the Subsidy) with and without Export Subsidies ($ billions)**

		Great Britain	
		No subsidy	Subsidy
United States	No subsidy	(40, 40)	(32.5, 50)
	Subsidy	(50, 32.5)	(42.5, 42.5)

Profits: (Amcoal, Britcoal)

Amcoal and Britcoal will each earn $32 billion in profits from their domestic sales and $8 billion from their exports, or $40 billion overall. From Section 3.4 we know that the optimal export subsidy is $0.75 billion per unit. If the United States is the only country to adopt this optimal subsidy, then we know from Section 3.3 that Amcoal continues to earn $32 billion in profits from its domestic sales, but now earns $18 billion in profits (including the subsidy payments) from its exports to Great Britain. Total Amcoal profits equal $50 billion. Britcoal's total profits fall to $32.5 billion ($24.5 billion domestically and $8 billion from its exports to the United States). Because the two markets are assumed to be symmetric, the numbers are simply reversed if Britain is the only country to adopt an optimal subsidy. That is, net of the subsidy, Britcoal's profits increase to $50 billion and Amcoal's profits fall to $32.5 billion. Finally, if both countries adopt the optimal subsidy, then each company earns $24.5 billion from its domestic sales and $18 billion from its exports. As a result, each firm's total profits equal $42.5 billion.

The profits in Table 3.3 are not the payoffs to the United States and Great Britain for the Subsidy Wars Game since they do not factor in consumer welfare. As classical economists pointed out long ago, it is the consumers *overseas* who benefit from the adoption of an export subsidy, and it is domestic consumers who pay for it. Table 3.4 shows consumer welfare—defined as domestic consumer surplus minus export subsidy payments.

Table 3.4 **Consumer Surplus Minus Subsidy Payments in Both Countries ($ billions)**

		Great Britain	
		No subsidy	Subsidy
United States	No subsidy	(36, 36)	(42.25, 27)
	Subsidy	(27, 42.25)	(33.25, 33.25)

Consumer welfare: (United States, Great Britain)

Table 3.5 Payoff Matrix for Subsidy Game Between the United States and Great Britain

		Great Britain	
		No subsidy	Subsidy
United States	No subsidy	(76, 76)	(74.75, 77)
	Subsidy	(77, 74.75)	**(75.75, 75.75)**

Payoffs: (United States, Great Britain)

The payoff matrix for the Subsidy Game is given in Table 3.5. The entries are the sum of the entries in Tables 3.3 and 3.4. The equilibrium strategies and outcome are shown in bold. The reader can readily verify that each government has a dominant strategy: adopt an export subsidy. Yet both countries would be better off if they could make a binding agreement not to impose any export subsidies at all! Simply put, the two governments are caught in a Prisoner's Dilemma.

Since World War II, many of the world's trading nations have reduced their export subsidies and tariffs through the General Agreement on Tariffs and Trade (GATT). U.S. tariffs, for example, are currently one tenth what they were at the beginning of the 1940s. Negotiations continue under the rules of the World Trade Organization. These negotiations provide indirect evidence in favor of our admittedly simple Prisoner's Dilemma model: no country will unilaterally reduce its export subsidies, yet all countries would and do benefit from simultaneous *multilateral* reductions.

3.6   Increasing Returns to Scale

We have so far retained the neoclassical assumption that both producers have constant returns to scale. Yet monopoly is usually associated with increasing returns to scale. Fortunately, allowing increasing returns to scale (declining average cost) only strengthens our results.

Starting from autarky, each monopoly now has *two* incentives to enter the foreign market. First, even if prices in both markets are initially the same, marginal revenue in the foreign market will be above marginal revenue in the domestic market. Second, exports, by increasing output, drive down the firm's unit production costs. The equilibrium of the two Cournot games played between the two monopolists will, therefore, involve cross-hauling. Finding the equilibrium of this game, though, is more complicated because the two markets can no longer be studied in isolation.

Increasing returns also increase the incentive for the government to impose an export subsidy. Not only does the subsidy shift monopoly rents in the foreign market away from the foreign producer and toward the domestic producer, but

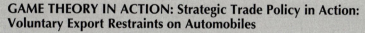

GAME THEORY IN ACTION: Strategic Trade Policy in Action: Voluntary Export Restraints on Automobiles

This chapter has concentrated on the use of export subsidies to extract monopoly profits from a foreign firm to a domestic one so as to leave the home economy better off. But governments are not limited to such policies. Other policies include import tariffs, import quotas, and regulations. From 1981 to 1994 a voluntary export restraint (VER) was placed by Japan on the export of automobiles from Japan into the United States. This was a very important policy, involving as it did the largest manufacturing industry in the United States. Initially the limit was 1.68 million cars, which was gradually raised to 2.30 million in 1992. This VER was deliberately structured so that cars produced by Japanese firms at plants in the United States were excluded, while cars produced in Japan and sold in the United States under an American brand were included. Both aspects of the VER were important. Japanese firms responded immediately by building manufacturing plants in the United States so that by 1990 five Japanese auto firms had American auto plants.

Steven Barry, James Levinsohn, and Ariel Pakes (BLP) used a Bertrand model to estimate the effect of this policy on prices and welfare in both the United States and Japan ("Voluntary Export Restraints on Automobiles: Evaluating a Strategic Trade Policy," NBER Working Paper 5235, August 1995). As was expected, the VER increased the price of Japanese cars dramatically. In contrast, the price of domestically produced cars in the United States actually fell a small amount over this period. BLP hypothesized that as Japanese firms raised their prices, it was primarily price-sensitive consumers who switched to domestic cars. As a result, domestic auto firms did not increase their markups. Although prices stayed constant, between 1986 and 1990 U.S. auto makers earned $9.6 billion more than they would have if no VER had been in place. In comparison total profits of the U.S. auto industry in 1990 were about $22 billion. Japanese auto producers' profits were hardly affected. Although sales were restricted, the increase in prices offset this.

The cost of the VER was borne by U.S. consumers, particularly those who bought Japanese cars during this period. BLP estimated that consumer welfare declined by over $12 billion. So on balance, the VER caused a *decline* in U.S. welfare. Had an equivalent tariff been placed on Japanese cars, it would have generated $13 billion in revenue, easily compensating for the loss in consumer welfare—assuming no retaliation by Japan. The VER amounted to a tariff in which the tariff revenue was given to the *Japanese auto companies* in the form of higher U.S. prices. BLP noted that this can be interpreted as a *bribe* paid to obtain Japanese cooperation with this policy to avoid retaliation.

by increasing the domestic firm's output, the subsidy once again reduces the subsidized firm's costs. In the two-stage Subsidy Game, both governments will award export subsidies to their coal producers. The game may no longer be a Prisoner's Dilemma, though. It is possible that the benefit due to the lower costs offsets the loss caused by the cross-hauling of coal between the two countries enough for the subsidy to Pareto dominate no subsidy.

3.7   Summary

In this chapter, we have sought to account for two apparent empirical refutations of neoclassical trade theory: (1) the general popularity of export subsidies and the simultaneous desire of governments to negotiate bilateral subsidy reductions with their main trading partners, and (2) the extensive cross-hauling of similar goods between countries with similar factor endowments, technologies, and consumer tastes.

Both puzzles can be explained by the existence of extensive market power in some markets. For example, two firms, Boeing and Aerobus, dominate the international market for large commercial aircraft, and seven firms dominate the international market in crude oil. Domestic monopolists will find it to their advantage to enter foreign markets, even if foreign firms are entering the domestic market. The pro-competitive effect of the resulting competition in all markets may increase consumer welfare enough to compensate for the cost of all the wasteful transporting of goods between trading countries.

Furthermore, export subsidies can provide a strategic tool for shifting monopoly rents away from foreign producers to domestic producers. The size of the shift can be large enough to "pay" for the subsidy. When this occurs, a subsidy is a rational strategy for a government to pursue even if its goal is to maximize total national income and not just the welfare of the exporting industry. Unfortunately, all countries have this tool at their disposal. If the countries cannot make binding agreements with each other, then the resulting noncooperative subsidy-setting game played between them can in certain cases resemble a multilateral Prisoner's Dilemma: although no country benefits from unilaterally reducing its subsidies, all would benefit from simultaneous reductions.

3.8   Further Reading

A good, although advanced, survey of the recent literature on trade theory in the presence of imperfect competition is Paul Krugman's contribution to the *Handbook of Industrial Organization, Vol. II* (edited by R. Schmalensee and R. Willig, Elsevier Science Publishers B.V., 1989, Chapter 20). A much simpler summary can be found in Krugman's article "Is Free Trade Passe?" (*Journal of Economic Perspectives* 1 (1987), pp. 131–44). Our model of trade with export subsidies is based on the work of James Brander and Barbara Spencer ("Export Subsidies and International Market Share Rivalry," *Journal of International Economics* 18 (1985), pp. 83–100).

3.9   Discussion Questions

1. In this chapter we have made the assumption that the government's objective is to maximize Amcoal's profits minus the subsidy. What empirical evidence can you find that either supports or refutes this assumption?

2. What do you think the government should be trying to maximize?

3.10   New Terms

autarky

comparative advantage

consumer surplus

cross-hauling

export subsidy

Hecksher-Ohlin-Samuelson model

producer surplus

3.11   Exercises

Exercises 3.1–3.8 are based on the Cournot model of Sections 3.2–3.5.

EXERCISE 3.1

Use the profit functions given in Eqs. [3.3a] and [3.3b] to derive algebraic expressions for Amcoal's and Britcoal's best response functions in the U.S. market. Find the Nash equilibrium, which is the *free trade* equilibrium for the United States.

EXERCISE 3.2

Suppose there is free trade and the U.S. government "busted up" Amcoal into a large number of price-taking firms (in both markets) with constant marginal production costs of $1 billion/unit. What will happen to the market equilibrium in both the United States and Great Britain? Is the United States better off with a "competitive" coal industry or a duopoly? Is Great Britain better off if the U.S. coal industry is competitive or not?

EXERCISE 3.3*

Suppose there is initially free trade in coal between the United States and Great Britain and there are no export subsidies. Now, suppose the United States imposes a tax, called a *tariff*, of $0.75 billion/unit on Britcoal's imports into the United States. This means that if the U.S. price of coal is P_{US}, then on every unit of coal Britcoal sells in the United States the company receives only P_{US} − $0.75 billion and the government receives $0.75 billion. Calculate the new best response function for Britcoal and the new Cournot-Nash equilibrium. By how much do Amcoal's profits go up compared to the free trade equilibrium? How much tariff revenue is collected by the government? How much does consumer surplus go down? Assuming that the tariff revenue is rebated to consumers and the rebate has an insignificant effect on the domestic demand for coal, is national welfare—as measured by the sum of consumer surplus, Amcoal profits, and tariff revenue—increased by the tariff or not?

EXERCISE 3.4

Suppose the demand for coal falls and the price of coal in both the United States and Great Britain is given by:

$$P_k(Q_k) = 4 - \tfrac{1}{8} \cdot Q_k \qquad [3.11]$$

---

*Indicates a difficult exercise.

where $Q_k = Q_k^B + Q_k^A$ and $k = US, GB$.

(a) Find the Cournot equilibrium in the British coal market. Symmetry implies that this is also the Cournot equilibrium in the U.S. coal market.

(b) Determine the optimal export subsidy for the United States. This is also the optimal export subsidy for Great Britain.

(c) Determine the payoffs in the Subsidy War Game and find its Nash equilibria. Show that the game is a Prisoner's Dilemma.

EXERCISE 3.5

Suppose that Britcoal and Amcoal engage in Bertrand competition. What is the Nash equilibrium in each market under free trade and no subsidies?

EXERCISE 3.6

Suppose that Amcoal and Britcoal are Cournot competitors but have capacity constraints on their output. Specifically, neither can produce more than 10 units of output. The Cournot equilibrium derived in Section 3.2 is no longer feasible. Determine the new Cournot equilibrium. (Hint: Assume that the output constraint is binding, so that $Q_{GB}^A = 10 - Q_{US}^A$ and $Q_{US}^B = 10 - Q_{GB}^B$. The profit functions of each firm can then be written as functions only of Q_{US}^A and Q_{GB}^B. For example, Amcoal's profit function is now

$$\pi^A(Q_{US}^A, Q_{GB}^B) = P_{US}(Q_{US}^A + (10 - Q_{GB}^B)) \cdot Q_{US}^A + P_{GB}(Q_{GB}^B$$
$$+ (10 - Q_{US}^A)) \cdot (10 - Q_{US}^A) - 2 \cdot Q_{US}^A - 4 \cdot (10 - Q_{US}^A).$$

Use the profit functions to determine the two firms' best response functions, $Q_{US}^{A*}(Q_{GB}^B)$ and $Q_{GB}^{B*}(Q_{US}^A)$, and find their common solution.

EXERCISE 3.7

In deriving the optimal export subsidy in Section 3.4, we assumed that each government's objective was to maximize domestic producer surplus minus the subsidy. Suppose, instead, that the government's objective is to maximize consumer welfare. Now the optimal policy is to *tax* exports and distribute the new revenue to consumers either in cash or services.

(a) Who, exactly, is affected (Amcoal, Britcoal, U.S. consumers, or British consumers) by the unilateral imposition of a tax on U.S. coal exports?

(b) Determine the optimal export tax rate assuming that the government's objective is to maximize export tax revenue.

EXERCISE 3.8

In analyzing the Subsidy War Game, we assumed that the objective of both governments was to maximize the sum of consumer and producer surplus (firm profits) net of the export subsidy. This welfare measure weights consumers and producers equally. Use the result of Sections 3.2–3.4 and Exercise 3.7 to find the Nash equilibrium of the Subsidy War Game assuming the following two alternative welfare measures:

(a) consumer surplus plus export tax revenue, and

(b) producer surplus minus export subsidy expenditure.

CHAPTER 4

Property Rights and Efficiency

OVERVIEW OF CHAPTER 4

4.1 Introduction

4.2 Undefined Property Rights and Fishing

4.3 Well-Defined Property Rights and the Coase Theorem

4.4 Summary

4.5 Further Reading

4.6 Discussion Questions

4.7 New Terms

4.8 Exercises

4.1 Introduction

Most of us have been in the following situation: We are at someone's house with a group of friends, just about to watch a movie, when the host brings out a big bowl of popcorn. The popcorn is put down on a central table and everyone is invited to share in this communal offering. We are normally civilized human beings, yet the ravenous manner in which we devour the popcorn is Neanderthal. The popcorn is gone before the plot even begins to thicken. Contrast that scenario with this one: You are spending a quiet evening alone, just you and a bowl of popcorn and a favorite movie. You eat the popcorn a fluffy kernel or two at a time and even a small bowl lasts throughout the movie.

Different social scientists would undoubtedly offer a variety of explanations for the contrast between our gluttonous behavior when sharing popcorn with friends and the relaxed eating that takes place when we are alone. Most economists, however, would argue that the gluttony in the earlier setting was caused by a lack of well-defined property rights for the bowl of popcorn. The spirit behind sharing a communal bowl of popcorn—namely, the fostering of a sense of community and friendship—is laudable. The sad fact seems to be that as we "compete" for the fixed amount of popcorn, we tend to shove as much into our mouths as fast as we can lest someone else deprive us of our "just" allocation. Of course, while eating popcorn alone, you need not have such concerns, and can eat at a more leisurely pace.

The problems associated with undefined property rights extend to a wide variety of economic applications. Currently the most important of these applications concern the environment. In this particular example we will suppose that two firms use a common input: a lake containing fish. Neither firm owns the lake. Instead, the lake is community property. Our objectives are to make some predictions about how the two firms will behave and to determine whether the resulting resource allocation is Pareto optimal.

In 1991, the Nobel Prize in economics was awarded to Ronald Coase of the University of Chicago. While Professor Coase has made many contributions to economics, the greatest derive from an article written in 1960, entitled *The Problem of Social Cost*. Over the last 30 years, this has become one of the most cited academic articles ever written. In this paper, Coase discusses the role of property rights and civil liability rules in determining alternative resource allocations, cutting to the quick of the interaction between the public and private sectors. Various insights that Coase presented in this article have come to be known as "the Coase theorem." Surprisingly, economists have tended to dwell on one portion of this article that was alluded to 186 years earlier in Adam Smith's *Wealth of Nations* and was based on a set of assumptions that are frequently unrealistic. Simply put, this part of the article says that if there are no legal or strategic barriers to efficient bargaining, and if property rights are well defined, then people can always negotiate to a Pareto optimal outcome. Furthermore, civil liability rules (the establishment of property rights) will have no effect on the allocation of economic resources. These rules can only affect the distribution of income. Once it is recognized, however, that bargaining may not be efficient, the establishment of property rights may affect behavior and resource allocation.

Hence, the role of property rights becomes central to issues of efficiency. In this chapter, we begin with a model in which property rights are not defined. We then move to a model in which property rights are defined but bargaining is costless and conclude with a model in which property rights are defined but bargaining is costly.

4.2   Undefined Property Rights and Fishing

Any fisherman knows the problems with overfishing. Although more fishing effort will result in more fish being caught, the stock of fish may be so diminished by the extra effort that the future catch is substantially reduced, if not eliminated. If one fisherman owned the lake, we would expect him to take into account the future cost of pulling one more fish out of the water today when deciding whether that extra fish was worth the effort. When more than one fisherman have the right to fish the lake, each of them will only bear a fraction of the future costs of pulling

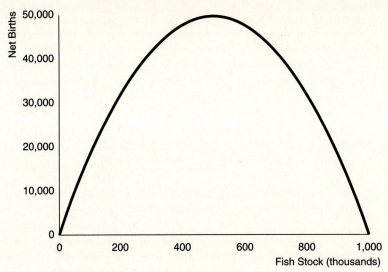

FIGURE 4.1 The net birth rate is plotted against the fish stock.

a fish out today. Because no one bears the full cost, they will overfish. This fundamental problem has become known as the **tragedy of the commons.**[1]

While the intuition seems fairly straightforward, we seek in this section to formalize the logic. As noted, the analysis and conclusions found in this application apply to a wide variety of important economic situations. You should therefore think of this application as a metaphor for the general problem of sharing a common resource.

Suppose the stock of fish in a lake is very low. A lusty fish looking for a mate will have a difficult time finding one. While the net birth rate in these circumstances may be positive, it will probably be low. This means the stock of fish will grow, but slowly. As the stock of fish gets larger, however, it becomes easier to find a mate and the increase in net births will cause the stock of fish to grow faster and faster. Once the fish stock becomes large enough, finding a mate will no longer be such a problem, but the competition for food will become increasingly fierce. As a result, the number of deaths will rise. Once this happens, net births, though still positive, will start to fall and the stock of fish will grow more slowly. Deaths will continue to climb, until net births equal zero, at which point the stock of fish will stop growing. This point of zero population growth is a **steady-state equilibrium.** In this equilibrium, the flow of fish into the stock (births) matches the flow of fish out of the stock (deaths); that is, net births are zero. This equilibrium stock of fish is called the **carrying capacity** of the lake. Our biological story is captured in Figure 4.1. Since equilibrium occurs when the net birth rate is zero, there are two equilibrium stocks of fish in this lake: zero and 1 million. That is, the carrying capacity of the lake is 1 million fish.

---

[1]See Garrett Hardin, "The Tragedy of the Commons," *Science* (December 13, 1968) for a brilliant and important discussion of this issue applied to common pasture fields.

An equation that describes the relationships identified above is:

$$B = N \cdot (1 - N) \qquad\qquad [4.1]$$

where B is net births and N is the stock of fish, both measured in millions of fish.

Fishing, of course, upsets the natural equilibrium by increasing the death rate. We will continue to define B as natural births of fish minus natural deaths. Although fishing does not affect the biological relationship between B and N, it will affect the equilibrium values of B and N. If B is zero and some number of fish, say C, begin to be caught on a regular basis, then the stock of fish will fall. As we saw earlier, a steady-state equilibrium exists when there is neither growth nor decay in the stock of fish. This will occur when the net birth rate exactly equals C, the rate of fishing. In Figure 4.2, we see that if the number of fish caught per unit of time equals C, then the equilibrium stock of fish must be either N_1 or N_2. At these two stocks, the net birth rate equals C.

Of course, with possible rare exceptions, fish don't just magically get caught. Resources must be devoted to catching them. We define a variable E to denote *fishing effort*. The higher the value of E, the greater the resources devoted to fishing. E incorporates, among other things, the number of boats, the number of crewmen, and the amount of time each boat is out in the lake fishing. Everything being equal, including the stock of fish, the more effort that goes into catching fish, the larger the catch. Furthermore, everything else being equal, including fishing effort, the larger the stock of fish, N, the larger the catch. We will measure fishing effort in millions of "effort units." When the lake is at its carrying capacity, a 1 unit increase in effort results in an additional unit of fish. We can capture these assumptions in the following equation:

$$C = N \cdot E. \qquad\qquad [4.2]$$

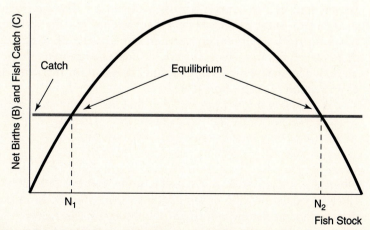

FIGURE 4.2 If the rate of fishing equals C, then the steady-state equilibrium stock of fish will either be N_1 or N_2.

In steady-state equilibrium, recall, net births just offset the number of fish caught, or $B = C$. Algebraically, this means

$$N \cdot (1 - N) = N \cdot E. \qquad [4.3]$$

Solving this equation for N yields the functional relationship between the steady-state equilibrium of the fish population and the level of fishing effort:

$$N = 1 - E. \qquad [4.4]$$

Eq. [4.4] says, if E goes up by 1 unit, then the equilibrium stock of fish goes down by 1 unit.

We will assume that the stock of fish adjusts rapidly toward a steady-state equilibrium to any changes in the level of fishing effort. As a result, we obtain an expression for the size of the catch of fish as a function of the effort devoted to catching fish by substituting the right-hand side of Eq. [4.4] for N in Eq. [4.2].

$$C = E \cdot (1 - E) \qquad [4.5]$$

Eq. [4.5] relates the fish catch (output) to fishing effort (input). As such, it is simply the production function for fishing the lake.

Suppose there are two fishing firms who are deciding how much fishing effort to put into fishing for lobsters: "Lobsters 'R Us" and "Lobster World." The two firms are rational, forward looking, and choose their fishing efforts, E_{LRU} and E_{LW}, independently and in ignorance of the other firm's decision. That means they play a static, two-player, continuous-strategy Fishing Game. Their current fishing catch generates immediate profits. Yet both firms also know that today's fishing, by altering the steady-state fishing population, can alter the profitability of fishing in the future. There are many ways the firms could balance current and future profits. Since we are interested in exploring how the lack of property rights, and not myopia, causes overfishing, we will assume that the firms wish to maximize their **steady-state profits**. Steady-state profits are the stream of profits earned when the fishing population is in a steady-state equilibrium. In a sense, this is the opposite of myopia since current profits are ignored; the long run is all that matters. It remains for us to find an expression for the firms' steady-state profits as a function of their effort levels.

We already know from Eq. [4.5] that the steady-state equilibrium catch rate, C_T, depends on the total effort of both firms. That is,

$$C_T = E_T \cdot (1 - E_T) \qquad [4.6]$$

where $E_T = E_{LRU} + E_{LW}$. We will assume that the ratio between the two firms' catches equals the ratio of their fishing efforts. So, for example, if Lobster World engages in no fishing effort, then Lobsters 'R Us receives the entire catch. If, however, Lobster World engages in 30% of the total effort, then Lobsters 'R Us receives only 70% of the total catch. Algebraically, this means that

$$C_{LW} = \frac{E_{LW}}{E_T} \cdot C_T$$

$$= \frac{E_{LW}}{E_T} \cdot E_T \cdot (1 - (E_{LW} + E_{LRU})) \qquad [4.7]$$

$$= E_{LW} \cdot (1 - E_{LRU}) - E_{LW}^2$$

and

$$C_{LRU} = \frac{E_{LRU}}{E_T} \cdot C_T$$

$$= \frac{E_{LRU}}{E_T} \cdot E_T \cdot (1 - (E_{LW} + E_{LRU})) \qquad [4.8]$$

$$= E_{LRU} \cdot (1 - E_{LW}) - E_{LRU}^2.$$

Eqs. [4.7] and [4.8] are the production functions for the two firms. They show that the productivity of each firm depends on the fishing effort of both. This is very different from the production of manufactured goods, where the productivity of a firm depends only on its technology and the mix of inputs it uses.

So far we have kept the analysis in terms of units of effort and units of fish. But the payoffs in the Fishing Game are steady-state profits. Suppose the price of fish is \$1 per fish, fishing effort costs \$0.10 per unit, and profits are measured in millions of dollars. Then the profit function for Lobsters 'R Us is given by:

$$\pi_{LRU}(E_{LRU}, E_{LW}) = ((1 - E_{LW}) \cdot E_{LRU} - \cdot E_{LRU}^2) - 0.10 \cdot E_{LRU} \qquad [4.9]$$
$$= (0.9 - E_{LW}) \cdot E_{LRU} - \cdot E_{LRU}^2.$$

Because of the symmetry between the two firms' production functions, we have a similar expression for Lobster World's profit function:

$$\pi_{LW}(E_{LRU}, E_{LW}) = (0.9 - E_{LRU}) \cdot E_{LW} - \cdot E_{LW}^2. \qquad [4.10]$$

Since the strategies are not a finite set but a continuum, in order to find the Nash equilibrium, we must calculate each firm's best response function. Recall that this function gives the optimum level of effort for each firm *at every possible effort level chosen by the other firm* and is found by maximizing the profit function, holding the other firm's effort constant. Recall from Section 1.8 that a payoff function of the form $a \cdot x - x^2$ has a maximum at $x^* = \frac{1}{2}a$. So the best response functions are:

$$E_{LRU}^{BR}(E_{LW}) = \tfrac{1}{2}(0.9 - E_{LW}) = 0.45 - \tfrac{1}{2} \cdot E_{LW} \quad \text{and}$$
$$E_{LW}^{BR}(E_{LRU}) = \tfrac{1}{2}(0.9 - E_{LRU}) = 0.45 - \tfrac{1}{2} \cdot E_{LRU}. \qquad [4.11]$$

These best response functions bear a remarkable similarity to the best response functions derived for Cournot duopolies in Chapter 2. The unique Nash equilibrium effort levels correspond to the intersection of the graphs of these best response functions:

$$E^*_{LRU} = E^*_{LW} = 0.3. \qquad\qquad [4.12]$$

At the Nash equilibrium, the level of fishing effort for each firm equals 0.3 million units, so the total fishing effort equals $0.3 + 0.3 = 0.6$ million units. Eq. [4.6] says that the equilibrium total catch equals $0.6 \cdot (1 - 0.6) = 0.24$ million fish. But Eq. [4.6] also implies that the same number of fish could have been caught by expending an effort of only 0.4 million units, since $0.4 \cdot (1 - 0.4) = 0.24$ also. This means that 0.2 million units of effort are being wasted. As a result, about 33% of the total cost of harvesting the 240,000 fish brought in by the two firms could be avoided if the strategic interaction between the two firms could be avoided.[2] This is in stark contrast to usual case, where intense competition between producers leads to *increased* productivity.

The prediction that competing firms or individuals will "waste" common resources is an important conclusion of game theory. It has implications for dinner party hosts (how to set up a table so that party-goers get maximum enjoyment), city planners (how to reduce rush hour traffic costs), and international lawyers (how to reduce the probability of conflicts when natural resources cross international boundaries).

A similar problem exists when there is a common output. For example suppose that the output of a good or service can be shared by a number of people. Defense services are a case in point. If an F-14 fighter jet is based near a community, then all members of the community simultaneously get the benefits the F-14 provides. Any single person's consumption of the defense capabilities of the F-14 fighter does not in any way diminish their neighbor's consumption of these services. Defense is said to be a **public good.** There is a serious question as to whether private firms will provide goods in which the output can be shared in this way. The reason is that it may be difficult for firms to induce people to buy their product. If you have a choice of whether to buy a public good or wait until one of your neighbors buys it, you might very well choose to wait. Unlike situations in which there is a common input—as with the fishery problem, where there will likely be too many resources devoted to fishing—when there is a common output, there are will be too few private resources devoted to producing it.

The Fishing Game assumed only two players, so you might wonder if the problem is diminished by having more firms. Unfortunately, in general, the inefficiencies associated with the use of common resources only become more severe as the number of users increases.

---

[2]One way in which this strategic behavior could be avoided, at least in the short run, is if the two fishing companies merge into one fishing company. But this would begin to undermine the extent of competition in the fish market.

4.3   Well-Defined Property Rights and the Coase Theorem

The problem treated in the previous section is one of a larger class of problems in which private costs and benefits diverge from social costs and benefits. Each fishery's decision about how much to fish affected the profits of the other fishery, resulting in a spillover effect from one firm to the other. Consider another example: a paper mill that is located along the banks of a river. The mill uses lumber, labor, and the power provided by the river's current to produce paper. In the process, the mill also produces chemical wastes, which are dumped into the river and carried downstream. In deciding how much paper to produce, the mill will take into account the cost of the lumber and the labor, but will ignore the use of the river for power and waste disposal. That is, it treats the river as a "free" resource. The use of the river may be "free" to the mill's owners in the sense that there is no explicit charge for using it, but the mill's use of the river may be very costly to the households downstream. The point is that people other than the owners of the paper mill bear a cost from the paper mill's use of the river. This cost is called an **externality.** Since the paper mill does not bear this cost, it cannot be expected to take the externality into account when choosing its output or its production process. In fact, if the paper industry is very competitive, then the only way the paper mill can stay in business in the long run is to ignore the cost of any resources for which the firm is not explicitly charged.

You have learned in your Principles of Economics class that freely competitive markets lead firms to choose outputs where **marginal private benefits** equal **marginal private costs,** because this is where private benefits to the firm (profits) are maximized. But net social benefits are maximized when outputs are chosen where **marginal social benefits** equal **marginal social costs.** As long as private costs and social costs are the same, competitive markets and voluntary exchange would result in an efficient allocation of resources (Pareto optimality). But when there is a divergence—at least, at the margin—then competitive markets might fail to achieve the necessary conditions for efficiency, namely, the production of outputs where marginal social benefit equals marginal social cost.

The simple solution to situations where this divergence between private and social marginal benefits and costs might arise is to do something that forces the relevant firms or consumers to **internalize the externality.** That is, if firms are forced to bear the full cost of their use of the river, they will no longer treat it as a free resource and will choose the efficient use of that resource. Professor Ronald Coase's insight was to show how this internalization of externalities might be accomplished via bargaining. In particular, he stressed the role of appropriately establishing property rights. We will demonstrate Coase's argument with the use of an example familiar to all.

An unintended by-product of jet airplane travel is noise. With few exceptions, people do not like the noise produced by jets and, in fact, would be willing to pay money to avoid it if necessary. When a jet flies over a neighborhood, a transaction takes place. The residents near the flight path of the jet "consume" the noise generated by the jet. What makes this "consumption" different from consuming a can of peas bought at the grocery store is that the consumption is involuntary. When markets work well, all voluntary exchanges (making all parties affected by the exchange better off) take place. But what about all the involuntary exchanges that occur on a day-to-day basis, from jet noise near a residential neighborhood to the germs passed from one student with a cold to another student in a classroom to the wonderful scent one smells when walking past a neighbor's rose garden? Coase wanted to know whether these involuntary transactions take place in an efficient manner. In terms of the example of noise pollution, is there an efficient amount of noise being exchanged between airlines and residents living beneath flight paths?

A fundamental insight is generated by thinking of an externality as an *involuntary* exchange. Any exchange requires two parties. In the noise pollution example, the cost of the noise increases with each additional flight over the houses. But it also increases with each additional housing unit placed within earshot of the jets. It may seem obvious to you that jets *cause* noise. But, in truth, jets are only partly responsible for noise. What the jet produces is air vibrations. Human ears are needed to convert the air vibrations into the psychological experience called noise. Although most people assume that the best way to reduce the jet noise problem is to run fewer flights, it may well be less costly to move the houses and apartments somewhere far from the airport. What is important at this stage is that you not naively jump to the conclusion that the "jets cause the damage." The jets only produce noise if there are people living near the flight path. The decision to live near the flight path "causes the damage" just as much as the jets do. As with any exchange, voluntary or not, "it takes two to tango."

Consider the hypothetical case of Lake Vue Development Corporation, an apartment construction firm that is interested in putting up apartment buildings on a parcel of land it owns next to the Smallville Regional Airport. Lake Vue owns enough land to build between zero and three apartment buildings. The Smallville airport is served by a small airline, Puddlejump Express, that runs flights between Smallville and its hub at the Metropolis International Airport (Metro) located 300 miles away. Puddlejump is deciding how many flights to run per day between Smallville and Metro. Due to limited availability of gates at Metro, Puddlejump can run no more than three flights per day between Smallville and Metropolis.

The rent Lake Vue can charge households for their apartments depends on three factors: (1) the number of apartment buildings the firm chooses to build; (2) the number of planes Puddlejump chooses to fly into the airport nearby; and (3) the legal liability rules identifying who must bear the cost of any noise pollution. The first determinant of rent reflects the downward sloping demand that Lake Vue faces for apartments in this area. The second determinant captures the damages caused by noise pollution. The third determinant is the essence of the Coase theorem.

Each apartment building that Lake Vue builds contains 50 homogeneous units. Column 3 of Table 4.1 lists the monthly rents that Lake Vue could charge if Puddlejump did not fly into Smallville. The rents reflect the fact that as more

Table 4.1   Lake Vue's Potential Profits in the Absence of Puddlejump

(1) Number of Apartment Buildings	(2) Number of Apartments	(3) Maximum Potential Rent per Apartment	(4) Annual Potential Rental Income	(5) Annualized Construction and Maintenance Costs	(6) Annual Potential Profit
0	0	0	$0	$0	$0
1	50	$590	$354,000	$300,000	$54,000
2	100	$550	$660,000	$600,000	$60,000
3	150	$510	$918,000	$900,000	$18,000

apartments are built, Lake Vue will be required to lower the price per apartment; that is, the demand for apartments in this location is downward sloping. Specifically, each additional apartment building lowers maximum monthly rent by $40 per apartment. The annual rental income Lake Vue receives from the apartments it builds, assuming 100% occupancy, is given by multiplying the monthly rent it can earn on each apartment by 12 (the months in one year) and then by the number of units it builds (50 times the number of buildings). The annualized cost that Lake Vue incurs from building and maintaining the apartments is $300,000 per building.[3] So if Lake Vue builds two apartment buildings and Puddlejump generates no noise pollution, then Lake Vue can earn 2 × 50 × $550 × 12 = $660,000 in rents and incur 2 × $300,000 = $600,000 in expenses for a profit of $60,000. You can see that in the absence of Puddlejump's noisy flights, Lake Vue would build two apartment buildings and earn a profit of $60,000.

Now we must take into account the fact that Puddlejump's flights make these apartments less attractive. Furthermore, the greater the number of flights overhead, the more unattractive the apartments become. The first daily flight overhead lowers every apartment's rental value by $40 per month; the second flight lowers the rental value by an additional $15 per month; and the third flight lowers it by an additional $10 per month. The resulting rent Lake Vue can charge, which depends on the number of apartments it builds and rents and the number of flights Puddlejump runs, is shown in Table 4.2.

Since building and operational expenses are not affected by Puddlejump's operations, Lake Vue's drop in profit is due entirely to its loss in revenue. If Lake Vue has one apartment building and Puddlejump runs one flight per day, then Lake Vue loses $40 per month per apartment or $24,000 per year. Table 4.3 lists Lake Vue's losses for other possible combinations of apartment buildings and flights. The table makes it clear that the losses can be reduced two ways: (1) by reducing the number of flights, *and* (2) by reducing the number of apartments.

Puddlejump's annual revenue equals the fare charged per passenger times the number of passengers carried per flight times the number of flights run per

---

[3]These costs consist of maintenance and depreciation plus the interest income foregone on the initial capital used to build the units.

Table 4.2 *Monthly Rent Lake Vue Can Charge when Puddlejump Flies Overhead*

		Number of apartment buildings built by Lake Vue		
	0	1	2	3
0	NA	$590	$550	$510
1	NA	$550	$510	$470
2	NA	$535	$495	$455
3	NA	$525	$485	$445

Number of flights run by Puddlejump (labels for rows 0–3)

Table 4.3 *Lake Vue's Lost Profits Resulting from Puddlejump's Operations*

		Number of apartment buildings built by Lake Vue		
	0	1	2	3
0	$0	$0	$0	$0
1	$0	$24,000	$48,000	$72,000
2	$0	$33,000	$66,000	$99,000
3	$0	$39,000	$78,000	$117,000

Number of flights run by Puddlejump (labels for rows 0–3)

year. As Table 4.4 shows, Puddlejump has to lower its price in order to attract more customers. We assume that the firm prices its flights so as to ensure all seats are sold, that each plane has a 100 seat capacity, and that the firm operates 250 days a year (it does not run on weekends or holidays). Similarly, the firm's annual costs equal their operating costs per flight times the number of flights they run per year. Because of economies of scale, operating costs per flight decline as the number of flights run per year increases. Left to itself, Puddlejump would operate two flights per day.

4.3.1 RESOURCE ALLOCATION BY A BENEVOLENT DICTATOR

Suppose there were a benevolent dictator capable of specifying the number of apartment buildings that would be built by Lake Vue and the number of daily flights run by Puddlejump. This dictator is interested in maximizing the net social benefit from both activities. She can choose zero, one, two, or three apartment buildings and zero, one, two, or three flights per day. The net social benefit equals the potential profit Lake Vue could earn from its apartments (Table 4.1) plus the profit Puddlejump earns from its flights (Table 4.4) minus the losses associated with Puddlejump's noise on Lake Vue's rents (Table 4.3). For example, suppose Lake Vue were to build one apartment building and Puddlejump were to run one flight per day. Then, the net social benefit would equal $54,000 (Lake Vue's *poten-*

Table 4.4   *Puddlejump's Profits, Ignoring the Effect on Lake Vue*

(1) Number of Flights per Day	(2) Fare per Passenger	(3) Passengers Served per Day	(4) Flying Days per Year	(5) Annual Revenues	(6) Operating Costs per Flight	(7) Annual Operating Costs	(8) Annual Profit
0	*NA*	0	250	$0	NA	$0	$0
1	$200	100	250	$5,000,000	$19,690	$4,922,500	$77,500
2	$150	200	250	$7,500,000	$14,840	$7,420,000	$80,000
3	$100	300	250	$7,500,000	$9,990	$7,492,500	$7,500

tial profits) + $77,500 (Puddlejump's *actual* profits) − $24,000 (Lake Vue's lost profits due to Puddlejump's overflights) = $107,500. The net social benefit from each of the 16 possible choices is shown in Table 4.5. Obviously, the best option is for the benevolent dictator to allow Lake View to build only one apartment building and to allow Puddlejump to run only one flight per day.

4.3.2 RESOURCE ALLOCATION WHEN PROPERTY RIGHTS ARE WELL-DEFINED AND BARGAINING COSTS ARE ZERO

For a brief moment we will leave the rather brutal confines of noncooperative game theory and dwell on the greener meadows of cooperation. To many economists, the material presented in this section constitutes the most important of Coase's contributions and the conclusions generated here have come to be known as the Coase theorem.

Returning to the example above, suppose that Puddlejump is legally liable for all damage to Lake Vue's owners that results from noise associated with Puddlejump's jets. That is, Puddlejump must compensate Lake Vue for any damage resulting from the noise. In short, property rights to noise (or lack thereof) have been established. Also, suppose, *and this assumption is absolutely crucial to what follows,* that both parties can negotiate costlessly.

Under this legal arrangement, the profit to Lake Vue is independent of the number of flights being run by Puddlejump. We know from Table 4.2 that Lake

Table 4.5   *Annual Net Social Benefit for Different Production Decisions*

		Number of apartment buildings built by Lake Vue			
		0	1	2	3
Number of flights run by Puddlejump	0	$0	$54,000	$60,000	$18,000
	1	$77,500	$107,500	$89,500	$23,500
	2	$80,000	$101,000	$74,000	−$1,000
	3	$7,500	$22,500	−$10,500	−$91,500

Table 4.6 Lake Vue's Annual Profit If Puddlejump Is Fully Liable for Noise Pollution

		Number of apartment buildings built by Lake Vue			
		0	*1*	*2*	*3*
	0	0	$54,000	$60,000	$18,000
Number of flights run by Puddlejump	*1*	0	$54,000	$60,000	$18,000
	2	0	$54,000	$60,000	$18,000
	3	0	$54,000	$60,000	$18,000

Vue suffers a $40 per apartment decline in rent each month if Puddlejump runs one flight, a $55 per apartment decline in rent per month if Puddlejump runs two flights, and a $65 per apartment decline in rent per month if Puddlejump runs three flights per day. Compensation by Puddlejump means that if Lake Vue builds only one apartment building, it will earn $590 per apartment per month regardless of the number of flights run by Puddlejump. Lake Vue's profits when Puddlejump is fully liable are shown in Table 4.6.

Puddlejump's profits, however, *do* depend now on the number of apartment buildings that Lake Vue builds, since Lake Vue suffers damage with every tenant that Lake Vue rents to. Taking the compensation it must pay to Lake Vue into account, Puddlejump's profits are shown in Table 4.7.

Notice that Lake Vue apparently will choose to build two apartment buildings because that maximizes its profits. Given this choice by Lake Vue, Puddlejump will run one flight per day. But this is not a very imaginative solution since there remain potential gains to both firms from bargaining. Lake Vue makes only $6,000 of *marginal* profit on the second apartment building, meaning that it could be bribed by any amount over $6,000 per year to reduce the number of buildings from two to one. Puddlejump's profits would rise by $24,000 if Lake Vue would reduce the number of buildings from two to one, meaning that it would be willing to pay up to $24,000 to have this happen. Recalling the Coase assumption that

Table 4.7 Puddlejump's Annual Profit If Puddlejump Is Fully Liable for Noise Pollution

		Number of apartment buildings built by Lake Vue			
		0	*1*	*2*	*3*
	0	$0	$0	$0	$0
Number of flights run by Puddlejump	*1*	$77,500	$53,500	$29,500	$5,500
	2	$80,000	$47,000	$14,000	−$19,000
	3	$7,500	−$31,500	−$70,500	−$109,500

bargaining is costless, Lake Vue and Puddlejump should strike a deal to reduce the number of apartment buildings from two to one.

Are there additional gains from further bargaining? Lake Vue values the first apartment building at $54,000. That is, it needs to be paid at least $54,000 to not build any buildings versus building one. Puddlejump's annual profits would rise by $26,500 if this were to happen (notice that Puddlejump would switch to two flights per day if the number of buildings went to zero). Hence, Puddlejump would be willing to pay up to $26,500 to bribe Lake Vue to reduce its apartment buildings from one to zero. But, since the most Puddlejump is willing to pay is less than the minimum Lake Vue will accept, no additional deals remain. Our prediction is that after all bargaining is done, one apartment building will be built and one flight per day will be run. *This is exactly the same outcome that the benevolent dictator would have chosen.*

An alternative legal arrangement is that Puddlejump is not liable for any noise pollution associated with its jets. Again, property rights have been assigned, but this time to the airline. Lake Vue must simply accept the reduced revenue it can collect from tenants as a result of jet noise overhead. Now, Lake Vue's annual profit equals the potential profits from Table 4.1 minus the lost profits given in Table 4.3. This is recorded in Table 4.8. Puddlejump's profit no longer depends on Lake Vue's activities and is shown in Table 4.9.

Without bargaining, we would expect Puddlejump to choose two flights per day, resulting in a net profit of $80,000. Given Puddlejump's choice, Lake Vue would choose to build one apartment building yielding net profits of $21,000. If Lake Vue were able to convince Puddlejump to reduce the number of daily flights from two to one, then Lake Vue could make an additional $9,000 per year. Puddlejump, for its part, only values the second flight per day at $2,500 per year. Therefore, a deal should be struck in which Lake Vue pays Puddlejump somewhere between $9,000 and $2,500 per year to run only one flight per day. We leave it as an exercise for you to show that Lake Vue will not be willing to pay enough to get Puddlejump to reduce the number of daily flights all the way to zero. The predicted outcome of the bargaining is that one apartment building will be built and one daily flight will be run. *Once again, this is the same result that the benevolent dictator would have chosen.*

Let us generalize what we have discovered using our simple example: As

Table 4.8 **Lake Vue's Annual Profit If It Is Fully Liable for Noise Pollution**

| | | Number of apartment buildings built by Lake Vue | | | |
		0	1	2	3
	0	0	$54,000	$60,000	$18,000
Number of flights run by Puddlejump	1	0	$30,000	$12,000	−$54,000
	2	0	$21,000	−$6,000	−$81,000
	3	0	$15,000	−$18,000	−$99,000

*Table 4.9 Puddlejump's Annual Profit If
Lake Vue Is Fully Liable for Noise Pollution*

		Number of apartment buildings built by Lake Vue			
		0	1	2	3
	0	$0	$0	$0	$0
Number of flights run by Puddlejump	1	$77,500	$77,500	$77,500	$77,500
	2	$80,000	$80,000	$80,000	$80,000
	3	$7,500	$7,500	$7,500	$7,500

long as bargaining costs are very low, information is perfect, and property rights for all resources have been defined, then bargaining will take place until no more mutually advantageous exchanges are possible. But if no more mutually beneficial exchanges are possible, then by definition the economy must be at a point of Pareto optimality, since no one can be made better off without making someone else worse off. Adam Smith argued in *The Wealth of Nations* that a laissez-faire economy with no externalities would be led by an invisible hand to produce greater wealth. Coase's article clarified the important role of bargaining and property rights in ensuring Pareto optimality in the presence of externalities. Where property rights are not well-defined—as we saw in the fishery example—it will be impossible for people to bargain over these rights. In the end, a nonoptimal allocation of resources may result, even if bargaining is very cheap.

This, of course, has a number of important policy implications. Among them is that as long as the assumptions of the Coase theorem are met, including the establishment of property rights, no policymaker need worry about the existence of external costs or benefits, since mutually advantageous exchanges will result in a Pareto optimal outcome for the economy. Furthermore, if we are interested only in efficiency and not in distribution, then how property rights are allocated is unimportant. The production decisions of firms will be unaffected.

4.3.3 RESOURCE ALLOCATION WHEN PROPERTY RIGHTS ARE WELL-DEFINED AND BARGAINING COSTS EXIST

One of the crucial assumptions of the previous analysis was that bargaining costs were zero. Keeping all the specifics of the previous example intact, we will now assume that bargaining costs are high enough that it never pays Lake Vue and Puddlejump to negotiate. Although this assumption is extreme, weakening it does not alter our conclusions but does greatly complicate our analysis. Our assumption means that the two producers simply take the legal rules as given and make their production decisions independently of each other. Since the decisions made by Lake Vue may affect Puddlejump and the decisions by Puddlejump may affect Lake Vue, the two firms are playing a noncooperative game.

There is one other player in this game besides Lake Vue and Puddlejump whom we will call the "legislator." Her objective is to maximize net social welfare by altering the legal environment.

The order of moves in this game is fairly simple. The legislator decides what fraction of damage from noise pollution will be paid by Puddlejump, α, and what fraction will be paid by Lake Vue, β. For simplicity, we will constrain the legislator to values of α and β that add up to 1. That is, the legislator cannot subsidize the two parties by setting $\alpha + \beta$ less than 1, nor can she impose a tax by having $\alpha + \beta$ add up to more than 1.

At one extreme, the legislator could have Puddlejump pay all damages ($\alpha = 1$, $\beta = 0$); at the other extreme, she could have Lake Vue pay for any damages ($\alpha = 0$, $\beta = 1$); or she could have the airline and the developer share the cost of the noise pollution, for example ($\alpha = 0.5$, $\beta = 0.5$).

If the legislator sets ($\alpha = 1$, $\beta = 0$), then the payoff matrix for the resulting static game is given in Table 4.10. We already solved this game in Section 4.3.4. Notice that Lake Vue has a strictly dominant strategy to build two apartment buildings. While Puddlejump has no strictly dominant strategy, it does have an iterated strictly dominant strategy of running one flight per day. The resulting iterated strictly dominant strategy equilibrium is shown in bold in Table 4.10.

At the other extreme, if the legislator sets ($\alpha = 0$, $\beta = 1$), then the payoff matrix is given in Table 4.11. In this case, Puddlejump has an obvious strictly dominant strategy of flying two jets per day, implying that Lake Vue has an iterated strictly dominant strategy of building one apartment building. Again, the iterated strictly dominant strategy equilibrium is shown in bold.

If the legislator were limited to only extreme liability rules, then she would choose to have Lake Vue completely liable for the noise pollution, absolving Puddlejump of any financial responsibility. This will generate a net social benefit of $101,000 versus $89,500 if liability were reversed.

Alternatively, the legislator may choose to have the affected parties share the liability from the noise pollution. If the legislator sets ($\alpha = 0.5$, $\beta = 0.5$) then the payoff matrix is shown in Table 4.12. The iterated strictly dominant strategy equilibrium is for Puddlejump to run one flight per day and Lake Vue to build one apartment building. Let's take a moment to verify this. First, constructing

Table 4.10   *Payoff Matrix If Puddlejump Is Fully Liable for Noise Pollution*

		Number of apartment buildings built by Lake Vue			
		0	*1*	*2*	*3*
	0	(0.0, 0.0)	(0.0, 54.0)	(0.0, 60.0)	(0.0, 18.0)
Number of flights run by Puddlejump	*1*	(77.5, 0.0)	(53.5, 54.0)	**(29.5, 60.0)**	(5.5, 18.0)
	2	(80.0, 0.0)	(47.0, 54.0)	(14.0, 60.0)	(−19.0, 18.0)
	3	(7.5, 0.0)	(−31.5, 54.0)	(−70.5, 60.0)	(−109.5, 18.0)

Payoffs ($1,000s): (Puddlejump, Lake Vue)

Table 4.11 *Payoff Matrix If Lake Vue Is Fully Liable for Noise Pollution*

| | | *Number of apartment buildings built by Lake Vue* | | | |
		0	*1*	*2*	*3*
Number of flights run by Puddlejump	0	(0.0, 0.0)	(0.0, 54.0)	(0.0, 60.0)	(0.0, 18.0)
	1	(77.5, 0.0)	(77.5, 30.0)	(77.5, 12.0)	(77.5, −54.0)
	2	(80.0, 0.0)	**(80.0, 21.0)**	(80.0, −6.0)	(80.0, −81.0)
	3	(7.5, 0.0)	(7.5, 15.0)	(7.5, −18.0)	(7.5, −99.0)

Payoffs ($1,000s): (Puddlejump, Lake Vue)

zero buildings and constructing three buildings are strictly dominated strategies for Lake Vue, and running zero flights and running three flights a day are strictly dominated strategies for Puddlejump. So we can delete these columns and rows from Table 4.12. In the simplified game, constructing two buildings is strictly dominated, as is running two flights a day. After these strategies are deleted, each player has only one strategy remaining, which is its iterated strictly dominant strategy. From Chapter 1 we know that this strategy profile is also the only Nash equilibrium (in both pure and mixed strategies).

The advantage, of course, to the legislator of having the two firms share the liability in the manner described above is that it induces the outcome with the highest net social benefit: that is, the Pareto optimal solution. The importance of selecting the correct liability rule when bargaining is very costly stands in sharp contrast to what we found when we assumed that bargaining was costless. In the case of costless negotiation and exchange, after all mutually beneficial exchanges had been negotiated between Puddlejump and Lake Vue, the number of jets flown each day and the number of apartment buildings constructed were independent of the liability rule. But once bargaining is costly, who is liable for the damages may matter greatly. Decentralization no longer works. In fact, the Coase theorem

Table 4.12 *Payoff Matrix If Lake Vue and Puddlejump Share the Cost of Noise Pollution ($\alpha = 0.5$, $\beta = 0.5$)*

| | | *Number of apartment buildings built by Lake Vue* | | | |
		0	*1*	*2*	*3*
Number of flights run by Puddlejump	0	(0.0, 0.0)	(0.0, 54.0)	(0.0, 60.0)	(0.0, 18.0)
	1	(77.5, 0.0)	**(65.5, 42)**	(53.5, 36)	(41.5, −18.0)
	2	(80.0, 0.0)	(63.5, 37.5)	(47, 27)	(30.5, −31.5)
	3	(7.5, 0.0)	(−12, 34.5)	(−31.5, 21)	(−50, −40.5)

Payoffs ($1,000s): (Puddlejump, Lake Vue)

GAME THEORY IN ACTION: The Coase Theorem and Baseball

One of the implications of the Coase theorem is the **invariance hypothesis:** in the absence of transaction costs and imperfect information, the outcome of bargaining will be independent of the distribution of property rights. A natural experiment with which to test this hypothesis appears to have occurred in the Major League Baseball labor market. First, a little background. Until 1976 the reserve clause banned a player from playing on any team other than the one that owned his contract. The team could sell the player's contract to any other team whenever it wished on whatever terms it wished. This ended in 1976 with the institution of free agency. The reserve clause remained in place for players with fewer than six years of Major League experience. But after six years were up, the player became a "free agent" and could negotiate with any team he wanted on any terms he and the team agreed to. That is, ownership of a player's baseball-playing services were suddenly transferred from the teams to the players. In addition, there is a wealth of public information on the "productivity" of players and their contribution to team performance and team revenue. The Coase theorem predicts that we should observe the same movements of players between the teams under free agency as under the reserve clause. The incentives every team had under the old system to transfer its players to teams in which they would be more productive will lead free agents to make exactly the same choices about the teams on which they want to play.

Timothy Hylan, Maureen Lage, and Michael Treglia used data on the mobility behavior of pitchers to test this hypothesis ("The Coase theorem, free agency, and Major League Baseball: a panel of pitcher mobility from 1961 to 1992," *Southern Economic Journal,* April, 1996). They found that the mobility patterns changed significantly. Older pitchers, better pitchers, and pitchers on teams with high winning percentages or in large markets moved less under free agency than they did before free agency.

is stood on its head. Although the airline and the developer cannot attain Pareto optimality on their own, they can be steered there by the proper actions of the all-knowing legislator.

4.3.4 BUREAUCRACY VERSUS THE MARKET

We argued at the beginning of this chapter that the claims of some Coase theorem advocates should be treated with a great deal of skepticism. You should be equally skeptical of the conclusion just reached that the legislator can attain Pareto optimality when the market fails. The legislator can determine the best liability rule only if she can determine how the parties will behave under every possible rule. This requires a lot of information, much of which may be known only to the affected parties. For example, our hypothetical legislator would have to know the marginal costs and benefits of both the airline and the developer.

But if the legislator has access to all this information, then so should the two affected parties. But then bargaining is far more likely to be efficient and the Coase theorem may actually hold. Precisely when we look to the legislator to repair the damage caused by inefficient bargaining, we find that the legislator may not know enough to choose the optimal liability rule.

If the payoffs are not known with certainty to the legislator, she may be able to devise a way for the airline and the developer to truthfully provide this information to her. They will be truthful only if she makes it in their own interests to be truthful. But this limits what the legislator can do with the payoff information provided. She may have to convince the two parties that this information will be kept confidential and used in only a limited way. Now we have a much more complicated game than any we have considered so far. We cannot begin to study it until we have learned how to analyze games in which information and knowledge play central roles. This is the subject of Parts IV and V of this book.

4.4 Summary

This chapter has analyzed one of the most important theorems in the economics of the public sector. We have seen that the outcome of a situation in which one party engages in activities that inadvertently affect another party depends on many factors. Among these are the legal rules on property rights and the potential for efficient bargaining. The role of the legislator in determining which games are played out between firms and consumers is both subtle and important. To quote Coase:

> It would clearly be desirable if the only actions performed were those in which what was gained was worth more than what was lost. But in choosing between social arrangements within the context of which individual decisions are made, we have to bear in mind that a change in the existing system [that] will lead to an improvement in some decisions may well lead to a worsening of others. . . . In devising and choosing between social arrangements we should have regard for the total effect. This, above all, is the change in approach which I am advocating.[4]

Sounds like a pitch for game theory to us!

4.5 Further Reading

Anyone interested in the common resource problem should begin their studies with Garrett Hardin, "The Tragedy of the Commons," *Science* (December 13, 1968). An early non–game-theoretic treatment of the fishery problem is found in Gordon Scott's article, "Economic Theory of a Common Property Resource: The Fishery," *Journal of Political Economy*, 62 (1954), pp. 124–42. A more modern, dynamic treatment of the same problem is found in Gordon Munroe's "Economics of Fishing: An Introduction," in *Economics of Environmental and Natural Resource Policy*, edited by John Butlin (Boulder, Colorado: Westview Press, 1981).

The reader is strongly encouraged to take a close look at Ronald Coase, "The Problem of Social Cost," *Journal of Law and Economics*, 3 (1960), pp. 1–44. Aside from its relevance to this chapter, it should simply be part of your general edu-

---

[4]Ronald Coase, "The Problem of Social Cost," *Journal of Law and Economics* 3 (1960), p. 44.

cation. Coase's ideas have received a great deal of attention. Other articles that clarify or extend the notion of property rights and resource allocation include R. Turvey, "On Divergences Between Private and Social Costs," *Economica* (1963), and Harold Demsetz, "The Exchange and Enforcement of Property Rights," *Journal of Law and Economics* (1964). For a more modern view of the Coase theorem, see the compilation of articles in Ronald Coase, *The Firm, the Market, and the Law* (Chicago: University of Chicago Press, 1988). The effects of imperfect information on the conclusions of the Coase theorem are clearly set forth in Joseph Farrell's article, "Information and the Coase Theorem," *Journal of Economic Perspectives*, 2 (1987), pp. 113–44). Two articles that have shown the relevance of the cooperative results embedded in the Coase theorem are Steven Cheung, "The Fable of the Bees: An Economic Investigation," *Journal of Law and Economics*, 16, 1973, pp. 11–34), and Ronald Coase, "The Lighthouse in Economics," *The Journal of Law and Economics*, 17 (1974).

4.6   Discussion Questions

1. Make a list of goods produced with common inputs.
2. Based on casual observation, are there tragedy of the commons problems associated with the inputs you describe in question 1?
3. Construct an experiment that would test the empirical validity of the tragedy of the commons problem.
4. Under what conditions is it more likely that bargaining costs among individuals or firms will be low?
5. What types of informational difficulties might a legislator face when trying to determine optimal liability rules?
6. In the example in the text one airline and one developer were affected by the noise pollution. In most real instances there will be many airlines and many homeowners who are all interconnected. What new issues arise?

4.7   New Terms

carrying capacity	marginal social benefits
externality	marginal social costs
internalized externality	public good
invariance hypothesis	steady-state equilibrium
marginal private benefits	steady-state profits
marginal private costs	tragedy of the commons

4.8   Exercises

EXERCISE 4.1

This problem concerns the common fishery example in Section 4.2. Suppose Lobsters 'R Us is more efficient than Lobster World. This is equivalent to Lobsters 'R-

Us having lower fishing effort costs. In particular suppose fishing effort costs Lobsters 'R Us $0.05 per unit, but it costs Lobster World $0.10 per unit. Assume everything else is the same.

(a) Rederive the two firms' best response function.

(b) Find the new Nash equilibrium effort levels and catch rate.

(c) What is the smallest total effort level that will yield the same size catch as in the new equilibrium?

EXERCISE 4.2

(a) Suppose only Lobster World fished the lake. What would be the profit-maximizing effort level and catch rate? Show that at this level of effort Lobster World could not catch the same amount of fish with any lower effort.

(b) Now suppose both firms fish the lake but that they pay a fishing tax of $0.225 per unit of fishing effort (*not* per fish caught). This means that their costs increase from $0.10 per unit of effort to $0.325 per unit. Show that the new Nash equilibrium results in the two firms catching the same amount of fish they would have caught if there were only one firm. The tax is said to have *internalized* the externality.

EXERCISE 4.3*

Suppose that Jerry and Linda are eating popcorn while watching a movie video. Each person eats the popcorn at the rate r_i. Each person's utility depends on the quantity of popcorn eaten, Q_i and the time it takes to eat it, which equals $\frac{Q_i}{r_i}$.

Specifically, the utility function takes the form $U_i = Q_i - \left(\frac{Q_i}{r_i} - 100\right)^2$. The second term of this utility function captures the idea that the "ideal" duration for popcorn eating is 100 minutes (the length of the movie they are watching).

(a) Suppose each person is given his or her own bowl with 1,800 popcorn kernels in it. What is the optimal rate of consumption and the utility attained at this maximum?

(b) Now suppose that 3,600 popcorn kernels are placed in a communal bowl and the amount of popcorn Jerry or Linda eats is proportional to the speed with which he or she eats it. So, $Q_i = \frac{r_i}{r_{Jerry} + r_{Linda}} \cdot 3{,}600$. Determine the payoff function for each person in the communal popcorn game in terms of the strategic variables r_{Jerry} and r_{Linda}. Find the two symmetric Nash equilibria of this game and calculate the utility attained at each. (Hint: Since the payoff functions are highly nonlinear in the strategic variables, you will not be able to derive a simple expression for the best response functions, much less determine where these functions intersect. Instead, you must make

---

*Indicates a difficult exercise.

use of the fact that at any symmetric equilibrium, where $r^*_{Jerry} = r^*_{Linda} = r^*$, Jerry (or Linda) must be maximizing his (or her) utility. That is,

$$\left.\frac{\partial U_{Jerry}(r_{Jerry}, r_{Linda})}{\partial r_{Jerry}}\right|_{r_{Jerry}=r_{Linda}=r^*} = \left.\frac{\partial U_{Linda}(r_{Jerry}, r_{Linda})}{\partial r_{Linda}}\right|_{r_{Jerry}=r_{Linda}=r^*} = 0.$$

These expressions will give you one equation in only one variable, r^*. This expression can be algebraically transformed into a quadratic equation in r^*. The two roots of this equation are the two symmetric Nash equilibria of the game.)

(c) Which one of the equilibria found in (b) do you think best exemplifies the "tragedy of the commons"?

Exercises 4.4 to 4.8 are based on the noise pollution problem from Section 4.3.

EXERCISE 4.4

Suppose the state imposes an apartment tax that reduces the revenue (net of the tax) that Lake Vue earns on its apartments by 5% and suppose Puddlejump is not liable for its noise pollution. Recalculate the entries in the payoff Table 4.11 and find all the Nash equilibria.

EXERCISE 4.5

What is the payoff matrix if the legislator has Lake Vue and Puddlejump share the cost of the noise pollution unequally? That is, the legislator chooses the biased rule ($\alpha = 0.8$, $\beta = 0.2$).

EXERCISE 4.6*

The payoff matrix for the game played between Puddlejump and Lake Vue depends on the legal liability parameters, α and β, where α is the proportion of the pollution costs allocated to Puddlejump and β is the proportion allocated to Lake Vue. Assume there are no subsidies or taxes, so that $\alpha + \beta$ must equal one or $\alpha = 1 - \beta$. Use Tables 4.1, 4.3, and 4.4 to calculate the entries in the payoff matrix as functions of the single parameter β. For example, if Lake Vue builds one building and Puddlejump runs two flights per day, then Puddlejump's payoff is $\$47,000 + \beta \cdot \$24,000$ and Lake Vue's payoff is $\$54,000 - \beta \cdot \$33,000$. Use the payoff matrix you constructed to show that the Nash equilibrium will be Pareto optimal if and only if $\beta > 0.25$ or $\beta < 0.722$.

EXERCISE 4.7

Suppose the rental value of every apartment is reduced by $15 per month for each additional flight that Puddlejump runs per day. That is, the rent is reduced by $15/month if there is one flight per day; by $30/month if there are two flights per day, and so on. Recalculate the noise pollution costs in Table 4.3. What is the Pareto optimal number of flights and number of apartment buildings? How much does society lose by adopting a "fair" liability rule that splits damages 50/50 between Lake Vue and Puddlejump rather than the optimal liability rule?

*Indicates a difficult exercise.

CHAPTER 5

Voting Games

OVERVIEW OF CHAPTER 5

5.1   Introduction

You may be surprised at finding a chapter on voting in a textbook that is aimed at economists. Economists usually confine their attention to the operation of markets. Yet voting is an important part of our lives and is used to make many important economic decisions such as:

> The acceptance or rejection by a corporation's board of directors of the merger offer tendered by a competing firm.

> The acceptance or rejection by a union's rank and file of the labor contract negotiated by the union's officers.

> The acceptance or rejection by a state's voters of a proposal to issue new bonds with which to build new roads and bridges.

The outcome of any vote depends on the voting rules and the ballots submitted by the voters. Voting is, therefore, a type of game and amenable to game-theoretic analysis. If secret ballots are used, then the voters are playing a static game. Strategically sophisticated voters realize that it may not always be optimal to vote sincerely. By "sincerely" we mean voting for the candidate or the ballot choice one truly believes is the best. When voters are sophisticated, small changes in the voting mechanism (e.g., making ballots secret) can significantly alter the ballots submitted.

Besides providing a framework for predicting how people and institutions interact, game theory has shown how seemingly fair and intelligent voting mechanisms can generate perverse voting outcomes. Such voting "paradoxes" are the subject of this chapter.

In this chapter, we will employ two different models of voters. We will refer to a voter as **naive** if he always casts his ballot honestly, even when it is not in his best interest to do so. We will refer to a voter as a **strategic voter** if she always casts her ballot so as to obtain the best outcome possible given her information, the voting rules, and her beliefs about how the other voters will behave.

5.2   Choosing Among Voting Mechanisms

Every second Tuesday in November in even-numbered years, U.S. voters elect members of the House of Representatives. Those eligible voters who find it worthwhile to cast their vote go to a designated polling location, are presented with a ballot listing the candidates for the House of Representatives seat for their district, and are asked to designate on the ballot which *one* of the candidates they prefer. These ballots are tallied and the person receiving the largest number of votes is declared the winner. This procedure is called **plurality voting** and is the voting mechanism most commonly used to make public decisions or to elect political candidates. Yet plurality voting is just one of many voting decision mechanisms that have been used or proposed. For example, voters could be allowed to vote for as many candidates as they *approve of.* The ballots are tallied and the candidate receiving the highest number of approval votes is declared the winner. This voting mechanism is called, unsurprisingly, **approval voting,** and is currently used to determine elections held by the American Statistical Association, the Mathematical Association of America, and the Institute of Electrical and Electronics Engineers.[1]

If we take a step back for a minute, we can see that voting is just one procedure the members of a group could use to form a "collective" ranking of a group of candidates on the basis of their individual rankings. We will refer to any such mechanism as a **social choice mechanism** or SCM. An SCM can be thought of as a computer program. Its input is the candidate rankings of every member of the group, however disparate these rankings are; its output is a single ranking of the candidates.

In 1954, Kenneth Arrow proposed four normative axioms that he thought any "democratic" and "rational" SCM ought to possess. This landmark work was the main reason he was awarded the Nobel Prize in 1972. Arrow's requirements:

---

[1]See Steven J. Brams and Peter C. Fishburn, *Approval Voting* (Boston: Birkhauser, 1983).

1. No candidate is ranked higher by *every* member of the group than the candidate ranked highest by the SCM.

2. The ranking provided by the SCM is always complete and transitive whenever the ranking of every member of the group is complete and transitive.

3. The relative ranking of any two candidates that is provided by the SCM depends only on the individual rankings of these two candidates. It does not depend on how these two candidates are ranked against any other candidates.

4. The social choice mechanism is *not* a dictatorship. That is, there is no individual whose ranking *always* matches the ranking of the SCM, whatever the rankings of the other members of the group.

The first condition simply requires that the SCM never generate a top candidate who would be unanimously defeated by another candidate in a head-to-head election. This requirement is often called the **Pareto condition.** If every voter in an election prefers a specific alternative outcome to the one that was chosen in the election, then surely the choice was a bad one and the mechanism giving rise to that choice should be changed. The second condition is called **transitivity with unlimited domain** and has four important features. First, it requires that the SCM be complete or "decisive." There is little point in elections that do not result in a decision. Second, it requires the SCM to rank candidate x better than candidate z whenever it also ranks candidate x better than candidate y, and candidate y better than candidate z. Third, it allows for any possible set of complete and transitive preferences among voters. Fourth, it requires the SCM to be complete and transitive *only* if the individual rankings of the group are complete and transitive. If any of the individual rankings are incomplete or intransitive, then the SCM can behave strangely. This is a variation of the old line: "garbage in; garbage out."

The third condition—and the most controversial of the four—is known as the **independence of irrelevant alternatives** condition. It implies that if the SCM ranks candidate A above candidate B, this ranking is independent of whether or not candidate C is on the ballot. Plurality voting is notorious for violating this condition. With plurality voting, two candidates, say Dem and Rep, might be ranked by as many as two thirds of the voters above the third candidate, Rad. That is, if either Dem or Rep ran head to head against Rad, she would win by a resounding two-to-one margin. But in a three-way race, Dem and Rep could (and have in a number of instances) split the anti-Rad vote, resulting in the election of the relatively unpopular Rad! The final condition simply defines and then rules out dictatorships. Remember that Arrow was trying to characterize the essential normative features of "democratic" mechanisms.

In what is one of the most remarkable works of logic ever written, Arrow proved that any SCM satisfying the first three conditions must necessarily run afoul of the fourth.[2] That is, any voting mechanism—repeat, *any* voting mecha-

---

[2]See Kenneth Arrow, *Social Choice and Individual Values* (New York: John Wiley & Sons, 1951).

nism—that meets conditions 1, 2, and 3, all of which appear eminently desirable and reasonable, is inconsistent with democracy—not just American democracy, *any* democracy. This result is now called **Arrow's impossibility theorem.**

> **THEOREM 5.1 (ARROW'S IMPOSSIBILITY THEOREM):** There is no social choice mechanism that simultaneously satisfies the Pareto condition, the independence of irrelevant alternatives condition, and the transitivity with unlimited domain condition, and is also nondictatorial.

Depressing as this result is, social choices must be made and voting mechanisms must be selected. We will consider several below. You will not be surprised, however, when in evaluating the merits of alternative SCMs we find they are all somehow fundamentally flawed. This is just the practical implication of Arrow's insight.

5.3 Majority Rule with Two Choices

Consider the choice between two candidates, x and y, by an odd number of voters using **majority rule:** the winner is the candidate who receives more than half of the votes cast. Each voter is allowed to express which of the two candidates he or she prefers, but there is no mechanism for expressing the intensity of this preference. The winner of the election is that candidate who receives the most votes. Since there are only two candidates and an odd number of voters, one of the two candidates is guaranteed to receive a majority of the ballots cast and win the election. As we have seen above in our discussion of the independence of irrelevant alternatives, such decisiveness is no longer guaranteed if there are more than two candidates.

Suppose a voter prefers candidate x over candidate y. Also assume that the vote is by secret ballot, so that the voter is playing a static game with other voters. If the election ends in a tie, then the winner is determined by a coin toss. She only has three strategies available to her: vote for x, vote for y, or abstain. Her vote matters only when it either causes a tie or breaks what would otherwise be a tie. In either case a vote for x weakly dominates a vote for y. In addition, if voting is costly, a vote for x weakly dominates abstaining. Only when voting is costly might it be rational to abstain.

In an election between two candidates decided by a majority rule, all voters will rationally abstain or vote honestly for their most preferred candidate. Abstentions aside, the incentive to vote honestly when casting a ballot seems like a good thing. Notice, however, that we have begged at least five important questions: (1) How was the voting mechanism chosen in the first place? (2) Why are only two candidates standing for election? (3) How have the two candidates staked out their positions so that the voters can choose between them? (4) Since voting is costly, what incentives does the voter have to actually go to the polling location to cast her ballot? (5) Since gathering information about candidates is costly, what incentive does the voter have to become informed about the candidates? For the rest of this chapter we will study the behavior of voting rules assuming that all voters are well informed, that their preferences are common knowledge, and that they take the voting mechanism and the slate of candidates as given.

One of the questions that we sidestepped above concerns the positioning of candidates. It would be hopelessly naive to believe that candidate positions reflect their heartfelt convictions and are independent of the preferences of the voters. In this section, we will demonstrate an important result in two candidate elections with majority rule and a large number of voters. Namely, candidates will tend to choose positions in accord with the median preferences of voters. First, a comment about voter behavior.

The expected benefit from voting strategically instead of honestly depends in part on the probability of one person's vote influencing the outcome of an election. With majority rule, one person's vote only matters if the vote would have been a tie or decided by one vote without this person's ballot. With a large number of voters, this probability is close to zero. Hence, in these circumstances, the expected gains from voting strategically are close to zero. If there is any nontrivial payoff from casting one's ballot honestly, then we would expect voters in these circumstances to vote honestly. In what follows in this section, we will presume that this is precisely what voters do. Later on we will discuss strategic voting when there are only a few voters and the expected gains from behaving strategically are much larger.

Suppose that candidate positions are captured by a univariate scale ranging from 0 to 1. See Figure 5.1. We can think of the position of 0 as being far to the left on public issues and a position of 1 as being an extreme right-wing position. Both candidates in this model are assumed to stake out positions on this scale simultaneously. Each candidate's objective is to win the election. There are 101 voters whose preferences also range from 0 to 1 on the same univariate scale. The preferences are uniformly distributed, meaning in this case that one voter is located at 0.0, another at 0.01, another at 0.02, and so on, with voter 101 being located at 1.0. Each voter will simply vote for the candidate who is positioned closest to his or her preferences. If the candidates are in exactly the same position, the voter will flip a coin. For example, if a voter is located at 0.35 and candidate A chooses to locate at 0.30 while candidate B chooses to locate at 0.39, this voter will cast her ballot for B because B is located only 0.04 units from her while A is located 0.05 units away. Voters such as these are said to have **single-peaked** preferences. Alternatively, if a voter preferred candidates located both to the left and to the right of some candidate, then this voter would *not* have single-peaked preferences. Economists have shown that if the domain of voter preferences is restricted to those that are single-peaked, then Arrow's theorem loses much of its teeth. The candidates are assumed to choose their positions simultaneously and cannot budge from that choice once it is made. We will also suppose that voter preferences and candidate objectives are common knowledge. We will refer to the resulting game as the **Candidate Positioning Game.**

Consider candidate A's position decision. Suppose candidate B positions

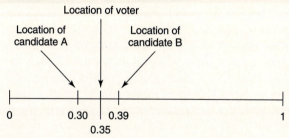

FIGURE 5.1 Candidate and voter locations on left-to-right scale.

himself at 0.30. Candidate A will guarantee herself a win by locating at any point from 0.31 to 0.69. In particular, she can win by positioning herself at 0.50. By doing so, A will receive all votes from voters ranging from 0.41 to 1.0 (60 votes) and B will receive at most all the votes from voters located less than or equal to 0.40 (41 votes). In fact, candidate A can guarantee herself a win by positioning herself at 0.50 if candidate B positions himself anywhere to the left of 0.50. The reverse is also true. If B positions himself to the right of 0.50, A can guarantee herself a win by locating at 0.50. If B positions himself directly on 0.50 then A will lose the election if she positions herself anywhere else but at 0.50 also. At least there she has a 50% chance of winning. Any other position guarantees B at least 51% of the votes. We have just shown that positioning at 0.50 is a weakly dominant strategy for both candidates, and so both candidates positioning themselves at 0.50 is a weakly dominant strategy equilibrium. This is also the unique Nash equilibrium for this game. But 0.50 is the position of the median voter. So we have shown that in the Candidate Positioning Game, both candidates' positions converge to the position of the median voter.

All uniform distributions with odd numbers of voters, however, have the property that the preferences of the median voter equal the mean of all the voters' preferences. To show that candidates will converge toward the median voter and not the mean of all the voters, we need to consider a distribution of preferences where the mean and the median are not equal.

Suppose the 101 voters have preferences as shown in Table 5.1.

The mean position across all 101 voters is approximately 0.31. The median position is 0.10. Is locating at the mean a reasonable strategy for a candidate to choose? If A positions herself at 0.31, then B can guarantee himself a win by positioning himself at 0.30 and getting 69 votes. But if B positions himself at 0.3, then A can guarantee herself a win by positioning herself at 0.20. So positioning at 0.31 is not an equilibrium strategy for either player.

Table 5.1 A New Distribution of Voter Preferences

Voter position	0.0	0.1	0.2	0.3	0.4	0.5	0.6	0.7	0.8	0.9	1.0
Number of voters	36	15	10	8	5	3	1	2	3	5	13

However, if A positions herself at 0.10, then B has a chance of winning the election only if he copies her and positions himself there as well. If B positions himself to the left of 0.10, he wins at most 36 votes and if he locates to the right of 0.10, he wins at most 50 votes, not quite enough to win. By locating at 0.10, B has a 50% chance of winning as opposed to a guaranteed loss. Positioning at 0.10, the median voter's position, is the unique weakly dominant strategy equilibrium. This conclusion is quite general and is known as the **median voter theorem.**

> **THEOREM 5.2 (THE MEDIAN VOTER THEOREM):** If there are two candidates, the two candidates' political positions can be represented by their location on a continuous linear scale, each voter's preference over these positions is single-peaked, the distribution of voter preferences is common knowledge, and the election is decided by majority rule; then the unique Nash equilibrium strategy in the Candidate Positioning Game is for both candidates to position themselves at the median voter's position.

5.4   Plurality Rule and the Condorcet Candidate

Consider an election among three candidates, x, y, and z, for the position of mayor of Tinytown. If a voter prefers candidate x to y and candidate y to candidate z, we display his preference symbolically as $x > y > z$. There are 300 voters whose preferences are shown in Table 5.2.

If all voters vote naively, then 95 votes will be cast for x, 95 for y, and 110 for z. Hence, z will win. One important problem with this outcome is that if z were put up against either x or y in head-to-head elections, z would lose badly. The vast majority of voters in this case detest z, yet he is the one elected. One way of describing this situation is that x and y are "splitting" the large anti-z vote.

If the election of candidate z seems a particularly bad outcome, then candidate x's election would appear to be particularly meritorious. If x were to go head to head against y, x would win 205 to 95. If x were to go head to head against z, x would win 190 to 110. Candidate x wins any head-to-head race against every other candidate. A candidate who is preferred by a majority of voters to any other alternative in a series of pairwise comparisons is called a **Condorcet candidate**

Table 5.2   Hypothetical Voter Preferences in Tinytown

Voter Type	Number of Voters with That Type	Preference
A	95	$x > y > z$
B	95	$y > x > z$
C	110	$z > x > y$

Table 5.3 ***Voter Preferences That Produce No Condorcet Candidate***

Voter Type	Number of Voters with That Type	Preference
A	1	$x > y > z$
B	1	$y > z > x$
C	1	$z > x > y$

after the Marquis de Condorcet. The Marquis argued that any voting system that did not elect the Condorcet candidate whenever one exists is flawed and should not be used. The fact that the plurality rule very often does not result in the election of the Condorcet candidate is a fairly strong argument against its use.[3] There are numerous examples in U.S. political history where a situation qualitatively identical to the one described in Table 5.2 has resulted in an extreme candidate such as z being chosen. In 1970, James Buckley won one of the two New York U.S. Senate seats over two other candidates, Charles Goodell and Richard Ottinger, by gathering just 39% of the vote (Goodell received 24% and Ottinger 37%). Polls suggested that either losing candidate would have beaten Buckley in a head-to-head election. Also in New York, in 1980, Alphonse D'Amato defeated Elizabeth Holtzman and Jacob Javits, both liberals, for a U.S. Senate seat by gathering 45% of the vote compared with Holtzman's 44% and Javits's 11%. Almost without doubt, Holtzman was the Condorcet candidate even though she lost the election.

There are many circumstances, however, in which there is no Condorcet candidate. Consider the preferences of voters depicted in Table 5.3.

In this case, if x goes head to head with y, x wins 2 to 1. If x goes head to head with z, z wins 2 to 1. And, if z goes head to head with y, y wins 2 to 1. No one candidate can muster a majority of votes against *all* alternatives, hence there is no Condorcet candidate. Voter preferences such as those listed in Table 5.3 are called a **cyclical majority.**

5.5 A Modified Plurality Rule: The Single Transferable Vote

In many elections, plurality rule is modified in some fashion so as to increase the likelihood that a majority will favor the winner. One way to do this is via a

---

[3]Without knowing the intensity of voters' preferences, we really cannot say with any certainty that x is the best option, hence our reluctance to give too much weight to this criteria.

GAME THEORY IN ACTION: Verdict Voting

In many voting situations where there are more than two options, the outcome is often heavily influenced by the order in which items are brought to a vote. In formal committees or legislatures, the order in which votes are taken is called the *agenda*. He who controls the agenda can often control the outcome. One of the oldest examples is recorded in the letters of Pliny the Younger, a Roman lawyer in the first century.[1] Pliny was the presiding officer of the Roman Senate when the case of Afranius Dexter was brought to the Senate for resolution. Consul Afranius Dexter had been found dead (probably from poisoning). The death could have been a self-inflicted suicide, a suicide at the hands of one of his servants, or a criminal murder by his servants. The Senate was called on to decide the fate of his free servants, or *freemen* (his slaves were probably executed wholesale). Before the Senators were three options—*acquittal (A), banishment (B),* and *execution (E)*—and there were supporters of each option. The size of these three groups and their preferences over the three options are given in the table below.

Factions in the Roman Senate

Decision	Size of the Faction	Preference
Acquittal (A)	45%	$A > B > E$
Banishment (B)	35%	$B > A > E$
Execution (E)	20%	$E > B > A$

If you examine the table carefully, you will see that banishment is a Condorcet candidate. As a result, any decision procedure in which the options are voted on in pairs (a *binary* procedure) will result in a verdict of guilt and banishment. This would be the outcome, for example, if the Senate used the procedures of a modern court and decided on guilt or innocence before deciding on the sentence. In the case at hand, the accused would have been found guilty by a vote of 55% to 45%. Banishment would then have been selected on a vote of 80% to 20%. Pliny, who sided with the acquitters, foresaw the outcome of a binary procedure and demanded that the Senate select the verdict using a single three-way plurality vote. In this three-way election, acquittal (with 45% of the vote) would be elected over banishment, the Condorcet option (with only 35% of the vote).

Pliny almost got the outcome he sought. The leader of the execution faction was as crafty as Pliny, however, and outmaneuvered him by joining the banishment faction. Pliny's strategem depended for its success on all the Senators voting truthfully, rather than strategically. By joining forces with the banishers, the executioners were able to get their second-most preferred option rather than their least preferred. As a result, Pliny was defeated even though he controlled the agenda.

[1]This story has appeared in many places. Our account is based on that of William Riker in *The Art of Political Manipulation* (New Haven: Yale University Press, 1986, Chapter 7).

mechanism called the **single transferable vote.** In this system, voters are given a slate of candidates and are asked to vote for one. If no one candidate receives a majority of the votes cast, a second ballot is taken in which the candidate receiving the smallest number of votes from the first ballot is dropped from the list of eligible candidates. This process is continued until a majority votes for one candidate. Assuming that voter preferences are unaffected by the sequential dropping of candidates (which will be true if voters are naive), the single transferable vote can be implemented most easily by asking the voters to rank the candidates rather than just selecting their favorite. Election officials would count the number of voters who ranked each candidate first. If a candidate is ranked first by a majority of the voters, he wins the election. Otherwise, the candidate who was ranked first by the fewest number of voters is scratched from every voter's preference ranking. Let us call this candidate Mr. D. On those voter lists where Mr. D was previously ranked first, his ranking is "transferred" to the second-best candidate. The officials now recount the number of voters who rank each candidate first (among eligible candidates). This continues until someone receives a majority and is elected. We will hereafter assume that the single transferable vote is implemented this way, and will refer to the candidate rankings submitted by each voter as a "ballot." This is precisely how public officials are elected in Australia, for example.

Suppose a corporation holds a shareholder election to choose a public accounting firm to act as that corporation's auditor. There are four voting owners of the corporation and each owner has as many votes as he or she has shares. Three public accounting firms are competing for the job. The preferences of the four voters are depicted in Table 5.4.

Each voter is asked to rank the three candidates on his ballot. The candidate receiving the smallest number of "most preferred" votes is eliminated and those voters casting ballots for that candidate now have their votes transferred to their "second most preferred" candidate. The voting ends when one candidate receives a majority of votes cast, in this case 13 votes. Since there are only three candidates, at most two rounds are required to find a winner.

If all voters cast their ballots honestly, then in the first round y receives 9

Table 5.4 **Shareholder Preferences**

Voter	Number of Shares/Votes	Preference
A	8	$z > y > x$
B	7	$x > z > y$
C	6	$y > x > z$
D	3	$y > z > x$

most preferred votes, z receives 8, and x receives 7. Hence, x is dropped. In the second round, B's votes are now transferred to z (B's second most preferred candidate). Candidate z now receives a majority of the votes cast in the second round and wins the election.

The single transferable vote can produce some odd and disturbing results. First, as is the case with the plurality rule, the Condorcet candidate is not always chosen. More subtly, however, suppose that voter D has a change of heart. Specifically, voter D decides that she does not really like accounting firm y all that much after all and really has a preference for z over y and both of those over x. In short, accounting firm z has risen in D's estimation. Now, if all voters cast their ballots honestly, the first round of ballots results in 11 votes for z, 7 for x, and 6 for y. Therefore, y is eliminated. This means that C's votes are transferred to candidate x. In the second round, x gets 13 votes and wins the election. The oddity, of course, is that when D did not have such a strong preference for z, z won. As D's preferences for z strengthened, z went from winning to losing. Many voting systems suffer from this **monotonicity paradox.**

Having discussed some attributes of the single transferable vote when voters cast ballots naively, we turn to the issue of how voters might behave when they can cast their ballots strategically. In particular, is voting honestly a Nash equilibrium under this system?

In our shareholder example, each voter has six possible strategies. Each strategy consists of the submission of one of the six possible preference orderings the shareholders can have over the three accounting firms. We have just seen that if all the other voters cast their ballots honestly, then z will win. Since this is voter A's preferred outcome, she cannot unilaterally improve her well-being by reporting her preferences dishonestly. Now, consider voter B. Given that the other voters submit their true preference rankings, Table 5.5 shows how the outcome of the election varies with B's ballot.

B cannot unilaterally get x, his most preferred choice, elected. The only possible outcomes are y or z, but y is B's worst option. B can do no better voting dishonestly than he can by voting honestly. Now consider voter C. Since z is the

Table 5.5 The Outcome of the Election As B's Vote Changes When the Other Voters Are Honest

Voter B's Ballot	Winner
$x > z > y$ (honest)	z
$x > y > z$	y
$z > x > y$	z
$z > y > x$	z
$y > x > z$	y
$y > z > x$	y

Table 5.6   A Nash Equilibrium for the Shareholder
Election under the Single Transferable Vote

Voter	Number of Shares/Votes	True Preference	Nash Equilibrium Strategy (Ballot)
A	8	$z > y > x$	$z > y > x$ (true)
B	7	$x > z > y$	$z > x > y$ (false)
C	6	$y > x > z$	$y > x > z$ (true)
D	3	$y > z > x$	$y > z > x$ true)

accounting firm C likes least, C is most likely to benefit from voting dishonestly. If the other three voters were to vote honestly, C could insure the selection of x by marking x as his most preferred option on his ballot. The fact that C can improve his well-being unilaterally means that voting honestly is *not* a Nash equilibrium in this election with these voter preferences.

This simple game has many Nash equilibria. One equilibrium is shown in Table 5.6. This set of ballots results in z winning on the first round with 15 votes out of 24 cast, regardless of what C and D do. Let us verify that this is an equilibrium. Since the election of z is A's preferred outcome, she gains nothing by altering her ballot. Since C and D are outvoted, their ballots have no effect on the outcome. Since z wins on the first ballot, the second and third rankings submitted also have no effect on the outcome. So it remains to verify that B cannot do better by changing the candidate he ranks first. If B ranks y first, then y wins, which B considers the worst outcome of all. If he reports $x > z > y$, then z is elected in the second round. Finally, if he reports $x > y > z$, then no one wins the first round, x is dropped, and y wins on the second ballot, which is B's worst outcome. This proves that these collections of ballots constitute a Nash equilibrium of this game. We encourage you to find the other Nash equilibria.

5.6   Strategic Voting with Plurality Rule

We already know that voting under both majority and plurality rule can produce some unsettling results. One of the more interesting results is one we will call the **chairman's paradox.** This example challenges most people's (untutored) ideas of "voting power." Very simply, one member of a committee—we'll refer to him as the chairman—is given the "power" to break ties. As a consequence of this "power," the resulting plurality-rule voting game has a unique iterated dominant strategy equilibrium whose outcome is the one considered the worst by the "powerful" chairman. Paradoxically, the "power" to break ties turns out to be a handicap that every member on the committee will want to shun.

Three economists at a college, Paul, Mary, and Sue, have been asked by the economics department to choose the mathematics requirement for economics majors. They are considering three options. The first option is to require no math courses for students majoring in economics. The second option is to require one term of univariate calculus. The third option is to require two terms of calculus: one of univariate calculus and one of multivariate calculus. We will denote the first option as *L* (low requirement), the second option as *M* (medium requirement) and the third option as *H* (high requirement).

Each member of the committee has a preference ranking of the three options that is common knowledge to everyone on the committee. In a small department such as this it would seem likely that these views would be known by others in the department. Concern over curriculum is a common lunch topic, and goodness knows, faculty members are rarely shy about expressing their opinions on issues of pedagogy. In short, over the years, each of the committee member's views about the importance of mathematics in an economics curriculum have been expressed, and these views are not likely to be changed by a committee discussion.

Paul is very sympathetic with those students who are math phobic and would prefer to have no math requirement. He argues that the math required for rigorous theoretical analysis can be taught at graduate school to those few students choosing that route and has only a limited role in an undergraduate curriculum. In fact, Paul would always rather have fewer math courses required than more math courses.

In contrast, were multivariate calculus required for an economics major, Sue would make good use of it in the upper-level courses she teaches. It is her sense that virtually all interesting economic relationships are multivariate and, therefore, one term of univariate calculus alone is not of much use to her. As a result, she prefers the *H* option, followed by the *L* option, followed by the *M* option.

Finally, Mary is not as strident as either of her colleagues. She certainly recognizes the value of calculus in economics, but is also aware that many students might be dissuaded from choosing economics as a major if they must take two terms of calculus. It is her view that a simple version of multivariate calculus can be added to an upper-level economics class at little cost, at least as long as the students have already had some univariate calculus training. She prefers option *M*. If she were asked to choose between *H* and *L*, she would reluctantly choose *H*.

The preferences of the three economists are summarized in Table 5.7.

Table 5.7 **Voter Preferences**

Voter	Preference
Paul	$L > M > H$
Sue	$H > L > M$
Mary	$M > H > L$

Because of his seniority in the department, Paul is chosen to chair the committee. Each member of the committee hopes that a consensus will develop, making a vote unnecessary. Knowing the past history of each of the other members, though, such a consensus seems unlikely. Indeed, we will assume that a consensus does not emerge. Instead, the matter is put to a vote. There are, of course, many voting procedures they could use, but we will suppose this vote takes place using plurality rule. The vote is by secret ballot with each committee member casting one ballot. The option receiving the greatest number of votes wins. In the event of a tie between two or more options, the Chair's vote will break the tie. With only three voters, a tie will occur only if all three voters vote for different options, thereby creating a three-way tie. When this happens, the option chosen by the Chair will be the one reported out by the committee.

To summarize: There are three members of a committee who are trying to choose among three options. There is a decided lack of agreement about which option is best for the department. One of the committee members, Paul, has been designated the Chair of the committee. The Chair carries with it the ability to cast a tie-breaking vote. It would seem that by virtue of the extra voting power, it is more likely that Paul's preferred outcome will be chosen. This intuition is confirmed by the naive voting model presented below.

5.6.1 THE NAIVE VOTING MODEL

If all three members of the committee vote naively, then the outcome of the vote is straightforward and intuitive: Paul will vote for L, Mary will vote for M, and Sue will vote for H. By virtue of being Chair, Paul will be able to break the deadlock. Therefore, L is chosen by the committee and economics majors will not be required to take any math courses. Furthermore, Paul ends up with the option that he thinks is the best of the three. The power of being Chair brings with it a very desirable outcome—from the Chair's perspective of course! There are no surprises.

5.6.2 THE STRATEGIC VOTING MODEL

Aside from the moral conviction to ''tell the truth,'' there is no obvious reason why each person should vote with their heart. The members of the committee are really interested in the outcome of the vote, not whether their vote accurately reflects their view of the way the economics major ought to be structured. From this perspective, we would expect each of the committee members to vote truthfully if and only if it is rational for them to do so.

Since the voting is by secret ballot, each committee member votes without knowledge of how anyone else voted. Paul gets to make a second move (to break the tie) in the event of a three-way tie. It is obvious, though, that he will cast his second vote for the option he considers the best: option L. So the game essentially reduces to a static game in which the set of strategies and the set of moves coincide. The concept we will employ to make predictions about strategic voting behavior

Table 5.8 **Payoff Matrix Assuming Paul Votes for L**

			Mary's vote	
		H	M	L
	H	(**Best, Middle,** Worst)	(**Middle,** Worst, Best)	(**Middle,** Worst, Best)
Sue's vote	M	(Middle, Worst, Best)	(Worst, **Best,** Middle)	(**Middle,** Worst, Best)
	L	(Middle, **Worst,** Best)	(**Middle, Worst,** Best)	(**Middle, Worst,** Best)

Payoffs: (Sue, Mary, Paul)

Best responses are in **bold**.

is Nash equilibrium. But, if we can find dominant strategies and/or iterated dominant strategies, we will use them as our predictors. Because of Paul's voting power, it is likely that he has dominated strategies that can be removed from the game. Let's find them.

Consider Paul's best response to every possible pair of votes by Mary and Sue. If Mary and Sue vote for the same candidate, then Paul's vote is irrelevant and all three of Paul's strategies are equally good. If Mary and Sue split their vote, then Paul's vote determines the outcome. Hence, Paul has a weakly dominant strategy of voting for *L*. We would predict, and so presumably would Mary and Sue, that he will vote for *L*. Based on this prediction, we can now reduce the game to a static game between Mary and Sue. The payoff matrix of this game is shown in Table 5.8. The best response of each player to the other's strategy is shown by displaying the player's payoff in boldface.

Table 5.8 shows that there are three pure-strategy Nash equilibria. We will now see if we can use dominance to pare these equilibria down to one. Since Mary is the voter who most vehemently dislikes option *L*, it makes some sense to see what we can say about her vote. Mary, you may recall, prefers *M* to *H* and *H* to *L*. Given that Paul will vote for *L*, Mary must vote with Sue for either *H* or *M*, or *L* will be chosen. Notice, this means that voting for *L* is weakly dominated by voting for *H* or *M*, but at this stage we cannot say which Mary will prefer. Table 5.9 shows the payoff matrix after we eliminate Sue's weakly dominated strategy.

Two Nash equilibria survive our paring. Recall that Sue has a preference for *H* over *L* and her least preferred outcome is *M*. If Mary votes for *H*, Sue is clearly best off voting for *H*. If Mary votes for *M*, the worst thing that Sue can do is vote for *M*, but it doesn't matter whether she votes for *H* or *L*. Therefore, Sue has an iterated weakly dominant strategy of voting for *H*. This allows us to pare down the game one more time, which we do in Table 5.10.

Having deduced that Paul will vote for *L* and Sue will vote for *H*, it is clearly in Mary's interest to vote for *H*. The Nash equilibrium that has survived is also an iterated (weakly) dominant strategy equilibrium. If you feel breathless, we are sympathetic. Take a moment to come to grips with the bottom line. We can, after all the going back and forth, predict the outcome of the voting. Paul will vote for

Table 5.9   Payoff Matrix Assuming Paul Votes for L *and Mary Does Not Vote for* L

		Mary's vote	
		H	*M*
Sue's vote	*H*	(**Best**, **Middle**, Worst)	(**Middle**, Worst, Best)
	M	(Middle, Worst, Best)	(Worst, **Best**, Middle)
	L	(Middle, **Worst**, Best)	(**Middle**, Worst, Best)

Payoffs: (Sue, Mary, Paul)

Best responses are in **bold**.

Table 5.10   Payoff Matrix Assuming Paul Votes for L, *Mary Does Not Vote for* L, *and Sue Votes for* H

		Mary's vote	
		H	*M*
Sue's vote	*H*	(**Best**, **Middle**, Worst)	(Middle, **Worst**, Best)

Payoffs: (Sue, Mary, Paul)

Best responses are in **bold**.

L, Mary will vote for *H*, and Sue will vote for *H*. Remarkably, *H* wins, even though the Chair of the committee, Paul, considers this his *worst outcome*. The "power" to break ties turns out to be a bad thing for the person who is unlucky enough to be saddled with it. Oddly enough, once the committee is assigned, there should be a fight among the members *not* to be chosen as Chair, even though the Chair brings with it extra voting "privileges."

Of course, what drives the result is that Mary does not vote "naively." She recognizes that if she were to do so, then she would end up with what she considers to be the worst outcome. Therefore, she votes strategically.[4]

5.6.3 OTHER EQUILIBRIA

We are not done with our analysis of this game. Although the "paradoxical" equilibrium is the only iterated weakly dominant equilibrium of this game, there are four other pure-strategy Nash equilibria.

---

[4]To single out Mary as acting strategically is unfair. We have assumed that all three committee members vote strategically. It just so happens that Mary's strategic vote differs from her naive vote while the strategic votes for the other two members of the committee coincide with their naive votes.

First, there are the three "unanimity" Nash equilibria in which all three committee members vote for the same outcome. These are clearly equilibria, since no member can alter the outcome by unilaterally changing his or her vote. But we dismissed these equilibria at the very beginning of this application as very unlikely. Each equilibrium requires one of the players to vote for his or her worst option and this action is weakly dominated by voting for either of the other two options. If it were possible for the committee to arrive at a unanimous decision when their preferences are so disparate, then there would be no need to undertake a game-theoretic analysis. The problem here is precisely that a consensus decision seems so unlikely.

The fourth pure-strategy Nash equilibrium has Paul voting for L (his preferred option), Mary voting for M (her most preferred option), Sue voting for L (her second most preferred option), and the committee selecting option L. The problem with this equilibrium is that *both* Sue and Mary are worse off at this equilibrium than at the "paradoxical" equilibrium. The only player who gains is Paul, even though he behaves the same in both instances. Assuming that the equilibria of the game are common knowledge, this knowledge should lead Sue and Mary to focus on the "paradoxical" equilibrium rather than this one. Although the outcome is consistent with rational behavior, it would seem to be less likely than the "paradoxical" equilibrium.

5.6.4 A CONCERN: THE LIMITS OF RATIONALITY

Predicting the voting patterns in the previous scenario was not a straightforward task. Not many people would look at the preference orderings and immediately conclude that Mary and Sue would end up voting for H while Paul would vote for L. Indeed, if it were obvious, it probably would not be considered a "paradox"!

Part of the reason for the subtlety of the outcome is that the iterated weakly dominant strategies for Mary and Sue require a fairly large number of iterations. As you were (painfully) aware, our analysis kept bouncing back and forth until we finally arrived at iterated dominant strategies. Do people actually go through these iterations to find their rational strategies? It is hard to imagine that this sort of thinking occurs (consciously) in the heat of a committee meeting. Unfortunately, the analysis of games under the assumption of limited rational ability is still in its infancy. We cannot answer the question we raised, but it is certainly a concern.

How frequently might this paradox arise?[5] If we think of the set of preference rankings of three people over three alternatives, then there are 6^3 or 216 distinct sets of preference orderings. Of these, 48 orderings result in the potential for some form of the Chairman's paradox. So, in small committees using plurality voting with tie-breaking by the Chair, the paradox could be expected to occur about 20% of the time.

---

[5]We have refrained from referring to the paradox as an economic problem since it is unclear which of the three options is the most "efficient."

5.7   Summary

Economists are interested in the allocation of resources in a variety of settings. Frequently, those settings are characterized by markets, but not always. In this chapter, we were concerned with social decisions made by some form of voting mechanism. All social decision rules meeting criteria hypothesized by Professor Arrow will invariably run afoul of his impossibility theorem. Hence, anomalies will tend to be the rule rather than the exception.[6] We considered some of the most widely used voting mechanisms: majority rule, plurality rule, and the single transferable vote.

Under majority rule, assuming that voters cast their ballots secretly and honestly and that there are two candidates with common knowledge of voters' preferences, the candidates will choose policy positions very close to each other. Plurality rule is fraught with potential problems, regardless of whether voters cast their ballots honestly or strategically. And the single transferable vote is not obviously any better.

Finally, we saw a result that occurs with some frequency in strategic situations: power can be a bad thing for the possessor of it. Even though the Chair is granted the power to break a tie with his vote, in some circumstances that power can work against the Chair, perhaps dramatically. In our example, the outcome that the Chair views as being the least desirable is the one that eventually gets voted into place. This is true even though the Chair's preferred outcome would be chosen if everyone naively voted for their true preferred option.

5.8   Further Reading

In the last twenty years a large literature on strategic voting has developed. Some good surveys of this literature at the undergraduate level are *Public Choice* (New York: Cambridge University Press, 1979) by Dennis Mueller, *Game Theory and Political Theory: An Introduction* (Cambridge University Press, 1986) by Peter Ordeshook, and *Rational Politics* (Washington: CQ Press, 1985) by Steve Brams. A sophisticated treatment of preference revelation can be found in J. Green and J. J. Laffont, *Individual Incentives in Public Decision-Making* (Amsterdam: North Holland, 1979). The journal *Public Choice* carries many articles in this area as well, many of them nontechnical enough for an undergraduate reader.

5.9   Discussion Questions

1. Find out what voting procedures are used at your college or university: (a) to elect members to the student government, (b) to decide motions at

---

[6]Itself a paradox!

general faculty meetings, (c) to decide motions at board of trustee meetings, (d) to elect officers of professional organizations, and (e) to vote on tenure or promotion decisions at departmental meetings.

2. Why do people vote in national elections?

3. Why do people become informed about candidates in elections?

4. What anecdotal evidence is there supporting or contradicting the median voter theorem.

5. What are the pros and cons of Professor Arrow's normative axioms that any SCM should possess?

5.10 New Terms

approval voting
Arrow's impossibility theorem
Candidate Positioning Game
chairman's paradox
Condorcet candidate
cyclical majority
independence of irrelevant
    alternatives
majority rule
median voter theorem

monotonicity paradox
naive voting
Pareto condition
plurality voting
single-peaked preferences
single transferable vote
social choice mechanism
strategic voting
transitivity with unlimited domain

5.11 Exercises

EXERCISE 5.1

Suppose three candidates are playing the Candidate Positioning Game (see Section 5.3). Their political positions are represented by points on the interval from 0 to 1. There are eleven voters, whose preferred positions are located at 0, 0.1, . . . , 0.9, 1. Each voter votes for the candidate that locates closest to him or her. If two candidates are both closest to a voter, then she splits her vote between them. If two or more candidates tie with the greatest fraction of the vote, the winner is chosen at random. The candidates choose their positions so as to maximize the probability of winning the election. Show that this game has *no* pure-strategy Nash equilibrium.

EXERCISE 5.2

This is a continuation of Exercise 5.1. Show that the Political Position Game has a pure-strategy Nash equilibrium when there are four candidates. (Hint: Two candidates locate at one point and two candidates locate at a second point).

EXERCISE 5.3

Suppose there are two candidates in an election decided by majority rule. Both must locate somewhere on the periphery of a circle (see Figure 5.2). The voters

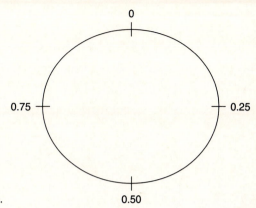

FIGURE 5.2   Location choices around a circle.

are uniformly distributed along the rim of the circle and vote for the candidate closest to them. Where will the two candidates locate?

Exercises 5.4–5.6 are based on the Chairman's Paradox Game from Section 5.6.

EXERCISE 5.4

Suppose Sue's preferences change so that she prefers H to M and M to L. That is, Sue likes Paul's preferred option, L, *less* than she did before. Show that there no longer exists an iterated weakly dominant strategy equilibrium, but there does exist a pure-strategy Nash equilibrium in which Paul votes for L and option M, Paul's second most preferred outcome, is adopted. That is, Paul can do better if he can get Sue to like his preferred option, L, *less*.

EXERCISE 5.5

Suppose Paul alters the game by credibly precommitting himself to voting for option M in the event of a tie, and the players have the preferences in Table 5.7. Show that the unique iterated weakly dominant strategy equilibrium is for Paul and Sue to vote for option L and for Mary to vote for option M.

EXERCISE 5.6

Suppose the committee uses the tie-breaking procedure used in the U.S. Senate. The Chair (Paul) does not get to vote unless there is a tie on the basis of the votes cast by the other committee members (Mary and Sue). The Chair can break the tie only by voting for one of the two options that are tied. For example, if Mary votes for M and Sue votes for H, then Paul gets to break the tie by voting for *either M or H, but he cannot now vote for L.* Find all the pure-strategy Nash equilibria of the resulting game.

PART II
Dynamic Games with Complete Information

CHAPTER 6

Subgame Perfect Equilibrium

6.1   Introduction

In Part I we considered situations in which the players moved "simultaneously"; that is, without knowing the moves of the other players in the game. In Part II we consider games in which the players move in a fixed sequence. In such **dynamic games,** the players who move later in a game do so knowing the moves others have made before them. Those who move earlier must take this into account in devising their optimal strategy. One well-known example of a dynamic game is chess. This should serve as a warning that predicting behavior in dynamic games is not always straightforward. Bargaining for a wage contract or a new car often takes place with sequential offers and counteroffers. The decision about where to purchase a residence often depends on who has made earlier decisions to live in a neighborhood and who can be expected to move in later. Hence, it, too, is a dynamic game.

6.2   An Example: Software Game I

Consider the following strategic situation: The Macrosoft Corporation, a computer software firm, is deciding what marketing strategy to use for a new computer game it has recently developed. After much research, the company has pared its choices to two: (1) A Madison Avenue ("slick") campaign or (2) a Word-of-Mouth ("simple") campaign.

Macrosoft knows that total sales of the computer game will be unaffected by the ad campaign chosen, but the *timing* of these sales will be very different. As long as Macrosoft is the sole provider of the game, employing a slick campaign results in very high sales in the first year as a result of a Madison Avenue advertising "blitz," but much smaller sales in the second year because of near saturation of the market. A simple campaign results in relatively small sales in the first year, but large sales in the second year as early users of the game tell their friends ("by word of mouth") how good the game is. In both campaigns there are no further sales after the second year due to complete saturation of the market. The net profits generated each year under the two ad campaigns are shown in Table 6.1.

On the basis of Table 6.1, it appears that Macrosoft's optimal decision is to use the cheaper simple campaign and rely on the reputation of the game to boost sales in the second year. But this conclusion ignores potential competition with *legal clones* of Macrosoft's game. A legal clone of a computer program is a second program that mimics the first, but whose code is sufficiently different that the clone's owner cannot be sued for copyright infringement. Unfortunately for Macrosoft, a second company, Microcorp, possesses the technical capability to produce a legal clone of Macrosoft's program within a year of the game's introduction at a cost of $300,000. If Microcorp produces a clone, then the two firms will split the market in the second year. This assumption sweeps under the rug other strategic issues such as the outcome of price competition between the two firms in the second year. Tables 6.2 and 6.3 display Macrosoft's and Microcorp's profits if the latter enters the market. It appears that the simple campaign is still optimal.

Because of the interdependency between the two companies, Macrosoft and Microcorp are playing a game. In order to analyze this game, we need to know the strategies available to the players and the payoffs they both attain when they

Table 6.1 **Macrosoft's Profits**

	Slick campaign	Simple campaign
Gross profit in year 1	$900,000	$200,000
Gross profit in year 2	$100,000	$800,000
Total gross profit	$1,000,000	$1,000,000
Advertising cost	−$570,000	−$200,000
Total net profit	$430,000	$800,000

Table 6.2 **Macrosoft's Profits If Microcorp Enters the Market**

	Macrosoft adopts the slick campaign	Macrosoft adopts the simple campaign
Gross profit in year 1	$900,000	$200,000
Gross profit in year 2	$50,000	$400,000
Total gross profit	$950,000	$600,000
Advertising cost	−$570,000	−$200,000
Total net profit	$380,000	$400,000

Table 6.3 **Microcorp's Profits If It Enters the Market**

	Macrosoft adopts the slick campaign	Macrosoft adopts the simple campaign
Gross profit in year 1	$0	$0
Gross profit in year 2	$50,000	$400,000
Total gross profit	$50,000	$400,000
Cloning costs	−$300,000	−$300,000
Total net profit	−$250,000	$100,000

play these strategies against each other. The first step in constructing the list of possible strategies is to list the **moves** available to the two players. Macrosoft can make one of two moves: (1) adopt the slick campaign; (2) adopt the simple campaign. We will refer to these moves as *slick* and *simple*. Microcorp also has two moves: (1) clone the game and enter the market; or (2) don't clone the game and stay out of the market. These two moves will be referred to as *enter* and *stay out*. If this were a static game, each player's set of strategies would be equivalent to its set of moves. But this is not a static game. In this game, Macrosoft moves first and this move is known to Microcorp before it makes its entry decision. A shorthand way of describing the **order of play** in this game is to say that Macrosoft is the **first mover** and Microcorp is the **last mover.** Because of this order of play, Microcorp can *condition* its move on Macrosoft's move. So a strategy for Microcorp—that is, a *complete* description of how to play this game—states what move Microcorp will take *if* Macrosoft adopts the *slick* campaign and what move the firm will take *if* Macrosoft adopts the *simple* campaign. These two moves need not be the same. The fact that play is now dynamic severs the simple one-to-one correspondence between moves and strategies. Since moves are easier to list than strategies, you are undoubtedly wondering, why bother with listing strategies? You will see below.

6.2.1 GAME TREES

In order to determine the set of strategies for either firm, we need to carefully specify not only the moves the players have but also the order in which they choose these moves and the information they have when they make their decisions. A powerful way to organize this information is with a **game tree.** A game tree is a picture composed of **nodes** and **branches.** Each node in the game tree represents a decision point for one of the players and is said to **belong** to the player that moves at that point. Decision nodes are represented by boxes, inside of which is the name of the player who moves at that node. A branch represents a possible move by a player. Every branch connects two nodes and has a direction. The direction is depicted by an arrowhead. If a branch points from a node N_1 belonging to player A to a node N_2 belonging to player B, then player A moves before player B and node N_1 *immediately precedes* N_2. In this book, game trees will always progress either from top to bottom or from left to right.

Figure 6.1 displays the game tree for Software Game I. The game begins at the far left of the diagram where Macrosoft chooses the ad campaign for its new product. Two branches lead right from the root, each one representing the choice of campaign. The move represented is listed next to the branch. Each branch points to a decision node for Microcorp since this firm makes its entry decision *after* it learns the type of ad campaign Macrosoft has adopted. From each of the two decision nodes extend two branches representing the two possible moves Microcorp can now make. At the end of these four arrows are small circles. These circles are special nodes called **terminal nodes.** At these nodes, the game ends. To the right of each terminal node are two numbers. The first number is the payoff of the first mover (Macrosoft) and the second number is the payoff of the last mover (Microcorp). The game tree, along with payoffs at all the terminal nodes, constitutes the **extensive form** of the game.

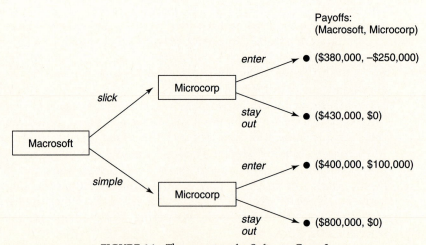

FIGURE 6.1   The game tree for Software Game I.

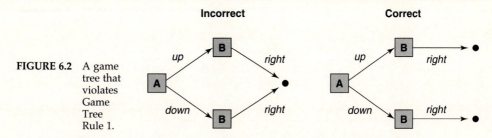

FIGURE 6.2 A game tree that violates Game Tree Rule 1.

In order to avoid ambiguity, game trees must follow four rules.

Game Tree Rule 1: Every node is immediately preceded by at most one other node.

Figure 6.2 shows a game tree that violates Rule 1. Player B has two decision nodes and the branches from them point to the same terminal node. If player A's move has no effect on the payoffs, then that player's decision node should be eliminated as inconsequential. And if player A's move does affect the payoffs, then two terminal nodes need to be added to the tree, one for each of A's moves.

When Rule 1 is satisfied, it makes sense to speak of one decision node "coming after" another. Informally, node B is a **successor** of node A if it is possible, starting at A, for the players to make a sequence of moves that gets the game to node B. Formally, node B is a successor of node A if and only if there exists some sequence of nodes, $N_1, N_2, \ldots, N_K$, such that $A = N_1$, $B = N_K$, and each node immediately precedes the next node in the sequence. This sequence of nodes will be referred to as the **path** from A to B. Rule 1 implies that there is at most one path between any two nodes. We will say that Node A is a **predecessor** of node B if and only if node B is a successor of node A. A terminal node has no successors and an **initial node** has no predecessors. We will reserve the term **decision node** for a node that is not terminal.

Figure 6.3 shows a game tree that satisfies Game Tree Rule 1, but in which there is a "loop": If player A moves down, then player B gets to move; and if player B moves down, then player A gets to move. So who moves first? In order to eliminate such ambiguities, we will avoid decision trees that have circular loops. The bottom half of Figure 6.3 shows one resolution of the ambiguity: Player A gets to move twice, once before player B and once after player B.

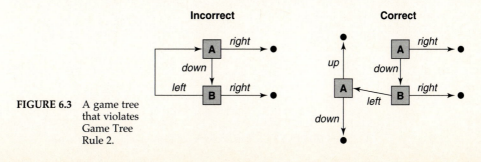

FIGURE 6.3 A game tree that violates Game Tree Rule 2.

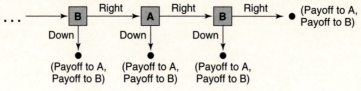

FIGURE 6.4 A game tree with no initial node.

Game Tree Rule 2: No path in a tree connects a decision node to itself.

Figure 6.4 shows a game tree that satisfies Rules 1 and 2 but has no initial node. Unfortunately, as you are asked to show in an exercise at the end of this chapter, "headless" decision trees can create ambiguity about the outcome of some strategy profiles. For this reason, we require our decision trees to satisfy Rule 3.

Game Tree Rule 3: Every node is the successor of a unique initial node.

Rules 1, 2, and 3 imply that every node has exactly one initial node among its predecessors. But the overall tree may have more than one initial node. Fortunately, whenever this happens, the nodes can be partitioned into disjoint sets according to which initial node they come after. We claim (and you are asked to prove in an exercise) that each of these disjoint subsets of nodes (together with the branches that connect them) can be viewed as separate game trees that satisfy Rules 1, 2, and 3. Yet each of these "subtrees" has only one initial node by construction (See Figure 6.5). As Figure 6.5 also shows, any game whose game tree has more than one initial node can be split up into independent games, each of which has exactly one initial node. We will refer to this unique initial node as the **root** of the tree. So there is no loss of generality, but a gain of simplicity, in our final requirement.

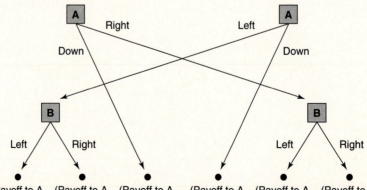

FIGURE 6.5 A decision tree with two initial decision nodes.

Game Tree Rule 4: Every game tree has exactly one initial node.

6.2.2 STRATEGIES

Recall from Chapter 1 that a strategy is a detailed set of plans for playing the game. This means that a strategy for a player must specify the move to make at each of that player's decision nodes. Since Macrosoft has only one decision node, a strategy for Macrosoft simply consists of choosing one of its two moves, *simple* and *slick.* Recall from Chapter 1 that moves are italicized and uncapitalized while strategies are italicized and capitalized. In keeping with this convention we will denote Macrosoft's strategies as *Simple* and *Slick.*

Microcorp has two decision nodes. As a result, a strategy for Microcorp consists of a decision to enter or stay out of the market *conditional* on Macrosoft's prior choice of ad campaign. One possible strategy for Microcorp would be: *enter* if Macrosoft adopts *Slick* and *stay out* if Macrosoft adopts *Simple.* We will write this strategy: *(enter, stay out).* The first part, *enter,* states what Microcorp will do *if* Macrosoft adopts *Slick;* the second part, *stay out,* states what Microcorp will do *if* Macrosoft adopts *Simple.* This is just one of four possible strategies. We leave it as an exercise for you to determine the other three.

It is common to confuse strategies and moves. In part, this is because almost all the games encountered in undergraduate textbooks are static. But it is crucial to understand that strategies are *not* the same as moves. A strategy maps out a plan of attack under *all* eventualities. Different strategies can give rise to the same sequence of moves. For example, both of the following strategy profiles result in Microcorp cloning Macrosoft's game: {*Simple,* (*enter, enter*)}, and {*Slick,* (*enter, stay out*)}.

6.2.3 INFORMATION

If a player knows where she is on the game tree whenever it is her turn to move, then the player is said to have **perfect information.** A game has perfect information if every player has perfect information. Most board games, such as chess or checkers, are games of perfect information. Software Game I is a game with perfect information. Alternatively, a player may have to move *without* knowing the previous move of another player. Such a player is said to have **imperfect information.** A game has imperfect information if at least one player has imperfect information. Static games are games with imperfect information, as are almost all card games. We will look at dynamic games with imperfect information in Part V.

6.2.4 OUTCOMES AND PAYOFFS

Macrosoft's and Microcorp's payoffs in Software Game I are shown in Table 6.4. Recall that Macrosoft's actions and strategies are identical but that Microcorp's are not. Note that Table 6.4 lists Microcorp's actions, not its strategies. Table 6.4

Table 6.4 **The Payoffs for Software Game I**

		Macrosoft's ad campaign	
		Slick	Simple
Microcorp's entry decision	enter	(−$250, $380)	($100, $400)
	stay out	($0, $430)	($0, $800)

Payoff (in $1,000s): (Microcorp, Macrosoft)

tells us, for example, that if Macrosoft chooses *Slick* and Microcorp chooses *enter* (conditional on Macrosoft choosing *Slick*), then Macrosoft will earn a profit of $380,000 and Microcorp will suffer a *loss* of $250,000.

6.3 Nash Equilibrium and Backward Induction

Having described the strategic situation, we want to predict the strategic choices of the two players. A **solution concept** is a methodology for predicting player behavior. Although there does not yet exist a universally accepted solution concept that can be applied to every game, there is wide agreement about some of the properties that any acceptable solution concept must have.

First, any solution of a noncooperative game must be a Nash equilibrium for that game. Recall from Chapter 1 that a Nash equilibrium for a game is a strategy profile in which every player's strategy is optimal *given that the other players use their equilibrium strategies.* We use italics here to emphasize the limited sense in which each player's strategy is optimal. Change the strategy of any single player and the proposed strategies of the other players will often become suboptimal.

We are now in a position to understand why it is more useful to consider players' strategies than just their actions. Suppose you were to try to use Table 6.4 to derive a Nash equilibrium. If Macrosoft adopts the *Simple* campaign, the best that Microcorp can do is to *enter*; $100,000 is better than $0. Also, if Microcorp chooses to *enter*, the best thing that Macrosoft can do is adopt the *Simple* campaign; $400,000 is better than $380,000. It would *appear* that Macrosoft adopting the *Simple* campaign and Microcorp *entering* in response is a Nash equilibrium. Furthermore, you can verify from Table 6.4 that this *appears* to be the only Nash equilibrium. Hence, if you believe that Nash equilibrium strategies constitute good predictors of how people behave, you would now be in a position to make these predictions.

Alternatively, consider the strategic form of the game in Table 6.5. Recall that the strategic form is a table that displays the payoffs earned by the players for every possible strategy profile. If Microcorp chooses to *enter* regardless of the campaign Macrosoft chooses, then Macrosoft will choose *Simple*. If Macrosoft chooses *Simple*, Microcorp is at least as well off choosing (*enter, enter*) as any other strategy. So the strategy profile {*Simple, (enter, enter)*} is a Nash equilibrium.

Table 6.5 **Strategic Form of the Software Clone Game**

		Macrosoft	
		Slick	*Simple*
	(Enter, Enter)	(−$250, $380)	**($100, $400)**
Microcorp	*(Enter, Stay Out)*	(−$250, $380)	($0, $800)
	(Stay Out, Enter)	**($0, $430)**	($100, $400)
	(Stay Out, Stay Out)	($0, $430)	($0, $800)

Payoffs (in $1,000s): (Microcorp, Macrosoft)

Alternatively, if Macrosoft chooses *Slick*, then Microcorp can do no better than to choose (*stay out, enter*). But if Microcorp chooses (*stay out, enter*), Macrosoft should choose *Slick*. This makes the strategy profile {*Slick*,(*stay out, enter*)} a Nash equilibrium as well. Microcorp does better at the first equilibrium and Macrosoft does better at the second. Which of the two outcomes is more likely?

A procedure we propose for selecting among multiple Nash equilibria is **backward induction.** This procedure has six steps.

1. Start at the terminal nodes of the game and trace each one to its immediate predecessor, which will be a decision node for some player. These decision nodes are either "trivial," "basic," or "complex." A decision node is **basic** if each of its branches leads to exactly one terminal node. A basic node with only one branch is **trivial.** A decision node is **complex** if it is not basic. If you reach a trivial decision node, then keep moving up the tree until you reach either a complex or nontrivial basic decision node or until you can go no further.

2. Find the optimal move at each basic decision node reached in step 1 by comparing the payoffs the player obtains at each terminal node reached from this decision node.[1] Notice that every path between a basic decision node A and a terminal node B starts at a unique branch of A. The branch that leads to the highest payoff for the player is the optimal move to make at that node.

3. Erase all the nonoptimal branches that originate from each of the basic decision nodes you examined in step 2. Each of these basic decision nodes becomes trivial.

---

[1]If there is more than one optimal decision, then we need to reevaluate the payoff assignments and find a way to break the tie. If the modeler believes that the tie is a correct formulation of the game, then we next need to determine whether or not there are "social conventions" that would make one choice much more likely than the other. If so, we use these social conventions to break the tie. Finally, if there are no conventions to fall back on, then we must acknowledge that the player's behavior at this node will be unpredictable.

4. You now have a new game tree that is simpler than the original one. If in step 1 you arrived at the root of the tree, you are now done.

5. If you have not yet reached the root, then go back to step 1 and start all over again. In this way, you work your way step by step toward the root.

6. For each player, collect together the optimal decisions at each of the player's decision nodes. This collection of decisions constitutes that player's optimal strategy in the game.

We will now apply this method to Software Game I. The last two decision nodes belong to Microcorp and both are basic. If Macrosoft chooses *Slick*, then Microcorp earns a $0 profit if it *stays out* and suffers a loss of $250,000 if it *enters*. Clearly, the optimal move in this case is *stay out*. If Macrosoft chooses *Simple*, then Microcorp earns a profit of $100,000 if it *enters*, and, of course, $0 if it *stays out*. The optimal decision for Microcorp in this case is *enter*. Since these are Microcorp's only decision nodes, we have found its optimal strategy: *(stay out, enter)*.

By pruning the nonoptimal moves from both of Microcorp's decision nodes, we are left with only one nontrivial decision node, which belongs to Macrosoft. The new game tree is displayed in Figure 6.6. In the figure, instead of erasing the nonoptimal moves we have grayed them out. We now "loop back" and evaluate the consequences of Macrosoft's possible moves *under the assumption that Microcorp subsequently plays its optimal strategy*. If Macrosoft chooses the *Slick* strategy, then Microcorp will *stay out* and Macrosoft will earn a profit of $430,000. If Macrosoft chooses the *Simple* strategy, then Microcorp will *enter* and Macrosoft will earn a profit of $400,000. Clearly, the optimal strategy for Macrosoft is *Slick*. Looking ahead and taking Microcorp's entry decision into account prevents it from making a $30,000 mistake.

Note that confusing actions with strategies when making predictions, as we did when we used Table 6.4 to make forecasts about behavior, can lead to very bad predictions. This is why the solution concept of Nash equilibrium has to be applied to the strategic form of the game. Furthermore, using backward induction

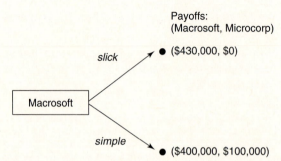

FIGURE 6.6 The Game Tree of Software Game I after the first round of "pruning."

to select among Nash equilibria will keep us from predicting behavior that is contrary to the best interests of the players in the game.

The strategy profile that results when both players adopt their optimal strategies is {*Slick*, (*stay out, enter*)}. We have already seen that this is a Nash equilibrium. If Microcorp believes Macrosoft will choose *Slick*, then it can do no better than to adopt (*stay out, enter*). Similarly, if Macrosoft believes Microcorp will adopt the strategy (*stay out, enter*), then Macrosoft will do best by adopting *Slick*. Therefore, when both players adopt their Nash equilibrium strategy, their beliefs about each other are confirmed. It is an important proposition in game theory that the strategy profile constructed by applying backward induction is always a Nash equilibrium.

> **THEOREM 6.1:** In a game with perfect information, the strategy profile selected using the process of backward induction is always a Nash equilibrium.

In Software Game I, the costly *Slick* campaign is best *precisely* because it induces Microcorp not to enter the market. To see this more clearly, consider what would happen if it cost Microcorp only $10,000 to clone the game. It would now be profitable for Microcorp to enter the market regardless of the ad campaign chosen by Macrosoft. So Microcorp's optimal strategy would be (*enter, enter*). Since Microcorp will clone the software as long as Macrosoft develops it, Macrosoft might as well choose the cheaper advertising campaign. So Macrosoft's optimal strategy would be *Simple*. Similarly, suppose the cost of cloning the program were $500,000. Then Microcorp would always suffer a loss if it entered and its optimal strategy would be (*stay out, stay out*). In this case, Macrosoft should ignore the threat of entry and choose its advertising campaign solely on the basis of cost. Once again, the optimal strategy would be *Simple*.

6.4 Threats and Credible Threats

Implicit in our analysis of the software game was the assumption that Microcorp and Macrosoft never talk with each other. But suppose they *do* talk with each other about their strategies. It turns out that our previous conclusions remain unchanged. The conclusions depend only on the players' inability to make *enforceable* commitments to each other. This is called **cheap talk.** Suppose, for example, that Microcorp tells Macrosoft that it will clone the software regardless of the advertising choice made by Macrosoft. In other words, Microcorp tries to convince Macrosoft to believe that it will adopt the strategy (*enter, enter*). We will sometimes refer to such a statement as a **threat.** Clearly, the threat is intended to induce Macrosoft to adopt a word-of-mouth campaign. If Macrosoft were to believe Microcorp's threat, then it would believe that it would earn $400,000 by adopting *Simple* and only $380,000 by adopting *Slick.* But should Macrosoft actually adopt

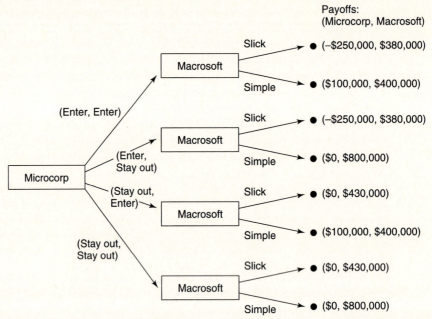

FIGURE 6.7 The new game tree if Microcorp can commit itself to an entry strategy prior to Macrosoft adopting its advertising strategy.

Slick, there is nothing to stop Microcorp from backing away from its threat and not entering after all.[2] From Microcorp's perspective there is nothing to be gained and much to be lost by carrying out the threat. Macrosoft would be wise to ignore this threat by Microcorp. This example reveals that the method of backward induction incorporates the following principle:

> **A credible threat** exists only if it is in the player's own interest to carry out the threat when given the option. Threats that are not credible are ignored by all rational players.

It is important to note the words "when given the option." If Microcorp *cannot* back down from its threat, then it is a **binding threat.** The proper way to model Software Game I if Microcorp can make binding threats is to have Microcorp move *first* and issue its threat and then to have Macrosoft move second and choose its ad campaign knowing Microcorp's threat. The game tree that corresponds to this new game is shown in Figure 6.7.

---

[2]It is tempting to say that Microcorp might want to make the threat real so that future threats to Macrosoft will be taken seriously. But then the terminal nodes in Figure 6.2 are not the real terminal nodes. The game goes on. We will examine such "repeated games" in Chapter 9.

In the new game, Microcorp moves once and selects its entry rule. Each move corresponds to a strategy in the original game. Macrosoft now has four decision nodes. A strategy for Macrosoft consists of the advertising campaign to adopt in response to each of Microcorp's four possible threats. We will denote its strategy by a four-tuple: (c_1, c_2, c_3, c_4), where c_1 is the ad campaign to launch when Microcorp threatens (*enter, enter*); c_2 is the campaign to adopt if Microcorp threatens (*enter, stay out*); c_3 is the campaign to adopt if Microcorp threatens (*stay out, enter*); and c_4 is the campaign to adopt if Microcorp threatens (*stay out, stay out*). In the exercises at the end of the chapter you will be asked to confirm that Macrosoft's optimal strategy in this new game is: (*simple, slick, simple, simple*). That is, Macrosoft should adopt the *slick* campaign only if Microcorp threatens (*stay out, enter*); otherwise it should adopt *simple*. Microcorp's optimal strategy is to threaten (*enter, enter*), that is, *enter* no matter what campaign Macrosoft adopts. The outcome when both firms adopt their optimal strategies is that Macrosoft chooses the cheaper word-of-mouth campaign and Microcorp enters and clones the software. Microcorp ends up $100,000 better off by becoming the first mover, while Macrosoft loses $30,000. Both firms would prefer to move first rather than second. That is, in this strategic situation, there is a **first-mover advantage.**

6.5   Subgames and Subgame Perfect Equilibrium

The idea, attributed to Reinhard Selten, that any Nash equilibrium incorporating incredible threats will be a poor predictor of human behavior is almost universally accepted by game theorists. Selten formalized his idea by inventing the concept of a **subgame** and the solution concept called **subgame perfect equilibrium.** For this innovation he was awarded the Nobel Prize in Economics in 1994, along with John Nash and John Harsanyi.[3]

In a game with perfect information, a subgame consists of a subset of the nodes and branches of the original game that, when taken together, constitute a game in themselves. Since a subgame must be a game, it has a unique initial node, which is called a **subroot** of the larger game. The first requirement of a subgame is that it consists of the subroot and all its successors. This implies that once the players begin playing a subgame, they will continue to play the subgame for the rest of the game.

We will now state this more formally. The subgame G_S of the game G_T is a game constructed as follows:

1. G_S has the same players as G_T, although some of these players may not make any moves in G_S.

2. The initial node of G_S is a subroot of G_T and the game tree of G_S consists of this subroot, all its successor nodes, and the branches between them.

---

[3]John Nash and John Harsanyi were awarded the prize for the invention of the concept of Nash equilibrium and Bayesian equilibrium. The second equilibrium concept is central to the analysis of games with incomplete information and will be introduced in Part V.

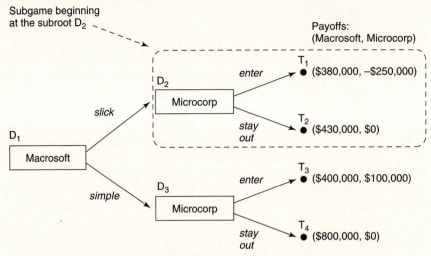

FIGURE 6.8 Software Game I and one of its two proper subgames.

3. Each player's payoffs at the terminal nodes of G_S are identical to the payoffs in G_T at the same terminal nodes.

These three conditions amount to saying that the set of players, the order of play, and the set of possible moves in the original game are preserved in the subgame. This definition implies that every game is a (trivial) subgame of itself. Nontrivial subgames of a game are called **proper subgames.** We will extend the concept of a subgame to games with imperfect information in Part V.

One subgame of Software Game I is shown in Figure 6.8. This subgame begins with the node labeled D_2 and includes the two subsequent terminal nodes T_1 and T_2, the two branches between these three nodes, and the payoffs ($380,000, $-$250,000) and ($430,000, $0). In games with perfect information, such as Software Game I, every decision node is a subroot of the game. Software Game I has two proper subgames.

Whenever the players begin playing any subgame of a game, this fact is common knowledge. As a result, rational behavior for the players in the overall game should also appear rational when viewed from the perspective of this subgame. Return for a moment to Software Game I. We know that the game has a second Nash equilibrium strategy profile: {*Simple*, (*enter, enter*)}. But this Nash equilibrium involves an incredible threat by Microcorp to *enter* if Macrosoft adopts the *Slick* campaign. Consider now the subgame in Figure 6.8 that begins at D_2. This subgame has only one Nash equilibrium; at this equilibrium, Microcorp chooses *stay out*. But the Nash equilibrium strategy profile {*Simple*, (*enter, enter*)} requires Microcorp to choose *enter* at D_2. The nonoptimality of this strategy profile in the subgame makes the threat incredible. Microcorp's incredible threat is eliminated in equilibrium once we demand that Nash equilibrium strategies remain Nash equilibria when applied to any subgame. A Nash equilibrium with this property is said to be *subgame perfect*.

*A strategy profile is a **subgame perfect equilibrium** of a game, G, if this strategy profile is also a Nash equilibrium for every proper subgame of G.*

In games with perfect information, the subgame perfect equilibria consist precisely of those selected using backward induction. The reason is straightforward. If we look at any subgame that begins at the last decision node for the last player who moves, the only Nash equilibrium of that subgame is the move that results in the highest payoff for the last decision maker. But this is precisely the move chosen using backward induction. As we move up the game tree, backward induction eliminates all the incredible threats, so that the collection of moves selected constitutes not only a Nash equilibrium, but a subgame perfect equilibrium.

THEOREM 6.2: A strategy profile is a *subgame perfect equilibrium* of a dynamic game, *G*, with perfect information if and only if it is the Nash equilibrium selected by the process of backward induction.

6.6   A Second Example: Software Game II

Suppose that Macrosoft and Microcorp play the dynamic game diagrammed in Figure 6.9. The story behind this hypothetical game is this: Macrosoft has developed a clever new computer game that is certain to be very popular. Although Microcorp can clone the game with its own engineers and compete against

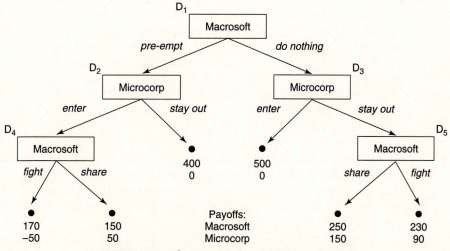

FIGURE 6.9   The extensive form of Software Game II.

Macrosoft, it can do it cheaper and better if it can hire away some of Macrosoft's engineers. Recognizing this, Macrosoft can choose to include in its contracts with its software engineers a clause that bars them from working for another software company for a certain period of time if they resign from Macrosoft. A move such as this is sometimes called a **preemptive move.** Its purpose is to alter its rivals' payoffs in order to alter their strategies. Preemptive moves are usually costly, and this one is no exception. Inserting a restrictive clause in its employment contracts makes Macrosoft a less attractive place to work. As a result, Macrosoft must pay its engineers above the going market salary if it adds this clause to its employment contracts.

Should Microcorp clone the game, Macrosoft must decide how to react. It can choose to *fight* Microcorp by aggressively advertising its game, which is costly but gives it a larger market share, or it can can forego the expense of an ad campaign and simply *share* the market 50/50 with Microcorp.

As you can see from Figure 6.9, Microcorp has two decision nodes, with two moves at each one, resulting in the four strategies listed below. The first word within parentheses is Microcorp's move if Macrosoft *preempts,* and the second is its move if Macrosoft *does nothing.*

S_{Micro}^1: (*enter, enter*) S_{Micro}^3: (*stay out, enter*)
S_{Micro}^2: (*enter, stay out*) S_{Micro}^4: (*stay out, stay out*)

Macrosoft has three decision nodes and two moves at each node, resulting in the eight strategies listed below. The first phrase within parentheses is Macrosoft's move at node D_1, the second is its reaction to Microcorp's entry at node D_4, and the third is its reaction to Microcorp's entry at node D_5.

S_{Macro}^1: (*preempt, fight, fight*) S_{Macro}^5: (*preempt, fight, share*)
S_{Macro}^2: (*preempt, share, fight*) S_{Macro}^6:(*preempt, share, share*)
S_{Macro}^3: (*do nothing, fight, fight*) S_{Macro}^7: (*do nothing, share, fight*)
S_{Macro}^4: (*do nothing, fight, share*) S_{Macro}^8: (*do nothing, share, share*)

Tables 6.6 and 6.7 provide the cost and revenue information needed to determine the game's payoffs. Over its lifetime, the computer game will generate $500,000 in net revenues (revenues minus production costs) for all the firms producing it or its clones. Macrosoft must pay its software engineers an additional $100,000 to get them to agree to accept a contract containing an anticompetition clause. It costs Microcorp $100,000 to develop the software if it can hire Macrosoft's engineers and $200,000 otherwise. Aggressive advertising costs Macrosoft $80,000 and has the effect of giving it a 70% market share if it restricts its engineers' employment and a 62% market share if it does not. The fall in market share is caused by the fact that without some of Macrosoft's engineers to guide its construction, Microcorp's clone is an imperfect substitute for Macrosoft's game, a fact that can be exploited by Macrosoft's advertisements. If, however, Macrosoft passively acquiesces to Microcorp's entry and shares the market, then both firms end up with a 50% market share.

The strategic form of Software Game II is shown in the Table 6.8.

There are four Nash equilibria. These have been identified by bold payoffs in Table 6.8. In this game, Microcorp would desperately like to make Macrosoft

Table 6.6   *Payoffs for Macrosoft in Software Game II (in $1,000s)*

Scenario	Revenue-Production Costs	Advertising Costs	Additional Engineer Costs if Restrict Other Employment	Profits for Macrosoft
Macrosoft restricts engineers; Microcorp clones software; Macrosoft aggressively advertises.	350	80	100	170
Macrosoft restricts engineers; Microcorp clones software; Macrosoft passively acquiesces.	250	0	100	150
Macrosoft restricts engineers; Microcorp does not clone software.	500	0	100	400
Macrosoft does not restrict engineers; Microcorp clones software; Macrosoft aggressively advertises.	310	80	0	230
Macrosoft does not restrict engineers; Microcorp clones software; Macrosoft passively acquiesces.	250	0	0	250
Macrosoft does not restrict engineers; Microcorp does not clone software.	500	0	0	500

believe that it will clone the software regardless of what contracts Macrosoft writes with its software engineers (i.e., it would like to convince Macrosoft that it will choose S^1_{Micro}). If it believes Microcorp will choose S^1_{Micro}, then Macrosoft's best response is to adopt S^4_{Macro} or S^8_{Macro}. As you can see, these combinations of strategies are Nash equilibria. But, are these equilibria subgame perfect? There are five subgames in Software Game II: the entire game, which begins at node D_1; the two subgames that begin at nodes D_2 and D_3; and the two subgames that begin at decision nodes D_4 and D_5. Beginning at the end of the game tree, Macrosoft's optimal move at D_4 is *fight*, and its optimal move at D_5 is *share*. Given this, Microcorp's optimal move at D_2 is *stay out*, while its optimal move at D_3 is *enter and clone*. Macrosoft can now see that if it preemptively adds noncompetitive clauses to its employment contracts, then it will pay to fight Microcorp's entry and so Microcorp will stay out, resulting in a payoff of $400,000. If Macrosoft does nothing, then it won't pay to fight entry and Microcorp, anticipating this, will enter, resulting in a payoff of $250,000. So Macrosoft will *preempt*. Putting

Table 6.7   Payoffs for Microcorp in Software Game II (in $1,000s)

Scenario	Revenue-Production Costs	Development Costs	Profits for Microcorp
Macrosoft restricts engineers; Microcorp clones software; Macrosoft aggressively advertises.	150	200	−50
Macrosoft restricts engineers; Microcorp clones software; Macrosoft passively acquiesces.	250	200	50
Macrosoft restricts engineers; Microcorp does not clone software.	0	0	0
Macrosoft does not restrict engineers; Microcorp clones software; Macrosoft aggressively advertises.	190	100	90
Macrosoft does not restrict engineers; Microcorp clones software; Macrosoft passively acquiesces.	250	100	150
Macrosoft does not restrict engineers; Microcorp does not clone software.	0	0	0

Table 6.8   The Strategic Form of Software Game II

		Microcorp			
		S^1_{Micro}	S^2_{Micro}	S^3_{Micro}	S^4_{Micro}
	S^1_{Macro}	(170, −50)	(170, −50)	**(400, 0)**	(400, 0)
	S^2_{Macro}	(150, 50)	(150, 50)	(400, 0)	(400, 0)
Macrosoft	S^3_{Macro}	(230, 90)	(500, 0)	(230, 90)	(500, 0)
	S^4_{Macro}	**(250, 150)**	(500, 0)	(250, 150)	(500, 0)
	S^5_{Macro}	(170, −50)	(170, −50)	**(400, 0)**	(400, 0)
	S^6_{Macro}	(150, 50)	(150, 50)	(400, 0)	(400, 0)
	S^7_{Macro}	(230, 90)	(500, 0)	(230, 90)	(500, 0)
	S^8_{Macro}	**(250, 150)**	(500, 0)	(250, 150)	(500, 0)

Payoffs: (Macrosoft, Microcorp)

this together, the strategy profile $\{S^5_{Macro}, S^3_{Micro}\}$ is subgame perfect and the other three Nash equilibria are not.

In equilibrium Macrosoft engages in the "wasteful" exercise of paying its software engineers above the market wage in order to prevent them from leaving to work for the rival firm, even though the potential rival never enters the market. This salary premium, however, is necessary to credibly deter entry.

6.7 Dynamic Games with Continuous Strategies: The Stackelberg Duopoly Game

So far we have only considered strategies that involve discrete choices. In Software Games I and II, for example, both Macrosoft and Microcorp have only two moves available at each decision node. Many decisions, however, involve choosing among a continuum of options. For example, it would be more realistic to recast the Software Game as one in which Macrosoft chooses *how much to spend* on advertising with sales depending continuously on the amount spent. Other examples of continuous choices include: the productive capacity of an electrical power plant; the salary to offer a prospective employee; or the insurance premium to charge a prospective policyholder. The six-step solution procedure outlined in Section 6.3 assumes that the game tree has a finite number of decision nodes. If the choice set of one of the players is infinite, however, then the game tree must have an infinite number of paths as well. One way to handle the problem of continuous strategies is to approximate the continuous set of choices with a large, but discrete, set. Fortunately, there is a simpler and more elegant way to solve such games that does not resort to discrete approximations.

As an illustration, we will examine a duopoly model based on the groundbreaking work by Heinrich von Stackelberg in 1934. Stackelberg did not have access to modern game theory, so we have taken the liberty to clean up the game theory imbedded in his duopoly model. The general ideas in this section, though, are his. Our duopolists are the Sparkling Water Co. and Clear Water Inc. They sell the exact same product, bottled water, in the same market. Both firms are private suppliers of bottled water to a community that has no municipal water company. They constitute the strategic players in the game. Both firms must decide how much water to put up for sale. We will denote Clear Water's choice by Q_C and Sparkling Water's choice by Q_S. Subsequently, the price of water is set "by the market" so as to equate the quantity supplied with the quantity demanded by consumers.[4] Since both firms produce a homogeneous product, they receive the same price for it. Output is measured in millions of bottles per year; price is quoted in dollars per bottle; and profit is reported in millions of dollars per year.

The technology for producing bottled water requires firms to set production

---

[4]The price-setting mechanism will not be formally modeled, although we could have cast the process of price determination as a static subgame of our game.

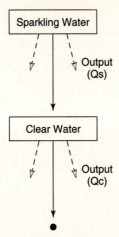

(Payoffs to Sparkling Water, Payoffs to Clear Water)

FIGURE 6.10   The Stackelberg duopoly game tree diagram showing continuous strategies.

levels and then contract with input suppliers to hire the necessary resources to meet the production target. Prior to hiring inputs, each firm has an unlimited production capacity. Once these contracts are set, changes in output are prohibitively expensive. Sparkling Water has superior management and can contract with input suppliers before Clear Water can. Therefore, Sparkling Water can effectively set its production target before Clear Water. This fact is common knowledge. Furthermore, there are enough corporate leaks so that once an output target has been set, it immediately becomes common knowledge. Therefore, the order of play is: Sparkling Water chooses its output first; this is observed by Clear Water, which then chooses its output. Figure 6.10 shows how to display such a game with a game tree diagram.

A strategy for Sparkling Water can be represented by a positive number, Q_S. A strategy for Clear Water is more complicated. It consists of a *function*, $Q_C(Q_S)$ from the positive numbers into themselves. Each function $Q_C(Q_S)$ provides a possible response by Clear Water to every possible initial move by Sparkling Water.

We complete our description of the game by stating the payoffs. The firms are profit maximizers. The inverse market demand function for bottled water can be written as

$$P = \begin{cases} 10 - (Q_S + Q_C) & \textit{if } Q_S + Q_C < 10 \\ 0 & \textit{if } Q_S + Q_C \geq 10 \end{cases} \qquad [6.1]$$

where P is the price received by both firms. Each firm can produce any output at a total cost of

$$TC_i = 3 \cdot Q_i. \qquad [6.2]$$

Profit for each firm is the difference between total revenue and total cost, so

$$\Pi_i(Q_S, Q_C) = \begin{cases} (10 - (Q_S + Q_C)) \cdot Q_i - 3 \cdot Q_i & \text{if } Q_S + Q_C < 10 \\ -3 \cdot Q_i & \text{if } Q_S + Q_C \geq 10 \end{cases} \qquad [6.3]$$

Inspection of this function reveals that all output levels above 7 units generate losses no matter what output is chosen by the opponent and, so, are strongly dominated by a strategy of never producing anything, thereby guaranteeing the firm zero profits. So we know that $Q_S^* \leq 7$ and $Q_C^*(Q_S) \leq 7$ for every Q_S. Furthermore, $Q_C^*(Q_S) = 0$ *if* $Q_S \geq 7$.

In many respects, this game seems quite similar to the Cournot model presented in Chapter 2. Of course, the crucial difference here is that play takes place sequentially instead of simultaneously. If outputs were chosen simultaneously, you could use techniques from Chapter 2 to find the Nash equilibrium outputs for both firms. This results in both firms producing an output of $\frac{7}{3}$ and both firms earning a profit of \$5.44. Given the output choice of the other firm, neither firm can do any better than to produce at this output level. Hence, the strategies $Q_S = \frac{7}{3}$ and $Q_C(Q_S) \equiv \frac{7}{3}$ are a Nash equilibrium of the Stackelberg game as well.

Be clear about the difference between $Q_C(Q_S) \equiv \frac{7}{3}$ and $Q_C(\frac{7}{3}) = \frac{7}{3}$. The first is a complete strategy for Clear Water and says that regardless of the output chosen by Sparkling Water, Clear Water will choose an output of $\frac{7}{3}$. The second is an incomplete strategy and only says that when Sparkling Water chooses an output of $\frac{7}{3}$, Clear Water will also choose an output of $\frac{7}{3}$, but is silent about Clear Water's response to any other output choice by Sparkling Water.

The problem is that Clear Water's proposed strategy $Q_C(Q_S) \equiv \frac{7}{3}$ implies an incredible threat. Suppose, for example, that Sparkling Water were to produce an output of 3. Since Clear Water can observe Sparkling Water's choice, its only credible response is to choose the profit-maximizing output conditional on Sparkling Water's choice of 3 units of output. The reader can confirm that this is 2 units of output, not $\frac{7}{3}$. Under these conditions, Sparkling Water earns a profit of \$6 and Clear Water earns a profit of \$4. Clearly, Sparkling Water can choose a better output, from its perspective, than the Cournot equilibrium output, and it does so at Clear Water's expense. Clear Water's problem is that it cannot credibly commit to the Cournot equilibrium output. Hence, larger outputs by Sparkling Water will, in fact, induce Clear Water to reduce its output.

The real problem for Sparkling Water, then, is to choose the output that, when combined with Clear Water's best response, results in the highest profits for itself. We want to find the subgame perfect equilibrium strategy profiles, $\{Q_S^*, Q_C^*(Q_S)\}$. Nash equilibrium requires that Q_S^* maximize the function $\Pi_S(Q_S, Q_C^*(Q_S))$ and that $Q_C^*(Q_S^*)$ maximize the function $\Pi_C(Q_S^*, Q_C)$. That is, both firms cannot unilaterally make themselves better off given their rival's output choice. Nash equilibrium places no other constraints on the function $Q_C^*(\cdot)$ other than that $Q_C^*(Q_S^*)$ be an optimal response to the choice of Q_S^* by Sparkling Water. Subgame perfection places the further requirement that *for every value of Q_S*, not only Q_S^*, the output level $Q_C^*(Q_S)$ maximize the function $\Pi_C(Q_S, Q_C)$. This means that $Q_C^*(\cdot)$ is precisely the *best response function* introduced in Chapter 1. In Chapter 1, the derivation of the best response function was used to determine the firm's strategy; here, the best response function *is* a strategy. We proceed by determining Clear Water's best response function and then use this to determine Sparkling Water's optimal output. The two optimal strategies determine Clear Water's optimal output, namely $Q_C^*(Q_S^*)$.

To find Q_C^* we employ calculus. The quantity $Q_C^*(Q_S)$ is the value at which the *partial derivative* of $\Pi_C(Q_S, Q_C)$ with respect to Q_C equals 0, unless that would make Q_C negative. In the latter case, Clear Water's optimal output would be zero. Since

$$\frac{\partial}{\partial Q_C} \Pi_C(Q_S, Q_C) = 7 - Q_S - 2Q_C, \qquad [6.4]$$

it follows that

$$7 - Q_S - 2Q_C^*(Q_S) = 0. \qquad [6.5]$$

The solution to Eq. [6.5] is

$$Q_C^*(Q_S) = \begin{cases} 3.5 - \frac{1}{2}Q_S & \text{if } Q_S < 7 \\ 0 & \text{if } Q_S \geq 7 \end{cases} \qquad [6.6]$$

Now we only need to determine Sparkling Water's optimal strategy, Q_S^*. We first substitute Clear Water's optimal strategy into Sparkling Water's profit function to get a "concentrated" profit function that depends only on Q_S, which we will denote $\Pi_S^*(Q_S)$.

$$\Pi_S^*(Q_S) = (10 - (3.5 - \frac{1}{2}Q_S) - Q_S) \cdot Q_S - 3Q_S \qquad [6.7]$$
$$= (3.5 - \frac{1}{2}Q_S) \cdot Q_S$$

We now take the derivative of the concentrated profit function. Q_S^* is the value at which this derivative equals zero. Since

$$\frac{d}{dQ_S} \Pi_S^*(Q_S) = 3.5 - Q_S, \qquad [6.8]$$

it follows that

$$Q_S^* = 3.5. \qquad [6.9]$$

The optimal output is 3.5 million bottles per year. At this output level, Sparkling Water will earn a profit of \$6.125 million. Clear Water reacts to this decision by producing 1.75 million bottles per year, on which it earns a profit of $3.063 million. Sparkling Water earns more than twice the profit of Clear Water. So the **first-mover advantage** in this game results in additional profit of $3.062 million per year.

When Stackelberg was writing about this model, he referred to the firm that chooses its output first as the industry *leader* and the firm choosing its output second as the *follower*.[5] Since the leader in a Stackelberg game has a first-mover advantage over the follower, what bars the follower from moving first and becoming the leader? In our example, the barrier was assumed to be contracting difficulties. Another way that one firm could gain a leadership position would be if the firm was particularly innovative in introducing new products. In this case, the leader would be a monopolist in the short run who faces the threat of entry from another firm. In order to maintain its Stackelberg leadership, though, this innovating firm must find it prohibitively costly to alter its output. Otherwise, the entrant would expect a reaction by the monopolist to its entry and, therefore, would no longer act as a Stackelberg follower. One way the leader could make it very costly to alter its own output would be to enter into long-term contracts with suppliers and/or consumers. Such contractual obligations reduce the leader's flexibility and make it more credible that it will not alter its output in response to entry. Of course, long-term contracts are risky since they make the firm more vulnerable to changes in tastes or technology. As a result, Stackelberg competition is more likely where the technology is mature and demand is stable (for example, steel), and much less likely where the technology is changing quickly or where demand is highly variable (computer games).

6.8   Summary

In this chapter, we discussed the analysis of dynamic games. These are games in which players make decisions sequentially, with later movers knowing the moves chosen earlier. In such games, first movers often have an advantage over those who move later, but not always. There are often Nash equilibria that involve incredible threats. Incredible threats are threats that the issuer will not, in fact, carry out when given the chance. Most game-theoretic analyses assume that such threats are ignored by all rational players. The procedure of backward induction will eliminate such "bad" Nash equilibria.

Reinhard Selten's concept of subgames and subgame perfect equilibrium formalizes the notion of backward induction. A subgame consists of a subset of the larger game with the following two properties: (1) Once the players start playing a subgame, they continue to play it until the game ends and (2) once the

---

[5]Stackelberg actually thought of the two firms as being run by managers with different temperaments, one of which was a leader and the other a follower. We have followed modern convention in recasting Stackelberg's model as a game of perfect information in which both players are rational.

players begin playing the subgame, this fact becomes common knowledge. A subgame perfect equilibrium is a Nash equilibrium strategy profile that continues to be a Nash equilibrium in every subgame. Such equilibria never involve incredible threats.

We noted that many games in which a player chooses among a continuum of moves are not easily analyzed using game trees. As an example, we considered a game-theoretic rendering of the Stackelberg model of duopoly. In the Stackelberg model, one player is the leader and moves first, while the other player is a follower and moves second. A strategy for the follower is now a function. The subgame perfect equilibrium strategy for the follower turns out to be the best response function. You may recall that the graph of the best response function is the player's best response curve. The Stackelberg leader's optimal output is the profit-maximizing point on the follower's best response curve.

6.9   Further Reading

The idea that players should never invoke threats that they will not want to carry out when forced to do so is credited to Reinhard Selten ("Reexamination of the perfectness concept for equilibrium points in extensive games," *International Journal of Game Theory*, 4 (1975), pp. 25–55). It is now a standard assumption in game theory.

For those of you with strong German skills, the original development of subgame perfection by Reinhard Selten is in "Spieltheoretische Behandlung eines Oligopolodells mit Nachfragetragheit" (*Zeitschrift für die gesamte Staatswissenschaft*, 121 (1965), pp. 301–24, 667–89).

Stackelberg first put forth his duopoly models in *Marktform und Gleichgewicht* (Vienna: Julius Springer, 1934), which has been reprinted in *The Theory of the Market Economy*, translated by A. T. Peacock (London: William Hodge, 1952).

6.10   Discussion Questions

1. Find a story in the newspaper that describes a strategic situation in which two or more players are playing a dynamic game. Can you determine the game tree from the details given in the story? If so, can you determine the subgame perfect equilibrium?

2. Some political scientists believe that the "all pay auction" described in Exercise 6.5 is a good model for the "arms race" between the United States and the Soviet Union during the cold war. What do you think of this application?

6.11   New Terms

backward induction	nodes
basic node	order of play
binding threat	path
branches	perfect information
cheap talk	predecessor
complex node	preemptive move
credible threat	proper subgame
decision node	root
dynamic games	solution concept
extensive form	subgame
first mover	subgame perfect equilibrium
first-mover advantage	subroot
game tree	successor
imperfect information	terminal node
initial mode	threat
last mover	trivial node

6.12   Exercises

EXERCISE 6.1

The standard Ultimatum Game is played as follows: There are two players who are strangers to each other and do not communicate with each other. Player A moves first and proposes a division of $1 between herself and player B. Player B moves second and either approves the proposed division or vetoes it. If B approves, then the $1 is divided between them as player A proposed. If B vetoes the proposed division, then both players get nothing. Draw the game tree, determine the strategies for each player, and find the subgame perfect Nash equilibria.

EXERCISE 6.2

The Nash equilibrium of Software Game I depends, in part, on how much it costs Microcorp to clone Macrosoft's game. Denote this cost by C. For what values of C will Macrosoft's Nash equilibrium strategy be *Slick* and for what values of C will its equilibrium strategy be *Simple*? What is Microcorp's Nash equilibrium strategy in each case?

EXERCISE 6.3

Verify the subgame perfect strategies for Microcorp and Macrosoft for the game depicted in Figure 6.1.

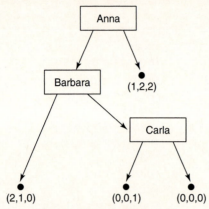

Payoffs: (Anna, Barbara, Clara)   **FIGURE 6.11**   The game tree for Exercise 6.4.

EXERCISE 6.4

Anna, Barbara, and Clara are playing the dynamic game whose game tree is shown in Figure 6.11.

(a) Find all the subgames of this game.

(b) Find all the Nash equilibria of each subgame, including the entire game. (Hint: The entire game has three Nash equilibria.)

(c) Which decision nodes are basic and which are complex?

(d) Apply the backwards induction algorithm outlined in Section 6.3 to find the subgame perfect equilibrium of this game.

EXERCISE 6.5

Prof. Brown announces in class that he is going to auction off an envelope containing $1.25 using an All Pay Auction. The rules of the auction are:

(1) The bidders take turns bidding. At each turn, the bidder can *accept* the current bid price or *pass*. The first acceptable bid price is 50 cents.

(2) Subsequent bid prices are increments of 50 cents.

(3) Bidders cannot bid twice in a row.

(4) The bidding ends once either bidder passes, except at the first bid, where if the first bidder passes, the second bidder is given the option of accepting the bid.

(5) The highest bidder gets the envelope.

(6) *All* bidders must pay Prof. Brown the amount of their last bid.

(a) Draw the game tree of the resulting game under the assumption that it is common knowledge that Mary and Tom are the only two bidders; that they each have only $1.50 in their wallets to bid with; and that Mary gets to make the first bid.

(b) Use backward induction to determine the subgame perfect equilibrium strategies for the two bidders. When Tom and Mary play these strategies, what moves do they make and what is the auction outcome?

EXERCISE 6.6

This is a continuation of Exercise 6.5. Suppose Prof. Brown amends rule (2) of the all pay auction:

(2') subsequent bids are in increments of *either* 50 cents **or** $1.00.

A bid that is greater than the minimum increment of 50 cents is called a *jump bid*. For example, suppose Mary bids $0.50, Tom bids $1.00, and then Mary bids $2.00. Mary made a jump bid. Find subgame perfect equilibrium strategies for the new game.

Exercises 6.7 and 6.8 are based on the Stackelberg Duopoly Game between Clear Water and Sparkling Water, in which Sparkling Water is the Stackelberg leader and Clear Water is the Stackelberg follower.

EXERCISE 6.7

Suppose the demand for bottled water is given by

$$P = \begin{cases} a - b \cdot (Q_C + Q_S) & \text{if } Q_C + Q_S < \frac{a}{b} \\ 0 & \text{if } Q_C + Q_S \geq \frac{a}{b} \end{cases}$$ [6.10]

and the total cost function is given by

$$TC_i = c + dQ_i.$$ [6.11]

Find the subgame perfect equilibrium strategies of both firms as functions of the four parameters a, b, c, and d.

EXERCISE 6.8

Suppose that Sparkling Water and Clear Water can independently set the prices of their bottled water. The marginal cost of production at both firms is $1. At least some consumers are willing to pay more than $1 for bottled water, and they will buy from the firm charging the lowest price. Sparkling Water must choose its price before Clear Water does. This price is revealed to Clear Water before it makes its pricing decision. Find a Nash equilibrium pricing strategy for each firm that involves only credible threats. (Hint: The number of consumers who are willing to pay more than $1 for the water is irrelevant.)

EXERCISE 6.9

The Centipede Game is a two-person dynamic game that is played as follows: There is a pot of money. Initially, the pot has $1.00 in it. Player 1 moves first. He can either stop the game and take all the money in the pot ($1) or let the game go to round two. In round two, a dollar is added to the pot and player 2 moves. She can either stop the game and take all the money in the pot ($2) or let the game go on to round three. And so on. Player 1 moves in odd-numbered rounds, player 2 moves in even-numbered rounds, and at the beginning of every round, a dollar is added to the pot; in round N there are N in the pot. The game ends when a player stops it or when round 100 is reached. In round 100, player 2 gets all the money in the pot ($100) and the game ends.

(a) Draw the game tree for the Centipede Game for the first and last three moves.

(b) Determine the subgame perfect equilibrium strategies for both players. What is the equilibrium outcome?

(c) In experiments with real subjects playing for real money, many games go as long as 50 rounds before one of the players stops the game and takes what is in the pot. How does this compare with the equilibrium outcome you found in (b)? How would you account for the experimental results?

CHAPTER 7

Bargaining

OVERVIEW OF CHAPTER 7

7.1   Introduction

Bargaining is an extremely important part of economic life. You may have already been confronted with the need to haggle with a potential employer over your starting salary and with an automobile salesperson over the selling price of a car. Firms are constantly negotiating contract terms with their input suppliers. While competition among buyers and sellers limits the possible terms of trade, there are pockets of local monopoly and monopsony power throughout the economy that allow these terms to vary. The rational behavior of economic agents in bilateral (that is, two-person) bargaining situations is the focus of this chapter.

In a market in which there are a large number of small suppliers and de-manders, it has proved fruitful to assume that every trader is a price-taker and does not engage in any real bargaining. Even in a market where there is a mo-nopolistic seller and a large number of buyers, it is generally assumed that the monopolist sets a single, profit-maximizing price, and the buyers take that price as given. In situations where neither side of the market can be thought of as a price-taker, such as a monopolist selling to a monopsonist, economists have not

149

been able to say much about the price and output that will likely result from their bargaining with each other. For example, a leading intermediate microeconomics textbook reads "Analysts find it difficult to predict the . . . decisions that will emerge when both the buying and selling side of a market are monopolized."[1] In recent years, game theorists have made great strides in reducing the degree of indeterminacy and making it far clearer what factors will affect bargaining outcomes.

7.2   Bargaining Without Impatience

Consider two parties negotiating a contract whereby a service is exchanged for a price. It is common knowledge between them that the buyer (Bill) is willing to pay up to $300 for the service, and that the seller (Sally) will not accept anything below $200. The $300 maximum price the buyer is willing to pay is the **buyer's reservation price,** and the $200 minimum price the seller is willing to accept is the **seller's reservation price.** The difference between the negotiated price and the reservation price is each trader's gain from trade. It follows that, as long as an agreement can be reached, Bill's and Sally's gains from trade will add to $100. It might be helpful to think of this $100 as a pie to be divided between the two parties.

We will model their negotiations as a dynamic game in which Bill makes the first move and offers a price for the service, P_1. Sally can then either accept or reject the offer. If Sally accepts, the game is over and the bargain is completed at the offered price. If, however, Sally rejects the first offer, then she makes a counteroffer, P_2. Bill can either accept or reject the counteroffer. The negotiations then end. The extensive form for this game is shown in Figure 7.1.

Once an offer is accepted, the payoff to each player equals that player's gains from trade. If no offer is ever accepted, then trade does not take place and the payoff to both players equals $0. Whenever a player is indifferent about accepting or rejecting an offer, we will assume that the offer is accepted.

Using backward induction, as long as Sally's last offer is not over $300, Bill will accept it. The reason is simple; Bill can do no better than to accept any offer that is not over $300. If we move up the game tree one more node, it is also clear that Sally will reject any offer made by Bill that is anything less than $300. To accept any other offer would be to ignore her ability to make a more lucrative counteroffer at the next round. This means that Bill, depressing as this might seem to him, might as well offer to buy her service for $300 at the start of the game because he is going to end up paying $300 anyway. There is a **last-mover's advantage.** Being able to make the last offer gives Sally the ability to extract the entire surplus, or in other words, "to eat up all the pie."[2]

---

[1]William J. Baumol and Alan S. Binder, *Economics, Principles and Policy*, 6th edition, Harcourt, Brace and Company, 1994, p. 410.

[2]Strictly speaking, Bill actually has the last move, namely to accept or reject the offer. Nevertheless, it is usually asserted that Sally has the last "real" move.

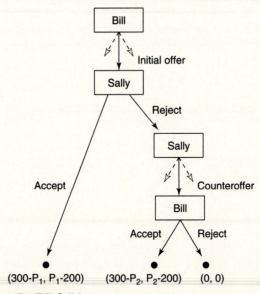

Payoffs: (Bill, Sally)

FIGURE 7.1   The game tree for bargaining between Bill and Sally with alternating offers.

This game, as you can probably already see, is very sensitive to the number of rounds of offers and to who moves first. For example, if there were only one round to this game, so that Sally did not have the chance to present a counteroffer, then the best strategy for Bill would be to offer to buy Sally's service for $200. This would be accepted by Sally since she is indifferent about accepting or rejecting the offer. In this case, Bill is able to extract the entire $100 surplus. We leave it as an exercise for you to show that if Bill makes the first offer and the number of rounds of offers is an odd number, then Bill will get a payoff equal to the entire surplus; but if the number of rounds of offers is an even number, then Sally will receive all of the surplus. If this strikes you as an odd and unrealistic result, we agree with you.[3] Read on.

7.3   Bargaining with Symmetric Impatience

Suppose that instead of only one or two rounds of offers, there are 100. Furthermore, suppose that delay in reaching an agreement imposes a cost on the negotiators. This cost could be related to the discounting of future earnings relative to present earnings. When a trader's time has a large opportunity cost, even a few days' worth of negotiating delays can be very expensive. For many people, this

---

[3]Note that we have begged the question of how the number of rounds in the game is determined. We have done so because we will eventually show that the number of rounds is largely irrelevant, unless there are very few.

Table 7.1 **Nash Equilibrium Outcome of Bargaining Game with Alternating Offers and Symmetric Impatience**

Round Number	Offer Maker	Seller's (Sally's) Share	Buyer's (Bill's) Share
100	Seller	100.0%	0.0%
99	Buyer	97.0%	3.0%
98	Seller	97.1%	2.9%
97	Buyer	94.2%	5.8%
⋮	⋮	⋮	⋮
4	Seller	53.4%	46.6%
3	Buyer	51.8%	48.2%
2	Seller	53.2%	46.8%
1	Buyer	51.7%	48.3%

cost may largely consist of the annoyance of having to deal with an unsettled and potentially pressure-filled situation. Who, for example, would not pay something to avoid haggling with a used car salesperson?

To make matters concrete, suppose the cost of delaying agreement by one round reduces the gains from trade to both players by 3%. That is, the players have **symmetric impatience.** As before, we will continue to assume that Bill and Sally will accept an offer whenever they are indifferent about accepting or rejecting it.

With 100 rounds of offers it is ridiculous to think of drawing a complete game tree, but we can still use backward induction to figure out Bill and Sally's rational strategies. Consider the subgame beginning with Sally's 100th and final offer. Just as in the previous section, Sally will offer to perform the service for $300 and Bill will accept it. Now move back to the subgame beginning with Bill's offer in the 99th round. As before, Bill knows what subgame perfect offer he can expect from Sally in the 100th round when he has to decide in the 99th round what to offer her. Unlike before, however, he will offer to buy the service from Sally for $297 and Sally will accept this. This number is derived from calculating the cost to Sally of delaying agreement for one round. Recall that the surplus to be divided has a value of $100, but a delay of one round costs the recipient of the offer 3% of his or her share of the surplus. Sally, by waiting until the 100th round can receive the entire surplus, but because of her impatience, she would be willing to accept 3% less to have the bargaining end in the 99th round. Therefore, Sally will accept any 99th round offer that is greater than or equal to $297 and reject anything less. From Bill's perspective, something today ($3) is better than nothing tomorrow; Bill offers $297.

But Sally knows that Bill is impatient as well. Since Bill receives a payoff in the 99th round of $3, Bill ought to be willing to accept a surplus 3% less than $3 ($0.09 less) in the 98th round. Therefore, Sally should offer her service for $297.09

in round 98, thereby receiving a surplus of $97.09. This is not only $0.09 more than she earns when she waits another round, but the offer allows her to avoid the cost of waiting. Once again, Bill knows that Sally ought to be willing to accept an offer by Bill of $294.16 in the 97th round (leaving her a 3% smaller surplus than she gets in the 98th round). Bill, in turn receives a larger surplus than he would by waiting ($5.84).

As you can see, each round of the negotiating process imposes a cost on both buyer and seller. This cost can be avoided only by making the split of the surplus attractive enough to the other player. The shares when the players make optimal offers are shown in Table 7.1. By using backward induction, we eventually find that Bill's best initial move is to offer Sally $251.65 for her service and that Sally should accept this offer. Bill ends up with a gain from trade of $48.35 while Sally gets $51.65. Notice that the surplus is split nearly 50/50, but that the last mover, Sally, continues to have a small advantage over Bill.

7.4 Bargaining with Asymmetric Impatience

The exact sharing of the surplus using this analysis depends on the number of rounds of offers and the magnitude of the transaction costs. A 50/50 split will occur if the cost of delay is the same for the two parties, the number of rounds is large, and the cost of a one-period delay is small. Although casual empiricism suggests that a 50/50 split is often chosen, this is not always the case. Those of you who have seen or heard the musical production of *Les Miserables* may recall the following exchange between Cosette's mother, Fantine (destitute, and in need of money to help her young daughter, Cosette), and an unsavory arbitrageur:

> *Arbitrageur: Come here my dear, let's see that trinket you wear. This bagatelle . . .*
>
> *Fantine: Madame I'll sell it to you.*
>
> *Arbitrageur: I'll give you four.*
>
> *Fantine: That wouldn't pay for the chain.*
>
> *Arbitrageur: I'll give you five. You're far too eager to sell. It's up to you.*
>
> *Fantine: It's all I have.*
>
> *Arbitrageur: That's not my fault.*
>
> *Fantine: Please make it ten.*
>
> *Arbitrageur: No more than five, my dear we all must stay alive.*

Clearly, we are left with the sense that the gains from exchange will be far removed from a 50/50 split. In fact, we are left with the impression that Cosette's mother has put herself in a very bad bargaining position by revealing her impatience. Back to Bill and Sally.

Suppose delay is more costly to Sally than to Bill, say because she is more impatient to receive the income than he is to receive her service. In particular, suppose delay reduces Sally's gains from trade by 6%, but reduces Bill's by only

Table 7.2 **Nash Equilibrium Outcome of the Bargaining Game with Alternating Offers but Asymmetric Impatience**

Round Number	Offer Maker	Seller's (Sally's) Share	Buyer's (Bill's) Share
100	Seller	100.0%	0.0%
99	Buyer	94.0%	6.0%
98	Seller	94.2%	5.8%
97	Buyer	88.5%	11.5%
96	Seller	88.9%	11.1%
.	.	.	.
.	.	.	.
.	.	.	.
4	Seller	34.8%	65.2%
3	Buyer	32.7%	67.3%
2	Seller	34.7%	65.3%
1	Buyer	32.6%	67.4%

3%. In this case, the players have **asymmetric impatience.** It remains optimal for Sally to offer a price of $300 in the 100th round, since she knows Bill will accept it, but now Bill's optimal offer to Sally in the 99th round is $294, not $297. In the 98th round, Sally knows that Bill will accept a gain from trade of $5.82 (97% of $6), so she will offer to supply her service to him for $294.18, and so on. The shares from some of the optimal offers are given in Table 7.2.

Bill's optimal initial offer is now $232.60, which Sally accepts rather than needlessly delay settlement. Notice that the split of the surplus is approximately 2:1 in Bill's favor, which matches the inverse of the ratio between their delay costs (6:3). This is no coincidence, as we will show below.

7.4.1 A GENERAL MODEL OF BARGAINING WITH IMPATIENCE

The impatience we have been talking about is often expressed as a **discount factor.** To say that it costs someone x percent of their portion of the surplus to wait one more round is equivalent to saying that the gains from a deal that is struck in round $t + 1$ should be discounted $1 - x$ percent from the previous round to account for the delay. The $1 - x$ percent is that player's discount factor. The greater the impatience (the higher the value of x), the lower the discount factor (the more the future is discounted). We will denote the buyer's discount factor by δ_B and the seller's discount factor by δ_S. In the bargaining example in Section 7.4, $\delta_B = 0.97$ and $\delta_S = 0.94$.

Each of the previous examples assumed that the number of rounds was fixed. In most bargaining circumstances, though, the number of rounds of offers and counteroffers is essentially unbounded. An important result in modern bargaining theory, attributed to Ariel Rubenstein, is that this type of game has a unique subgame perfect equilibrium. The result is important enough to state it formally.

> THEOREM 7.1: Suppose two players, S and B, are bargaining over the division of a surplus using alternate offers. Player B makes the first offer; there is no limit to the number of offers that can be made; both players have discount factors of $0 < \delta_S < 1$ and $0 < \delta_B < 1$; and players accept offers when they are exactly indifferent about accepting or rejecting them. Then this bargaining game has a unique subgame perfect equilibrium in which player B immediately offers S the fraction $\dfrac{\delta_S \cdot (1 - \delta_B)}{1 - \delta_S \cdot \delta_B}$ of the surplus retaining $\dfrac{1 - \delta_S}{1 - \delta_S \cdot \delta_B}$ for himself and S accepts.

The proof of Rubenstein's theorem is a testimony to the value of clear and logical thought. But thinking clearly and logically is not always easy.

The buyer moves first and proposes that a fixed sum of money be split in the proportions (w_B, w_S), where w_B and w_S are the proportions of the money retained by the buyer and seller respectively. For simplicity, we will suppose that this sum is \$1. The seller then accepts or rejects the split and the round ends. If the seller rejects the split, she makes a subsequent counteroffer, which the buyer can accept or reject. So far, this sounds identical to the previous models we have discussed. What is different, however, is that the game continues as long as the players keep rejecting offers. In theory, the game could last forever.

This game has an infinite number of subgames. As we learned earlier, one of those subgames is the game itself. Denote this game by G_1. Suppose this game has at least one subgame perfect equilibrium. Among the subgame perfect equilibria of G_1, let Q_B denote the largest payoff for the buyer and let q_B denote the smallest payoff for the buyer. Another subgame of the entire game begins at the subroot where the seller makes her first counteroffer to the buyer. Call this game G_2. Let Q_S denote the highest payoff the seller can obtain among all the subgame perfect equilibria of G_2 and let q_S denote the smallest payoff the seller obtains among these equilibria. A third subgame begins at the subroot where the buyer makes his second offer to the seller. Call this game G_3. These subgames are diagrammed in Figure 7.2. Stop for a minute and think about this game: it begins the same way as G_1, with the buyer making an offer to the seller. As with G_1, the game then consists of alternating offers with no limit to the number of offers. And finally, the payoffs decline each period by δ_B and δ_S, as in G_1. This means that G_3 is strategically equivalent to G_1. If the players get this far into the game, it is as if they start all over from the beginning. This implies that Q_B is the largest payoff for the buyer and q_B is the smallest payoff for the buyer among all the subgame perfect equilibria of G_3.

Consider some constraints on the buyer at the first round of G_1. In order for the offer to have any chance of acceptance (that is, in order for it to be subgame perfect), the seller must receive at least $\delta_S \cdot q_S$. This is because the seller can be guaranteed a payoff of q_S once the game reaches the subgame $G_{2,}$, but since this

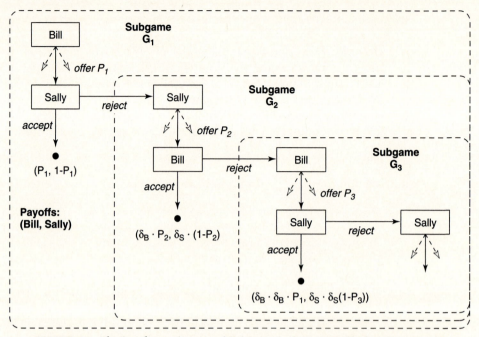

FIGURE 7.2   The first three subgames of Rubinstein's alternating offer bargaining game.

game is one round in the future, the payoff has to be discounted by δ_S to make it comparable to an immediate payoff. Of course, if the seller gets at least $\delta_S \cdot q_S$, and the total amount to be split is \$1, then the most the buyer can receive is $1 - (\delta_S \cdot q_S)$. This means

$$Q_B \leq 1 - (\delta_S \cdot q_S). \tag{7.1}$$

Using similar logic, we can find a bound for q_B. If the buyer offers the seller anything greater than or equal to $\delta_S \cdot Q_S$, she will take it. This is because she knows she can receive at most Q_S once the subgame G_2 is reached. Hence, it makes no sense for the buyer to offer more than $\delta_S \cdot Q_S$ when the game is G_1. This means the buyer can get at least $1 - (\delta_S \cdot Q_S)$ immediately, or

$$q_B \geq 1 - (\delta_S \cdot Q_S). \tag{7.2}$$

If the buyer rejects the seller's counteroffer, then the game continues on to the subgame G_3 where the buyer makes his second offer. We leave it as an exercise for you to show that by reversing the position of the buyer and the seller in the earlier logic, two further constraints can be placed on the payoffs Q_B, Q_S, q_B, and q_S. These constraints are

$$Q_S \leq 1 - (\delta_B \cdot q_B) \tag{7.3}$$

and

$$q_S \geq 1 - (\delta_B \cdot Q_B). \qquad [7.4]$$

Multiplying both sides of Eq. [7.4] by $-\delta_S$ and adding 1 results in the inequality

$$1 - (\delta_S \cdot q_S) \leq 1 - \delta_S \cdot (1 - \delta_B \cdot Q_B) = 1 - \delta_S + \delta_S \cdot \delta_B \cdot Q_B. \qquad [7.5]$$

The inequalities shown in Eqs. [7.5] and [7.1] imply

$$Q_B \leq 1 - \delta_S + \delta_S \cdot \delta_B \cdot Q_B. \qquad [7.6]$$

Rearranging Eq. [7.6] leads to the inequality

$$Q_B \leq \frac{1 - \delta_S}{1 - (\delta_S \cdot \delta_B)}. \qquad [7.7]$$

Similarly, multiplying both sides of Eq. [7.3] by $-\delta_S$ and then adding 1 implies

$$1 - (q_S \cdot Q_S) \geq 1 - \delta_S \cdot (1 - \delta_B \cdot q_B). \qquad [7.8]$$

Combining Eq. [7.2] with Eq. [7.8] and rearranging them results in the inequality

$$q_B \geq \frac{1 - \delta_S}{1 - (\delta_S \cdot \delta_B)}. \qquad [7.9]$$

But Eqs. [7.7] and [7.9] imply

$$Q_B \leq \frac{1 - \delta_S}{1 - (\delta_S \cdot \delta_B)} \leq q_B. \qquad [7.10]$$

By definition, Q_B and q_B are the highest and lowest payoffs to the buyer over all the subgame perfect equilibria for this game. This means

$$Q_B \geq q_B. \qquad [7.11]$$

For Eqs. [7.10] and [7.11] to both be true requires that

$$Q_B = q_B = \frac{1 - \delta_S}{1 - (\delta_S \cdot \delta_B)}. \qquad [7.12]$$

Similar logic (which we urge you to verify) leads to the conclusion that

$$Q_S = q_S = 1 - \frac{1 - \delta_S}{1 - (\delta_S \cdot \delta_B)} = \frac{\delta_S \cdot (1 - \delta_B)}{1 - (\delta_S \cdot \delta_B)} \qquad [7.13]$$

Thus, when the number of possible rounds is unbounded, the equilibrium payoffs of the two players are determinate and depend only on the discount factors of the two players and who moves first. Usually the "more patient" player—that is, the player with the largest discount factor—gets more than half of the surplus. This isn't always true because the first player to make an offer has a (small) **first-mover's advantage.** For example, when $\delta_S = 0.75$ and $\delta_B = 0.70$, the buyer is predicted to receive 53% of the pie even though the seller is more patient.

The fact that there is a first-mover advantage in this game poses a problem, since in many situations who goes first is not predetermined but is negotiated between the two parties. If this aspect of the bargaining determines the outcome of the bargaining, then the preliminary negotiations concerning who goes first are important. What now determines the outcome of this "prebargaining bargaining"? It is easy to see that we can get into an infinite regression of bargaining stages here. Fortunately, in most cases, who goes first is *not* important. The reason is that the first-mover's advantage goes to zero as the discount factors of the two players goes to one. The time between offers is an important determinant of the discount factor. The shorter the time interval between offers, the less costly is delaying the settlement for one more period. This implies that as the time interval between offers decreases, the discount factors of both players will approach one, but they may do so at different rates.

Suppose that the discount factors of the buyer and the seller are decreasing functions of the time interval between offers, t. We will denote the discount factors by $\delta_B(t)$ and $\delta_S(t)$ and the subgame perfect equilibrium split of the surplus by $(w_S^*(t), w_B^*(t))$. It follows from Theorem 7.1 that the ratio $\dfrac{w_B^*(t)}{w_S^*(t)}$ equals $\dfrac{1 - \delta_S(t)}{\delta_S(t) \cdot (1 - \delta_B(t))}$. We want to determine the limit of $\dfrac{w_B^*(t)}{w_S^*(t)}$ as the time interval between offers goes to zero. Clearly, it must be the case that $\delta_B(0) = \delta_S(0) = 1$. Suppose, furthermore, that both discount factor functions are differentiable and $-\delta_B'(0) = r_B > 0$ and $-\delta_S'(0) = r_S > 0$. The numbers r_B and r_S are the buyer's and seller's instantaneous delay costs. Then it follows (using L'Hopital's rule) that as t goes to zero, $\dfrac{w_B^*(t)}{w_S^*(t)}$ converges to $\dfrac{r_S}{r_B}$. That is, the players will agree to divide up the surplus in a ratio that exactly equals the inverse of the ratio of the instantaneous delay costs. Who goes first no longer matters.

7.5 Experimental Evidence on Sequential Bilateral Bargaining

Not surprisingly, given the importance of bargaining, a fairly large number of experiments have attempted to shed light on how people bargain in simple situations. Unfortunately, these experiments have often raised more questions than they have answered.

The simplest of the bargaining experiments are **dictator games.** One participant—the dictator—is asked to split a fixed sum of money between herself and an anonymous second participant. The split designated by the dictator is final. The obvious rational strategy for a purely self-interested person is to take the entire sum for herself. Unfortunately for believers in self-interested behavior, this strategy is typically chosen by far fewer than half of the dictators.[4]

Slightly more complicated are experimental games that allow the second player some discretionary power. **Ultimatum games** require the first participant to propose a split of a fixed sum of money. The second player can accept or reject the split. If the split is rejected, neither player gets anything. The rational subgame perfect, self-interested strategy profile is for the first player to propose a split that takes nearly the entire sum of money, leaving only a minimal amount for the second player. The second player, faced with the choice of a small positive sum (accepting the split) or nothing (rejecting the split), should choose to accept. In experiments of this sort, however, a 50/50 split is typically the modal response by the first player.[5] Furthermore, it is not uncommon for the second player to reject non-zero splits. Researchers have devoted much effort to trying to explain these results. They have learned that modifying the structure of the experiment (for example, by using market language instead of neutral language, or by making the players "earn" the right to be the first player) can significantly alter the outcome. But much research is still needed to understand these results.

A third class of experiments has been carried out that allows for alternating offers combined with discounting. An important paper by Binmore, Shaked, and Sutton (1985) reported the results of an experiment in which the first player was asked to divide 100 pence between himself and a second player.[6] The second player could either accept the division, thereby ending the game with the payoffs proposed by the first player, or reject the split. If the second player rejected the split, then the second player proposed a split of only 25 pence. The first player could accept this new split, ending the game with payoffs proposed by the second player, or reject the split, in which case neither player got anything. In essence, future payoffs are discounted 75%. The subgame perfect (self-interested) outcome is for the first player to offer a 75/25 split, which is accepted by the second player.[7] Participants in these experiments expected to play only once, but those who drew the role of the second mover were unexpectedly allowed to play a second time as

---

[4]For example, see Forsythe, R., Horowitz, J., Savin, N. E., and Sefton, M., "Fairness in Simple Bargaining Experiments," *Games and Economic Behavior* 6 (1994), pp. 347–69. It is worthwhile noting that this is not evidence that people are not rational, just that their utility depends, at the very least, on more than personal income.

[5]Ibid. See also Guth, W., Schmittberger, R., and Schwartz, B., "An Experimental Analysis of Ultimatum Bargaining," *Journal of Economic Behavior and Organization* 3 (1982), pp. 367–88.

[6]Binmore, K., Shaked, A., and Sutton, S., "Testing Noncooperative Bargaining Theory: A Preliminary Study," *American Economic Review* 75 (1985), pp. 1178–80.

[7]This subgame perfect equilibrium assumes that players will reject any offer they are indifferent about accepting or rejecting.

a first mover. In the first game, the average proposed split was 57 pence for the first player, while the modal proposal was 50 pence. In the second game (where the second player becomes the first player), the average increased to 67 pence with a mode near the subgame perfect equilibrium. While seeming to provide some confirming evidence of the subgame perfect prediction, further research has shown these results to be quite sensitive to experimental structure. For example, altering the discount factor can profoundly modify the results.

A commonly reported observation of experimental bargaining games is the high frequency with which players will make decisions that are guaranteed to make them financially worse off. The most obvious example is the decision second players make in the ultimatum game to reject non-zero splits proposed by the first player. Binmore, Shaked, and Sutton found similar behavior in their experiments. They found that a surprisingly large number of first-round offers were rejected by the second player, followed by second-round proposals by the second player that resulted in less money than they had originally been offered in the first round. This is obviously not subgame perfect self-interested behavior. One possible explanation is that players in these games found extreme payoff differentials abhorrent and were willing to give up cash to even out the payoffs. An experiment designed by Prasnikar and Roth looked at behavior in what is called a **best shot game** to see, in a different experimental setting, how willing players were to avoid payoff disparities.[8] In this dynamic game, player 1 is first asked to choose the integer quantity she is willing to provide. Denote this by Q_1. Having observed this quantity, player 2 must then choose the integer quantity he is willing to provide. Denote this by Q_2. Each unit provided by either player costs that player \$0.82. The revenue returned to each player is given by:

$$
R(Q_1, Q_2)_i = \begin{cases} \max\{Q_1, Q_2\} - 0.05 \cdot \displaystyle\sum_{j=1}^{\max\{Q_1,Q_2\}-1} i & \text{if } \max\{Q_1, Q_2\} > 1 \\ 1 & \text{if } \max\{Q_1, Q_2\} = 1 \\ 0 & \text{if } \max\{Q_1, Q_2\} = 0 \end{cases} \quad [7.14]
$$

We leave it as an exercise for you to show that the subgame perfect, self-interested equilibrium is for player 1 to provide a quantity of zero and for player 2 to provide a quantity of 4. The payoff to player 1 at the equilibrium is \$3.70 but is only \$0.42 for player 2. Hence, there is great disparity in the payoffs assuming subgame perfect behavior. It costs player 2 relatively little to equalize the payoffs fairly dramatically. For example, by providing an output of 2 instead of an output of 4, player 2 will reduce his own payoff by just \$0.11 while reducing player 1's payoff by \$1.75. And, of course there is the extreme option of providing nothing which will equalize payoffs at zero (a fairly regular occurrence in ultimatum games). Nevertheless, the actual behavior of the players in the best shot game corresponds closely to the subgame perfect equilibrium prediction.

---

[8]Prasnikar, V., and Roth, A., "Considerations of Fairness and Strategy: Experimental Data from Sequential Games," *Quarterly Journal of Economics* (August 1992), pp. 865–88.

As you can see, the evidence from bargaining experiments is difficult to interpret. The message appears to be that subtle issues of fairness in bargaining experiments seem to matter, but they are tempered by self-interested rationality.

7.6 A Bargaining Example: Sharing Sunk Costs

Consider the owner of a natural gas field trying to decide how to market her product. The gas she owns is a potentially valuable product to people living in a community some distance from the gas field, but in order for its value to be realized, it has to be piped and a pipeline does not currently exist. The residents of the community value the gas enough that they are willing to pay the cost of the pipeline as well as the cost of drilling the well and pumping the gas through the pipe. Clearly this is a situation in which mutually beneficial exchange is possible.

Certain characteristics of the pipeline investment are noteworthy. First, the construction of a pipeline is a large investment that must be undertaken prior to the delivery of any natural gas. Second, should the residents of the community decide in the future to buy their gas from some other source, the salvage value of the pipeline will be a small fraction of the cost of installing it. In the jargon used by economists, the delivery of gas to this community has a large *fixed cost* (a cost that does vary with the magnitude of the output), which is also a *sunk cost* (a cost that is largely unrecoverable should the gas producer decide to shut down operations because of low demand).

Unfortunately, *once the investment is made,* the residents of the community will recognize that they are paying natural gas prices far in excess of the marginal cost of delivery. Recall that the *marginal cost* of delivering the gas includes only the cost of pumping the gas through the pipeline, not the cost of building the pipeline. From the gas producer's perspective, however, she may only be charging a price high enough to allow her to recover the pipeline cost and the marginal cost of producing gas. The difference between the marginal cost of delivering the gas *after* the pipeline is built and the marginal cost of delivering the gas *before* the pipeline is built is crucial to what follows.

The customers have the producer over a barrel. As any Principles of Economics student will confirm, businesses only need to recover their *variable costs* to continue in operation. Once the pipeline is built, the producer will be willing to accept a price equal to the marginal cost of production rather than the average cost of production (inclusive of the pipeline costs). The difference between the marginal and average cost is due to the large sunk costs of the pipeline. It is perfectly reasonable to suspect that residents of the community will do what they can to "hold up" the producer, that is, only pay the producer a price equal to the marginal cost of production, or at the very least to lobby their local regulatory agency to reduce the natural gas rates to their community.[9]

---

[9]Ironically, the customers will almost certainly argue their point by citing evidence that the gas company is making an abnormal profit, or in other words "holding up" the consumers.

The producer, while looking toward the future, will certainly recognize how vulnerable she is to being held up once the pipeline is built. If these fears are great enough, and if contracts about natural gas pricing cannot be airtight enough and written far enough into the future to greatly reduce the chances of being held up, then it seems likely that the pipeline will never be built. This implies that the large mutually beneficial exchange never materializes.

You may be wondering if the community can simply build the pipeline itself and thereby avoid the "hold up" problem. There are many reasons why this is unlikely to occur, among them is the following: While the community as a whole might be willing to pay a great deal for the pipeline, no individual is likely to have the inclination or the means to carry out such a major investment. Someone with a publicly spirited bent might serve as an instigator to get the community together to contribute to make the investment, but the sad (and realistic) fact is that many individuals will prefer not to be included in the group. They would rather take a *free ride* off the ones who do join up. As a result, this approach is almost certain to fail.

Much of the preceding was filled with "probably" and "likely." To be more certain about the outcome of a situation such as the one described above, we need a more concrete example.

7.6.1 A MORE SPECIFIC EXAMPLE

There are two essential elements to the preceding example concerning the gas producer. One is that the investment decision must be made prior to contracting for the benefits of that investment. Another is that the investment is only of value to a small set of people; that is, the investment has little value in its next best alternative use.

Suppose the new Siberia Gas Company, a privately owned gas producer and distributor in Russia, is considering building a pipeline to Tomsk, a city in central Russia, which is currently not serviced by a gas producer. Residents in the community are collectively willing to pay 90 rubles per acre-foot of gas. In any given year they would demand a total of 10,000 acre-feet, implying an annual willingness to pay for gas of 900,000 rubles. At an interest rate of 10%, the present value of the consumers' collective willingness to pay for gas is 9 million rubles.

The Siberia Gas Company can build a pipeline to Tomsk for 3 million rubles. If it is built, we will suppose that the pipeline lasts forever. Once it is built, the cost per acre-foot of providing gas is constant and equal to 50 rubles. Satisfying the demand for gas in Tomsk would generate an annual operating cost of 500,000 rubles. At an interest rate of 10%, the present value of the stream of operating costs over the lifetime of the pipeline would be 5 million rubles. Therefore, building the pipeline and providing gas to residents of Tomsk will cost 8 million rubles. To complete the model, we will finally suppose that the pipeline has no scrap value, and that the Siberia Gas Company and citizens of Tomsk *cannot* reach a binding agreement *before* the pipeline is built.

Building the pipeline and shipping gas to the residents of Tomsk results in a net gain of 1 million rubles. This surplus must be split between the citizens of Tomsk and the owners of the Siberia Gas Company. Clearly, both the citizens of Tomsk and the Siberia Gas Company can be better off if the pipeline is built. Recall, however, that the pipeline must be built before a binding contract can be written between the citizens of Tomsk and the gas company. *Once the pipeline is built*, the minimum amount that the Siberia Gas Company is willing to accept per acre-foot is 50 rubles while the maximum amount that people in Tomsk are willing to pay is 90 rubles. The net gain per acre-foot is 40 rubles. At 10,000 acre-feet per year, the total present value equals 4 million rubles.

We have here a dynamic game. The players in the game are the citizens of Tomsk and the Siberia Gas Company. The order of play is: the Siberia Gas Company moves first and decides whether to build a pipeline to Tomsk; the citizens of Tomsk and the Siberia Gas Company then bargain over the terms of trade for the gas. We will suppose that the bargaining game is itself a dynamic game, much as we discussed in the previous sections of this chapter. As we have seen in the beginning of this chapter, when two parties present each other with alternating offers in quick succession, and when they know each other's instantaneous delay costs, they will agree to divide the surplus in a ratio that is the inverse of the ratio of these costs.[10] In this case, let us assume that these costs of delay are the same and that this is common knowledge. Then we know that the citizens of Tomsk and the Siberia Gas Company will agree to divide the net gains equally between them.

The implications of this bargaining process are profound. In order to break even on the pipeline before having built it, the Siberia Gas Company must be certain of a price per acre-foot of 80 rubles. By receiving this price, the firm can be assured of 800,000 rubles per year in revenues, which translates into a present value of the stream of revenue equal to 8 million rubles. Since this exactly matches the cost of laying the pipeline and providing the gas to Tomsk, the Siberia Gas Company will just break even.

If, however, the Siberia Gas Company builds the pipeline, it can expect a price that splits the 40 ruble per acre-foot surplus equally between Tomsk and itself. This means the price that the Siberia Gas Company *can rationally expect* to negotiate with Tomsk is 70 rubles per acre-foot. Since this is 10 rubles per acre-foot below their break-even price (calculated prior to building the pipeline), they will choose not to build the pipeline.

Even though both parties can be made better off through the construction of a pipeline, the inability to establish a binding contract before the pipeline has been laid results in the pipeline not being built. Had it been possible to negotiate a contract successfully *prior* to the investment decision, the minimum price that the Siberia Gas Company would have required to provide gas would have been 80 rubles per acre-foot. The maximum amount the citizens of Tomsk would have been willing to pay would still have been 90 rubles per acre-foot and the resulting

---

[10]You should go back and review some of the conditions that generated this result.

negotiated price would have been 85 rubles per acre-foot. The pipeline, in these circumstances, would have been built and no further gains from trade would be left unexploited.

7.7   Summary

A great many decisions that we make include bargaining in one form or another. How much we pay for a car, how much you will get paid by an employer, how much a firm producing electricity will pay for coal from another producer, and how much the Pentagon will pay for military equipment are all examples. Economists have historically said a great deal about the welfare gains from trade, but have had very little to say about how those gains are shared between the transactors. Game theory applied to bargaining begins to provide a mechanism to better understand the deals that will be struck.

In this chapter, we have developed a theory of bargaining from a very simple model in which there is no time discounting to a relatively complex model. This model predicts that the gains two bargainers split from trade depend on who makes the first offer, the number of rounds of offers, and the relative impatience of the two bargainers. While there is a great deal more to be said about bargaining, we now have a framework with which to structure the future reasoning, and we have developed empirically testable hypotheses.

Understanding how the gains from trade are split has a wide variety of applications. We have highlighted what has become known as the "hold-up problem": When an investment such as a gas pipeline generates benefits to a specific demander, the costs of the investment are unrecoverable, and the costs of contracting prior to the investment taking place are sufficiently high, then the investment will not take place, even when everyone could benefit from it.

7.8   Further Reading

Ariel Rubinstein presented the first model of bargaining as a dynamic game in "Perfect Equilibrium in a Bargaining Model," *Econometrica* 50(1) (1982), pp. 97–109. This paper is very difficult. Fortunately, the results are presented in a much more readable form in *Bargaining and Markets* by Martin Osborne and Ariel Rubinstein (New York: Academic Press, 1990). Our proof of Rubinstein's bargaining result is due to Ken Binmore, *Fun and Games: A Text on Game Theory* (Lexington, MA: D. C. Heath, 1992, pp. 209–11).

The experimental literature on bargaining is summarized in John H. Kagel and Alvin E. Roth, eds., *The Handbook of Experimental Economics* (New Jersey: Princeton University Press, 1995, pp. 253–348). Some of the more important experimental research on bargaining is contained in Forsythe, R., Horowitz, J., Savin, N. E., and Sefton, M., "Fairness in Simple Bargaining Experiments," *Games and*

Economic Behavior, 6 (1994), pp. 347–69; Guth, W., Schmittberger, R., and Schwartz, B., "An Experimental Analysis of Ultimatum Bargaining," *Journal of Economic Behavior and Organization*, 3 (1982), pp. 367–88; Binmore, K., Shaked, A., and Sutton, S., "Testing Noncooperative Bargaining Theory: A Preliminary Study," *American Economic Review*, 75 (1985), pp. 1178–80; and Prasnikar, V., and Roth, A., "Considerations of Fairness and Strategy: Experimental Data from Sequential Games," *Quarterly Journal of Economics* (August 1992), pp. 865–88.

7.9   Discussion Questions

1. Describe real-life bargaining situations that might be modeled by the alternating offer game presented in this chapter.

2. Identify reasons why discounting between alternate offers might exist, even when the time between offers is short.

3. Provide explanations for the experimental results outlined in Section 7.5.

7.10   New Terms

asymmetric impatience	last-mover's advantage
best shot game	seller's reservation price
buyer's reservation price	symmetric impatience
dictator games	ultimatum games
discount factor	

7.11   Exercises

EXERCISE 7.1

Suppose that Bill and Sally are bargaining over the division of a $100 surplus. They make alternating offers and do not discount the future at all. That is, they consider the receipt of a dollar at any time in the future equivalent to the receipt of a dollar today. The number of offers is fixed in advance. Show that the last person to make an offer gets all of the surplus.

EXERCISE 7.2

Prove the inequalities in Eqs. [7.3] and [7.4] in Section 7.5.1.

EXERCISE 7.3

Show that in the best shot game described in Section 7.5, the subgame perfect strategy profile is for player 1 to provide 0 units and for player 2 to provide 4 units.

EXERCISE 7.4

Suppose that Bill, a buyer, and Sally, a seller, are bargaining over the price at which Sally will perform a service for Bill. It is common knowledge that the maximum price Bill will pay is $300 and the minimum price Sally will accept is $200. They bargain over the price in the following manner: Bill offers a price to Sally, who can either accept or reject it. If she accepts Bill's first offer, the game ends and they exchange at this price, P_1. Bill's payoff is $300 − P_1$ and Sally's payoff is $P_1 − \$200$. If Sally rejects the offer, then Bill offers *another* price, P_2, which Sally can again accept or reject. And so on. Both players discount future income by 50% per period. So, if Sally accepts Bill's Nth offer, P_n, then Bill's payoff is $\dfrac{\$300 − P_n}{2^{n-1}}$ and Sally's payoff is $\dfrac{P_n − \$200}{2^{n-1}}$. Sally will accept an offer if she is indifferent about accepting or rejecting it.

(a) Draw the game tree for this bargaining under the simplifying assumption that Bill's only possible offers are $200, $250, or $300 and that they bargain for only two rounds. That is, if Sally rejects Bill's second offer, then they do not trade, and each receives a payoff of $0. Be careful to label the action taken along each branch, to label who moves at each decision node (Bill or Sally), and to label the payoff of both players at each terminal node.

(b) Use backward induction to determine the equilibrium strategies for both players if the game ends after two rounds and if Bill can offer Sally anything.

(c) Use backward induction to determine the equilibrium strategies for both players if the game ends after 400 rounds and if Bill can offer Sally anything.

CHAPTER 8

Time-Consistent Macroeconomic Policy

OVERVIEW OF CHAPTER 8

8.1   Introduction

You have probably learned in your Principles of Economics class that the growth rate of the money supply determines the inflation rate in the long run. The inflation rate can also affect the growth of output and employment. It is reasonable to suppose that a country's central bank cares about both the inflation rate and the level of employment.[1] Worker and employer behavior, obviously, also have an impact on the aggregate economy. It is the interdependency among these three groups—the central bank, workers, and employers—that we will explore in this chapter.

Workers and employers tend to write long-term labor contracts that are expressed in terms of dollars (called *nominal value*) rather than in terms of purchasing power (called *real value*). This means that workers, when establishing a nominal wage contract, must predict the central bank's choice of the rate of

---

[1]In the United States, it is not only reasonable, it is the law!

inflation and the real value of their wages. In a model of perfect information and rational behavior, one in which subgame perfect equilibrium strategies are chosen, workers will be able to predict the behavior of the central bank even though the central bank chooses the inflation rate after the workers sign their labor contracts.

We will present a model in which the central bank chooses a higher level of inflation than it would like. The central bank's inability to credibly commit to a lower inflation rate is at the heart its problem. The question then arises as to how the central bank might possibly precommit to a lower and more preferable inflation rate.

8.2 Inflation

One of the most commonly used economic terms in the popular press is **inflation.** Unfortunately, the word is often used in ways that lead to confused analysis and ridiculous policy prescriptions. To economists, inflation consists of a *persistent* increase in the *general* price level. A one-time jump in the price level is not inflation, nor is an increase in the price of a single commodity, even one as important as oil. Whether an unexpected increase in the price of one commodity, such as oil, will be followed by inflation depends on how employers, households, and the government respond to the increase.

During the late 1960s, most of the 1970s, and the early 1980s, many industrialized countries experienced historically high rates of inflation. Figure 8.1 displays the so-called "core" inflation rate in the United States for the period 1955–1996. The **core inflation** rate is the average percentage increase in prices of all consumer commodities *other than* food and energy. The elimination of these two classes of goods reduces the distortion caused by the large one-time changes in world energy and food prices in 1973, 1974, 1979, and 1986.

Figure 8.1 has some striking features. The first is the steady acceleration in the inflation rate over the period 1965–1981. Starting from a stable core inflation rate in 1965 of under 2%, the inflation rate began accelerating in the late 1960s until by 1981 it was over 12%. The second feature of Figure 8.1 is the sudden deceleration in the inflation rate between 1981 and 1983, from 12% to less than 5%.

The accelerating inflation of the 1960s and 1970s led many economists during this period to hypothesize that modern economies possessed an **inflationary bias.** It was argued that central banks are under great political pressure to use inflationary monetary policies to stimulate economic growth and reduce unemployment. We will demonstrate that such a policy will stimulate economic activity only if the public does not anticipate the resulting inflation. But persistent underestimation of persistent inflation is inconsistent with rational behavior. Once the public catches on to what the central bank is doing, the policy will not stimulate economic growth or higher employment.

It has also been argued that oligopolistic firms can pass on to consumers, in the form of higher output prices, any wage increases demanded by their unionized

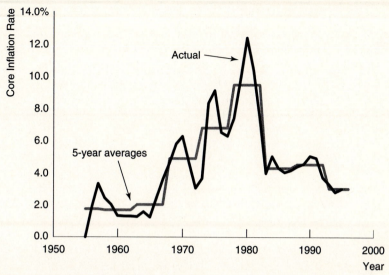

FIGURE 8.1 The "core" inflation rate for the United States during the period 1955–1996, excluding energy and food prices.

workers. This, it is claimed, will result in a vicious cycle of wage and price escalation. This explanation, too, has a serious flaw. Although market power can account for why the wages of unionized workers in monopolistic or oligopolistic industries are *relatively* higher than the wages of other workers, market power can account for *persistent increases* in the wages of these workers only if there is a *persistent increase* in their market power. Over the last 40 years, the unionized sector of the labor force has been *declining* in relative size and importance, not growing. And the largest oligopolistic industries, notably steel and automobiles, have experienced a steady increase in competition (most of it foreign).

8.3   A Simple Macroeconomic Model

Wages are almost always negotiated in terms of money, even though workers and employers are ultimately interested in purchasing power. Occasionally, wage contracts will be indexed to prices, but this is relatively rare and almost never complete. This has two important implications. First, the money wage that clears the labor market will depend on the rate of inflation expected over the period covered by the contract. Second, if the inflation rate actually differs from what was expected when the money wage was negotiated, then workers will be forced by their contracts to supply either more or less labor than they would have supplied had the inflation rate been correctly foreseen.

The inflation rate workers and employers are trying to forecast is not completely random, like the weather, but is influenced by the rate of growth of the money supply, which is under the control of the central bank. So the wage and

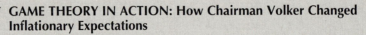

GAME THEORY IN ACTION: How Chairman Volker Changed Inflationary Expectations

Between 1965 and 1980 inflation in the United States accelerated from 2% to more than 12%. According to our model, the Federal Reserve Board is mostly to blame because the equilibrium inflation rate is an increasing function of the Fed's inflation and employment targets. We will show that, to lower the equilibrium rate of inflation, two things have to change: (1) the Federal Reserve Board's employment and inflation targets have to decline and (2) the public has to believe that the Federal Reserve Board's targets have declined.

The first condition was met when Paul Volker was appointed chairman of the Federal Reserve Board in 1979. Volker was known to believe that accelerating inflation was a very serious problem that had to be stopped. He was also a very strong personality who quickly took control of the Board and its important policy arm, the Federal Open Market Committee (FOMC), of which he was also the chair. Volker's task was to convince the public that the Fed had new targets. He went about this in an ingenious way. First, Volker announced that the Federal Reserve would no longer try to control interest rates but would, instead, seek to control the rate of growth of the money supply. The hidden message in this announcement was that the Federal Reserve was changing. Second, he "allowed" short-term interest rates to rise to over 20%, until they finally triggered a recession. But when the recession ended nine months later and inflation was still above 10%, Volker forced interest rates up a second time, generating a second recession. This recession was the worst since the 1930s. But by the time it ended in late 1982, the public was convinced that the Federal Reserve's inflation and unemployment targets had indeed changed, and the reward was a core inflation rate of less than 5%. This low inflation rate has now been maintained for 15 years, through one mild recession and two very long expansions.

Volker's strategy was ingenious in that the announced change in operating procedures was used to hide the real agenda, which was to create a recession with which to alter the public's inflationary expectations. When interest rates surged in 1979 and again in 1981, the Federal Reserve was able to avoid blame by arguing that increased interest rate volatility could be expected from a policy of controlling money supply growth. The reason why the Federal Reserve's "cover story" is not credible is that money supply growth became *more* erratic, not less, after 1979. Money growth was erratic because the money supply was repeatedly manipulated to boost interest rates and generate a recession. If only one recession had been needed to do the job, Volker might have succeeded in fooling everyone.

employment decisions of workers and employers depends on the bank's money growth decision. But the bank's performance, in turn, depends on the wage and employment decisions of the workers and employers. This interdependence means that the three groups are embroiled in a game. Under very general conditions, this game has a Nash equilibrium in which the central bank chooses a growth rate for the money supply that results in inflation above its target. Unfortunately for the central bank, in our dynamic game, a low-inflation monetary policy is not **time consistent**: When the time comes for the central bank to choose the rate of inflation, it will no longer find it optimal to follow a low-inflation policy. A high-inflation policy will be optimal instead.

8.3.1 IDENTITIES

Macroeconomic modeling emphasizes the aggregate behavior of the economy and ignores the behavior of individual markets. The model we will present below involves the following aggregates: the level of employment, L_t; the price level, P_t; the money supply, M_t; the money wage, W_t; the real wage, R_t; and the expected price level, P_t^e.

We will measure all price and quantity aggregates in natural logarithms. It is customary to denote these by lowercase letters. So, for example, m_t represents the natural logarithm of the money supply, M_t. Measuring our variables in natural logarithms has many advantages. First, the difference between the natural log of a variable at time t and the natural log of that variable at time $t - 1$ is approximately the rate of growth of the variable between $t - 1$ and t. That is,

$$\ln(X_t) - \ln(X_{t-1}) = x_t - x_{t-1} \approx \frac{X_t - X_{t-1}}{X_{t-1}}. \qquad [8.1]$$

Second, the logarithm of the ratio of two variables equals the difference of their logarithms. That is, $\ln\left(\dfrac{X}{Y}\right) = \ln(X) - \ln(Y) = x - y$. Third, the natural logarithm of one equals zero. This last property of logarithms means the choice of a unit for the original variable X determines the zero point for the transformed variable $\ln(X) = x$.

In our discussion, we will make use of the following definitions:

$$\pi_t \equiv p_t - p_{t-1} \quad \text{rate of price inflation,}$$

$$\pi_t^e \equiv p_t^e - p_{t-1} \quad \text{expected rate of price inflation, and} \qquad [8.2]$$

$$g_t \equiv m_t - m_{t-1} \quad \text{rate of growth of money supply;}$$

the following identity:

$$r_t \equiv w_t - p_t \quad \text{the real wage (in logarithms); and} \qquad [8.3]$$

the following normalizations:

$$m_1 = 0$$
$$\qquad\qquad\qquad\qquad\qquad\qquad\qquad [8.4]$$
$$p_1 = 0.$$

From Eqs. [8.2] and [8.4] it follows that

$$\pi_2 = p_2$$
$$\pi_2^e = p_2^e \tag{8.5}$$
$$r_2 = w_2 - \pi_2.$$

8.3.2 ACTIONS AND ORDER OF PLAY

To avoid inessential technical details, we will model the economy using a highly stylized dynamic game played out over two time periods. During the first time period, the workers choose the money wage at which they will work in the second period. They make this decision without knowing what the price level will be in the second period. At the beginning of the second period, the central bank chooses the rate of inflation. Employers then choose the level of employment. The game tree is shown in Figure 8.2.

The central bank controls the inflation rate indirectly through its control of the growth in the money supply. Although the causal linkage between money growth and inflation is not yet settled among economists, we will take an extreme monetarist position and assume that all price inflation is caused by money growth. That is,

$$\pi_2 = \phi(g_2), \tag{8.6}$$

where $\phi(\cdot)$ is a strictly increasing function.

Evidence in favor of a causal relationship between money growth and inflation can be found in the cross-national survey data graphed in Figure 8.3. Because

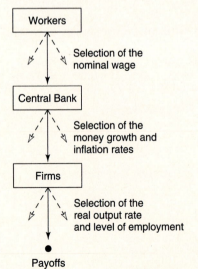

FIGURE 8.2 The game tree for the Macroeconomic Policy Game played between workers, employers, and the central bank.

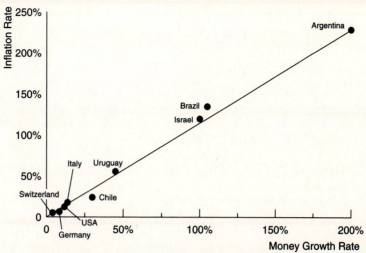

FIGURE 8.3 Average rates of inflation during the period 1977–1987 plotted against the average rate of growth of the money supply over the same period.

of the presumed causal link, we will hereafter assume that the central bank chooses the inflation rate π_2 directly.

8.3.3 STRATEGIES

A strategy for the workers consists of a money wage, w_2. A strategy for the central bank consists of an **inflation policy** of the form $\pi_2(w_2)$. The fact that the rate of inflation can depend on the wage selected by the workers turns out to be an important reason for the central bank's poor performance in this game. A strategy for employers consists of an **employment rule** of the form $l_2(w_2, \pi_2)$.

8.3.4 PAYOFFS

Workers are utility maximizers who value both real income and leisure. For a given real wage, increasing employment leads to increasing real worker income, but decreasing leisure. Decreasing marginal utility from both income and leisure implies that for any real wage, r_t, there is a utility maximizing level of labor supplied, $l^s(r_t)$. This is just a labor supply curve. We will assume for simplicity that

$$l^s(r_t) = \alpha \cdot r_t, \tag{8.7}$$

where α is simply a constant. It equals the percentage change in labor supply induced by a 1% change in the real wage. That is, α is the elasticity of labor supply with respect to the real wage. We will assume the workers want to minimize the difference between the level of employment eventually chosen by employers, l_2, and the utility-maximizing level of employment, $\alpha \cdot r_2$. Specifically, we assume that the workers' payoff function, v_W, takes the form

$$v_W(w_2, l_2, \pi_2) = -(l_2 - \alpha \cdot (w_2 - \pi_2))^2. \tag{8.8}$$

The central bank's goal is simple. It has target values for employment and inflation, denoted $\tilde{l}_2$ and $\tilde{\pi}_2$, and wants to steer l_2 and π_2 toward its two targets using its one policy instrument: π_2. Assume that the central bank's goal is to maximize the payoff function

$$v_{FR}(w_2, l_2, \pi_2) = -(l_2 - \tilde{l}_2)^2 - \mu \cdot (\pi_2 - \tilde{\pi}_2)^2, \tag{8.9}$$

where the exogenous constant μ in Eq. [8.9] measures the relative importance the central bank places on its employment target versus its inflation target. The larger μ is, the more weight is given to the inflation target and the less weight is given to the employment target. The fact that the two terms in Eq. [8.9] are squared implies that as l_2 or π_2 gets further away from the target values, there are increasing marginal losses in utility. Big misses are proportionately more painful than small misses.

Employers are profit-maximizing price-takers. At the profit-maximizing level of employment, the marginal physical product of labor will equal the real wage rate. This condition defines the labor demand function, $l^d(r_t)$. For simplicity, we will assume that the demand for labor (in logarithms) can be written as:

$$l^d(r_t) = -\eta \cdot r_t. \tag{8.10}$$

When interpreting the parameter η it is important to remember that the variables are in logarithmic form. In general, η is the elasticity of labor demand with respect to the real wage rate. Using the expression for the real wage rate, Eq. [8.5], we can write the labor demand function in the second time period as

$$l^d(r_2) = \eta \cdot (\pi_2 - w_2). \tag{8.11}$$

Employers want to minimize the difference between their level of employment and the profit-maximizing level of employment. Specifically, we assume that the employers' payoff function is

$$v_E(w_2, l_2, \pi_2) = -(l_2 - \eta \cdot (\pi_2 - w_2))^2. \tag{8.12}$$

The labor market is in equilibrium when the amount of labor supplied equals the amount of labor demanded. Eqs. [8.7] and [8.10] imply that this will occur when r_t (the logarithm of real wage) is zero. The level of employment at this equilibrium real wage is the **natural level of employment.** We have chosen our units so that the natural level of employment is 1, which means that its logarithm is zero. You might expect that when the labor market is in equilibrium no one is unemployed. But that is not correct. Even when the labor market is in equilibrium, some workers will continue to look for jobs that pay more than they have been offered so far. These workers are **voluntarily unemployed** and their unemployment is called **frictional unemployment.** It remains an important open question as to whether a modern competitive economy can have a macroeconomic equilibrium in which employment is below the natural level. At such an equilibrium some workers would be willing to take any job paying the current real wage, yet employers would not hire them. These workers would be *involuntarily unemployed.* In Chapter 12 we examine some circumstances under which involuntary unemployment can exist in equilibrium.

8.3.5 EQUILIBRIUM

Since this is a dynamic game with perfect information, we can determine the subgame perfect equilibrium using backward induction.

Employers move last. Given the money wage chosen by the workers and the rate of inflation chosen by the central bank, the employer's profit-maximizing strategy maximizes $v_E(l_2, w_2, \pi_2)$ for the only variable in their payoff function over which they have discretion, l_2. It is easy to see that the optimal level of employment, $l_2^*(w_2, \pi_2)$ equals $\eta \cdot (\pi_2 - w_2)$. This is the economy's **aggregate employment function,**

$$l_2^*(w_2, \pi_2) = \eta \cdot (\pi_2 - w_2). \qquad [8.13]$$

The central bank moves second. Its optimal strategy maximizes

$$v_{FR}(w_2, l_2^*(w_2, \pi_2), \pi_2).$$

That is, it chooses π_2 so as to minimize

$$(\eta \cdot (\pi_2 - w_2) - \tilde{l}_2)^2 + \mu \cdot (\pi_2 - \tilde{\pi}_2)^2. \qquad [8.14]$$

We leave it as an exercise for you to verify that the central bank's optimal inflation policy is

$$\pi_2^*(w_2) = \frac{\mu \cdot \tilde{\pi}_2 + \eta \cdot \tilde{l}_2 + \eta^2 \cdot w_2}{\mu + \eta^2}. \qquad [8.15]$$

The workers move first. Their choice of wage contract depends on their forecasts about employment and inflation rates. The inflation forecasts, π_2^e, are called **inflationary expectations** in the macroeconomic literature. What inflation forecast should the workers use? Rationality dictates that workers form their expectations by looking ahead and foreseeing the inflation rate that will be generated by the central bank's optimal inflation policy. This means

$$\pi_2^e = \pi_2^*(w_2). \qquad [8.16]$$

If the workers behave this way, they are said to have **rational inflationary expectations.** Professor Robert Lucas at the University of Chicago won the Nobel Prize in economics in 1995 for his pioneering work using rational expectations.[2] Incorporating the subgame perfect strategies into the workers' payoff function yields

$$v_W(w_2, l_2^*(w_2, \pi_2^*(w_2)), \pi_2^*(w_2))$$
$$= -(l_2^*(w_2, \pi_2^*(w_2)) - \alpha \cdot (w_2 - \pi_2^*(w_2)))^2$$
$$= -(\eta \cdot (\pi_2^*(w_2) - w_2) - \alpha \cdot (w_2 - \pi_2^*(w_2)))^2 \qquad [8.17]$$
$$= -(\eta + \alpha)^2 \cdot (\pi_2^*(w_2) - w_2)^2.$$

This expression is maximized when $\pi_2^*(w_2^*) = w_2^*$, or

$$w_2^* = \tilde{\pi}_2 + \frac{\eta}{\mu} \cdot \tilde{l}_2. \qquad [8.18]$$

Substituting Eq. [8.18] into Eq. [8.15] you can verify that

$$\pi_2^*(w_2^*) = \tilde{\pi}_2 + \frac{\eta}{\mu} \, \tilde{l}_2. \qquad [8.19]$$

Since $\pi_2^*(w_2^*) = w_2^*$, the equilibrium real wage rate (in logarithms) in the second time period, r_2^*, will equal zero. The equations for labor supply and labor demand then imply that

$$l_2^d(r_2^*) = l_2^s(r_2^*) = 0, \qquad [8.20]$$

which means that the labor market is in equilibrium.

So the central bank can reach its inflation and employment targets if, and only if, $\tilde{l}_2 = 0$. It turns out, however, that there are many reasons why the central bank might consider the natural level of employment to be socially suboptimal and would target a level of employment above the natural level. Some of these reasons include:

1. Income taxes reduce the effective wage rate earned by workers, creating a disincentive to work and a possible reduction in labor supply.

2. Unemployment compensation reduces the cost of searching for new employment, making the effective unemployment rate artificially high.

3. Monopolistic unions push for wages above the market clearing level, thereby reducing the quantity of labor demanded.

4. Monopsonistic employers pay wages below the competitive level, thereby reducing the quantity of labor supplied.

---

[2]Evidence that people are rationally foresighted comes from Professor Lucas's ex-wife, who included as part of their divorce settlement a provision giving her 50% of the $1 million Nobel Prize award if he were to win prior to 1996. He was awarded the prize only a few months before this provision expired.

Whenever $\tilde{l}_2$ is strictly positive, the central bank misses its employment target, $\tilde{l}_2$, *and* its inflation target, $\tilde{\pi}_2$. The central bank's inability to alter the level of employment is a very important result of this model. Since the worker's inflationary expectations turn out to be correct, this equilibrium is also said to be characterized by **perfect foresight.** Perfect foresight is a consequence of our assumption that there is no uncertainty. When uncertainty is present, then worker's inflationary expectations are correct *on average*. Such forecasts are called **unbiased forecasts.**

8.3.6 A NUMERICAL EXAMPLE

Suppose the central bank sets a target inflation rate of 2% and a target employment level 2% above the natural level of employment, and that both goals have equal weight. This means $\tilde{\pi}_2 = 0.02$, $\tilde{l}_2 = 0.02$, and $\mu = 1$. Suppose also that the wage elasticity of labor demand is unity, or $\eta = 1$. We can display the central bank's payoff function in two dimensions (employment and inflation) by drawing contour lines associated with different payoff levels. This is done in Figure 8.4. The contour lines are the central bank's indifference curves. The smaller the radius of the contour line, the higher the payoff. The highest payoff occurs, obviously, at the target values, $\tilde{\pi}_2$ and $\tilde{l}_2$.

The central bank announces both targets to the national media. If the workers naively believe the central bank's announcement, that is, $\pi_2^e = 0.02$, then workers will contract for $w_2 = 0.02$. If the central bank keeps its promise and holds the inflation rate to 2%, employers will respond according to the aggregate employment function and the economy will be at the natural level of employment.

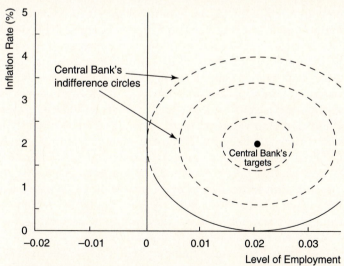

FIGURE 8.4 The central bank's indifference curves. Higher payoffs are associated with circles with smaller radii.

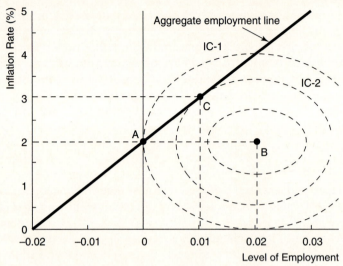

FIGURE 8.5 If workers naively believe the central bank's promise to keep inflation to 2%, then the central bank will renege on its promise and choose a higher inflation in order to boost employment above the natural employment level.

This outcome is represented by the point labeled A in Figure 8.5. Inflation is measured on the vertical axis and employment is measured (in logarithms) on the horizontal axis. The aggregate supply curve is drawn under the naive assumption that $w_2 = 0.02$. The central bank's inflation and employment targets correspond to the point labeled B.

The problem with this outcome is that although the central bank may promise to keep inflation to 2%, once the workers set the nominal wage to 0.02, it is not rational for the central bank to keep its promise. The central bank's promise is **time inconsistent.** If the central bank were to keep its promise, it would be on the indifference circle labeled IC-1. Indifference circles closer to point B are associated with higher payoffs to the central bank. Since the central bank can only control the inflation rate and must wait for employers to set employment, the central bank is constrained to end up with an inflation rate/employment combination along the aggregate employment line. The "highest" indifference circle the central bank can be on subject to the aggregate supply curve constraint is labeled IC-2. The central bank can end up on this circle by choosing an inflation rate of 3% and waiting for employers to set employment (in logarithms) equal to 0.01. Therefore, the economy will end up at point C. This means that the real wage in period two will be lower than workers thought it would be when they initially negotiated the money wage. Employers will respond to the lower real wage by hiring above the natural level of employment.

At the natural level of employment and equilibrium wage, the workers are maximizing their utility and employers are maximizing their profits based on their forecasts about the price level. Once the money wage is fixed, though, the employer is free to alter the level of employment and the workers have to acquiesce and provide this level of employment. Those are the contractual terms. When employment is above the natural level, the workers are providing *more* labor at a lower real wage than they initially expected. Conversely, when employment is below the natural level, workers are providing *less* labor at a higher real wage than they initially expected. In both instances, the workers regret the contract they voluntarily entered into with employers in period one. When workers are naive, the central bank can have an impact on the level of employment.

Because the central bank's promise that inflation will be held to 2% is not binding and it is in its interests to stimulate a higher inflation rate than this, the workers should not believe the central bank's announcements. The only promises they should believe are those that the central bank will actually carry out. These are limited to inflation and employment combinations where the central bank's indifference curves are tangent to the employers' aggregate supply function. In our example, there is only one such point. We have labeled this point D in Figure 8.6. If the central bank were to promise to set an inflation rate of 4% and the workers were to believe this, then the nominal wage would be set at 0.04. The aggregate supply curve under the assumption that $w_2 = 0.04$ is the upward sloping line in Figure 8.6. The best the central bank can do, given the aggregate supply curve, is to set the inflation rate at 0.04—just what the workers expected. Employers will then choose the natural level of employment. The subgame perfect equilibrium outcome is the natural level of employment with a 4% inflation rate.

The central bank's promise to hold inflation to 4% is, therefore, *credible.* So it must resign itself to overshooting its inflation target by 2% and undershooting its employment target by 2%. This outcome is the only one that is consistent with

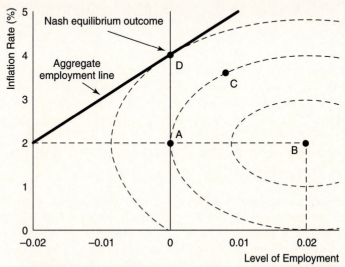

FIGURE 8.6 At a subgame perfect equilibrium for the Macroeconomic Policy Game, employment is at the natural level and workers' forecasts about the rate of inflation turn out to be correct.

> ## GAME THEORY IN ACTION: Optimal Central Bank Performance
>
> A key insight provided by the macroeconomic model presented in this chapter is the recognition that central bankers respond to incentives just like everyone else. This raises the question of whether it is possible to find incentives for the central bank that eliminate the bank's inflationary bias without eliminating its ability to respond optimally to unexpected aggregate demand or supply shocks. "Incentives" can be as explicit as cash bonuses to the members of the bank's governing board and its chairman or as subtle as the process for reappointment to the board. For example, in 1989 the New Zealand government actually considered giving the head of the central bank a bonus payment if the bank's inflation target was reached.
>
> Professor Carl Walsh at the University of California at Santa Cruz has shown that optimal incentive contracts exist under a wide range of conditions ("Optimal Contracts for Central Bankers," *American Economic Review*, 85 (1995), pp. 150–67). In particular he shows that optimal incentives exist when: (1) the bank has private information about the economy that the government can never verify, (2) the bank's preferences about the inflation/employment trade-off differ from that of the government (and the public who elect the government), (3) the bank's choice of instruments affects the informational content of financial-market and macroeconomic indicators of monetary policy that the government can monitor, and (4) where the candidates to head the central bank differ in their competency, and this competency is observed only imperfectly.
>
> Walsh's optimal performance contract resembles a "targeting rule" with a reporting requirement. The central bank is "paid" an amount that depends on how close the economy comes to achieving inflation and employment targets set by the government. The payment to the bank can take the form of explicit cash bonuses to governing board members as well as an increased budget for more staff, more comfortable offices, more travel allowances, and so forth.

rational behavior on the part of all the players. From the central bank's perspective, this results in a significantly worse payoff than it could have attained if it had been able to commit themselves to a 2% inflation rate.

8.4   One Solution to the Central Bank's Problem: Precommitment

The inflationary outcome of the simple policy game discussed above results in part from the central bank's inability to fix its money growth policy *before* the workers and employers settle on the money wage. The central bank could reach its inflation target (although not its employment target) if the workers could be sure that such an inflation choice were in the central bank's own best interests. This means that the game's payoffs would have to be altered so that choosing the low-inflation policy would be an equilibrium strategy of the new game.

For example, suppose the members of the Board of Governors of the central bank offered to resign if the inflation rate exceeded the announced target value. This would make it in the central bank's interest not to exceed this target. However, since the central bank does not have perfect control over the rate of inflation, the members of the Board might find such a promise very risky. As an empirical matter, no central bankers are known to have made such a promise either in the United States or elsewhere. This suggests that the degree of control over the inflation rate may simply be too low.

As a result, penalties probably need to be imposed on the central bank from the outside. Once again, governments seem to be unwilling to impose such penalties. One reason may be that, in many countries (the United States being an important exception), the head of the central bank is a member of the government in power (and usually a member of the executive cabinet). In such cases, the central bank's "preferences" over employment and inflation are simply those of the government of which it is a part. This means that no disinterested "outside authority" exists to discipline the bank.

8.5   Summary

The establishment of central banks by most governments during the last century has been for the express purpose of achieving rates of inflation and employment that are set by the politicians in power rather than by the marketplace. This chapter calls into question the central bank's ability to achieve such goals. Workers and employers who anticipate the behavior of the central bank may undermine its best laid plans. Under a reasonable set of conditions, the central bank may be led to a monetary growth policy that results in its missing *both* its inflation and employment targets. This is not because central bankers are stupid or foolish, but because the bank's actions are constrained by its strategic interactions with workers and employers. The strategic behavior of workers and employers simply makes the bank's targets unobtainable. This may explain why inflation persists in many countries despite cries from all sides for a lower rate.

8.6   Further Reading

The macro-policy model in this chapter is based on a paper by Matthew Canzoneri, "Monetary Policy Games and the Role of Private Information," *The American Economic Review*, 75 (1985), pp. 1056–70. The first part of this paper is very readable, but the second half is quite difficult. A more general model (and more difficult paper) is that of Robert Barro and David Gordon, "A Positive Theory of Monetary Policy in a Natural Rate Model," *The Journal of Political Economy*, 91 (1983), pp. 589–601. The more empirically minded are encouraged to read William Poole's analysis of the 1970–1980 period from a game-theoretic perspective in "Monetary Policy Lessons of Recent Inflation and Disinflation," *Journal of Economic Perspectives* 2 (1988), pp. 90–98. A particularly useful and complete summary of central bank credibility problems is contained in Alex Cukierman, *Central Bank Strategy, Credibility, and Independence: Theory and Evidence*, MIT Press, 1992. This book is reviewed by Charles Goodhart in "Game Theory for Central Bankers: A Report to the Governor of the Bank of England," *Journal of Economic Literature*, 32 (1994), pp. 101–14.

One of the first discussions of the problem of "time consistency" in dynamic games was by Finn Kydland and Edward Prescott, "Rules Rather Than Discretion: The Inconsistency of Optimal Plans," *Journal of Political Economy*, 85 (1977), pp. 473–80. Although this paper looks at the problem abstractly, it is not that mathematically advanced.

8.7 Discussion Questions

1. In what ways can central banks make their announcements more credible? In what ways can laws be written that make central bank announcements more credible?

2. In light of the results in this chapter, why don't workers write their long-term contracts in real terms rather than nominal terms?

3. Parents often do not follow through on the punishments they promise to inflict on their children for some transgression. Construct a model where parental threats are not credible.

8.8 New Terms

aggregate employment function
core inflation
employment rule
frictional unemployment
inflation
inflation policy
inflationary bias
inflationary expectations

natural level of employment
perfect foresight
rational inflationary expectations
time consistent
time inconsistent
unbiased forecast
voluntarily unemployed

8.9 Exercises

EXERCISE 8.1

A father has to do some errands for an hour. He has two children, Lauren and Emily (ages 13 and 9), who do not want to go with him. Lauren is put in charge of looking after Emily. Dad has promised Lauren that he will take her to a basketball game that evening, something he would very much like to do, if she does a good job babysitting. But she will be punished by not going to the game if she annoys Emily too much. Dad will find out how Lauren behaved from Emily after he returns from his errands, since Emily always tells the truth. As Dad leaves he yells back a nonbinding threat, "Lauren, you bug your sister at all and you are not going to the game." Let A represent the proportion of the hour that Lauren spends annoying Emily. Lauren's utility function is given by:

$$U_L = B_L + \sqrt{A}$$

where B_L equals $\frac{1}{5}$ if Lauren goes to the basketball game and 0 if she is punished and doesn't. Dad's utility function is

$$U_D = B_D - A^2$$

where B_D equals $\frac{1}{3}$ if he takes Lauren to the game and equals $\frac{A}{2}$ if he does his duty as a father and punishes her for teasing her sister (the worse she behaves the better he feels for punishing her). Both utility functions are common knowledge. Lauren chooses A. Dad observes A after the fact and chooses whether or not to take Lauren to the game.

(a) Draw a game tree for this situation, including payoffs.

(b) What are the subgame perfect Nash equilibrium strategies?

(c) What will be the outcome of the game?

(d) Is Dad's threat credible?

EXERCISE 8.2

This problem is a variation of the Macroeconomic Policy Game developed in Section 8.3. Suppose the central bank sets a target inflation rate of 0% and a target employment level 1% above the natural employment level, the inflation target is twice as important as the employment target and the elasticity of employment with respect to inflation equals 0.5. Find the subgame perfect equilibrium.

EXERCISE 8.3

Consider a two-player, sequential-move game with perfect information and certainty. One player is the government, which has a utility function given by: $y - (m - 1)^2$, where y is the logarithm of output and m is the logarithm of the money supply. The government has discretion over m. The other player is a "price-setter," with a utility function given by: $p - \dfrac{p^2}{2 \cdot m}$, where p is the logarithm of price and is set by the price-setter. Suppose that y equals $m - p$. Assume that the government moves first and the price-setter moves second.

(a) Find the price-setter's optimal price function, $p(m)$.

(b) Find the government's optimal money supply.

(c) Find the equilibrium value of y.

EXERCISE 8.4

Suppose all the conditions of Exercise 8.3 hold except that the price-setter makes the first move.

(a) Find the government's optimal money supply function, $m(p)$.

(b) Is an announcement that m will equal 1 credible? Explain.

(c) Find the optimal price level.

(d) Find the equilibrium value of y.

CHAPTER 9

Repeated Games and Dynamic Competition

OVERVIEW OF CHAPTER 9

9.1   Introduction

You have probably been bothered by the "one-shot" nature of the strategic situations we have considered so far. In the real world, most interactions between people or firms are repeated. We negotiate with the same employer repeatedly; we shop at the same food store repeatedly; and we buy the same brands repeatedly. Other examples of repeated interactions are a sequence of new firms assessing whether to enter a market and compete against an established monopolist; a group of countries negotiating tariff reductions under the GATT; and an economy in which workers and firms must constantly try to predict the inflation rate that will be chosen by the country's central bank.

Games in which players meet in strategic interactions repeatedly are referred to as **repeated games.** Consider the following example: Two vegetable stands are located near each other on the same highway. The owner of each stand must simultaneously choose her vegetable prices each morning. Once the prices are chosen, they cannot be changed until the next day. Therefore, each day, both stands must choose among the same set of actions, although they may not choose the same actions all the time. For example, the weather may influence the prices they charge. Yet each day, the structure of the daily pricing game is the same. The information they have on any morning will be different from the information they have on other mornings, but the sequence of moves, the timing of those moves, and the actions that can be taken are the same every day. We will refer to the play that takes place in the course of a day as a **stage** of the repeated game. The *entire sequence of stages* constitutes the complete game being played by the two stands. One stage in the game described above is shown in Figure 9.1.

We have introduced a new element into Figure 9.1. Notice that Vegetable Stand 2's decision nodes are encircled by a dashed line. Decision nodes within a dashed line are said to be within the same **information set.** Information sets allow us to specify what each player knows whenever she is called on to move in the game. When we encircle some player's decision nodes so that they lie in the same information set, we mean to say that when the game reaches one of these nodes the player doesn't know which node was reached. All she knows is that she is making her move at some node in the set. Figure 9.1 shows the owner of Vegetable Stand 1 setting her price before the owner of Vegetable Stand 2. This ordering implies that the first player does not know the second player's price when she sets hers. The diagram also shows that the second owner's two decision nodes are in the same information set. This means that the second owner must make her pricing decision without knowing her competitor's price. In the terminology of Chapter 1 the two players are moving "simultaneously." In Part V we will show how to use information sets to represent other types of knowledge and ignorance. For now, we will use them solely to depict on our game tree diagrams in which two or more players move simultaneously.

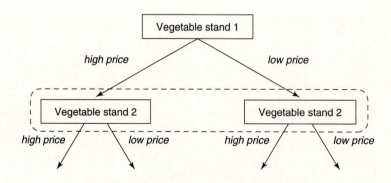

End of stage 1.
Next stage begins with all actions in
stage 1 being common knowledge.

FIGURE 9.1   A stage in a daily Vegetable Pricing Game.

As you might imagine, drawing a game tree for a repeated game with even a relatively small number of stages can be an absurdly tedious task. Frequently, the portion of the game tree that describes any single stage will be sufficient to clarify the game. Sometimes the number of stages is infinite. When the game is infinite, all the players are strategic, and they are all informed about each other's past actions, then the game is called a **supergame.**

The techniques developed in Chapter 6 to find a subgame perfect equilibrium of a single-stage game apply just as well to repeated games. When one player is deciding what action to take at any stage of a game, that player will rationally take into account the ramifications that this action has on the behavior of her opponents in future stages of the game. The central feature of subgame perfect equilibrium is that only credible strategies are chosen. If a player wants to make it clear to her opponents that she will retaliate if her opponents choose a particular course of action, *this retaliation must be credible.* The test for credibility is the same as always: is it in the player's best interests to carry out the threat if deterrence fails?

9.2   Example: Duopoly Revisited

Let us begin by looking at a one-stage duopoly game between two specialty American jean manufacturers: Rip Jeans (R) and Torn Jeans (T). The "worn" jeans manufactured by the two firms are perfect substitutes that sell at a common world market dollar price, P. The inverse market demand function, which states the market clearing price as a function of the output of the two firms, is

$$P(Q_R + Q_T) = \begin{cases} 22 - (Q_R + Q_T) & \text{if } Q_R + Q_T < 22 \\ 0 & \text{if } Q_R + Q_T \geq 22, \end{cases} \qquad [9.1]$$

where the output of the two firms, denoted Q_R and Q_T, is measured in millions of jeans per year. Both firms face the same marginal cost of $10 per jean and fixed costs of $9 million per year. These fixed costs are not sunk costs, though. Should the firm shut down completely, the firm could reduce its costs to zero. If we measure costs in millions of dollars, the cost functions for Rip Jeans and Torn Jeans, denoted $C_R(Q_R)$ and $C_T(Q_T)$, is given by

$$C_i(Q_i) = \begin{cases} 9 + 10 \cdot Q_i & \text{if } Q_i > 0 \\ 0 & \text{if } Q_i = 0, \end{cases} \qquad [9.2]$$

$i = R, T$. It follows that the profit functions of the two firms, denoted $\Pi_R(Q_R, Q_T)$ and $\Pi_T(Q_R, Q_T)$, have the form

$$\Pi_T(Q_R, Q_T) = P(Q_R + Q_T) \cdot Q_i - C_i(Q_i) =$$
$$\begin{cases} 0 & \text{if } Q_i = 0 \\ Q_i \cdot (22 - (Q_R + Q_T)) - (9 + 10 \cdot Q_i) & \text{if } Q_i > 0 \text{ and } Q_R + Q_T < 22 \\ -(9 + 10 \cdot Q_i) & \text{if } Q_i > 0 \text{ and } Q_R + Q_T \geq 22. \end{cases}$$
$$[9.3]$$

If the two firms could collude (a big *if*), they could maximize their combined profits,

$$\Pi_R(Q_R, Q_T) + \Pi_T(Q_R, Q_T) =$$
$$\begin{cases} (22 - (Q_R + Q_T)) \cdot (Q_R + Q_T) \\ \quad - (18 + 10 \cdot (Q_R + Q_T)) & \text{if } Q_R > 0 \text{ and } Q_T > 0 \\ (22 - Q_R) \cdot (Q_R) - (9 + 10 \cdot Q_R) & \text{if } Q_T = 0 \text{ and } Q_R > 0 \\ (22 - Q_T) \cdot (Q_T) - (9 + 10 \cdot Q_T) & \text{if } Q_R = 0 \text{ and } Q_T > 0, \end{cases}$$
[9.4]

by having one firm produce 6 million jeans per year and the other nothing. Since the marginal cost of producing a jean is constant and is the same for both firms, the variable costs of producing 6 million jeans do not depend in the slightest on the output mix between the two firms. The two firms, however, can reduce their joint fixed costs by $9 million by having one of them sell its assets and halt production. We will hereafter refer to this output level as the *cartel output*, and will denote it as $Q_{R,T}^*$. When the two firms produce the cartel market output, the world market price for "worn jeans" is $P(Q_{R,T}^*) = 16$ dollars per jean and the two firms earn a combined annual profit of $(16 - 10) \cdot Q_{R,T}^* - 9 = \$27$ million or (if split equally) $13.5 million each.

Of course, any such cartel agreement would not only be unenforceable in American courts, but would also be illegal! Therefore, the firms cannot rely on the courts to help them enforce such agreements. If a commitment to produce at the cartel output level by one firm is to be believable to the other firm, it must be in the best interest of the first firm to produce the cartel output. That is, the commitment must be a subgame perfect equilibrium strategy for the firm. This type of multiplayer agreement, in which all the players agree to a particular behavior, and in which the behavior is consistent with a subgame perfect equilibrium, is said to be a **self-enforcing agreement.**[1]

Suppose both jean companies must sign binding one-year contracts for factory space, fabric, and labor at the beginning of the year. Then both firms will be forced to choose their annual output at the beginning of the year without prior knowledge of the other firm's decision. Both firms are assumed to maximize the present value of the stream of profits (long-run profits). Since we are temporarily limiting ourselves to a one-stage game, short-run and long-run profits are the same. As we saw in Chapter 2, where we studied the simultaneous-move Cournot duopoly game, this game has a unique Nash equilibrium. To find it, we proceed in two steps. First, we note that both firms can guarantee themselves zero profits simply by shutting down. Using Eq. [9.3], you should verify that output levels above 12 million jeans/year will guarantee a loss. It follows that output levels above 12 million jeans are strictly dominated by zero output, and can be hereafter disre-

---

[1]It must also be executed in such a manner that the firms cannot be successfully prosecuted by the U.S. Justice Department under antitrust laws. We will ignore this complication in what follows.

garded. The second step is to derive both firms' best response functions. Recall that the best response function for a firm gives the level of output that maximizes the firm's profit *given* the other firm's output level. Since the two firms are identical, it is enough to determine Rip's best response function. Torn's will have the same functional form.

Because Rip has the option of shutting down completely, the best response function Q_R^{BR} satisfies the profit-maximizing condition:

$$\frac{\partial \Pi_R(Q_R, Q_T)}{\partial Q_R}\bigg|_{Q_R = Q_R^{BR}(Q_T)} = 12 - Q_T - 2Q_R^{BR}(Q_T) = 0 \qquad [9.5]$$

or, equivalently,

$$Q_R^{BR}(Q_T) = 6 - \tfrac{1}{2}Q_T \qquad [9.6]$$

as long as Rip's profits are nonnegative at $Q_R^{BR}(Q_T)$. If Rip's profits are negative at $Q_R^{BR}(Q_T)$, then Rip's optimal output level is zero. Since

$$\Pi_R(Q_R^{BR}(Q_T), Q_T) = (6 - \tfrac{1}{2}Q_T) \cdot (22 - ((6 - \tfrac{1}{2}Q_T) + Q_T)) - (9 + 10 \cdot (6 - \tfrac{1}{2}Q_T))$$

$$= (6 - \tfrac{1}{2}Q_T)^2 - 9, \qquad [9.7]$$

Rip's profits are negative at Q_R^{BR} if and only if $6 - \tfrac{1}{2}Q_T < 3$ or $Q_T > 6$ million jeans. So Rip's and Torn's best response functions are

$$Q_R^{BR}(Q_T) = \begin{cases} 6 - \tfrac{1}{2}Q_T & \text{if } Q_T \leq 6 \\ 0 & \text{if } Q_T > 6 \end{cases} \qquad [9.8]$$

and

$$Q_T^{BR}(Q_R) = \begin{cases} 6 - \tfrac{1}{2}Q_R & \text{if } Q_R \leq 6 \\ 0 & \text{if } Q_R > 6. \end{cases} \qquad [9.9]$$

Finding the intersection of Eqs. [9.8] and [9.9] yields the Cournot-Nash output levels $Q_T^* = Q_R^* = 4$ million jeans for a total of 8 million jeans. We will refer to this output level as the *Cournot output*. At this equilibrium, the jeans sell for $P(4 + 4) = \$14$ per jean, and each firm earns an annual profit of $14 \cdot Q_T^* - (9 + 10 \cdot Q_T^*) = \$7$ million. This is $6.5 million per year less than when the two firms collude.

Let us now analyze this game from a different angle. To make our example more vivid, let us imagine that the CEOs (Chief Executive Officer) of the two companies, Bob Sharp of Rip and Ruth Lessing of Torn, meet in December at a holiday party. Off in a corner, Ruth quietly points out to Bob that "producing 4 million jeans each, which we are bound to do if we do not cooperate, is in neither firm's self-interest. If," she goes on, "we were to both cut our production to 3

Table 9.1   *Cournot Duopoly Game between Rip Jeans and Torn Jeans*

		Rip Jeans	
		Cooperation ($Q_R = 3$)	Defection ($Q_R = 4$)
Torn Jeans	Cooperation ($Q_T = 3$)	(9, 9)	(6, 11)
	Defection ($Q_T = 4$)	(11, 6)	(7, 7)

Payoffs: (Torn Jeans, Rip Jeans)

million jeans, we would force the market price up to \$16 and boost our profits by 28%!'' Bob says that her implicit proposal sounds like a great idea to him and that he will advise his firm to reduce its output for the coming year. Talk, however, is cheap!

Notice that Ruth does not propose that one of them shut down and that the two firms split the much larger profits that result when just one firm produces the 6 million jeans. Since any agreement Ruth and Bob make along those lines would clearly not be legally binding, this agreement is not credible and the firm that chose to shut down could expect to actually earn \$0 in profits while the other firm enjoyed \$27 million. Already, Ruth is limiting the options to ones that are potentially credible.

As soon as Bob gets home from the party he calls his CFO (Chief Financial Officer), Sam Shade, and tells him about his conversation with Lessing. What should they do? Should they go ahead with their plan to produce 4 million jeans, or should they reduce their output to 3 million jeans as Lessing has proposed? Of course there are many other output options the two executives could also consider, but for simplicity, we will limit the choice to just these two. We will call the decision to reduce output to 3 million jeans per year *cooperation* and the decision to keep output at the Cournot-Nash equilibrium level *defection*. The payoffs associated with these two output choices, assuming Torn Jeans is also only considering these same two options, are given in Table 9.1.[2]

If Torn Jeans believes Rip Jeans will cooperate, then the optimal action is to defect. On the other hand, if Torn Jeans expects Rip Jeans to defect, then Torn Jeans should defect as well. Torn Jeans has a strictly dominant strategy to defect, as does Rip Jeans. Therefore, there is a unique strictly dominant strategy Nash equilibrium in which both firms defect, produce 4 million jeans apiece, and earn only \$7 million dollars each in profits. These firms are stuck playing a Prisoner's Dilemma first discussed in Chapter 1.

The problem with this purported equilibrium is that it seems to depend on the assumption that the firms make one output decision and then never meet again. It is, of course, much more realistic to suppose that Rip Jeans and Torn

---

[2]It may have occurred to you that if a player is going to cheat on his cooperating opponent, then the optimal cheating output is higher than the Cournot output level. We have chosen to ignore this and limit ourselves to two output levels, rather than three, in the interest of simplicity.

Jeans do not interact only once, but meet in the marketplace year after year. Unless the CEOs are congenitally myopic, they should be interested not only in their current profits, but also in their future profits. What is the equilibrium if the game described in this section is just one stage of a repeated game? In particular, is it possible to find an equilibrium in which the two firms cooperate? If so, what are the strategies that sustain such cooperation?

9.3 Finitely Repeated Games

As our story goes, Rip and Torn share a duopoly in the "worn jean" market because they foresaw the advent of a fad ahead of other jean manufacturers. This good fortune will last only as long as the fad. Suppose that experience suggests the fad will last only two years. Then the Cournot stage game will be repeated exactly twice. The extensive form of the repeated game is shown in Figure 9.2. Rip's first two decision nodes are within the same information set. This means that in the first year Rip and Torn move simultaneously. The two players know these first two moves when they move in year two. This is why Torn has four decision nodes, one for each combination of moves that could have been taken in year one and none of which lie in an information set. Rip moves last at one of eight possible decision nodes, but these eight nodes are collected together into four information sets, one set for each combination of moves that could have been taken in year one. This means that Torn and Rip are ignorant of each other's decisions in year two. Putting it all together, Figure 9.2 shows a game in which Torn and Rip move twice, each time simultaneously, and the moves made by each player in year one are common knowledge in year two.

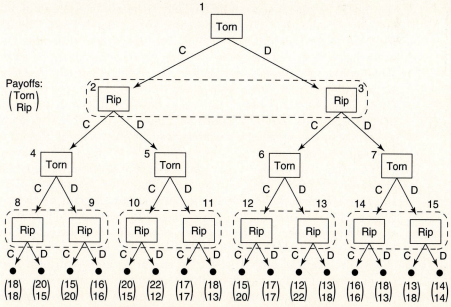

FIGURE 9.2 A game tree for a two-stage repeated game.

In the first stage of this two-stage repeated game, Rip and Torn simultaneously decide whether to cooperate or defect. The respective outputs are observed and the first stage comes to an end. The second stage is qualitatively the same as the first stage. Rip and Torn again simultaneously choose whether to cooperate or defect. Then the game ends. Payoffs are listed at the end of the game, not because that is when they are realized, but because it is assumed that the firms care about long-run profits, not short-run profits. We have ignored discounting over the two time periods in order to simplify the arithmetic. Consider the payoffs to the two firms if they both choose a strategy in which they cooperate in both stages. In that case, they can both expect to earn $9 million per year, or $18 million over the two years. Alternatively, if Rip chooses to cooperate in the first time period, but defect in the second, while Torn always chooses to cooperate, then Rip will earn $9 million in the first year and $11 million in the second, for a total of $20 million. Torn will earn $9 million in the first year and $6 in the second for a total of $15 million. We leave it as an exercise for you to verify the other payoffs.

As you can see, this game involves both sequential play (between stages) and simultaneous play (at each stage). A strategy consists of a choice of output for stage one (in ignorance of the output chosen by the opponent) and a choice of output for stage two (in ignorance of the output chosen by the opponent for that stage), *where the choice in stage two can depend on both players' output choices in stage one.* We wish to determine whether one player can affect the other player's behavior by threatening the other player. A *threat* consists of the promise to choose some action in the second stage of the game if the opponent takes a particular action in the first stage of the game. Of course, in order for the threat to affect the opponent's behavior, it must be *credible*. That is, it must be in the player's interest to actually carry out the threat if it fails to deter the opponent.

Since this repeated game is partially sequential, the technique of backward induction can be used to find a subgame perfect equilibrium. Therefore, we will try to solve the second stage of the game first, prune the game tree, and then solve the first stage of the game. Even though the subgame played in the second stage involves simultaneous moves, it has a unique (strictly dominant strategy!) Nash equilibrium in which both players defect and choose the Cournot output levels. Each will earn only $7 million in the second year. It is important to note that the optimality of these actions is independent of what happened in the first stage. Regardless of what transpires in stage one, rational play in stage two is now known. The game tree can be pruned back. When this is done, we are left with the first stage, which is now just a single-stage simultaneous-move Cournot game. The payoffs of this game consist of the first-stage payoffs plus the second-stage payoffs of $7 million. Since the same amount is being added to all the first-stage payoffs, maximizing these new payoffs is equivalent to maximizing the first-stage payoffs. So the "reduced" game is equivalent to a one-stage Cournot game. But we know that the only Nash equilibrium for such a game is for both firms to choose the Cournot output levels. So in equilibrium, both firms defect in both stages. Repetition does not generate cooperation.

You may think the problem is that we did not repeat the game enough times.

GAME THEORY IN ACTION: Cooperation in the Trenches of World War I

A prediction of this chapter is that self-interested players of a repeated Prisoner's Dilemma game will cooperate as long as they attach a high enough value to future payoffs. An unusual "natural experiment" testing this prediction was performed in the early years of World War I. The players in this experiment were the Allied and German troops who faced each other in the trenches along the 500-mile Western Front. Anatol Rapaport, in *The Evolution of Cooperation,* has argued that these troops played a repeated Prisoner's Dilemma game. His reasoning is as follows: Whenever a soldier on one side of "no man's land" spotted a soldier on the other, the choice was simple: aim and shoot to kill ("defect") or aim and shoot to miss ("cooperate"). Because weakening the enemy would promote survival in the next battle, in the short run defecting was always a dominant strategy. But mutual cooperation was preferable to mutual defection because the killing of troops on *both* sides did not alter *relative* troop strength.

Sociologist Tony Ashworth, in his seminal study of infantry life in the trenches, found that a "live-and-let-live" system of cooperation quickly sprang up between the Allied and German infantry troops. "Live-and-let-live" was Ashworth's name for the pattern of tacit restraint exercised between enemy troops facing each other during WWI. For example, a British staff officer reported that he was "astonished to observe German soldiers walking about within rifle range behind their own line. Our men appeared to take no notice. . . . These people evidently did not know there was a war on. Both sides apparently believed in a policy of 'live-and-let-live.' " This behavior flourished despite repeated efforts by the officer staffs on both sides to stop it.

Cooperation appears to have been enforced by a strategy similar to that of tit-for-tat (TFT). The TFT strategy is as follows: initially cooperate; thereafter, cooperate if the opponent cooperated last period and defect if the opponent defected last period. If both sides adopt this strategy, then the outcome is sustained cooperation. As one soldier put it, "It would be child's play to shell the road behind the enemy's trenches, crowded as it must be with ration wagons and water carts. . . . After all, if you prevent your enemy from drawing his rations, his remedy is simple: he will prevent you from drawing yours." Retaliation was usually more severe than what was called for by the standard tit-for-tat strategy. Instead, two or three "tits for a tat" was the more common response to a defection. During periods of restraint by both sides, each side often did things that showed the other that retaliation was possible and that it was acting from a position of military strength rather than weakness.

Rapaport hypothesizes that the live-and-let-live system was eventually destroyed by the invention of the *raid.* A "raid" was a carefully prepared attack on the opposing trenches, involving 10 to 200 men, whose objective was to capture enemy troops in their own trenches. These raids were incessant, random, and easily monitored by headquarters. That is, the troops could not pretend to stage a raid because at a raid's conclusion the raiding party had to have either prisoners or casualties. This eliminated the front-line troops' ability to reciprocate cooperation by the enemy and, thereby, eliminated cooperation.

For example, suppose both firms expect the market to evaporate in two years, but they choose their outputs only a week in advance. The simultaneous-move stage game is now repeated 104 times. Remarkably, backward induction selects the same type of subgame perfect equilibrium as before. At the last stage in the game, both firms will find it to their advantage to choose the Cournot output regardless of their earlier output. Pruning the tree back one stage leaves us at stage 103. Now that the 103rd stage is the last stage of the (sub-)game, it is still in both firms' best interest to choose the Cournot output, allowing us to prune back the tree yet another layer. This process, of course, keeps being repeated all the way to the first stage of the game, where it is still in both firms' best interest to choose the Cournot output. The only subgame perfect equilibrium, solvable using backward induction, has both firms choosing the Cournot output at every stage. The argument is valid no matter how many times the game is repeated.

Besides being counterintuitive, the prediction that both players will never cooperate when playing a finite number of repetitions of a Prisoner's Dilemma-type stage game is inconsistent with the outcomes of numerous experiments. When people play repeated Prisoner's Dilemma games in experimental settings, they usually cooperate until near the end of the game, at which point cooperation finally breaks down.

The backward induction argument we used above is valid only if: (1) neither player can fix his second-period output at the same time he sets his first-period output, *and* (2) both players know each other's payoffs, *and* (3) both players know how many times they will repeat the stage game. These three conditions are quite strong and are frequently violated. We can rarely be *certain* how frequently we will interact with an opponent; we can never be *certain* about our opponent's subjective assessment of his payoffs or about our opponent's beliefs about our assessment of our payoffs; and it is possible sometimes to make binding commitments about our future actions. We will now examine how the relaxation of these three conditions can make it rational to cooperate with an opponent—at least to some extent.[3]

9.4   A First Modification: Precommitment

We return to the example in which Rip Jeans and Torn Jeans are embroiled in a repeated game with just two stages. Each stage is a Prisoner's Dilemma. We now make the following change: in the first stage of the game, the two firms make simultaneous announcements about their output in *both* periods. These announcements are binding. The announced output in period two may depend on the opponent's choice of output in period one. For example, a firm could adopt a **tit-for-tat** policy. That is, it promises to cooperate in period two if the opponent cooperates in period one, but to defect in period two if the opponent defects in period one.

---

[3]More is not better here. Too much uncertainty can actually destroy the incentives for cooperation.

Table 9.2 "Noncooperative" Nash Equilibrium Strategies for the Repeated Cournot Game with Precommitment

	Rip Jeans	Torn Jeans
$Q_{1i} =$	4 million	4 million
$Q_{2i}(\cdot, \cdot) \equiv$	4 million	4 million

When binding commitments are possible, the two-stage repeated game is transformed into a one-stage static game. The strategies of the two firms in this one-stage game consist of: (a) a level of output in stage one, denoted Q_{1R} and Q_{1T}, and (b) a level of output in stage two that depends on the output of the two firms in stage one, denoted $Q_{2R}(Q_{1T}, Q_{1R})$ and $Q_{2T}(Q_{1R}, Q_{1T})$. Since the output commitment in stage two is binding, the firms choose their strategies simultaneously at the beginning of stage one and cannot alter them in stage two. In stage two they simply play the strategy out.

This game has many Nash equilibria. One of these equilibrium profiles is for both firms to set output at 4 million jeans in both stages regardless of what the rival does in the first stage. This pair of strategies is shown symbolically in Table 9.2.

To verify this, imagine that you are the CEO of Rip Jeans and that you believe that Torn Jeans is irrevocably committed to producing 4 million jeans in both stages. We start with the second stage. Regardless of what has happened in the first stage and regardless of the strategy you think your opponent is following, it is a strictly dominant strategy to produce 4 million jeans. We now consider the move to make in the first stage. Since you believe your move will have no effect on your opponent's move in stage two, your best move is to choose the Cournot output level (at least it is dominant in the stage game).

Consider now the strategies in Table 9.3. If both firms follow these strategies, then each will produce 3 million jeans in the first stage and 4 million in the second. The price will be $16/jean in stage one and $14/jean in stage two. Although they are not cooperating in the second stage, they do cooperate in the first stage. Profits for each firm will be $9 million in the first stage and $7 million in the second

Table 9.3 "Cooperative" Nash Equilibrium Strategy for the Repeated Cournot Game with Precommitment

	Output			
$Q_{1i} =$	3 million			
$Q_{2i}(Q_{1i}, Q_{1j}) =$	$\begin{cases} 0 \\ 4 \text{ million} \\ 6 \text{ million} \end{cases}$	$\begin{array}{l} \text{if } Q_{1i} > 3 \text{ million} \\ \text{if } Q_{1j} \leq 3 \text{ million} \\ \text{if } Q_{1j} > 3 \text{ million} \end{array}$	$\begin{array}{l} \\ and \\ and \end{array}$	$\begin{array}{l} \\ Q_{1i} \leq 3 \text{ million} \\ Q_{1i} \leq 3 \text{ million} \end{array}$

stage, or $16 million overall. To verify that this is indeed a Nash equilibrium of the game, we need to show that neither firm can unilaterally alter its strategy and earn total profits of more than $16 million.

Because the two firms are identical and the proposed equilibrium strategies are the same, we need only show that Rip Jeans cannot earn more than $16 million when Torn follows the "cooperative" strategy. First, suppose Rip produces 3 million jeans in the first stage; then it knows that Torn will produce 4 million in the second stage, to which its best response is to defect and produce 4 million jeans as well. Given Torn's proposed first-stage move, suppose Rip decides to consult its best response function, shown in Eq. [9.8] and maximize its first-stage profits by increasing production to 4.5 million jeans. It will boost its first-stage profit to $11.25 million, but it will also trigger retaliation by Torn in the second stage. Indeed, it knows that Torn will flood the market with 6 million jeans in the second stage, driving down the price so much that Rip cannot make a profit at any output level! Rip's best response to Torn's threat is to shut down completely and earn nothing in the second stage. Its profit over the two stages is $11.25 million, which is less than the $16 million it earns when it (partially) cooperates with Torn.

9.5   A Second Modification: Discounting the Future

When we showed earlier that Rip Jeans and Torn Jeans would never cooperate, we assumed not only that the number of interactions was finite, but also that the number of interactions was fixed and common knowledge. Suppose, instead, that the number of interactions is infinite, but that profits earned today are worth more than profits earned in the distant future. Specifically, $1 in profits N periods from now has a present value of δ^N dollars today, where $0 < \delta < 1$. The constant δ is the player's **discount factor.** So, for example, if the discount factor equals 50%, then $1 next period is worth $0.50, $1 two periods from now is worth $0.25, and so forth. If either Rip or Torn earns the stream of profits $\{\pi_1, \pi_2, \ldots, \pi_t, \ldots\}$, where period one means "now," then the present value of this profit stream is given by $\sum_{t=1}^{\infty} (\delta^{t-1} \cdot \pi_t)$. We will find it convenient to renormalize the utility function by multiplying it by the constant $1 - \delta$. This ensures that the receipt of $1 every period has a present value of $(1 - \delta) \cdot \sum_{t=1}^{\infty} (\delta^{t-1} \cdot \$1) = 1$, whatever the discount factor. More generally, if the decision maker is given M dollars in profit every time period, then the present value would equal $M = (1 - \delta) \cdot \sum_{t=1}^{\infty} (\delta^{t-1} \cdot M)$

An unfinished game tree for our new game is presented in Figure 9.3. There

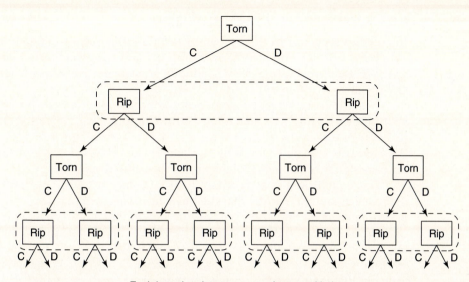

Each branch points to a new subgame with the same moves and information structure.

FIGURE 9.3 The game tree for an infinitely repeated Cournot game with discounted payoffs.

are now an infinite number of stages, which are one period apart. At each stage, Rip and Torn simultaneously determine their outputs knowing the complete history of the game up to that point.

Call the sequence of choices the two firms have made previous to stage t, the *history* of the game up to t, and denote it by H_t. Since the game goes on indefinitely, a pure strategy for firm i consists of the following sequence of output choices:

1. A choice of output in stage one, Q_{i1};

2. A choice of output in stage two, which may depend on what the players produced in stage one, $Q_{i2}(H_2)$;

3. A choice of output in stage three, which may depend on what the players produced in stage two, $Q_{i3}(H_3)$;
   $\vdots$

t. A choice of output in stage t, which may depend on the history up to that point, $Q_{it}(H_t)$; and so on.

The sequence of output choices $\{Q_{i1}, Q_{i2}(H_2), \ldots, Q_{it}(H_t), \ldots\}$ will be denoted by S_i. So S_R is Rip Jeans' strategy and S_T is Torn Jeans' strategy. Every strategy profile determines a sequence of outputs for both firms, resulting in a sequence of profits. For example, suppose Rip and Torn select strategies that result in both producing the Cournot output of 4 million jeans at every stage. Then both will earn $7 million at every stage. Although the number of profit payments is infinite, this infinite stream provides a *finite* utility of exactly 7 million.

9.5.1 A "NONCOOPERATIVE" EQUILIBRIUM

In previous sections, the noncooperative equilibrium output—often referred to as the *Cournot output*—frequently ended up being a subgame perfect equilibrium. Consider two firms that *stubbornly* adopt a noncooperative strategy. Such a strategy is shown in Table 9.4.

When playing against a stubbornly noncooperative opponent, the best response at each stage is to choose the Cournot output level. Any other choice leads to lower profits in the current stage and has no offsetting future benefit since it does not affect the behavior of the opponent. Therefore, the strategy pair in Table 9.4 constitutes (once again) a subgame perfect equilibrium.

This equilibrium is somewhat disturbing since it relies on completely dogmatic behavior. No matter what the other firm does, neither firm will change its beliefs about what the other firm will produce at the next stage. If your opponent were to produce at the cooperative output level for 10 years in a row, it would appear silly to ignore this history and conclude that they will be noncooperative from now on. It seems more likely that either they don't know what they are doing or that they are trying to tell you something (such as "cooperate with me"). In both cases, you can probably increase the likelihood of future cooperation by cooperating today.

9.5.2 A "COOPERATIVE" EQUILIBRIUM

We now will consider a "cooperative" equilibrium in which the threats made are credible. The equilibrium strategy of both players is rather vindictive: Each player cooperates only as long as its rival cooperates. Once the opponent breaks rank, the other player never cooperates again and produces the Cournot output forevermore. Such a strategy is, rather accurately, referred to as a **grim strategy.**

Suppose that Rip and Torn both expect to make simultaneous output decisions under the same circumstances every time period out into the foreseeable future. That is, they are in a supergame. Let δ denote the discount factor both firms use each time period into the future and, as we did in the previous section, suppose that each additional dollar of profit generates $1 - \delta$ additional units of utility.

In order to state the grim strategy more rigorously, let HC denote the collection of all histories (of whatever length) in which both firms have always chosen

Table 9.4   A Stubbornly Noncooperative Strategy

	Output
$Q_{i1} =$	4 million
$Q_{ti}(H_t) \equiv$	4 million

the cooperative output level (3 million jeans). Then the *grim strategy* is described in Table 9.5.

Suppose both firms adopt the grim strategy. Then at stage one both firms produce 3 million jeans. At stage two, since both firms cooperated at stage one, both firms will again cooperate and choose 3 million jeans. The same will be the case at stage three, and at stage 4. Since profits to either firm are $9 million as long as they both produce the cooperative quantity, the discounted stream of profits has a present value of utility equal to 9 million.

Let us suppose Rip believes that Torn has adopted a grim strategy. Then Rip will expect Torn to initially cooperate. Rip will also expect that should it ever defect, then Torn will defect forever after. Since cooperation is a sensible move in this game only if it is expected to elicit cooperation from the opponent in the future, Rip's optimal response to Torn's strategy is to defect forever after as well—which is precisely what the grim strategy dictates.

We will now show the conditions under which Rip can expect to do better by cooperating at any stage in the game than by defecting. We make explicit use of the fact that at any stage in the game, the future payoffs look identical since the game keeps extending out to infinity. Suppose Rip defects at a particular stage. At that stage, Rip will earn a profit of $11 million, but, since both firms defect from then on, Rip's profits will be $7 million per year from the next stage until the end of time. Hence, the present value of the utility stream from defecting at any stage,

$$(1 - \delta) \cdot (11 \text{ million} + \sum_{j=2}^{\infty} \delta^{t-1} \cdot 7 \text{ million})$$

$$= (1 - \delta) \cdot 11 \text{ million} + \delta \cdot 7 \text{ million}, \quad [9.10]$$

must be compared to the utility from not defecting. Rip will *not* defect if

$$9 \text{ million} > (1 - \delta) \cdot 11 \text{ million} + \delta \cdot 7 \text{ million}. \quad [9.11]$$

As long as δ is greater than 0.5, Rip will find it in its best interest not to defect at any stage.

Table 9.5 **The Grim Strategy**

	Output
$Q_{i1} =$	3 million
$Q_{ti}(H_t) =$	$\begin{cases} 3 \text{ million} & \text{if } H_t \in HC \\ 4 \text{ million} & \text{otherwise} \end{cases}$

In summary, as long as Torn's discount factor is high enough (i.e., Torn is not too impatient), Torn might as well be cooperative unless Rip is uncooperative, at which point Torn might as well be unforgiving and not cooperate ever again. But this is just the grim strategy! This proves the grim strategy is a best response to an opponent who has also adopted the grim strategy—as long as the prospect of future profits has a high value today. It follows that a subgame perfect equilibrium for this game is for both firms to use the grim strategy.

9.5.3 AND NOW THE BAD NEWS: THE FOLK THEOREM

In a neat world, there would be a relatively small number of equilibria from which to choose. In the repeated duopoly game we have been describing, we have already found two subgame perfect equilibria. Are there more? Are there a great deal more? To begin to answer this very important question, let us try to limit the set of possible strategies either firm might choose to reasonable ones.

Take a look at this game from a somewhat different perspective. By employing the grim strategy, both firms are opening themselves up to the possibility of low profits in period one. Alternatively, each firm can guarantee itself an expected profit of zero by choosing not to produce in every period. In a repeated game, deviations from cooperative equilibrium play must be punished. The lowest utility level the other players can force on a player is that player's **minimax utility level.** Formally, it is defined as $U_i \min_{S_{-i}} \max_{S_i} U_i(S_1, \ldots, S_N)$ where U_i is player i's utility

and $S_{-i} = \{S_1, \ldots, S_{i-1}, S_{i+1}, \ldots, S_N\}$ is the strategy profile of every player except player i. This is the lowest utility level player i's opponents can hold her to if she foresees their move and plays her best response to it. For Rip and Torn, the worst each can do to the other is to drive the price so low as to make it unprofitable to produce any output. Since both firms have the option of shutting down and earning nothing, their minimax utility level is zero. Any payoff combination, for both players, that gives both of them no less than their minimax utility is said to be **individually rational.**

A payoff schedule for the two players that *can* be achieved by the adoption of *some* strategy profile (not necessarily a Nash equilibrium strategy profile!) is said to be **feasible.** In the case of the Jean Duopoly Game, we leave it as an exercise for you to show that the feasible present utility levels, (π_T, π_R), are precisely those in the set $\{(\pi_T, \pi_R): \pi_R + \pi_T \le 18 \text{ million}\} \cup \{(27 \text{ million}, 0), (0, 27 \text{ million})\}$.

We have drawn the feasible and individually rational payoff vectors for the Jean Duopoly Game in Figure 9.4.

As you can see, there are a large number of feasible and individually rational payoffs. Now for the answer to our question about the number of subgame perfect equilibria. It turns out that—subject to some technical restrictions[4]—any given individually rational and feasible payoff schedule is also a subgame perfect equi-

---

[4]These can be found in Fudenberg and Maskin (1986), but this paper is very difficult.

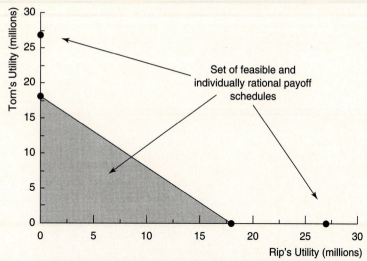

FIGURE 9.4   The set of feasible and individually rational payoffs.

librium payoff schedule for the repeated game as long as δ, the discount factor, is sufficiently close to one. This result is known as the **Folk theorem** because early versions of it have been around for so long that no one quite remembers who first stated it or proved it.

How bad a problem is the Folk theorem? There is some evidence that the Folk theorem may not be as bad a problem as was once thought. In many applications, it is possible to pare down the number of reasonable equilibria by using criteria such as symmetry between the players. In addition, when the discount factor is *not* close to one, then the set of equilibrium payoff vectors may be *much smaller* than the set of all feasible and individually rational payoffs. Indeed, if δ is sufficiently small—that is, if the players are sufficiently impatient—then the repeated game is almost a one-shot game, and its set of subgame perfect equilibrium payoff schedules will simply coincide with the Nash equilibrium payoff schedules of the one-shot stage game.

9.6   The Bertrand Game Revisited

You will recall from Chapter 2, Section 4 that the static, Bertrand (price-setting) Duopoly Game in which marginal cost is constant and equal to average cost has a unique Nash equilibrium in which both firms charge a price equal to marginal cost. Suppose, however, that the firms meet repeatedly under these same circumstances. You can easily see that if the number of meetings is finite and common knowledge, then the only subgame perfect equilibrium results in the same outcome as in the static game: both firms charge a price equal to marginal cost.

But if the game is repeated an infinite number of times, and the two firms do

Table 9.6 *The Grim Strategy in the Bertrand Game*

	Price
$P_{1i} =$	P_m
$P_{ti}(H_t) =$	$\begin{cases} P_m & \text{if } H_t \in HC \\ c & \text{otherwise} \end{cases}$

not discount the future too much, then, as with the Cournot model, the results can change dramatically. Denote the profit-maximizing monopolistic price by P_m, marginal cost by c, and the set of game histories in which both firms charge P_m every period by HC, and consider the strategy described in Table 9.6.

In the Bertrand model, consumers will purchase from the firm charging the lowest price. If both firms charge the same price, it is assumed that the market is divided equally between the two firms. Denote monopoly profits by Π_m. We will now find conditions under which the grim strategy is a subgame perfect equilibrium strategy for both firms. We will do this by showing that the grim strategy is a best response by firm 1 to the adoption of the grim strategy by firm 2. If both firms adopt the grim strategy, then they will both charge the monopolistic price at every stage, split the market, and obtain the utility payoff $\frac{1}{2}\Pi_m$. Now suppose firm 2 adopts the grim strategy and firm 1 deviates from the monopolistic price by undercutting it by the smallest amount possible, thereby capturing the market. This results in profits at the first stage of (slightly less than) Π_m. But because of retaliation by firm 2, profits at every subsequent stage equal zero. Hence, the present value of the utility stream for firm 1 equals $(1 - \delta) \cdot (\Pi_m + \delta \cdot 0 + \delta^2 \cdot 0 + ...) = (1 - \delta) \cdot \Pi_m$. The deviation in strategy results in the same or lower utility than playing the purported equilibrium strategy if and only if $(1 - \delta) \cdot \Pi_m \leq \frac{1}{2}\Pi_m$, which holds if and only if $\frac{1}{2} \leq \delta$. This shows that if $\frac{1}{2} \leq \delta$ and firm 2 has adopted the grim strategy, then at least at the first stage, firm 1 will choose the monopoly price also. Furthermore, the same logic shows that firm 1 should always charge the monopoly price whenever the grim strategy calls for firm 2 to charge the monopoly price. In addition, if the grim strategy calls for firm 2 to set its price at marginal cost, then the firm will do so thereafter. It follows that a best response by firm 1 is to set its price exactly at marginal costs forever after.

You can test your understanding of the Folk theorem by showing that the strategy of charging a price between the monopolistic price and marginal cost and charging marginal cost forever if either firm ever charges anything else is a subgame perfect Nash equilibrium.

9.7 Summary

We have proceeded far from the simple one-shot simultaneous-move games we first analyzed in Chapter 1. We can now incorporate in our models repeated interaction between players. This allows us to find conditions under which it is rational for selfish players to cooperate with their opponents and ignore the incentives to cheat. These conditions are not surprising: the players must place a high value on the future so that they are sufficiently fearful of future retribution by an opponent. Retribution need not be due to any "psychic" desire for revenge. Instead, retribution simply provides the proper incentives for cooperation. If you do not punish noncooperative behavior, you invite this behavior in the future.

Unfortunately, although cooperation is consistent with subgame perfect equilibrium, the Folk theorem shows that *many* other outcomes of a repeated game are also generated by subgame perfect equilibrium strategies. In the worst case, almost any payoff vector that is both feasible (attainable by the execution of some set of strategies) and individually rational (gives to each player at least what each can guarantee for him- or herself) can be attained as the outcome of some subgame perfect equilibrium of the game. Paring down this huge set of possible outcomes is a problem receiving great attention by game theorists at the moment.

9.8 Further Reading

There are many statements of the Folk theorem. One of the more recent is by Drew Fudenberg and Eric Maskin, "The Folk Theorem in Repeated Games with Discounting or with Incomplete Information," *Econometrica*, 54 (1986), pp. 533–54. This paper is very difficult. A less general, but more readable discussion of the Folk theorem can be found in Chapter 5 of Eric Rasmusen's *Games and Information* (New York: Basil-Blackwell, 1989).

9.9 Discussion Questions

1. Find a real-world example in which a strategy approximating the grim strategy has been applied.

2. In Section 9.4, Rip Jeans and Torn Jeans can precommit to an output level in the future in the current time period. Explain how a firm might credibly be able to do this.

3. The Folk theorem implies that there are typically many subgame perfect Nash equilibria in repeated stage games. Are there focal point equilibria among these?

9.10 New Terms

feasible
Folk theorem
grim strategy
individually rational
information set
minimax utility level

repeated games
self-enforcing agreement
stage
supergame
tit-for-tat

9.11 Exercises

EXERCISE 9.1

Verify the payoffs for the two-stage game displayed in Figure 9.2.

Exercises 9.2 and 9.3 are based on the infinitely repeated Cournot Stage Game between Rip Jeans and Torn Jeans presented in Section 9.5. The payoffs of the stage game are given in Table 9.1.

EXERCISE 9.2

According to the Folk theorem, as long as the discount factor is high enough, then any payoff vector lying in the shaded region of Figure 9.4 can be attained by playing some pair of Nash equilibrium strategies. Which of these many equilibria do you consider most likely to be observed in practice? Does the notion of a "focal point" apply?

EXERCISE 9.3

Use Eq. [9.4] to show that the feasible payoff schedules, (π_T, π_R), in the repeated Jean Duopoly Game with discounting (Section 9.5) are those for which $\pi_T + \pi_R \le \$18$ million, plus the two payoff schedules ($27 million, $0) and ($0, $27 million).

PART III
Games with Uncertain Outcomes

CHAPTER 10

Uncertainty and Expected Utility

OVERVIEW OF CHAPTER 10

10.1 Introduction

All of the games we have considered so far have been **deterministic.** This means that all the players know with certainty the outcome of any strategy profile. Clearly, the world is much more complicated than this. Firms never know exactly how much more they will sell when they reduce their prices. Union labor negotiators are never certain which contracts will be accepted by the union membership. Stock market traders do not know the liquidation value of every company in whose shares they trade. In this chapter, we will show how to incorporate *uncertainty* into a game and determine its Nash and subgame perfect equilibria.

We will also examine in some detail the fundamental behavioral assumption on which all the analysis in this book is based: the *expected utility hypothesis*. This hypothesis implies that for each player in a game, each outcome of the game can be assigned a number—called the outcome's *von Neumann-Morgenstern utility* to that player—such that the player acts as if he or she is maximizing his or her expected utility. We explain how the expected utility hypothesis is related to five weaker assumptions about how players choose strategies when there is uncertainty about the outcome of their choices.

10.2 Exogenous Uncertainty in Static Games

We return to the Oil Drilling Game presented in Chapter 1. In this game, two firms, Clampett and TEXplor, are deciding whether and how to drill wells into an oil deposit that lies under their adjacent land tracts. To this we now add a new wrinkle: the two firms do not know for sure whether there is oil under their land or not. As a result, the consequence of their actions now depends on something beyond their knowledge and control. All the factors that affect the outcome of the game but are not under any player's control will be lumped together and called the **state of the world.** The state of the world is unpredictable or *random*. We will hereafter employ the fiction that there is a player, whom we will call **Nature,** who is indifferent to the outcomes and ''selects'' the state of the world randomly according to fixed probabilities. These probabilities are common knowledge to all the players. We will distinguish the other players from Nature by referring to them as the **strategic players.** The outcome of the game depends on the strategies chosen by the strategic players and the state of the world chosen randomly by Nature.

Table 10.1 **The Payoff Matrix of the Oil Drilling Game II**

State of the world: *Gusher*		Clampett		
		Don't drill	Narrow	Wide
	Don't drill	(0, 0)	(0, 44)	(0, 31)
TEXplor	Narrow	(44, 0)	(14, 14)	(−1, 16)
	Wide	(31, 0)	(16, −1)	(1, 1)

State of the world: *Dry hole*		Clampett		
		Don't drill	Narrow	Wide
	Don't drill	(0, 0)	(0, −16)	(0, −29)
TEXplor	Narrow	(−16, 0)	(−16, −16)	(−16, −29)
	Wide	(−29, 0)	(−29, −16)	(−29, −29)

Payoffs ($ millions)̸ (TEXplor, Clampett)

We will assume that there are two possible states of the world: either (1) there is a 4 million barrel oil deposit under the land and any well will be a *gusher*, or (2) there is no oil under the land and any well will be a *dry hole*. The probability of a gusher is 60% and the probability of a dry hole is 40%. The two states of the world and the nine possible strategy profiles result in eighteen possible outcomes displayed in Table 10.1.

We will assume that both Clampett and TEXplor want to maximize their *expected payoff*. The expected payoff equals the payoff of a gusher times the probability of a gusher plus the payoff of a dry hole times the probability of a dry hole. For example, if both firms adopt the *Narrow* strategy, then they both earn $14 million if there is a gusher and both suffer a loss of $16 million if there is a dry hole. The expected payoff to each one equals $14 million $\times$ 0.60 $-$ $16 million $\times$ 0.40 = $2 million. The other expected payoffs are calculated the same way and are shown in Table 10.2. You can easily verify that {*Narrow, Narrow*} is the unique Nash equilibrium of this game. The assumption that the players maximize their expected payoffs is not a trivial one and is a source of debate among game theorists. We will look at this assumption more carefully in Section 10.4.

10.3   Exogenous Uncertainty in Dynamic Games

In the Software Game introduced in Chapter 6, an incumbent monopolist, Macrosoft, must decide on the advertising campaign for its new computer game. The choices are a Madison Avenue ad campaign (*Slick*) or a word-of-mouth ad campaign (*Simple*). It does this knowing that its ad decision may affect whether its potential competitor, Microcorp, enters the market with a clone or not. The consumer demand induced by each marketing campaign was assumed to be known ahead of time with certainty to both players. In the real world, of course, such certainty is unlikely.

Suppose, instead, that Macrosoft has to make its marketing decision without knowing with certainty how consumers will respond. Demand for its game could

Table 10.2   *The Expected Payoff Matrix of the Oil Drilling Game II*

		Clampett		
		Don't drill	Narrow	Wide
TEXplor	Don't drill	(0, 0)	(0, 20)	(0, 7)
	Narrow	(20, 0)	**(2, 2)**	(−7, −2)
	Wide	(7, 0)	(−2, −7)	(−11, −11)

Expected payoffs ($ *millions*): (TEXplor, Clampett)

Table 10.3 **Macrosoft's Profits with No Competition (in thousands)**

	Slick		Simple	
	High demand	Low demand	High demand	Low demand
Gross profit in year 1	$900	$600	$200	$200
Gross profit in year 2	$700	$200	$1,200	$400
Total gross profit	$1,600	$800	$1,400	$600
Advertising cost	−$600	−$600	−$200	−$200
Net profit	$1,000	$200	$1,200	$400

be *high* or *low*. The probability of each level of demand is 0.50. Profits now depend on both the state of demand and on the marketing campaign used. Table 10.3 shows the four possibilities. If it faced no competition, then Macrosoft would obtain a higher profit using the *Simple* campaign, regardless of whether demand were high or low.

Of course Macrosoft faces potential competition from Microcorp. As in Chapter 6, it costs Microcorp $300,000 to clone the game and enter the market. And when Microcorp enters, both firms split the profits in the second year. Tables 10.4 and 10.5 show the effect of the level of demand and the type of ad campaign on the profits of both firms. If both firms knew the state of demand with certainty before they moved, Microcorp would enter when demand was high and stay out when demand was low, regardless of the campaign chosen by Macrosoft. As a result, Macrosoft would use the *Slick* ad campaign if demand were high and would use the *Simple* ad campaign if demand were low.

The game changes radically when the firms do not know the level of demand in advance of playing. Figure 10.1 displays one way of modeling the new game. We incorporate uncertainty into the game by adding a nonstrategic player, Nature. Macrosoft moves first, chooses an ad campaign, and begins selling the software. Nature and Microcorp move next, the order depending on which ad campaign

Table 10.4 **Macrosoft's Profits If Microcorp Enters the Market (in Thousands)**

	Slick		Simple	
	High demand	Low demand	High demand	Low demand
Gross profit in year 1	$900	$500	$200	$200
Gross profit in year 2	$350	$100	$600	$200
Total gross profit	$1,250	$600	$800	$400
Advertising cost	−$600	−$600	−$200	−$200
Net profit	$650	$0	$600	$200

Table 10.5 *Microcorp's Profits If It Enters the Market (in Thousands)*

	Slick		Simple	
	High demand	Low demand	High demand	Low demand
Gross profit in year 1	$0	$0	$0	$0
Gross profit in year 2	$350	$100	$600	$200
Total gross profit	$350	$100	$600	$200
Entry cost	−$300	−$300	−$300	−$300
Net profit	$50	−$200	$300	−$100

Macrosoft selected. If Macrosoft adopts a *Slick* ad campaign, its profits in the first year are higher when demand is high than when it is low. As a result, Microcorp can determine the state of demand before it decides whether to clone the game and condition its entry on this data. This informational advantage is captured by having Microcorp move after Nature randomly chooses the state of demand. When Macrosoft adopts the *Simple* ad campaign, though, its profits during the first year are the same whether demand is low or high. Since Macrosoft's profits are Microcorp's only source of information about demand, Microcorp must make its entry decision ignorant of the level of demand. We can model this ignorance by having Nature select the state of demand *after* Microcorp moves, since what matters is when Nature's move is revealed to Microcorp.

In both Software Game I and Software Game II, Macrosoft moves first and its strategies are limited to two: adopt the *Slick* campaign or adopt the *Simple*

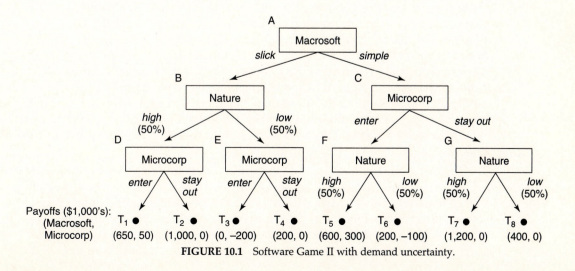

FIGURE 10.1 Software Game II with demand uncertainty.

Table 10.6 **Strategic Form for Software Game II**

		Macrosoft	
		Slick	*Simple*
	(stay out, stay out, stay out)	($0, 550)	($0, $800)
	(stay out, stay out, enter)	($0, $550)	($100, $400)
	(stay out, enter, stay out)	(−$100, $500)	($0, $800)
	(stay out, enter, enter)	(−$100, $500)	($100, $400)
Microcorp	(enter, stay out, stay out)	($25, $425)	($0, $800)
	(enter, stay out, enter)	**($25, $425)**	($100, $400)
	(enter, enter, stay out)	(−$75, $325)	($0, $800)
	(enter, enter, enter)	(−$75, $325)	**($100, $400)**

Expected payoffs (in thousands):
(Microcorp, Macrosoft)

campaign. But Microcorp's decision nodes increase from two to three, and so its strategies expand from four to eight. A strategy now consists of a three-tuple: (‹Entry decision if *Slick* is adopted and demand is high›, ‹Entry decision if *Slick* is adopted and demand is low›, ‹Entry decision if *Simple* is adopted›). For every strategy profile, say {(enter, stay out, stay out), *Slick*}, two payoffs are possible, depending on the level of demand. In the case of {(enter, stay out, stay out), *Slick*}, the payoffs are $50,000 for Microcorp and $650,000 for Macrosoft if demand is high and $0 for Microcorp and $100,000 for Macrosoft if demand is low. The *expected payoffs* to Microcorp and Macrosoft are $0.5 \times \$50,000 + 0.5 \times \$0 = \$25,000$ and $0.5 \times \$650,000 + 0.5 \times \$200,000 = \$425,000$, respectively. This gives us one of the entries in the strategic form. The rest are found in Table 10.6, which also displays each player's best response in boldface. You can readily see that there are two pure-strategy Nash equilibria. The first is {(enter, stay out, stay out), *Slick*}, in which Microcorp enters the market only if demand is high. The second is {(enter, enter, enter), *Simple*}, in which Microcorp always enters the market. Microcorp does better at the second equilibrium and Macrosoft does better at the first.

Only one of these Nash equilibria is subgame perfect, however. But before we can find it, we must modify our backward induction algorithm so that it can handle moves by Nature. The necessary modification is straightforward and is given below.

1. Start at the terminal nodes of the game and trace each one to its immediate predecessor, which will be a decision node for some player. These decision nodes are either "trivial," "basic," or "complex." A decision node is *basic* if from each of its branches you can either reach exactly one terminal node or a basic decision node belonging to Nature. A basic node with only one branch is *trivial*. A decision node is *complex* if, starting from one of its

branches, you can reach one or more decision nodes of strategic players or a complex decision node belonging to Nature. If you reach a trivial decision node, then keep moving up the tree until you reach either a complex or nontrivial basic decision node or you can go no further.

2. a. If the basic node belongs to Nature, then when this node is reached, the outcome is determined at random using predetermined probabilities. Calculate the expected payoff for each player using these probabilities.

   b. If the basic node belongs to a strategic player, then find the optimal move by comparing the payoffs the player obtains at each terminal node reached from this decision node.[1] Note that every path between a basic decision node A and a terminal node B starts at a unique branch of A. The branch that leads to the highest payoff for the player is the optimal move to make at that node.

3. a. Erase all the branches of the basic decision nodes belonging to Nature that you examined in step 2a. Each of these decision nodes now becomes a terminal node. Assign to these terminal nodes the expected payoffs you calculated in step 2a.

   b. Erase all the nonoptimal branches that originate from each of the basic decision nodes you examined in step 2b. Each of these basic decision nodes becomes trivial.

4. You now have a new game tree that is simpler than the original one. If in step 1 you arrived at the root of the tree, you are now done.

5. If you have not yet reached the root, then go back to step 1 and start all over again. In this way, you work step by step toward the root.

6. For each player, collect the optimal decisions at each of the player's decision nodes. This collection of decisions constitutes that player's optimal strategy in the game.

Let us apply this algorithm to Software Game II as illustrated in Figure 10.1. There are eight terminal nodes leading back to four decision nodes, labeled D, E, F, and G. The first two belong to Microcorp. At D, the best move is to *enter*, while at E, the best move is to *stay out*. The last two belong to Nature. At F, the expected payoff to Microcorp is $0.50 \times \$300,000 + 0.50 \times -\$100,000 = \$100,000$ and to Macrosoft is $0.50 \times \$600,000 + 0.50 \times \$200,000 = \$400,000$; at G, the expected payoffs are $0 and $800,000. So we now prune from the tree the two nonoptimal branches from nodes D and E and all the branches from nodes F and G. Nodes D and E become trivial and nodes F and G become terminal. This results

---

[1] If there is more than one optimal decision, then we need to reevaluate the payoff assignments and find a way to break the tie. If the modeler believes that the tie is a correct formulation of the game, then we need to determine whether there are "social conventions" that would make one choice much more likely than the other. If so, we use these social conventions to break the tie. Finally, if there are no conventions to fall back on, then we must acknowledge that the player's behavior at this node will be unpredictable.

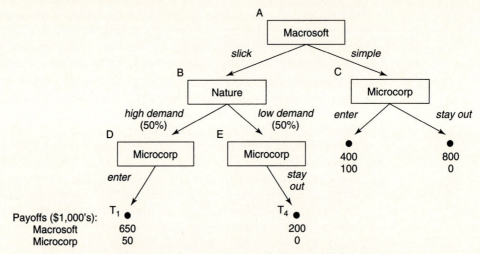

FIGURE 10.2 The game tree after the first round of pruning.

in the new tree shown in Figure 10.2. This new tree has four terminal nodes leading back to two basic (nontrivial!) nodes, B and C. Since B belongs to Nature, we calculate the expected payoffs, which are $0.50 \times \$50{,}000 + 0.5 \times \$0 = \$25{,}000$ for Microcorp and $0.50 \times \$650{,}000 + 0.5 \times \$200{,}000 = \$425{,}000$ for Macrosoft. Node C belongs to Microcorp. The firm's optimal move at this node is *enter*. We prune away both branches from B and the nonoptimal branch from C. This turns B into a terminal node and C into a trivial node. We now have the tree displayed in Figure 10.3. This tree has only one nontrivial decision node, A, which belongs to Macrosoft. Macrosoft's best move at A is to adopt the *Slick* campaign.

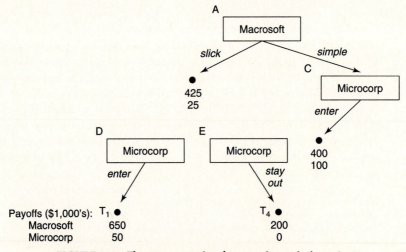

FIGURE 10.3 The game tree after the second round of pruning.

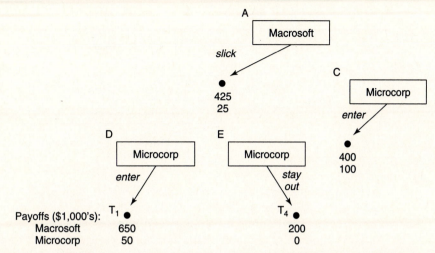

FIGURE 10.4 The game tree after all the pruning, showing the subgame perfect equilibrium strategies.

If we delete the nonoptimal branch from A, we are left with a tree consisting entirely of trivial nodes belonging to strategic players, shown in Figure 10.4. This tree displays the subgame perfect equilibrium strategies of both players. The subgame perfect equilibrium is {(*enter, stay out, enter*), *Slick*}. This reveals that the second Nash equilibrium strategy profile, {(*enter, enter, enter*), *Simple*}, in which Microcorp threatens to enter when Macrosoft adopts the *Slick* campaign and demand is *low*, is not credible since it is not in Microcorp's best interests to carry it out.

10.4 Endogenous Uncertainty in Static Games

Up to this point we have been entirely concerned with *pure strategies*. A pure strategy is one that calls for the selection of exactly one action at each decision node. Unfortunately, many simultaneous-move games do not have a Nash equilibrium if the players are restricted to pure strategies.

One of the simplest examples of a game with no pure-strategy Nash equilibrium is Matching Pennies. In this two-person game, each player, we will call them Simon and Antonia, places a penny in his or her hand either heads up (*Heads*) or tails up (*Tails*) out of sight of the opponent and then makes a fist. Simon and Antonia simultaneously open up their fists and reveal their pennies. If the two pennies match—both are heads up or both are tails up—then Antonia pays Simon a dollar. If the pennies do not match—one is heads up and the other is tails up—then Simon pays Antonia a dollar. The strategic form of this game is shown in Table 10.7. You should verify that none of the four possible pure-strategy profiles is a Nash equilibrium. For example, {*Heads, Heads*} is not a Nash equilibrium since

Table 10.7 **Matching Pennies**

		Simon	
		Heads	Tails
Antonia	Heads	(−1, 1)	(1, −1)
	Tails	(1, −1)	(−1, 1)

Payoffs: (Antonia, Simon)

if Antonia believes that Simon chose *Heads*, her best response is *Tails*, not *Heads*. Since there is no Nash equilibrium, neither is there a dominant strategy equilibrium nor an iterated dominant strategy equilibrium.

If we demand of any acceptable solution for a game that it be a Nash equilibrium, but no pure strategy Nash equilibrium exists, then we are unable to predict how the players will behave in such games. The resolution to this impasse is to expand the set of possible strategies and allow players to choose among their actions randomly. Such a strategy is called a **mixed strategy.** A standard assumption of noncooperative game theory is that when more than one player adopts a mixed strategy, these players randomize *independently* of each other. **Independence** means that knowledge of the strategy chosen by one player provides no new information about the strategy that will be chosen by any other player who has adopted a mixed strategy. The assumption of independence makes sense in situations in which the players cannot communicate with each either before or during the game. If there is substantial preplay communication, though, then it may be possible for the players to agree on some method for correlating their strategies. Throughout the rest of this book, we will assume that whenever two or more players adopt mixed strategies, they randomize independently.

In order to display mixed strategies, we must introduce some new notation. If $\{S_1, \ldots, S_K\}$ is the set of pure strategies for a player in a game, a mixed strategy is written as $M = (S_1:p_1, \ldots, S_K:p_K)$, where the number p_j is the probability of selecting the pure strategy S_j. The laws of probability require that these probabilities lie between 0 and 1 and add up to 1. For example, if there are three pure strategies, $\{S_1, S_2, S_3\}$, then a possible mixed strategy is $(S_1:0.25, S_2:0.40, S_3:0.35)$. The **support** of the mixed strategy $M = (S_1:p_1, \ldots, S_K:p_K)$ consists of those pure strategies S_j for which $p_j > 0$. If the support of the mixed strategy M contains all of a player's pure strategies, then M is said to be a **completely mixed strategy.**

When players adopt mixed strategies, the outcome of the game becomes unpredictable. So the player's payoffs become unpredictable. We will assume that, in such cases, the players seek to maximize their **expected payoffs.** We will define this term rigorously for the two-person case and leave it as an exercise for you to extend this definition to the case of games with more than two players. Suppose player 1 adopts the mixed strategy $(S_1:p_1, \ldots, S_K:p_K)$, player 2 adopts the mixed strategy $(T_1{:}q_1, \ldots, T_L{:}q_L)$, and player 1's payoff when player 1 adopts strategy S_i and player 2 adopts strategy T_j equals V_{ij}. Then player 1's expected payoff, EV_{ij}, is given by

$$\mathbf{E}V = \sum_{i=1}^{K} \sum_{j=1}^{L} V_{ij} \cdot p_i \cdot q_j.$$

In Matching Pennies, the mixed strategies take the form (*Heads*: p, *Tails*: $1 - p$); that is, choose *Heads* with probability p and choose *Tails* with probability $1 - p$. We claim that in the unique Nash equilibrium of the Matching Pennies game, both players adopt the mixed strategy (*Heads*: 0.5, *Tails*: 0.5). The players can implement this mixed strategy very easily: flip a coin into the air and catch it. When the players open their hands, half the time the coin will lie heads up and half the time it will lie tails up. Many of you probably guessed this right off. The players in this game want to maximize their unpredictability. Using a "fair coin"— a coin that comes up heads exactly half the time—to select their strategy accomplishes this.[2]

Poker players will have no problem understanding the importance of mixed strategies. Poker is the name given to a group of card games that involve betting. One simple version of this game begins with the players being dealt five cards. Play proceeds clockwise around the table. In every round, every player still in the game has the choice to drop out of the game ("fold"), increase the amount of money all players must put in the pot in order to stay in the game ("raise"), or place in the pot the amount of money announced by the last person who raised ("see"). Play continues around the table until everyone but one person folds, or no one raises. Once betting stops, the players still in the game reveal their cards. The player with the best hand wins all the money that has been placed in the pot.

Poker players know that "bluffing," that is, betting a lot of money on a hand that is unlikely to win, can be helpful in keeping opponents off balance. If you only raise when you have a very good hand, then your opponents will soon figure this out. Armed with this information, their optimal strategy is to "fold" the minute you start raising the stakes. Since very little money will be in the pot if everyone folds quickly, you will win only a small amount of money. On the other hand, if you occasionally bluff by betting on a lousy hand, your opponents can no longer be sure of the quality of your hand from the way you bet. As a result, you can lure them into betting against you when you have a good hand, thereby winning more money.

Good tennis players are also aware of the power of mixed strategies. If your opponent runs up to the net, your best responses are either to hit the ball hard to

---

[2]For those with some familiarity with statistics, this statement can easily be proven. Let X be a Bernoulli random variable: one which takes on two values, 1 and 0, with probabilities p and $1 - p$. The variance of X is a measure of the unpredictability of X. For the case of a Bernoulli random variable, the variance equals $p \cdot (1 - p)$, which is maximized at $p = 0.5$.

Table 10.8 **The Battle of the Sexes**

		Rhett	
		Saloon	Dinner club
Scarlett	Saloon	**(5, 12)**	(0, 0)
	Dinner club	(0, 0)	**(10, 4)**

Payoffs: (Scarlett, Rhett)

one side of the court (a "passing shot") or to loft the ball softly over your opponent's head (a "lob"). The best defense against a passing shot is to intercept the ball right at the net and hit it where the opponent cannot reach it (a "volley"). The best defense against a lob is to halt well short of the net and hit an "overhead smash" that the opponent cannot return. Well-executed volleys and overhead smashes are almost always winning shots. The aggressiveness with which your opponent rushes to the net depends on how confident she is that she can anticipate your response. If you always hit passing shots or always hit lobs, then your opponent will be able to adjust her strategy accordingly and win the game. Even if you are very good at hitting passing shots and not very good at hitting lobs, hitting an occasional lob will make your passing shots more effective by keeping your opponent away from the net.

Consider another famous game introduced in Chapter 1, Battle of the Sexes. Recall that this game involves a couple, Rhett and Scarlett, who are making independent decisions about how to spend the evening. Rhett would prefer to spend an evening in a low-life saloon. Scarlett would prefer to spend the evening at posh dinner club. Obviously, they could go their separate ways but this is not as appealing to either of them as being together. The payoff matrix is shown in Table 10.8. This game has two pure-strategy Nash equilibria. The payoffs of these equilibria are shown in Table 10.8 in **boldface**.

This game also has a third Nash equilibrium in mixed strategies. The equilibrium strategy profile is {(*Saloon*: $\frac{1}{4}$, *Dinner club*: $\frac{3}{4}$), (*Saloon*: $\frac{2}{3}$, *Dinner club*: $\frac{1}{3}$)}, where the first mixed strategy is Scarlett's and the second is Rhett's. Table 10.9 reports the likelihood of the four possible outcomes of this game if the players adopt this equilibrium. The most likely outcome is that each player goes to his or her preferred event—even though this results in a much worse outcome than going together to one person's preferred event. Furthermore, in the event they both go to the same place, it is 50% more likely to be Scarlett's first choice (the dinner club) than Rhett's (the saloon).

To see how we found this equilibrium, let p_S and p_R denote the probability of Scarlett and Rhett choosing *Saloon*. Since the two players are assumed to randomize independently, the probability that both choose *Saloon* equals $p_R \cdot p_S$; the probability that Scarlett chooses *Saloon* and Rhett chooses *Dinner club* equals $p_S \cdot (1 - p_R)$; and so forth. If the two players adopt the mixed strategy profile

Table 10.9 *Probability of Outcomes in the Battle of the Sexes When Mixed Strategy Equilibrium Is Adopted*

		Rhett	
		Saloon ($p_R = \frac{2}{3}$)	*Dinner club* ($1 - p_R = \frac{1}{3}$)
Scarlett	*Saloon* ($p_S = \frac{1}{4}$)	$\frac{1}{6}$	$\frac{1}{12}$
	Dinner club ($1 - p_S = \frac{3}{4}$)	$\frac{1}{2}$	$\frac{1}{4}$

{(*Saloon*: p_S, *Dinner club*: $1 - p_S$), (*Saloon*: p_R, *Dinner club*: $1 - p_R$)}, then Scarlett's expected payoff, denoted $EV_S(p_S, p_R)$, equals

$$EV_S(p_S, p_R) = 5 \cdot p_S \cdot p_R + 0 \cdot p_S \cdot (1 - p_R) + 0 \cdot (1 - p_S) \cdot p_R +$$
$$10 \cdot (1 - p_S) \cdot (1 - p_R) \qquad [10.1]$$
$$= 10 \cdot (1 - p_R) + 15 \cdot p_S \cdot (p_R - \tfrac{2}{3})$$

and Rhett's expected payoff $EV_R(p_S, p_R)$, equals

$$EV_R(p_S, p_R) = 12 \cdot p_S \cdot p_R + 0 \cdot p_S \cdot (1 - p_R) + 0 \cdot (1 - p_S) \cdot p_R +$$
$$4 \cdot (1 - p_S) \cdot (1 - p_R) \qquad [10.2]$$
$$= 4 \cdot (1 - p_S) + 16 \cdot p_R \cdot (p_S - \tfrac{1}{4}).$$

The completely mixed strategy profile {(*Saloon*: p_S^*, *Dinner club*: $1 - p_S^*$), (*Saloon*: p_R^*, *Dinner club*: $1 - p_R^*$)} is a Nash equilibrium if and only if both $0 < p_R^* < 1$ and $0 < p_S^* < 1$, and p_R^* maximizes the function $EV_R(p_S^*, p_R)$ and p_S^* maximizes the function $EV_S(p_S, p_R^*)$ among numbers in the interval $(0, 1)$. Looking at Eq. [10.1], we see that $EV_S(p_S, p_R^*)$ is a strictly increasing function of p_S when $p_R^* > \frac{2}{3}$, is a strictly decreasing function when $p_R^* < \frac{2}{3}$, and is constant when $p_R^* = \frac{2}{3}$. Therefore, it must be the case that $p_R^* = \frac{2}{3}$, in which case, Scarlett is indifferent about adopting *Saloon* or *Dinner club*. This indifference makes her unpredictable. Given the symmetry in their situation, the same must be true of Rhett: he must be indifferent about his two pure strategies, which makes him unpredictable as well. This is only possible if $p_S^* = \frac{1}{4}$. So the only possible mixed-strategy Nash equilibrium of this game is {(*Saloon*: $\frac{1}{4}$, *Dinner club*: $\frac{3}{4}$), (*Saloon*: $\frac{2}{3}$, *Dinner club*: $\frac{1}{3}$)}. If the two players adopt this profile, then they will be indifferent about all their strategies, both pure and mixed! This means that neither player can do *strictly better* by unilaterally switching from his or her Nash equilibrium strategy to another strategy. But this is the definition of a Nash equilibrium. So {(*Saloon*: $\frac{1}{4}$, *Dinner club*: $\frac{3}{4}$), (*Saloon*: $\frac{2}{3}$, *Dinner club*: $\frac{1}{3}$)} is the unique mixed-strategy Nash equilibrium of this game.

You probably feel a bit uneasy about assuming that players use mixed strategies. You may well be thinking: Do people really make important decisions by tossing coins, throwing dice, or picking numbers out of a hat? Probably not. Then what can it mean to say that a player is using a mixed strategy? One interpretation of a mixed strategy is that it represents the *beliefs of the other players as to what a given player is going to do.* If we adopt this interpretation, then the profile $\{Saloon: \frac{1}{4}, Dinner\ club: \frac{3}{4}), (Saloon: \frac{2}{3}, Dinner\ club: \frac{1}{3})\}$ means that Scarlett believes Rhett is unpredictable and is twice as likely to choose *Saloon* as *Dinner club;* and that Rhett believes Scarlett is unpredictable and is three times as likely to choose *Dinner club* as *Saloon.* There is no need for explicit randomization. For example, suppose Scarlett chooses *Saloon* if she got up on the right side of the bed and chooses *Dinner club* if she got up on the left side of the bed. Then Scarlett's decision is not random, but is deterministic. Yet, as long as Rhett does not know her decision rule, Scarlett will *appear* unpredictable to him. We will examine this interpretation of a mixed strategy in Chapter 13.

Mixed strategies are necessary to ensure the existence of a Nash equilibrium for some games. But is this enough? Are there games for which there is no Nash equilibrium even when mixed strategies are allowed for? Happily, under very general conditions, a Nash equilibrium is known to exist as long as the players have mixed strategies at their disposal. We conclude with the simplest of the known *Nash equilibrium existence theorems.*

> **THEOREM 10.1:** Every game with a finite number of players, each of whom has a finite number of pure strategies, possesses at least one Nash equilibrium, possibly in mixed strategies.

The proof of this important theorem is beyond the level of this book. References to the proof, as well as more general equilibrium existence theorems, are listed in Section 10.9.

10.5   The Expected Utility Hypothesis[3]

In this textbook, we assume that when players face uncertain outcomes, they seek to maximize their *expected payoffs.* This assumption is known as the **expected utility (EU) hypothesis** and has been controversial since it was first proposed by John von Neumann and Oscar Morgenstern in 1944.

Before we can go further, however, we need a theoretical framework in which to discuss choice over random outcomes. You are probably familiar with *lotteries* in which people buy tickets with a number printed on them; at an appointed time, one number is chosen publicly at random; and the owner of the lucky ticket wins

---

[3]This section is more mathematically advanced than the other material in this chapter. The section is self-contained and is not used in the remainder of the book.

a prize (money, a car, a Caribbean cruise, etc.). There are many variations on this description of a lottery. In some lotteries, ticket buyers can choose their lottery number; in some lotteries, the prize money increases with the number of tickets sold; and in some lotteries, the winner is automatically entered in a second special lottery with an even bigger prize. Lotteries have been used to determine the order in which men were drafted into the army, to ration tickets to the first Beatles concerts in the United States, and to select which applicants would receive state-subsidized mortgages. Any uncertain outcome can be modeled as if it were a type of "lottery." As a result, in order to find out how a rational player will rank different uncertain outcomes, it is enough to know how she will rank different lotteries.

Given a set of possible outcomes $X = \{T_1, T_2, \ldots, T_N\}$, a **simple lottery** over X is simply a random selection from the elements of X with fixed probabilities $\{p_1, p_2, \ldots, p_N\}$. These probabilities are nonnegative numbers that add up to one and p_i is the probability that the outcome T_i is chosen. A simple lottery will be represented as follows: $(T_1:p_1, T_2:p_2, \ldots, T_N:p_N)$. For example, suppose you are offered a lottery in which you pay \$2 to roll a die and you win \$1 for each dot on the die. If you pay and roll a 5, then you will be \$3 wealthier, but if you roll a 1, you will be \$1 poorer. In this case, $X = \{-\$1, \$0, \$1, \$2, \$3, \$4\}$. If the die is "fair," then all outcomes are equally likely with a probability of $1/6$. This means the lottery is $(-\$1:\frac{1}{6}, \$0:\frac{1}{6}, \$1:\frac{1}{6}, \$2:\frac{1}{6}, \$3:\frac{1}{6}, \$4:\frac{1}{6})$. Even a certain outcome, say a gift of \$10, can be expressed as a type of lottery: $(\$10:1)$.

We can also construct **compound lotteries** in which some of the outcomes are themselves lotteries. An example of a compound lottery is the process of applying to American colleges. In the first round of the lottery, high school students (and their parents) apply to colleges for admission and the colleges then inform the students whether they have been accepted, rejected, or put on the school's "waiting list." A student who has been accepted at one college but wait-listed at another, more preferred, college must decide whether to accept the first college's offer by the cutoff date or wait and hope to be accepted later at the second college. If she chooses to wait, she has essentially entered herself in a second lottery. The entire process, from initial application to eventual enrollment, is a compound lottery.

In general, the first round of a compound lottery determines which of the lotteries $\{L_1, L_2, \ldots, L_k\}$ will be played next. If the lottery chosen in the first round of a compound lottery is a simple lottery, then in the second round this lottery is played, an outcome is selected, and the lottery ends. If the lottery chosen in the first round is itself a compound lottery, then the second round results in the selection of a *third* lottery. This third lottery is played in the third round, and so forth. Compound lotteries will be denoted as $(L_1:p_1, L_2:p_2, \ldots, L_k:p_k)$, where the numbers $\{p_1, p_2, \ldots, p_k\}$ are positive numbers that add up to 1. The number p_i is the probability of selecting the lottery L_i in the first round.

The expected utility hypothesis is a model of choice over simple and compound lotteries.

Expected Utility Hypothesis: There exists a function $U(\cdot)$ over the final outcomes $\{T_1, \ldots, T_N\}$ such that: (1) a simple lottery $L_1 = (T_1:p_{11}, T_2:p_{12}, \ldots, T_N:p_{1N})$ is preferred to a simple lottery $L_2 = (T_1:p_{21}, T_2:p_{22}, \ldots, T_N:p_{2N})$ if and only if $EU(L_1) \geq EU(L_2)$, where $EU(\hat{L}_i) = \Sigma_k\, p_{ik} \cdot U(T_k)$ for $i = 1, 2$; (2) a compound lottery $\hat{L}_1 = (L_{11}:q_{11}, \ldots, L_{1N}:q_{1N})$ is preferred over a compound lottery $\hat{L}_2 = (L_{21}:q_{21}, \ldots, L_{2N}:q_{2N})$ if and only if $EU(\hat{L}_1) \geq EU(\hat{L}_2)$, where $EU(\hat{L}_i) = \Sigma_j\, q_{ij} \cdot EU(L_{ij})$ for $i = 1, 2$.[4]

The function $U(T_i)$ is called a **von Neumann-Morgenstern utility** (VNMU) for the decision maker's lottery preferences and the number $EU(L)$ is the **expected utility** of the lottery L based on the von Neumann-Morgenstern utility U.

In order to illustrate the expected utility hypothesis, consider your purchase of a \$2 State Lottery ticket. If it is your lucky day, you win \$10 million; otherwise you are out the \$2. The chances of your winning are 1 in 15 million. If losing the \$2 only results in a loss in utility of 0.01 "utils" while the winning of \$10 million results in a gain in utility of 12 million "utils," then the expected gain in utility from buying the lottery ticket equals $-0.01 \cdot \left(\dfrac{14{,}999{,}999}{15{,}000{,}000}\right) + 12{,}000{,}000 \cdot \left(\dfrac{1}{15{,}000{,}000}\right) = 0.79$. Since, on average, your utility will be higher by 0.79 utils if you buy the ticket than if you don't, we assume that you will buy the ticket. That is, we assume that you will choose the option with the highest expected utility.

The expected utility hypothesis requires that preferences over lotteries satisfy certain conditions. The restrictions on preferences implied by the expected utility hypothesis are strong and controversial. As a result, the empirical validity of this hypothesis is an area of great research interest among economists.

Because choosing among lotteries confronts a decision maker with subtle tradeoffs between the various outcomes, such choices reveal more information about his preferences than would a simple ordinal ranking of them. In particular, when a VNMU utility function exists, it reveals, in a limited sense, *how much* he prefers one alternative over another. Such information is called a **cardinal measure** of his preferences. Other examples of cardinal measures are temperature, acidity, and pressure. Two cardinal measures are equivalent if they differ only in their choice of units and origin. An example of equivalent measures are the Celsius and Fahrenheit temperature scales. Temperature in the Celsius scale can be converted to the Fahrenheit using the conversion formula $F = 32 + \frac{9}{5}C$.

Since the VNMU function cannot be observed directly, the expected utility

---

[4]This definition is to be understood recursively. If the lotteries that make up the compound lottery are all simple, then the expected utility of each is defined by part one of the definition. If any of these lotteries are themselves compound lotteries, then part two of the definition should first be applied recursively to each of them in order to obtain $EU(L_{ij})$. Then their weighted average can be calculated.

hypothesis cannot be tested directly. What can be observed are the choices people make when they have to choose among pairs of lotteries. Fortunately, in 1949 mathematician John von Neumann and economist Oscar Morgenstern showed that the expected utility hypothesis is satisfied if and only if the decision maker's preferences over lotteries satisfy five directly testable conditions. Not surprisingly, these five conditions are known as the **von Neumann-Morgenstern axioms** and the mathematical theorem that establishes their equivalence with the expected utility hypothesis is called the **expected utility theorem.** We will discuss the axioms, the theorem, and its proof in Section 10.6. Although this material is somewhat technical and dry, the expected utility hypothesis forms the behavioral foundations on which much else in this book rests.

The expected utility hypothesis simply says that there is *some* von Neumann-Morgenstern utility representation for the decision maker's lottery preferences. It says nothing about how many such representations there are or what relation, if any, each one has to the normalized von Neumann-Morgenstern utility function. It is easy to see that if U is a VNMU, then so is the function V obtained from U by multiplying U by some positive constant, b, and then adding another constant, a.

The surprising fact is that these alterations of scale and origin are the *only* transformations of the utility function that will completely preserve the decision maker's preferences. That is, if the VNMU function U cannot be transformed into the VNMU function V by a simple change of scale or origin, then it is possible to construct two lotteries L_1 and L_2 such that $EU(L_1) > EU(L_2)$ but $EV(L_1) < EV(L_2)$. This second, stronger property of a VNMU means the function is a *cardinal measure* of the decision maker's preferences in the same way that temperature is a cardinal measure of the heat a body radiates.

Take the hypothetical VNMU for profits labeled "Utility 1" in Table 10.10. Any other VNMU for its preferences, say the one labeled "Utility 2," will differ from the function tabulated in Table 10.10 only by the addition or subtraction of a constant and multiplication or division by a positive constant. In particular,

$$\frac{\left(\dfrac{85 - 78}{\$1.5 - \$1}\right)}{\left(\dfrac{78 - 57}{(\$1) - (-\$4)}\right)} = \frac{10}{3} = \frac{\left(\dfrac{256 - 235}{\$1.5 - \$1}\right)}{\left(\dfrac{235 - 172}{(\$1) - (-\$4)}\right)} \qquad [10.3]$$

This ratio measures the *marginal* utility of an increase in profits from $1 million to $1.5 million (per dollar of increase) relative to the *marginal* utility of an increase in profits from $-\$4$ million to $1 million (per dollar of increase). This ratio must be the same for every VNMU representation of the preferences in Table 10.10. Since the ratio in this case is greater than one, we can say that in this range of profits, the marginal utility of an additional dollar of profit is increasing as profits increase.

More generally, if V and U are two VNMUs for an expected utility maximizer,

Table 10.10 **Two Equivalent VNMU Functions over Profits**

Outcome (profit)	Utility 1	Utility 2
$1.5 million	85	256
$1 million	78	235
−$4 million	57	172
−$7 million	50	151

then there exist constants a and b such that $V(x) \equiv a + b \cdot U(x)$. If $x_1 < x_2 < x_3 < x_4$ are four outcomes, then

$$\frac{\dfrac{V(x_4) - V(x_3)}{x_4 - x_3}}{\dfrac{V(x_2) - V(x_1)}{x_2 - x_1}} = \frac{\dfrac{[a + bU(x_4)] - [a + bU(x_3)]}{x_4 - x_3}}{\dfrac{[a + bU(x_2)] - [a + bU(x_1)]}{x_2 - x_1}}$$

$$= \frac{\dfrac{U(x_4) - U(x_3)}{x_4 - x_3}}{\dfrac{U(x_2) - U(x_1)}{x_2 - x_1}}.$$

[10.4]

Contrast what we can say about marginal utility when we know the decision maker's VNMU with what we can say when we only know the ranking of the outcomes. Marginal utility is meaningless if all we know is the ranking of some outcomes. However, when someone's preferences are described by a VNMU, we can talk intelligently about whether marginal utility is increasing or decreasing.[5] In Section 10.7 we will relate the shape of the VNMU to the degree to which the decision maker avoids risky situations.

10.6   The Expected Utility Theorem[6]

The expected utility hypothesis implies that the decision maker's preference ranking of lotteries is complete and transitive. A preference ranking of a set of outcomes is **complete** if, for any two outcomes, T_1 and T_2, either T_1 is preferred to T_2 or T_2 is preferred to T_1. If T_1 is preferred to T_2 *and* T_2 is preferred to T_1 then the decision-maker is *indifferent* between them. The preference ranking is **transitive** if, given any three outcomes, T_1, T_2, and T_3, if T_1 is preferred to T_2 and T_2 is

---

[5]We still cannot talk intelligently about how much it absolutely increases or decreases, nor can we make utility comparisons across people.

[6]This section is more mathematically advanced than the other material in this chapter. It is self-contained and is not used in the remainder of the book.

preferred to T_3, then T_1 is preferred to T_3. These two properties, therefore, must be satisfied in order for the expected utility hypothesis to hold. This is the first von Neumann-Morgenstern axiom.

Axiom 1 (Consistency): There is a complete and transitive preference ordering over the elements of the set L of lotteries constructed from the finite set of outcomes X.

The consistency axiom implies that it is possible to order the elements of X from worst to best. The reason is that every outcome in X, say T, can be identified with the "trivial" lottery $L_T = (T{:}1)$ in which the outcome T occurs with certainty. As a result, any preference ordering over lotteries implies the obvious preference ordering over elements of X: the outcome T is preferred to the outcome T' if and only if the lottery L_T is preferred to the lottery $L_{T'}$. It is easy to see that if the preference ordering over lotteries is complete, and transitive, then so is the implied preference ordering over the outcomes in X. Since X is finite, there exists a best and worst outcome in X. We will denote the worst outcome in X as T_W and the best outcome in X as T_B. For example, among the four outcomes in Table 10.10, a profit of $1.5 million is the best outcome and a loss of $7 million is the worst.

Consider a special lottery $L(u) = (T_B{:}u, T_W{:}1 - u)$ in which only the best or worst outcomes are selected with probabilities u and $1 - u$, respectively. As we increase u from 0 to 1, T_B becomes increasingly more likely to occur and T_W becomes increasingly less likely to occur. As a result, it seems reasonable that as u increases, the lottery $L(u)$ becomes more desirable. This is the second von Neumann-Morgenstern axiom.

Axiom 2 (Monotonicity): $L(u)$ is preferred to $L(v)$ if and only if $u > v$.

If T is any other outcome in the set X, then, by assumption, the trivial lottery $(T_B{:}1, T_W{:}0) = L(1)$ is preferred to T, and T is, in turn, preferred to the trivial lottery $(T_B{:}0, T_W{:}1) = L(0)$. Monotonicity implies that as u increases, $L(u)$ becomes more and more preferred. The third von Neumann-Morgenstern requirement is that as u increases, eventually there comes a point at which the decision maker is exactly indifferent between the lottery $L(u)$ and any given outcome T. Otherwise, a discontinuity in the preference ordering would exist.

Axiom 3 (Continuity): For every outcome T in X, there exists a unique number, $U(T)$, called the *normalized von Neumann-Morgenstern utility* of T, such that the decision maker is indifferent between the (certain) outcome T and the lottery $L(U(T))$.

To see what the continuity axiom implies, let T_1, T_2, T_3, T_4 be the profits (losses) of $1.5 million, $1 million, $-$4 million, and $-$7 million listed in Table

Table 10.11 **Normalized von Neumann-Morgenstern**
Utility Function for Clampett

Outcome (profit)	Utility
T_1: \$1.5 million	1
T_2: \$1 million	0.70
T_3: −\$4 million	0.30
T_4: −\$7 million	0

10.11. The outcomes T_1 and T_4 are, respectively, the best and worst. As a result, we assign to T_1 the normalized von Neumann-Morgenstern utility of one and to T_4 a normalized von Neumann-Morgenstern utility of zero. Suppose that you are indifferent about the outcome T_2 with certainty and the lottery (T_4:30%, T_1:70%)—a 30% chance of having a loss of \$7 million and a 70% chance of having a profit of \$1.5 million—then T_2 has a normalized von Neumann-Morgenstern utility of 0.70. Likewise, if you are indifferent about T_3 and the lottery (T_4:70%, T_1:30%), then the normalized von Neumann-Morgenstern utility of T_3 equals 0.30.

The final two von Neumann-Morgenstern axioms concern "inconsequential" changes in a lottery. By this we mean changes that do not alter the lottery's relative attractiveness. These last two axioms are much more controversial than the first three. The first type of "inconsequential" change is the substitution of one outcome in a lottery for another outcome that the decision maker finds equally attractive.

Axiom 4 (Substitution): Suppose the decision maker is indifferent between the certain outcome T and the lottery L, and two lotteries L_1 and L_2 differ only in that wherever T appears in one, L appears in the other. Then the decision maker is also indifferent between L_1 and L_2.

The second type of "inconsequential" change involves the replacement of a compound lottery by a simple one. This fifth axiom implies two things: (1) the decision maker is interested only in the probability that each outcome will occur, not in the specifics of the mechanism by which the final outcomes are selected; and (2) the decision maker believes the random selections that occur at each stage of a compound lottery are independent events.

Axion 5 (Simplification): Suppose L is the compound lottery (L_1:q_1, L_2:q_2, ..., L_M:q_M), where each of the lotteries L_i is simple and $L_i = (T_1$:p_{i1}, T_2:p_{i2}, ..., T_K:p_K), $i = 1, ..., M$. Then the decision maker is indifferent between L and the simple lottery (T_1:r_1, T_2:r_2, ..., T_K:r_K), where $r_j = \Sigma_i p_{ij} \cdot q_i$.

The whole point of specifying the von Neumann-Morgenstern utility function and the von Neumann-Morgenstern axioms is to prove

> **THE EXPECTED UTILITY THEOREM:** The expected utility hypothesis holds if and only if the five von Neumann-Morgenstern axioms are satisfied.

PROOF: The proof that the expected utility hypothesis implies the five von Neumann-Morgenstern axioms is left as an end-of-chapter exercise. We will show here that the von Neumann-Morgenstern axioms imply that the normalized von Neumann-Morgenstern utility function is a von Neumann-Morgenstern utility representation of the decision maker's preferences over lotteries. But this means the expected utility hypothesis holds.

Suppose the five von Neumann-Morgenstern axioms are satisfied and the set of final outcomes is $X = \{T_1, \ldots, T_K\}$. The consistency axiom implies that these outcomes can be ordered from the worst, T_W, to the best, T_B. Let $L(u)$ denote the simple lottery $(T_B{:}u, T_W{:}1 - u)$ and let S be an arbitrary simple lottery $(T_1{:}p_1, \ldots, T_K{:}p_K)$ where p_i is the probability of the outcome T_i. The continuity axiom implies that for every outcome T_i there exists a number $U(T_i)$ such that T_i is equivalent to the lottery $L(U(T_i)) = (T_B{:}U(T_i), T_W{:}1 - U(T_i))$. The heart of the proof is the demonstration that every simple lottery S is equivalent to the simple lottery $L(EU(S))$, where $EU(S) = \Sigma_i p_i \cdot U(T_i)$. Once this is shown, the monotonicity and consistency axioms imply that any simple lottery L_1 is preferred to another simple lottery L_2 if and only if $EU(L_1) \geq EU(L_2)$. This is the first part of the expected utility hypothesis. The second part of the hypothesis now follows from the first part and the simplification axiom. We leave this as an end-of-chapter exercise for the reader.

Since T_i is equivalent to the lottery $L(U(T_1))$, the substitution axiom implies that S is equivalent to the lottery $(L(U(T_1)){:}p_1, T_2{:}p_2, \ldots, T_K{:}p_k)$. Repeated use of the substitution axiom implies that S is equivalent to the lottery $(L(U(T_1)){:}p_1, L(U(T_2)){:}p_2, \ldots, L(U(T_K)){:}p_k)$. The only final outcomes of this compound lottery are T_B and T_W. It follows from the simplification axiom that this compound lottery is equivalent to the simple lottery $(T_B{:}\Sigma_i p_i \cdot U(T_i), T_W{:}\Sigma_i p_i(1 - U(T_i)))$. But $\Sigma p_i \cdot U(T_i) = EU(S)$ and $\Sigma_i p_i \cdot (1 - U(T_i)) = \Sigma_i p_i - \Sigma_i p_i \cdot U(T_i) = 1 - \Sigma_i p_i \cdot U(T_i) = 1 - EU(S)$, since the outcomes T_i are exclusive and mutually exhaustive events. It follows from the transitivity of indifference that S is equivalent to the lottery $(T_B{:}EU(S), T_W{:}1 - EU(S)) = L(EU(S))$, as we claimed.

10.7 Attitudes Toward Risk

Suppose that people's utility depends only on their purchasing power, that is, on their real income.[7] The marginal utility of income is defined as the *additional* utility

---

[7]Traditionally, utility depends on a set of consumable goods and services. To describe utility as a function of real income amounts to assuming that the individual's ability to buy bundles of goods and services is a good proxy for the vector of individual goods and services themselves.

received from an *additional* dollar of income. This number will normally be different at different levels of income. For example, if your income is very low and you are often hungry, then an additional dollar with which to buy food may result in a large increase in your utility. On the other hand, if your income is high enough that you are never deficient in food, shelter, or seasonally correct clothing, then an additional dollar of income may well be frittered away on minor amusements that improve your welfare only slightly. A person's aversion or love of risk turns out to be directly related to whether the person's marginal utility of income decreases or increases as income increases.[8]

Let us be more concrete. Suppose Mr. Swiss is invited to participate in a simple lottery. A fair coin is flipped and if it comes up heads, Mr. Swiss wins $100, but if it comes up tails, he loses $100. Call this lottery L_1. Alternatively, Mr. Swiss can choose not to participate. This riskless option can also be cast as a lottery, which we will call L_2. Now suppose we learn that Mr. Swiss is perfectly indifferent between the two lotteries. Assuming that his preference over lotteries satisfies the expected utility hypothesis, this indifference implies that $EU(L_1) = EU(L_2)$. Since expected values carry with them a precise mathematical meaning, we can express the previous equation as

$$0.5 \cdot U(Y_0 + \$100) + 0.5 \cdot U(Y_0 - \$100) = U(Y_0) \qquad [10.5]$$

where Y_0 is Mr. Swiss's current income. The left-hand side of Eq. [10.5] simply says that there is a 50% chance that Mr. Swiss's income will rise by $100 and a 50% chance that it will fall by $100 if he participates in L_1. Arbitrarily set $U(Y_0) = 100$ and $U(Y_0 - \$100) = 50$.[9] Using this calibration, we find that $U(Y_0 + \$100) = 150$. As Mr. Swiss's income rises from $Y_0 - \$100$ to Y_0, his utility rises by 50. That is, his marginal utility equals $\frac{50}{100}$, or 0.5. Similarly, as his income rises from Y_0 to $Y_0 + \$100$, his utility increases by 50, implying a marginal utility of $\frac{50}{100}$ or 0.5. Therefore, Mr. Swiss, through his preference among lotteries, has shown that he has a *constant marginal utility of income*. Figure 10.5 shows that as income rises between $Y_0 - \$100$ and $Y_0 + \$100$, his utility increases along a straight line.

Suppose there is a second "gambler," Ms. Safe, who is not indifferent between the two lotteries, but prefers not to participate in lottery L_1. Once again, as long as Ms. Safe's preference over lotteries satisfies the expected utility hypothesis, we know that $EU(L_1) < EU(L_2)$, which says that the expected utility from lottery one is less than the expected utility from lottery two. Therefore,

$$0.5 \cdot U(Y_0 + \$100) + 0.5 \cdot U(Y_0 - \$100) < U(Y_0). \qquad [10.6]$$

---

[8]Once again, a warning is in order. It does make sense to compare the marginal utility of real income *of a single individual* at different income levels. It does *not* make sense to compare the marginal utility of different individuals at different income levels. For example, we cannot logically argue that because person A is poor and therefore has a high marginal utility of income and B is rich and has a low marginal utility of income, that a redistribution of income from B to A will make the world a better place. That argument relies on ethics.

[9]Remember that a VNMU is only defined up to a linear transformation, so you can arbitrarily set the origin and the scale.

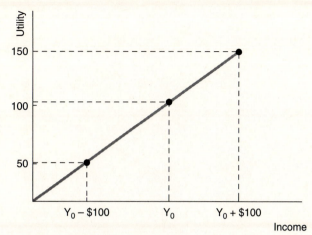

FIGURE 10.5   Mr. Swiss's von Neumann-Morgenstern utility function.

Once again, arbitrarily setting $U(Y_0) = \$100$ and $U(Y_0 - \$100) = 50$ reveals that $U(Y_0 + \$100)$ is less than 150. As Ms. Safe's income rises from $Y_0 - \$100$ to Y_0, her utility rises by 50, implying a marginal utility of $\frac{50}{100}$, or 0.5. As her income rises from Y_0 to $Y_0 + \$100$, however, her utility must rise by less than 50, implying that her marginal utility of income is less than 0.5. We can determine from Ms. Safe's choice between the two lotteries that, as her income rises, her marginal utility of income must fall. A possible utility function with this property is shown in Figure 10.6.

The lottery L_1 offers a 50% chance of winning $100 and a 50% chance of losing $100. On average, across many bets, you would break even playing this lottery. More formally, the expected additional income from this lottery is zero. Such a lottery is called a **fair lottery.** In an **unfair lottery,** the expected additional income from a lottery is negative; in a **superfair lottery,** the expected additional income is positive.

If a person is indifferent between playing a fair lottery and doing nothing (what we have been calling lottery L_2), then that person has a constant marginal utility of income in that income range. Conversely, a person with a constant marginal utility of income will be indifferent between participating in a fair lottery and not participating. This person will also jump at the chance to play any superfair lottery and will steer clear of any unfair lottery. Anyone who behaves this way is said to be **risk neutral.** If, however, this person is not willing to play any fair lottery, but only superfair ones, then, as we have seen, she must have a diminishing marginal utility of income. In this case, she would be said to be **risk averse.**[10] A third possibility is that the person is willing to accept unfair lotteries. Such an individual must have an increasing marginal utility of income and is

---

[10]A common misconception is the belief that risk-averse people do not take any risks. This is not correct. Risk-averse people simply must be compensated before they will agree to assume additional risk. The more risk averse people are, the more they must be compensated.

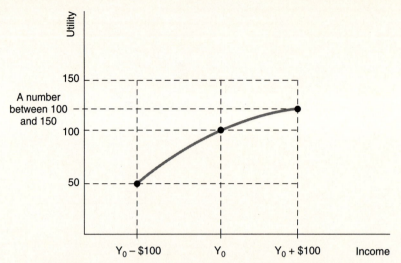

FIGURE 10.6   Ms. Safe's von Neumann-Morgenstern utility function.

called **risk loving.** A risk lover gets some type of "thrill" from increasing his exposure to risk.

We can be a little more general about the implications of being risk neutral, risk averse, or risk loving. So far we have considered only comparisons of two lotteries where one of the lotteries was really just the status quo. Unfortunately, life is filled with situations where the status quo is not an option. Even by doing nothing, the world moves on around you, time passes, and your wealth and income change through no fault of your own. Consider the following two lotteries: In lottery one, a fair coin is flipped and if it lands heads up, you win $10; if it lands tails up, you lose $10. In lottery two, the same coin is flipped and if it is heads, you win $1,000 and if it is tails, you lose $1,000. In both lotteries, the expected change in wealth is $0. But as you can see, there is a big difference between them. Lottery one involves relatively modest gains or losses, while lottery two results in much more dramatic changes in wealth.

Consider a risk-neutral, expected utility–maximizing gambler, such as Mr. Swiss. We know Mr. Swiss will be indifferent between either lottery and doing nothing. It follows that he is also indifferent between the two lotteries themselves. What about a risk-averse gambler? Recall that risk aversion is characterized by a diminishing marginal utility of income. In this example, there are four possible levels of income. In order of magnitude they are:

$$Y_1 = Y_0 - \$1{,}000,$$

$$Y_2 = Y_0 - \$10,$$

$$Y_3 = Y_0 + \$10, \text{ and}$$

$$Y_4 = Y_0 + \$1{,}000. \tag{10.7}$$

Because the marginal utility of income is assumed to fall as income increases, we know that

$$\frac{U(Y_4) - U(Y_3)}{Y_4 - Y_3} < \frac{U(Y_2) - U(Y_1)}{Y_2 - Y_1}.$$ [10.8]

Since $Y_4 - Y_3 = Y_2 - Y_1 = \$900$, this inequality implies that

$$U(Y_4) - U(Y_3) < U(Y_2) - U(Y_1).$$ [10.9]

Rearranging Eq. [10.9] and multiplying both sides by 0.5 results in

$$0.5 \cdot U(Y_4) + 0.5 \cdot U(Y_1) < 0.5 \cdot U(Y_2) + 0.5 \cdot U(Y_3).$$ [10.10]

The left-hand side of Eq. [10.10] is the expected utility of lottery two, while the right-hand side is the expected utility of lottery one. Since lottery two has a larger dispersion in its outcomes than lottery one (while the expected dollar gains are the same for both lotteries), lottery two is said to be *riskier* than lottery one. The expected utility hypothesis, combined with risk aversion, implies that the less risky lottery one is preferred. The intuition behind this result makes a great deal of sense. Lottery two will result in either a large gain or a large loss. Because of the diminishing marginal utility of income, the gain in utility from the large gain in income is small compared to the large loss in utility from the large loss in income. A risk-averse person wants to minimize the swings in her income. As a result, she worries about more than the expected income from playing a lottery. She also is interested in how much her lottery income will deviate from this expected income.

When a player's preferences over money lotteries satisfies the expected utility hypothesis, the player can assign to every lottery L a monetary value called the lottery's **certainty equivalent,** or $CE(L)$. $CE(L)$ satisfies the following equation:

$$U(CE(L)) = \mathbf{E}U(L).$$ [10.11]

When $CE(L)$ is positive, it is the least amount of money the player will accept as compensation for not playing the lottery. When $CE(L)$ is negative, its absolute value is the most the player is willing to pay to avoid playing the lottery. For lotteries that involve relatively small changes in wealth, the certainty equivalent can be expressed as a simple function of the lottery's expected payoff and a measure of its risk, called its **variance,** and a number that measures the player's attitude toward risk. The variance of a lottery measures how far the payoffs deviate from the expected payoff. A lottery with a high variance has a wide range of payoffs, while one with a low variance has a narrow range of payoffs. If $L = (T_1{:}p_1, \ldots, T_K{:}p_K)$ is the lottery, its expected payoff is $\mathbf{E}(L) = \sum_i p_i \cdot T_i$ and variance $\mathbf{V}(L)$ is given by

$$\mathbf{V}(L) = \sum_{i=1}^{K} (T_i - \mathbf{E}(L))^2 \cdot p_i. \tag{10.12}$$

A very useful mathematical fact is that the certainty equivalent is approximately,

$$CE(L) \approx \mathbf{E}(L) + \rho \cdot \mathbf{V}(L). \tag{10.13}$$

The constant ρ is the player's **risk-aversion coefficient.** It can also be thought of as the person's price for risk. A risk-averse person has a negative risk-aversion coefficient; a risk-neutral person has a zero risk-aversion coefficient; and a risk lover has a positive risk-aversion coefficient. The magnitude of ρ measures the person's degree of risk aversion.

10.8   Summary

Frequently, players must choose their strategies without knowing the outcome for certain. Another way of expressing this uncertainty is that they make their choices without knowing the state of the world. We can incorporate this lack of knowledge into both the strategic form and the extensive form by assuming that the state of the world is chosen by a special player whom we call Nature. Nature is indifferent to the game's outcome and chooses its action randomly. As a consequence, the players must choose among different random selections of the final outcomes. These random selections we call lotteries.

If the expected utility hypothesis is satisfied, then the decision maker can rank these lotteries according to their expected utility. The expected utility of a lottery is simply the weighted sum of the utility of each lottery outcome, where the weights are the lottery probabilities. The utility function is called a von Neumann-Morgenstern utility (VNMU) function because of the early research by these two game theory pioneers. John von Neumann and Oscar Morgenstern showed that the expected utility hypothesis is satisfied if and only if the decision maker's preferences over lotteries satisfy five conditions, called the von Neumann-Morgenstern axioms. When the expected utility hypothesis is satisfied, the VNMU is a cardinal measure. That is, like the temperature, the VNMU is completely determined once you choose the scale and point of origin.

When the final outcomes consist of changes in the decision maker's wealth, the VNMU is often referred to as the utility of wealth. The decision maker's preferences over wealth-altering lotteries reveal whether the decision maker's marginal utility function is constant, increasing, or decreasing in wealth. If the marginal utility decreases as wealth increases, then the person is risk averse and will not accept gambles whose expected payoff is zero; if the marginal utility is constant, then the person is risk neutral and is exactly indifferent between accepting and rejecting gambles whose expected payoff is zero; and if the marginal utility is increasing as wealth increases, then the person is risk loving and will accept any gamble whose expected payoff is zero.

10.9   Further Reading

The expected utility hypothesis is due to John von Neumann and Oscar Morgenstern, *Theory of Games and Economic Behavior* (Princeton University Press, 1944, Chapter 3). The proof given here is based on those in C. J. McKenna, *The Economics of Uncertainty* (New York: Oxford University Press, 1986) and R. D. Luce and H. Raiffa, *Games and Decision* (New York: John Wiley, 1957).

Experimental evidence against the expected utility hypothesis was first reported by M. Allais, "Le Comportement de L'homme Rationnel Devant le Risque: Critique des Postulates et Axiomes de L'ecole Americaine," *Econometrica* 21 (1953), pp. 503–46. A summary of this research is surveyed in M. Allais and O. Hagens, eds., *Expected Utility Hypothesis and the Allais Hypothesis* (Boston: Reidel, 1979).

The experimental evidence has led theorists to formulate alternatives to expected utility. These include the *regret theory* of G. Loomes and R. Sugden, "Regret Theory: An Alternative of Rational Choice under Uncertainty," *Economic Journal* 92 (1982), pp. 805–24, and the *prospect theory* of D. Kahneman and A. Tversky, "Prospect Theory: An Analysis of Decisions under Risk," *Econometrica* 47 (1979), pp. 263–91. Measures of risk aversion have been developed by Kenneth Arrow, *Some Aspects of the Theory of Risk Bearing* (Helsinki: Yrjo Jahnssonin saatio, 1965) and John Pratt, "Risk Aversion in the Small and in the Large," *Econometrica* 32 (1964), pp. 122–36.

10.10   Discussion Question

1. It has been argued that experimental evidence against the expected utility hypothesis is irrelevant because what matters is not how people behave in artificial experimental environments with highly stylized problems that are divorced from everyday experience, but how they behave in the real world where decision problems have real consequences and where there is extensive feedback to weed out "bad" decision rules. Do you agree or disagree?

10.11   New Terms

cardinal measure	expected utility
certainty equivalent	expected utility (EU) hypothesis
complete ranking	expected utility theorem
completely mixed strategy	fair lottery
compound lotteries	independence
deterministic	mixed strategy
expected payoffs	

Nature	superfair lottery
risk averse	support
risk-aversion coefficient	transitive ranking
risk loving	unfair lottery
risk neutral	von Neumann-Morgenstern utility
simple lottery	von Neumann-Morgenstern axioms
state of the world	variance
strategic players	

10.12 Exercises

EXERCISE 10.1

In each example below, a group of players are trying to predict some future event. In each case, provide an example of variables that affect the probability that the event occurs and is (1) under the players' control and (2) under no player's control.

(a) Players: Automobile commuters using the same freeway to get to work. Event: Heavy congestion on the freeway at 8 A.M.

(b) Players: Stores in a suburban shopping mall the week before Christmas. Event: Low sales.

(c) Players: Two dominant grocery store chains in a city. Event: Heavy response by households to one grocery store chain's store coupons, but light response to the other chain's coupons.

(d) Players: American wheat farmers. Event: Record crop yields.

(e) Players: Two college football teams competing against each other. Event: A tied game.

EXERCISE 10.2

(a) Pearl believes that the Democratic candidate, whom she favors, has a $\frac{2}{3}$ chance of winning the next presidential election, while Denise believes it is the Republican candidate, whom she favors, who has the $\frac{2}{3}$ chance of winning the election. They agree that all the third-party candidates have no chance of winning. Each is willing to accept any bet on the election's outcome that assures a nonnegative expected payoff, given her beliefs about the election's outcome. So, for example, Pearl is willing to wager as much as $10 that the Democratic candidate will win against $5 that the Republican will win since her expected payoff equals $\frac{2}{3} \cdot \$5 - \frac{1}{3} \cdot \$10 = \$0$, and Denise is willing to bet as much as $10 that the Republican candidate will win against $5 that the Democratic candidate will win since her expected payoff equals $\frac{2}{3} \cdot \$5 - \frac{1}{3} \cdot \$10 = \$0$. Pearl and Denise bet each other $5 at even odds that their candidate will win, which means that Denise pays Pearl $5 if the Democratic wins and Pearl pays Denise $5 if the Republican wins. What does each believe is the expected payoff of her bet?

(b) Find a pair of bets that *both* women would accept from you that *guarantee* you will win a total of $5 *regardless* of which candidate wins the election—assuming it is not a third party.

EXERCISE 10.3

Hilga is a contestant on the television show *Let's Make a Deal* and stands before three curtained partitions on a stage. Behind one of the curtains is a brand new luxury car. Behind each of the other two curtains are "booby" prizes worth very little. The curtain hiding the car was chosen completely at random, with each curtain having the same chance of being chosen. The host, Monty Hall, asks Hilga to choose one of the curtains and she chooses curtain #1. Monty then opens up curtain #2 to reveal that behind it is a booby prize. Before he reveals what is behind curtain #1 Monty gives Hilga the opportunity to switch curtain #1 for the unopened curtain #3. He then opens curtains #1 and #2 and Hilga gets her prize. Should she switch or not?[11] Proceed as follows:

(a) Hilga and Monty are playing a game against each other. Model this game as follows: Since Hilga is the last to learn where the car is located, have her go first and choose her curtain *and* whether or not she will switch curtains. It is as if Hilga decided which curtain she would choose and whether she would switch curtains before she ever appeared on the show. This gives Hilga six strategies. Nature moves second and places the car behind one of the three curtains; each curtain has a one third chance of being chosen. Monty moves last. Knowing where the car is located, he opens up one of the two unopened curtains. *He is not allowed to open the curtain that hides the car.* This means that if Hilga chooses curtain #1 and the car is behind curtain #2, then Monty *must* open curtain #3. Hilga is then allowed to switch curtains. Hilga's payoff is 1 if she wins the car and 0 otherwise. Monty's payoff is 1 if Hilga gets a booby prize and 0 otherwise. Draw the game tree for this game.

(b) Find Hilga and Monty's optimal strategies using backward induction. If at any decision node either player is indifferent between two or more moves, assume that they choose between them at random. What is your conclusion: Should Hilga switch or not?

(c) Why do you think most people who are presented with this problem conclude that it makes no difference whether Hilga switches or not?

EXERCISE 10.4

Table 10.12 shows the strategic form of a hypothetical game played between the San Francisco 49ers and the New York Jets in the waning seconds of the Super Bowl. SF has possession of the ball on New York's 30 yard line, New York is ahead 20–17, and there is time for only one more play. The payoffs for each team are the probability (in percent) of winning the game. If the VNMU of each team

---

[11]This problem has been the source of quite a bit of controversy. See Section 10.9 for a few sources.

is normalized so that the utility of winning equals 1 and the VNMU of losing equals 0, then the expected utility of winning the game with a probability of p equals $p \cdot 1 + (1 - p) \cdot 0 = p$. Find the mixed strategy equilibrium of this game, assuming that the teams are expected utility maximizers.

Table 10.12 *The Touchdown Game*

		San Francisco	
		Pass	Run
New York	Defend against the pass	50, 50	60, 40
	Defend against the run	90, 10	20, 80

Payoffs: (San Francisco, New York)

EXERCISE 10.5

An executive at a publishing house has just been given two *stock options* as a bonus. Each option gives the executive the right (but not the obligation) to purchase one share of the publishing company's stock for $50, as long as she does it before the close of the stock market tomorrow afternoon. When the executive exercises either option, she must immediately sell the stock bought from the company at the market price in effect at the time. An option can only be exercised once. The stock's price today is $55, so if she exercises either option today she is guaranteed a profit of $5 per option exercised. The stock price tomorrow will either be $45 or $65 with equal probability. This means that if she waits until tomorrow and the stock price rises to $65, she can exercise any remaining options for a profit of $15 per option exercised. On the other hand, if the stock price falls to $45, then exercising either option results in a loss of $5 per option exercised. Today the executive can: (1) exercise both options, (2) exercise one option today and wait until tomorrow to decide about the second one, or (3) exercise neither option today and wait until tomorrow to decide what to do about both. Tomorrow the executive must either exercise any option(s) not already cashed in or let it (them) expire unused. Draw the game tree for this Option Game between the executive and Nature. Remember to label the action taken along each branch, who moves at each decision node (the executive or Nature), and the change in the executive's wealth at each terminal node. Assume that there are no brokerage commissions or taxes. Use the game tree to enumerate the executive's six strategies and the expected profit for each one.

EXERCISE 10.6

This is a continuation of Exercise 10.5. Suppose the executive has the VNMU displayed in Table 10.13. Use backward induction to determine the optimal course of action.

Table 10.13 **Executive's VNMU of Wealth**

Change in Wealth	Utility	Marginal Utility
$0	0	
		2.0
$5	10	
		1.6
$10	18	
		1.4
$15	25	
		1.2
$20	31	
		1.0
$25	36	
		0.8
$30	40	

EXERCISE 10.7*

This is a continuation of Exercise 10.5. Draw a second game tree to depict the executive's decision problem when she *knows today* what the firm's stock price will be tomorrow. Such knowledge is sometimes called "insider information." Use backward induction to determine the executive's optimal decision in this case. Combine your answer with that from Exercise 10.6 to determine (a) whether the executive's actions today could be used to predict the firm's stock price tomorrow and (b) whether her actions today and tomorrow could be used to show she had insider information at the time she acted.

EXERCISE 10.8

A randomly chosen college student is presented with the following three lotteries:

(1) a 30% chance of winning $5 and a 70% chance of winning nothing.

(2) a 20% chance of winning $10 and an 80% chance of winning nothing.

(3) an 80% chance of winning $3.33 and a 20% chance of winning nothing.

The student prefers 1 to 2 and prefers 2 to 3. Assume that the student is an expected utility maximizer and let U be his VNMU function. Setting $U(\$0) = 0$ and $U(\$10) = 1$, use his reported lottery preferences to find a lower bound for $U(\$5)$ and an upper bound for $U(\$3.33)$. Use these bounds to draw a plot of the VNMU through the four points ($0, U(\$0)$), ($3.33, U(\$3.33)$), ($5, U(\$5)$), and ($10, U(\$10)$). What can you say about the risk aversion of this student from your plot? Where must the function be concave? Where must it be convex?

EXERCISE 10.9 (Uses Section 10.5)

Show that if the expected utility hypothesis is satisfied, then the decision maker's preferences over lotteries must satisfy the five von Neumann-Morgenstern axioms.

---

*Indicates a difficult exercise.

EXERCISE 10.10* (Uses Section 10.5)

Karen's preferences over lotteries satisfy the von Neumann-Morgenstern axioms; the set of possible outcomes $\{T_1, \ldots, T_K\}$ is ordered from best (T_1) to worst (T_K); and for every simple lottery L, Karen is indifferent between L and the lottery $(T_1:EU(L), T_K:1 - EU(L))$, where $EU(L) = \Sigma_i p_i \cdot U(T_i)$. Let $\hat{L}$ denote the compound lottery $(L_1:q_1, \ldots, L_m:q_m)$ in which each lottery L_i is simple. Show that Karen is indifferent between $\hat{L}$ and the simple lottery $(T_1:EU(\hat{L}), T_K:1 - EU(\hat{L}))$, where $EU(\hat{L}) = \Sigma_i q_i \cdot EU(L_i)$.

---

*Indicates a difficult exercise.

CHAPTER 11

Moral Hazard and Incomplete Insurance

OVERVIEW OF CHAPTER 11

11.1   Introduction

Because the future is inherently uncertain, all people find themselves faced with risk. Most families risk having their house destroyed by a fire or other natural disaster. On a brighter note, many families risk winning their state lottery. Insurance markets consist of buyers and sellers of risk. An insurance policy is a contract in which a household or firm transfers all or part of some risk it faces to someone else, typically an insurance company. For example, almost all families face the risk that one of the family's breadwinners will die while still young and productive, leaving the rest of the family with little or no income. A **life insurance** contract allows a family to transfer this risk to an insurance company, thereby reducing the uncertainty surrounding its future income. Similarly, a **futures contract** allows a farmer to reduce his uncertainty about the price he will be paid for his crops. The seller of the futures contract commits to buying the farmer's future crop at a predetermined price. This commitment transfers the price risk from the farmer to the investor who sells him the futures contract.[1]

A family with only one income earner and no other sources of income will typically be willing to pay a high price, relative to the income at risk, to protect itself against the sudden loss of this income. Such a household is said to be **poorly diversified.** In contrast, an insurance company that already owns a large collection of similar risks—only a few of which will eventually result in claims—will be willing to sell an additional policy for a relatively low price. The insurance company is said to be **highly diversified.** As a result, a deal can be struck between the family and the company. This suggests that there should be mutually acceptable terms under which large insurance companies will buy most of the risks facing households.

Casual empiricism suggests, however, that many types of insurance coverage are not provided at all by private insurers, even though we would expect buyers to be willing to pay more for the insurance coverage than the sellers would need to be paid to provide it. For example, workers cannot purchase private insurance against the risk that they will be laid off. College students cannot insure themselves against the risk that they will fail their college courses and will have to leave school or retake some of their classes. And businesses cannot insure themselves against bankruptcy. Furthermore, where privately provided insurance protection does exist, it is often incomplete. For example, almost all insurance policies against the risk of an auto collision limit the extent of coverage through the use of deductible clauses or expenditure limits. The purpose of this chapter is to explain why insurance coverage is so incomplete, that is, why so many apparently mutually beneficial exchanges are not completed.

One reason for the lack of complete insurance protection is the existence of **moral hazard:** the ability of insurance buyers to take actions that are unobservable to the insurance company and that alter the amount of risk they transfer to the insurance companies.[2] To see what we have in mind, consider the risk to a student from failing his college courses. The probability that this will happen depends, in part, on how hard the student tries to prevent this from happening. One thing the student could do, for example, is to study more. Unfortunately, monitoring the student's study effort is prohibitively expensive, if not impossible. As a result, any insurance company that agrees to compensate the student in the event of failure will have to provide the same compensation whether the student studies a lot or a little. Since a contract of this form partially shields the student from the adverse consequences of failure, the insurance reduces the marginal benefit from spending a lot of time studying. As a result, we would expect the student to reduce his effort as the amount of insurance protection purchased increased. This

---

[1]This does not mean that the farmer may not eventually be unhappy that he purchased this contract. It simply means that the farmer can be certain of the price he will receive.

[2]Another reason is *adverse selection:* a market situation in which the insurance buyer is better informed of the likelihood and magnitude of the loss than is the insurer. When there is adverse selection, the buyer's willingness to buy an insurance policy on some terms, but not others, allows the company to infer some of the buyer's private information. The problem of adverse selection requires new concepts and tools and will be examined in Part V.

reduction in the student's effort is the "moral hazard" to which the insurance company is exposed. The insurance company must take this into account in determining whether to offer insurance, what price to charge for it, and whether to restrict the amount of insurance the student can buy.

11.2   Insurance in the Absence of Moral Hazard

Consider Melissa, a hypothetical stockroom worker for a hypothetical grocery store. On the first of every month, the store decides how many people it will employ that month. Sometimes the store reduces its employment and lays off workers who worked for it the previous month. Sometimes the store increases its employment, calls back workers who were laid off the previous month, and advertises for new workers. Because of Melissa's low seniority at the store, she faces a 50% chance of being laid off in any given month. Layoffs last only one month, since the firm has a policy of calling back any laid-off worker the following month. As we will see in Chapter 12, if Melissa is laid off, she may not be able to find another job immediately. For the moment we will suppose that if she is laid off, she has no chance of finding another job for a month. Whenever she is not laid off, Melissa earns $1,000 per month. It follows that each month Melissa has a 50% chance of earning $1,000 and a 50% chance of earning nothing. For the moment, we will assume that the probability of a layoff is a fixed number outside Melissa's control and known to everyone. Since our goal is to understand why unemployment insurance is provided by the government rather than by private insurers, we will assume that Melissa has no government-provided unemployment insurance benefits.

Melissa has a von Neumann-Morgenstern utility function (VNMU), which depends on her monthly income Y, denoted $U(Y)$. We will measure income in thousands of dollars per month. So an income of 0.5 means an income of $500 per month. U is increasing in income but at a decreasing rate. The latter implies that Melissa is *risk averse*.[3] Without insurance, her expected utility each month equals $0.5 \cdot U(0) + 0.5 \cdot U(1)$. We will refer to this expected utility as her **reservation utility** and denote it by U_0. This is the expected utility she can obtain on her own without trading away any of her income uncertainty. Since she is assumed to maximize expected utility she will never enter into any trades that result in an expected utility lower than U_0.

At the end of each month, Melissa can buy an **unemployment insurance policy** from the Allcounty Insurance Company. This insurance policy reimburses her some fraction of her monthly income if she is unemployed the following month. The size of the reimbursement, denoted by I, is called the policy's **indemnity.** In return for the insurance company's commitment to pay Melissa I in the event she is unemployed, the company requires Melissa to pay it a nonrefundable **premium,** P. An unemployment insurance policy is, therefore, completely specified by two numbers: the premium, P, and the indemnity, I. We will refer to a policy by the ordered

---

[3]If you have forgotten what risk aversion means, review Section 10.7.

pair (P, I). We will quote the indemnity and premium in thousands of dollars per month. For example, the policy $(0.1, 0.8)$ requires Melissa to immediately pay Allcounty a premium of $100 ($= 0.1 \cdot \$1,000$) and Allcounty to pay Melissa $800 ($= 0.8 \cdot \$1,000$) in the event that she is unemployed the following month.

If Melissa purchases the policy (P, I), then her expected utility for the following month at the time of the purchase equals

$$EU(P, I) = 0.5 \cdot U(I - P) + 0.5 \cdot U(1 - P). \qquad [11.1]$$

Melissa will buy the policy (P, I) only if the expected utility from this policy is greater than or equal to her reservation utility: $EU(P, I) \geq U_0$. Any policy that promises to pay Melissa her full month's wages if she is laid off, a policy in which $I = 1$, is said to provide Melissa with **full insurance** against the risk of unemployment. Such a policy guarantees that Melissa's income in the coming month will equal $1 - P$, regardless of whether she is unemployed. If $1 > I$, then the policy **underinsures** Melissa against the risk of unemployment; and if $1 < I$, then the policy **overinsures** her against the risk of unemployment.[4]

If Melissa buys the policy (P, I) from Allcounty, then—assuming no administrative costs[5]—the company gets the premium income P, regardless of whether Melissa is laid off or not, but only has to pay the indemnity I if she is laid off. The probability of having to pay out money is 0.5. The company's expected profit from the policy, denoted $ER(P, I)$ equals

$$ER(P, I) = P - 0.5 \cdot I. \qquad [11.2]$$

If $ER(P, I) = 0$, then the policy is **actuarially fair.** If $ER(P, I) > 0$, then the policy is **actuarially unfair;** and if $ER(P, I) < 0$, the policy is **actuarially superfair.** Clearly, a policy is actuarially fair if and only if $P = 0.5 \cdot I$.

Price competition between insurance companies, coupled with their ability to diversify away all risk, will cause them to offer only actuarially fair policies. In order to keep our analysis simple, we will assume that the unemployment insurance market is a *contestable monopoly*.[6] Recall that a market is *contestable* if entry into and exit from the market are costless regardless of the size of the firm and there are potential competitors who will enter if there is any profit to be made from doing so. Although Allcounty is the only company offering insurance, in equilibrium it offers only actuarially fair insurance.[7]

---

[4]At this stage of the analysis you should not apply a pejorative meaning to the terms "underinsurance" and "overinsurance." Perhaps better terms would be "less-than-full insurance" and "more-than-full insurance." Later on, however, there will be a normative sense to these terms, which will make them well-chosen.

[5]There are three possible sources of administrative costs: (1) the cost of writing a new policy; (2) the cost of processing a claim; and (3) the cost of paying a validated claim by selling the asset bought initially with the premium income. Insurance companies refer to this as their **load factor.**

[6]You may want to review Chapter 2, Section 4 on the theory of contestable monopoly before going further.

[7]Actually, since in reality there are administrative costs, the contract must be slightly unfair in order for the firm to break even.

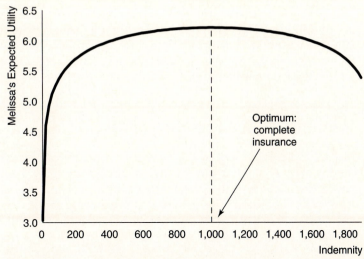

FIGURE 11.1 Melissa's expected utility from fair insurance as a function of the level of indemnity.

Melissa's expected utility after buying an actuarially fair policy $(0.5 \cdot I, I)$ equals

$$\mathbf{E}U(0.5 \cdot I, I) = 0.5 \cdot U(I - 0.5 \cdot I) + 0.5 \cdot U(1 - 0.5 \cdot I). \qquad [11.3]$$

Figure 11.1 shows the graph of $\mathbf{E}U(0.5 \cdot I, I)$ when $U(Y) = \ln(Y)$. From this plot it is clear that, if offered the entire set of actuarially fair insurance policies, Melissa's optimal decision is to purchase a policy with an indemnity of 1 ($1,000) in return for a premium of $0.5 \cdot 1 = 0.5$ ($500). That is, Melissa will choose to buy full insurance against the risk of unemployment. With this policy, Melissa is guaranteed an income of $500 regardless of whether she is laid off or not. We leave it as an exercise for you to show that Melissa's decision to buy full insurance does not depend on the functional form we assumed for her VNMU. It only depends on the fact that she is being offered actuarially fair insurance and that she is risk averse. For future reference, we will state the general result as a formal proposition.

> **THEOREM 11.1:** Suppose a risk-averse decision maker faces the loss of a fixed amount of wealth, X, with a fixed probability, π. Suppose further that this decision maker can purchase any amount of indemnity, I, at the actuarially fair price of $P = \pi \cdot I$. Then the decision maker's best decision is to fully insure herself and choose an indemnity level of X.[8]

---

[8]This proposition can be extended to situations where the size of the loss is itself random. In such cases, the level of reimbursement will, in general, depend on the size of the loss. If the insurance premium charged is actuarially fair—meaning now that the premium equals the probability of a loss times the expected size of the loss—then the insurance buyer will choose a policy that reimburses her fully for her loss whatever its size.

Since she is risk averse, Melissa is willing to pay more than the fair premium to buy full insurance. The insurance company, being forced to charge an actuarially fair premium, is also willing to sell her insurance at a fair rate. An exchange that benefits her and does not hurt the insurance company will take place and there will be no market failure.

11.3   Insurance in the Presence of Moral Hazard

Moral hazard is present in the market for unemployment insurance if two conditions hold: First, after purchasing an insurance policy, the insurance buyer can take actions that alter the probability of the loss or the size of the loss. Second, it is so costly to observe these actions that monitoring the buyer's actions is economically infeasible. Because of these high monitoring costs, the insurance company cannot make the terms on which they will pay the indemnity depend on the buyer's subsequent actions. They can't do this because they will not be able to determine when these terms have been met.

Both of these conditions hold in the market for unemployment insurance. First, when Melissa learns that she has been laid off from her current job, she does not have to wait passively until she is recalled by the grocery store. She can, instead, search for another job. The more effort she puts into her search, the higher her probability of finding another job. Second, although Allcounty can costlessly verify Melissa's employment status, the company cannot monitor her search effort at all. Melissa knows her search effort, of course, but the insurance company would never trust her to report it truthfully. As a result, Allcounty's unemployment insurance policies must indemnify Melissa if she is unemployed regardless of the amount of effort she puts into finding another job.

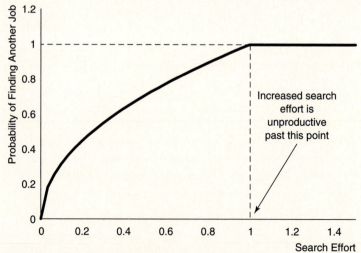

FIGURE 11.2   The probability that Melissa will find another job after she is laid off.

We will denote her job search effort by E and will denote by $\pi(E)$ the probability that she finds another job after she is laid off. The probability of finding a job increases as her search effort increases, but at a decreasing rate, and she will not find another job if she does not search at all. The second requirement means $\pi(0) = 0$. We will assume that $\pi(E) = \min\{\sqrt{E}, 1\}$. This function is graphed in Figure 11.2. Since searching for a job is costly, Melissa will never expend an effort greater than 1. We will assume hereafter, therefore, that $E \leq 1$.

For the sake of simplicity, we will assume that if Melissa does not immediately go out and find another job on the first of the month, she will remain unemployed the rest of the month. This allows us to ignore the complication of random lengths of unemployment. Either she is employed all month and earns $1,000 or she is unemployed all month and earns nothing.

Since searching for a job is costly, Melissa must balance the marginal cost of additional searching with the marginal expected net benefit. This means that her von Neumann-Morgenstern utility function no longer depends solely on her income, Y, but also on the level of effort, E, she puts into her search. To simplify our calculations, we will assume that this utility function takes the form $U(Y, E) = \log_2(Y) - E.$[9]

The net financial benefit of a successful search equals the difference between her income if she finds another comparable job (paying $1,000) and the indemnity, I, paid by her policy. The higher the indemnity, the smaller the net benefit from finding another job. Hence, Melissa will search less the higher the indemnity paid by her policy.

Full unemployment insurance, which provides her the same income if she is unemployed as she would get if she found another job, reduces the net benefit of immediately finding another job to zero. If Melissa has full unemployment insurance, then she will not search for another job when she is laid off and so will not work that month for sure. As a result, the probability that she is unemployed for a month will be 50%. On the other hand, if Melissa's policy offers her only partial indemnity against the loss of income, she may find it worthwhile to engage in some search. This will reduce the probability of being unemployed in any given month to $0.5 \cdot \pi(E)$. Since the probability of being unemployed affects the insurance company's expected profit or loss on any policy, the insurance company must look ahead and foresee how Melissa will behave *after* she buys one of its policies, before it knows how to price the policies. Notice that this is very different from a commodity such as bread. Most bakers are uninterested in what their customers do after they sell them a loaf of bread.

Melissa and Allcounty are playing a **principal–agent game** in which the company is the "principal" and Melissa is the "agent." The game tree is shown in Figure 11.3. There are five moves in this game. Allcounty moves first and announces its **premium schedule** $P(I)$. The premium schedule lists the price

---

[9]At the cost of added complexity, we could have made her utility function depend on income and leisure and measured her job search effort by the amount of leisure she has to give up to search for another job.

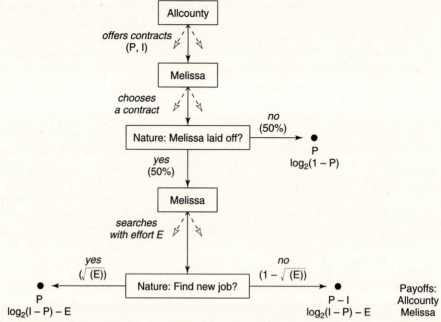

FIGURE 11.3 Game tree for the principal–agent game played between Allcounty Insurance Company and Melissa.

charged for every level of indemnity. Melissa moves second and decides how much insurance to buy. Nature moves third and chooses whether Melissa is laid off or not. If she is not laid off, the game ends. Otherwise, Melissa moves again and chooses how hard to search for a job. Nature moves last and determines whether she finds another job or not. If she finds another job, she takes it and the insurance policy becomes void. If she fails to find a job, the policy comes into force and the firm pays her the amount specified in her contract.

A strategy for Allcounty consists of a premium schedule $P(I)$ that lists the price charged for each level of indemnity. We will continue to assume that the insurance market is a contestable monopoly. In equilibrium, Allcounty must earn an expected profit of zero on each policy it sells.

Since Melissa moves twice, a strategy for Melissa has two components: the first is an *indemnity level* for each possible premium schedule and the second is her *job search effort level* for each possible insurance contract chosen. A subgame perfect equilibrium requires that: (1) Melissa's choice of search effort be optimal given the insurance policy chosen; (2) Melissa's choice of indemnity level be optimal for the given insurance schedule, assuming that she will then engage in the optimal search effort; and (3) Allcounty's premium schedule allows it to break even at every indemnity level, assuming that Melissa buys the indemnity and engages in the job search effort that maximizes her expected utility.

If Melissa buys the policy (P, I), is laid off, puts in an effort of E searching for another job, and finds another job, her payoff is $\log_2(1 - P) - E$. If she doesn't find another job, then her insurance policy comes into force and her payoff is $\log_2(I - P) - E$. So, if she purchases the policy (P, I) and is laid off, then the expected utility from expending an effort of E searching for another job is

$$\mathrm{E}U(P, I, E) = \sqrt{E} \cdot \log_2(1 - P) + (1 - \sqrt{E}) \cdot \log_2(I - P) - E. \qquad [11.4]$$

Consider the choice of effort level that maximizes $\mathrm{E}U(P, I, E)$. We will denote this level of effort by E^*. You are asked to verify in the exercises that

$$E^*(P, I) = \begin{cases} 0 & \text{if } I \geq 1 \\ \left(\frac{1}{2}\log_2\left(\frac{1 - P}{I - P}\right)\right)^2 & \text{if } \dfrac{1 + 3P}{4} < I < 1 \\ 1 & \text{if } I \leq \dfrac{1 + 3P}{4}. \end{cases} \qquad [11.5]$$

Six of Melissa's isoeffort curves—insurance polices that induce her to put in the same amount of effort searching for another job when she is laid off—are graphed in Figure 11.4. We argued earlier that the optimal search effort would equal zero if Melissa were to buy complete insurance. We see from Figure 11.4 that optimal effort is also zero for policies that overinsure her. The set of insurance policies that result in zero search effort lie in the shaded region in Figure 11.4.

Recall that if Allcounty sells the policy (P, I) to Melissa, then the only time it will have to pay out I is when Melissa loses her job and does not find another

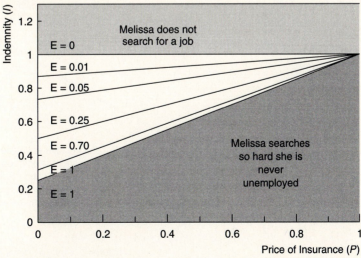

FIGURE 11.4 Optimum search effort as a function of indemnity and the price of insurance if Melissa is laid off.

one. The probability that both events occur equals $0.5 \cdot (1 - \pi(E^*(P, I)) = 0.5 \cdot (1 - \sqrt{E^*(P, I)})$. Allcounty's expected profits equals $ER(P, I) = P - 0.5 \cdot (1 - \sqrt{E^*(I)}) \cdot I$. Since the insurance market is a contestable monopoly, in equilibrium, Allcounty must exact break even on all of its contracts. This means that any break-even contract (P, I) must satisfy the identity

$$P = 0.5 \cdot (1 - \sqrt{E^*(P, I)}) \cdot I = 0.5 \cdot \left(1 - \tfrac{1}{2}\log_2\left(\frac{1 - P}{1 - P}\right)\right) \cdot I. \qquad [11.6]$$

If we define p as the cost of insurance per dollar of indemnity, which equals the ratio $\frac{P}{I}$, then Eq. [11.6] implies that the only contracts that break even are of the form $(\tilde{P}(p), \tilde{I}(p))$, where

$$\tilde{P}(p) = p \cdot \tilde{I}(p)$$
$$\tilde{I}(p) = (p + (1 - p) \cdot 2^{(2 - 4p)})^{-1}. \qquad [11.7]$$

The graph of the zero-profit level of coverage as a function of the price is displayed in Figure 11.5. An important property of these contacts is that as the level of indemnity goes up, so does the price. The more protection Melissa buys, the higher the cost per dollar of coverage. This is very different from buying tomatoes, where the cost per tomato usually does not depend on the amount purchased or, if it does, the cost per tomato goes *down* as the amount of tomatoes purchased goes up. The insurance company charges much more for higher levels of

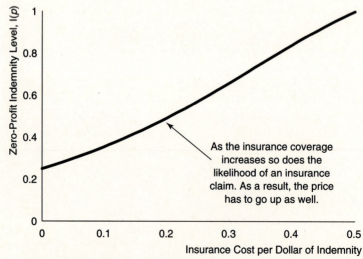

FIGURE 11.5 The actuarially fair price of insurance as a function of the amount of indemnity purchased, taking into account the moral hazard caused by Melissa's ability to alter the effort she puts into searching for another job when she is laid off.

protection, not because of monopolistic price discrimination, but because it can foresee that higher levels of insurance protection will result in more frequent insurance claims. If Melissa buys the policy $(\tilde{P}(p), \tilde{I}(p))$, then should she lose her job, her effort to find a new job rather than filing a claim for unemployment insurance is

$$
\begin{aligned}
E^*(\tilde{P}(p), \tilde{I}(p)) &= \left(\tfrac{1}{2}\log_2\!\left(\frac{1 - \tilde{P}(p)}{\tilde{I}(p) - \tilde{P}(p)}\right)\right)^2 \\
&= \left(\tfrac{1}{2}\log_2\!\left(\frac{\tilde{I}(p)^{-1} - p}{1 - p}\right)\right)^2 \qquad\qquad [11.8] \\
&= (\tfrac{1}{2}\log_2(2^{(2-4p)}))^2 \\
&= (1 - 2p)^2.
\end{aligned}
$$

It only remains to determine how much insurance Melissa purchases when she is offered the actuarially fair set of policies, $(\tilde{P}(p), \tilde{I}(p))$. If there were no moral hazard, we know that Melissa would purchase complete insurance. Will that still be true when there is moral hazard?

Melissa must purchase her insurance before she knows whether she is going to be laid off. So the purchase of the policy $(\tilde{P}(p), \tilde{I}(p))$ is essentially the purchase of a lottery ticket with three possible outcomes: (1) she is not laid off; (2) she is laid off but finds a new job; or (3) she is laid off and does not find a new job. The probability that each of these events will occur and Melissa's payoff if they do are shown in Table 11.1.

Melissa chooses the break-even contract that maximizes her expected utility

$$
\begin{aligned}
\mathrm{E}U(\tilde{P}(p), \tilde{I}(p), E^*(\tilde{P}(p), \tilde{I}(p))) &= 0.5 \cdot (1 - p \cdot \tilde{I}(p)) + (0.5 - p) \cdot (1 - p \cdot \tilde{I}(p) \\
&\quad - (1 - 2p)^2) + p \cdot (\tilde{I}(p) - p \cdot \tilde{I}(p) - (1 - 2p)^2) \\
&= 0.5 + p - 2p^2. \qquad\qquad [11.9]
\end{aligned}
$$

Table 11.1   *A Summary of Melissa's Situation Prior to Purchasing Insurance*

Melissa's Situation	Probability of Occurring	Melissa's Payoff
Not laid off	0.5	$1 - \tilde{P}(p) = 1 - p \cdot \tilde{I}(p)$
Laid off but finds another job	$0.5 \cdot \pi(E^*(p \cdot \tilde{I}(p), \tilde{I}(p)))$ $= 0.5 \cdot \tfrac{1}{2}\log_2\!\left(\dfrac{\tilde{I}(p)^{-1} - p}{1 - p}\right)$ $= 0.5 - p$	$1 - \tilde{P}(p) - E^*(\tilde{P}(p), \tilde{I}(p))$ $= 1 - p \cdot \tilde{I}(p) - (1 - 2p)^2$
Laid off but does not find another job	$0.5 \cdot (1 - \pi(E^*(p \cdot \tilde{I}(p), \tilde{I}(p)))$ $= 0.5 \cdot \left(1 - \log_2\!\left(\dfrac{\tilde{I}(p)^{-1} - p}{1 - p}\right)\right)$ $= p$	$\tilde{I}(p) - \tilde{P}(p) - E^*(\tilde{P}(p), \tilde{I}(p))$ $= (1 - p) \cdot \tilde{I}(p) - (1 - 2p)^2$

GAME THEORY IN ACTION: The S&L Mess: Double Moral Hazard

Between 1981 and 1986, 530 savings and loan associations ("thrifts"), 12% of all thrifts in existence at that time, failed or were forced to merge to avoid failure. This exceeded the number of thrifts that failed during the Great Depression of the 1930s. By 1986 more than 450 additional thrifts were insolvent, using generally accepted accounting principles (GAAP)—which greatly overvalued the fixed rate as mortgages held by thrifts by valuing them at face value, rather than at market value—and as many as a quarter of the thrifts were probably insolvent by stricter "market-to-market" accounting rules. By 1992 the cost to the taxpayers from the losses suffered by the Federal Savings and Loan Insurance Corporation (FSLIC) had a present value of between $100 and $200 billion.

Unlike the banking panics of the Great Depression, the thrift "meltdown" was not initially caused by a deep economic depression or some unanticipated wave of foreclosures and bankruptcies. The problem was deeply structural. The typical thrift balance sheet had a severe case of what bankers call "mismatched maturities": Their assets consisted almost entirely of 30-year fixed-rate home mortgages, most of which would not come due for 10 to 20 years, and their liabilities consisted almost entirely of passbook savings accounts, all of which could be closed in a few minutes. This is all right as long as interest rates are stable, as was the case between the 1930s, when thrifts were created, and the early 1960s. But between 1965 and 1982 short-term interest rates in the United States increased gradually from 4% to 16%. Thrifts were forced to pay higher and higher interest rates to their depositors but were saddled with loans whose interest income was frozen at the levels that prevailed in the 1950s and 1960s. This resulting financial hemorrhaging was matched by a drop in the thrifts' net worth. Net worth fell because of the steep decline in the market value of the mortgages thrifts owned.

When the market value of a thrift's assets fell below the value of its liabilities, the banking authorities should have closed the firm's doors, sold off the assets, and paid off the depositors using the funds from the asset sales and those accumulated over the years by the FSLIC. But this was not done. Instead, the FSLIC and the Federal Home Loan Bank Board (FHLBB) engaged in **regulatory forbearance** and allowed the insolvent thrifts to continue to operate. Many accounting gimmicks were used to hide the growing losses of the SLA industry, among them allowing thrifts to value their loans at their "book" rather than at their market value and allowing them to include among their assets a hard-to-value intangible asset called "goodwill." The result was that the losses of the insolvent thrifts grew with every uptick in interest rates.

Why did the FSLIC and FHLBB do this? Here are at least three reasons: First, the FHLBB, besides being a bank regulator and overseer, was also the industry's promoter and spokesperson in Washington. As a result, it became too enmeshed in the industry. Second, as early as the mid-1970s the FSLIC no longer had enough funds to close all the insolvent thrifts. Third, the FSLIC and FHLBB regulators did not want to publicly admit that their agencies were in trouble. There was a lot of wishful thinking that if they just waited long enough interest rates would come down and the crisis would disappear. The misuse by the thrift regulators of their authority to supervise and close insolvent thrifts is one of the ways in which moral hazard figures in this tale.

Regulatory forbearance exposed taxpayers to a new form of moral hazard and the insolvent thrifts took full advantage of it. They aggressively sought out new deposits and used the funds to make increasingly risky loans for increasingly doubtful projects. If the projects succeeded, then the rewards could be used to make the institution solvent again. And if the projects failed and the loans were defaulted, these thrifts were already insolvent and the depositors were insured, so the depositors and shareholders were no worse off than before. In essence, the insolvent thrifts tried to use the federal government's high credit rating to gamble their way out of their financial hole.

In this endeavor they were aided by an increase in FSLIC insurance coverage in 1980 and bank and thrift deregulation in 1982. The increase in insurance coverage from $40,000 per *account* (*not* per person) to $100,000 made it possible for large depositors to break up their funds and spread them among many thrifts to get complete insurance protection. These **brokered deposits** allowed even small thrifts in out of the way places to obtain billions of dollars in new deposits. The bank and thrift deregulation allowed thrifts to loan funds for a much wider—and riskier—spectrum of activities than simple home mortgages. Thrifts built shopping centers in the middle of the Arizona desert, bought billions of high-yield, high-risk "junk" bonds, and lent funds to start up old Colorado gold mines and to breed Kentucky racing horses. Although some of this activity was deliberately fraudulent, much of it was completely legal. Thrift managers were simply trying to maximize shareholder value with the financial tools that had been put at their disposal. Contrary to common opinion, fraud of the kind committed by Charles Keating of Lincoln Savings and Loan, through headline grabbing (Lincoln's losses were more than $2 billion), played a minor role in the S&L debacle.

This quadratic function is maximized at the price $p^* = 0.25$ ($25 per $100 of coverage). At this price, Melissa can purchase a utility-maximizing indemnity of

$$I^* = \tilde{I}(p^*) = \frac{1}{0.25 + 0.75 \cdot 2^{(2-4\cdot0.25)}} = \frac{4}{7} \approx 0.57 \text{ (57\% coverage). For this much}$$

coverage, she pays the premium $P^* = \tilde{P}(p^*) = 0.25 \cdot 0.57 = 0.14$ ($140). With this amount of coverage, when Melissa loses her job, she searches for a new one with effort $E^* = E^*(\tilde{P}(p^*), \tilde{I}(p^*)) = (1 - 2 \cdot 0.25)^2 = 0.25$, and she finds a new one with probability $\pi(0.25) = \sqrt{0.25} = 0.50$. Even though she is being offered actuarially fair insurance, Melissa will not buy complete insurance. If she could buy more insurance at a price of $0.25, she would. She cannot obtain more insurance at this price, however, because it is common knowledge that if Melissa bought more insurance, her behavior would change. Specifically, she would no longer search as hard for a new job when she was unemployed and, therefore, would be more likely to file a claim. With only 57% coverage, she willingly searches so hard for another job whenever she is laid off that the probability of finding one is 50%. Nevertheless, 25% (= 0.5 × 0.5) of the time she will find herself unemployed and suffer an income loss of $430.

11.4   Welfare Effects of Moral Hazard

We have just seen that moral hazard can cause Melissa to choose incomplete insurance. But she does this in order to get the benefit of a lower price. As a result, it is not immediately clear whether Melissa is hurt by moral hazard or not. We will now show that, in general, she is hurt.

Suppose Allcounty could observe Melissa's job search effort at no cost. In this case, Allcounty can make its price, P, depend on *both* E and I. Since only search effort affects the risk of unemployment, there is no longer any reason to make the price depend on the amount of indemnity purchased. The principal–agent game changes. Allcounty still moves first and announces its premium schedule, but the price schedule depends now on the search effort promised, E, not the amount of coverage bought, I. Melissa continues to move second and choose an indemnity level, I. But now she must also precommit herself to a search effort, E. If she loses her job but then fails to search as hard as she has promised to, then she voids the contract and Allcounty does not have to pay her anything. You may think this is harsh treatment, but without such strong measures, Melissa will have an incentive to promise a high search effort. She will do this in order to get a low insurance price. But when she is actually thrown onto the job market, she will put out a lower search effort and Allcounty will find itself paying out in claims more than it collects in premium revenue.

Suppose again that Allcounty is constrained to offering only actuarially fair insurance contracts—say by the threat of entry by competitors—then the equilibrium premium schedule $\tilde{\tilde{P}}(E)$ must satisfy the equation

$$\tilde{\tilde{P}}(E) = 0.5 \cdot (1 - \pi(E)) \cdot I = 0.5 \cdot (1 - \sqrt{E}) \cdot I. \qquad [11.10]$$

Since the price per dollar of indemnity no longer depends on the level of I, she can buy as much insurance as she wants. For example, if she commits to an effort level of 0.25, she will pay a price per dollar of indemnity of 0.25. At this price she *could* choose to buy $570 of indemnity for a total premium of $140. In short, if she wants to, she *could* put herself in precisely the same circumstances she was in when there was moral hazard. What she *can* do, and what she *will* do, however, are not the same things. Since every policy offered is fair, we know from Theorem 11.1 that Melissa will choose complete insurance, whatever her choice of effort. If she were to commit to an effort level of 0.25, she would not choose $570 of indemnity but $1,000. Melissa could choose the effort and indemnity levels that are optimal when there is moral hazard, but she need not. This means she is no worse off when Allcounty can monitor her search effort and eliminate the moral hazard. She can do strictly better, however. We leave it as an exercise for the reader to show that Melissa's optimal effort level, E^*, maximizes

$$\log_2(1 - \tilde{\tilde{P}}(E)) - \tfrac{1}{2}E = \log_2(0.5 + 0.5 \cdot \sqrt{E}) - \tfrac{1}{2}E. \qquad [11.11]$$

You will be asked in the exercises to find E^* and to show that $\pi(E^*) \approx 48\%$. So in equilibrium, in any month, Melissa has about a 50% × (1 − 48%) = 26% chance of being unemployed.

11.5 Government Responses to Market Failure in the Unemployment Insurance Market

We have identified a possible instance of *market failure,* that is, a market equilibrium in which there is an inefficient allocation of resources. In this instance, the resources are job search effort and income risk. It is tempting to conclude from this that the government should intervene and provide public unemployment insurance. But this is a mistake. Unless the government can observe Melissa's job search effort at much lower cost than can a private insurance company, the government cannot get out of the moral hazard game. And unless it can do this, it cannot improve on the market allocation, inefficient though it might be. There do not appear to be any efficiency gains from having unemployment insurance provided by a government agency rather than by private firms through a competitive insurance market. Indeed, government-provided unemployment insurance provides the same disincentives for searching.

11.6 Summary

In the insurance game, the principal (in our game, the insurance company), offers a policy to the agent (in our game, the consumer). The policy is completely defined by the premium and the indemnity value. Unfortunately, the firm faces moral hazard since the consumer can alter the probability of being unemployed after she takes out a contract. Since it is too costly for the insurance company to distinguish between workers who don't bother looking for another job and workers who do but are merely unlucky, the insurance company finds itself in a delicate position. It can't offer a complete insurance policy, for example, without eliminating all incentive to search for another job when the consumer is laid off. As a result, the consumer will often end up being underinsured.

The problem of moral hazard exists in a variety of risky situations. Life and medical insurance providers, for example, cannot easily observe the efforts taken by their policyholders to reduce their risk from various costly diseases such as stroke, heart attack, cancer, or diabetes. As a result, the insurance providers cannot reward policyholders for changing their diets, increasing their amount of exercise, or breaking their smoking habits.

The source of Melissa's problem is her inability to credibly commit herself to searching hard for another job when she is laid off at her current one. It has been suggested that one way Melissa could solve this problem would be by posting a bond, a contract in which one party promises to do something under penalty of losing money or property. Unfortunately, bonding does not resolve the problem of observability, because "search effort" may be interpreted differently by Melissa and the insurance company.

11.7 Further Reading

Economists have known for some time that insurers are exposed to moral hazard. Excellent non–game-theoretic discussions are those by Mark Pauly's "Overinsurance and Public Provision of Insurance: The Roles of Moral Hazard and Adverse

Selection," *Quarterly Journal of Economics,* 87 (1974), pp. 44–54, Michael Spence and Richard Zeckhauser's "Insurance, Information, and Individual Action," *American Economic Review,* 61 (1971), pp. 380–87, and Kenneth Arrow's "Uncertainty and the Welfare Economics of Health Care," *American Economic Review,* 53 (1963), pp. 941–69. These three articles can also be found in the collection of readings by Peter Diamond and Michael Rothschild, *Uncertainty in Economics* (New York: Academic Press, 1978).

11.8 Discussion Questions

1. Identify real-world situations in which moral hazard might be a problem.
2. What policy suggestions might be reasonable to help deal with moral hazard problems?
3. What functional forms for Melissa's utility function might be realistic?
4. What functional forms for Melissa's probability of getting a job function might be realistic?

11.9 New Terms

actuarially unfair/fair/superfair
brokered deposits
futures contract
highly/poorly diversified
indemnity
life insurance
load factor
moral hazard

over/under/fully insure
premium
premium schedule
principal–agent game
regulatory forbearance
reservation utility
unemployment insurance

11.10 Exercises

EXERCISE 11.1*

Suppose that Melissa is offered unemployment insurance at the fair price of $0.50 per dollar of indemnity and there is no moral hazard. Then Melissa's problem is to determine the indemnity level that maximizes $EU(0.25, I) = 0.5 \cdot U(0.5 \cdot I) + 0.5 \cdot U(1 - 0.5 \cdot I)$.

(a) Suppose Melissa's VNMU is $I(Y) = \sqrt{Y}$. Show that Melissa's best action is to purchase full insurance.

(b) Show that it is optimal for Melissa to purchase full insurance as long as the VNMU is increasing and concave.

EXERCISE 11.2

Show that $EU(P, I, E)$, defined in Eq. [11.4], is a concave function of E, and that Eq. [11.5] is the value of E that maximizes Melissa's expected utility as a function of the policy terms I and P.

---

*Indicates a difficult exercise.

EXERCISE 11.3

Suppose Melissa's effort can be costlessly observed by Allcounty and, therefore, the firm can make the price it charges her for unemployment insurance depend on E. If Allcounty breaks even on every insurance policy it sells, so that $\tilde{P}(E) = 0.5 \cdot (1 - \pi(E)) = 0.5 \cdot (1 - \sqrt{E})$, show that Melissa's best strategy is to insure herself fully and to choose the effort level that maximizes Eq. [11.8].

EXERCISE 11.4

Suppose that Joe has a VNMU utility function that depends on his income for the term and the number of waking hours he spends studying. He has 1,260 waking hours in the term. Specifically, $U(Y, S) = Y - (\frac{S}{126})^2$, where S is the number of hours he spends studying and Y is his income. Joe currently has an income of $2,000 per term. As an incentive to study, Joe's parents have offered him the following deal: If Joe passes his economics course, he will be given an additional $100; if he fails, he will be given nothing. The probability of his passing equals $\frac{S}{1,260}$. An insurance company is considering offering Joe income insurance. The insurance company cannot observe S.

(a) If Joe cannot buy insurance against the possibility of failing, what percentage of his waking hours will he spend studying?

(b) If the insurance company were for some reason to offer Joe complete insurance for a fair price, what percentage of his waking hours would he spend studying?

(c) If the insurance company is profit maximizing and has to offer fair policies, but does not have to offer complete insurance, what policy would they offer Joe?

EXERCISE 11.5

Suppose a worker can either wear safety goggles or not. The goggles are not 100% effective against the loss of an eye and the worker works alone so that no one knows whether he is wearing goggles or not. Losing an eye reduces the present value of the worker's future income by $1 million. The probability of losing an eye if safety goggles are worn is 10%; if goggles are not worn, it is 15%. An insurance company is considering offering insurance for eye injury. It cannot observe whether goggles are worn or not. Wearing goggles costs the worker (in present value terms) $10,000 in psychic income. The worker has a utility function given by $U(Y) = \ln(Y)$ and currently has an income stream whose present value is $2 million.

(a) Draw a game tree for this game.

(b) Consider an insurance policy that has a premium (in present value) of $100,000 and an indemnity of $1 million. What are the rational decisions for the worker to make? Is this a fair policy? Explain.

(c) Find what, if any, insurance policy would be written if an insurance company could only sell policies that broke even on average.

CHAPTER 12

Moral Hazard and Involuntary Unemployment

OVERVIEW OF CHAPTER 12

12.1   Introduction

At the heart of Keynesian macroeconomic theory is the notion of **involuntary unemployment.** A worker is said to be involuntarily unemployed if employers will not hire him or her at the current market wage rate even though the worker is willing and able to work at that wage. In the standard competitive model of wage determination, involuntary unemployment is inconsistent with market equilibrium. Keynesian macroeconomists have usually assumed that wages are "sticky downward"—meaning that firms do not lower wages when there is an excess supply of labor. This will certainly be true for firms that sign long-term contracts. If this is the case, then a downward shift in the demand for labor caused, say, by an increase in the price of oil will not reduce the wage rate and will create a spell of involuntary unemployment driven by disequilibrium in the labor market.

Here, we will modify the standard model in a very different fashion. Those of you who have seen the movie *On the Waterfront* may recall the scene in which actor Marlon Brando, playing Terry Malloy, a sometime boxer and dockyard worker in New York City, is offered a day's wages to unload the cargo of a newly arrived ship. Unlike his fellow workers, Terry does not spend the day lifting heavy cartons. Instead, he lounges in a corner reading magazines. At the end of the day all the workers, including Terry, have spent the same number of hours on the job, but the firm hiring them received very different levels of productivity. The central aspect of our modification of the standard model is the recognition that employees have control over the degree of energy they expend on the job. Of course, "cracking the whip" over the employees' heads can reduce the level of shirking, but hiring someone to crack the whip is costly. The firm has to balance the increased effort of its workforce from increased monitoring against the higher monitoring costs.

The consequences of introducing these simple and realistic features into the standard labor market model are dramatic. Even if wages are freely flexible, there is involuntary unemployment *in equilibrium*. As we alluded to above, this model has two central characteristics. First, labor productivity is determined partly by the firm's technology and partly by the "work effort" chosen by its workers. Second, it is costly for the firm to continually monitor the intensity with which its employees are working. The result is that each firm and its workers play a principal–agent game with moral hazard. The firm is the principal, the workers are the agents, and the unobservable action is work effort.

In the type of labor market we will consider, a market-clearing wage is not a stable equilibrium. If every firm were paying a market-clearing wage, then any one of them could increase its profits by unilaterally increasing the wage it pays. Profits rise because the higher wage makes it more costly for the firm's workers to shirk and run the risk of getting fired. The increased productivity from the reduction in shirking more than compensates for the higher wage. The firm is said to be paying an *efficiency wage* since it is using its wage as a strategic variable to affect its labor productivity.

If all firms adopt the strategy of paying an efficiency wage, then the market wage will rise above the market-clearing level and involuntary unemployment will appear in the labor market. In the new equilibrium, all firms pay the same wage. But the threat of being fired continues to motivate the workers to work hard since when a worker loses his current job, he risks a spell of unemployment. Workers who are out of work are not hired even though they offer to work for less than the current wage, since the employers expect such "cheap" workers to be less productive (shirk more often) than their current staff. This is an example of the old adage: "You get what you pay for."

12.2   A Simple Model of Moral Hazard in the Labor Market

We will use the following simple example to illustrate our ideas concretely. Smartshop, a trucking firm, employs workers at its single distribution warehouse. These workers load and unload delivery trucks, move pallets around the warehouse, keep inventory records, check for spoilage and vermin infestation, and, more generally, do "whatever needs to be done." Because the workers are constantly changing tasks, they have the opportunity to shirk. The fraction of the time that a worker is not shirking will be denoted by E ("effort"). By definition, E lies between 0 and 1. If there are L workers working for the firm, and every worker's effort level equals E, then $L \cdot E = L_E$ is the **effort-adjusted labor force.** The firm's revenue, R, depends on the output produced by its workforce and therefore is a function of L_E, not L. The revenue function strictly increases with L_E, but at a decreasing rate. We also assume that labor is essential, so that $R(0) = 0$. One functional form that has all these properties is $R(L_E) = \ln(1 + L_E)$. This is Smartshop's revenue function. Smartshop's costs, however, depend on the number of workers it contracts, L, and the contracted wage, W. Of course, Smartshop would prefer to pay wages for hours actually worked, L_E, but that is unobservable.

Smartshop's costs are $W \cdot L$. We define the firm's **efficiency wage** as $W_E = \dfrac{W}{E}$.

The efficiency wage is the amount of money paid per unit of time actually worked. This is in contrast to the **posted wage**, W, which is the amount of money paid per unit of time on the job. So, for example, if the posted wage is \$5/hr but only one hour of real work is done for every two hours on the job (that is, $E = \frac{1}{2}$), then the efficiency wage equals \$10/hr. The firm's profits, V, can be written as a function of the number of workers hired, the wage paid, and the workers' effort level.

$$V(W, L, E) = \ln(1 + L \cdot E) - W \cdot L \qquad [12.1]$$

The workers each have an identical von Neumann-Morgenstern utility function, U, which depends on the wage, W, and work effort, E. For the sake of simplicity, suppose the utility function takes the form

$$U(W, E) = W \cdot \left(1 - \frac{3}{8} \cdot E\right). \qquad [12.2]$$

If a worker leaves the firm, she obtains a reservation utility of $\overline{U}$. There is no reason for a worker to accept employment from a firm that generates a utility less than the reservation utility.

Smartshop disciplines workers by firing them if they are caught shirking "too often." Smartshop finds its shirkers by engaging in random spot checks. How often is "too often" is set by law. The probability that a worker is caught shirking too often and is fired is a decreasing function of E. This probability, denoted $\pi(E)$, is the same for every worker and takes the form

$$\pi(E) = 1 - E. \qquad [12.3]$$

More generally, we could have modeled the probability of being caught shirking as a function of the resources the firm devotes to catching shirkers. That extension of our model is beyond the scope of this book.

The strategic interaction between Smartshop and each of its workers can be modeled as a principal–agent game with moral hazard. The game tree is shown in Figure 12.1. The firm moves first and selects the wage it will pay its workers, W, and the number of workers it will try to hire, L. The workers move next, each making her or his decision independently and simultaneously. Since the workers are assumed to be identical, Figure 12.1 depicts the situation facing a "representative" worker, whom we will call Natalie. Natalie first decides whether to work for the firm. If she rejects the firm's wage offer, then the game ends. If she accepts it, then she moves a second time and chooses her level of work effort E. This move is not observed by the firm. All the information the firm gets about E is determined from its occasional spot checks. The result of these checks we will call "Nature," who moves last and decides whether Natalie is caught shirking too often and is fired.

Since Natalie's work effort is not directly observable, Smartshop cannot write a contract in which Natalie's wage depends on her effort. This means Smartshop's strategy consists simply of the selection of a single wage, W, and the number of laborers hired, L. Natalie's strategy is more complicated. It consists of a rule for rejecting or accepting the firm's wage and a rule for determining the intensity with which she works depending on the wage she is paid. The relationship between her wage and her effort is denoted $E(W)$.

This game has three possible outcomes. The first outcome is that the firm makes a contract offer that is rejected by Natalie. The firm's payoff is assumed to equal 0 and Natalie's payoff is assumed to equal her reservation utility, $\overline{U}$. The

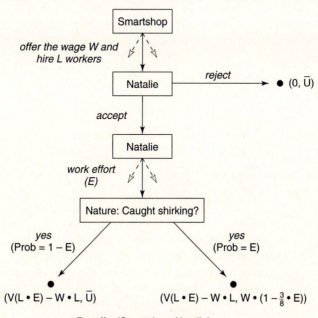

Payoffs: (Smartshop, Natalie)

FIGURE 12.1 The game tree for the principal–agent game played between Smartshop and Natalie.

value of $\overline{U}$ depends on Natalie's employment opportunities outside the firm or on the level of unemployment insurance the government might provide. This reservation utility is treated by both Natalie and the firm as exogenous. We will consider its determination later. The second possible outcome is that Natalie accepts the firm's offer and is not fired for excessive shirking. In this case, the firm's payoff equals $\ln(1 + L \cdot E) - W \cdot L$ and Natalie's payoff equals $W \cdot (1 - \frac{3}{8}E)$. The third outcome is that Natalie accepts the firm's offer, but is found to be shirking too often and is fired. We will, for the moment, assume the firm can immediately replace her with an identical worker at the wage it was paying Natalie. As a result, the firm is unaffected by her firing. The firm's payoff is, therefore, $\ln(1 + L \cdot E) - W \cdot L$, and Natalie's payoff is her reservation utility, $\overline{U}$.

We will solve this game using backward induction. Since Natalie moves last, she treats the firm's wage and the reservation utility as given. If Natalie accepts the firm's offer, she chooses her work effort, E, so as to maximize her expected utility, which is given by

$$\mathrm{E}U(W, E) = \pi(E) \cdot \overline{U} + (1 - \pi(E)) \cdot W \cdot (1 - \tfrac{3}{8}E). \qquad [12.4]$$

When we substitute the expression for $\pi(E)$ given in Eq. [12.3] into Eq. [12.4] we get

$$\begin{aligned}\mathrm{E}U(W, E) &= (1 - E) \cdot \overline{U} + W \cdot E \cdot (1 - \tfrac{3}{8}E) \\ &= \overline{U} + (W - \overline{U}) \cdot E - \tfrac{3}{8}W \cdot E^2.\end{aligned} \qquad [12.5]$$

We leave it as an exercise for you to show that the optimal level of effort $E^*(W)$ equals

$$E^*(W) = \begin{cases} 0 & \text{if } W \le \overline{U} \\ \dfrac{4}{3} \cdot \left(\dfrac{W - \overline{U}}{W}\right) & \text{if } \overline{U} < W \le 4 \cdot \overline{U} \\ 1 & \text{if } 4 \cdot \overline{U} < W. \end{cases} \qquad [12.6]$$

You can verify that $0 \le E^*(W) \le 1$ for every wage, and that $E^*(W)$ is an increasing function of the posted wage.

Natalie accepts the firm's offer if and only if her expected utility from doing so is greater than or equal to her reservation utility, or $\mathrm{E}U(W, E^*(W)) \ge \overline{U}$. You can verify that this will be the case if and only if $W \ge \overline{U}$.

Having determined the workers' optimal strategy, we now look at Smartshop's optimal response to it. Our assumption that the game being played is common knowledge implies that the firm knows exactly how the workers will react to any posted wage. First we look for dominated strategies. For example, if the firm offers a posted wage of $\overline{U}$, then it will attract workers. But notice that $E^*(\overline{U}) = 0$. That is, the workers will refuse to do any work! The firm is unequivocally better off offering a wage of 0 rather than a wage of $\overline{U}$, assuming that $\overline{U} > 0$. So offers of $\overline{U}$ or below are dominated strategies and can be discarded. From now on we will only consider wages that are strictly above $\overline{U}$. Furthermore, offering a wage rate of $4 \cdot \overline{U}$ will induce the workers not to shirk at all. By offering any wage above $4 \cdot \overline{U}$ the firm gains no productivity while increasing its costs. All wages in excess of $4 \cdot \overline{U}$ are dominated.

Earlier we wrote Smartshop's profits as a function of the wage, the size of the labor force, and the effort given by the workers. Incorporating the workers' optimal effort level into this function allows us to rewrite profits as a function only of the posted wage and the number of workers.

$$V(W, L) = \ln(1 + L \cdot E^*(W)) - W \cdot L. \qquad [12.7]$$

The firm has discretion over both W and L. Maximizing profits means solving

$$\frac{\partial V(W, L)}{\partial W} = 0 \text{ and } \frac{\partial V(W, L)}{\partial L} = 0 \qquad [12.8]$$

simultaneously, and checking to see that the optimum values, W^* and L^*, result in positive profits. Substituting the optimal effort function into the profit function, while eliminating the dominated strategies, results in

$$V(W, L) = \ln\left(1 + \frac{4}{3} \cdot \left(\frac{L \cdot (W - \overline{U})}{W}\right)\right) - L \cdot W. \qquad [12.9]$$

Therefore,

$$\frac{\partial V(W, L)}{\partial W} = \frac{4 \cdot L \cdot \overline{U}}{W \cdot (3 \cdot W + 4 \cdot L \cdot (W - \overline{U}))} - L \qquad [12.10]$$

and

$$\frac{\partial V(W, L)}{\partial L} = \frac{4 \cdot (W - \overline{U})}{3 \cdot W + 4 \cdot L \cdot (W - \overline{U})} - W. \qquad [12.11]$$

We leave it as an exercise for you to show that the optimal posted wage equals

$$W^* = 2 \cdot \overline{U} \qquad [12.12]$$

and the optimal number of workers equals

$$L^* = \begin{cases} \dfrac{1 - 3 \cdot \overline{U}}{2 \cdot \overline{U}} & \text{if } \overline{U} \leq \frac{1}{3} \\ 0 & \text{otherwise.} \end{cases} \qquad [12.13]$$

GAME THEORY IN ACTION: Did Henry Ford Pay Efficiency Wages?

On January 5, 1914, the Ford Motor Company, a firm employing 14,000 workers, announced that it would "inaugurate the greatest revolution in the matter of rewards for its workers ever known to the industrial world." Ford's "revolution" consisted of reducing the work day from 9 to 8 hours and more than doubling its minimum daily wage from $2.34 to $5.00 a day. The reaction was swift. The *New York Times* reported that in the days following the announcement, "Twelve thousand men, more than congregated around the plant on any day last week celebrated the [five-dollar day] with a rush on the plant which resulted in a riot. . . . The crowd began forming at 10 o'clock last night in spite of a blizzard."

Why did Henry Ford do this? Economists Daniel Raff and Lawrence Summers ("Did Henry Ford Pay Efficiency Wages?" *Journal of Labor Economics,* Vol. 5[2], [October, 1987], pp. S57–S86) find that the most plausible reason was to reduce high labor turnover and absenteeism and increase the labor efficiency of its workers. Raff and Summers offer many forms of evidence. First, there are Henry Ford's own words, "There was . . . no charity in any way involved. . . . We wanted to pay these wages so that the business would be on a lasting foundation. . . . A low wage business is always insecure. . . . The payment of five dollars a day for an eight hour day was one of the finest cost cutting moves we ever made." This was no idle boast, as Table 12.1 shows.

*Table 12.1 **Ford Motor Company Real Net Income (1910 Dollars)***

Year	Ford Net Income (millions of 1910 dollars)	Model T Prices (1910 dollars)
1910	4.1	950
1911	7.4	787
1912	13.1	669
1913	26.4	585
1914	30.4	526
1915	36.9	448

Source: Raff and Summers, Tables 2 and 5, pp. S75–S77.

How was it possible to increase the wage bill by $10 million, cut (real!) prices by 15%, and increase profits by 20%? Raff and Summers believe the answer is simple: Ford's supracompetitive (efficiency) wage resulted in long queues for jobs and a substantial increase in labor productivity. They estimate (albeit somewhat crudely) that labor productivity increased by 40–70% between 1914 and 1915. The increased productivity was accomplished in a number of ways: a 75% fall in absenteeism, a 90% decline in discharges, and a decline in the turnover rate from 370% just before the 8-hour day was introduced to 16% a year after. Although other auto makers did not immediately copy Ford's example, as the industry adopted Ford's manufacturing technological innovations, it also gradually copied his high-wage policies. By 1928, well before the United Auto Workers had any market clout, wages in the auto industry were 40% greater than in the rest of manufacturing.

Note that the firm is deliberately paying its workers "more than it has to" (that is, more than the workers' reservation utility) in order to get the workers to work harder. We will hereafter assume that $\overline{U} \leq \frac{1}{3}$. The optimal wage results in a subgame perfect effort level of

$$E^*(W^*) = \frac{4}{3} \cdot \left(\frac{W^* - \overline{U}}{W^*} \right) = \frac{2}{3}. \qquad [12.14]$$

That is, any individual worker will be shirking one third of the time. This relatively high level of shirking is due to the firm's limited ability to monitor its workers. It can get a higher effort level only by paying a higher wage. At some point, this is no longer cost effective. As a result, the firm's optimal efficiency wage equals

$$W_E^* = \frac{W^*}{E^*} = 3 \cdot \overline{U}. \qquad [12.15]$$

12.2.1 MORAL HAZARD AND INCREDIBLE PROMISES

At the subgame perfect equilibrium, the expected utility of any employed worker, including Natalie, equals

$$EU(W^*, E(W^*)) = \frac{1}{3} \cdot \overline{U} + \frac{2}{3} \cdot (2 \cdot \overline{U}) \cdot \left(1 - \frac{3}{8} \cdot \frac{2}{3}\right) = \frac{4}{3} \cdot \overline{U}. \qquad [12.16]$$

So by accepting a job offer from Smartshop, she earns $\frac{1}{3} \cdot \overline{U}$ more than her next best option. Suppose, however, that Smartshop never makes her an offer. It would appear that there is room for a mutually beneficial exchange. Specifically, Natalie would be willing to take any offer that generates an expected utility level of $\overline{U}$ or above. At the effort level expected of the rest of the workforce, $\frac{2}{3}$, she would be willing to accept a posted wage of $\frac{4}{3} \cdot \overline{U}$ or more. Smartshop would be happy to replace one of its existing workers, who the firm is paying $2 \cdot \overline{U}$, with someone who provides the same level of effort at a lower wage. The problem is that Natalie is unable to credibly commit to the effort level of $\frac{2}{3}$. Once she contracts for the lower wage, the firm hiring her must rationally expect her to expend less effort than its other workers. Hence, the firm will not get as much output from her as they will from their other employees. But, is the lower wage worth it? We still need to show that there is *no* wage offer between $\overline{U}$ and $2 \cdot \overline{U}$ that increases the firm's profits.

There are two cases to consider. First, Smartshop might simply add Natalie to their workforce. Second, they might replace an existing worker with Natalie. Without hiring Natalie, subgame perfect equilibrium profits for Smartshop equal

$$V(W^*, L^*) = \ln\left(1 + \frac{1 - 3 \cdot \overline{U}}{3 \cdot \overline{U}}\right) - (1 - 3 \cdot \overline{U}). \qquad [12.17]$$

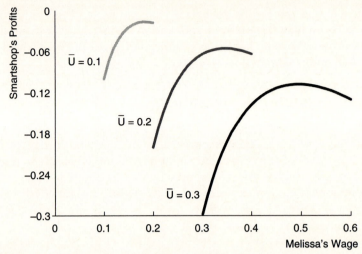

FIGURE 12.2 The net gain to Smartshop from hiring Natalie as an additional worker.

If Smartshop hires Natalie at a wage W_{Nat} without firing anyone else, their profits will equal

$$V(W^*, W_{Nat}, L^* + E^*(W_{Nat}))$$

$$= \ln\left(1 + \frac{1 - 3 \cdot \overline{U}}{3 \cdot \overline{U}} + \frac{4 \cdot (W_{Nat} - \overline{U})}{3 \cdot W_{Nat}}\right) - (1 - 3 \cdot \overline{U}) - W_{Nat}. \qquad [12.18]$$

The net gain from hiring Natalie as an additional worker is the difference between Eq. [12.17] and [12.18], which simplifies to

$$\ln\left(1 + 4\overline{U} - \frac{4\overline{U}^2}{W_{Nat}}\right) - W_{Nat}. \qquad [12.19]$$

The graph of this function for different values of $\overline{U}$ and $\overline{U} \leq W_{Nat} \leq 2\overline{U}$ is shown in Figure 12.2. The important thing to notice is that the net gain from hiring Natalie as a new employee is always negative.

Alternatively, Smartshop could fire one of their current employees and hire Natalie in his or her place. You can verify that the net gain to Smartshop under these circumstances equals

$$\ln\left(1 + 2\overline{U} - \frac{4\overline{U}^2}{W_{Nat}}\right) + (2\overline{U} - W_{Nat}). \qquad [12.20]$$

The graph of this function appears in Figure 12.3. It, too, never rises to a value above zero, and only equals zero when $W_{Nat} = 2 \cdot \overline{U}$.

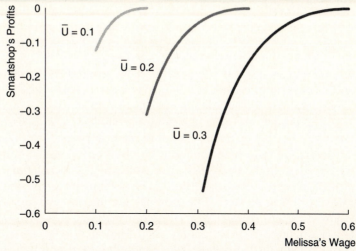

FIGURE 12.3 The net gain to Smartshop from replacing an existing worker with Natalie.

This leaves us with the counterintuitive result that unemployed workers will not be able to offer to work for Smartshop at a lower wage than existing employees and have that offer accepted by the firm. This result would be uninteresting if there were never any unemployment, but such is not the case.

12.3 Completion of the Model: The Necessity of Involuntary Unemployment

The equilibrium we have just derived is deficient in one important respect: it treats the workers' reservation utility, $\overline{U}$, as exogenous. In reality, of course, this variable is determined by the labor market. We need to complete the model by deriving $\overline{U}$. We begin with an obvious question: What are Natalie's alternatives to working for Smartshop? Clearly, either she works for some other firm or she is unemployed. Suppose there are a number of other trucking firms competing with Smartshop for warehouse workers like Natalie. To keep things simple, we will suppose that these firms are identical to Smartshop. This means they have the same revenue function, the same objectives (maximizing expected profits), and the same worker-monitoring technology. We will also suppose that the firms make their wage and employment decisions independently and simultaneously.

Recall that the subgame perfect expected utility for Natalie if she takes employment at Smartshop, or for that matter at any trucking firm, is $\frac{4}{3} \cdot \overline{U}$. In equilibrium, all firms will pay the same wage. If this wage clears the market, then any worker who is fired from one job can obtain immediate employment at another job. This is what the term "market-clearing wage" normally means in economics, at least from the labor suppliers' perspective. But if this is the case, then the workers are always employed and the reservation utility, $\overline{U}$, must equal the subgame perfect expected utility from being employed at the other firm. But we have just seen that the subgame perfect expected utility from being employed is $\frac{4}{3} \cdot \overline{U}$. This implies a contradiction, assuming that $\overline{U} > 0$. A market-clearing wage is not consistent with subgame perfect equilibrium behavior. This shows that guaranteed employment at the market wage is not an equilibrium, so, there must be unemployment—*involuntary unemployment*.

The existence of unemployment *in equilibrium* implies that every firm faces an excess supply of labor. There are more applicants for jobs than there are jobs available. One way of rationing these jobs is on a first-come-first-serve basis. Those just fired go to the back of the unemployment line and those in the front go into a firm to replace those just fired. The spell of unemployment is what gives the threat of firing its sting and provides the impetus for greater effort. Unemployment is more unattractive, and the reservation utility, $\overline{U}$, is lower, the longer the spell of unemployment, denoted T_U. That is, $\overline{U}$ is an increasing function of the length of unemployment. Let L_T denote the total number of workers (which we will assume for simplicity is a fixed number). If there are n firms, each employing L^* workers, then the number of unemployed workers will be $L_T - n \cdot L^*$. We also know that each firm will catch one third of their workers shirking too much and will fire them. They will immediately pull exactly the same number of workers off the unemployment roles. This means that $\frac{n \cdot L^*}{3}$ people previously unemployed will find work. The number of periods workers can expect to be unemployed, once they are fired, is given by

$$T_U = \frac{\text{Stock of unemployed workers}}{\text{Flow of new hires}} = \frac{L_T - n \cdot L^*}{\dfrac{n \cdot L^*}{3}} = \frac{3 \cdot L_T}{n \cdot L^*} - 3. \qquad [12.21]$$

Since $L^* = \dfrac{1 - 3 \cdot \overline{U}}{2 \cdot \overline{U}}$, we find

$$T_U = \frac{6 \cdot \overline{U} \cdot \left(L_T + \dfrac{3}{2} \cdot n - \dfrac{n}{2 \cdot \overline{U}} \right)}{n \cdot (1 - 3 \cdot \overline{U})}. \qquad [12.22]$$

So, for example, if there are 100 workers and each of two firms employs 30 people in equilibrium, then 40 people are unemployed at any time and 20 workers are being fired and replaced each period. As a result, it takes two periods for a newly fired worker to work his or her way to the front of the queue and be rehired. We leave it as an exercise for you to show that T_U is an increasing function of $\overline{U}$.

The equilibrium reservation utility depends on the length of unemployment spells; at the same time, the length of unemployment spells depends on the reservation utility. The equilibrium occurs when the reservation utility, $\overline{U}^*$, pro-

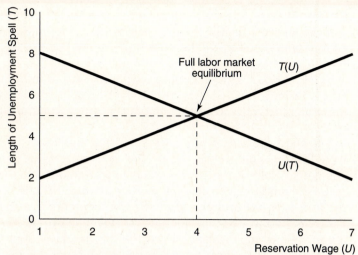

FIGURE 12.4 The determination of the equilibrium reservation utility $\overline{U}^*$.

duces the length of unemployment, $T_U(\overline{U}^*)$, that makes being fired sufficiently unattractive to produce the reservation utility $\overline{U}$. Mathematically, this is the solution to the following "fixed-point" equation:

$$\overline{U}^* = \overline{U}(T_U(\overline{U}^*)). \qquad [12.23]$$

Equation [12.23] can be expressed diagrammatically as the intersection of the graphs of the reservation utility function and the length of unemployment function. Hypothetical functions are shown in Figure 12.4.

We lack only the function $\overline{U}(T_U)$ to complete the model. Unfortunately, deriving this function requires us to move from the static framework in which we initially modeled this market to an explicitly dynamic one. The correct dynamic model must address the fact that a worker's work history will consist of alternating spells of unemployment and employment, with a random transition between them. This requires advanced analytical tools, such as *dynamic programming*, which is beyond the mathematical level of this book.

12.4   Summary

A recurring theme in game theory is the importance of information in determining how rational players behave. Information is at the heart of the problem of moral hazard and principal–agent games in general. In the game considered in this chapter, the principal, a trucking firm, offers a wage contract to employees. The employee (the agent) accepts or rejects the contract and then decides how much effort to put into the job. The firm cannot directly observe the level of effort costlessly. As a result, it must use imperfect devices such as random spot checks to deter shirking. In these circumstances, we showed that involuntary unemployment is not only consistent with a competitive labor market equilibrium, but that equilibrium also requires the existence of some positive level of unemployment. Essentially, the unemployment spell gives the sting to the firm's threat to fire shirking workers. This, of course, flies in the face of traditional, non–game-theoretic economic thinking. As a result, the firm consciously pays its workers more than the minimally acceptable amount in order to induce them not to shirk as often.

If you believe that firing workers is an inefficient way of getting them to work harder, you are not alone. We share that belief with you. Indeed, one alternative method of getting workers to work more is to form a labor union and make the union responsible for policing its members.[1] In return for doing this, the firm pays the (more productive) workers more than they would otherwise. One reason for the decline in union membership during the last 30 years may be the increasing sophistication in monitoring workers using computers and new telecommunication devices such as pagers and portable phones.

12.5 Further Reading

The literature on the effect of moral hazard in the labor market has now grown quite large. Many of the seminal journal articles have been collected by George Akerlof and Janet Yellen in *Efficiency Wage Models of the Labor Market* (Cambridge: Cambridge University Press, 1986). The labor market model in this chapter borrows liberally from the pioneering work of Robert Solow ("Another Possible Source of Wage Stickiness"), Carl Shapiro and Joseph Stiglitz ("Equilibrium Unemployment as a Worker Discipline Device"), and James Foster and Henry Wan ("Involuntary Unemployment as a Principal–Agent Equilibrium"). All three articles are included in Akerlof and Yellen's collection.

12.6 Discussion Questions

1. What other ways could workers credibly commit themselves to putting in more work effort when this effort is imperfectly observed at best?

2. Have you or someone you know ever shirked on the job? How frequently? What were the penalties for shirking? How painful were they?

12.7 New Terms

efficiency wage	involuntary unemployment
effort-adjusted labor force	posted wage

---

[1]Ironically, in the movie *On the Waterfront*, alluded to at the start of the chapter, it is Terry Malloy's union bosses that makes sure he is not caught shirking.

12.8   Exercises

EXERCISE 12.1

Consider the unemployment game played between Smartshop and Natalie. Suppose that the probability of getting caught shirking is equal to $1 - E^2$.

(a) Find an expression for Natalie's expected utility.

(b) Find an expression for Natalie's optimal effort function.

(c) Find an expression for the optimum wage the firm pays Natalie.

(d) Find an expression for the optimum level of effort Natalie makes at the optimum wage.

(e) Show that the optimum wage is greater than $\overline{U}$.

EXERCISE 12.2

Suppose that $V(W, L, E) = \sqrt{L \cdot E} - W \cdot L$ and $E^*(W)$ is given by Eq. [12.6]. What does the model predict will happen to W^*, L^*, and Natalie's expected utility, $EU(W^*, E^*)$, if her reservation utility, $\overline{U}$, increases?

EXERCISE 12.3

What unilateral actions could an unemployed worker take that would convince the firm it could pay this worker less than its current workers, yet not experience a higher rate of shirking? (Hint: How could Natalie make it very costly for her to be caught shirking?)

PART IV

Static Games with Incomplete Information

CHAPTER 13

Bayesian Nash Equilibrium

OVERVIEW OF CHAPTER 13

13.1 Introduction

One of the most important new ideas in economics is that private information is a valuable resource whose use can affect economic and social welfare as much as the use of labor, land, or technology. By "private information" we mean knowledge about the state of the world possessed by some players but not by others. Examples of private information include the financial condition of a company that is known to some stockholders but not to others; the willingness of a new job applicant to work overtime on short notice that is not known to her potential employer; and the results of a survey of a union's members about a proposed new labor contract with a firm that is not shared with the firm's negotiators.

Unfortunately, economists cannot analyze the production and consumption of information the same way they study physical resources such as labor, steel, or wheat. Among its many anomalies, information tends to be indivisible, simultaneously consumable by many people, and capable of causing discontinuous changes in the behavior of those who come to possess it. Classical price theory,

273

with its reliance on marginal analysis and price-taking behavior, does not handle well goods that have such features. Fortunately, game theory has proved to be a powerful tool for modeling information and studying its economic role.

We saw in Part I that when one player is ignorant of the moves made by other players, the strategic form and Nash equilibrium are adequate tools for finding the mutually rational strategies of the players. Nash equilibrium "only" requires that every player's available strategies and payoffs be common knowledge. Unfortunately, this requirement rules out many important strategic situations such as auctions, labor contract negotiations, and corporate takeover battles. In situations such as these, some players often do not know the values others place on the possible outcomes. For example, a firm may not know the labor contract terms its labor union would accept rather than strike. An oil company bidding for the right to drill for oil on federal land may not know what another bidding company believes this right is worth. This means that the payoffs are not common knowledge. Such games are known as games of **incomplete information.**

To see the problem that incomplete information creates, consider your search for a job when you graduate from college. You will have a better sense of what activities you would like to be engaged in than will any potential employer. In the hopes of securing a job offer with some employer, you might very well find it in your interest to try to convince her that the job she has described to you is exactly what you are looking for. The employer's problem is to determine whether to believe you, and your problem is to make your claim believable. This is clearly a strategic situation. Yet neither you nor your interviewer know exactly whom you are dealing with. If you do not express concern over the relatively low initial salary offer the interviewer proposes, will this be interpreted as a signal that you like the job a lot and are confident that you will do well and quickly secure raises; will the interviewer interpret this to mean that you are desperate and will accept anything; or will she decide that your response tells her nothing at all about how much you like the job? Her interpretations of your actions depend on the strategy she thinks you are following. In order to figure out your strategy, she has to know your motives. But your motives (that is, your preferences or payoffs) are precisely what she doesn't know!

Fortunately, John Harsanyi found a way to model and study games in which the players have incomplete information. His solution, one of the things for which he was awarded the Nobel Prize in economics, is to transform games with incomplete information into games with complete but *imperfect* information. The **Harsanyi transformation** treats players who have different payoffs as being of distinct **types.** Harsanyi proposed that such games be modeled by having Nature move first and "choose" each player's type. Players start out knowing their type but not that of their competitors. Players share a common **belief** as to how Nature makes its probabilistic choice. The new game is called a *Bayesian game* and can be analyzed using the tools we have introduced so far. The Harsanyi transformation is described in Section 13.2, along with the associated notion of a *Bayesian Nash equilibrium.* In Section 13.3, we go on to show how mixed strategies can be reinterpreted as uncertainty about the opponent's type. Finally, in Section 13.4, we present the surprising *revelation principle,* which has enabled game theorists to design games that have particularly nice properties—such as auction rules that maximize the seller's expected revenue.

13.2   The Harsanyi Transformation

A very simple example of a game with incomplete information is the **Entry Deterrence Game.** There are two players, an *Incumbent* firm and a potential *Entrant.* The Incumbent must decide whether to expand the capacity of his plant. Simultaneously, the Entrant must decide whether to enter and compete against the Incumbent or stay out of the market. The added capacity will allow the Incumbent to produce more output at lower cost. Because of this, it is profitable for the Entrant to enter if and only if the Incumbent does not expand. The Incumbent's payoffs, however, depend on two things: whether the Entrant enters and the cost of expanding his plant. These costs can be *high* or *low.* If the costs are low, then the payoffs of both players are given in Table 13.1A; if the costs are high, the payoffs are those shown in Table 13.1B. These costs are known to the Incumbent, but not to the Entrant. That is, the Entrant has *incomplete* information about which game is being played. Is it the game on the left or the game on the right?

Regardless of which game is being played, the Entrant, if he could enter based on the Incumbent's expansion decision, would want to enter if and only if the Incumbent did not expand. From the payoffs, she can see that the Incumbent has a dominant strategy when his costs are high: *Don't expand.* The Incumbent also has a dominant strategy when his costs are low: *Expand.* We can go no further with the facts at hand.

Harsanyi's insight was to see that just as the players must form beliefs about how their opponents will play, they must also form beliefs about which game they are playing. Harsanyi proposed modeling strategic situations such as the Entry Deterrence Game as follows: The new game has three players, an Entrant, an Incumbent and Nature. The Incumbent can be of two **types,** "low cost" or

Table 13.1   ***Payoffs in the Entry Deterrence Game***

		(A) *Expansion costs are low*		(B) *Expansion costs are high*	
		Incumbent		*Incumbent*	
		Expand	*Don't expand*	*Expand*	*Don't expand*
Entrant	*Enter*	(−1, 2)	(1, 1)	(−1, −1)	(1, 1)
	Stay out	(0, 4)	(0, 3)	(0, 0)	(0, 3)

Payoffs: (Entrant, Incumbent)

"high cost," where cost refers to the cost of expanding capacity. The Incumbent's payoffs depend on this cost and, hence, on his type. In the new game Nature moves first and determines the Incumbent's type. The Incumbent knows his type (that is, he knows his payoffs), but the Entrant doesn't. The Entrant's payoffs remain common knowledge. The probability that Nature chooses the high-cost Incumbent is called the *prior belief* about this type and is common knowledge. In this example, we will assume that this probability is 1/3. One interpretation of the new game is that Incumbents and Entrants are randomly paired and that the proportion of high-cost Incumbents is 1/3. We will refer to the new model as Entry Deterrence Game II.

A strategy for the Entrant remains a move, either *Enter* or *Stay out.* A strategy for the Incumbent, however, now consists of a *pair* of moves, the move to take when his type is *low cost,* and the move to take when his type is *high cost.* An example of a strategy is (*expand, don't expand*), meaning expand when costs are low and don't expand when costs are high. If the Entrant's strategy is *Enter* and the Incumbent's strategy is (*expand, don't expand*), then with probability $\frac{2}{3}$, the Entrant's payoff is -1 and with probability $\frac{1}{3}$, the payoff is 1. The expected payoff is therefore $\frac{2}{3} \cdot (-1) + \frac{1}{3} \cdot 1 = -\frac{1}{3}$. Similarly, the expected payoff from *Staying out* is 0. We already determined that this strategy is the optimal one for the Incumbent, in the sense that it gives the Incumbent the highest payoff in each of the two possible states of the world. Although the Entrant can predict what the Incumbent will do in each state of the world, she doesn't learn the state of the world until after she moves. Using the terminology introduced in Chapter 10, the Entrant is choosing a lottery. If the Entrant is an expected utility maximizer and the payoffs in Table 13.1 are her von Neumann-Morgenstern utilities of the outcomes, then she will choose the lottery that yields the highest expected payoff. Clearly, *Stay out* is the best response to (*expand, don't expand*). So it seems safe to conclude that {*Stay out*, (*expand, don't expand*)} is a Nash equilibrium for this game, even though we have not yet formally extended this concept to games with incomplete information.

When these equilibrium strategies are played, two outcomes result. If the Incumbent has low costs, then he expands his capacity, but when the Incumbent's costs are high, he does not expand his capacity.

In general, every player may be of more than one type. This would be the case, for example, in an auction in which the bidders' valuations of the object being sold was private knowledge. Furthermore, the players' types may be **stochastically dependent,** meaning that knowledge about one player's type reveals information about another player's type. Again, this would be expected in an auction if the object has a resale value on which the bidders have independent assessments. The assessment of the object's resale value constitutes each bidder's type. If one bidder's assessment is higher than normal, then it probably means that the object's resale value is higher than normal. As a result, we would expect every other bidder's assessment to be higher than normal. The two assessments are said to be positively **correlated.**

Recall that a static game of complete information can be described by its strategic form, which consists of three lists: a list of players, a list of (pure) strategies for each player, and a list of payoffs for each player for every possible collection of strategies, or a strategy profile. In static games, (pure) strategies correspond identically to moves. In a similar fashion, a **static Bayesian game** consists of five lists, all of which are common knowledge: First is the list of players. Second is the list of moves for each player. Moves will be written in lowercase *italics*. A list of moves, one for each player, is a **move profile** and will be enclosed in curly brackets { }. Third is a list of possible types for each player. Types will also be written in lowercase *italics*. Every player knows his own type but may not know the type of the other players. We will denote the "other players" by the index -*i*. A list of types, one for each player, is a **type profile** and is enclosed within square brackets [ ]. The players have a common **prior belief** about the probability of each possible type profile. The probability that the player profile is $[t_1, \ldots, t_N]$ is denoted $P[t_1, \ldots, t_N]$. These probabilities comprise the fourth list. Every move profile $\{m_1, \ldots, m_N\}$ and type profile $[t_1, \ldots, t_N]$ results in a payoff for each player; player *i*'s payoff will be denoted in general as $U_1(m_1, \ldots, m_N, t_1, \ldots, t_N)$. The payoffs make up the fifth list. Notice that a player's payoffs can depend on another player's type as well as her own. For example a firm's profits will in general depend on its workers' productivities (their types) as well as how hard they work (their moves).

The Entry Deterrence Game has two players: Entrant and Incumbent. The Entrant has two possible moves—*enter* and *stay out*—as does the Incumbent—*expand* and *don't expand*. While the Entrant has only one type, *normal*, the Incumbent can be of two types, *low cost* or *high cost*. This means there are two possible type profiles: [*normal, low cost*] and [*normal, high cost*]. If the Entrant had two possible types, four type profiles would have been possible. The prior belief is that the probability of the type profile [*normal, low cost*] is 2/3, while the probability of [*normal, high cost*] is 1/3. The payoffs in the entry deterrence game were given in Tables 13.1. For example, you should verify that $U_{Entrant}(enter, expand, normal, high cost) = -1$.

In general, what can we say about player *i*'s behavior in a static Bayesian game? Clearly player *i*'s move may depend on her type. So a pure strategy for *i* consists of a move as a function of the player's type and will be denoted in general as $S_i(t_i)$. We will write strategies in *italics* and capitalize the first letter. A list of strategies, one for each player, is a *strategy profile* and will be enclosed within curly brackets. Since the players' types are randomly selected, the outcome of a strategy profile will be uncertain. In the terminology of Part III, every strategy profile defines a *lottery* over the set of outcomes. We assume the players are expected utility maximizers and choose among strategies on the basis of *conditonal expected utility*.

Before we can say what we mean by conditional expected utility we must introduce the concept of *conditional probability*. Let t_{-i} be the type profile of the players other than *i*. That is, $t_{-i} = [t_1, \ldots, t_{i-1}, t_{i+1}, \ldots t_N]$. Then $P_i[t_{-i} \mid t_i]$ will denote the probability that the other players have the type profile t_{-i} given that player i has the type t_i. This is an example of a **conditional probability.** This conditional probability can be calculated from the prior belief using the formula

$$P[t_{-i} \mid t_i] = \frac{P[t_1, \ldots, t_{i-1}, t_i, t_{i+1}, \ldots, t_N]}{P_i[t_i]} \qquad [13.1]$$

where $P_i[t_i]$ is the **marginal probability** of player i's type and equals

$$P_i[t_i] = \sum_{t_{-i}} P[t_1, \ldots, t_{i-1}, t_i, t_{i+1}, \ldots, t_N]. \qquad [13.2]$$

In most of the games in this book, the player types will be *stochastically independent* of each other. Informally, player A's type is stochastically independent of player B's type if A cannot learn anything about player B's type from knowledge of his own type. Formally, player i's type is **stochastically independent** of his opponent's types if for every type profile $[t_1, \ldots, t_i, \ldots, t_N]$, we have

$$P[t_{-i} \mid t_i] = P[t_1, \ldots t_{i-1}, t_{i+1}, \ldots, t_N] = \sum_{t_i} P[t_1, \ldots t_{i-1}, t_i, t_{i+1}, \ldots, t_N]. \qquad [13.3]$$

The **conditional expected utility (CEU)** of player i of type t_i when the players adopt the strategy profile $S = \{S_1(t_1), \ldots, S_N(t_N)\}$ is

$$\mathbf{EU}_i(S, t_i) = \sum_{t_{-i}} U_i(S_1(t_1), \ldots S_i(t_i), \ldots, S_N(t_N), t_1, \ldots, t_i, \ldots, t_N) \cdot P_i[t_{-i} \mid t_i], \qquad [13.4]$$

where the summation is over all the possible type profiles of the other players.

The concepts of dominant strategy (both strict and weak), dominant strategy equilibrium, iterated dominant strategy equilibrium, and Nash equilibrium all extend naturally to this new class of games if we replace the word "payoff" with "conditional expected utility." As an example, below we formally define the extension of Nash equilibrium to static Bayesian games, which we will refer to as a *Bayesian Nash equilibrium.*

A strategy profile $S^* = \{S_1^*(t_1), \ldots, S_N^*(t_N)\}$ *is a **Bayesian Nash equilibrium** of a static Bayesian game if and only if for every player* i, *every type* t_i *of player* i, *and every alternative strategy of player* i, *say* $\hat{S}_i(t_i)$, $\mathbf{EU}_i(S^*, t_i) \geq \mathbf{EU}_i(S_1^*(t_1), \ldots, \hat{S}_i(t_i), \ldots, S_N^*(t_N), t_i)$. *That is, the player's strategy is a best response to the strategies of the other players, whatever the player's type.*

We will now confirm that the strategy profile {*Stay out, (expand, don't expand)*} is the only (pure-strategy) Bayesian Nash equilibrium of Entry Deterrence Game II. In order to find all the pure-strategy Bayesian Nash equilibria we have con-

Table 13.2   *Strategic form of the Entry Deterrence Game II.*

		Incumbent			
		(expand, expand)	*(expand, don't expand)*	*(don't expand, expand)*	*(don't expand, don't expand)*
Entrant	Enter	$((-1), (2, -1))$	$((-\frac{1}{3}), (2, 1))$	$((\frac{1}{3}), (1, -1))$	$((1), (1, 1))$
	Stay out	$((0), (4, 0))$	**$((0), (4, 3))$**	$((0), (3, 0))$	$((0), (3, 3))$

Conditional Expected Utilities: ((Entrant), (*low-cost* Incumbent, *high-cost* Incumbent))

structed the strategic form for the game in Table 13.2. This table has a new look. Rows and columns still correspond to strategies of the two players, but the cell entries are different. The number enclosed within the pair of parentheses to the left of the comma is the CEU of the Entrant. The CEU consists of only one number beause the Entrant has only one type. The two numbers enclosed within the parentheses to the right of the comma are the CEU's of the Incumbent. The first number in the pair is the CEU of a *low-cost* Incumbent, and the second is the CEU of a *high-cost* Incumbent. The CEU of the unique Bayesian Nash equilibrium, {*Stay out*, (*expand, don't expand*)}, is displayed in **boldface**.

We will now verify that each player's equilibrium strategy is a best response to the other player's equilibrium strategy, whatever the player's type. Given the Incumbent's strategy (*expand, don't expand*), the Entrant's CEU is $-\frac{1}{3}$ if it *Enters* and 0 if it *Stays out*, implying that the best response is *Stay out*. Given the Entrant's strategy *Stay out*, if the Incumbent is *low cost*, then it maximizes its CEU by adopting either the strategy (*expand, expand*) or (*expand, don't expand*). If the Incumbent is *high cost*, then it maximizes its CEU by adopting either (*expand, don't expand*) or (*don't expand, don't expand*). The strategy (*expand, don't expand*) is the only strategy that is a best response to *Stay out* whatever the Incumbent's type.

13.3   Mixed Strategies Reinterpreted[1]

When we introduced the concept of mixed strategies in Chapter 10, Section 4, you probably felt it odd to assume that players would ever choose their moves randomly. We noted at that time that another interpretation of a mixed strategy is that it represents *uncertainty about what a player is going to do.* We left the origin of this uncertainty vague. John Harsanyi suggested that the uncertainty could be due to the existence of a small amount of uncertainty about the opponent's payoffs. He conjectured that any mixed-strategy Nash equilibrium could always be interpreted as the pure-strategy equilibrium of a very similar game with a small

_____

[1]This section is more mathematically advanced and can be skipped.

Table 13.3 **The Battle of the Sexes (complete information)**

		Rhett	
		Saloon	Dinner club
Scarlett	Saloon	(5, 12)	(0, 0)
	Dinner club	(0, 0)	(10, 4)

Payoffs: (Scarlett, Rhett)

amount of incomplete information, rather than as a belief that the other player was choosing her moves randomly, say by rolling a die or flipping a coin. How can a small amount of ignorance have such an effect? Recall that if it is optimal for a player to use a mixed strategy, then she must be indifferent among some of her moves. The smallest change in any of the payoffs associated with these moves will destroy her indifference. Some move will now be clearly inferior or superior. So if an opponent is even the slightest bit uncertain about these payoffs, he will be uncertain about which move she will make—even if he believes that she is not moving randomly. So she becomes unpredictable—which is the strategic purpose of a mixed strategy. We will now flesh out this idea using a familiar example, the Battle of the Sexes Game first introduced in Chapter 1, Section 7.

Recall that this game involves a couple, Rhett and Scarlett, who are making independent decisions about how to spend the evening. Its strategic form is reproduced in Table 13.3. In Chapter 10, Section 4 we showed that this game has the mixed-strategy Nash equilibrium {(Saloon: $\frac{1}{4}$, Dinner club: $\frac{3}{4}$), (Saloon: $\frac{2}{3}$, Dinner club: $\frac{1}{3}$)} where the first strategy is Scarlett's mixed strategy and the second is Rhett's.

Suppose, however, that these two players are not exactly sure about the other's payoffs. Instead, suppose that Scarlett is somewhat unsure about how much Rhett dislikes the dinner club and Rhett is somewhat unsure exactly how much Scarlett dislikes the saloon. The other payoffs are common knowledge. We can model this by assuming that the payoffs are those given in Table 13.4.

Table 13.4 **The Battle of the Sexes (incomplete information)**

		Rhett	
		Saloon	Dinner club
Scarlett	Saloon	$(5 + \varepsilon_S, 12)$	(0, 0)
	Dinner club	(0, 0)	$(10, 4 + \varepsilon_R)$

Payoffs: (Scarlett, Rhett)

Scarlett knows ε_S but is unsure about the value of ε_R, while Rhett knows ε_R, but is unsure about the value of ε_S. So ε_S is Scarlett's type and ε_R is Rhett's type. Suppose that it is common knowledge that ε_S and ε_R are independent random variables and uniformly distributed between $-\delta$ and $+\delta$. This implies that $E(\varepsilon_R) = E(\varepsilon_S) = 0$. In this variation of our original game, a pure strategy for each player is a function, say $S(\varepsilon)$, from the set of possible types, $[-\delta, \delta]$, to the set of possible moves {*Saloon, Dinner club*}. In general, these functions can be complicated. Fortunately, the Nash equilibrium strategies of each player, $S_S^*(\varepsilon)$ and $S_R^*(\varepsilon)$, are simple and are representable by two numbers, τ_S and τ_R, which we will refer to as *switching parameters*, as follows:

$$S_S^*(\varepsilon) = \begin{cases} Saloon & \text{if } \varepsilon > \delta \cdot \tau_S \\ Dinner\ club & \text{if } \varepsilon \leq \delta \cdot \tau_S \end{cases}$$

$$S_R^*(\varepsilon) = \begin{cases} Saloon & \text{if } \varepsilon < \delta \cdot \tau_R \\ Dinner\ club & \text{if } \varepsilon \geq \delta \cdot \tau_R. \end{cases}$$

[13.5]

The reason that Scarlett's equilibrium strategy takes this form is that as ε increases, the saloon option becomes more attractive, and as ε decreases the dinner club becomes more attractive. So if it is optimal to go to the saloon for some value of ε, say $\tilde{\varepsilon}$, then it remains optimal for all values of ε greater than $\tilde{\varepsilon}$. Likewise, if it is optimal to go to the dinner club for some value of ε, say $\tilde{\varepsilon}$, then it remains optimal for all values of ε less than $\tilde{\varepsilon}$. The reverse holds for Rhett. We will refer to the equilibrium strategies by their switching parameters.

Because the players' moves depend on a variable that the opponent does not know, each will be uncertain about the other's move—*even though the two players are not explicitly randomizing*. Since the players' types are uniformly distributed on the interval $[-\delta, \delta]$, it is easy to show that the equilibrium strategy profile causes Rhett to perceive that Scarlett chooses *Saloon* with probability $\dfrac{1 - \tau_S}{2}$ and causes Scarlett to perceive that Rhett chooses *Saloon* with probability $\dfrac{1 + \tau_R}{2}$. Again, note that neither player is making their move randomly. The uncertainty about their behavior is due to uncertainty about their preferences. We will show that as the parameter δ goes to zero, $\dfrac{1 - \tau_S}{2}$ converges to $\frac{1}{4}$ and $\dfrac{1 + \tau_R}{2}$ converges to $\frac{2}{3}$. These two limits are the equilibrium mixing probabilities in the original complete information game. So the pure-strategy equilibrium behavior of the players in our modified game is very close to that of the players in the mixed-strategy equilibrium of the original Battle of the Sexes.

When ε equals the player's threshold, $\delta \cdot \tau$, the expected utility of choosing *Saloon* exactly equals the expected utility of choosing *Dinner club*. This implies that the two thresholds satisfy the following two equations

$$(5 + \delta \cdot \tau_S)\left(\frac{1 + \tau_R}{2}\right) = 10\left(\frac{1 - \tau_R}{2}\right) \text{ and}$$

[13.6]

$$12\left(\frac{1 - \tau_S}{2}\right) = (4 + \delta \cdot \tau_R)\left(\frac{1 + \tau_S}{2}\right).$$

When δ equals zero, the two equations become linear with solutions $\tau_R = \frac{1}{3}$ and $\tau_S = \frac{1}{2}$, implying that Scarlett perceives that Rhett chooses *Saloon* with probability $\frac{1 + \tau_R}{2} = \frac{2}{3}$ and Rhett perceives that Scarlett choose *Saloon* with probability $\frac{1 - \tau_S}{2} = \frac{1}{4}$. It then follows from the implicit function theorem from calculus that Eq. [13.6] has solutions for values of δ sufficiently close to 0.

13.4   The Revelation Principle and Game Design

Up until now, we have taken all our games as givens and sought their equilibria. The reverse question can be also be asked: Given a set of players, their payoffs over a set of outcomes, and their private information about these payoffs, is it possible to construct a static Bayesian game whose Bayesian Nash equilibrium satisfies certain specified properties? For example, what auction format will maximize the seller's expected revenue? The answer is difficult since so many auction formats are possible. Should the auction be oral or by sealed bid? Should the winner pay her bid or should the price depend, in part, on the bids submitted by the losing bidders? More radical still, should the highest bidder win the auction—or should criteria besides the bids made be used to decide the winner? Should the bidders be charged a fee beforehand? Should the seller set a lower bound on the winning bid, and if so, should this reservation price be announced beforehand or kept secret?

The branch of game theory concerned with such questions is referred to as **mechanism design.** Designing games so that their equilibria have certain nice properties is much more difficult than determining the equilibrium of a single game. Roger Myerson of Northwestern University is responsible for one of the most important tools for designing games. It is called the **revelation principle.** The revelation principle allows the game designer to break the problem into two much more manageable pieces. First, the designer restricts herself to a very simple class of Bayesian games called *incentive compatible direct mechanisms* (ICDM). A **direct mechanism** (DM) is a static Bayesian game in which the players simply report their type to a "referee," and these reports determine the players' payoffs. A DM is **incentive compatible** if truthfully reporting one's type is a Bayesian Nash equilibrium strategy. The designer now searches among this much smaller set of games for the ones with the desired properties. The game designer's work is not done, though, since the ICDM implicitly requires a disinterested "referee" to whom the players report their types. The second step is to find a game format that does not require a referee and has the same equilibrium as the ICDM. This is the optimal game.

Myerson's contribution to mechanism design was to realize that any Bayesian Nash equilibrium of any Bayesian game can always be "represented" by a properly constructed ICDM. By "represented" we mean that for every type profile, the players' moves and payoffs in the equilibrium of the ICDM are identical to those in the equilibrium of the original game. This result is known as the **revelation theorem.** We state and prove it here for static games, but it can be readily extended to encompass dynamic games as well.

> **THEOREM 13.1 (REVELATION THEOREM):** Any Bayesian Nash equilibrium of any static Bayesian game can be represented by an incentive compatible direct mechanism.

Here, we will quickly sketch the argument for the case of two players. For a more rigorous proof, see the articles cited in Section 13.6. Suppose we have a static Bayesian game with two players, Ann and Bart. We will denote their types by t_A and t_B, their moves by m_A and m_B, their strategies by $S_A(t_A)$ and $S_B(t_B)$, and their payoff functions by $U_A(m_A, m_B, t_A)$ and $U_B(m_A, m_B, t_B)$. The common prior belief about the player types is $P(t_A, t_B)$. Suppose $\{S_A^*(t_A), S_B^*(t_B)\}$ is a Bayesian Nash equilibrium strategy profile for this game. We will construct an ICDM that gives both players the same expected payoff as they receive at this equilibrium.

In the ICDM, each player reports his or her type to a neutral referee. These reports will be denoted r_A and r_B. When the players report r_A and r_B, Ann receives the payoff $\tilde{U}_A(r_A, r_B, t_A) = U_A(S_A^*(r_A), S_B^*(r_B), t_A)$ and Bart receives the payoff $\tilde{U}_B(r_A, r_B, t_B) = U_B(S_A^*(r_A), S_B^*(r_B), t_B)$. Note that the DM has been constructed so that if both players report their true types, then they receive the same payoff they would have received in the equilibrium of the original game. So, assuming that the DM is incentive compatible, the DM gives the players the same payoff they would have received in the Bayesian Nash equilibrium of the original Bayesian game. This is the sense in which the DM "represents" that equilibrium. The incentive compatibility of the DM is easy to see. Suppose one player, say Ann, adopts the strategy of always reporting her type truthfully, but the other player, Bart, lies and reports that his type is t' instead of truthfully reporting that his type is t_B. Then, whatever Ann's type, Bart gets the payoff he would have gotten in the original game from making the move $S_B^*(t')$ rather than the move $S_B^*(t_B)$. Since $\{S_A^*(t_A), S_B^*(t_B)\}$ is a Bayesian Nash equilibrium strategy profile for the original game, Theorem 13.2 says that Bart cannot do better by making such a move, and may do worse. It follows that Bart does not do better by misreporting his type than by telling the truth. Since this is true whatever his type, it follows that truthful reporting is a best response to truthful reporting by Ann. It also follows that truthful reporting is Ann's best response to truthful reporting by Bart. So the DM we have constructed to represent the original Bayesian game is incentive compatible.

The revelation theorem allowed Myerson to answer our question about the auction format that maximizes the seller's expected revenue. If each buyer's valuation is known only to that buyer and would not be altered by information about any other buyer's valuation—an auction environment referred to in the auction literature as *independent private values*—then the standard sealed-bid auction will yield to the seller the highest expected bid. We will explore this more in Chapter 14 where we will look at auctions in more detail.

Myerson and Satterthwaite also used the revelation theorem to study bilateral trade, the quintessential economic interaction. They asked the following question: Are there trading rules that ensure that a good will always be voluntarily traded from a seller to a buyer whenever the trade would make them both better off, assuming that each trader's reservation price is known only to that trader? Myerson and Satterthwaite showed that in general the answer is: *No!* Whatever the trading rules used—whether it be take-it-or-leave-it offers, alternating offers, or bilateral auctions, to name just a few—there will always exist reservation prices in which the buyer and seller could both be made better off by trading, yet trading does not take place in equilibrium.

13.5   Summary

We have shown in this chapter how to model and analyze games in which some of the players are unsure about how their opponents will behave. This uncertainty arises because the players have private information about the game's payoffs. Such games are called games of incomplete information and cannot be analyzed using any of the tools we have developed so far.

Fortunately, John Harsanyi found a way to model and study such games. The Harsanyi transformation converts this game with incomplete information into a game with complete but imperfect information. In the new game, players can be of different types. Each player type corresponds to a particular payoff schedule. The game begins with Nature selecting each player's type. Initially, each player knows only his or her type, but not that of any other player. Nature "chooses" the players' types according to probabilities that are common knowledge. These common probabilities are the players' initial beliefs about the game. A game with this structure is called a Bayesian game. A Bayesian Nash equilibrium is a Nash equilibrium of a Bayesian game.

This new type of game provides another interpretation for a mixed strategy of a standard static game with complete information. Instead of explicit randomization by a player, a mixed strategy can be thought of as uncertainty about what the player is going to do. John Harsanyi suggested that this uncertainty could be due to the existence of a small amount of incomplete information about the opponent's payoffs. He conjectured that any mixed-strategy Nash equilibrium could be interpreted as the pure-strategy equilibrium of a similar game with a small amount of incomplete information. We showed how this is possible using the Battle of the Sexes game introduced in Chapter 1.

Bayesian games can also be used to design games with particular properties—or to show that games with certain properties do not exist. This is the domain of mechanism design and the revelation principle. The revelation principle says that the equilibrium outcome of any static Bayesian game can be obtained as an outcome of a simpler game called an incentive compatible direct mechanism. A direct mechanism is a static game in which the players simply report their type to a neutral referee and then each receives a payoff based on these reports. The mechanism is incentive compatible if truthful reporting by every player is a Bayesian Nash equilibrium of the game. We concluded by summarizing a few of the more important results that have been learned about auctions and bilateral trading using the revelation principle.

13.6   Further Reading

A more advanced treatment of the material in this chapter can be found in Chapter 5 of Eric Rasmusen's *Information and Games* (New York: Basil-Blackwell, 1989). Many interesting games involving information are discussed in a nontheoretical way in Avinash, Dixit, and Nalebuff, *Thinking Strategically: The Competitive Edge in Business, Politics, and Everyday Life* (New York: Norton, 1991). An excellent but more advanced analysis of games with incomplete information can be found in Part III of David Kreps's *A Course in Microeconomic Theory* (Princeton: Princeton University Press, 1990). Kreps's book is meant for mathematically adept graduate students. Our definition of Bayesian Nash equilibrium is based on that in Robert Gibbons, *Game Theory for Applied Economists* (Princeton University Press, 1992).

Two seminal papers on mechanism design are by Roger Myerson ("Optimal Auction Design," *Mathematics of Operations Research*, 6 (1981), pp. 58–73), and Roger Myerson and Mark Satterthwaite ("Efficient Mechanisms for Bilateral Trading," *Journal of Economic Theory*, 28 (1983), pp. 265–81). A nice review of the literature is given by R. Preston McAfee and John McMillan ("Auctions and Bidding," *Journal of Economic Literature*, 25 (1987), pp. 699–738).

13.7   Discussion Question

1. Can you recall playing a two-person game with incomplete information? What strategy do you recall using? Was there a better strategy? Did your opponent choose a good strategy? What was the outcome?

13.8   New Terms

Bayesian Nash equilibrium	conditional probability
belief	correlated
conditional expected utility	direct mechanism

Entry Deterrence Game	revelation principle
Harsanyi transformation	revelation theorem
incentive compatible	static Bayesian game
incomplete information	stochastically dependent
marginal probability	stochastically independent
mechanism design	type profile
move profile	types
prior belief	

13.9 Exercises

EXERCISE 13.1

Apply the Harsanyi transformation to the Job Interviewing Game described in Section 13.1.

EXERCISE 13.2

Find all the Nash equilibria, both in pure strategies and in mixed strategies, for the Entry Deterrence Game introduced in Section 13.2.

EXERCISE 13.3

In the Entry Deterrence Game, the entrant is able to enter exactly once. Suppose the Entrant and the Incumbent play the Entry Deterrence Game twice in succession. What does the game tree look like now? What are the players' strategies? Determine the normal form for this game and find a pure strategy equilibrium in that case that $\pi < \frac{1}{2}$.

EXERCISE 13.4

Recall the Battle of the Bismark Sea from Exercise 3.6. At the time of this battle, the United States had secretly broken the Japanese Navy's code for encrypting radio messages and could intercept and read Imamura's radio messages to and from Tokyo. Suppose that Kenney knew Imamura's plans ahead of time. This means that Imamura thought he was playing a simultaneous-move game against Kenney (and also thought that Kenney thought he was playing a simultaneous-move game against Imamura), whereas Kenney knew the game was actually a sequential one in which he knew Imamura's plans ahead of time. Assume that it is common knowledge that both commanders believe the probability the opponent can read its radio messages is 1 in 100,000. How would you propose modeling this game of incomplete information? Does this information alter Kenney's choice of strategy? Explain why or why not.

EXERCISE 13.5

This is a continuation of Exercise 13.4. Suppose you were in charge of the United States' war against Japan. Why might you deliberately *not* let American field commanders such as Captain Kenney know important tactical facts gleaned from decoded radio messages such as Imamura's route to New Guinea? How might you defend such a decision game-theoretically?

EXERCISE 13.6

Suppose HAL is a monopolist in the market for scientific computer workstations. This market is a "natural monopoly," meaning that only one firm can survive in the long run. HAL faces only one potential competitor, MOON. HAL and MOON move simultaneously. HAL chooses one of two prices for its computers: *high* or *low*. MOON chooses whether to *Enter* the market or *Stay out*. These moves are made simultaneously. It is costly for MOON to *enter*. If MOON *stays out*, then HAL enjoys a monopoly forever. If MOON *enters*, then they compete for a while, but the firm with the higher costs is eventually forced out and the firm with the lower costs enjoys a monopoly forever after. There is a 50% chance that HAL's costs are lower than MOON's and this is common knowledge. HAL knows its costs when it sets its prices, but MOON does not. MOON's costs are common knowledge. Table 13.5 shows the discounted profits of the two firms as a function of their decisions and their relative costs.

Table 13.5 **Payoff Matrix of the Workstation Game**

		HAL's costs are higher than MOON's		HAL's costs are lower than MOON's	
		HAL		**HAL**	
		high	*low*	*high*	*low*
MOON	*Enter*	(100, 20)	(100, 5)	(−20, 60)	(−20, 20)
	Stay out	(0, 90)	(0, 30)	(0, 120)	(0, 70)

Payoffs: (MOON, HAL)

(a) This is a static game with incomplete information. How would you propose applying the Harsanyi transformation to make this a game of complete but imperfect information?

(b) What constitutes a strategy for HAL? What constitutes a strategy for MOON?

(c) Construct the strategic form for this game and find all the pure-strategy Bayesian Nash equilibria.

CHAPTER 14

Auctions

OVERVIEW OF CHAPTER 14

14.1   Introduction

A raucous crowd of people in bright blazers scream and gesture to each other in a trading pit at the Chicago Board of Trade. A knot of dark-suited men talk on phones and to each other on the floor of the New York Stock Exchange below suspended banks of green television monitors. A quiet gathering of well-dressed men and women sit in antique chairs in the main gallery at Sotheby's in London. A hundred or so road construction contractors sip coffee in the cafeteria at the Minnesota Department of Transportation as state officials open sealed envelopes. A woman in a business suit stands before a bank of microphones and TV cameras in the lobby of the Federal Communications Commission headquarters in Washington, D.C. What do these people all have in common? They are all participating in auctions.

The **auction** is a system for allocating property based on price competition by buyers and/or sellers for the right to purchase and/or sell a good. It is the primary alternative to take-it-or-leave-it pricing. Auctions have been used for thousands of years. The Greek historian Herodotus reports the auctioning off of brides-to-be in Babylonia about 2,500 years ago. Imperial Roman soldiers used auctions to sell the loot they plundered in the course of military conquests. Indeed, for this reason, business agents accompanied the Roman Legions during their military expeditions in order to bid for this war booty. The emperor Marcus Aurelius is reported to have held an auction of royal furniture and used the proceeds to finance a state deficit. Apparently it was as difficult to raise taxes then as it is now. This auction is reported to have taken a month to complete! One of the stranger auctions took place in A.D. 193 when the Praetorian Guard auctioned off the Roman emperorship to the highest bidder. Didius Julianus won with a bid of 6,250 drachmas per soldier. It proved to be a poor purchase. Emperor Julianus was beheaded two months later by Septimius Severus.

In the United States, auctions are the primary method for selling tobacco leaf, livestock, used cars, art, and Treasury bills. They have also been used to sell everything from airplanes and antique furniture to unclaimed baggage. So-called "open cry" auctions are the basis of all trading in futures and options on the floor of the Chicago Board of Trade, while a "negotiated" auction is used to buy and sell stocks on the New York Stock Exchange. The federal government has awarded off-shore oil drilling rights using auctions for many years and has recently used a new type of auction format to award licenses for newly available radio spectrum. State governments routinely conduct monthly auctions to purchase road construction and repair services from private contractors.

When most people think of auctions, they picture an auctioneer holding a mike, trying to encourage a sea of poker-faced buyers to accept higher and higher bids. Yet auctions need not have ascending bids nor involve yelling. In Dutch tulip auctions, the price *descends* until the first bidder electronically signals to the auctioneer that he wants to buy at the current price. The bidders in many Japanese fish auctions use hand signals to communicate their bids *simultaneously* to the auctioneer—who is capable of determining the high bidder in the sea of waving hands in a few seconds! Bidders are not always buyers, either. In order to minimize favoritism, many government bodies in the United States award supplier contracts—from computers to construction materials—using sealed-bid auctions. In these auctions, the bids are *selling* prices, not purchase prices, and the *low* bidder wins the contract.

Auctions would seem to be a natural testing ground for game theory. Unlike bargaining, auctions have clearly defined players and carefully followed procedures. However, even carefully specified auctions allow a mind-numbing number of strategies, making analysis difficult. Only recently have game theorists been able to cut through the thicket of detail to find the strategically important aspects of these games. A successful theory of auctions should be capable of explaining such things as: Why does the English oral auction predominate? Why did bidders in the early U.S. off-shore oil lease auctions "overbid" for the leases? When can bidding profiles be used to uncover antitrust behavior? What types of goods are most likely to be auctioned?

Game theorists have recently gone beyond explaining observed auction bidding behavior to active *auction design.* The goal of auction design is to ensure that the auctioned object is won by the bidder who values it the most while at the same time getting the highest price for the seller or the lowest price for the buyer. The most recent fruits of this new research have been the Federal Communications Commission's spectacularly successful radio spectrum auctions in 1994 and 1995 (see the box). Every aspect of these auctions was developed in close consultation with leading game theorists. The success of these auctions has led members of Congress to suggest that *all* government licenses should be awarded through auctions.

In this chapter, we will show how your relatively small game-theoretic toolkit can uncover interesting and far from obvious properties of the most common auction games. We will show how to calculate optimal bidding strategies, give an example of the surprising revenue equivalence theorem, and explain how to avoid the "winner's curse."

GAME THEORY IN ACTION: Game Theorists Design a Historic Auction for the FCC

July 25, 1994, marks an important milestone in the history of game theory. On that day, the Federal Communications Commission began the first auction of radio licenses in the nation's history. After 46 rounds of bidding spanning five days, 10 nationwide licenses for new radio frequencies on which to provide "personal communication services (PCS)" sold for a total of over $600 million. This was over 10 times the highest estimates that had appeared in the press.

The auctions were mandated by Congress after a concerted lobbying effort by academic economists and the telecommunications industry. During most of its history, the FCC allocated new broadcast licenses using very lengthy and costly "comparative hearings." In 1984, Congress authorized the FCC to forego the hearings and award cellular phone licenses using lotteries. Given the value of many of these licenses, it is not surprising that over 400,000 individuals and firms applied! It is also not surprising that the lottery winners were *not* the firms best positioned to develop cellular phone service. It has taken 10 years for the cellular phone industry to aggregate these licenses into efficient cellular phone networks through reselling. Determined not to repeat the cellular phone fiasco, the paging industry lobbied Congress hard to allow the FCC to award the PCS licenses using competitive bidding. PCS consists of a new generation of portable phones, pagers, and other wireless devices still on the drawing boards. This is a fast-moving area in which firms wanted to be able to build up networks to compete against cellular, satellite-based, and other communications technologies.

Once given the authorization by Congress, the FCC decided to start small by auctioning off 10 nationwide licenses for so-called "narrowband" frequencies.

This was done so as to eliminate the complications of geographic aggregation and allow the bidders to concentrate on simpler questions of substitutability and complementarity among the licenses. Some of the license frequencies were more efficient for transmitting messages to handheld PCS devices and some were more efficient for transmitting messages from small, low-power devices. The strategic questions facing the bidders included: What was the demand for PCS services and how fast would it grow? Which frequencies were substitutes and which were complements? At what point in the auction would it be better to withdraw and wait either for the later, regional PCS auctions or for resale of the national licenses? How much cash and lines of credit were needed?

While the firms set about determining the value of the licenses and consulted with game theorists about strategy, the FCC developed the auction rules. On the advice of a number of game theory and auction experts, the FCC decided to adopt a *simultaneous, multiple-round auction* format. This format would allow bidders in each round to simultaneously submit bids on more than one license. The rules were: No firm could purchase more than three licenses. Before bidding began, every firm had to put up $350,000 for each license it wanted to be able to bid on simultaneously. In the early rounds of the auction, every firm could bid on any combination of licenses it wished; in the later rounds, each firm could bid on no more than three. To stay in the auction, firms had to submit a bid on at least one license in every round, and this bid had to be at least 5% higher than the high bid on the previous round. The auction ended when no new bids were submitted on any license.

The auction surprised most outsiders from the very start. Four firms put up $3,500,000, allowing them to bid on all 10 licenses simultaneously—even though they could eventually own only three. *On the first round,* the sum of the 10 high bids exceeded $100 million. *Jump bidding* was common. A **jump bid** is a bid that exceeds the previous high bid by more than the minimum. Almost half of new high bids were jump bids and almost a quarter of new high bids were *raises of the bidder's own high bid on the previous round!* It appears that firms used jump bids to signal that they had a high valuation for a particular license. The message was "don't bother bidding against me for this license because I am prepared to outbid you." Game theorists had previously shown that jump bidding could be a credible way of signaling such messages between bidders.

Since the narrowband auction in 1994, the FCC has used a similar simultaneous, multiple-round auction format to allocate regional broadband licenses for frequencies with which to provide even more advanced PCS products. Most of the bidders for these licenses are interested in purchasing groups of licenses with which to create regional or national networks. Because of this, a license for, say, New York City is more valuable when it is combined with a license for Boston than when it is owned alone. These auctions were much more complex because of the need for bidders to consider geographic aggregation and took over three months to complete. Total winning bids were about *$8 billion.*

The PCS auctions have been judged so successful that there is now discussion in Washington about using auctions to allocate other government assets such as airport landing rights and hazardous waste disposal rights. The FCC auctions stand to date as one of the most successful uses of game theory since its inception 50 years ago.

14.2   A Primer for Auctioneers

In our discussion, we will distinguish the *auction rules* from the *auction environment*. The **auction rules** state who can bid, what bids are acceptable, how bids are submitted, what information is made public during the course of the auction, when the auction ends, how the winner is determined, and what price the winner pays for the item being auctioned off. The **auction environment** consists of the population of potential bidders, the values these bidders place on the object being auctioned, their attitudes toward risk, and the information they possess about each other's valuations and risk attitudes.

Auctions are either **open,** meaning that anyone can submit a bid, or **closed,** meaning that bidders must be invited or approved by the seller. Art auctions are often closed, as are almost all auctions involving financial assets. Bidders may be required to have a license, to pay a nonrefundable fee, and even to post a bond against timely payment for items purchased. Both fees and bonds were required of bidders in the FCC spectrum auctions. In many auctions there is also a **reserve price.** This is the minimum price for which the seller will allow the item to be sold. In many road construction contracts, this reserve price is not known until after the bidding has ended. If the highest bid submitted is less than the reserve price, then the item is withdrawn and not sold. Reserve prices can help protect the seller against collusion by bidders—known as "bidding rings"—as well as low bidder turnout.

In a **sealed-bid auction,** the bidders submit a single bid in secret to the auctioneer in writing. The bids are only revealed after the auction is over and the winner has been declared. Many government contracts are awarded this way, as are timber and mineral rights on public lands and leases for off-shore oil drilling. In an **oral auction,** on the other hand, the bidders submit their bids by announcing them publicly during the course of the auction. One obvious difference between sealed-bid and oral auctions is the visibility of the bidders. Yet in oral auctions, bidders often try to hide their identities by using others to submit their bids for them or calling their bids in to the auctioneer by phone.

Bids can be **ascending, descending,** or **simultaneous.** One advantage of descending or simultaneous bids over ascending bids is the greater speed with which the auction can be conducted. In Japanese fish auctions, bidders have only a few seconds to show their bids to the auctioneer. In the Dutch fresh-cut flower auctions, a continuously moving "Dutch clock" is used to "countdown" the price and bidders signal the auctioneer electronically. Again, each round of bidding often takes less than a minute.

The winner of an auction is the bidder who submits the highest bid—or the lowest bid in the case of procurement auctions. But the bid need not equal the price the winner pays for the auctioned object. When the price paid equals the winning bid, the auction is called a **first-price auction.** First-price auctions are by far the most common. Almost all other auctions are **second-price auctions.** As the name implies, in these auctions, the price paid equals the second-highest price submitted. Another way of saying this is that the price paid equals the highest bid submitted among the *losing* bidders. Second-price auctions are of great interest to game theorists because of their remarkable "truth-revelation" properties (see Theorem 14.2). They are sometimes called **Vickrey auctions** in honor of William Vickrey, an American economist who first discovered their truth-revelation properties over 30 years ago. For this work, Vickrey was awarded the Nobel Prize in 1996.

An **English auction** is an ascending-bid, first-price, oral auction. If there is a reserve, then the bidding begins at the reserve price and ends when no more bids are made. Otherwise, the first bid is often called out from the floor. The termination of bidding is usually at the discretion of the auctioneer. A **Dutch auction** is a descending-bid, first-price, oral auction. The price starts out high and is lowered until the first bid is made, at which point the auction ends.

An auction can be *single unit* or *multi unit.* In a **single-unit auction,** there is only one item at auction and the bids apply only to that item. The archetypal example of a single-unit auction is the art auction. Each painting sold is unique and is sold separately. In a **multi-unit auction,** a stock of essentially identical items is sold. Bidders typically submit both a desired purchase price and the desired quantity of units they want to purchase. The largest multi-unit auctions in the world are the weekly U.S. Treasury bill auctions, in which tens of billions in U.S. government securities may be sold at a single time.

14.3 Auctions with Perfect Information

Before we consider the problem of bidding in an auction where the players do not know each other's valuations for the good being auctioned, let us begin by asking how the bidders would behave under various auction rules if their valuations were common knowledge.

Let us assume that Larry and Mary are bidding on a small painting by an unknown artist. Larry is willing to pay up to \$54 for it, while Mary is willing to pay only up to \$34 for it. This is common knowledge. If Larry wins the auction with a bid b_{Larry}, his payoff is equal to \$54 $- b_{Larry}$; if he loses, his payoff is zero. Similarly, if Mary wins the auction, her payoff equals \$34 $- b_{Mary}$; and if she loses, it equals zero. Suppose the auction is a sealed-bid, first-price auction and all bids are in multiples of \$10. In the event of a tie, the winner is decided by the toss of a fair coin. Bids above \$54 are obviously strongly dominated for Larry as are bids above \$34 for Mary. The strategic form of this static game is displayed in Table 14.1. You should verify that this game has exactly one weakly iterated dominant strategy equilibrium: Larry bids \$40 and Mary bids \$30. We have highlighted these equilibrium strategies and the associated payoffs in the table. That is, Mary, the loser, bids truthfully, while Larry, the winner, bids less than his true valuation.

The \$10 spread between Larry's and Mary's bids is an artifact of the requirement that the bids have to be multiples of \$10. If the bids were multiples of \$1, the equilibrium would be: Mary bids \$34 and Larry bids \$35. And if the bids were

Table 14.1 *The Strategic Form of the Sealed-Bid, First-Price Art Auction*

		Larry				
		$10	$20	$30	**$40**	$50
	$10	(12, 22)	(0, 34)	(0, 24)	(0, 14)	(0, 4)
Mary	$20	(14, 0)	(7, 17)	(0, 24)	(0, 14)	(0, 4)
	$30	(4, 0)	(4, 0)	(2, 12)	**(0, 14)**	(0, 4)

Expected payoff: (Mary, Larry)

multiples of $0.01, then the equilibrium would be: Mary bids $34 and Larry bids $34.01. If we let the bid unit shrink to zero, we have the result: *The winner is the bidder who values the painting the most (Larry) and the winner pays what the painting is worth to the loser ($34).*

A second type of auction is the sealed-bid, second-price auction. The rules of this auction are almost the same as for the first-price auction discussed above, except for the payoffs. In this auction, the painting goes to the bidder who submits the highest bid, but the winner pays what the loser bid. For example, if Larry bids $40 and Mary bids $30, then Larry wins the painting, but he pays $30 for it, not $40. There are many Nash equilibria, one of which is highlighted in Table 14.2. This particular equilibrium reveals an interesting property of this auction format: bidding honestly—bidding what the painting is really worth to you—is a weakly dominant strategy. One of the more surprising things about second-price auctions is that under certain circumstances, bidding honestly remains a weakly dominant strategy for every player, even when no one knows what the painting is worth to any other player. As long as the increment between allowable bids is very small, all the Nash equilibria of this auction game result in the same outcome: *The winner is the bidder who values the painting the most (Larry) and the winner pays what the painting is worth to the loser ($34).*

Table 14.2 *The Strategic Form of the Sealed-Bid, Second-Price Art Auction*

		Larry				
		$10	$20	$30	$40	**$50**
	$10	(12, 22)	(0, 44)	(0, 44)	(0, 44)	(0, 44)
Mary	$20	(24, 0)	(7, 17)	(0, 34)	(0, 34)	(0, 34)
	$30	(24, 0)	(14, 0)	(2, 12)	(0, 24)	**(0, 24)**

Expected payoff: (Mary, Larry)

Let us now suppose that the painting is auctioned off to Larry and Mary using a "modified" English auction. In the auction, the auctioneer calls out prices in ascending order. A portion of the game tree is displayed in Figure 14.1. Each time he calls out a new price, the two bidders simultaneously decide whether to *Pass* or *Accept*. In a standard English auction, the players can pass on one price and accept the next. In order to simplify the analysis, we will assume that once a player passes, he or she can no longer bid. So if one player passes and the second accepts, then the auction ends and the player who accepted wins the painting and pays the current auction price. If both accept, then the auctioneer raises the current price by $10 and the auction continues for another round. The auction ends as soon as one player passes.

This is a dynamic game in which a new subgame begins every time the auctioneer raises the price. A pure strategy consists of a bidding decision (*Pass* or *Accept*) at every possible price. We can denote the bidding decision as an infinite sequence of the form $(D_1, D_2, \ldots D_n, \ldots)$, where D_n is the decision taken when the current price reaches $10 \cdot n$. A sample strategy is (*Accept, Accept, Accept, Pass, Pass, . . .*), where the player accepts prices of $10, $20, and $30, but passes once the price goes higher than $30. Another is (*Accept, Pass, Accept, Pass, Pass, . . .*). This strategy calls for the player to accept a price of $10 but to pass when the price rises to $20. Under the auction rules, the auction will end at this point—if it does not end in the first round. The strategy, though, has to specify what the player will do if the auction continues and the price rises to $30 and beyond. Without this information, the player may not be able to tell whether she should pass when the price reaches $20 or not. Table 14.3 displays the unique subgame perfect equilibrium.

The equilibrium outcome is that Larry wins the auction and pays $40. As we saw earlier, as the increment between successive prices drops to zero, the price Larry pays falls to Mary's valuation of $34. *The winner of the lottery is the player*

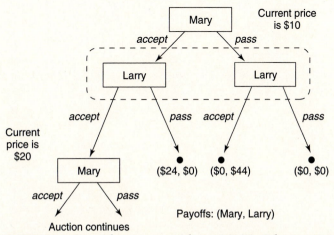

FIGURE 14.1 Part of the game tree of the modified English art auction.

Table 14.3 *The Subgame Perfect Equilibria of the (Modified) English Art Auction*

Current Price	Larry's Strategy	Mary's Strategy
$10	*Accept*	*Accept*
$20	*Accept*	*Accept*
$30	*Accept*	*Accept*
$40	*Accept*	*Pass*
$50	*Accept*	*Pass*
$60	*Pass*	*Pass*
⋮	⋮	⋮

who values the painting the most (Larry) and he pays what the painting is worth to the losing bidder ($34).

The last type of auction format we will consider is the Dutch auction. In a Dutch auction, the auctioneer begins with a high price, say $100, and lowers it by $10 decrements. Each time he calls out a new price, the two bidders simultaneously decide whether to Pass or Accept. The first time a player accepts the current price, the auction ends and that player gets the painting for the price accepted. In the event that both players accept the same price, the winner is chosen by tossing a fair coin. A portion of the game tree is displayed in Figure 14.2.

A strategy consists of a bidding decision at each possible price and can be represented by a finite sequence of the form $(D_1, D_2, \ldots D_{10})$, where D_n is the decision made when the current price reaches $10 \cdot (11 - n)$. If the price drops to $10 and there are still no takers, the painting is not sold and the auction ends.

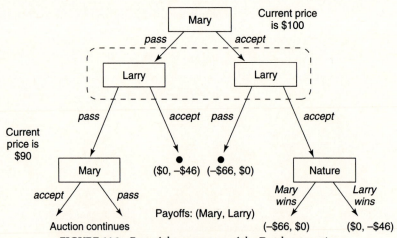

FIGURE 14.2 Part of the game tree of the Dutch art auction.

Table 14.4 **The Subgame Perfect Equilibria of the (Modified) Dutch Art Auction**

Current Price	Larry's Strategy	Mary's Strategy
$100	Pass	Pass
$90	Pass	Pass
$80	Pass	Pass
$70	Pass	Pass
$60	Pass	Pass
$50	Pass	Pass
$40	Accept	Pass
$30	Accept	Accept
$20	Accept	Accept
$10	Accept	Accept

Table 14.4 displays the unique subgame perfect equilibrium. Larry passes when the price reaches $50—which is below the painting's worth to him—since he anticipates that when the price falls to $40, Mary will continue to pass. He accepts at $40 since he anticipates that Mary will accept a price of $30 and $14 ($54 − $40) is better than a 50% chance of $24 ($54 − $30). If we let the bidding unit fall to zero, then the outcome is the same as for the other auction formats: *The painting is sold to the bidder who values it the most (Larry) and he pays what it is worth to the losing bidder ($34).*

In summary, when the bidders' valuations of the object being auctioned are common knowledge, under all four auction formats—first-price sealed bid, second-price sealed bid, English oral, and Dutch oral auctions—the good is bought by the bidder with the highest valuation and he or she pays what the object is worth to the second-highest bidder. As a result, the seller is paid the same amount regardless of the auction format used. Surprising as it may seem, even when the bidders' valuations are known only to them, as long as the valuations are independent of each other and the bidders are risk neutral, the *expected revenue* to the seller is the same (in equilibrium) under all four auction formats. This result is known as the **revenue equivalence theorem** and is the subject of the next two sections.

14.4 Sealed-Bid Auctions with Independent Private Values

Bidding strategies have been most extensively studied where the bidder valuations are **independent private values** (IPV). In this auction environment, the number of bidders is fixed and each bidder knows the value of the object to herself, denoted V_i, but does not know the value placed on the object by the other N bidders. Clearly this is a game in which the players have incomplete information about the payoffs. Applying the Harsanyi transformation, we will model this by having Nature move first and assign valuations to each bidder. The bidders have a common *belief* about the N valuations, $(V_1, \ldots, V_N)$, namely, that they are independent, identically distributed, random variables with a known distribution function F. This common belief is common knowledge. This is the key assumption of the IPV model. The IPV model is most appropriate when the bidders desire the auctioned object solely for personal consumption and are uninterested in its resale value.

In a sealed-bid auction, the bidders simultaneously submit bids, denoted $b_1, \ldots, b_N$. So this auction is an example of a static Bayesian game. A pure strategy consists of a **bidding function,** $b_i(V_i)$. This function states the bid, b_i, to be submitted when the object is worth V_i to the bidder.

The **ex post payoffs** are those earned after the auction is over and the winner is declared. Let $b_{(1)}$ denote the highest bid submitted and let $b_{(2)}$ denote the second-highest bid submitted. If bidder i is the winner, his ex post payoff equals $V_i - b_i$ in a first-price auction and equals $V_i - b_{(2)}$ in a second-price auction. The losing bidders get an ex post payoff of zero. Because the valuations of other bidders are random variables, even if any single bidder knows the other players' bidding strategies, the bids they actually submit will be perceived to be random variables. The bidders can't maximize their ex post payoffs since these payoffs depend on information they don't have at the time they make their decisions. Instead, we will assume that *the bidders are risk neutral, expected utility maximizers and select their strategies so as to maximize their conditional expected payoff.* This is an important assumption.

14.4.1 AN EXAMPLE

Veronica has decided to sell her comic book collection in order to help pay for a new car. The only people interested in bidding for the collection are her friends, Archie and Betty. In order to get a good price and yet be fair to her friends, she has decided to have a first-price, sealed-bid auction with no reserve. In the event that Archie and Betty submit the same bid, the winner will be determined by tossing a fair coin. Archie considers the collection worth V_A and Betty considers it worth V_B. For Archie, Betty's valuation is an independent random variable uniformly distributed between \$0 and \$1,000. Similarly for Betty, Archie's valuation is an independent random variable uniformly distributed between \$0 and \$1,000. In order to simplify our calculations, we will use \$1,000 as our monetary unit. So a valuation or a bid of 0.5 will represent 0.5 of \$1,000 or \$500. This choice of units implies that the two bidders' valuations are uniformly distributed between 0 and 1.

This static game has a unique symmetric, pure-strategy Nash equilibrium: $b_A^*(V_A) = \frac{1}{2}V_A$ and $b_B^*(V_B) = \frac{1}{2}V_B$. That is, both Betty and Archie submit a bid equal to half what they consider the collection worth. In order to prove that this is an equilibrium strategy for both players, it is sufficient to show that b_A^* is Archie's best response to the belief that b_B^* is Betty's strategy. Suppose Archie submits the bid b and Betty bids $b_B^*(V_B) = \frac{1}{2}V_B$, then Archie's conditional expected payoff equals

$$\Pi_A(b) = 0 \cdot P\{b < \tfrac{1}{2}V_B\} + (V_A - b) \cdot P\{b > \tfrac{1}{2}V_B\}$$
$$+ \; 0.5 \cdot (V_A - b) \cdot P\{b = \tfrac{1}{2}V_B\} \qquad \text{[14.1]}$$

where $P\{X\}$ means the probability of the event X. Since V_B is continuously distributed, the probability that Archie's bid exactly equals Betty's is zero. An important property of a random variable that is uniformly distributed between 0 and 1 is that the probability of falling between 0 and x, where x is a number between 0 and 1, is exactly equal to x. Since V_B is uniformly distributed, $P\{b > \frac{1}{2}V_B\} = P\{2b > V_B\} = \min\{2b, 1\}$. Therefore,

$$\Pi_A(b) = (V_A - b) \cdot \min\{2b, 1\}. \qquad \text{[14.2]}$$

Increasing b when it is already greater than $\frac{1}{2}$ will have no effect on $\min\{2b, 1\}$ but reduces $(V_A - b)$. Therefore, the optimal bid must be less than 0.5. Restricting b to this range, Eq. [14.2] simplifies to $\Pi_A(b) = (V_A - b) \cdot 2b$. This function has a unique maximum at $b = \frac{1}{2}V_A$, implying that $b_A^*(V_A) = \frac{1}{2}V_A$, proving this is a Bayesian Nash equilibrium strategy. This optimal bid balances the gain from bidding low (a larger surplus $V - b$) with the gain from bidding high (a higher probability of winning the auction). The fact that $b_A^*(V_A) < V_A$, meaning that it is not optimal to bid truthfully, is not particular to this example but is a general result in first-price auctions.

> **THEOREM 14.1:** A first-price sealed-bid auction in which risk-neutral bidders have independent private values results in bids that are strictly below the bidders' true valuations.

When Archie and Betty adopt this strategy, Veronica is paid one half of the maximum of the two valuations. Since both players always bid one half their valuation, Veronica can expect Betty and Archie's bids to be uniformly distributed between zero and one half. If you are not careful, you might conclude that her expected earnings will be one fourth, but the fact that she always gets the higher of the two bids means that her expected earnings will be above one fourth. In fact, her expected revenue equals

$$R = \mathbf{E}(\tfrac{1}{2}\max\{V_A, V_B\}) = \tfrac{1}{2}\int_0^1\!\!\int_0^1 \max\{V_A, V_B\}\, dV_A\, dV_B = \tfrac{1}{3}. \qquad \text{[14.3]}$$

(See Section 14.13 if you are interested in this calculation.) Recalling that our units are thousands of dollars, we see that Betty can expect to receive \$333 from the auction.

Before Veronica conducts her auction, however, she runs into her friend Jughead. Jughead tells her that she should seriously consider having a *second-price* auction. He has just read in his game theory textbook that in a second-price auction, the optimal strategy for all the bidders is to bid their true values. Although Veronica would have to accept the losing bid in a second-price auction, the losing bid will be twice what it would be in a first-price auction. As a result, she may actually get a higher price for her collection.

Since you may doubt Jughead's claim that Archie and Betty would bid truthfully in a second-price auction, let us take a minute to see whether it is true. We'll look at the situation from Betty's point of view this time. In a second-price auction, what Betty pays for the collection if she wins the auction depends not on what she bids, but on what *Archie* bids, since his bid will be the second-highest. Let us consider what Betty should do *if she knew ahead of time what Archie was going to bid*. With such inside information, Betty can determine exactly what the payoff from any bid will be. If Archie plans to submit a bid that is less than she thinks the collection is worth, then she should submit a higher bid—how much higher is irrelevant—which will guarantee that she wins the auction. If Archie plans to submit a bid that is exactly equal to what she thinks the collection is worth, then she gets the same payoff—zero—whether she wins the auction or not. So her bid can be anything. And if Archie plans to submit a bid that is higher than she considers the collection worth, then she should submit a lower bid than his and let him win. This is summarized in Table 14.5. The table makes it clear that Betty has a weakly dominant strategy: Bid her true value, V_B. (Why isn't this strategy *strictly* dominant?)

Notice that in our proof of Jughead's claim we made no use of our assumption that the bidders' valuations are independent of each other or are uniformly distributed. Truthfulness remains the optimal strategy even if the two bidders' valuations are correlated. What matters is that each bidder's valuation of the object is predetermined, known with certainty, and not affected by the valuations the bidders have for the object.

> **THEOREM 14.2:** In a second-price sealed-bid auction with risk-neutral bidders, bidding truthfully is a dominant strategy for every bidder.

Table 14.5 **Betty's Optimal Bids When She Knows Archie's Bid Ahead of Time**

Archie's Bid	Betty's Best Response	Betty's Resulting Payoff
$b_A < V_B$	Bid anything above b_A (for example, V_B)	$V_B - b_A$
$b_A = V_B$	Bid anything (for example, V_B)	0
$b_A > V_B$	Bid anything less than b_A (for example, V_B)	0

So Jughead was correct. If Veronica uses a second-price auction, then both Archie and Betty will bid exactly what they consider the collection is worth. Veronica's expected revenue, going back to our assumption that the bidders' valuations are independent and uniformly distributed, now equals

$$R = \mathbf{E}(\min\{V_A, V_B\}) = \int_0^1 \int_0^1 \min\{V_A, V_B\}\, dV_A\, dV_B = \tfrac{1}{3} \qquad [14.4]$$

or \$333—exactly what she can expect to get from the first-price auction! Although the bidders in the second-price auction are submitting higher bids, this is offset by the fact that Veronica is now paid the *losing* bid rather than the winning bid. This turns out not to depend on the assumption that the valuations are all uniformly distributed. That is, in an IPV environment, the first-price auction and the second-price auction always generate exactly the same expected revenue to the auctioneer when the bidders are risk neutral. This is generally known as the revenue equivalence theorem.

> **THEOREM 14.3 (REVENUE EQUIVALENCE THEOREM):** In an independent private values environment with risk-neutral bidders, the expected price paid for the object is the same under the first-price and second-price sealed-bid auctions.

14.5   Oral Auctions with Independent Private Values

In the previous section we assumed that Veronica used a sealed-bid auction. Can she do better by switching to an oral auction format? In light of the revenue equivalence theorem, it may not surprise you to hear that the answer is no. But you may be surprised by the reason. Dutch and English oral auctions result in the same expected revenue as the two sealed-bid auction formats because the Dutch and English oral auctions are **strategically equivalent** to the first-price and second-price sealed-bid auctions in IPV environments.

Recall that in a Dutch auction the price is lowered until the first bidder signals that he accepts it, at which point the auction stops and that bidder gets the object auctioned at the price signaled. When the bidding starts, each bidder knows only the object's value to him or her, V_i, and no more information is revealed until the auction is stopped. That is, during the course of the auction, all that each bidder knows is his or her private value V_i. A strategy, therefore, consists of a price $b_i(V_i)$ at which to stop the bidding when the good is worth V_i. The winner is the bidder with the highest stopping price. The ex post payoff to the losing bidders is 0, while the payoff to the winning bidder is $V_i - b_i$. This shows that the set of strategies and the ex post payoffs in the Dutch oral auction are the same as those in the first-price sealed-bid auction. This is the sense in which these two games are *strategically equivalent*. In these two games, rational bidders will behave the same and the equilibrium outcome will be the same. Although we will not do so here, it is possible to show that this equivalence holds even in the most general auction environments where the bidders' ex post values for the object are correlated and are not known with certainty beforehand.

> **THEOREM 14.4:** The Dutch auction is strategically equivalent to the first-price, sealed-bid auction, whatever the auction environment.

The relationship between the English auction and the second-price, sealed-bid auction is more delicate, since there are a number of ways that such an auction can be carried out. We will assume that the procedure is one that is used in Japan. There is a screen in front of all the bidders on which the current price is displayed. The price is increased in small increments starting from the reserve price. Each bidder has a button which she holds down as long as the price displayed is acceptable to her. Once she releases the button, she drops out of the bidding and cannot reenter it. The auction stops the instant only one bidder remains. That bidder wins the auction and pays the price that has been frozen on the screen.

In this auction, each bidder has to make one decision: select the price at which to drop out of the auction, b_i. The winner is the bidder with highest dropout price. The ex post payoff to the losing bidders is 0 and the payoff to the winning bidder is $V_i - b_2$, where b_2 is the second-highest dropout price. Initially, each bidder knows only V_i. As the auction progresses, bidders drop out, revealing their dropout bids and, indirectly, the values they place on the object. However, because the bidders' values are independent of each other, this provides no information about when the remaining bidders will drop out. So the bidders do not know anything during the auction other than V_i. A strategy, therefore, consists of a dropout price function $b_i(V_i)$. You can see that strategies and the ex post payoffs in this version of the English oral auction are the same as those in the second-price, sealed-bid auction. We will leave it as an exercise for you to consider other variations of the English auction format and show that the strategic equivalence of these games with the second-price sealed-bid auction game continues to hold.

> **THEOREM 14.5:** In an independent private values environment, the English auction is strategically equivalent to the second-price, sealed-bid ("Vickrey") auction.

The strategic equivalence of the English and Vickrey auctions breaks down once bidders' valuations are correlated and they do not initially know with certainty the value of the good being sold. In this environment, the very act of bidding now reveals to the other bidders the bidder's current assessment of the object's value—thereby possibly altering their assessment of this value and their subsequent bidding behavior. Bidders must take this into account in devising their strategies.

14.6   Common Value Auctions and the "Winner's Curse"

The IPV model does not apply to many important auction settings. For example, it does not apply to the auction of mineral extraction rights or financial assets. In these auctions, the goods being auctioned are worth the same to all of the bidders—the problem is that this common value is both uncertain and something about which the bidders have differing beliefs and information. This is the **common value (CV) environment.** The behavior of bidders in a common value environment differs dramatically from that in an IPV environment. In a CV auction, rational bidders realize that they win only if their initial estimate of the object's value turns out to be higher than everyone else's. This implies that the winner probably overestimates the object's true value and risks paying more for the object than it will turn out to be worth. This risk is known as the **winner's curse.**

> **THEOREM 14.6 (WINNER'S CURSE):** In a common value environment, the auction winner will be the bidder who initially overestimates the object's value the most. Rational bidders take this into account in forming their bids.

14.6.1 OUR EXAMPLE REVISITED

We previously assumed that Archie and Betty desire Veronica's collection for themselves and have independent private valuations. Suppose, however, that this is not the case. Suppose the two friends aren't interested in adding Veronica's comic books to their own collections, but rather want to resell them to other collectors who are coming into town next week for a comic book collector's convention. In addition, Veronica's collection actually consists of two subcollections: her collection of early-edition Marvel comic books and her collection of mint-condition Disney comics. Archie knows nothing about the value of the Disney comics, but he knows exactly what the Marvel comics are worth. For Betty, the opposite is true. She has no idea what the Marvel comic books are worth, but she is an expert on Disney artifacts and knows exactly what the Disney comic books will sell for. Veronica knows neither market values.

We will refer to the ex post value of the Marvel comics as V_A and the ex post value of the Disney comics as V_B. The ex post value of the entire collection to both Archie and Betty is $V_A + V_B$. So we are in a common values environment. Our unit of accounting will be \$1,000. So, for example, $V_A = 0.3$ means that Archie estimates the Marvel subcollection is worth \$300. Archie knows V_A and believes V_B is uniformly distributed between 0 and 0.5. Betty knows V_B and believes V_A is uniformly distributed between 0 and 0.5. Let us call the expected value of $V_A + V_B$, conditional on Archie's knowledge of V_A, Archie's *ex ante valuation* of the collection's ex post value. It follows from the formulas for conditional expected values that Archie's ex ante valuation equals $V_A + 0.25$. Similarly, we will refer to the expected value of $V_A + V_B$, conditional on Betty's knowledge of V_B, her ex ante valuation of the collection's ex post value. Betty's ex ante valuation equals $V_B + 0.25$.

Veronica decides to use a Vickrey auction. If this were an IPV environment, then it would be a dominant strategy equilibrium for both Archie and Betty to bid their true private valuations. The natural analogue of a bidder's "private value" in this CV setting is the bidder's ex ante valuation. Suppose that Archie and Betty both submit these as their bids. What will be the outcome? Consider Archie. Suppose he believes the Marvel comics are only worth 0.1 (\$100). Then his ex ante valuation of the collection is 0.35 (\$350). If both he and Betty bid their ex ante valuations and he wins the auction, then he pays Betty's bid of $V_B + 0.25$ for a collection he knows is worth $V_B + 0.1$. This much he can determine, even though he doesn't know the value of V_B. But $V_B + 0.1$ is 0.15 less than $V_B + 0.25$, whatever the value of the Disney comics. This means that if he wins, he is *guaranteed to lose \$150!* Archie has suffered the *winner's curse.*

So how should Betty and Archie bid in this auction? A Nash equilibrium of this game is for Archie to bid $2 \cdot V_A$ and for Betty to bid $2 \cdot V_B$. Before we prove that this is an equilibrium, we will show how these strategies enable both players to avoid the winner's curse. Suppose again that Archie believes the Marvel comics are worth only 0.1 and both bidders use our proposed strategies. Archie will submit a bid of 0.2. If he wins the auction, he gets a collection worth $V_B + 0.1$ and he must pay Betty's losing bid of $2 \cdot V_B$. His profit (or loss) will be $0.1 - V_B$. But he only wins the auction if $0.2 > 2 \cdot V_B$ or $0.1 > V_B$. So a positive profit is *guaranteed* if he wins. So playing this strategy is profitable and the winner's curse is avoided.

It remains only to show that bidding $2 \cdot V_A$ is Archie's optimal strategy if Betty adopts the strategy of bidding $2 \cdot V_B$. Symmetry will then imply that bidding $2 \cdot V_B$ is Betty's optimal strategy if Archie's strategy is to bid $2 \cdot V_A$. This will then prove that the two strategies are a Nash equilibrium. If Archie bids b and wins the auction, then his ex post profit equals $(V_A + V_B) - 2 \cdot V_B = V_A - V_B$. He wins the auction when his bid, b, exceeds Betty's bid of $2 \cdot V_B$ or $\frac{1}{2}b > V_B$. So his expected profit equals

$$\Pi_A(b) = \int_0^{\frac{1}{2}b} (V_A - V_B)\, dV_B + \int_{\frac{1}{2}b}^1 0\, dV_B = V_A \cdot \tfrac{1}{2}b - \tfrac{1}{2}(\tfrac{1}{2}b)^2. \qquad [14.5]$$

We leave it as a calculus exercise for you to show that Π_A is maximized at $b = 2 \cdot V_A$, as we claimed.

The winner's curse is harder to avoid if Veronica uses a first-price, sealed-bid auction since now the winner pays his (winning) bid, not the losing bid. We leave it as an exercise for you to show that it is a Nash equilibrium strategy for each player to bid V_i. Note that this means that both bidders act as if the part of the collection they are uninformed about is worth nothing! If Archie follows this strategy, then when he wins the auction, his profit equals $(V_A + V_B) - V_A = V_B \geq 0$, so he avoids the winner's curse. Note that it would not always be profitable to bid his ex ante valuation of $V_A + 0.25$. Were he to do this, and were Betty to play her equilibrium strategy and submit a bid of V_B, then he would win only when $V_A + 0.25 > V_B$. The expected value of V_B, conditional on it being less than $V_A + 0.25$, equals $\frac{1}{2}(V_A + 0.25)$. So the expected value of the collection—*conditional on winning the auction*— is $V_A + \frac{1}{2}(V_A + 0.25)$. But Archie would have to pay his bid of $V_A + 0.25$, resulting in an expected profit or loss of $\frac{1}{2}(V_A - 0.25)$. If Archie knows the Marvel subcollection is worth less than 0.25 ($V_A < 0.25$), then he can expect to take a loss.

In this example, Veronica's expected revenue is $333 whether she uses a first-price or a second-price auction. This equality, however, is not generally true. Usually, the seller can expect a higher selling price if she uses an English auction than if she uses a Dutch or sealed-bid auction format. The reason is that in an English auction, the bidders gradually reveal their private assessments of the object's worth. This reduces the size of the winner's curse and allows them to bid more aggressively. Since most auctions take place in environments that lie somewhere between an IPV and CV setting, this may account for the English auction's popularity among auctioneers.

14.7   The Efficiency of Auctions

In an IPV setting, an auction is said to be **efficient** if in equilibrium the object being auctioned is always won by the bidder who values it the most. Efficiency is assured as long as the auction has a symmetric, pure-strategy equilibrium bidding function that is strictly increasing in the private value V_i. Although we showed this was true for the four different auction formats when bidders valuations are uniformly distributed, it can be shown that it holds for any distribution with a continuous density.

> **THEOREM 14.7:** In an independent private values environment in which the valuations have a distribution with a continuous density, the English oral auction, Dutch oral auction, first-price, sealed-bid auction, and second-price, sealed-bid auction are all efficient.

Defining efficiency in a common values setting is far from obvious. Efficiency no longer has anything to do with who wins the auction. What we want the auction to do now is to provide an incentive for the bidders to invest the optimal amount of resources in determining the worth of the good. An overinvestment in information is wasteful and an underinvestment in information results in too many unexploited opportunities. This is a complicated question with no clear-cut answers.

14.8   Summary

In this chapter, we have looked at one of the oldest and most important types of games in economics: auctions. Although auctions can have a bewildering variety of rules, game theorists have isolated four idealized formats that can be used to approximate almost all auctions in use: the first-price and second-price sealed-bid auctions, and the English and Dutch oral auctions. The first-price, sealed-bid auction and English oral auction are by far the most common formats used. In both those two auctions and the Dutch auction, the high bidder gets the object being auctioned for the amount bid. The second-price auction is distinguished by the fact that the winning bidder does *not* pay the amount of his bid, but instead pays the *second-highest* bid. An initially surprising game theoretic fact about auctions is that the Dutch auction is strategically equivalent to the first-price, sealed-bid auction. That is, the two auction formats can be modeled by the same strategic form.

The auction environment can be very complex as well. Nevertheless, theorists have concentrated on two extreme auction environments—the independent private values model and the common value model—that bracket real-world auctions. In an IPV setting, the object being auctioned has an idiosyncratic value to every bidder and each knows only what the good is worth to her. In the CV case, the reverse is true; the good has the same value to every bidder, only they have differing initial opinions about what this common value is. In both cases, though, every bidder has private information (the value he believes the object to be worth) on which to base his bid. A strategy is, therefore, not a bid, but rather a bidding function that tells what to bid given the value he places on the object.

Using the notions of dominance and best response, we were able to find the equilibrium bidding strategies for a simple example with two bidders and uniformly distributed valuations. This example illustrated four important game-theoretic generalizations about bidding behavior in an independent private value framework:

1. A first-price, sealed-bid auction in which risk-neutral bidders have independent private values results in bids that are strictly below the bidders' true values.

2. In a second-price, sealed-bid auction with private values, bidding truthfully is a dominant strategy for every bidder.

3. In an IPV environment with risk-neutral bidders, the expected price paid for the object is the same under the first-price and second-price, sealed-bid auctions; this is known as the revenue equivalence theorem.

4. The English oral auction is strategically equivalent to the Vickrey sealed-bid auction in an IPV environment.

The common value model has been successfully used to model auctions for offshore oil leases and federal timber sales. An important new problem that surfaces in these auctions is the winner's curse.

5. In a common value environment, the auction will be won by the bidder who initially overestimates the object's value the most. Rational bidders take this into account in forming their bids.

The way bidders can avoid the winner's curse is to take advantage of the fact that the very act of winning the auction reveals some of the other bidders' private information. Optimal bidding takes this additional information into account in forming the bid. As a result, rational bidders in a common values environment will act conservatively and submit bids well below their *initial* valuation of the object's true worth.

We concluded by examining the question of the economic efficiency of auctions as resource allocation mechanisms. The meaning of "efficiency" is different in the two auction environments considered. In an IPV setting, an auction is efficient if it is always the case that the auction winner is the bidder who values the auctioned object the most. All four auction formats are efficient in this sense.

In a common value setting, "efficiency" means that the bidders have the incentive to gather the optimal amount of information about the object's value before bidding. At the optimum, the expected benefit from additional information is exactly offset by its expected cost. This is a complex problem that is beyond the level of this book.

14.9   Further Reading

Though somewhat dated, a good account of the history of auctions and pointers on conducting and participating in them is Ralph Cassidy's *Auctions and Auctioneering* (Berkeley: University of California Press, 1967). The original account of the Babylonian bride auction can be found in Herodotus's *The Histories of Herodotus*, of which many English translations exist. Roman auctions are described in Will Durant's *Caesar and Christ* (New York: Simon and Schuster, 1944).

A classic discussion of auction strategy from a non–game-theoretic perspective is W. Vickrey's article, "Counterspeculation, Auctions, and Competitive Sealed Tenders," *Journal of Finance*, 16 (1961), pp. 8–37. A more game-theoretic analysis of Vickrey's ideas is A. Ortega-Reichert's dissertation "Models for Competitive Bidding under Uncertainty," Department of Operations Research Technical Report no. 8, (1968), Stanford University.

A very informative discussion of the FCC's auction of PCS licenses is John McMillan's "Analyzing the Airwaves Auction," *Journal of Economic Literature*, 10 (1996), pp. 159-75.

14.10   Discussion Questions

1. Look through the business and classified section of your local newspaper and locate an announcement of a recent public auction. What types of items are being sold? What type of auction format is being used—sealed bid, open cry, first price, second price? If possible, try to attend the auction and see how it is conducted. (But be careful what you do with your hands!)

2. Cassidy reported in 1967 that about 75% of all auctions in the United States were English auctions. Given the strategic equivalence of the English auction to the second-price, sealed-bid auction and the revenue equivalence theorem, why do you think the English auction is so much more popular than the other three formats we have considered?

3. Is there some way to detect collusive bidding by a group of bidders (a "bidding ring") in a sealed-bid auction? In an English auction?

4. What strategies could an auctioneer use to counter a bidding ring in an English oral auction? What about in a Dutch auction?

14.11   New Terms

ascending/descending/simultaneous
   bids
auction
auction design
auction environment
auction rules
bidding function
common value environment
Dutch auction
efficient auction
English auction
ex post payoffs
first-price auction

independent private values
jump bid
multi-unit auction
open and closed auctions
oral auction
reserve price
revenue equivalence theorem
sealed-bid auction
second-price auction
single-unit auction
strategically equivalent
Vickrey auction
winner's curse

14.12   Exercises

All the exercises concern Veronica's comic book auction to her friends Archie and Betty. The units are thousands of dollars. That is, 1 = $1,000, 0.8 = $800, etc. In Exercises 14.1–14.3, it is common knowledge that Veronica's collection is worth 0.8 ($800) to both Archie and Betty.

EXERCISE 14.1

What is the Nash equilibrium of (a) a first-price, sealed-bid auction, and (b) a Vickrey auction?

EXERCISE 14.2

Suppose Veronica decides to sell her collection using an *all-pay auction* format. In an all-pay auction, the collection goes to the highest bidder, but *all the bidders— both the winner and the loser(s)*—have to pay the amount they bid. Find the unique mixed-strategy Nash equilibrium of this auction. Proceed as follows: A mixed strategy is a random variable on the interval [0, 0.8] with a distribution function $F(b)$. If Betty uses the mixed strategy $F_B(b)$, then $F_B(b)$ is the probability that Betty's bid will be less than the bid b. The expected payoff to Archie from submitting the bid b equals $0.8 \cdot F_B(b) - b$. Archie will adopt a mixed strategy only if he gets the same expected payoff from every possible bid. That is, Betty's mixed strategy must satisfy the identity $0.8 \cdot F_B(b) - b \equiv$ constant. Use this identity and the fact that $F_B(0.8) = 1$ to determine $F_B(b)$.

EXERCISE 14.3

This is a continuation of exercises 14.1 and 14.2. What is Veronica's expected revenue from (a) a first-price, sealed-bid auction; (b) a second-price, sealed-bid auction; and (c) an all-pay auction? What can you say about Veronica's attitude toward risk if she prefers format (c) to either (a) or (b)?

EXERCISE 14.4

Suppose Veronica uses a first-price auction but that Archie and Betty have independent, private valuations that take on only two values, 0 and 1, with equal probability. A pure strategy now consists of two numbers, $b(0)$ and $b(1)$, where $b(V)$ is the bid when the collection is worth V to the bidder. Find a symmetric Nash equilibrium strategy b^* of this game. (*Hint:* Clearly $b^*(0) = 0$. So the problem reduces to determining how to bid when the collection is worth 1. Next convince yourself that there is no Nash equilibrium in pure strategies by graphing the expected payoff from submitting a bid when the collection is worth 1, given an arbitrary hypothesized value of $b^*(1)$. The equilibrium therefore involves choosing $b^*(1)$ according to some probability distribution, F. This distribution is continuous on the interval $[0, B]$, with $B < 1$, and $F(0) > 0$. Furthermore, F makes Archie and Betty indifferent to any bid within the interval $[0, B]$ whenever he or she believes the collection is worth 1.)

Exercises 14.5–14.8 assume the independent private value environment of Section 14.4: Archie values the collection at V_A, Betty values it at V_B, and the two valuations are independent random variables uniformly distributed on the unit interval [0, 1].

EXERCISE 14.5

Suppose Veronica uses a Vickrey auction, but sets a reserve price of 0.5 ($500).

This means that the payoff function of both players is

$$\Pi_i(b_A, b_B) = \begin{cases} V_i - \max\{0.5, b_j\} & \text{if } b_i > \max\{0.5, b_j\} \\ \$0 & \text{otherwise.} \end{cases} \qquad [14.6]$$

(a) Show that it is a dominant strategy for both players to bid their true values for the collection.

(b) What is Veronica's expected revenue at this equilibrium? (*Hint:* Veronica's revenue, R, depends on Betty and Archie's valuations of the collection as follows:

$$R(V_A, V_B) = \begin{cases} 0 & \text{if } V_A < 0.5 \text{ and } V_B < 0.5 \\ 0.5 & \text{if } V_A < 0.5 \leq V_B \\ 0.5 & \text{if } V_B < 0.5 \leq V_A \\ \min\{V_A, V_B\} & \text{if } 0.5 \leq V_A \text{ and } 0.5 \leq V_B. \end{cases}$$

The expected value of $R(V_A, V_B)$ equals

$$\int_0^{0.5} \int_0^{0.5} 0 \, dV_A \, dV_B + \int_{0.5}^1 \int_0^{0.5} 0.5 \, dV_A \, dV_B$$

$$+ \int_0^{0.5} \int_{0.5}^1 0.5 \, dV_A \, dV_B + \int_{0.5}^1 \int_{0.5}^1 \min\{V_A, V_B\} \, dV_A \, dV_B$$

Use the integral formulas in Section 14.13 to evaluate this integral.

EXERCISE 14.6*

This exercise is a continuation of 14.5. Suppose Veronica uses a Vickrey auction, but sets a reserve price of $\overline{R}$. Find an expression for Veronica's expected revenue in terms of the variable $\overline{R}$ when both Archie and Betty bid truthfully. Use this expression to determine the optimal reservation price if Veronica is risk neutral. In general, the seller should set a reservation price above zero.

EXERCISE 14.7

Suppose Veronica tries to sell her comics by giving Archie and Betty a take-it-or-leave-it price of 0.5 ($500). If exactly one of the two potential buyers accepts this offer, then the collection goes to him or her at that price. If both accept the offer, then they flip a fair coin and the winner of the toss gets the collection at that price. If neither of them accepts, then neither gets the collection and the collection is left unsold. Veronica considers the collection worth nothing to her and is risk neutral.

(a) What constitutes a pure strategy for Archie and Betty?

(b) What are equilibrium strategies for Archie and Betty?

(c) What is Veronica's expected revenue from her take-it-or-leave-it offer, and how does it compare with her revenue from using an English auction?

---

*Indicates a difficult exercise.

(d) Is Veronica's "threat" not to sell the collection if Betty and Archie turn down her offer credible? Why or why not?

(e) Suppose that Veronica makes a sequence of "take-it-or-leave-it" offers, each time reducing the price. How does this compare to the auction formats we have studied in this chapter?

EXERCISE 14.8

This is a continuation of Exercise 14.7. We now want to determine Veronica's optimal take-it-or-leave-it price. So the game is now: Veronica announces a take-it-or-leave-it price, P. Archie and Betty then move simultaneously and announce whether they want to buy the collection at that price.

(a) What constitutes a strategy for Archie and Betty now?

(b) What are equilibrium strategies for Archie and Betty?

(c) What is the expected revenue to Veronica as a function of P?

(d) What is the optimal price for Veronica to charge and what is her revenue when she charges this price?

Exercises 14.9–14.11 concern the common value environment of Section 14.6.1. That is, the collection is worth $V_A + V_B$, where V_A is known only to Archie, V_B is known only to Betty, and V_A and V_B are independent and uniformly distributed on the interval [0, 0.5].

EXERCISE 14.9

Show that the function Π_A defined in Eq. [14.5] has a unique maximum at $b = 2V_A$.

EXERCISE 14.10

Show that if Veronica uses a first-price, sealed-bid auction, then the Nash equilibrium strategy is for each bidder to bid V_i.

EXERCISE 14.11

Show that since there are only two bidders, the second-price, sealed-bid auction is strategically equivalent to the English auction even when the bidder's valuations of the collection are not independent. (*Hint:* Show the equivalence for the Japanese version of the English auction in which the bidders cannot reenter the auction once they leave.)

EXERCISE 14.12*

Suppose Veronica uses a first-price, sealed-bid auction to sell her collection. Show that the linear bidding functions $b_A = \alpha \cdot V_A$ and $b_B = \beta \cdot V_B$ are Nash equilibrium strategies for Archie and Betty whenever $\frac{1}{\alpha} + \frac{1}{\beta} = 2, \frac{1}{2} < \alpha < 2$, and $\frac{1}{2} < \beta < 2$.

---

*Indicates a difficult exercise.

14.13 Appendix: A Guide to Working with Uniformly Distributed Random Variables

We will begin with some basic definitions. The distribution function F_X equals the probability that the random variable X is less than or equal to x. The derivative of F_X is called the *density* of X and will be denoted by f_X. We are interested in random variables that are *uniformly distributed* on the unit interval [0, 1]. The distribution function for a uniformly distributed random variable X is given by

$$F_X(x) = \begin{cases} 1 & \text{if } 1 < x \\ x & \text{if } 0 \leq x \leq 1 \\ 0 & \text{if } x > 1. \end{cases} \qquad [14A.1]$$

Its density is given by

$$f_X(x) = \begin{cases} 0 & \text{if } x < 0 \ \text{ or } \ x > 1 \\ 1 & \text{if } 0 \leq x \leq 1. \end{cases} \qquad [14A.2]$$

The *expected value* of X equals

$$\int_0^1 x \, f_X(x) \, dx = \int_0^1 x \, dx = \tfrac{1}{2} \qquad [14A.3]$$

and the expected value of X conditional on X lying in the subinterval $[a, b]$ of [0, 1] equals

$$\frac{\int_a^b x \, f_X(x) dx}{\int_a^b f_X(x) dx} = \frac{\int_a^b x \, dx}{\int_a^b dx} = \frac{\tfrac{1}{2}b^2 - \tfrac{1}{2}a^2}{b - a} = \frac{b + a}{2}. \qquad [14A.4]$$

In studying auctions, we are often not interested in the expected value of a valuation, but usually in some function of a valuation. If g is a real-valued function of the uniformly distributed random variable X, then the *expected value* of $g(X)$, or $\mathbf{E}g(X)$, is equal to $\int_0^1 g(x) dx$. In evaluating expected values, the following integral formulas are useful, where $0 \leq a \leq b \leq c \leq 1$ and A, B, and C are constants.

$$\int_a^c g(x) dx = \int_a^b g(x) dx + \int_b^c g(x) dx \qquad [14A.5]$$

$$\int_a^b (A \cdot f(x) + B \cdot g(x)) dx = A \cdot \int_a^b f(x) dx + B \cdot \int_a^b g(x) dx \qquad [14A.6]$$

$$\int_a^b C \, dx = C \cdot (b - a) \qquad\qquad [14A.7]$$

$$\int_a^b x^n \, dx = \frac{1}{n+1} \cdot (b^{n+1} - a^{n+1}) \qquad\qquad [14A.8]$$

We are also interested in the expected value of events that depend on more than one random variable. Two random variables X and Y are *independent* if for any two intervals $[a, b]$ and $[c, d]$ $P(a \leq X \leq b \text{ and } c \leq Y \leq d) = P(a \leq X \leq b) \cdot P(c \leq Y \leq d)$. If $g(X, Y)$ is a real-valued function of two independent uniformly distributed random variables, then the expected value of g equals

$$\int_0^1 \int_0^1 g(x, y) \, dx \, dy = \int_0^1 \left(\int_0^1 g(x, y) \, dx \right) dy = \int_0^1 \left(\int_0^1 g(x, y) \, dy \right) dx. \qquad [14A.9]$$

In evaluating such expected values, the following integral formulas are useful.

$$\int_a^b \int_a^b \max\{V_A, V_B\} dV_A dV_B = \int_a^b \int_{V_B}^b V_A \, dV_A \, dV_B + \int_a^b \int_{V_A}^b V_B \, dV_B \, dV_A \qquad [14A.10]$$

$$= \tfrac{2}{3}b^3 + \tfrac{1}{3}a^3 - ab^2$$

$$\int_a^b \int_a^b \min\{V_A, V_B\} dV_A dV_B = \int_a^b \int_a^{V_B} V_A \, dV_A \, dV_B + \int_a^b \int_a^{V_A} V_B \, dV_B \, dV_A \qquad [14A.11]$$

$$= \tfrac{2}{3}a^3 + \tfrac{1}{3}b^3 - ba^2$$

PART V

Dynamic Games with Incomplete Information

CHAPTER 15

Perfect Bayesian Equilibrium

OVERVIEW OF CHAPTER 15

15.1   Introduction

In a dynamic game, ill-informed players may be able to learn something about the game being played by observing the moves of better-informed opponents. Since incorporating such learning into the analysis is difficult, we begin this chapter by introducing two important tools: *information sets* and *Bayes' theorem*.[1]

In Section 15.3 we show that Nash equilibria exist that are implausible precisely because they implicitly assume that information imbedded in another player's moves is not being used intelligently. This is analogous to the implausibility of equilibrium strategies that involve incredible threats. One obvious solution is to impose the stronger criterion of subgame perfection. Unfortunately, the games that are generated by applying the Harsanyi transformation usually do not have any proper subgames—that is, subgames other than the entire game. As a result,

---

[1]Readers who studied Chapter 9 have already been introduced to information sets.

every Nash equilibrium in these games is subgame perfect. The solution is to extend the concept of subgame perfection so that it regains its "bite," and to require players to "rationally update" their beliefs about the game being played using a procedure known as *Bayesian updating*. The resulting equilibria are known as *perfect Bayesian equilibria*. Section 15.5 examines the important concept of *signaling*. This is contrasted with the related concept of *screening* in Section 15.6.

15.2   Information Sets

When players possess private information in dynamic games, it is crucial to keep track of who knows what and when. **Information sets** are tools economists use to keep track of decision nodes that are different but appear the same to the decision maker. We will illustrate the notion of an information set using the Software Game presented in Chapter 6. The game tree is reproduced in Figure 15.1. Macrosoft moves first, Microcorp moves second, and four outcomes are possible. If Microcorp does not know Macrosoft's decision before it moves, then it cannot tell whether it is making its decision at decision node D_2 or at D_3. We will say that D_2 and D_3 are in the same *information set*. Simply put, an information set is a set of decision nodes among which a player cannot distinguish. When a player reaches a decision node lying within an information set containing more than one node, she does not know exactly where she is on the game tree.

When two decision nodes are in an information set we will display this in the game tree by encircling the two nodes with a dotted line. This new feature can be found in Figure 15.1. The collection of information sets constitutes the **information partition** for the game.

Having defined what an information set is and how it will be depicted, we will now consider some *invalid* information sets. What makes these information sets invalid is that in each case it is possible for the player to logically deduce which node he or she has reached using his or her knowledge of the game tree

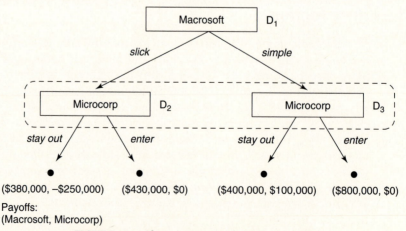

Payoffs:
(Macrosoft, Microcorp)

FIGURE 15.1   The game tree for the Software Game.

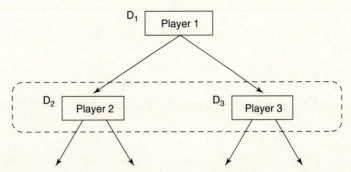

FIGURE 15.2 An information set that contains nodes belonging to different players.

and his or her memory of previous moves. The first example of an invalid information set is shown in Figure 15.2, where nodes belonging to two different players are shown within the same information set. When Player 3 reaches node D_3, he knows he is not at D_2 since he does not move at that node. Similarly, when Player 2 reaches this information set, she knows she is not at D_3. So to be valid, an information set must follow:

Information Set Rule 1: All the nodes in any information set must belong to the same player.

In Figure 15.3, nodes D_1 and D_2 are designated as members of an information set. By definition, this means that the player who moves at these nodes should not be able to distinguish between node D_1 and node D_2. But node D_2 can only be reached from node D_1—and then only if Player 1 moves down. The player will know if she has reached node D_2 by dint of her knowledge of the game tree and her move at node D_1. Therefore, nodes D_1 and D_2 cannot be in the same information set. Similarly, it would be incorrect for Figure 15.3 to show nodes D_1 and D_3 within the same information set. And it would be incorrect for nodes D_1, D_2, and D_3 to be included in a common information set. The point is that an

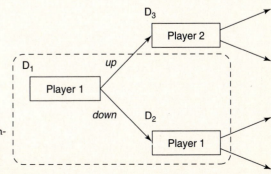

FIGURE 15.3 An information set containing two nodes that follow each other on the decision tree.

information set cannot contain nodes that the players could distinguish by reason of their *following* one another on the game tree.

Information Set Rule 2: If decision node D_1 is a predecessor of node D_2, then D_1 and D_2 cannot be contained in the same information set.

Consider now the somewhat different situation shown in Figure 15.4. Suppose the decision node D_2 allows player 1 to choose only between moves 1 or 2 and the decision node D_3 allows player 1 to choose only between moves 1 and 3. If the player reaches the node D_2, then she knows her options are moves 1 or 2. Since she knows 3 is *not* an option, she knows she *cannot* be at D_3. Therefore, D_2 and D_3 are logically distinguishable and cannot be in the same information set.

Information Set Rule 3: Exactly the same set of moves can be taken at each of the decision nodes in an information set.

Almost all games used in economics are games with **perfect recall.** These are games in which no player forgets any information she once knew, including hers and any other player's earlier observed moves. Perfect recall implies two further restrictions on information sets. Consider the game tree displayed in Figure 15.5. In this diagram, decision nodes D_1, D_2, D_3, and D_4 all belong to player 1, and the information sets are {D1}, {D2}, and {D3, D4}. This means that player 1 can distinguish between nodes D_1 and D_2, but she cannot distinguish between nodes D_3 and D_4. But D_3 can only be reached if player 1 moves Right at node D_1, and D_4 can only be reached if player 1 moves Left at node D_2. The diagram implies that when player 1 gets to D_3 or D_4, she has "forgotten" her previous action at D_1 or D_2, respectively. So this is not a game of perfect recall.

Eliminating game trees such as Figure 15.5 is not enough. Perfect recall also rules out game trees such as the one shown in Figure 15.6. In this game, player 2's decision nodes D_4 and D_5 are contained within the same information set. The

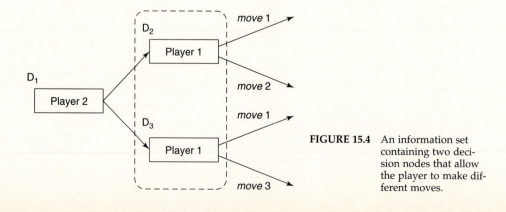

FIGURE 15.4 An information set containing two decision nodes that allow the player to make different moves.

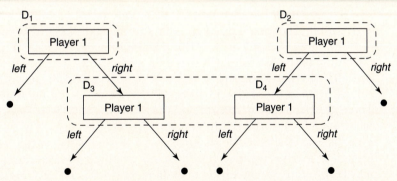

FIGURE 15.5 A game tree diagram that implies a player has forgotten a move previously taken.

game reaches player 2's decision node D_4 only if player 1 moves Left at D_1 and player 2 moves Down at D_2. Similarly, the game reaches player 2's decision node D_5 only if player 1 moves Right at D_1 and player 2 moves Down at D_4. Since D_2 and D_3 are in different information sets, player 2 knows what player 1 chose at D_1 when he moves at either D_2 or D_3. Yet D_4 and D_5 are shown as being in the same information set, which implies that when player 2 reaches D_4 or D_5, he has forgotten player 1's earlier move.

15.3 Bayes' Theorem

In dynamic games with incomplete information, players' moves can sometimes reveal the private information on which they were based. When that happens, the other players will want to take this new information into account. We will use a tool known as *Bayesian updating*, applying it first to a simple decision-theoretic problem. We will postpone its application to a game until later.

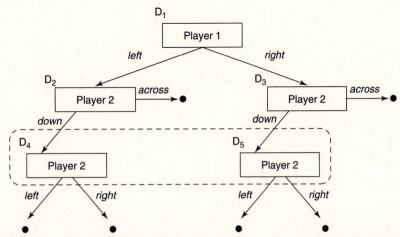

FIGURE 15.6 A game tree diagram that implies a player has forgotten something he knew earlier in the game.

Let us revisit the Clampett Oil Company (see Chapter 1) and its decision to drill for oil. Clampett's problem is that it does not know whether there is an oil deposit under its land or not. The firm believes the chance of a deposit is 10%. Given the high costs of drilling a well, such a low probability of success makes drilling too risky. Fortunately, before it makes its decision, Clampett can conduct seismic tests to detect the presence or absence of oil, although not without error. There are two types of error: (1) the test can suggest the presence of oil when in fact there is none, and (2) the test can suggest the absence of oil when a deposit in fact exists. The first error is known as a **false positive** result, and the second is known as a **false negative** result. In this example, the conditional probability of a false positive result, given that there is no oil, is 25%; and the conditional probability of a false negative result, given there is oil, is 5%.

Clampett's decision tree is displayed in Figure 15.7. Nature first chooses the state of the world, that is, whether there is oil or not. This move is not observed by Clampett. Nature then moves again and determines the outcome of the seismic test. Clampett then has to decide whether to drill. Not drilling has a payoff of $0, drilling a dry hole results in a loss of $10 million, and drilling a gusher results in a profit of $20 million. Without the test results, the expected payoff from drilling equals $0.10 \cdot \$20\ million - 0.90 \cdot \$10\ million = -\$7\ million$. However, suppose Clampett tests for oil and the test is positive. What should Clampett do? Not drilling results in a certain payoff of $0, while the payoff from drilling results in the lottery ($20 *million*:$\pi$, $-$10 *million*:$1 - \pi$), where π is the conditional probability of an oil deposit given a positive test result. Note that this is *not* the same thing as the conditional probability of a *positive test* given an *oil deposit*. The problem is to calculate π from the data at hand. The necessary tool is a theorem concerning conditional probabilities called **Bayes' theorem.** See Section 15.12 for a mathematical proof of Bayes' theorem.

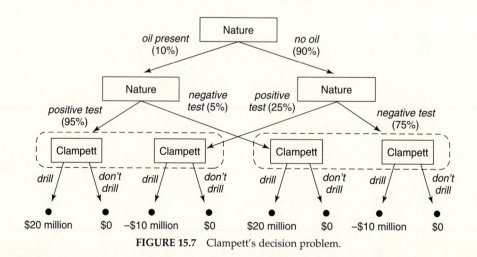

FIGURE 15.7 Clampett's decision problem.

> **BAYES' THEOREM:** Suppose the events $E_1, \ldots, E_N$ are mutually exclusive, exhaustive, and have nonzero probability. Suppose further that the event F has a nonzero probability. Then for each event i
>
> $$P(E_i|F) = \frac{P(F|E_i) \cdot P(E_i)}{P(F)} \text{ and } P(F) = \sum_{i=1}^{N} P(F|E_i) \cdot P(E_i),$$
>
> where $P(E_i|F)$ is the probability the event E_i will occur given that the event F has occurred.

Bayes' theorem allows a player to reassess the probability of the event E_i after learning that F has occurred using only the conditional probabilities that F will occur given E_i and the unconditional probabilities of E_i. The probability $P(E_i)$ is called the **prior probability** of E_i, since it represents the player's beliefs before learning that the event F has occurred. Similarly, the probability $P(E_i|F)$ is the **posterior probability** of E_i, since it represents the player's beliefs after learning about F. **Bayesian updating** during a game consists simply of replacing the prior probability of a state of the world with its posterior probability after observing the moves of a better-informed player.

In order to apply Bayes' theorem to Clampett's problem, we will let E_1 be the event "there is an oil deposit," E_2 be the event "there isn't an oil deposit," and F be the event "the seismic test is positive." We want to know the posterior probability $P(E_1|F)$ (i.e., the probability there is oil given that the test is positive) from our knowledge of the prior probability of an oil deposit and the conditional probabilities of false negative and false positive test results. Bayes' theorem implies that

$$
\begin{aligned}
P(E_1|F) &= \frac{P(F|E_1) \cdot P(E_1)}{P(F|E_1) \cdot P(E_1) + P(F|E_2) \cdot P(E_2)} \\[2mm]
&= \frac{0.95 \cdot 0.10}{0.95 \cdot 0.10 + 0.25 \cdot 0.90} \qquad\qquad [15.1] \\[2mm]
&= 0.30.
\end{aligned}
$$

So, when the test is positive, there is only a 30% chance that drilling will produce a strike. You are probably surprised that the conditional probability of oil given a positive test result is so low since the test seems to be fairly accurate. Your reasoning has been confounded by ignoring the second way that a positive test result can occur: there is no oil, but the test produces a false positive result. Because the probability of a dry well is very high (90%) and the conditional probability of a false positive is not so low (25%), the product of these two probabilities is fairly large (23%). Since this number is in the denominator of Eq. [15.1], it leads to a small quotient. The expected profit from drilling a well when the test is positive equals $0.30 \cdot \$20$ *million* $- 0.70 \cdot \$10$ *million* $= -\$0.10$ *million*. Even a risk-neutral drilling company will find it unprofitable to drill. We leave it as an exercise for you to show that a negative test implies an even larger expected loss.

Bayes' theorem often yields results that are counterintuitive. An example arises in the current debate over universal screening for infection by the virus that causes AIDS, known as HIV ("human immunodeficiency virus"). HIV screening consists of a laboratory test for the presence of antibodies to the HIV virus using a blood sample. This test is not foolproof. Like nearly all medical tests, there is a chance of "false negative" and "false positive" results. The test generates a "false negative" result if the laboratory detects no antibodies to the HIV virus when the person is, in fact, infected. This can occur if the person has been infected only recently, since it takes time for the body to manufacture antibodies to the virus. The current false negative error rate is so low that we can assume it to be zero. The test is said to generate a "false positive" result if the test detects the presence of antibodies to the HIV virus when the person is, in fact, not infected. This can happen through contamination of the sample or error on the part of the lab staff. The probability of a false positive result depends on the test used. For example, the ELIZA test has a false positive error rate of about 7%. But when this test is combined sequentially with the Western blot test, the error rate can be reduced to 0.005%.

It is currently estimated that less than 1% of the adult population in the United States is infected with the HIV virus. But this overall infection rate disguises sizable differences among subgroups. For example, screening of military recruits and blood donors has shown an infection rate among women of between 0.01% and 0.06%, respectively. Assume that the infection rate among all women is 0.01% and we institute universal HIV testing using a test with a false positive error rate of 0.005% and a false negative error rate of 0%. What is the probability that a woman randomly chosen from the general population will *not be infected* with the HIV virus, even though the test result is positive? Before you go further, write down your guess. Let us now use Bayes' theorem to find the answer.

Let E be the event "not infected with the AIDS virus" and let F be the event "the test is positive." We want to compute $P(E|F)$, the probability of no infection given a positive test result. We know the probability of testing positive when the person is infected, $P(F|not\ E)$, equals 100% and the probability of testing positive when the person is not infected, $P(F|E)$, equals 0.005%. Finally, we assume that the probability the person is infected, $P(E)$, equals 0.01%. It now follows from Bayes' theorem that

$$P(E|F) = \frac{P(F|E) \cdot P(E)}{P(F|E) \cdot P(E) + P(F|not\ E) \cdot P(not\ E)}$$

$$= \frac{0.005\% \cdot 99.99\%}{0.005\% \cdot 99.99\% + 100\% \cdot 0.01\%} \qquad [15.2]$$

$$= \frac{1}{3}$$

This means that *one third* of all women who test positive for the HIV virus will, in fact, not be infected! If you don't believe this answer, check the arithmetic. Furthermore, this is actually a *lower bound* on the error rate since it assumes a zero probability of a false negative. This assumption has the effect of inflating the denominator, thereby reducing the value of $P(E|F)$.

Figure 15.8 may help you visualize why the probability of infection is so small among those who test positive. The figure shows three concentric disks

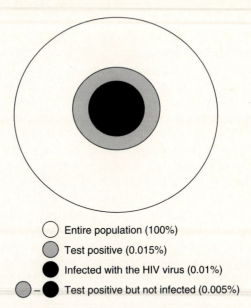

- ◯ Entire population (100%)
- ⬤ Test positive (0.015%)
- ⬤ Infected with the HIV virus (0.01%)
- ◯ – ⬤ Test positive but not infected (0.005%)

(Note: Areas are not drawn exactly to scale)

FIGURE 15.8 The size of the group of HIV-infected women relative to all women who will test positive for the virus.

colored white, gray, and black. The white disk represents the entire population of adult women. The gray disk represents all those who will obtain a positive test result. The black disk represents those who are infected with HIV. The black disk lies entirely within the gray disk because of the negligible number of false negative test results. The uninfected women who will get false positive test results is represented by the gray doughnut-shaped area that lies between the white and black regions. The probability of non-infection among those who test positive, $P(E|F)$, is the ratio between the area of the gray doughnut and the area of entire gray disk (which equals the area of the gray doughnut plus the area of the black disk). As you can see from Figure 15.8, this ratio can be large, even if the gray disk is small.

15.4 Perfect Bayesian Equilibrium

You saw in Chapter 13 that once a game with incomplete information is transformed into a game with complete but imperfect information, its Bayesian Nash equilibria can be determined. Such games often have many Bayesian Nash equilibria. When dynamic elements are added some of them involve incredible threats and are implausible. We dealt with this problem in Chapter 6 where we proposed a solution: Eliminate from consideration all Nash equilibria that are not subgame perfect. Unfortunately, games with incomplete information usually have only one subgame—namely, the entire game. As a result, the implausible equilibria are subgame perfect as well. In order to "weed them out" we will have to be more subtle.

In Chapter 6, section 5, we defined a subgame for a game of perfect information. In these games every decision node lies in its own information set. When games contain information sets consisting of more than one decision node, the definition of a subgame needs to be modified. Fortunately, the modification is easy. Recall from our earlier definition that the subgame G_S of the game G_T is constructed as follows: (1) G_S has the same players as G_T, although some of these players may not make any moves in G_S; (2) the initial node of G_S is a subroot of G_T; and (3) the game tree of G_S consists of this subroot, all its successor nodes, and the branches between them. We need to modify the second and third conditions so as to ensure that whenever a player makes a move in a subgame, the player can logically deduce this from knowledge of the game tree. This means that whenever a decision node in a subgame lies in an information set that contains other decision nodes, these other nodes must also be part of the subgame. Suppose that a player had an information set that contained two decision nodes, one that was part of the subgame and the other that wasn't. If that information set were reached during the play of the game, the player that moves at that information set could not be sure whether he was playing the subgame or not. A logical corollary is that every initial node of a subgame must lie in its own information set. Otherwise the subgame has more than one initial node and is not a well-defined game.

To illustrate both the problem and its solution, we will modify the Entry Deterrence Game introduced in Chapter 13. An Incumbent firm must decide whether to expand the capacity of its plant and an Entrant must decide whether to enter and compete against the Incumbent or stay out of the market. The added capacity will allow the Incumbent to produce more output at lower cost. Because of this, it is profitable for the Entrant to enter if and only if the Incumbent does not expand. Suppose that the Entrant can decide whether to enter only *after* observing the Incumbent's choice of capacity but she does not know the Incumbent's costs. The game tree for this dynamic game is displayed in Figure 15.9.

In the new game, the Incumbent has the same strategies as before. His strategy

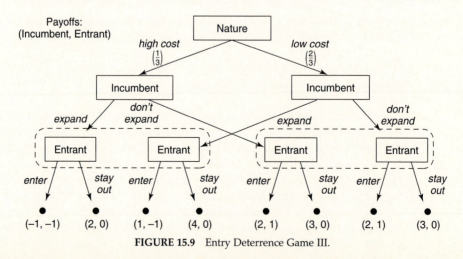

Payoffs:
(Incumbent, Entrant)

FIGURE 15.9 Entry Deterrence Game III.

Table 15.1   **Normal Form of Entry Deterrence Game III**

		Entrant			
		(enter, enter)	(enter, stay out)	(stay out, enter)	(stay out, stay out)
Incumbent	(expand, expand)	$((-1, 1), (-1))$	$((-1, 1), (-\frac{1}{3}))$	$((1, 4), (0))$	$((1, 4), (0))$
	(expand, don't expand)	$((-1, 2), (\frac{1}{3}))$	$((-1, 3), (-\frac{1}{3}))$	$((1, 2), (\frac{2}{3}))$	$((1, 3), (0))$
	(don't expand, expand)	$((2, 1), (-\frac{1}{3}))$	$((3, 1), (-\frac{2}{3}))$	**$((2, 4), (\frac{1}{3}))$**	$((3, 4), (0))$
	(don't expand, don't expand)	**$((2, 2), (1))$**	$((3, 3), (0))$	$((2, 2), (1))$	$((3, 3), (0))$

Conditional Expected Payoffs: ((*high cost* Incumbent, *low cost* Incumbent), (Entrant))

specifies the move to make for each of his two types. A pure strategy is represented by a pair of moves, such as (*expand, don't expand*). The first word corresponds to the move made when the costs are high and the second to the move made when the cost is low. The Entrant, however, now has two information sets, each corresponding to a move by the Incumbent. A pure strategy is now a pair of moves, such as (*enter, stay out*). The first move is made when the Incumbent expands and the second is taken when he doesn't. The normal form for the game is shown in Table 15.1. Each column corresponds to a strategy of the Entrant and each row corresponds to a strategy of the Incumbent. To see how the conditional expected payoffs were calculated, consider the first row and column. The Entrant always enters and the Incumbent always expands. The Entrant gets a payoff of -1 whatever the Incumbent's costs; hence, her conditional expected payoff equals -1. The Incumbent, on the other hand, earns a payoff of -1 when he is a *high cost* type and 1 when he is a *low cost* type. So his conditional expected payoff is $(-1, 1)$.

This game has two pure-strategy Nash equilibria. The equilibrium payoffs are displayed in boldface. At one equilibrium, the Incumbent expands when he has *low costs* and the Entrant *enters* if and only if the Incumbent *does not expand*. At the second equilibrium, the Incumbent never *expands* and the Entrant always *enters*. This equilibrium is highly implausible. Although the Incumbent's strategy calls for him never to *expand*, if the Entrant were ever to observe the Incumbent *expanding*, she would not want to carry out her threat to *enter* since she knows she would face a loss, while *staying out* insures her against any loss.

As Figure 15.9 shows, this game has no proper subgames. As a result, all Nash equilibria are subgame perfect by default. This is true not only of this game, but also of almost all games with incomplete information to which the Harsanyi transformation is applied. However, all is not lost. Although the Entrant's two information sets cannot be the starting nodes to a well-specified game subtree, this does not prevent us from finding the Entrant's optimal move at each information set. The reason is that in this game, the Entrant's payoff depends only on the Incumbent's capacity, not on the cost of installing this capacity. The game-theoretic meaning is that the Entrant can determine her payoff after observing the Incumbent's move without also having to know the state of the world. So, *in this special case,* the Entrant can determine her optimal move at either information set without having to guess which node within the set she has reached. In general, though, her optimal move at an information set *will* depend on her assessment of the probability of reaching each of the decision nodes within that information set. Like Sherlock Holmes, she must form a probabilistic inference about the state of the world from observing the moves of her better-informed opponents.

This collection of probability assessments, one for each information set, is called the player's **belief profile.** In Entry Deterrence Game III, there are four information sets, although two of them are trivial. The nontrivial information sets are labeled *Expand* and *Don't expand.* Beliefs are displayed using the same format we use for lotteries. For example, the belief "(*high:* 0.50, *low:* 0.50)" means the player believes that the chance of the Incumbent firm being a "high cost" type is 50% and the chance of it being a "low cost" type is 50%. A belief profile is represented as follows: {*Expand:* (*high:* 0.50, *low:* 0.50), *Don't expand:* (*high:* 0.8, *low:* 0.2)}.

A perfect Bayesian equilibrium consists of a strategy profile that is consistent with optimization on the part of the players and a belief profile that respects the laws of probability, particularly Bayes' theorem. This means, first of all, that the strategy profile must be a Nash equilibrium, given the player's beliefs. But more than that is needed. Using the strategy profile and her beliefs, a player can calculate the expected utility of making any move at any information set—even information sets that will not be reached if the equilibrium strategies are played. In contrast, Nash equilibrium places no constraints on players' moves at such information sets. We will require, therefore, that each player's strategy always selects moves that maximize the player's expected utility given her knowledge of the game up to that move, her beliefs, and the strategies of all the players. We will refer to this complex notion as "no incredible threats." Secondly, wherever possible, the players must use Bayesian updating to form their beliefs based on the common prior beliefs and the strategy profiles. When we considered Nash equilibrium strategies, we required them to be mutually consistent. Now we are requiring the same mutual consistency of beliefs. Such mutually consistent strategies and beliefs constitute a **perfect Bayesian equilibrium.**

A **perfect Bayesian equilibrium** *consists of a strategy profile and a belief profile such that:*

(1) *The collection of strategies constitute a Nash equilibrium, given the players' beliefs.*

(2) *At each player's information set, the move required by the player's strategy maximizes that player's expected utility, given the player's beliefs about the state of the world at that information set and the other players' strategies.*

> (3) Wherever possible, every player's beliefs can be derived from the equilibrium strategy profile and the common prior beliefs using Bayesian updating.

If we apply our definition to Entry Deterrence Game III, we see that the following is a perfect Bayesian equilibrium: the strategy profile {(Don't expand, Expand), (Stay out, Enter)}, and the belief profile {Expand: (high: 0, low: 1), Don't expand: (high: 1, low: 0)}. We leave it as an exercise for you to show that there is no belief profile for which the strategy profile {(Don't expand, Don't expand), (Enter, Enter)} is part of a perfect Bayesian equilibrium. So our definition, although complicated, eliminates the implausible Nash equilibrium.

At this point, you may be bothered by a certain circularity in the reasoning behind a Bayesian equilibrium. The optimal strategies of the players depend on the evolution of their beliefs about each other's type during the course of the game. But these beliefs depend, in turn, on the players' strategies via Bayes' theorem. This circularity is not that different from what we encountered in Chapter 1 when we looked at the Nash equilibrium for static games. This should not be too surprising since static games are also games of imperfect information.

It is one thing to define a Bayesian equilibrium. It is quite another to find one. In many instances in economics, finding an equilibrium involves the use of an "algorithm." For example, one algorithm for finding the equilibrium price in a perfectly competitive market is to plot the supply and demand curves and find where the curves intersect. In Chapter 6, to give another example, we presented the algorithm of backward induction for finding the subgame perfect equilibria of a game with perfect information.

Unfortunately, there is no well-established algorithm for finding Bayesian equilibria. One crude (i.e., not very helpful) algorithm for finding a Bayesian equilibrium has three steps: (1) propose a possible set of strategies and beliefs; (2) check to see if the proposed strategies satisfy the first and second conditions of the definition; and (3) check to see if the beliefs satisfy the third condition of the definition. Since there are frequently a very large number of possible strategies and beliefs, this algorithm can take a long time. There are better ways of searching for equilibria. Chapter 16 provides many tips for finding perfect Bayesian equilibria.

15.5 Signaling Games

One type of game with incomplete information has proven to be enormously useful in economics. This is the *signaling game*. Economist Michael Spence is credited with discovering and first studying this type of strategic situation.[1] Con-

---

[1]For this and other important research, he was awarded the John Bates Clark medal by the American Economics Association.

sider a publishing firm that is producing a new principles of economics textbook and deciding how much to spend on advertising. The firm is well aware that the consumers it would be advertising to are cynical economists who are unlikely to be swayed by a lot of cheap talk about the qualities of the new text they are touting. Instead, these economists must experience the book—try it out on their classes—before they can judge how good it is.

The publisher has done enough class testing of early drafts of the book that it has no doubts that this will be the best book on the market. The publisher is certain that if it could get enough economists to adopt the book as soon as it came out, the good word-of-mouth reviews would make the book a commercial success. Unfortunately for the publisher, the economists who are considering adopting the book are very uncertain about its quality. Because of this uncertainty, only a few of them will initially try it out. Even if the early adopters like the book and tell their friends and colleagues, there will be so few of them that the publisher won't recoup the money it must spend up front to bring the book to market. As a result, the publisher won't produce it.

The publisher appears to have no way to credibly *signal* to the academic community its private assessment of the book's quality. To be credible, any such signal must have the property that the publisher will *signal* that the book is good if and only if the book *is* good. We claim that an expensive advertising campaign may have this property. Suppose the book is not good, but the firm publishes it anyway with a large ad campaign and many economists adopt it immediately, expecting it to be a good textbook. Although sales will be good during the first year, they will plummet once the early adopters discover that the book is mediocre and share their experience with their colleagues. If the fall-off in sales is steep enough, the publisher won't be able to profit from this "deception" strategy. On the other hand, if the book is good and if the book's potential adopters interpret an expensive ad campaign as a signal that the book is good, then sales will grow quickly and the book will be a commercial success. This implies that adopters can infer the book's quality from the publisher's ad budget for the book. The ability of advertisement spending to allow the publisher to credibly reveal its private knowledge about the book's quality makes it rational for the firm to engage in this otherwise seemingly wasteful behavior.

Many other seemingly wasteful activities could be signals. For example, have you ever wondered whether your college classes are really making you more productive? Or do colleges exist primarily to "separate the sheep from the goats"? Michael Spence hypothesized that education might be functioning largely as a signal of a person's innate labor productivity. To see how, read on.

15.5.1 EDUCATION AS A SIGNAL

The following game involves an employer, Jorge, and a potential new employee, Carla. Jorge has to decide whether to hire Carla to work in his factory. Carla is asking for a wage of w. Her marginal productivity, which will be denoted by θ, is either 20 (*high*) or 10 (*low*). Jorge does not know θ, but Carla does. Carla's next best alternative to working for Jorge is to work for herself, where she earns $\frac{3}{4}\theta$, so this is the opportunity cost of working in Jorge's factory. If Jorge hires Carla and pays her w, then his payoff equals $\theta - w$ and her payoff equals $w - \frac{3}{4}\theta$. If Jorge does not hire Carla, then both earn a payoff of zero. Were Carla's productivity common knowledge, then the Pareto optimal outcome would be for Jorge to hire Carla and pay her a wage between $\frac{3}{4}\theta$ and θ.

Let us now examine this situation as a game with incomplete information. We will assume that it is common knowledge that Jorge has a prior belief about Carla's productivity, namely, that it is *high* with probability $\frac{1}{3}$ and *low* with probability $\frac{2}{3}$. Perhaps this arises from past observations that $\frac{1}{3}$ of all previous workers hired by Jorge have been high productivity workers and $\frac{2}{3}$ have been low productivity workers. This assumption allows us to apply the Harsanyi transformation and turn the game into one of complete but imperfect information. In the new game, Nature moves first and chooses Carla's type—*high* (productivity) with probability $\frac{1}{3}$ or *low* with probability $\frac{2}{3}$. Carla observes this move, but Jorge does not. Carla moves next and either quits the labor market or proposes a wage, w, to Jorge. If Carla quits, then the game ends and both players get a payoff of zero. If she makes a wage offer to Jorge, then he moves last and either hires Carla or does not. We will refer to this game as the Hiring Game. The game tree for the Hiring Game is displayed in Figure 15.10.

A pure strategy for Carla consists of a function $w(\theta)$ that states the wage Carla demands when her type is θ. A **pooling strategy** is one in which Carla behaves the same regardless of her type, that is, $w(10) = w(20)$. A **separating strategy** is one in which Carla behaves differently depending on her type, that is, $w(10) \neq w(20)$. After hearing Carla's wage demand w, Jorge forms an updated belief $p(w)$ about the probability that Carla's type is *high*. With this belief, the expected payoff from hiring her equals

$$(10 - w) \cdot (1 - p(w)) + (20 - w) \cdot p(w). \qquad [15.3]$$

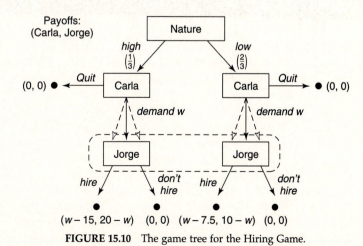

FIGURE 15.10 The game tree for the Hiring Game.

A pure strategy for Jorge consists of a hiring decision $h(w)$ for each wage w that Carla might propose.

The strategies and beliefs constitute a perfect Bayesian equilibrium only if

1. For each θ, $w^*(\theta)$ maximizes Carla's expected utility over all wage offers w given Jorge's strategy;

2. the hiring decision $h^*(w)$ maximizes Jorge's expected utility given his updated beliefs and Carla's announced wage demand; and

3. $p^*(w)$, Jorge's updated beliefs, can be derived from Carla's equilibrium strategy $w^*(\theta)$ using Bayesian updating.

The following strategies and beliefs form a perfect Bayesian equilibrium for our game:

Carla's strategy: Carla demands a wage of 10 when she is a low productivity type and quits the market when she is a high productivity type.

Jorge's strategy: Jorge hires her if and only if she demands a wage less than or equal to 10.

Jorge's belief: Carla is certainly a low productivity type whenever she applies for a job, regardless of the wage she demands.

Now we will show that these strategies and belief profiles satisfy the conditions for a perfect Bayesian equilibrium. We will start with Jorge's beliefs. Given Carla's wage demand of 10, the conditional probability that she is a *high* productivity type is

$$P(\theta = 20 | w = 10)$$

$$= \frac{P(w = 10 | \theta = 20) \cdot P(\theta = 20)}{P(w = 10 | \theta = 20) \cdot P(\theta = 20) + P(w = 10 | \theta = 10) \cdot P(\theta = 10)}$$

$$= \frac{0 \cdot \frac{1}{3}}{0 \cdot \frac{1}{3} + 1 \cdot \frac{2}{3}}$$

$$= 0. \qquad\qquad\qquad [15.4]$$

Bayes' theorem places no restrictions on Jorge's beliefs when Carla offers a wage other than 10, so it is perfectly all right to propose that Jorge believes that any wage demand other than 10 also implies that Carla is certainly a low productivity type. This implies that condition (3) above is satisfied.

Now consider Jorge's expected utility, given his updated beliefs and Carla's wage offer. Jorge's proposed strategy is clearly optimal. He would be willing to pay up to what he believed she was worth to him (10) and he would be thrilled to pay less. This means that condition (2) is satisfied.

Finally, we need to evaluate Carla's strategy. Since Jorge will only accept a wage less than or equal to 10, Carla should only make a wage offer if she is a low productivity type. If she is, then she clearly should get the highest wage she can. Hence, Carla's strategy is optimal and condition (1) is satisfied.

The outcome of this equilibrium is that Carla is hired if and only if she is a low productivity type. This is an example of what economist George Akerlof has termed a **lemon's market.** The presence of low productivity workers (the "lemons") pulls down the wage paid, causing the highest productivity workers to leave the market. As these workers leave, the wage falls even more, which causes the next most highly productive workers to leave. In the worst case scenario, the process continues until the only workers who remain in the market are the least productive ones, the "lemons."

When Carla has a high productivity she earns less than she would if Jorge knew her productivity beforehand. This suggests that when she has a high productivity, Carla might be willing to spend something to "certify" this fact. But if such certification is to work—which means it allows Carla to get a higher wage when she is a high type than when she is a low type—something must ensure that she doesn't get certification when she has a low productivity. Michael Spence is credited with first describing how high-value sellers like Carla can "self-certify" their quality. He called the procedure **signaling.** We will refer to the underlying game as a *signaling game.*

In order to see what Spence had in mind, we will modify our game so that before Carla makes her wage offer to Jorge, she has the option of obtaining an "education." While Jorge cannot observe Carla's productivity prior to hiring her, he can observe her level of education. This is why it might serve as a signal. We will let y denote the amount of education Carla acquires. She can acquire either 0 or 1 units of education. In order to highlight the role of education as a signal, we will also assume that education has no effect on Carla's productivity, yet is costly for her to acquire. This cost may depend on the worker's productivity and will be denoted as $c(\theta)$. After Carla chooses her education, she either quits the labor market or proposes a wage w to Jorge. If Carla quits, then the game ends and both players get a payoff of zero. If she makes a wage offer to Jorge, then he either hires Carla or he doesn't. The game then ends and Jorge earns a payoff of $(\theta - w)$ if he hires Carla and 0 if he does not. Carla earns a payoff of $(w - \frac{3}{4} \cdot \theta) - c(\theta) \cdot y$ if she is hired and $-c(\theta) \cdot y$ if she is not. Note that education is a sunk cost. Carla cannot recover the cost of acquiring it in the event that Jorge does not hire her. We will refer to this game as the Educational Signaling Game. The game tree is displayed in Figure 15.11.

In the new game, a pure strategy for Carla consists of two decisions based on her productivity: her education level, $y(\theta)$, and her wage demand, $w(\theta)$. As before, Carla's pure strategies can be characterized as either pooling ($y(10) = y(20)$ and $w(10) = w(20)$) or separating ($y(10) \neq y(20)$ or $w(10) \neq w(20)$). A pure strategy for Jorge consists of a decision whether to hire Carla when she acquires y units of education and demands the wage w. A belief for Jorge consists of a function $p(y, w)$, where $0 \leq p(y, w) \leq 1$, that states the probability that Carla is a high productivity type when she acquires y units of education and demands the wage w.

Spence showed that education will never be acquired unless *high productivity*

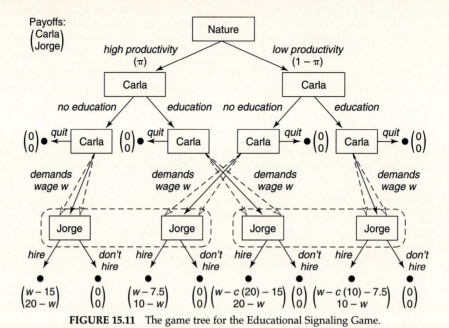

FIGURE 15.11 The game tree for the Educational Signaling Game.

workers can acquire it at lower cost than low productivity workers. That is, a necessary condition for education to serve as a signal is

$$c(10) > c(20). \tag{15.5}$$

In order to see what Eq. [15.5] implies about Carla's preferences, look at Figure 15.12. In this diagram, the level of education is measured along the horizontal axis and the wage rate is measured along the vertical axis. A point (y, w) represents a level of education and a wage demand. The solid parallel lines are three of Carla's indifference curves when she is a low productivity type; the dotted parallel lines are three of Carla's indifference curves when she is a high productivity type. Because of Eq. [15.5], the solid indifference curves are steeper than the dotted ones. As a result, each solid indifference curve intersects each of the dotted ones exactly once. For this reason, Eq. [15.5] is often referred to in the economics literature as the **single-crossing condition.**

We will assume that $c(10) = 11$ and $c(20) = 4$. With these costs, the following strategies and beliefs form a perfect Bayesian equilibrium:

Carla's strategy: Carla does not acquire an education and demands a wage of 10 when she is a low productivity type and acquires an education and demands a wage of 20 when she is a high productivity type.

Jorge's strategy: Jorge hires Carla if and only if she either doesn't get an education and demands a wage less than or equal to 10 or gets an education and demands a wage less than or equal to 20.

Jorge's beliefs: Jorge believes Carla is certainly a high productivity type when she gets an education and believes she is certainly a low productivity type when she doesn't.

To see why this is a perfect Bayesian equilibrium, we will start with Jorge's beliefs. If Carla's wage demand is 20, she has acquired an education, and she employs the proposed equilibrium strategy, the conditional probability that she is a *high* productivity type is

$$P(\theta = 20 | w = 20, y = 1) = \frac{P(w = 20, y = 1 | \theta = 20) \cdot P(\theta = 20)}{P(w = 20, y = 1)}, \qquad [15.6]$$

where

$$P(w = 20, y = 1) = P(w = 20, y = 1 | \theta = 20) \cdot P(\theta = 20)$$
$$+ P(w = 20, y = 1 | \theta = 10) \cdot P(\theta = 10).$$

Or,

$$P(\theta = 20 | w = 20, y = 1) = \frac{1 \cdot \frac{1}{3}}{1 \cdot \frac{1}{3} + 0 \cdot \frac{2}{3}} = 1. \qquad [15.7]$$

You can verify that Bayes' theorem also implies that when Carla offers a wage of 10 and has not acquired an education, a rational belief for Jorge is that she is a low productivity type with certainty.

With these beliefs, it is easy to verify that Jorge's strategy is rational. Carla offers a wage of 20 and has acquired an education only if she is a high productivity type. Therefore, accepting any wage less than or equal to 20 is better than rejecting

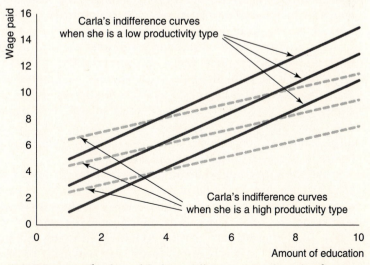

FIGURE 15.12 The slope of Carla's indifference curves depend on her type.

it. He will always, of course, reject any wage offer above 20. If she offers a wage of 10 and does not have an education, then the highest acceptable wage is 10.

Now, let's look at Carla. If she is a high productivity type, then getting an education will yield her a payoff of $20 - 4 = 16$. This move is better than self-employment since it is greater than her self-employment payoff of $\frac{3}{4} \cdot 20 = 15$. It is also better than working for Jorge without having an education since then Carla's payoff is only 10. If, on the other hand, she is a low productivity worker, then getting an education will result in a payoff of $20 - 11 = 9$. Self-employment will only yield a payoff of $\frac{3}{4} \cdot 10 = 7.5$. The best option for her in these circumstances would be to not get an education, resulting in a payoff of 10. Note that Carla's strategy, Jorge's strategy, and Jorge's beliefs are all self-confirming. This is an example of a separating equilibrium.

Other equilibria are possible depending on the cost of signaling, the opportunity cost of self-employment, and the probability of having a high productivity. These other cases are the subject of some of the end-of-chapter exercises.

15.6 A Screening Game

Notice that in signaling games the better-informed player makes a move before the less-informed player. That, of course, is the whole point of a signal, namely, for the better-informed player to send information to the less well-informed player. In **screening games,** the better-informed player can move only *after* the less well-infomed player. For example, the education signaling game presented above can be modified by having the uninformed firm (Jorge) offer a potential worker (Carla) a wage contract that might depend on the worker's subsequent choice of education. The worker then chooses a level of education and subsequently accepts or rejects the contract. In short, the screen is essentially a set of hoops set by the uninformed player that the informed player can choose to jump through or not, depending on the rewards offered by the uninformed player.

Consider the same underlying conditions used in our analysis of Spence's education signaling game. Jorge can hire workers that are high productivity ($\theta = 20$), or low productivity ($\theta = 10$). There is a $\frac{1}{3}$ chance that any worker drawn at random is high productivity and a $\frac{2}{3}$ chance that she is low productivity. It costs a high productivity worker 4 to get educated and a low productivity worker 11. A second employer is also able to hire workers under the same conditions as Jorge. Unlike in Spence's signaling game, however, Jorge makes the wage offer before he observes Carla's choice of education.

In finding an equilibrium, note that we no longer need worry about updating Jorge's beliefs. He no longer makes any decisions after he has the opportunity to observe Carla's decisions. Consider a fairly obvious strategy for Jorge. Offer a wage of 20 to Carla if she gets an education and a wage of 10 if she does not. If Carla is low productivity, getting an education is still too expensive to warrant doing so, but if Carla is high productivity, it will make sense to do so. Can Jorge get away with offering Carla a lower wage if she is high productivity? Not as long as a second firm is willing to pay her 20 if she is educated. So Carla has a best response to Jorge's strategy: get an education and accept Jorge's wage offer if she has a high productivity and don't get an education but accept Jorge's wage offer if she has a low productivity. Hence, we have described a Bayesian Nash equilibrium.

It is also worth checking for a pooling equilibrium. If Jorge tries to offer a pooling wage below the one that yields a zero payoff, he will be vulnerable to a slightly higher wage offer by the other employer, resulting in no employees. The pooling wage that results in zero payoff for Jorge is 13.33. But at this wage, the other employer can offer a wage of 20 to workers who get an education and 10 to workers who don't. The other employer will get all the high productivity workers and Jorge will get only low productivity workers. Since screening models do not make use of Bayesian updating, we will not consider them further in this section.

15.7 Summary

We have shown in this chapter how uninformed players can learn from the behavior of other players. Starting from a state of relative ignorance, it may be possible for a player to update her beliefs about the game being played based on data gleaned from other players' moves. As a result, the formation of beliefs becomes a central concern. Fortunately, Bayesian updating can be used to revise players' beliefs during the course of play. This leads to the notion of a perfect Bayesian equilibrium as a collection of beliefs and strategies with two properties: (1) each player's strategy is an optimal response to the other players' strategies and the players' beliefs about the game, and (2) each player's beliefs can be derived from the other players' strategies using Bayes' theorem. We showed how to use this new equilibrium concept to solve an entry deterrence game.

Next we looked at a class of games with incomplete information called signaling games. These games were first studied by Michael Spence and have been used to successfully model such disparate economic phenomena as credit rationing, strikes, and predatory pricing. In the simplest two-person signaling games, one player, the sender, has perfect information about the game's payoffs and the other player, the receiver, does not. The sender, however, moves first and signals her private information to the receiver. Spence showed how workers might be able to use costly education credentials to signal their value to firms *even if* such education had no effect on the workers' productivity. We concluded by contrasting signaling games with screening games, that is, games in which the uninformed player must move *before* the better-informed player, thereby rendering Bayesian updating useless.

15.8 Further Reading

A more advanced treatment of the material in this chapter can be found in Eric Rasmusen's *Information and Games* (New York: Basil-Blackwell, 1989, Chapter 5). Many interesting games involving information are discussed in a nontheoretical way in Dixit and Nalebuff's *Thinking Strategically: The Competitive Edge in Business, Politics, and Everyday Life* (New York: Norton, 1991). An excellent but more advanced analysis of games with incomplete information can be found in *A Course in Microeconomic Theory* by David Kreps (Princeton: Princeton University Press, 1990, Part III). Kreps's book is meant for mathematically adept graduate students. Michael Spence's original labor market signaling model—which he did not analyze as a game—appears in the paper "Job Market Signaling," *Quarterly Journal of Economics* (August 1973), pp. 355–74.

Our definition of Bayesian equilibrium and perfect Bayesian equilibrium are based on those in Drew Fudenberg and Jean Tirole, *Game Theory* (Cambridge, MA: MIT Press, 1991). A very good treatment of perfect Bayesian equilibrium is contained in Robert Gibbons' *A Primer in Game Theory* (New York: Harvester Wheatsheaf, 1992, Chapter 4).

15.9   Discussion Questions

1. Name a real-world example of an action that has no seeming merit other than that it is a signal.

2. If education is pursued primarily because it adds to productivity, how would we expect the wage rate to change with respect to small changes in education? If, alternatively, wages change dramatically in response to relatively small changes in education (e.g., someone age 22 who is just shy of a college degree earns significantly less than someone with a college degree), what does this say about the signaling model of education?

15.10   New Terms

Bayesian updating	perfect recall
Bayes' theorem	pooling strategy
belief profile	posterior probability
false negative	prior probability
false positive	screening games
information partition	separating strategy
information set	signal
lemon's market	signaling
perfect Bayesian equilibrium	single-crossing condition

15.11   Exercises

EXERCISE 15.1

This is a variation of Exercise 13.6. Suppose HAL is a monopolist in the market for scientific computer workstations. This market is a "natural monopoly," meaning that only one firm can survive in the long run. HAL faces only one potential competitor, MOON. HAL *moves first* and chooses one of two prices for its computers: *High* or *Low*. MOON moves second and decides whether to *Enter* or *Stay out* knowing HAL's price. It is costly for MOON to enter. If MOON stays out, then HAL enjoys a monopoly forever. If MOON enters, then they compete for a while, but the firm with the higher costs will eventually be forced out and the firm with the lower costs will enjoy a monopoly forever after. There is a 50% chance that HAL's costs are lower than MOON's and this is common knowledge. HAL knows its costs when it sets its prices, but MOON does not. Table 15.2 shows the discounted profits of the two firms as a function of their decisions and their relative costs.

Table 15.2 **Payoff Table of the Workstation Game**

		HAL's costs are higher than MOON's		HAL's costs are lower than MOON's	
		HAL		HAL	
		High price	*Low price*	*High price*	*Low price*
	Enters	(100, 20)	(100, 5)	(−20, 60)	(−20, 20)
MOON					
	Stays out	(0, 90)	(0, 30)	(0, 120)	(0, 70)

Payoffs: (MOON, HAL)

(a) This is a game with incomplete information. How would you apply the Harsanyi transformation to make this a game of complete but imperfect information?

(b) Draw a game tree for the game derived from applying the Harsanyi transformation. Carefully label the information sets of both players.

(c) What constitutes a strategy for HAL? What constitutes a strategy for MOON? What constitutes a belief for HAL? What constitutes a belief for MOON?

EXERCISE 15.2

Find a perfect Bayesian equilibrium for the Workstation Game described in Exercise 15.1.

EXERCISE 15.3

Suppose Beverly wants to sell her 1985 Tiger sports coupe in order to pay her college tuition bill and Jim wants to buy a 1985 Tiger in order to commute to college. Suppose the following is common knowledge to both:

(1) 50% of used 1985 Tiger coupes will need extensive repairs in the near future (they are "lemons"), and 50% will need no repairs (they are "good cars").

(2) If the car is a lemon, it is worth $2,000 to the buyer and $1,000 to the seller; if the car is good, it is worth $6,000 to the buyer and $4,500 to the seller.

(3) The seller knows the condition of the car at the time she sells it, but the buyer only finds out the condition after he buys it.

(4) The buyer and seller are both risk neutral.

Beverly places a newspaper ad and offers a take-it-or-leave-it price, P, and Jim sees the ad. If he buys the car from Beverly, Jim's payoff equals $V_J - P$, where V_J is the true value of the car to Jim. Conversely, if she sells the car to Jim, Beverly's payoff equals $P - V_B$, where V_B is the true value of the car to her.

(a) This is a game with incomplete information. How would you apply the Harsanyi transformation to make this a game of complete but imperfect information?

(b) Draw a game tree for the game derived from applying the Harsanyi transformation. Carefully label the information sets of both players.

(c) What constitutes a strategy for Beverly? What constitutes a strategy for Jim? What constitutes a belief for Beverly? What constitutes a belief for Jim?

EXERCISE 15.4

Show that the Car Buying Game in Exercise 15.3 is a "Lemon's Market." That is, the game has a perfect Bayesian equilibrium in which the car is sold if and only if it is a lemon.

EXERCISE 15.5

The following strategies and beliefs constitute another Bayesian equilibrium of the Car Buying Game described in Exercise 15.3.

Beverly's strategy: If the car is good, always offer to sell the car for $5,000; if the car is a lemon, offer to sell it for $5,000 with probability p and offer to sell it for $2,000 with probability $1 - p$.

Jim's strategy: Always reject a price above $5,000; accept a price of $5,000 with probability q; always reject a price between $2,000 and $5,000; always accept a price at or below $2,000.

Jim's beliefs: If the price is below $5,000, then the car is a lemon for sure; if the price is $5,000 or higher, then the car is a lemon with probability θ.

Find the values of p, q, and θ as follows:

(1) Given Beverly's strategy, use Bayes' theorem to find an expression for θ in terms of p, denoted $\theta(p)$.

(2) If Jim rejects a price of $5,000, his expected payoff equals zero. If he accepts the price, his expected payoff equals $(\$6,000 - \$5,000) \cdot (1 - \theta) + (\$2,000 - \$5,000) \cdot \theta = \$1,000 - \$3,000 \cdot \theta$. Since his equilibrium strategy calls for him to randomize when Beverly offers to sell for $5,000, these two expected payoffs must be equal. Use this fact to solve for θ.

(3) Now use the value for θ you found in (2) and the expression for $\theta(p)$ you found in (1) to solve for p.

(4) If Beverly's car is a lemon and she offers a price of $2,000, then her expected payoff equals $2,000 − $1,000 = $1,000. If she offers a price of $5,000, then her expected payoff equals $0 \cdot (1 − q) + q \cdot (\$5,000 − \$1,000) = q \cdot \$4,000$. Since Beverly's equilibrium strategy calls for her to randomize when her car is a lemon, these two expected payoffs must be equal. Use this fact to solve for q.

What is the probability that the car is sold if it is a lemon? What is the probability if the car is good?

15.12 Appendix: Bayes' Theorem

Here is a proof of Bayes' theorem: Since F and E_i both have nonzero probabilities by assumption, the definition of conditional probability in Section 15.5 implies that

$$P(E_i|F) = \frac{P(E_i \text{ and } F)}{P(F)} \tag{15.A1}$$

and

$$P(F|E_i) = \frac{P(E_i \text{ and } F)}{P(E_i)}. \tag{15A.2}$$

Equations [15.A1] and [15.A2] can be rewritten as

$$P(F|E_i) \cdot P(E_i) = P(E_i \text{ and } F) \tag{15A.3}$$

and

$$P(E_i|F) \cdot P(F) = P(E_i \text{ and } F). \tag{15A.4}$$

Substituting the left-hand side of Eq. [15.A3] for $P(E_i \text{ and } F)$ in Eq. [15.A1] yields the first conclusion of Bayes' theorem. Summing both sides of Eq. [15.A4] over the index i and collecting common terms yields the relation

$$\left(\sum_{i=1}^{N} P(E_i|F) \right) \cdot P(F) = \sum_{i=1}^{N} P(E_i \text{ and } F). \tag{15A.5}$$

Since the events $\{E_1, \ldots, E_N\}$ are mutually exhaustive and exclusive by assumption, the term within brackets on the left-hand side of Eq. [15.A5] equals 1. As a result, Eq. [15.A5] reduces to the second conclusion of the theorem.

CHAPTER 16

Bargaining with Private Information

OVERVIEW OF CHAPTER 16

16.1   Introduction

In Chapter 7 you were introduced to bilateral bargaining over the division of a fixed sum of money between two fully informed players. We modeled the bargaining as a game in which the players made alternating offers to each other, stopping once either accepted the other's offer. If a delay in reaching agreement is costly, this game has a unique, subgame perfect equilibrium in which the first offer made is immediately accepted and protracted and costly haggling is avoided. The ratio of the surplus each player receives equals the inverse of the ratio of cost of delay. Relatively impatient players get less and relatively patient players get more. If the two players are equally impatient, then they both get exactly half. Although it is admittedly highly idealized, the predicted simple relationship between impatience and "bargaining power" is not obvious and is empirically testable.

The model is less successful at predicting the speed of negotiations. Negotiations over new labor contracts are often lengthy and sometimes end in costly strikes or company lockouts. And it is not unusual for international multilateral trade agreements to "break down" at the last minute. These negotiation breakdowns suggest some violation of our underlying assumptions, the most suspect being the assumption of perfect information about the game being played. As you will see in this chapter, uncertainty about who the opponents are can cause traders to walk away from mutually beneficial gains from trade.

16.2 Bargaining When the Uninformed Player Moves First

A common business news item in the newspaper is the acquisition of one company by another. Companies do this for many reasons: to acquire important patents or established and respected tradenames, or well-developed distribution systems, or new client lists, or new lines of business. Such a purchase often follows lengthy and difficult negotiations over the terms of the purchase, particularly the price. Such negotiations are tricky precisely because both sides possess relevant private information that they are reluctant to share. For example, the firm being bought may have potentially valuable "trade secrets" that it may not want to show to the potential buyer prior to sale for fear that they will be stolen.

Consider the problem facing Bill Raider, who is considering the purchase of Bull's Eye Inc. Bull's Eye is wholly owned by Janet Target. Janet values her firm at either $10 million or $100 million, depending on the outcome of a secret project code-named "Crapshoot." She claims that the project has been a big success, but she refuses to reveal anything more to Raider about the project because of the fear that he might be able to steal the project's ideas before she can get them to market. Of course, she could be lying and the project may have been a complete failure.

Raider has concluded from his investigations that there is a 50% chance that the project was successful. Synergies between the two firms make Bull's Eye worth 50% more to Raider than to Target, whatever the outcome of the project. For example, if Bull's Eye is worth $100 million to Target, then it is worth $150 million to Raider. And if Bull's Eye is worth $10 million to Target then it is worth $15 million to Raider. All of this is common knowledge. Raider wants to maximize the difference between the value of the firm (to him) and the price he pays for it. This is his payoff. Similarly, Target wants to maximize the difference between what she sells the firm for and the value of the firm (to her). So if the firm is worth $100 million to Target and $150 million to Raider and he pays $120 million to acquire it, his payoff is $30 million and hers is $20 million. Both Target and Raider are risk-neutral expected utility maximizers.

Raider's bargaining style is to make a single take-it-or-leave-it offer for the firm he wants to acquire, in this case Bull's Eye. If Target turns him down, he will simply go elsewhere. As you saw in Chapter 7, this type of game is sometimes known as an *ultimatum game*. Raider's reputation for "toughness" has been gained over a long period of time and Raider has no desire to undermine that reputation here. So Target knows she will get only one offer from Raider. This is the critical assumption. If Target doubts that Raider will just walk away from a first refusal, then the game changes dramatically. We will return to this issue later.

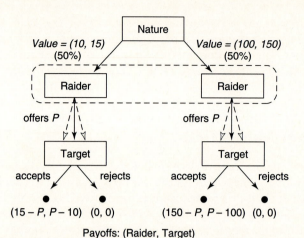

Payoffs: (Raider, Target)

FIGURE 16.1   The game tree for the Raider–Target Bargaining Game.

Figure 16.1 displays the game tree for the Raider–Target Bargaining Game. As is usual in games with incomplete information, Nature moves first and determines the true value of the firm to each player. We will denote these values by the ordered pair (V_{Target}, V_{Raider}). Nature can select one of two valuations: (10, 15) or (100, 150), where all monetary values are in millions of dollars. Raider moves second and offers to buy the firm from Target for an amount, P. Since Raider doesn't know the firm's true value, he has only one information set containing two decision nodes. One decision node corresponds to a high value for the firm and one corresponds to a low value for the firm. When he moves, all he knows is that there is a 50% probability the firm is worth 15 to him and 10 to Target and a 50% probability it is worth 150 to him and 100 to Target. A pure strategy for him is an offer price P. Target moves last and either accepts or rejects Raider's offer. She has perfect information about Raider's offer and the firm's true value to both players. As a result, a pure strategy for her is to either *accept* or *reject* the offer. When Target moves, she knows the firm's value and can therefore calculate the payoff from accepting the offer. If she rejects the offer, the payoff to each player is zero. If she accepts the offer, Raider's payoff equals $V_{Raider} - P$ and Target's equals $P - V_{Target}$.

This game can be solved by backward induction. The reason is that Target, who has perfect information and moves last, can determine her optimal strategy without knowing Raider's strategy. And although Raider moves second, his move follows that of a *nonstrategic* player, namely, Nature. As a result, Raider does not have to update his initial beliefs in order to calculate the expected payoff of any strategy. He can determine his optimal strategy from his knowledge of the game and Target's optimal strategy.

Tip 16.1 for Finding Perfect Bayesian Equilibria: If the incompletely informed player moves before the completely informed player and never after, then the game can be solved using backward induction.

Target has an obvious weakly dominant strategy: she accepts any price P that is greater than or equal to V_{Target} and rejects any price below V_{Target}. Although she knows that Raider values the firm more than she does, if she rejects any profitable price, the game with Raider ends, her payoff is zero and there is no second chance.

Target's strategy implies that Target always rejects offers under 10, accepts offers greater than or equal to 10 or less than 100 if and only if the firm's value is low, and always accepts offers of 100 or more. It follows that Raider's expected profit, as a function of his offer, P, is given by

$$E\Pi_{Raider}(P) = \begin{cases} 0.5 \cdot 0 + 0.5 \cdot 0 & \text{if } P < 10 \\ 0.5 \cdot (15 - P) + 0.5 \cdot 0 & \text{if } 10 \leq P < 100 \\ 0.5 \cdot (15 - P) + 0.5 \cdot (150 - P) & \text{if } 100 \leq P \end{cases}$$

[16.1]

$$= \begin{cases} 0 & \text{if } P < 10 \\ 0.5 \cdot (15 - P) & \text{if } 10 \leq P < 100 \\ 82.5 - P & \text{if } 100 \leq P \end{cases}$$

This profit function is plotted in Figure 16.2. If Raider offers anything below $10 million, he guarantees himself a zero profit, and if he offers anything above $15 million, he makes an expected *loss*. So his best strategy is to offer $10 million and earn an expected profit of $2.5 million. The surprising consequence is that *Target sells her firm only if it has a low value.* This is another example of a *lemon's market,* first introduced in Chapter 15. It can occur whenever there is uncertainty about the true value of a good or service, the seller has no incentive to be truthful about the value, and the seller cannot signal the good's value to the buyer. The equilibrium is summarized in Table 16.1.

You may have noticed that Target's response to Raider's $10 million offer reveals the firm's true worth since Target rejects Raider's offer if and only if

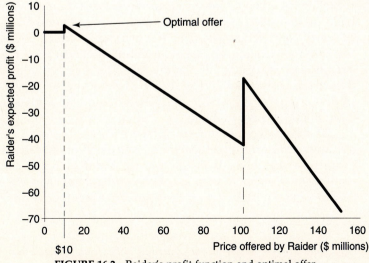

FIGURE 16.2 Raider's profit function and optimal offer.

Table 16.1 **Perfect Bayesian Equilibrium of the Raider–Target Bargaining Game**

Target's strategy	$A(P, V_{Target}, V_{Raider}) = \begin{cases} accept & if\ P \geq V_{Target} \\ reject & if\ P < V_{Target} \end{cases}$
Raider's strategy	$P = 10$

Crapshoot was successful. Raider knows this. So if Janet rejects his first offer, why doesn't Raider come back and offer her $100 million? He doesn't give in to the temptation because it would destroy his reputation as a tough take-it-or-leave-it bargainer. This reputation is valuable when bargaining over the sale price of companies whose true value is common knowledge and there is only one buyer. In these situations, the "tough" buyer will be able to get the seller to accept any price above the seller's minimum. Raider won't return with a second offer if the value of his reputation is greater than the value of making a second offer on this one transaction.

16.3 Bargaining When the Informed Player Moves First

In the previous example, the uninformed player moved first. But that is not always the case. In some negotiations, the first offers may come from the fully informed player. This is the case in the following hypothetical and highly simplified scenario: A surgeon, Dr. Green, performed an appendectomy on a young wife and mother, Mrs. Smith. During the operation, Mrs. Smith died. Her husband, Mr. Smith, has hired an attorney and sued Dr. Green for **malpractice,** which means not following accepted medical procedure. He is claiming damages of $1 million. Right up until the case goes to the jury, Mr. Smith and Dr. Green can negotiate an **out-of-court settlement.** This is a contract in which the doctor agrees to pay Mr. Smith a fixed sum of money in return for Smith dropping the lawsuit. As is often true in such cases, Mr. Smith's lawyer has agreed to take the case on a **contingent fee** basis: He will receive 25% of whatever Mr. Smith gets either through an out-of-court settlement or a jury award, but will receive nothing for his work if Mr. Smith receives nothing.

Dr. Green does not have malpractice insurance. As a result, she will have to pay any jury award or settlement as well as all of her legal expenses out of her own pocket. Her one advantage over Mr. Smith is that she was in the operating room when Mrs. Smith died and knows what happened. As a result, she knows the outcome of a trial.[1] If no malpractice occurred, then the doctor knows that Mr.

---

[1] In reality, juries are notoriously unpredictable. A more realistic assumption is that the doctor has a more accurate estimate of the probability of her being acquited than does Mr. Smith. Such a model is much more difficult to analyze.

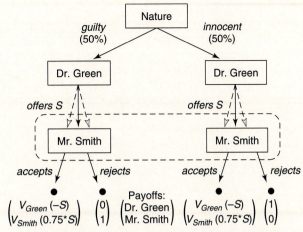

FIGURE 16.3 The game tree for the Lawsuit Game.

Smith will lose his case in court. On the other hand, if there was malpractice, then the doctor knows Mr. Smith will win the case and be awarded the $1 million he has claimed in damages. Her informational advantage is common knowledge to both players.

If the case goes to trial, Dr. Green must hire an attorney and incur a $100,000 legal bill. In order to simplify the analysis, we will assume that Mr. Smith has to reimburse her for this cost should the jury find the doctor innocent of malpractice.[2] This implies that the doctor has nothing to lose (besides her time and her good name) by going to court if she is innocent. But she will lose $1.1 million—$1 million to Mr. Smith and his attorney and $100,000 to her own attorney—if she is guilty. Dr. Green can avoid this large expense only by reaching an out-of-court settlement with Mr. Smith.

Dr. Green makes a single take-it-or-leave-it offer to Mr. Smith. If Mr. Smith rejects the offer, then the matter is decided by the jury. Even with this simplification, four scenarios are possible: (1) Dr. Green is *guilty*, she makes a settlement offer, and Mr. Smith *accepts*; (2) Dr. Green is *guilty*, she makes a settlement offer, and Mr. Smith *rejects* it; (3) Dr. Green is *innocent*, she makes a settlement offer, and Mr. Smith *accepts* it; (4) Dr. Green is *innocent*, she makes a settlement offer, and Mr. Smith *rejects* it.

The game tree is displayed in Figure 16.3. Since Mr. Smith has incomplete information, we have applied the Harsanyi transformation. Nature moves first and selects Dr. Green's *guilt* or *innocence* according to fixed probabilities. These probabilities are common knowledge. We will assume the probability that the doctor is guilty of malpractice is 50%. Only Dr. Green knows Nature's move. Dr.

---

[2]This is the rule in many countries, but not in the United States. In the United States, the losing party often has to pay "court costs," but not the opponent's legal bills.

Table 16.2 **Payoffs of the Settlement Game**

Outcome	Dr. Green	Mr. Smith
Out-of-court settlement in which Dr. Green pays Mr. Smith S.	$V_{Green}(-S)$	$V_{Smith}(\frac{3}{4}S)$
Out-of-court settlement in which Dr. Green pays Mr. Smith $0.	1	0.25
Out-of-court settlement in which Dr. Green pays Mr. Smith $1 million.	0.5	1
Jury trial in which Dr. Green is found guilty.	0	1
Jury trial in which Dr. Green is found innocent.	1	0

Green moves second and offers an out-of-court settlement, denoted by S. There are an infinite number of such offers. Offering Mr. Smith $0 is equivalent to refusing to settle. Mr. Smith moves last and either *accepts* or *rejects* Dr. Green's offer. Accepting an offer of $0 is equivalent to dropping the lawsuit. Each player has a strictly increasing VNMU function over his or her change in wealth. Dr. Green's VNMU function will be denoted V_{Green} and Mr. Smith's will be denoted V_{Smith}. The payoffs are summarized in Table 16.2. We have normalized both players' VNMU functions so that each player's worst court outcome has a utility of zero and the best court outcome has a utility of 1. This means

$$V_{Smith}(-\$100{,}000) = V_{Green}(-\$1{,}100{,}000) = 0$$

and   [16.2]

$$V_{Smith}(\$750{,}000) = V_{Green}(\$0) = 1.$$

By accepting any offer that Dr. Green makes, Mr. Smith can guarantee himself a utility of at least $V_{Smith}(\$0)$. Likewise, by offering to settle the case for the full $1 million Mr. Smith is seeking in damages, Dr. Green can guarantee herself a utility no lower than $V_{Green}(-\$1\ million)$. Our normalization of the two VNMUs implies that $0 < V_{Smith}(\$0) < 1$ and $0 < V_{Green}(-\$1\ million) < 1$. These two utility levels are related to the players' attitudes toward risk. This relationship is displayed in Figure 16.4, where $V_{Smith}(\$0)$ is shown for VNMUs having differing degrees of concavity, hence displaying differing levels of risk aversion. $V_{Smith}(\$0)$ is higher the more concave the utility function, hence, the more risk averse is Mr. Smith. We will assume that both players are risk averse and $V_{Smith}(\$0) = 0.25$ and $V_{Green}(-\$1\ million) = 0.5$.

Since Dr. Green has two decision nodes in separate information sets, a pure strategy consists of *two* offers, $(S_{guilty}, S_{innocent})$. The first offer is the one she makes when she is *guilty* and the second offer is the one she makes when she is *innocent*. One possible strategy for Dr. Green is ($1 million, $0), meaning she offers Mr. Smith $1 million when she is *guilty* and nothing when she is *innocent*. Mr. Smith

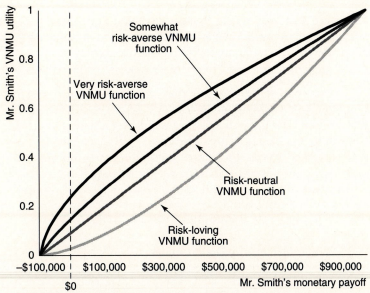

FIGURE 16.4 Mr. Smith's status quo utility levels for different VNMUs.

has an information set corresponding to each possible offer Dr. Green could make. Therefore, a pure strategy for him is a function $A(S)$ that takes on only two values, *accept* or *reject*. A possible pure strategy for Mr. Smith is

$$A(S) = \begin{cases} accept & \text{if } S \geq \$1 \text{ million} \\ reject & \text{if } \$100{,}000 < S < \$1 \text{ million} \\ accept & \text{if } S \leq \$100{,}000. \end{cases} \qquad [16.3]$$

Mr. Smith's belief as to the probability that the doctor is *guilty*, given that she offered him S to settle the lawsuit out of court, will be denoted by the function $\pi(S)$. Table 16.3 shows some possible beliefs for Mr. Smith.

All that remains is to solve this game. We will construct the equilibrium strategies and beliefs piece by piece. We begin by searching for dominated and iteratively dominated strategies.

Table 16.3 **Possible Beliefs for Mr. Smith**

Naive belief:

$\pi(S) = 0.5 \text{ for all } S$

Very sophisticated belief:

$$\pi(S) = \begin{cases} 1 & \text{if } S \geq \$1 \text{ million} \\ 0.5 & \text{if } \$100{,}000 \leq S < \$1 \text{ million} \\ 0 & \text{if } S < \$100{,}000 \end{cases}$$

Tip 16.2 for Finding Perfect Bayesian Equilibria: If backward induction cannot be used, then start by finding and eliminating all the dominated and iteratively dominated strategies for each player.

Common sense suggests that since the jury can award him at most the $1 million he is claiming as his loss, Mr. Smith should *accept* any pretrial offer over $1 million. The game-theoretic justification is that any strategy that calls for Mr. Smith to *reject* an offer greater than $1 million is weakly dominated by a strategy in which he *accepts* the offer. It is only *weakly* dominated because the second strategy does not result in a *strictly* higher payoff against *every* one of Dr. Green's strategies. In particular, it does not result in a strictly higher payoff if Dr. Green's strategy is to refuse to offer a settlement whether *guilty* or *innocent*. As a result, we can restrict our attention to strategies of the form:

$$A(S) = \begin{cases} ? & \text{if } S < \$1 \text{ million} \\ accept & \text{if } S \geq \$1 \text{ million.} \end{cases} \qquad [16.4]$$

Because Mr. Smith accepts all offers over $1 million, any strategy in which Dr. Green offers more than $1 million when she is guilty is iteratively dominated by a strategy in which she offers exactly $1 million. Common sense also tells us that Dr. Green will offer nothing if she is *innocent* of malpractice, since she has nothing to lose by going to court. In game-theoretic jargon, any strategy in which the doctor offers Mr. Smith money when she is *innocent* is weakly dominated by a strategy in which she refuses to settle. So we can restrict our attention to pure strategies of the form: $(S_{guilty}, \$0)$, with $S_{guilty} \leq \$1 \text{ million}$.

Tip 16.3 for Finding Perfect Bayesian Equilibria: Every time you learn something about the informed player's strategy, see what it implies about the uninformed player's beliefs.

If Dr. Green ever offers Mr. Smith a nonzero settlement offer, clearly Mr. Smith should infer that *Dr. Green is guilty for sure.* So Mr. Smith's updated beliefs take the form:

$$\pi(S) = \begin{cases} \theta & \text{if } S = \$0 \\ 1 & \text{if } S > \$0, \end{cases} \qquad [16.5]$$

where θ has still to be determined.

Tip 16.4 for Finding Perfect Bayesian Equilibria: Every time you revise the uninformed player's beliefs, find and eliminate any strategies that are now iteratively dominated.

Table 16.4   **Mr. Smith's Two Pure Iteratively Undominated Strategies**

Wimp Strategy	Tough Strategy
$A(S) = \begin{cases} accept & if\ S = \$0 \\ reject & if\ \$0 < S < \$1\ million \\ accept & if\ S \geq \$1\ million \end{cases}$	$A(S) = \begin{cases} reject & if\ S < \$1\ million \\ accept & if\ S \geq \$1\ million \end{cases}$

Mr. Smith knows he will win $1 million in court whenever the doctor offers him money to settle the lawsuit. So Mr. Smith should reject any offers between $0 and $1 million. We are left with only two iteratively undominated pure strategies, which we will call the *Wimp strategy* and the *Tough strategy*. See Table 16.4.

Tip 16.5 for Finding Perfect Bayesian Equilibria: Every time you eliminate iteratively dominated strategies for one player, check to see if this creates new iteratively dominated strategies for the other players.

Suppose Dr. Green knows she is *guilty*. Then she also knows that going to court will cost her $1.1 million. Since offers between $0 and $1 million will be *rejected*, any strategy that calls for her to offer a settlement in this range when she is *guilty* is iteratively dominated by a strategy in which she offers $1 million, thereby saving herself the $100,000 legal bill. We are left with only two iteratively undominated pure strategies, ($0, $0) and ($1 *million*, $0), which we will refer to as the *Bluff strategy* and the *Fold strategy*. The *Bluff* strategy is an example of a *pooling strategy:* a strategy in which the informed player behaves the same whatever the state of the world. This strategy is analogous to a poker player bidding the same way whether her cards are good or bad. The *Fold* strategy is an example of a *separating strategy:* a strategy in which the informed player acts differently in each state of the world. In poker, this is analogous to a player dropping out or *folding* whenever she has a weak hand of cards and bidding aggressively whenever she has a good hand.

Tip 16.6 for Finding Perfect Bayesian Equilibria: If you have eliminated all iteratively dominated strategies and thereby reduced the strategies of each player to a few, calculate the strategic form of the simplified game and find the Bayesian Nash equilibria. If there is only one, it is the perfect Bayesian equilibrium.

Table 16.5 displays the changes in Mr. Smith's and Dr. Green's wealth that results from every pure-strategy profile (of the reduced game) in each possible state of the world. For example, suppose Dr. Green adopts the *Bluff* strategy, Mr. Smith adopts the *Tough* strategy, and Dr. Green is *guilty*. Then Dr. Green will refuse to settle the case, Mr. Smith will call the bluff, go to court, and win.

Table 16.5 **Changes in Wealth for Mr. Smith and Dr. Green from Adopting Iteratively Undominated Strategies**

		Guilty Dr. Green		Innocent Dr. Green	
		Bluff	*Fold*	*Bluff*	*Fold*
	Wimp	($0, $0)	($750,000, −$1 million)	($0, $0)	($0, $0)
Mr. Smith	*Tough*	($750,000, −$1.1 million)	($750,000, −$1 million)	(−$100,000, $0)	(−$100,000, $0)

Change in wealth (Mr. Smith, Dr. Green)

Mr. Smith ends up $0.75 million wealthier and Dr. Green ends up $1.1 million poorer. Hence the entry ($750,000, −$1.1 million) in the lower left corner of Table 16.5. Stop and verify the other entries in the table before you go further.

Table 16.5 is not the strategic for the (reduced) game. Recall that the strategic form gives the *conditional expected utility* (CEU) of each player for every strategy profile. These are shown in Table 16.6.

Let's see how these numbers were calculated. Suppose Dr. Green adopts the *Bluff* strategy and Mr. Smith adopts the *Tough* strategy. Then the case will end up in court. Mr. Smith receives $750,000 if Dr. Green is *guilty* and has to pay Dr. Green $100,000 if she is *innocent*. So Mr. Smith's CEU equals $0.5 \cdot V_{Smith}(\$750,000) + 0.5 \cdot V_{Smith}(-\$100,000) = 0.5 \cdot 1 + 0.5 \cdot 0 = 0.5$. Dr. Green has two CEUs depending on her type. If she is *guilty*, then she gets her worst outcome and her CEU equals 0; if she is *innocent*, she gets her best outcome and her CEU equals 1. So the strategy profile {*Tough, Bluff*} results in the CEU profile ((0.5), (0, 1)). We leave it as an exercise for you to verify the other three entries in the payoff table.

You can now show that if Mr. Smith adopts the *Wimp* strategy, then Dr. Green's best response is *Bluff*, and if Mr. Smith adopts the *Tough* strategy, then Dr. Green's best response is *Fold*. Likewise, if Dr. Green adopts the *Fold* strategy, then Mr. Smith's best response is *Wimp*, while if Dr. Green adopts the *Bluff* strategy, then Mr. Smith's best response is *Tough*. As a result, there is no perfect

Table 16.6 **Mr. Smith's and Dr. Green's Conditional Expected Utilities in the Reduced Game**

		Dr. Green	
		Bluff	*Fold*
Mr. Smith	*Wimp*	((0.25), (1, 1))	((0.625), (0.5, 1))
	Tough	((0.50), (0, 1))	((0.50), (0.5, 1))

Payoffs: ((Mr. Smith), (*guilty* Dr. Green, *innocent* Dr. Green))

Table 16.7 **A Perfect Bayesian Equilibrium of the Lawsuit Game**

Dr. Green's strategy	*If guilty:* (*bluff* (offer \$0): p, *fold* (offer \$1 million): 1 − p). *If innocent:* always offer \$0
Mr. Smith's strategy	$A(S) = \begin{cases} accept\ wth\ probability\ q & if\ S = \$0 \\ reject & if\ \$0 < S < \$1\ million \\ accept & if\ S \geq \$1\ million \end{cases}$
Mr. Smith's beliefs	$\pi(S) = \begin{cases} \dfrac{p}{1+p} & if\ S = \$0 \\ 1 & if\ S > \$0 \end{cases}$

Bayesian equilibrium in pure strategies. Any perfect Bayesian equilibrium involves mixed strategies: Dr. Green adopts the *Bluff* strategy with probability p and adopts the *Fold* strategy with probability $1 − p$; and Mr. Smith adopts the *Wimp* strategy with probability q and adopts the *Tough* strategy with probability $1 − q$. If you are bothered by the notion that Dr. Green and Mr. Smith would choose their moves at random, recall that another interpretation of a mixed strategy is that it is a probabilistic belief held by *the opponents* about the strategy a player will adopt.

Mr. Smith's belief about Dr. Green's guilt when she refuses to settle equals

$$\pi(\$0) = P(guilty|S = \$0)$$

$$= \frac{P(S = \$0|guilty) \cdot P(guilty)}{P(S = \$0|guilty) \cdot P(guilty) + P(S = \$0|innocent) \cdot P(innocent)}$$

$$= \frac{p \cdot 0.5}{p \cdot 0.5 + 1 \cdot 0.5} \qquad [16.6]$$

$$= \frac{p}{p + 1}.$$

Not surprisingly, the less frequently Dr. Green bluffs (i.e., the smaller is p), the more informative her move is to Mr. Smith and the more his estimate of Dr. Green's guilt changes (i.e., moves toward either 0 or 1) after he observes her move. We have summarized our deductions in Table 16.7.

We are almost done. We have narrowed down our search to two numbers: p and q. As we saw when we introduced mixed strategies in Chapter 10, Mr. Smith's assessment of the probability that Dr. Green will adopt the *Bluff* strategy, p, must make Mr. Smith exactly indifferent between adopting the *Wimp* and the *Tough* strategies. Otherwise, Mr. Smith won't randomize between them. Using the entries in Table 16.6, we have

$$p \cdot 0.25 + (1 − p) \cdot 0.625 = p \cdot 0.50 + (1 − p) \cdot 0.50, \qquad [16.7]$$

or

$$p = \frac{1}{3}.$$ [16.8]

Similarly, Dr. Green's assessment of the probability that Mr. Smith will adopt the *Wimp* strategy, q, must make Dr. Green exactly indifferent between adopting the *Bluff* strategy and the *Fold* strategy whatever her type. Again using Table 16.6, we have

$$q \cdot 1 + (1 - q) \cdot 0.5 = q \cdot 0.75 + (1 - q) \cdot 0.75,$$ [16.9]

or

$$q = \frac{1}{2}.$$ [16.10]

Substituting the values of p and q into Table 16.7 results in Table 16.8. From our derivations, we know these beliefs and strategies form a perfect Bayesian equilibrium: Mr. Smith's strategy is optimal given his beliefs, Dr. Green's strategy is optimal given Mr. Smith's strategy, and Mr. Smith's beliefs are consistent with Bayes' theorem and Dr. Green's strategy.

In the exercises you are asked to show that the equilibrium of our game depends on two numbers, $V_{Green}(-\$1\ million)$ and $V_{Smith}(\$0)$. As we saw earlier, these two utility levels are positively related to the players' risk aversion. They are usually larger the more risk averse are the players. As a result, our model predicts that if it is common knowledge that Mr. Smith is very risk averse, then Dr. Green will always refuse to settle, even when she knows she is *guilty*, and Mr. Smith will drop the lawsuit rather than risk going to court. Once Mr. Smith's risk aversion falls below a certain threshold, Dr. Green will stop *Bluffing* all the time and will start to *Fold* with some positive probability. The less risk averse Mr. Smith is, the greater the probability that Dr. Green will *Fold* rather than *Bluff*

Table 16.8 *Perfect Bayesian Equilibrium of the Lawsuit Game*

Dr. Green's strategy	*If guilty:* (bluff (offer \$0): $\frac{1}{3}$, fold (offer \$1 million: $\frac{2}{3}$)) *If innocent:* always offer \$0
Mr. Smith's strategy	$A(S) = \begin{cases} accept\ wth\ probability\ \frac{1}{2} & if\ S = \$0 \\ reject & if\ \$0 < S < \$1\ million \\ accept & if\ S \geq \$1\ million \end{cases}$
Mr. Smith's beliefs	$\pi(S) = \begin{cases} \frac{1}{4} & if\ S = \$0 \\ 1 & if\ S > \$0 \end{cases}$

when she is *guilty*. Similarly, the more risk averse Dr. Green is, the greater the probability that Mr. Smith will not go to court when Dr. Green refuses to settle.

The purpose of the pretrial negotiations is to avoid a costly court trial. This fails whenever Dr. Green offers Mr. Smith nothing and Mr. Smith refuses to drop the lawsuit. Dr. Green offers Mr. Smith nothing if she is *innocent* or if she is *guilty* and *Bluffs*. The probability of either equals $\frac{1}{2} \cdot 1 + \frac{1}{2} \cdot \frac{1}{3} = \frac{2}{3}$. Since we are assuming that the two players randomize independently, the probability that Dr. Green offers Mr. Smith nothing and that Mr. Smith takes her to court equals $\frac{2}{3} \cdot \frac{1}{2} = \frac{1}{3}$. So a case such as this one will be settled out of court two thirds of the time.

16.4   Bargaining When Delay Is an Option

When negotiators have complete information about each other's payoffs, each can look ahead and calculate the consequences of refusing the opponent's last offer and delaying a settlement. A consequence is that nothing is gained by delay. The unique subgame perfect Nash equilibrium outcome is that the first offer made is accepted by the other player and wasteful back-and-forth haggling is avoided. When negotiators have *incomplete* information about each other's payoffs, however, delay is often rational. This is because delay can reveal information about the payoffs. We will explore this idea using a simple model of labor negotiation between a firm and a labor union.

Welmade Products, Inc. is a hypothetical unionized shirt manufacturer re-negotiating a new union labor contract with the Amalgamated Stitchcraft Union. The negotiation process is very simple: Welmade makes a take-it-or-leave-it wage offer to the Union. If the Union accepts the wage offer, it will be in force for the next two years. If the Union rejects this offer, Welmade will close down and resume negotiations with the Union next year. This action by the firm is known as a **lockout**. A year from now, the firm will make a second wage offer to the Union. If the Union accepts this offer, this wage will be in force for one year. If the offer is rejected, the firm will close permanently and the Union's workers will have to find other jobs.

Welmade's objective is to maximize its expected total profit over the next two years. The firm's profit each year it is in operation equals $\$10 - W$, where W is the annual wage paid to each worker, and wages and profits are in thousands of dollars per year. When it is not in operation, its profits are zero. All of this is common knowledge. The Union's objective is to maximize the expected total income of the "average worker" over the next two years. When Welmade locks the Union out, the workers have to find other temporary employment to tide them over until negotiations resume next year. The income of the average worker in his best alternative employment is his **reservation wage** and is denoted by $\underline{W}$. This reservation wage can be either *low wage* ($\underline{W} = \$4$) or *high wage* ($\underline{W} = \$8$). The Union's reservation wage is not known to Welmade.

The labor negotiation process can be modeled as a game with incomplete information among three players: Welmade, the Union, and Nature. The game tree is shown in Figure 16.5. Nature determines the Union's reservation wage, $\underline{W}$. Nature's choice is known to the Union but not to Welmade. Welmade's initial belief is that the probability that $\underline{W}$ is low equals 0.5 and the probability that it is high equals 0.5. Welmade makes at most two offers, which we will denote as W_1 and W_2. The Union either *accepts* an offer or *rejects* it. Three outcomes are possible: (1) the Union *accepts* Welmade's first offer and the game ends; Welmade's payoff is ($10 − W_1$) for each of two years, or $2 \cdot (\$10 − W_1)$ and the Union's payoff is $2 \cdot W_1$; (2) the Union *rejects* Welmade's first offer, but *accepts* the second, at which point the game ends; Welmade's payoff is $1 \cdot (\$10 − W_2)$ and the Union's payoff is $\underline{W} + W_2$; or (3) the Union *rejects* both wage offers; now Welmade's payoff is zero and the Union's payoff is $2 \cdot \underline{W}$.

If you are not careful, Figure 16.5 can mislead you into thinking that Welmade has only two information sets and that a pair of offers, W_1 and W_2, designates a pure strategy for the firm. This is not correct. A pair of offers represents a possible sequence of *moves* by Welmade in the game, but it does not come close to describing all of Welmade's *strategies*. Look at Figure 16.5 again. Notice that there is a *cluster of arrows* connecting Welmade's first information set with the second one. Such a cluster means that at the first information set, Welmade can choose from

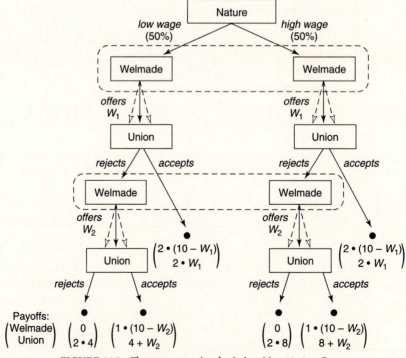

FIGURE 16.5 The game tree for the Labor Negotiation Game.

an *infinite number* of possible offers. *Each first offer* leads to a second information set. At this information set, Welmade must make a second offer following the Union's rejection of the first one. Welmade has an infinite number of information sets in addition to the first one. Each of these information sets corresponds to a different (rejected) first offer by the firm. A pure strategy for Welmade consists, therefore, of a first offer, denoted by W_1, and a second offer *function* $W_2(W_1)$. The latter states the second offer Welmade will make should the Union reject the first offer, W_1. So the strategy ($4, W_1 + $1) is one in which Welmade first offers the Union a wage of $4,000 per year for two years; and if the Union *rejects* the wage W_1, then, after locking the Union out for a year, the company returns to the bargaining table and increases its initial offer by $1,000.

The Union has complete information in this game. It makes its first decision knowing the firm's first offer and its reservation wage, and it makes its second decision knowing in addition the firm's second offer. As a result, a pure strategy for the Union gives the conditions under which the Union *accepts* or *rejects* the first offer, depending on its magnitude and the Union's reservation wage, and *accepts* or *rejects* the second offer, also depending on its magnitude and reservation wage.

If Welmade's first offer is *rejected*, the firm's second offer will be influenced by its assessment of the likely value of the Union's reservation wage. Welmade's probabilistic assessment of the Union's reservation wage at each of its information sets constitutes its belief in this game. Since Welmade moves before the Union, its belief at its first information set is simply the prior probabilities of low and high reservation wages, $\Pr\{low\ wage\} = \Pr\{high\ wage\} = 0.5$. Its beliefs at its other information sets are not set *a priori* but depend on the firm's belief about the Union's strategy (via Bayes' theorem). We will denote by $\pi(W_1)$ the firm's updated probability assessment that the Union's reservation wage is low, given that the Union rejected the first offer of W_1.

We will begin by finding and eliminating all the iteratively dominated strategies of both players. We will require that if the Union is indifferent between accepting and rejecting a wage offer, then the Union always accepts the offer. You can show that strategies with the following features are iteratively dominated:

1. Union strategies that *reject* a wage $W_2 > \underline{W}$ or *accept* a wage $W_2 < \underline{W}$.

2. Welmade strategies in which $W_2(W_1)$ equals a wage other than $4 or $8.

3. Union strategies that *reject* an initial wage $W_1 > $8 or *accept* an initial wage $W_1 < $4.

4. Welmade strategies that initially offer a wage $W_1 > $8 or $W_1 < $4.

Welmade's undominated pure strategies are those for which $4 \leq W_1 \leq $8 and $W_2(W_1)$ always equals either $4 or $8. The Union's undominated pure strategies are shown in Table 16.9.

Since Welmade, the incompletely informed player, moves after Nature but before the Union, the game between Welmade and the Union is strategically equivalent to the one in which Welmade moves first and then Nature selects the Union's reservation wage. This game is displayed in Figure 16.6. When we say

Table 16.9 **The Union's Undominated Pure Strategy Decisions**

Time Period	Union's Reservation Wage	Welmade's Offer	Union's Response
1	*low* or *high*	$W_1 \geq \$8$	*Accept*
1	*low* or *high*	$W_1 < \$4$	*Reject*
1	*low*	$\$4 \leq W_1 < \$8$	*?*
1	*high*	$\$4 \leq W_1 < \$8$	*Reject*
2	*low* or *high*	$W_2 \geq \underline{W}$	*Accept*
2	*low* or *high*	$W_2 < \underline{W}$	*Reject*

the games in Figures 16.5 and 16.6 are strategically equivalent, we mean that the two games can be modeled by the same strategic form. The two games have the same players, the players have the same sets of strategies, the relative order in which the *strategic players* move is the same and the payoff to both players from each strategy profile is the same. In the new game, Welmade moves first and the game that unfolds after it offers W_1 is a proper subgame of the original game. We will refer to this subgame as $G(W_1)$.

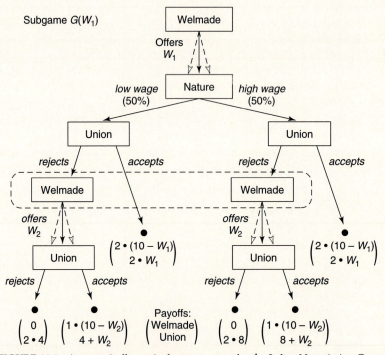

FIGURE 16.6 A strategically equivalent game tree for the Labor Negotiation Game.

With no loss of generality we will restrict our attention to first offers between $4 and $8, inclusive. For each first offer in this range, we will find a perfect Bayesian equilibrium of the subgame $G(W_1)$. At this equilibrium, Welmade's expected payoff equals $V(W_1)$. Welmade's optimal first offer is the one that maximizes $V(W_1)$. This will provide us with the solution to the entire game.

We begin by considering only first offers less than $8. In the subgame $G(W_1)$ Welmade has only two iteratively undominated pure strategies: the *Low wage* strategy in which its second offer equals $4 and the *High wage* strategy in which its second offer equals $8. A *high wage* Union will always *reject* a first offer that is less than $8. It might seem that a *low wage* Union would always *accept* any first offer that is greater than $4, but this isn't necessarily true. If by *rejecting* the first offer a *low-wage* Union can make itself indistinguishable from a *high wage* Union, then it might be able to get an offer of $8 in the second round. As a result, the Union has two undominated pure strategies: the *Honest* strategy, in which the Union *accepts* W_1 when $\underline{W}$ is low, *rejects* it when $\underline{W}$ is high, and *accepts* the second offer if and only if the offer is greater than or equal to $\underline{W}$; and the *Bluff* strategy, in which the Union always *rejects* W_1 and *accepts* the second offer if and only if it is greater than or equal to $\underline{W}$. The game tree for the Labor Negotiation Game, in which dominated (or iteratively dominated) strategies for Welmade have been eliminated is shown in Figure 16.7.

Suppose that the Union has a low reservation wage. If the Union accepts the

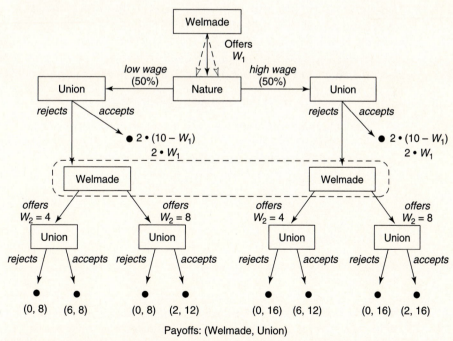

Payoffs: (Welmade, Union)

FIGURE 16.7 The Labor Negotiation Game in which iteratively dominated strategies for Welmade have been eliminated.

first offer, its payoff will be $2 \cdot W_1$; if the Union *rejects* the first offer, the best it can hope for is to earn its reservation wage of \$4 in the first period and to earn \$8 working at Welmade in the second, or \$12 in all. Therefore, if W_1 is greater than or equal to \$12 ÷ 2 = \$6, then this will always be accepted by a *low-wage* Union. Hence, an initial offer of between \$6 and \$8 will force the Union to reveal to Welmade whether its reservation wage is *high* or *low*. That is, if the Union *rejects* any offer between \$6 and \$8, the rational inference is that the Union has a high reservation wage. As a result, Welmade's optimal second wage offer is \$8.

If $\$4 \leq W_1 < \$6$, then there is no longer any pure-strategy Bayesian Nash equilibrium for the subgame $G(W_1)$, but there is a unique Bayesian Nash equilibrium in mixed strategies. In this equilibrium, Welmade adopts a *High wage* strategy with probability $q_W(W_1)$ and adopts a *Low wage* strategy with probability $1 - q_W(W_1)$. The Union adopts the *Honest* strategy with probability $p_U(W_1)$ and adopts the *Bluff* strategy with probability $1 - p_U(W_1)$. The Union's acceptance probability, $p_U(W_1)$, must make Welmade indifferent between offering a wage of \$8 and offering a wage of \$4 at the beginning of year two. The way the Union's unpredictability accomplishes this is by forcing Welmade to revise its assessment of the Union's reservation wage in the face of a rejection. Likewise, Welmade's unpredictability must make the Union indifferent between accepting and rejecting Welmade's initial offer. We now must determine $q_W(W_1)$ and $p_U(W_1)$.

Suppose Welmade initially offers the Union a wage of \$5 and the Union's reservation wage is *low*. If the Union *accepts* the offer, its payoff is certain and equals $2 \cdot \$5 = \$10$. But if the Union *rejects* the offer, then it is gambling. If Welmade comes back and offers \$8 in the second year, the gamble is successful and the Union's payoff is $\$4 + \$8 = \$12$. But if Welmade only offers \$4, then the gamble fails and the Union's payoff over the two years is only $\$4 + \$4 = \$8$. The Union's expected payoff from playing this gamble by rejecting the first offer equals

$$\$4 + (q_W(\$5) \cdot \$8 + (1 - q_W(\$5)) \cdot \$4) = \$8 + \$4 \cdot q_W(\$5). \qquad [16.11]$$

The Union is indifferent between *accepting* and *rejecting* the offer if $\$10 = \$8 + \$4 \cdot q_W(\$5)$ or $q_W(\$5) = 0.5$. In general, the Union is indifferent between accepting and rejecting the first offer when

$$2 \cdot W_1 = \$4 + (q_W(W_1) \cdot \$8 + (1 - q_W(W_1)) \cdot \$4) \qquad [16.12a]$$
$$= \$8 + \$4 \cdot q_W(W_1)$$

or

$$q_W(W_1) = \tfrac{1}{2}W_1 - 2. \qquad [16.12b]$$

We leave it as an exercise for you to verify that $0 \leq q_W(W_1) < 1$ as long as $\$4 \leq W_1 < \$6$.

If Welmade's first offer is *rejected* and its second offer is \$8, then the offer is always *accepted* and its payoff is $\$10 - \$8 = \$2$. But if it follows up the *rejection* with a \$4 offer, it is gambling. If the Union reservation wage is *low*, then it will *accept* the offer and Welmade will earn a profit of $\$10 - \$4 = \$6$. On the other hand, if the Union's reservation wage is *high*, then it will reject the offer and Welmade will earn nothing. The expected payoff from this gamble *equals*

$6 \cdot \pi(W_1) + \$0 \cdot (1 - \pi(W_1)) = \$6 \cdot \pi(W_1)$, where $\pi(W_1)$ is Welmade's assessment of the probability that the Union has a *low* reservation wage when it rejects the firm's initial offer of W_1. Welmade is indifferent between offering $4 and offering $8 if $\pi(W_1) \cdot \$6 \equiv \$2$ or $\pi(W_1) \equiv \frac{1}{3}$. Notice that this is the same for every wage between $4 and $6. In order to be rational, Welmade's assessment of the Union's type must be consistent with Bayes' theorem and the Union's strategy. Bayes' theorem implies that

$$\pi(W_1) =$$

$$\frac{\Pr\{W_1 \ rejected | \underline{W} = 4\} \cdot \Pr\{\underline{W} = 4\}}{\Pr\{W_1 \ rejected | \underline{W} = 4\} \cdot \Pr\{\underline{W} = 4\} + \Pr\{W_1 \ rejected | \underline{W} = 8\} \cdot \Pr\{\underline{W} = 8\}} \qquad [16.13]$$

$$= \frac{p_U(W_1) \cdot 0.5}{p_U(W_1) \cdot 0.5 + 1 \cdot 0.5}$$

$$= \frac{p_U(W_1)}{p_U(W_1) + 1}.$$

Since we have already determined that $\pi(W_1) \equiv \frac{1}{3}$, it follows that $p_U(W_1) \equiv \frac{1}{2}$.

We can now calculate Welmade's expected profit from offering a wage in the interval ($4, $6) and playing the subgame $G(W_1)$. If the Union's reservation wage is *high*, then it always *rejects* the offer, and *rejects* the second offer when it is $4 and *accepts* it when it is $8. Conditional on the Union having a high reservation wage, Welmade's expected payoff equals

$$\$0 + (\$0 \cdot (1 - q_W(W_1)) + (\$10 - \$8) \cdot q_W(W_1)) = \$2 \cdot (\tfrac{1}{2}W_1 - \$2) = W_1 - \$4. \qquad [16.14]$$

If the Union's reservation wage is *low*, then it *accepts* the first wage offer with probability 0.5 and always *accepts* the second wage offer. If the Union *accepts* the first offer, Welmade's payoff equals $2 \cdot (\$10 - W_1)$; if it *rejects* the first offer, then Welmade's payoff equals either $10 - \$8 = \$2$ or $10 - \$4 = \$6$ with probabilities $q_W(W_1)$ and $1 - q_W(W_1)$. So, conditional on the Union's reservation wage being low, Welmade's expected payoff equals

$$0.5 \cdot 2 \cdot (\$10 - W_1) + 0.5 \cdot ((\tfrac{1}{2}W_1 - 2) \cdot \$2 + (3 - \tfrac{1}{2}W_1) \cdot \$6) = \$17 - 2 \cdot W_1. \qquad [16.15]$$

Welmade's expected profit from offering W_1 *unconditioned* by the Union's type equals

$$\tfrac{1}{2} \cdot (W_1 - \$4) + \tfrac{1}{2} \cdot (\$17 - 2 \cdot W_1) = \tfrac{1}{2}(\$13 - W_1) = V(W_1), \text{ for } \$4 < W_1 < \$6. \qquad [16.16]$$

When $6 \le W_1 < 8$, we have already shown the unique perfect Bayesian equilibrium is {*Honest, High wage*}. The equilibrium outcome is that the Union *accepts* the first offer when the Union's reservation wage is *low*, but *rejects* it when its reservation wage is *high*. It follows that when the Union *rejects* the offer, Welmade

Table 16.10 **Perfect Bayesian Equilibria of $G(W_1)$**

	Perfect Bayesian Equilibrium Strategies in $G(W_1)$			
Initial Wage Offer	Welmade	Union	Welmade's Beliefs	Welmade's Expected Payoff $V(W_1)$
$\$4 \leq W_1 < \$6$	(High wage: $\frac{1}{2}W_1 - 2$, Low wage: $3 - \frac{1}{2}W_1$)	(Honest: 0.5, Bluff: 0.5)	$\pi(W_1) = \frac{1}{3}$	$\frac{1}{2}(\$13 - W_1)$
$\$6 \leq W_1 < \$8$	High wage	Honest	$\pi(W_1) = 0$	$\$11 - W_1$
$W_1 = \$8$	Low wage	Honest	$\pi(W_1) = \frac{1}{2}$	$\$4$

believes that the Union's reservation wage is *high* for sure. That is, $\pi(W_1) = 0$. A low second wage will, therefore, be *rejected* for sure. So a high wage is the best second offer. This confirms that the Bayesian Nash equilibrium strategy profile is also a perfect Bayesian equilibrium. Welmade's expected payoff at this equilibrium equals

$$\tfrac{1}{2}2(\$10 - W_1) + \tfrac{1}{2}(\$10 - \$8) = \$11 - W_1 = V(W_1), \text{ for } \$6 \leq W_1 < \$8.$$

[16.17]

Finally, suppose $W_1 = \$8$. The Union's weakly dominant strategy in $G(W_1)$ is to always *accept* this offer. This strategy implies that the first offer will never be *rejected*. As a result, Bayes' theorem places no restriction on Welmade's beliefs about the Union should the first offer ever be *rejected*. One belief is that rejection

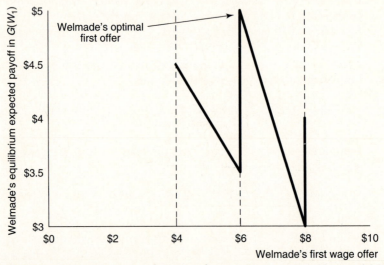

FIGURE 16.8 Welmade's expected payoff at the perfect Bayesian equilibrium of $G(W_1)$.

GAME THEORY IN ACTION: How Well Do Strategic Bargaining Models Explain Strike Data?

Strikes are one of the more interesting outcomes of collective bargaining and, as such, have been the object of much empirical research. Progress has accelerated in recent years, thanks to the creation of large data sets that combine information on contract expiration, wage agreements, and strikes and lockouts. Any successful theory of strikes must account for the following well-documented facts about strikes in the United States and Canada (John Kennan and Robert Wilson, "Can strategic bargaining models explain collective bargaining data?" *Papers and Proceedings of the American Economic Association,* 80 [1992], pp. 405–409; and David Card, "Strikes and bargaining: A survey of the recent empirical literature," *Papers and Proceedings of the American Economic Association,* 80 [1992], pp. 410–415):

1. Strikes are relatively rare, occurring in about 15 percent of labor bargaining negotiations.

2. Most strikes are short, 21 days being the median duration.

3. As the duration of the strike increases, (a) the likelihood of settlement falls and (b) the eventual negotiated wage falls.

4. During economic expansions (recessions) the frequency of strikes rises (falls) and the average duration falls (rises); that is, frequency is procyclical and duration is countercyclical.

Any strategic bargaining model that can explain strikes as an equilibrium phenomenon rather than as mistakes must assume incomplete information. Generally speaking, three types of games have been tested against the available data: games of attrition, signaling games, and screening games. In a *game of attrition* the players alternately decide whether to stay or quit. Staying in another round is costly, but the last player to quit wins everything. The reservation wages of the firm and union are common knowledge, but the cost of staying in is private information. Each side decides when to quit and give in to the other side as a function of the cost of delay; the smaller the cost of delay, the longer the player will wait. This model implies fact 3(a) is at odds with fact 1 and doesn't seem to have much to say about fact 4.

Signaling and screening models seem more promising. Both types of games assume asymmetric information. Usually the firm's reservation wage is assumed to be unknown to the union, rather than the reverse as we have assumed in this chapter. A strike, therefore, signals to the union that the firm's reservation wage is low. The longer the strike, the lower is the firm's reservation wage. This can account for fact 3(b). Recall that in a signaling model the informed player moves first, and in a screening model the uninformed player moves first. Kennan and Wilson show that even if both sides are very impatient, a signaling model usually implies far too long a delay until settlement. Such long delay is needed to prevent employers with high reservation wages from pretending to have low ones. Peter Cramton and Joseph Tracy have successfully fitted a signaling model to U.S. strike data by recognizing that when a contract expires before a new one is in place, work often continues under the terms of the old contract ("Strikes and holdouts in wage bargaining," *The American Economic Review,* 82 [1992], pp. 100–121).

> The screening model seems to be able to come closest to explaining facts 1 to 3 and with an additional assumption can explain fact 4 as well. The additional—and somewhat ad hoc—assumption is that in a recession the union can sustain each offer for a longer period of time than it can in an expansion. As a result, the negotiations are stretched out over a longer period of time during recessions than during expansions. In addition, the firm is willing to accept each offer if it knows that it will have to wait a while for the next one. As a result, the firm is more likely to accept the union's first offer in a recession. So we get both procyclical strike incidence and countercyclical strike duration.

of the offer provides no information about the Union's reservation wage. That is, $\pi(W_1) = \frac{1}{2}$. With this belief, Welmade's best response to an initial rejection is to offer \$4 the second time, since the expected payoff from this, $\frac{1}{2}(\$10 - \$4) + \frac{1}{2}\$0 = \$3$, is more than the certain payoff of \$2 from offering a wage of \$8. Welmade's payoff equals $2 \cdot (\$10 - \$8) = \$4 = V(\$8)$.

Our results are summarized in Table 16.10 and Welmade's expected payoff function, $V(W_1)$, is plotted in Figure 16.8. As can be seen from the graph, Welmade's optimal strategy is to initially offer a wage of \$6. The Union *accepts* the offer when its reservation wage is low and *rejects* it when its reservation wage is high. At this equilibrium, Welmade's expected payoff is \$5 and the Union's expected payoff is \$14. The equilibrium outcome is that there is no lockout when the Union has a low reservation wage and there is a one-year lockout when it has a high reservation wage. This is an example of a *separating equilibrium* since the Union's response to Welmade's first offer identifies its reservation wage. Welmade is able to get the Union to reveal this information by paying a wage *above the reservation wage* when that wage is low—which is precisely when it might be valuable to hide that fact from Welmade.

16.5   Summary

We have shown in this chapter how to model and analyze bargaining games in which one side has knowledge not possessed by the other side. In such situations, the moves made by the better-informed player may convey some private information to the less-informed player. When this is the case, rational play demands that this information be fully utilized.

First we examined the purchase of one firm by another. We assumed that there was uncertainty about the true value of the firm. The seller knew the firm's true value—both to herself and to the buyer, but the buyer didn't. We assumed that the buyer and seller played an ultimatum game in which the buyer moved first and made a take-it-or-leave-it offer to the seller, whose only options were to accept or to reject it. Although it was common knowledge that the buyer valued the firm much more than did the seller, the equilibrium of this game displayed the *lemon's market problem:* Even though the expected value of the firm is very high, the optimal strategy of the buyer is to offer a low price and for the seller to sell the firm only when it has a low value. If the firm has a high value, it remains unsold.

Next we studied a highly stylized model of a malpractice lawsuit. In our model, a patient dies on the operating table and the surviving spouse, Mr. Smith, sues the attending doctor, Dr. Green, for malpractice. Dr. Green knows whether the lawsuit has merit; Mr. Smith does not. If guilty, Dr. Green has an incentive to reach an out-of-court settlement and avoid the legal costs of a trial. Mr. Smith also has an incentive to avoid a court battle since the outcome is uncertain and if he loses, he will have to pay Dr. Green's sizable legal bill. This eliminates any incentive for Dr. Green to settle if she is innocent. As a result, Dr. Green's offer may reveal her private knowledge as to her guilt.

This bargaining game has two types of equilibria, depending on Mr. Smith's degree of risk aversion. If Mr. Smith is sufficiently risk averse—and this is common knowledge—then the equilibrium outcome is that Dr. Green never settles and Mr. Smith accepts this and drops the case rather than risk an adverse court outcome. The other equilibrium is more interesting. Dr. Green refuses to settle when she is innocent. But when she is guilty, sometimes she settles for the full amount of the damages, but occasionally she bluffs and refuses to settle, acting as if she were innocent. In doing this, she gambles on Mr. Smith dropping the lawsuit in the mistaken belief that Dr. Green is innocent. Mr. Smith always accepts a full settlement, but his response to a refusal to settle is uncertain. Sometimes he drops his lawsuit, but sometimes he presses on into court, gambling that Dr. Green is bluffing. In both equilibria there is a positive, and perhaps substantial, probability that the two will fail to reach a settlement and will take the costly path into the courtroom.

We concluded by examining a simple model of contract negotiations between a labor union and a manufacturer, Welmade. The workers' reservation wages— the minimum wages they are willing to accept—is not known to the firm, but is known to the Union negotiator. The reservation wage can be high or low with equal probability. The negotiation process is that Welmade makes at most two wage offers to the Union and imposes a lockout if its first offer is rejected. Welmade's equilibrium strategy is to offer a wage that is halfway between the two possible reservation wages. This is accepted only when the worker's reservation wage is low. As a result, when the offer is rejected, the firm learns that the workers' reservation wages are high and it returns later to the bargaining table with a high wage offer. The firm only gets the workers to reveal this information by offering an attractive wage initially. This is the benefit to the Union of its informational advantage over the firm.

Although we were unable to provide a foolproof algorithm for finding every perfect Bayesian equilibrium of every game, we were able to provide the following tips:

> If the incompletely informed player moves before the completely informed player and never after, then the game can be solved using backward induction.

If backward induction cannot be used, then start by finding and eliminating all the dominated and iteratively dominated strategies for each player.

Every time you learn something about the informed player's strategy, see what it implies about the uninformed player's beliefs.

Every time you revise the uninformed player's beliefs, find and eliminate any strategies that are now iteratively dominated.

Every time you eliminate iteratively dominated strategies for one player, check to see if this creates new iteratively dominated strategies for the other players.

If you have eliminated all the iteratively dominated strategies and reduced the strategies of each player to a few, calculate the strategic form of the simplified game and find the Bayesian Nash equilibria. If there is only one, it is the perfect Bayesian equilibrium.

16.6   Further Reading

A more advanced treatment of the material in this chapter can be found in Eric Rasmusen's *Information and Games* (New York: Basil-Blackwell, 1989, Chapter 5). Many interesting games involving information are discussed in a nontheoretical way in Dixit and Nalebuff's *Thinking Strategically: The Competitive Edge in Business, Politics, and Everyday Life* (New York: Norton, 1991). An excellent, but very advanced treatment analysis of games with private information can be found in David Kreps's *A Course in Microeconomic Theory* (Princeton: Princeton University Press, 1990, Part III).

The original inspiration for the game between Dr. Green and Mr. Smith was the article by Ivan Png, "Strategic Behavior in Suit, Settlement, and Trial," *Bell Journal of Economics*, 14(2) (Autumn 1983), pp. 539–50.

16.7   Discussion Questions

1. Suppose Dr. Green cannot predict the outcome of a court contest with certainty, but she has a better idea than Mr. Smith does of the probability of winning in court. How could the game be modified to incorporate this fact?

2. Suppose Dan inadvertently overhears two men in a washroom discuss a brilliant plot to assassinate the president of the United States the following week. Dan considers calling the Secret Service and offering to sell his information to them. Suppose the Secret Service gets calls like this from cranks all the time. Is there anyway Dan can "cash in" on his secret? Why or why not?

3. Suppose that instead of an assassination plot, Dan inadvertently overhears a rumor from a very knowledgeable source that a large corporation will

declare bankruptcy tomorrow. Now is there a way Dan can "cash in" on his secret? How is this secret different from the assassination secret?

4. Recall the Ultimatum Game discussed in Exercise 16.1. A subgame perfect Nash equilibrium of that game is that the first player offers to give nothing to the second player and the second player accepts anything that the first player offers. Yet when experimental subjects play the ultimatum game, the first player often offers a substantial portion of the dollar to the other player and the second player often vetoes divisions that are too one-sided. How might imperfect information account for these results without abandoning the assumption that it is common knowledge that the players are rational and self-interested?

16.8 New Terms

contingent fee   out-of-court settlement
lockout   reservation wage
malpractice

16.9 Exercises

Exercises 16.1–16.5 all concern the Raider–Target Bargaining Game analyzed in Section 16.2.

EXERCISE 16.1

What is the perfect Bayesian equilibrium of the Raider–Target Game if:

(a) It is common knowledge that Crapshoot has been successful?

(b) It is common knowledge that Crapshoot has a 75% chance of being successful?

EXERCISE 16.2

Let π denote the probability that Crapshoot is successful. For what values of π does the Target–Raider Game have a perfect Bayesian equilibrium in which Raider offers Target 100?

EXERCISE 16.3

Does the Raider–Target Game ever have a separating equilibrium?

EXERCISE 16.4

Suppose it is Target who makes a take-it-or-leave-it offer to Raider. The payoffs and the informational assumptions remain unchanged.

(a) Draw the game tree for the new Target–Raider Game.

(b) What are the two players' strategies in this new game?

Table 16.11   **A Perfect Bayesian Equilibrium of the Lawsuit Game When $V_{Smith}(0) \geq 0.5$**

Dr. Green's strategy	Always offer \$0
Mr. Smith's strategy	$A(S) = \begin{cases} accept & if\ S = \$0 \\ reject & if\ \$0 < S < \$1\ million \\ accept & if\ S \geq \$1\ million \end{cases}$
Mr. Smith's beliefs	$\pi(S) = \begin{cases} 0.5 & if\ S = \$0 \\ 1 & if\ S > \$0 \end{cases}$

EXERCISE 16.5*

Find a perfect Bayesian equilibrium of the new Target–Raider Game.

Exercises 16.6–16.11 all concern the Lawsuit Game analyzed in Section 16.3.

EXERCISE 16.6

(a) Show that if Mr. Smith is risk neutral and his VNMU satisfies the normalizations in Eq. [16.2], then $V_{Smith}(0) = \frac{1}{8.5}$. (*Hint:* If Mr. Smith is risk neutral, then his VNMU takes the form $V_{Smith}(S) = a + b \cdot S$).

(b) Show that if Dr. Green is risk neutral and her VNMU satisfies the normalizations in Eq. [16.2], then $V_{Green}(-1\ million) = \frac{1}{11}$.

EXERCISE 16.7

Show that as long as Mr. Smith is sufficiently risk averse so that $V_{Smith}(0) \geq 0.5$, then the strategies and beliefs in Table 16.11 are a perfect Bayesian equilibrium of the Lawsuit Game. The outcome is that Dr. Green refuses to settle and Mr. Smith then always drops the lawsuit rather than risk losing in court.

EXERCISE 16.8

Show that as long as $V_{Smith}(0) < 0.5$, then the strategies and beliefs in Table 16.12 are a perfect Bayesian equilibrium of the Lawsuit Game.

Exercise 16.9

Find a perfect Bayesian equilibrium of the Lawsuit Game if the VNMUs of Mr. Smith and Dr. Green are given by

$$V_{Smith}(S) = \sqrt{\left(\frac{S + 100{,}000}{850{,}000}\right)}$$

---

*Indicates a difficult exercise.

Table 16.12 *A Perfect Bayesian Equilibrium of the Lawsuit Game When $V_{Smith}(0) < 0.5$*

Dr. Green's strategy	*If guilty: bluff* and offer $0 with probability p or *fold* and offer $1 million with probability $1 - p$. *If innocent:* always offer $0.
Mr. Smith's strategy	$A(S) = \begin{cases} accept \ wth \ probability \ q & if \ S = \$0 \\ reject & if \ \$0 < S < \$1 \ million \\ accept & if \ S \geq \$1 \ million \end{cases}$
Mr. Smith's beliefs	$\pi(S) = \begin{cases} \dfrac{p}{1 + p} & if \ S = \$0 \\ 1 & if \ S > \$0 \end{cases}$

and

$$V_{Green}(S) = \sqrt{\left(\frac{1.1 \ million \ + \ S}{1.1 \ million}\right)}.$$

EXERCISE 16.10

Suppose the law is changed so that the defendant's legal fees are no longer paid by the plaintiff when the plaintiff loses his or her lawsuit in court. The monetary gains and losses of the lawsuit outcomes are now given by Table 16.13. All the other elements of the lawsuit game remain unchanged.

Table 16.13 *Changes in Wealth at Each Bargaining Outcome When Dr. Green's Legal Expenses Are No Longer Reimbursed by Mr. Smith*

Outcome	Dr. Green	Mr. Smith
Out-of-court settlement in which Dr. Green pays Mr. Smith $S.	pays S	gets $0.75 \cdot S$
Jury trial in which Dr. Green is found guilty.	pays $1.1 million	gets $750,000
Jury trial in which Dr. Green is found innocent.	pays $100,000	pays nothing and gets nothing

(a) Draw the new game tree.

(b) Show that the strategy and belief profiles in Table 16.8 no longer constitute a perfect Bayesian equilibrium.

Exercise 16.11

Suppose lawyers are banned from negotiating contingency fees. Under the new law, attorneys must charge their clients a fixed fee that does not depend on either the size of any out-of-court settlements they help negotiate for their clients or the size of damage awards made by juries. But these fixed legal fees are added to the damage award. Mr. Smith's lawyer charges $200,000 to represent Mr. Smith in his lawsuit against Dr. Green and Dr. Green's lawyer charges $100,000 to represent the doctor. The monetary gains and losses of lawsuit outcomes are now given by Table 16.14. All the other elements of the Lawsuit Game remain unchanged.

Table 16.14   *Changes in Wealth at Each Bargaining Outcome When Contigency Fees Are Banned*

Outcome	Dr. Green	Mr. Smith
Out-of-court settlement in which Dr. Green pays Mr. Smith $S.	S	$S - \$200{,}000$
Jury trial in which Dr. Green is found guilty.	$-\$1.1$ million	$\$800{,}000$
Jury trial in which Dr. Green is found innocent.	$\$0$	$\$300{,}000$

(a) Draw the new game tree.

(b) Show that the strategy and belief profiles in Table 16.8 no longer constitute a perfect Bayesian equilibrium.

Exercise 16.12 is based on the Labor Negotiation Game in Section 16.4.

EXERCISE 16.12*

Suppose Welmade's initial belief is that the probability that the Union's reservation wage is low equals 0.25, but all the other assumptions of the Labor Negotiation Game remain unchanged. Find a perfect Bayesian equilibrium of the new game.

---

*Indicates a difficult exercise.

CHAPTER 17

Corporate Takeovers and Greenmail

OVERVIEW OF CHAPTER 17

17.1   Introduction

There has been a great deal of popular interest in the most recent wave of corporate mergers. The stories of insider trading, of the gathering and losing of fortunes among investment bankers such as Ivan Boesky and Michael Miliken, and the collapse of firms such as Drexel Burnham have made for fascinating reading.

Interestingly, this expansive coverage of the corporate sector has given rise to a flowery new language. Twenty years ago, economists simply talked about "mergers" and the "market for corporate control," and students' eyes would glaze over. Now we can talk about "greenmail," "white knights," "raiders," and "poison pills."

In this chapter, we will first consider the conventional wisdom surrounding some of these strategies. We will then show some ways in which the conventional wisdom may be wrong. The credit for this unconventional viewpoint is due to two economists: Andrei Shleifer and Robert Vishny. We borrow liberally from their analysis.

17.2   The Current Lexicon and Conventional Wisdom

Outside of curiosity about the act of one firm taking over another firm, there is a great deal of debate among economists and businesspeople about two aspects of merger activity. First, how does the threat of a merger affect shareholders of corporations? It has long been recognized that managers of corporations may have different objectives than corporate owners (the shareholders). Since managers seem to be able to engage in behavior that discourages merger activity or takeover attempts (such as "greenmail" or "poison pills"), the question arises as to whether these managerial strategies are in the best interest of the owners of the corporation.

Second, what are the consequences of merger activity for the economy as a whole? Are mergers simply motivated by complicated tax laws or financial market gimmicks that make investment bankers rich at the expense of the rest of the world? Or do mergers serve the purpose of driving mediocre management and corporate structures out of existence and replacing them with more efficient managers and firms?

In this chapter, we will tackle only the first question. That is, we will concentrate on finding conditions under which certain types of managerial responses to a takeover attempt are actually in the best interest of the shareholders. One of the most controversial strategies managers have employed when confronted with "unfriendly" takeover attempts has become known as *greenmail*. The "unfriendly" acquirer is often called a **raider** and the firm the raider has set its sights on is known as the **target firm.** Suppose that someone perceives a firm as a target for a takeover attempt.[1] Perhaps this someone has reason to believe that better management could run the firm more profitably; or perhaps it is thought that the various operations that the firm performs could be sold off piecemeal at a profit; or perhaps it is thought that there will be a synergistic effect (one plus one equals more than two) by merging this firm with another. Whatever the reason, one possible move the acquirer might make is to begin buying up shares of the target firm (or to threaten to do so). At some stage the acquirer then announces, or threatens to announce, a tender offer for a majority of the outstanding shares. In a tender offer, the acquirer promises to buy all shares offered to it before a given date and time at a share price usually well above the current market price—as long as enough shares are tendered so as to transfer effective control of the corporation to the acquirer.

To combat the raider's tender offer, the management of the target firm can buy back the raider's shares at a price above what the raider paid for them; this is known as a **repurchase agreement.** In addition, the management of the target firm almost always requires in this agreement that the raider not buy any new shares in the target firm for some fairly lengthy time period. In short, the target firm's management bribes the potential acquirer to get away and stay away! The profit the raider makes from accepting such an agreement is **greenmail.**

---

[1]"Someone" can refer to an individual investor, a consortium of investors, or the management of another firm using the financial capital of their stockholders.

On the surface it seems that greenmail helps the managers of the firm, who are worried about their future employment, but is bad for the shareholders, who are prevented from selling their shares for a relatively high price. All the acquirer wants to do, so the conventional wisdom goes, is to offer the shareholders a share price above the current market price. The shareholders will only tender their shares if they perceive that it is in their interest to do so. So, they must be made better off if they choose to tender their shares. It follows, therefore, that self-interested management must be protecting its own narrow interests by engaging in greenmail. In what follows, we will challenge the validity of this conventional wisdom. In particular, we will present conditions under which it is in the best interests of the current shareholders of a takeover target to pay greenmail to a raider.

The reason shareholders of the targeted firm might be made better off if the management pays greenmail to a raider is that by doing so *they may be able to induce other firms to start bidding for ownership of the firm.* The entry of these other firms may result in a higher share price than would have resulted if only the raider made an offer. A **white knight** is a special type of bidder who has been invited by the target firm to submit a bid. The cynical view is that the white knight is invited in by the firm in distress in order to save the jobs of senior managers. But we will show that another possible reason for the invitation is that it can increase the level of competition for the rights of the distressed firm. The payment of greenmail turns out to be a signal to the white knight about the economic status of the target firm, which is known only to that firm.

17.3   Greenmail Without White Knights

Imagine a target firm, Bull's Eye Inc., which is being considered for acquisition by two potential acquirers, Carnivore, Inc. and Appetite UnLtd. Two important aspects of this model are that these two potential acquirers are *not* identical and that each is uncertain about the profitability of a takeover.

The owners of Carnivore have no concrete idea how they would go about making Bull's Eye more profitable. They do believe, however, that if they spend $12,000 on a consultant, there is a 50% chance the consultant will uncover some hitherto unknown scheme that will increase Bull's Eye's market value by $120,000.[2] There is also a 50% chance the consultant will come up empty and Carnivore will have spent $12,000 for nothing. The other potential acquirer, Appetite UnLtd. is in a similar, but not identical, position. They have access to another consultant who has a 50% chance of finding a way to increase the market value of Bull's Eye by $200,000. The cost of this consultant is $48,000. As with Carnivore, if the consultant fails, then Appetite will have spent $48,000 for nothing.

We will refer to the game played between Carnivore, Appetite, and Bull's

---

[2]This is the present value of the increased profits Bull's Eye would earn after reorganization. In a more general model, we would model the expected payoff as an increasing, continuous function of the amount spent by Carnivore for financial consulting services.

Eye as Takeover Game I. We will model this game as two static subgames played in succession: a Consultant-Hiring Game and a Bidding Game. In the first subgame, Carnivore and Appetite decide simultaneously whether to hire a consultant. Nature then decides whether the consultants hired are successful. Nature's moves are common knowledge. The two firms then bid for Bull's Eye's shares and the game ends. As usual, we begin at the end by analyzing the Bidding Game. From the equilibrium payoffs of this subgame, we then calculate the expected payoffs of the first static game. A slightly simplified game tree is displayed in Figure 17.1.

Carnivore and Appetite will bid for Bull's Eye's shares if and only if its consultant has successfully figured out how to increase the value of the target firm. So if both consultants fail, the game ends and everyone gets a payoff of zero. If both consultants are successful, then Appetite and Carnivore will get into a "bidding war." We will suppose that this takes the form of a first-price auction in which the shares of Bull's Eye are sold to the highest bidder. Under conditions of perfect information (remember that for the sake of simplicity we are assuming that each firm's valuation of Bull's Eye is common knowledge), it is recognized by all that the firm that is willing to pay the most for Bull's Eye must pay at least what the second highest bidder is willing to offer—but no more than this. Since at this stage the consultants' fees are sunk costs, the value to Carnivore of acquiring Bull's Eye equals $120,000, and the value to Appetite of acquiring Bull's Eye equals $200,000. It follows that Appetite will win the auction by paying $120,000 for Bull's Eye's shares. Bull's Eye's current shareholders gain $120,000, Appetite gains $200,000 − $120,000 = $80,000, and Carnivore gains nothing.

It is much less clear what the outcome will be if only one of the two potential acquirers makes a bid for Bull's Eye. Shareholders may rationally hold on to shares to participate in the increased value of the firm rather than sell them to a

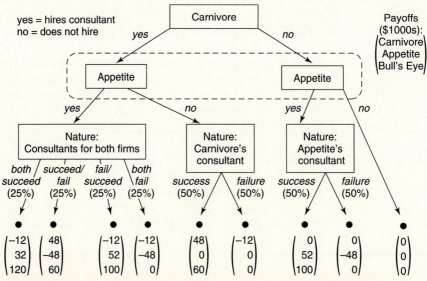

FIGURE 17.1 Game tree for Takeover Game I between Bull's Eye, Carnivore, and Appetite.

bidder. For simplicity, we will simply assume that if there is only one bidder, then Bull's Eye's increased value is split 50/50 between the acquirer and the current shareholders. So if Appetite is the sole bidder, it buys Bull's Eye for $100,000 over its current market value and both it and earlier owners of Bull's Eye get a payoff of $100,000. On the other hand, if Carnivore is the sole bidder, then it buys Bull's Eye for $60,000 over its current market value and both it and earlier owners of Bull's Eye end up with a payoff of $60,000. There are a wide variety of other splits that could also be rationalized. Although our specific numerical solutions depend on how these gains are divided, the qualitative features of the equilibria we will obtain below remain unchanged if other splits are used. What is important is that the acquirer and Bull's Eye's shareholders both gain something from the takeover.

With the bidding subgames solved, we turn our attention to the initial static game in which the firms decide whether to hire a consultant. A firm that does not hire a consultant gets a payoff of zero. A firm that hires a consultant receives an uncertain payoff that depends on whether the consultant is successful, as well as on whether the opponent's consultant is successful. That is, hiring a consultant is equivalent to playing a lottery. We will assume that both raiders make their decision on the basis of the expected payoffs to both of them from playing these lotteries. These expected payoffs are reported in Table 17.1.

It is worth verifying the four nonzero payoffs asserted in Table 17.1. If only one firm hires a consultant, then two equally likely outcomes are possible: either the consultant is successful and the firm splits the increased value of Bull's Eye with Bull's Eye's stockholders or the consultant fails, in which case nothing happens and all three players earn zero payoffs. If only Carnivore hires the consultant, then its expected payoff equals

$$0.5 \cdot (\tfrac{1}{2} \cdot \$120{,}000) + 0.5 \cdot \$0 - \$12{,}000 = \$18{,}000, \qquad [17.1]$$

and if only Appetite hires a consultant, then its expected payoff equals

$$0.5 \cdot (\tfrac{1}{2} \cdot \$200{,}000) + 0.5 \cdot \$0 - \$48{,}000 = \$2{,}000. \qquad [17.2]$$

Finally, suppose both firms hire a consultant. Then each firm ends up playing a lottery with four equally likely outcomes: both consultants are successful and

Table 17.1 *Expected Payoffs in Takeover Game I*

		Carnivore Inc.	
		Hire consultant	Don't hire consultant
Appetite UnLtd.	Hire consultant	(−$3,000, $3,000)	($2,000, $0)
	Don't hire consultant	($0, $18,000)	($0, $0)

Payoffs: (Appetite, Carnivore)

Appetite outbids Carnivore for Bull's Eye; only Carnivore's consultant is successful and it acquires Bull's Eye by splitting the gains with the shareholders; only Appetite's consultant is successful, in which case it, too, splits the gains with the shareholders; or both consultants are unsuccessful, in which case neither firm bids for Bull's Eye. Carnivore's expected payoff equals

$$0.25 \cdot \$0 + 0.25 \cdot (\tfrac{1}{2} \cdot \$120{,}000) + 0.25 \cdot \$0 + 0.25 \cdot \$0$$
$$- \$12{,}000 = \$3{,}000, \qquad [17.3]$$

and Appetite's expected payoff equals

$$0.25 \cdot \$80{,}000 + 0.25 \cdot \$0 + 0.25 \cdot (\tfrac{1}{2} \cdot \$200{,}000)$$
$$+ 0.25 \cdot \$0 - \$48{,}000 = -\$3{,}000. \qquad [17.4]$$

From Table 17.1 you can verify that Carnivore has a strongly dominant strategy: hire the consultant. Appetite does not have a dominant strategy, but it does have an iterated dominant strategy: don't hire the consultant. So this game has an iterated dominant strategy equilibrium (which is the unique Nash equilibrium) in which only Carnivore hires a consultant. This consultant has a 50% chance of successfully figuring out how Carnivore can make Bull's Eye more profitable. The expected payoff to Bull's Eye shareholders when Carnivore and Appetite play their equilibrium strategies equals

$$0.5 \cdot \tfrac{1}{2} \cdot \$120{,}000 + 0.5 \cdot \$0 = \$30{,}000. \qquad [17.5]$$

But now let us suppose that the management of Bull's Eye can "bribe" Carnivore not to play the takeover game we have just analyzed. The only way Bull's Eye could benefit from paying such a bribe is if doing so would induce Appetite to hire a consultant and explore the feasibility of taking over Bull's Eye. We already know that Appetite will hire a consultant if and only if Carnivore is removed from the game. But taking a potential acquirer out of the takeover game is exactly what greenmail is meant to do! What has been missed in the conventional analysis of takeovers is that the shareholders might actually benefit from removing an acquirer. They will benefit if doing so induces a *better* acquirer—meaning one willing to pay more to Bull's Eye's shareholders—to enter the picture.

Takeover Game II, in which Bull's Eye has the option to pay greenmail, is diagrammed in Figure 17.2. In the first stage, Bull's Eye offers Carnivore greenmail to stay out of the takeover game against Appetite. Carnivore can either accept or reject this offer. If Carnivore accepts the offer, then Appetite can decide whether to hire the consultant, confident that there will be no bidding war against Carnivore. If Carnivore rejects the greenmail offer, then Carnivore and Appetite play the takeover subgame we just analyzed. In Figure 17.2, we have replaced this entire subgame with a terminal node and assigned to this node the Nash equilibrium expected payoffs of the subgame.

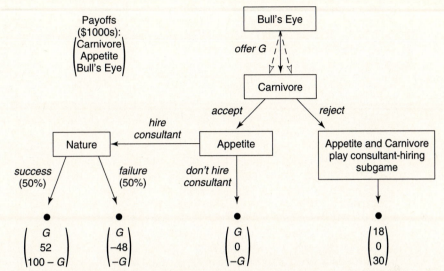

FIGURE 17.2 Game tree for Takeover Game II between Bull's Eye, Appetite, and Carnivore that allows Bull's Eye to pay greenmail.

Since this is a dynamic game, we can find its equilibrium using backward induction. We begin with Appetite's decision to hire the consultant knowing that Carnivore has accepted the greenmail offer. If Appetite hires the consultant and she is successful, then Appetite will take over Carnivore without getting into a bidding war with Carnivore. This increases the profitability of such a takeover. But Bull's Eye's market value is reduced by the amount of the greenmail payment, G. We will assume that in the subsequent negotiations between Appetite and Bull's Eye over the purchase price, Bull's Eye's shareholders absorb all of this loss in value. That is, Appetite buys Bull's Eye for $100,000 − G and its profit from the transaction is ($200,000 − G) − ($100,000 − G) = $100,000, as is the case when no greenmail is paid. The expected payoff from hiring the consultant equals

$$(0.5 \cdot \$100{,}000 + 0.5 \cdot \$0) - \$48{,}000 = \$2{,}000. \qquad [17.6]$$

Since this is positive, Appetite will hire the consultant. Moving up the game tree, the next decision node belongs to Carnivore. Since Carnivore's expected payoff in the takeover subgame is $18,000, Carnivore will only accept a greenmail offer at or above $18,000. If Bull's Eye offers $18,000 to Carnivore, the offer will be accepted and Appetite will hire the consultant. The expected payoff to Bull's Eye's shareholders equals

$$0.5 \cdot (\$100{,}000 - \$18{,}000) + 0.5 \cdot (-\$18{,}000) = \$32{,}000. \qquad [17.7]$$

On the other hand, if Bull's Eye offers less than $18,000 to Carnivore, the offer will be rejected, only Carnivore will hire a consultant, and the expected payoff to Bull's Eye's shareholders will equal $30,000. It follows that payment of $18,000 in greenmail to Carnivore is in the best interest of the shareholders!

GAME THEORY IN ACTION: Greenmail and Stockholder Well-Being: Some Evidence

The conventional wisdom is that the payment of greenmail (sometimes called "targeted repurchases") harms the firm's shareholders by eliminating a potential buyer but benefits the current management by saving their jobs. We have shown that it is *theoretically* possible for a management that acts in the best interest of shareholders to elect to pay greenmail to a raider. It does so to signal other investors that it may be profitable to take over the firm. But is this theoretical possibility observed in practice? Research carried out by Professors Wayne Mikkelson and Richard Ruback provides some evidence that greenmail both benefits shareholders and does not prevent managers from being replaced ("Targeted repurchases and common stock returns," *RAND Journal of Economics*, 4 [1991], pp. 544–561).

Mikkelson and Ruback studied 111 instances of greenmail payments made between 1978 and 1983. Consistent with earlier studies, they found that stock prices usually fall right after the greenmail payment. But they also found that the fall in price that occurs after the greenmail payment is less than the run-up in price that occurs when the raider initially purchases the firm's stock! So even though greenmail has an immediate depressing effect on the firm's stock price, the target's stock price ends up higher than it began. So, on average, a takeover attempt that results in a greenmail payment does not hurt the target firm's shareholders.

Perhaps more interesting was the history of the target firms in the three years after they paid greenmail. Of the 111 firms in the sample, 24 were taken over, 6 went private, and 2 had changes in the control of their boards of directors. This means that 29 percent of the firms in the sample eventually had changes in the control of the firm within three years of the greenmail payment. This is almost exactly the same proportion of changes in control that were observed in a control group of firms that did not make greenmail payments. The payment of greenmail does not appear to prevent managers and board members from being replaced.

17.4 Greenmail with White Knights

While the model presented above is logically sound, it does not conform well to empirical data. The model predicts that when the shareholders of a takeover target observe a raider accepting a greenmail offer from their firm, then they should infer that a more suitable acquirer exists and is being enticed into exploring the firm's takeover. As a result, the shareholders should immediately revise their evaluation of the firm's worth upward, and the firm's stock price should increase. Unfortunately, that is not what the data show. Instead, the acceptance of greenmail is usually followed by a *drop* in the target firm's stock price. Secondly, when a target refuses to pay greenmail to a raider, the target often seeks out a "white knight." Recall that a white knight is a potential acquirer that the targeted firm asks to make an offer for its shares.

In this section, we will try to account for these two stylized facts by introducing some private information into our takeover game. We will continue to assume that there are two potential acquirers for Bull's Eye: Carnivore and Appetite. Neither firm knows initially how to increase Bull's Eye's market value, but each can hire a consultant to find a way. The new wrinkle is that Bull's Eye *may already know* how Appetite can increase Bull's Eye's value by $200,000. When this is the case, we will say that Bull's Eye *has a white knight.* When Bull's Eye shares this information with Appetite, the latter can profitably take over the firm without having to hire a consultant. So Bull's Eye can be of two types: it either has a White Knight or it doesn't. Both Bull's Eye and Appetite know Bull's Eye's type, but Carnivore doesn't, so this is a game with incomplete information to which we apply the Harsanyi transformation. The resulting game is diagrammed in Figure 17.3.

If Nature moves right and fails to give Bull's Eye a white knight, then the three players play Takeover Game II. We have simplified the game tree in Figure 17.3 by replacing Nature's decision nodes in this subgame with the expected payoffs from Nature's moves. *If it were common knowledge that Bull's Eye did not have a white knight,* then we know from Section 17.2 that the three firms' equilibrium strategies are as follows: Bull's Eye pays Carnivore $18,000 in greenmail;

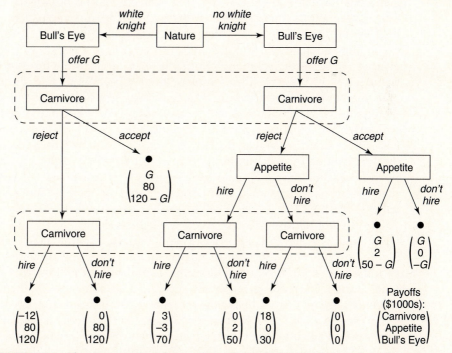

FIGURE 17.3 The game tree for Takeover Game III, in which Bull's Eye may know how Appetite can profitably take over the firm.

Carnivore only accepts greenmail offers of $18,000 or more; and Appetite hires a consultant if and only if Carnivore accepts Bull's Eye's greenmail offer.

If Nature moves left and gives Bull's Eye a white knight, then Appetite knows the target is worth $200,000 more than its current market value. It knows, therefore, that it is guaranteed to outbid Carnivore should the latter make a play for Bull's Eye. This means that Carnivore is guaranteed to take a $12,000 loss if it hires a consultant, regardless of whether or not the consultant is successful. It follows that *if it were common knowledge that Bull's Eye had a white knight,* then in the subgame, Carnivore's optimal strategy would be to accept any greenmail offer Bull's Eye makes and don't hire a consultant. It follows that Bull's Eye's optimal strategy is not to pay any greenmail (which is represented by an "offer" of $0). We will assume that because it has helped show Appetite how to profit from a takeover, Appetite and Bulls' Eye agree on a purchase price of $120,000 (which is what Bull's Eye would get if Carnivore were to bid against Appetite). This assumption implies that Bull's Eye has no incentive to make Carnivore believe it has a white knight when it does not.

Of course, Bull's Eye's type is not common knowledge in this game. Bull's Eye knows his type, but how can the firm credibly communicate this to Carnivore? The answer is simple: the greenmail offer reveals this information. For *if Carnivore believes that Bull's Eye will offer it greenmail if and only if there is no white knight,* then Bull's Eye's best strategy is to *offer greenmail* (of $18,000) to Carnivore if and only if there is no white knight! To see why, consider the consequence of failing to offer greenmail to Carnivore when there isn't a white knight. Since Carnivore believes no greenmail means that there is a white knight, it does not hire a consultant and nobody bids for Bull's Eye, even though there is a 75% chance that at least one of the consultants would have found a way for one of the two acquirer's to increase the firm's value. Now suppose Bull's Eye offers $18,000 in greenmail to Carnivore when there is a white knight. Carnivore will then believe there is no white knight and that it is playing Takeover Game II. So Carnivore will accept the greenmail. But Bull's Eye does not need to pay greenmail when it has a white knight since with Bull's Eye's help, Appetite will find a way to increase the firm's value by much more than it would ever be worth to Carnivore. This proves that Bull's Eye's optimal strategy is to offer greenmail only when it does not have private information about how Appetite can increase Bull's Eye's market value.

In this equilibrium, paying greenmail signals that Bull's Eye does *not* have a white knight. When Bull's Eye has a white knight, no greenmail is paid to Carnivore. Instead, Bull's Eye reveals its private information to Appetite and the two split the added value. Not only does this equilibrium reveal the role of the white knight, but it also shows why paying greenmail is "bad news" to the target firm's shareholders: in this equilibrium, the shareholders' expected payoff is higher when there is a white knight than when there isn't. Not only is the expected price paid for Bull's Eye's stock higher when there is a white knight, but no greenmail needs to be paid to Carnivore. So our model can explain the drop in the target firm's stock price after it announces that it will pay geenmail to the raider.

17.5   Summary

This chapter presented a game-theoretic analysis of corporate takeovers. Using this framework, we showed how the payment of greenmail to a corporate raider might be in the best interests of the firm's shareholders if it resulted in a better offer from another firm. The reason one acquirer might have to be eliminated in order to get another acquirer to make a bid is that the acquiring firm often has to first invest some time and money to see if taking over the target firm makes economic sense. A firm will not be willing to make this investment if there is too great a chance that it will face a bidding war against a raider.

Unfortunately, our first takeover model failed to conform to one well-documented fact about greenmail: The payment of greenmail to a raider is usually followed by a decline in the target firm's market value. Our first model, by contrast, predicted that greenmail would be associated with an *increase* in the firm's value. In order to make our model agree with the facts, we modified it by introducing asymmetric information. In our new model, the target firm may or may not have a white knight. The target has a white knight if it knows the identity of an acquirer that can make the firm much more valuable. In our model, the target firm uses the greenmail payment to the initial raider to signal whether it has a white knight. If the target has a white knight, then it does not pay greenmail and simply informs the white knight of its private information about how the white knight can make the target more valuable. If it does not have a white knight, though, then the target firm needs to signal this to the group of potential acquirers by paying greenmail to a raider. Once they see the greenmail payment, the potential buyers begin exploring the possibility of acquiring the firm. Without the greenmail payment, they would not be sure that they were not being "suckered" into a bidding war against the purported white knight and would not explore a takeover attempt.

17.6   Further Reading

This chapter is based in large measure on Andrei Shleifer and Robert W. Vishney, "Greenmail, White Knights, and Shareholders' Interest," *Rand Journal of Economics*, 17 (1986), pp. 293–309.

17.7   Discussion Questions

1. Consider a recent takeover attempt. Look at the details of the case and discuss why it does or doesn't seem to fit with this model.

2. As noted in this chapter, the standard explanation for greenmail is that it saves the hides of existing managers. What predictions would be made about firm and stock price behavior that are different if that model were correct versus the model presented here?

17.8   New Terms

greenmail   target firm
raider   white knight
repurchase agreement

17.9   Exercises

Exercises 17.1 and 17.2 are based on Takeover Game I presented in Section 17.4 and diagrammed in Figure 17.1.

EXERCISE 17.1

Takeover Game I assumes that if only one of the potential acquirers bids for Bull's Eye (either because it was the only firm to hire a consultant or because only its consultant was successful), then the shareholders get $\alpha = 50\%$ of Bull's Eye's increased value while the acquirer gets $1 - \alpha = 50\%$. Find all the values of α for which the Takeover Game I has a Nash equilibrium in which Carnivore hires its consultant and Appetite does not. (*Hint:* You know from Section 17.4 that one value is 50%.)

EXERCISE 17.2

Takeover Game I assumes that Carnivore's consultant charges a fee of $F_{Carnivore} = \$12,000$ and Appetite's consultant charges a fee of $F_{Appetite} = \$48,000$. Find the values of $F_{Carnivore}$ for which the takeover game has a Nash equilibrium in which Carnivore hires its consultant and Appetite does not. (*Hint:* You know from Section 17.4 that one value is $12,000.)

Exercises 17.3 and 17.4 are based on Takeover Game II presented in Section 17.4 and diagrammed in Figure 17.2.

EXERCISE 17.3

Takeover Game II assumes that if Carnivore rejects Bull's Eye's greenmail offer of G, then its expected payoff in the consultant-hiring subgame equals $P_{Carnivore} = \$18,000$. Find all the values of $P_{Carnivore}$ for which this game has a subgame perfect equilibrium in which Bull's Eye offers greenmail to Carnivore.

EXERCISE 17.4

Takeover Game II assumes that Carnivore's consultant charges a fee of $F_{Carnivore} = \$12,000$ and Appetite's consultant charges a fee of $F_{Appetite} = \$48,000$. Use your answers to Exercises 17.2 and 17.3 to find the values of $F_{Carnivore}$ for which the takeover game has a Nash equilibrium in which Bull's Eye offers greenmail to Carnivore.

Exercise 17.5 is based on Takeover Game III presented in Section 17.5 and diagrammed in Figure 17.3.

EXERCISE 17.5

Takeover Game III assumes that if only one of the potential acquirers bids for Bull's Eye (either because it is the only firm to hire a consultant or because only its consultant is successful), then the shareholders get $\alpha = 50\%$ of Bull's Eye's increased value while the acquirer gets $1 - \alpha = 50\%$. Find all the values of α for which the Takeover Game III has a perfect Bayesian equilibrium in which Bull's Eye offers greenmail to Carnivore if and only if it does not have a white knight.

CHAPTER 18

Adverse Selection and Credit Rationing

18.1   Introduction

In Part III, we showed how traders in the markets for insurance and labor are exposed to moral hazard. You will recall that in games with moral hazard one player cannot directly observe the move made during the game that another player can *and* this unobserved move is made *after* the uninformed player moves. One consequence of moral hazard is that some trades that would benefit both parties are not realized. In this chapter, we will examine the related phenomenon of *adverse selection*. A buyer faces **adverse selection** in a market if the profitability of a purchase depends on the seller's type and a lower price attracts not only fewer sellers but also less desirable sellers.

A stockbroker is exposed to adverse selection when she trades with someone who may have *inside information*. **Inside information** is any information about the future profitability of a company that is known only to a select few, who are usually referred to as "insiders." Similarly, an insurance company is exposed to adverse selection when it offers to sell life insurance to a group that includes people who know they have a higher-than-average chance of getting cancer because of their family history. A used car buyer is playing an adverse selection game if he does not know the quality of the used cars that are offered for sale, but the sellers do.

Figure 18.1 displays the prototypical game tree for a two-player game with adverse selection. Since adverse selection games are games with incomplete information, we use the Harsanyi transformation. Nature moves first and determines the informed player's *type*. Recall from Chapter 13 that a player's "type" is anything that affects the payoffs but is known only to that player. Players can differ in their risk aversion, discount rate, labor productivity, and/or risk of losing some of their wealth. The informed player knows his type, but the uninformed player does not. Another way of saying this is that the uninformed player does not know precisely against whom she is playing. In the game displayed in Figure 18.1, the type consists of the quality of the seller's product, which can be *good* or *bad*. The uninformed player, not knowing the product's quality, then moves and offers a price for the product, which can be *high* or *low*. The informed player moves last and either *accepts* the buyer's price or *rejects* it. Looking at the payoffs, you can see that the seller will always accept a high price, but will accept a low price only if the product is bad. Offering a high price attracts the "wrong" type of seller. The buyer does best if she can buy a good product for a low price and does worst if she buys a bad product for a high price. Of course, the buyer can see that the seller will never accept a low price if the product is good, so that outcome will never occur. The next best outcome is to pay a high price but get a good product. If the buyer offers a low price, the seller accepts only when the

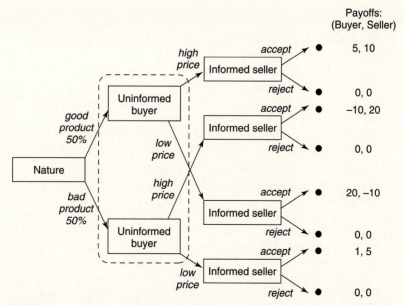

FIGURE 18.1 A prototypical game tree for a two-player game with adverse selection.

product is bad and the buyer's payoff is either 0 or 1. If the buyer offers a high price, the seller always accepts and the buyer's payoff is either 5 or −10. The buyer's best strategy now depends on the prior probability of the product being good and on her degree of risk aversion. Under a wide range of circumstances, the buyer will offer a low price and will obtain the product only if it is bad. Such a market equilibrium is usually referred to as a *lemon's market*, since only "lemons" (bad products) are bought and sold and the good products are withheld from the market and sold through other channels, such as to personal friends, colleagues, or relatives.

In this chapter, we will examine the market for bank loans. Potential borrowers differ in their "creditworthiness," that is, in the likelihood they will repay their bank loan. Unless the amount being borrowed is very high, the bank will not be willing to incur the costs to become well informed about the borrower's creditworthiness.

The bank's problem is that the interest it charges its borrowers will affect the creditworthiness of the borrowers who apply for a loan. Under a wide array of circumstances, an increase in the bank's interest rate will cause the average creditworthiness of the bank's borrowers to fall. If the bank does not know the creditworthiness of its borrowers, the bank has to offer the same interest rate to everyone. As a result, there may exist an excess demand for loans at the current market interest rate, yet no bank will be willing to eliminate this excess demand by increasing its rates for fear of reducing the creditworthiness of those borrowing from it. The result is a competitive market equilibrium in which credit is "rationed" on the basis of something other than price, such as the order in which borrowers apply for a loan.

18.2 Lending in the Absence of Adverse Selection

Consider the hypothetical case of a recent college graduate, Rebecca, who has decided to establish a printing business she calls Rebecca Printing. Because our budding entrepreneur has no previous business experience, Rebecca's suppliers demand to be paid in advance. She needs $1,000 in "working capital" simply to get her business off the ground. Since she has almost no funds of her own, she applies to a local bank for a one-year, $1,000 loan. We will treat the bank as single decision maker and refer to it hereafter as "the Bank." In what follows, we will measure all dollar values—revenues, losses, profits, and so forth—in thousands of dollars.

It is common knowledge to both Rebecca and the Bank that there is no guarantee the venture will be profitable. There is a probability π that Rebecca's services will be in high demand over the next year, and a probability $1 - \pi$ that the demand for her services will be low. If demand is high, then her revenues will be 1.5 ($1,500) and she can repay the loan. If demand is low, Rebecca's revenues will be 0.8 ($800) and she cannot repay the loan. We will refer to π as Rebecca's *creditworthiness*. Rebecca's expected revenue equals

$$1.5\,\pi + 0.8 \cdot (1 - \pi). \tag{18.1}$$

The Bank and Rebecca must negotiate the interest rate r_L for this one-year loan. The loan contract requires that all revenues earned by Rebecca must be used first to repay the bank loan. If the firm's revenue is greater than what it owes the Bank, then the Bank is paid principle and interest of $1 + r_L$ and Rebecca earns profits of

$$1.5 - (1 + r_L) = 0.5 - r_L. \tag{18.2}$$

The loan payment of $1 + r_L$ is the Bank's revenue from the loan. To calculate the Bank's profit, we must subtract from this the principal and interest the Bank must pay its depositors for the use of the funds it loaned out. We will suppose the Bank can obtain an unlimited supply of funds by paying an interest rate of 5%. This means that for every dollar the Bank obtains from its depositors (say by selling one-year certificates of deposit), it has to pay back $1 + 5\%$ one year from now. If the loan is repaid, the Bank's profits equal

$$(1 + r_L) - (1 + 5\%) = r_L - 5\%. \tag{18.3}$$

If Rebecca's revenue is less than what she owes the Bank, then she cannot pay back all of the loan. When Rebecca fails to repay, the Bank will declare her in **default** and force her to declare herself **bankrupt.** When a firm is declared bankrupt, a bankruptcy court oversees the sale of its assets and the orderly payment of its creditors. Bankruptcy is obviously a bad outcome for the Bank, since it means Rebecca will not pay back all that the Bank is owed.[1] When Rebecca defaults on the loan, the Bank is able to seize only her net income of 0.8. The loss to the Bank, when Rebecca declares bankruptcy, equals

$$0.8 - (1 + 5\%) = -0.25. \tag{18.4}$$

Bankruptcy is also a bad outcome for Rebecca. Not only will she fail to receive any compensation for her year of hard work, but she will also have to pay legal costs and will incur increased lending costs in the future. We will assume that the total cost of bankruptcy equals 0.2 ($200). The payoffs to the Bank and to Rebecca are summarized in Table 18.1.

The problem for both Rebecca and the Bank is that neither learns whether the demand for the firm's services is low or high until *after* they negotiate the terms of the loan. Figure 18.2 shows the game tree for the Lending Game I. The Bank moves first and offers to loan Rebecca $1,000 at an interest rate of r_L. There

---

[1]This means that the bank loan is unsecured. We will assume that all of the firm's capital assets— for example, the printing equipment, furniture, and space—are leased. Alternatively, the firm could have assets whose sale in the event of bankruptcy would just satisfy the firm's other, more senior creditors.

Table 18.1 *Profits to Rebecca and the Bank in Lending Game I*

	Rebecca	National Savings Bank
Loan Repaid	$0.5 - r_L$	$r_L - 5\%$
Loan Defaulted	-0.2	-0.25

is no bargaining over this rate; it is a take-it-or-leave-it offer. If Rebecca rejects the loan terms, then the game ends and both the Bank and Rebecca earn zero profits. If Rebecca accepts the loan terms, then Nature next determines whether Rebecca Printing's demand is high or low. The game then ends and profits are determined according to Table 18.1. We will assume that both Rebecca and the Bank are risk-neutral wealth maximizers.

A strategy for the Bank consists of an interest rate r_L. A strategy for Rebecca consists of a rule, $A(r_L)$, for deciding which interest rates are acceptable and which are not. If Rebecca accepts the loan at the interest rate r_L, then her expected payoff, denoted $V_{Rebecca}(r_L)$, equals

$$V_{Rebecca}(r_L) = (0.5 - r_L) \cdot \pi - 0.2 \cdot (1 - \pi) = \pi \cdot \left(0.5 - \frac{0.2 \cdot (1 - \pi)}{\pi} - r_L\right)$$

[18.5]

and the Bank's expected payoff, denoted $V_{Bank}(r_L)$, equals

$$V_{Bank}(r_L) = (r_L - 5\%) \cdot \pi - 0.25 \cdot (1 - \pi) = r_L \cdot \pi - 0.2 \cdot (1 - \pi) - 5\%.$$

[18.6]

Since the informed player moves last, the game can be solved using backward induction. Rebecca will accept the Bank's terms if and only if doing so results in

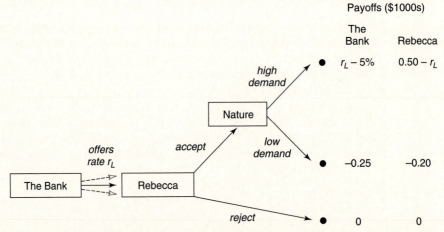

FIGURE 18.2 Game tree of Lending Game I played between the Bank and Rebecca when both are uninformed about the future demand for Rebecca's services.

a nonnegative expected profit. By rearranging the right-hand side of Eq. [18.5], you can show that her optimal strategy is

$$A(r_L) = \begin{cases} accept & if \ r_L \leq 0.5 - \dfrac{0.2 \cdot (1 - \pi)}{\pi} \\ reject & otherwise. \end{cases} \qquad [18.7]$$

The highest interest rate Rebecca will accept, $0.5 - \dfrac{0.2 \cdot (1 - \pi)}{\pi}$, is Rebecca's **reservation interest rate,** and will be referred to as $r^*_{Rebecca}$. Rebecca's reservation interest rate is a decreasing function of bankruptcy costs, and an increasing function of her creditworthiness, π. The latter means that the higher her creditworthiness, the higher the interest rate she is willing to pay the bank in order to borrow the working capital needed to start her firm.

Since $V_{Bank}(r_L)$ is an increasing function, the Bank's optimal strategy is to offer Rebecca her reservation interest rate, so long as doing so results in a nonnegative expected profit. The Bank's expected payoff is nonnegative if and only if

$$V_{Bank}\left(0.5 - \frac{0.2 \cdot (1 - \pi)}{\pi}\right) = \left(0.5 - \frac{0.2 \cdot (1 - \pi)}{\pi}\right) \cdot \pi - 0.2 \cdot (1 - \pi) - 5\% \geq 0 \qquad [18.8]$$

or, after rearranging terms,

$$\pi \geq 0.473. \qquad [18.9]$$

The number on the right-hand side of Eq. [18.9] is Rebecca's *creditworthiness threshold.* Not surprisingly, this threshold is an increasing function of the interest rate on deposits, and of her losses when demand is low, and is a decreasing function of her profitability when demand is high. This threshold is also an *increasing* function of the bankruptcy costs. The reason is that as the cost of bankruptcy increases, the maximum loan interest rate Rebecca is willing to pay falls. Holding all other variables constant, the probability of default must go down in order to keep profits unchanged.

18.3   Adverse Selection and Monopolistic Banking

In the previous section, we assumed that the firm and the Bank were symmetrically informed about the likelihood that the loan would be repaid. In most lending situations, however, the borrower has a more accurate estimate of the probability of default than does the lender. Typically, the higher the probability of default, the greater the returns to the firm taking out the loan if things go well. This fact is important to what follows since it implies that poor credit risks may accept higher loan interest rates than will good credit risks. The reason is simple. A poor credit risk is less likely to have to pay the interest on the loan, and when a poor credit risk does repay the loan, she has a high revenue from which she can do so.

In contrast, a good credit risk is not sheltered as much by bankruptcy. When she repays the loan interest, she does so out of more modest revenue. As a consequence, when the bank raises its interest rate, it will tend to drive out exactly the borrowers it would like to keep.

Suppose, as before, that the firm's revenue will be either *high* or *low*. Although Rebecca does not know what demand will be when she applies for a loan from the Bank, an informal market survey has allowed her to estimate the probability π that demand will be *high*. Because she did the survey herself, there is no way for Rebecca to credibly share this information with the Bank. The Bank knows it is in Rebecca's interest to claim that π is a high number and, therefore, that the loan is very safe, whether or not this statement is true.

The game tree for the adverse selection game played between Rebecca and the Bank is shown in Figure 18.3. We will refer to the new game as Lending Game II. Nature moves first and chooses Rebecca's creditworthiness, π. Rebecca knows π, but the Bank does not. The Bank then offers to loan Rebecca $1,000 at an interest rate r_L, which Rebecca can either *accept* or *reject*. Since the Bank does not know π, all of its decision nodes lie in a single information set. Since Rebecca does knows π, each of her decision nodes lie in separate information sets. As before, if the loan is rejected, then the game ends and both players get a payoff of zero. After Rebecca accepts the loan, Nature chooses demand. If demand is high, the loan is repaid; if demand is low, Rebecca defaults and is bankrupt. As before, the cost of declaring bankruptcy equals 0.2.

Since the Bank does not observe Nature's selection of π, a strategy consists of the selection of a single loan rate, r_L. Since Rebecca *does* observe π, a strategy

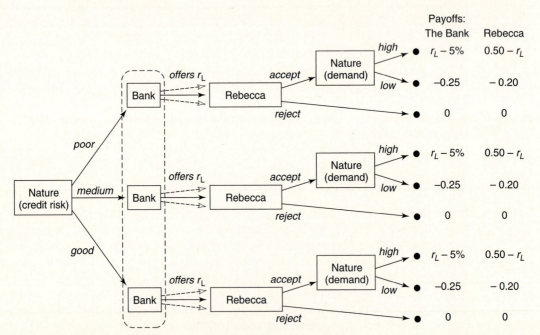

FIGURE 18.3 The game tree for the Lending Game II played between the Bank and Rebecca.

consists of a reservation interest rate for each value of π, denoted by the function $r^*_{Rebecca}(\pi)$.

The Bank has learned from previous experience that the riskier the business venture (i.e., the lower the value of π), the higher Rebecca's expected revenue. Such an inverse relationship between risk and expected reward is common in competitive financial markets. Specifically, when demand is high, revenue equals $1 + s_H(\pi)$, where

$$s_H(\pi) = \frac{0.5}{\pi} \qquad\qquad [18.10]$$

and when demand is low, revenue equals $1 - s_L$. Note that the latter does *not* depend on Rebecca's creditworthiness. Substituting Eq. [18.10] into Rebecca's expected profit function, Eq. [18.5], and rearranging terms results in the expression

$$V_{Rebecca}(r_L) = 0.3 + \pi \cdot (0.2 - r_L) = \pi \cdot \left(\frac{0.3}{\pi} + 0.2 - r_L\right). \qquad [18.11]$$

As was the case in the previous section, Rebecca's optimal strategy is to accept any interest rate less than or equal to her reservation interest rate, $r^*_{Rebecca}(\pi)$, which now depends on her creditworthiness, and is given by

$$r^*_{Rebecca}(\pi) = \frac{0.3}{\pi} + 0.2. \qquad\qquad [18.12]$$

Figure 18.4 provides a plot of Rebecca's reservation interest rate. The surprising property of $r^*_{Rebecca}(\pi)$ is that it is a *decreasing function* of Rebecca's creditworthiness. That is, as her creditworthiness increases, the interest rate she will accept *decreases*

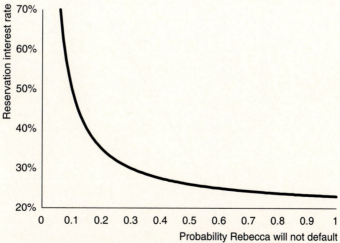

FIGURE 18.4 Rebecca's reservation interest rate as a function of her creditworthiness when her creditworthiness is private information.

instead of increases, as you might have expected. This is in stark contrast to the case where Rebecca's creditworthiness is common knowledge. The reason for this reversal is that now, as her creditworthiness increases, the firm's profitability when demand is high *declines*. That is the cost of lower risk. The probability of earning this profit, of course, increases as her creditworthiness increases. Holding everything else constant, as her creditworthiness increases, her expected profit declines.

Although Rebecca's reservation interest rate reveals information about her creditworthiness, the Bank finds this out only *after* it announces the interest rate at which it will lend. When the Bank announces the interest rate r_L, Rebecca accepts the loan if and only if $r_{Rebecca}^*(\pi) \geq r_L$, or

$$\pi \leq \overline{\pi}(r_L) \equiv \begin{cases} \dfrac{0.3}{r_L - 0.2} & r_L > 50\% \\ 1 & r_L \leq 50\%. \end{cases} \qquad [18.13]$$

In order to determine the probability that Rebecca will default, the Bank must have some initial belief about the likelihood that Rebecca's creditworthiness takes on any given value. We will assume that the Bank believes that every value of π is equally likely. This means that Nature draws π from a uniform distribution on the unit interval. It follows that if the Bank offers to lend at the interest rate r_L and Rebecca applies for a loan, then the bank knows that her creditworthiness is uniformly distributed within the interval $[0, \overline{\pi}(r_L)]$. As a result, her expected creditworthiness, *conditional on accepting the bank's interest rate*, equals the midpoint of the interval, or $\frac{1}{2}\overline{\pi}(r_L)$.

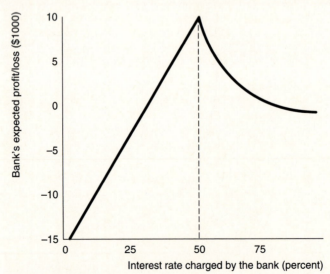

FIGURE 18.5 The Bank's expected payoff function taking account of the adverse selection problem.

The Bank's expected profit when it offers the interest rate r_L equals

$$P_{Bank}(r_L) = (r_L \cdot \tfrac{1}{2}\overline{\pi}(r_L) - 0.2 \cdot (1 - \tfrac{1}{2}\overline{\pi}(r_L)) - 5\%) \cdot \overline{\pi}(r_L) + 0 \cdot (1 - \overline{\pi}(r_L)).$$
$$[18.14]$$

The first term in Eq. [18.14] is the expected profit from making a loan to Rebecca, assuming that she accepts and taking her expected creditworthiness into account, multiplied by the probability that she accepts. The second term is the profit when she doesn't accept (which is zero) times the probability that she rejects the Bank's offer. The Bank's expected profit function is plotted in Figure 18.5. The Bank's profit is maximized at an interest rate of 50%. At this interest rate, Rebecca will always apply for a loan. As a result, her expected creditworthiness is 50%, which equals the Bank's risk of default. At this interest rate, the Bank's expected profit equals $100. Notice that because of the high probability of default, although the loan rate is very high, the Bank's expected profit is only 10% of the amount loaned.

18.4 Adverse Selection and Bertrand Banking Competition

So far we have been concerned with the relationship between one bank and one borrower. Suppose instead that there are two banks, the First Bank and the Second Bank, and 100 new entrepreneurs like Rebecca, all of whom want to borrow $100,000 in working capital. The two banks are identical. The 100 firms wanting to borrow from these two banks appear identical to both banks, but they really are not: Firm 1 has a creditworthiness of $\pi_1 = 0.01$, firm 2 has a creditworthiness of $\pi_2 = 0.02$, and so on. Each firm knows its own creditworthiness π_i and acts independently of the other firms. We know from the previous section that a firm will borrow from a bank only if it can obtain a loan rate at or below $r_L^*(\pi_i) = \left(\dfrac{0.3}{\pi_i}\right) + 0.2$. If the firm borrows, it does so from the bank offering the lowest loan rate. For simplicity, we will assume that if both banks offer the same loan rate, exactly half of the borrowers apply for a loan from one bank and exactly half apply for a loan from the other.[2]

As we have already noted, banks are financial intermediaries. This means the funds they loan out to the firms are obtained from depositors by paying these depositors interest. We will abstract from such complications as reserve requirements and capital adequacy ratios and assume that the bank lends out every dollar it obtains from depositors. The banking market, therefore, consists of two

---

[2]We are implicitly assuming that a firm cannot apply for a loan from both banks. If the firms can apply to both banks without either one knowing this, then there is a strong potential for fraud: If the firm gets both $100,000 loans, then its best strategy is to default, pay each bank the "bad revenue" of $50,000, pay the bankruptcy costs of $70,000 and pocket the remaining $30,000! Now there is moral hazard as well as adverse selection. For a hilarious example of what can happen when such a scheme backfires, see Mel Brooks's movie, *The Producers*.

interrelated submarkets: the market for deposits and the market for loans. The interest rates First Bank pays on deposits and charges for loans will be denoted r_D^1 and r_L^1, respectively; Second Bank's interest rates will be denoted r_D^2 and r_L^2. Because of the presence of adverse selection, the probability of any borrower defaulting on a loan depends on which types of borrowers accept the loan which, in turn, depends on the interest rate the bank charges. We know from the previous section that the bankruptcy rate will equal $1 - \frac{1}{2} \cdot \overline{\pi}(r_L^i)$, where the function $\overline{\pi}$ is defined in Eq. [18.13]. On every dollar that the First Bank obtains from its depositors and then lends out, its expected profit equals

$$V_{First}(r_L^1) = \tfrac{1}{2} \overline{\pi}(r_L^1) \cdot r_L^1 - s_L \cdot (1 - \tfrac{1}{2} \overline{\pi}(r_L^1)) - r_D^1. \qquad [18.15]$$

The first term in Eq. [18.15] equals the interest income per dollar of loan times the probability of repayment; the second is the loss per dollar of loan that results when the borrower defaults times the probability of default; and the third term is the interest paid per dollar of deposit to the depositor. A similar expression holds for the Second Bank.

There are 100 potential depositors, each with $1,000 to deposit with the two banks. As with the firms, although these depositors appear identical to both banks, they really are not. Like the firms, each depositor has a reservation interest rate. This interest rate is the *lowest* interest rate the depositor will accept before he or she will deposit funds in a bank. Depositors have different reservation interest rates, in part because they face different alternate investing opportunities and different investing horizons. One depositor will find a 30-day C.D. (certificate of deposit) paying 7% attractive while another depositor will not. These reservation interest rates are uniformly distributed between 0% and 20%, and this distribution is common knowledge. That is, one depositor will accept an interest rate of 0.2% or lower, 2 depositors will accept an interest rate of 0.4% or lower, 20 depositors will accept an interest rate of 4% or lower, and so on. Each depositor knows his or her reservation interest rate and acts independently of the other depositors. If the two banks offer the same deposit rate, every interested depositor deposits $500 with one bank and $500 with the other.

We will call the new game Lending Game III. Nature moves first and assigns a reservation interest rate to every depositor, and a level of credit worthiness, π_i, to every new firm. The two banks then simultaneously engage in Bertrand competition in the market for loans and deposits. That is, they simultaneously announce a loan and deposit rate. Depositors and borrowers then simultaneously apply to the banks for a loan or a deposit account. Finally, each bank simultaneously decides how many loan and deposit applications to accept. A greatly simplified sketch of the game tree is shown in Figure 18.6.

Although the game looks complicated, we can simplify our search for an equilibrium by restricting ourselves to symmetric equilibria—those in which both banks are charging the same loan and deposit rates. We will denote the deposit and loan rates at such an equilibrium by r_D^* and r_L^*. One characteristic of Bertrand competition is that in any Nash equilibrium, both banks must be earning zero

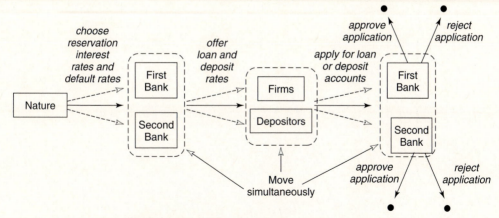

FIGURE 18.6   The game tree for the Lending Game III.

expected profits. The reason is simple: If both banks were earning positive expected profits, one bank can almost double its expected profits by cutting its loan rates very slightly, raising its deposit rates very slightly and, thereby, capturing both the loan and deposit markets from its competitor. Combining the zero-profit condition with Eq. [18.15] implies that r_D^* and r_L^* must satisfy the equation

$$r_D^* = R_D(r_L^*) = \tfrac{1}{2}\overline{\pi}(r_L^*) \cdot r_L^* - 0.2 \cdot (1 - \tfrac{1}{2}\overline{\pi}(r_L^*)). \qquad [18.16]$$

We will hereafter assume that the parameters are those in Table 18.2. For each loan rate, r_L, we will denote the deposit rate that results in zero profits for both banks by $R_D(r_L)$. For loan interest rates below 20% and above 140%, expected profits are negative, even if deposit interest rates are zero. So in any perfect Bayesian equilibrium, it must be the case that $20\% < r_L^* < 140\%$. Figure 18.7 provides a plot of the function R_D for loan interest rates in this interval. At any point above R_D, expected profits are negative and at any point below R_D, expected profits are positive. This function has a peculiar shape. For loan interest rates below 50%, the function is increasing, reflecting the fact that at these interest rates, every borrower wants to borrow and so the expected creditworthiness of the borrowers is constant. As a result, holding all other variables constant, as the loan interest rate rises, expected loan revenue increases and expected loan losses stay constant, so expected profits increases. Competition for deposits results in increased deposit rates. But as interest rates rise above 50%, the most creditworthy borrowers begin to drop out of the market. As a result, the probability of default increases. This increase in loan defaults is large enough that it more than offsets the higher income on the loans that are repaid. The result is that, holding the deposit rate constant, expected profits *decline* as the interest rate increases. As a result, R_D must decline.

The Bertrand equilibria are the pairs of interest rates between the points A and B in Figure 18.7. The points on the segment joining B and C are not Bertrand

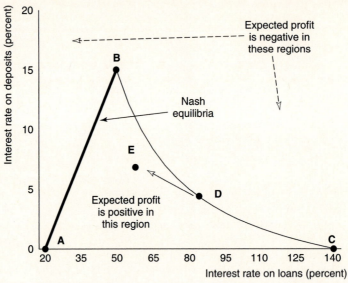

FIGURE 18.7 The Bertrand equilibrium deposit and loan rates for the Bank Loan Game III.

equilibria. To see why, suppose both banks offered the pair of interest rates denoted as D in Figure 18.7. Now suppose First Bank unilaterally changed its interest rates to those marked as E. E lies up and to the left of D. Since First Bank is offering lower loan rates and higher deposit rates, it will capture all the business from Second Bank. In addition, since E lies below the graph of R_D, First Bank is earning a positive expected profit on every dollar deposited and loaned out. So

Table 18.2 **Supply and Demand for Loanable Funds**

(1) r_L	(2) Loan Applications	(3) Loanable Funds demanded	(4) Default Rate	(5) $R_D(r_L)$	(6) Deposit Applications	(7) Loanable Funds Supplied	(8) Excess Demand for Funds
20%	100	$100,000	0.50	0%	0	$0	$100,000
30%	100	$100,000	0.50	5%	25	$25,000	$75,000
40%	100	$100,000	0.50	10%	50	$50,000	$50,000
50%	100	$100,000	0.50	15%	75	$75,000	$25,000
70%	60	$60,000	0.70	7%	35	$35,000	$25,000
90%	43	$43,000	0.79	3.5%	18	$18,000	$25,000
110%	33	$33,000	0.83	1.6%	8	$8,000	$25,000
130%	27	$27,000	0.87	0.4%	2	$2,000	$25,000
140%	25	$25,000	0.88	0%	0	$0	$25,000

First Bank is able to unilaterally increase its expected profits. This proves that none of the points on the segment BC is an equilibrium. You can confirm that, in contrast, at any point on AB no bank can unilaterally increase its deposit rate, decrease its loan rate, and make positive profits.

As Table 18.2 shows, at every one of these Bertrand equilibrium interest rates, the demand for loans exceeds the supply. The result is a competitive equilibrium in which there is **credit rationing.** If there were no adverse selection in the loan market and there were an excess demand for loans at the current loan rate, then every bank would have an obvious incentive to raise its loan rates. If it were receiving more income on its loans, the bank could offer a higher interest rate to its depositors, which would provide the bank with more funds to lend out. But notice what happens in our hypothetical bank market. Above a certain interest rate, as a bank raises its loan rate, it attracts the "wrong" type of borrowers—those more likely to default. If the default rate goes up faster than its interest rate, then in order to break even, the bank will have to turn around and *reduce* the interest rate it pays on deposits. But such a reduction will cause its deposits to shrink. As a result, the bank will find itself unable to increase its loans and must ration customers on some nonprice basis.

GAME THEORY IN ACTION: "Credit Crunches" and Lending Risk

The term "credit crunch" was coined in 1966 to describe a period of sharply increased nonprice credit rationing. Using this definition, economists Raymond Owens and Stacy Schreft ("Identifying credit crunches," *Contemporary Economic Policy,* 13 [1995], pp. 63–76) have identified four credit crunches since World War II. These episodes occurred in 1966, 1969, 1980, and 1991–92. According to Owens and Schreft, the 1966 and 1969 credit crunches were caused by direct appeals by the Federal Reserve, the President, and Congress to the banking industry to reduce its lending without increasing lending rates. The logic was that increased interest rates would lead to increases in prices as the higher cost of borrowing was passed forward by firms into the prices of their goods and services. The banking industry was threatened with "voluntary" credit restraint programs and congressional investigations into alleged "collusion." The banks responded by trying to comply. They began to take into account such nonprice criteria as whether or not the funds borrowed would be used for "speculation," whether the funds would affect the country's international trade balance, or whether the borrower was a new customer or not. The 1980 credit crunch was altogether different. It was caused by a surge in short-term interest rates above 20 percent. Although interest rates were high enough to equilibrate the market for business loans, they ran up against state usury ceilings in the consumer loan market, leading to nonprice rationing. In all three credit crunches—1966, 1969, and 1980—interest rates were prevented by political or regulatory forces from equilibrating the loan market.

The 1991–92 credit crunch was strikingly different from the other three. In that instance banks were encouraged by politicians and policy makers to *increase* their lending, not to restrict it. This "jawboning" was ineffectual precisely because it was not backed up with any credible threat. As Owen and Schreft point out, increased regulation would have only increased the cost of lending and made matters worse. Banks reduced their lending when they began to realize that they were overexposed to losses from their commercial real estate loans. Unfortunately, they acted too late. When real estate prices collapsed, first in New England and then in cities on both coasts, many banks found themselves with many bad commercial real estate loans. Worse, as commercial real estate prices plunged, it became very difficult for the banks to determine the market value of property borrowers were pledging as collateral. This exposed them to adverse selection risk of the type we have discussed in this chapter: the willingness by a borrower to pay a high interest rate becomes a signal of desperation, not of economic health. Banks, therefore, did the rational thing and used nonprice criteria to ration their funds to borrowers.

18.5   Other Examples of Adverse Selection

Adverse selection is a serious problem in many markets. For example, the amount a person is willing to pay for medical insurance increases with the probability that the person will face high medical bills in the near future. The model presented here suggests that unless the medical insurance company can obtain this information ahead of time through medical histories or testing, it will have to charge the same premium to everyone. In such a market, insurance companies will find that when they raise their premiums, their "good" policyholders will tend to cancel their policies or reduce their coverage, but their "bad" policyholders will not. As a result, the companies may find that after some point, increasing insurance premiums causes their profits to *decrease*, not increase. It is, therefore, theoretically possible for this market to have a competitive equilibrium in which every insurance company restricts the number of policies it sells, even though there is excess demand. As a result, there are people who cannot obtain medical insurance "at any price." It might also be possible for the insurance company to offer a menu of contracts in which low-risk consumers self-select contracts providing full coverage and high-risk consumers select contracts that do not result in complete coverage.

A second market in which adverse selection exists is the stock market. On most organized exchanges, such as the New York Stock Exchange, all stock transactions ultimately go through one of a small number of *specialists*. Each specialist trades only a limited group of stocks. In return for this monopoly, each specialist agrees to "make a market" in her group of stocks. This means she agrees to announce prices at which she will currently buy or sell these stocks before she knows with whom she is trading or what the demand will be at these prices. The specialist's problem is that there are two types of people in the market: traders wishing to change their liquidity and traders wishing to cash in on private information. When the specialist trades with a liquidity-motivated trader, she is at no informational disadvantage and will, on average, break even on the trade. But when she trades with an "inside trader," she will, on average, take a loss; either she will sell the stock at too low a price or buy the stock for too high a price. To cover her losses on her trades with inside traders, the specialist must widen the "bid–ask" spread: the difference between the price at which she will sell a stock and the price at which she will buy a stock. The bid–ask spread allows the specialist to break even after covering her occasional losses to inside traders. The result is that some investors are prevented from optimally adjusting the liquidity of their portfolios due to these higher transaction costs.

18.6   Summary

In this chapter, we examined the effect of adverse selection on the performance of competitive markets. Adverse selection exists when one participant in a transaction has more information about the game being played than does the other participant. The result is that some mutually beneficial trades are not made.

We used a simple model to show how adverse selection arises in the loan market. In this market, borrowers are often better informed about the probability of default than are the banks from whom they are borrowing. Under certain conditions, bad credit risks are willing to pay a higher interest rate to finance their riskier schemes than are good credit risks. When this is the case, banks will find that when they raise their interest rates, the good credit risks drop out of the market and the bad credit risks stay in. As a result, the default rate on their loans increases. After some point, further interest rate increases result in lower expected profits, rather than higher. We showed that if the banks are engaging in noncollusive Bertrand price competition in both the loan and deposit markets, it is possible for the market to be in equilibrium yet for there to exist borrowers who cannot borrow "at any interest rate." We concluded by sketching how this same phenomenon can arise in the market for medical insurance and corporate stocks.

18.7   Further Reading

The issue of adverse selection was first analyzed systematically by George Akerlof in his classic article "The Market for Lemons: Quality Uncertainty and the Market Mechanism," *Quarterly Journal of Economics* 89 (1970), pp. 488–500. The first paper to discuss credit rationing as an equilibrium outcome of the credit market is Joseph Stiglitz and Andrew Weiss, "Credit Rationing in Markets with Imperfect Information," *American Economic Review* 71 (1981), pp. 393–410. Other papers dealing with the topic include Besanko and Thakor, "Collateral and Rationing: Sorting Equilibria in Monopolistic and Competitive Credit Markets," *International Economic Review* 28 (1987), pp. 671–89, and Bester, "Screening vs. Rationing in Credit Markets with Imperfect Information," *American Economic Review* 75 (1975), pp. 850–55. If you are interested in exploring the potential importance of this topic, see Ben Bernanke's paper, "Nonmonetary Effects of the Financial Crisis in the Propogation of the Great Depression," *American Economic Review* 73 (1973), pp. 257–76. The seminal paper on adverse selection in the insurance market is Rothschild and Stiglitz, "Equilibrium in Competitive Insurance Markets: An Essay on the Economics of Imperfect Information," *Quarterly Journal of Economics*, 90 (1976), pp. 629–50.

18.8   Discussion Questions

1. In what market situations do you have information about yourself that is significantly different from the person/firm you are trying to contract with? Does this asymmetry appear to create an adverse selection problem?

2. In what real-world instances can you observe prolonged periods of excess demand or excess supply? Can these seemingly be explained by adverse selection problems?

18.9   New Terms

adverse selection	default
bankrupt	inside information
credit rationing	reservation interest rate

18.10   Exercises

EXERCISE 18.1

An insurance company is considering offering newly married couples insurance contracts covering some fraction of the medical costs associated with pregnancy. The couples can decide which of the insurance contracts offered to them, if any, they want to purchase. After purchasing insurance, the couples decide whether or not to use contraception. In each case, determine whether the insurance company faces adverse selection, moral hazard, or both and draw the appropriate game tree:

(a) It is common knowledge that contraception is not completely effective at preventing pregnancy. A recently published survey of newly married couples reveals that they are more likely to use contraception the more worried they are about the financial costs of having a baby.

(b) It is common knowledge that contraception is 100% effective at preventing pregnancy. A recently published survey of newly married couples reveals that 20% of them want to have a baby immediately and never use contraception, whereas the other 80% do not want to have a baby immediately and always use contraception.

(c) It is common knowledge that even among newly married couples who always use contraception the probability of pregnancy increases with the frequency of sexual intercourse. It is also common knowledge that there is a large variation in the frequency with which newly married couples have intercourse and not all newly married couples want to have children immediately.

EXERCISE 18.2

One way that a bank can try to get a borrower to reveal her assessment of her creditworthiness is to make her pledge some of her wealth as *collateral*. If she defaults on the loan, the bank can seize the collateral, which is denoted by *c*. Collateral increases the cost of bankruptcy. Suppose that in the Lending Game II, the Bank requires less collateral the higher the interest rate Rebecca is willing to pay so that if she defaults on the loan, the cost of bankruptcy equals $0.2 + c$. The collateral is worth less to the bank than it is to Rebecca. If Rebecca defaults on the loan, the bank receives $0.8 + \frac{1}{2}c$ back. The bank can now make the interest rate it charges Rebecca depend on the amount of collateral that Rebecca puts up, and a loan contract stipulates both an interest, r_L, and a collateral amount, *c*. Suppose that Rebecca's creditworthiness is either *high* ($\pi = 90\%$) or *low* ($\pi = 50\%$). Find two loan contracts the bank can offer *simultaneously*, (r_{high}, c_{high}) and (r_{low}, c_{low}), such that: (1) Rebecca chooses (r_{high}, c_{high}) when she has *high* creditworthiness and chooses (r_{low}, c_{low}) when she has *low* creditworthiness, and the bank's expected profit is positive whichever one she chooses. You will have shown that the bank can use collateral to get its borrowers to reveal their private information.

EXERCISE 18.3

A homeowner owns a $100,000 house. The probability that the house is completely destroyed by fire equals π. The homeowner knows π, but the fire insurance company does not. The insurance company offers to sell the homeowner as much fire insurance protection as he wants at the price of P dollars for every dollar of insurance coverage I purchased. The homeowner's expected utility when the probability of loss equals π and he buys I dollars of coverage at the price P is given by $(1 - \pi) \cdot \log(\$100,000 - P \cdot I) + \pi \cdot \log(I - P \cdot I)$.

(a) Draw the game tree for this strategic interaction.

(b) Find an algebraic expression for the amount of insurance protection I^* that maximizes the homeowner's expected utility as a function of P and π. Use calculus to show that I^* is an increasing function of π, that is, "risky" policyholders will buy more insurance protection than will "safe" policyholders.

EXERCISE 18.4

Until recently, it was common for employer-provided health insurance plans to refuse coverage of new employees with "preexisting medical conditions," meaning the employee had been diagnosed with serious medical conditions prior to working for the firm.

(a) Show how adverse selection would lead an employer to want to refuse to cover preexisting conditions in its insurance plan if all other employers refused to cover them.

(b) Explain why the firm would not object much to a law that required *all* health insurance plans to cover new employees with preexisting conditions.

CHAPTER 19

Limit Pricing and Entry Deterrence

OVERVIEW OF CHAPTER 19

19.1   Introduction

Adam Smith recognized over 200 years ago that the established firms in an industry might try to behave strategically in order to keep out new competitors:

> When by an increase in effectual demand, the market price of some particular commodity happens to rise above the natural price, those who employ their stocks in supplying that market are careful to conceal this change. If it was commonly known, their great profit would tempt so many new rivals to employ their stocks in the same way, that, the effectual demand being fully supplied, the market price would soon be reduced to the natural price, and perhaps for some time even below it.[1]

It has been understood since Smith that the benefits of long-run competition require that firms be able to enter and exit industries with low cost. Casual stories of the various means by which firms might stop or retard entry have given way

---

[1]Adam Smith, *The Wealth of Nations* (New York: The Modern Library, 1937), p. 60.

in the last 20 years to carefully articulated game-theoretic models that make far clearer the conditions under which entry-deterring behavior makes sense.

As Adam Smith makes clear above, potential entrants into an industry face a great deal of uncertainty about the prospects for future profits. Existing firms are in a better position to evaluate market conditions, both demand conditions and supply conditions, than is an outsider. Therefore, there is an asymmetry of information. As you saw in Chapter 15, the observable behavior of firms in an industry may signal market conditions to potential entrants. If such signals trigger entry, it may be in the interest of incumbents to give up short-run profits in order to deter entry and earn larger long-run profits. This is the essence of the phenomenon of *entry deterrence*, which we will address in this chapter.

One of the first economists to examine the problem of entry deterrence with the tools of modern price theory was Joe S. Bain. Bain was interested in how a monopolist might use price and output decisions to maintain its monopoly position. His work was soon extended by Modigliani in 1958 and Sylos-Labini in 1962. A simplified version of Bain's model, which has come to be known as *entry limit pricing*, is presented below. We will follow Bain's model with a modern game-theoretic reformulation.

19.2   Bain's Model of Entry Limit Pricing

Suppose a monopolist faces the industry demand curve shown in Figure 19.1. Because the demand curve is downward sloping, the marginal revenue curve will lie below it. The short-run, profit-maximizing output is determined by setting

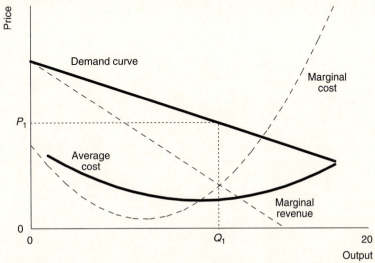

FIGURE 19.1   In the short run, a profit-maximizing monopolist will choose Q_1 and P_1 as its output and price.

marginal revenue equal to marginal cost. The profit-maximizing price is the highest price at which this output can be sold. The profit-maximizing price and output are labeled P_1 and Q_1 in Figure 19.1.

Suppose another firm is considering whether to enter the industry. It is traditional to refer to the existing firm as the **incumbent,** and its potential competitor as the **entrant.** Assume that the entrant can produce an identical product for the same cost as the incumbent. Because both firms produce the same homogeneous product, the market price will be determined by the quantity produced by both firms.

The models developed by Modigliani and Sylos-Labini assume that the potential entrant believes the incumbent firm will not alter its output or sales in response to entry. Furthermore, the incumbent firm believes the entrant believes this, and so on. In game-theoretic terms, the entrant's belief is common knowledge. If, prior to entry, the incumbent produces Q_1 units of the good, then the potential entrant believes the incumbent will continue to produce Q_1 units of the good after entry. Therefore, the only demand left for the entrant is that portion of the demand curve extending to the right of Q_1 in Figure 19.1. If we bring this leftover demand, or what is called the *residual demand*, back to the vertical axis, we obtain the demand curve that the entrant believes it will face if it enters. This is shown in Figure 19.2. Remember that profits equal the difference between price and average cost multiplied by output, or $(P(Q) - AC(Q)) \cdot Q$ where P is the inverse demand function and AC is the average cost function. As long as the residual demand curve lies above the average cost curve over some range of prices, the entrant can make a profit by entering.

Assuming that the entrant believes profits are possible, it will maximize those profits by setting the residual marginal revenue curve equal to marginal cost. As

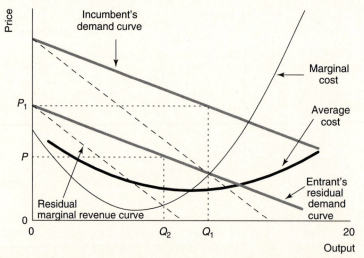

FIGURE 19.2 If the residual demand curve lies above average cost, then entry is profitable.

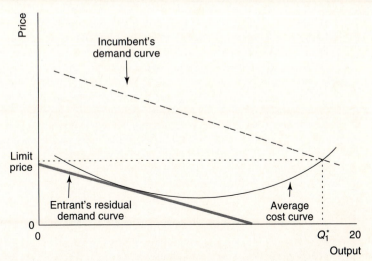

FIGURE 19.3   The limit pricing strategy is the smallest output at which entry is deterred.

you can see from Figure 19.2, when the incumbent produces Q_1, entry is believed to be profitable and the entrant's output will be Q_2. The resulting industry output of $Q_1 + Q_2$ lowers the future profits of the incumbent firm.

As Bain pointed out, however, if the incumbent firm knows the entrant's beliefs, the incumbent firm may have an incentive to produce a preentry output different from the output that maximizes short-run profits, Q_1. Consider Figure 19.3. Suppose that the incumbent firm produces an output of Q_1^*, somewhat greater than the short-run, profit-maximizing output of Q_1. Because of the higher level of output by the incumbent, the residual demand facing the entrant is farther to the left than it was in Figure 19.2. The residual demand, in this case, is never above average cost, making entry unprofitable. The highest price (smallest output) at which entry is deterred is referred to as the **limit price.** An incumbent firm charging this price is using a **limit pricing strategy.** This strategy allows the incumbent to increase its future profits by giving up some short-run profits.

If the present value of the incumbent's profit stream from using the limit pricing strategy and successfully deterring entry exceeds the present value of the profit stream from maximizing short-run profits and inducing entry, then it is obviously better to charge the limit price.

19.3   A Game-Theoretic Look at Limit Pricing

The Modigliani-Stylos-Labini model, while a tremendous improvement on what preceded it, leaves a lot to be desired. For example, it is hard to justify the belief that an incumbent firm will not alter its output after entry occurs. While the incumbent might *threaten* to do so, the threat is simply not credible. It is not hard to see that the incumbent, once entry has taken place, will have an incentive to modify the output chosen.

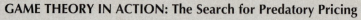

GAME THEORY IN ACTION: The Search for Predatory Pricing

For years the popular press has written stories about firms that charged customers below cost in order to drive out existing competitors or to deter new competitors from entering an industry. These writers have claimed that the "predatory" firms did this in the hope of raising prices and making greater profits later on. A particularly famous case involved the Standard Oil Company of New Jersey during the first decade of the twentieth century. It was alleged at the time that Standard Oil systematically drove regional competitors in the oil refining industry out of business by pricing below cost while subsidizing this behavior through monopoly profits in other regional markets. In 1958 Professor John McGee published a case study of Standard Oil's behavior and concluded that little or no evidence indicated that it had engaged in predatory pricing ("Predatory price cutting: The Standard Oil (N.J.) case," *Journal of Law and Economics,* 1 [1958], pp. 253–279). His empirical work was buttressed by strong theoretical arguments that predatory pricing could never be profitable.

McGee's research started a forty-year dispute among economists about the existence of predatory pricing. While most of the research has involved case studies, in 1985 Professors Mark Isaac and Vernon Smith of the University of Arizona offered new evidence using experimental laboratory techniques ("In search of predatory pricing," *Journal of Political Economy*, 93 [1985], pp. 320–345). They created a series of experimental environments that they claimed were conducive to predatory behavior, but their subjects did not appear to engage in such behavior.

As you have seen in this chapter, new theoretical models based on games with incomplete information can have equilibria in which rational firms engage in predatory entry deterrence. Professors Yun Joo Jung, John Kagel, and Dan Levin designed an experiment similar to that of Isaac and Smith in which imperfect information was an important element ("On the existence of predatory pricing: An experimental study of reputation and entry in the chain-store game," *RAND Journal of Economics,* 25, 1 [1994], pp. 72–93). In their experiment a monopoly and a series of entrants play a repeated stage game. The monopoly has either low production costs or high production costs. The monopolist knows whether its costs are low or high but the entrants don't. They know only that there is a prior probability of one-third that the monopolist has low costs. At each stage in the game an entrant chooses whether to enter the market or not. If there is entry, the monopolist must choose whether to fight or acquiesce. This stage game is repeated eight times. If there were only one stage, in the perfect equilibrium the monopolist with high costs would acquiesce to entry and the monopolist with low costs would fight. Entrants are better off not entering if they believe the monopolist will fight. Because of the repeated stages, however, it is possible for subsequent entrants to learn about the monopolist's costs from its previous behavior.

In one perfect Bayesian equilibrium of their repeated game the high-cost monopolist mimics the low-cost monopolist in the early stages of the game and fights entry even though it takes a loss. Rational entrants, of course, recognize this and stay out until the later stages when it no longer pays for the high-cost monopolist to build a reputation. Jung, Kagel, and Levin find that a good deal of entry is deterred in this game. When entry happens early in the game, high-cost monopolists almost always engage in predatory behavior. Given the earlier negative results by Isaac and Smith, it appears that asymmetric information is a crucial element in generating predatory behavior.

The model developed above was substantially improved on by Michael Spence in 1977 and Avinash Dixit in 1980. They argued that entrants were less concerned about the actual level of output in the preentry period and more concerned about the perceived ability of the incumbent to increase output in response to entry. The incumbent firm could rationally invest in capacity that *allowed* it to increase output in the face of entry. The firm may never expect to use this capacity; it exists solely to deter entry. Therefore, the incumbent need not actually produce a limit pricing output, only credibly threaten to do so.

19.3.1 THE SPENCE-DIXIT MODEL OF ENTRY DETERRENCE

Suppose that the small town of Oberlin, Ohio, currently has no pizza parlors. Joe, a budding restaurateur, is planning to build one and must decide what the parlor's capacity should be. Joe has gotten a fair amount of local press for his decision to build a pizza parlor. Maria, another potential restaurateur, is also thinking about opening a pizza parlor, but has not progressed far enough in the planning stages to be able to complete her restaurant before Joe has built his. If Maria builds the restaurant, she will not benefit as much as Joe from free local publicity and must advertise to let the community know about her restaurant. Once both restaurants are established, they both play a static Cournot quantity-setting game with capacity constraints.

The game tree—without the payoffs—is displayed in Figure 19.4. This game has up to four moves. The first move is Joe's choice of capacity. The second is

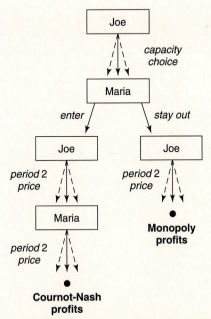

FIGURE 19.4   The game tree for Maria and Joe when they play the Spence-Dixit Entry Deterrence Game.

Maria's decision to enter and her capacity if she enters. If she enters, then Joe and Maria play a static Cournot (quantity-setting) duopoly game. If Maria stays out, then Joe has a last move in which he acts as a classical monopolist.

In order to calculate the payoffs, we need to fill in some details. The demand for pizza in Oberlin is common knowledge and is equal to

$$P(Q_t) = \begin{cases} 16 - \frac{1}{100} \cdot Q_t & \text{for } 0 \le Q_t \le 1{,}600 \\ 0 & \text{otherwise,} \end{cases} \qquad [19.1]$$

where $P(Q_t)$ is the price per pizza in Oberlin as a function of both firms' pizza output Q_t. Once either restaurant is built, both firms face constant pizza production costs of $7 per pizza up to their capacity. Capacity costs are incurred when the restaurant is built while the production costs are incurred only when the pizzas are produced. Capacity costs both firms $3 per pizza. Finally, Maria needs to incur $150 of advertising expenses to compete with Joe if she chooses to enter the market.

We can use backwards induction to solve this game. Suppose that Joe has chosen a capacity of $\overline{Q}_J$ and Maria has chosen not to enter the Oberlin pizza market. In that case, Joe will simply choose the pizza output that maximizes his profit. You can verify that if Joe has chosen a capacity in excess of 450 pizzas, he will produce 450 pizzas (remember that once capacity is chosen, Joe's marginal cost is just $7 per pizza). If he has chosen a capacity less than 450, he will produce at that capacity.

If Maria chooses to enter the pizza market, the situation is more complex. After she enters, Maria chooses her capacity, and then Joe and Maria play a static Cournot quantity-setting game. She will select a capacity exactly equal to the output she plans on producing in the Cournot subgame. Hence, in determining the Cournot solution to this subgame, we need to recognize that Maria effectively faces a marginal cost of $10 per pizza ($3 for the oven capacity and $7 for the ingredients). Joe, on the other hand, chose his capacity prior to Maria's entry decision. His capacity costs at this stage are sunk. So Joe faces a marginal cost of only $7 per pizza.

Maria's profits, inclusive of the $150 advertising expense she incurs when she enters, are given by

$$\Pi_M = P(Q_M + Q_J) \cdot Q_M - \$10 \cdot Q_M - \$150. \qquad [19.2]$$

As you recall from Chapter 2, her best response function gives the profit-maximizing output for each level of output Joe might produce. Using calculus you can verify that

$$Q_M^{BR}(Q_J) = 300 - \tfrac{1}{2} \cdot Q_J. \qquad [19.3]$$

For Maria, $Q_M^{BR}(Q_J)$ represents not only her best output for any level of Joe's output, but also her optimal capacity. Joe's net profit function, exclusive of his sunk capacity costs, is

$$\Pi_J^n = P(Q_M + Q_J) \cdot Q_J - \$7 \cdot Q_J, \tag{19.4}$$

where $Q_J \le \overline{Q}_J$. So Joe's best response function is

$$Q_J^{BR}(Q_M) = min[\overline{Q}_J, 450 - \tfrac{1}{2} \cdot Q_M]. \tag{19.5}$$

Equation 19.5 says that Joe's best response equals his normal Cournot best response function unless that output exceeds his earlier capacity choice, in which case he will choose to produce at capacity.

If Joe's capacity could be ignored, then Joe and Maria's traditional Cournot-type best response functions would intersect where Joe produces 400 pizzas and Maria produces 100 pizzas. The price of a pizza would be $11. Any choice of capacity for Joe greater than or equal to 400 pizzas will yield this same result. Hence, Maria's profits, exclusive of her advertising costs, will equal

$$\Pi_M = \$11 \cdot 100 - \$10 \cdot 100 = \$100. \tag{19.6}$$

Although her profits are positive, they are less than the $150 initial advertising expense that she incurred when she decided to enter this market.

Joe's gross profits (inclusive of his capacity costs) will equal

$$\Pi_J^g = \$11 \cdot 400 - \$7 \cdot 400 - \$3 \cdot \overline{Q}_J = \$1,600 - \$3 \cdot \overline{Q}_J \tag{19.7}$$

if $\overline{Q}_J \ge 400$. On the other hand, if Joe has chosen a capacity less than 400, he will produce at capacity and Maria will respond according to her best response function. In this case, the price of a pizza will equal

$$P(\overline{Q}_J + Q_M^*(\overline{Q}_J)) = 16 - \frac{1}{100} \cdot (\overline{Q}_J + (300 - \tfrac{1}{2} \cdot \overline{Q}_J)) = 13 - \frac{\overline{Q}_J}{200}. \tag{19.8}$$

This can be used to solve for Joe and Maria's profit function when Joe's capacity is less than 400.

$$\Pi_M = \begin{cases} \left(13 - \dfrac{\overline{Q}_J}{200}\right) \cdot (300 - \tfrac{1}{2} \cdot \overline{Q}_J) - \$10 \cdot (300 - \tfrac{1}{2} \cdot \overline{Q}_J) - \$150 & \text{if } \overline{Q}_J < 400 \\ \qquad\qquad\qquad - \$50 & \text{if } \overline{Q}_J \ge 400 \end{cases} \tag{19.9}$$

$$\Pi_J^g = \begin{cases} \left(13 - \dfrac{\overline{Q}_J}{200}\right) \cdot \overline{Q}_J - \$7 \cdot \overline{Q}_J - \$3 \cdot \overline{Q}_J & \text{if } \overline{Q}_J < 400 \\ 1,600 - \$3 \cdot \overline{Q}_J & \text{if } \overline{Q}_J \ge 400 \end{cases} \tag{19.10}$$

Now, we are in a position to make some predictions about Maria's entry decision. If she does not enter, she earns nothing. Hence, she will only enter if she can earn more than zero profit. All we need to do, then, is find which of Joe's capacity choices will make it profitable for Maria to enter. The answer is any capacity less than 319. If Joe chooses a capacity less than 319, then Maria will enter, and if Joe chooses a capacity of 319 or greater, she won't.

The first step of the game has Joe deciding what capacity to choose. If he chooses a capacity less than 319, he will invite entry. Joe needs to ask himself, then, if Maria were to enter, what capacity is the best from his perspective? Remember that if he selects a capacity less than 400, he will choose to produce at that capacity and Maria will respond by producing on her best response function. So Joe will want to select the capacity that maximizes his profits, inclusive of his capacity costs, subject to Maria's best response function. That is, Joe will simply behave as a Stackelberg first-mover in which his profit function is

$$\Pi_J^g = P(Q_M^{BR}(\overline{Q}_J) + \overline{Q}_J) \cdot \overline{Q}_J - 10 \cdot \overline{Q}_J. \qquad [19.11]$$

You can verify that this results in Joe choosing a capacity output level of 300. At this capacity level, Maria will enter and produce 150 units of output. The market price will be $11.50 and Joe's profits will equal $450.

Alternatively, Joe can deter entry by producing at a capacity greater than or equal to 319. If he chooses this output, the price will be $12.83 and Joe will earn profits of approximately $897. Deterring entry is clearly much better than accommodating entry. Joe might want to consider capacity levels in excess of 319. If, however, Joe faced no threat of entry, he would have chosen a capacity and an output of only 300. The further he is from this output, the lower his profits are, so a capacity of 319 is his best option in this case.

The equilibrium outcome of this game is that Joe chooses a capacity of 319, Maria decides not to enter, and Joe chooses an output level of 319. Under different demand and cost conditions, Joe might find it best to accommodate entry. But in this section, we wanted to show how rational entry deterrence might occur.

19.3.2 THE MILGROM-ROBERTS MODEL OF ENTRY DETERRENCE

In 1982, important articles on limit pricing and predatory pricing were written by Paul Milgrom, John Roberts, David Kreps, and Robert Wilson. For the first time, models were presented in which both incumbents and entrants are rational and far-sighted under conditions of asymmetric information. The incumbent has some private information that may or may not be signaled to the entrant depending on its price–output choice. In this section, we will present a modified version of the Milgrom and Roberts model that is credited to Jean Tirole.

We will make use of many of the elements of the pizza example from the previous section. Following the spirit of Milgrom and Roberts, we will suppose Joe's costs are unknown to Maria. Since Joe knows something that Maria does not (namely, his costs) this is a game with asymmetric information.

Joe would like to keep Maria out of the Oberlin pizza market. If he can make her believe that he has relatively low production costs then she will stay out. But how can he convince her of this? Simply telling her that his costs are low obviously will not work. Maria will be able to see that it is in Joe's interest to keep her out of the Oberlin pizza market, regardless of his costs. Therefore, she will be persuaded only if the information she gets about Joe's costs is *credible.* Herein lies the rub.

One possible way Joe might convince Maria that he has low costs is to *signal* this fact to her through some observable behavior, perhaps by charging a relatively low price for pizza. A lower price for a pizza at Joe's might be a credible way to tell Maria that his costs are low. But this signal will be credible only if the price is low enough so that a high-cost operation would be severely punished if it charged such a low price. That is, the signal must be *costly* in order to be persuasive.

The extensive form for this game is sketched in Figure 19.5. Using the Harsanyi transformation, Nature makes the first move, choosing whether Joe's costs are high or low. The probability that Joe's costs are high equals 10% and the probability they are low equals 90%. Nature's choice is observed by Joe but not by Maria. In the first time period, Joe's is the only pizza parlor in Oberlin. He must decide what price to charge and, therefore, how much pizza to sell. At the start of the second time period, it is Maria's turn to move. After observing Joe's price and quantity, *but not his costs,* she must decide whether to enter the Oberlin pizza market. If she decides not to enter, then Joe retains his monopoly and sets

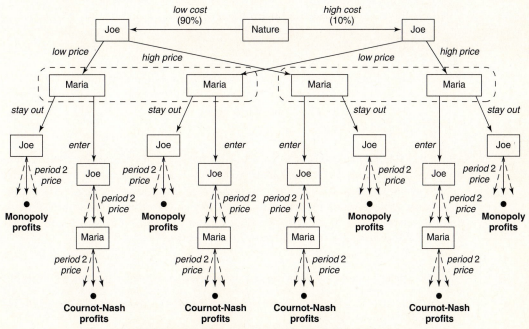

FIGURE 19.5 The game tree for the Limit Pricing Game.

his price and output in the second period. If she does enter, then Maria and Joe play a static Cournot duopoly game where they simultaneously choose their outputs and their common price is set "by the market." Maria's production costs are common knowledge. Joe's production costs become common knowledge only after Maria chooses to enter.[2] Missing from the game tree are the payoffs to each player, which we will now derive.

Since a general analysis of this game can get rather complex, we will proceed by specifying the cost and demand functions more completely. The demand for pizza in Oberlin is given by the inverse demand function,

$$P(Q_t) = \begin{cases} 16 - \dfrac{1}{100} \cdot Q_t & for\ 0 \le Q_t \le 1{,}600 \\ 0\ otherwise, \end{cases}$$

[19.12]

where Q_t is the total quantity of pizza sold in Oberlin and P is the price per pizza. This is common knowledge. Maria has heard rumors that Joe gets a deal on his tomato sauce from his brother-in-law who operates a tomato sauce plant outside of Toledo. She has done enough research to know that Joe really does have a brother-in-law running the plant in Toledo, which gives rise to her prior beliefs that there is a 90% chance that Joe gets a special deal. Maria's prior beliefs are also common knowledge. Joe's total costs depend on his output, Q_J, and are either

$$C_J^L(Q_J) = \$5 \cdot Q_J$$

[19.13]

if he gets the special deal from his brother-in-law, or

$$\mathbf{C}_J^H(Q_J) = \$7 \cdot Q_J$$

[19.14]

if he does not. Maria's total costs are common knowledge and equal

$$C_M(Q_M) = \begin{cases} \$600 + \$7 \cdot Q_M & if\ Q_M > 0 \\ 0\ otherwise. \end{cases}$$

[19.15]

Maria faces a $600 cost to enter the Oberlin market. This might represent a one-time license fee from the city of Oberlin, or some initial advertising expense to let people know she has arrived. Her marginal cost of making a pizza will be $7 if she enters, which equals Joe's marginal cost if he has to purchase tomato sauce at the market price she pays. The two time periods are close enough together that we need not worry about discounting future profits.

---

[2]This assumption makes the second-period duopoly game much easier to evaluate. Without this assumption, we have to consider separately how the players act when Maria's belief about Joe's best response function is correct and when her belief is not correct. This complication does not alter the overall properties of the equilibrium.

All perfect Bayesian equilibria will also be subgame perfect. Using backwards induction, we start at the end of the game tree and begin with the simplest case in which Maria chooses not to enter. Joe will simply select the simple, monopolistic, profit-maximizing output level and price in the second time period. The market marginal revenue, which now depends only on Joe's output, equals

$$MR(Q_J) = 16 - \frac{1}{50} \cdot Q_J. \qquad [19.16]$$

Setting marginal revenue equal to marginal cost gives Joe's optimal output. This means that when Joe's costs are high, he selects the output at which

$$MR(Q_J) = 16 - \frac{1}{50} \cdot Q_J = 7, \qquad [19.17]$$

or $Q_J = 450$, and then sets the price to clear the market or $P = P(450) = 11.50$. He does a similar calculation when his costs are low. The optimal price and output, along with Joe's payoffs depending on whether his costs are either high or low, are summarized in Table 19.1.

Consider any of the subgames that follow Maria's decision to enter the Oberlin pizza market. With two pizzerias, the market becomes a duopoly. Given our assumption that the two firms produce a homogeneous product, and that the market price depends only on the sum of their outputs, the best model of their interaction is the Cournot duopoly model. We therefore proceed the way we did in Chapter 2, where we studied Cournot and Bertrand equilibriums: First, we derive the firms' profit functions, from which we derive their best response functions, from which we find the Nash equilibrium outputs and market-clearing price.

Because the market demand in period two can be written as

$$P(Q_J, Q_M) = 16 - \frac{1}{100} \cdot (Q_J + Q_M), \qquad [19.18]$$

Table 19.1 *Outcome in Period Two If Maria Does Not Enter*

| | *Joe's Costs* | |
	High	*Low*
Joe's pizza output	450	550
Joe's pizza price	$11.50	$10.50
Joe's profit	$2,025	$3,025

Joe's second-period profits are

$$
\begin{aligned}
\pi_{J2}^H &= (P(Q_J, Q_M) - 5) \cdot Q_J \\
&= \left(11 - \frac{1}{100} \cdot (Q_J + Q_M)\right) \cdot Q_J
\end{aligned}
\qquad [19.19]
$$

if his costs are low, and

$$
\begin{aligned}
\pi_{J2}^L &= (P(Q_J, Q_M) - 7) \cdot Q_J \\
&= \left(9 - \frac{1}{100} \cdot (Q_J + Q_M)\right) \cdot Q_J
\end{aligned}
\qquad [19.20]
$$

if his costs are high. Maria earns profits only in the second period, so her profit function is

$$
\begin{aligned}
\pi_M &= (P(Q_J, Q_M) - 7) \cdot Q_M - 600 \\
&= \left(9 - \frac{1}{100} \cdot (Q_J + Q_M)\right) \cdot Q_M - 600.
\end{aligned}
\qquad [19.21]
$$

Joe's best response function, that is, his optimal output choice conditional on the output choice for Maria, is found by maximizing his profits with respect to his output; similarly for Maria. We leave it as an exercise for you to derive the Cournot-Nash equilibria of these subgames. Some outcomes associated with this subgame perfect behavior are summarized in Table 19.2.

Note that if Joe's costs are high, then Maria earns a profit of $300, but if Joe's costs are low, Maria suffers a loss of $55.56. This is an important result. It tells us (and Joe) that Maria will enter if she knows that Joe's costs are high but not if she knows Joe's costs are low. If, somehow, Joe can *signal credibly* to Maria that he has

Table 19.2 **Subgame Perfect Outcomes of Nash-Cournot Game in Period Two If Maria Enters**

| | Joe's Costs | |
	High	Low
Joe's pizza output	300	433.33
Joe's pizza price	$10.00	$9.33
Joe's profit	$900.00	$1,877.78
Maria's pizza output	300	233.33
Maria's pizza price	$10.00	$9.33
Maria's profit	$300.00	−$55.56

low costs, then he can keep her from entering the market. This is the central feature of any limit pricing model.

As you saw in Chapter 15, abstracting from the possibility of either player using mixed strategies, in games with asymmetric information there are two types of perfect Bayesian equilibria: **separating equilibria** and **pooling equilibria.** In a separating equilibrium, Joe will behave differently in the first period depending on whether his costs are high or low. In a pooling equilibrium, Joe will behave the same regardless of his costs.

19.3.3 FINDING A SEPARATING EQUILIBRIUM

The only means at Joe's disposal to signal to Maria whether he has high or low costs is the price he charges in the first period. In the separating equilibrium, Joe must convince Maria that he has low costs when he does have low costs. It is only by being convincing that he deters entry. But, in order to be convincing when his costs are low, he must be truthful when his costs are high.

Suppose Joe were to choose the short-run profit-maximizing price/output combination in period one. If Joe's costs were high, he would choose a price of $11.50 (and an output of 450) and if his costs were low, he would choose a price of $10.50 (and an output of 550). Furthermore, suppose that Maria believes that a price of $11.50 means that Joe has high costs and a price of $10.50 means that Joe has low costs. Could this be a separating equilibrium? At a minimum, we need to demonstrate that when Joe's costs are high, he would not have an incentive to charge a first-period price of $10.50. If Joe's costs are high and he charges the $11.50 price, he will earn first-period profits of $2,025. Maria will enter the industry and Joe will earn second-period profits of $900. His total profits are $2,925. If Joe charges the $10.50 price, he will earn profits in the first time period of $1,925. He will also deter entry in the second period, allowing him to earn $2,025 then. The total now is $3,950. Joe will rationally choose the $10.50 price, regardless of his costs. Clearly, the $10.50 price is *not low enough to credibly signal to Marie that Joe definitely has low costs.*

We could proceed by trial and error, but instead we will try to generalize from the thought process above. Let P^H and P^L represent the prices that Joe might charge in the first period if he has high or low costs, respectively. For these prices to be part of a separating equilibrium, if Joe has high costs, it must be the case that his payoff is higher by charging P^H in the first time period than by charging P^L. That is,

$$\pi_{j1}^H(P^H) + 900 > \pi_{j1}^H(P^L) + 2{,}025 \qquad [19.22]$$

where the second-period profits of either $900 or $2,025 take account of the entry decision of Maria and the subgame perfect behavior by both firms that follows. Rearranging terms,

$$\pi_{j1}^H(P^H) - \pi_{j1}^H(P^L) > 1{,}125. \qquad [19.23]$$

The low price has to be low enough so that the first-period profits Joe earns by charging a high price are at least $1,125 greater than what he would earn by charging the low price. If Joe has high costs and if the equilibrium is separating, then Joe must expect a price of P^H to signal to Maria that his costs are high. She will then enter the industry. But if he expects her to enter the industry, then he expects deterrence to fail so P^H should just equal the short-run, profit-maximizing price of $11.50, and $\pi_{J1}^H(P^H)$ will equal $2,025. This fact and Eq. [19.23] imply that $\pi_{J1}^H(P^L) < 900$, or

$$(P^L - 7) \cdot (1,600 - 100 \cdot P^L) < 900. \qquad [19.24]$$

This means that $P^L < 8.146$.

Rounding down to the penny results in a low price that must be less than $8.14. Any price below this level will satisfy the requirement established in Eq. [19.24]. If Joe has low costs, the highest low price that meets Eq. [19.24] will be the one that maximizes his profits. We can now make an educated guess about what prices might constitute a separating equilibrium, namely a price of $11.50 if costs are high and a price of $8.14 if costs are low. We can also begin to make educated guesses about Maria's beliefs. If she observes a price of $11.50, she should believe Joe has high costs, and if she observes a price of $8.14, she should believe Joe has low costs. We are left to determine her beliefs when she observes prices other than $11.50 or $8.14.

For example, suppose Maria believes that any price greater than $8.14 means that Joe has high costs, otherwise he has low costs. Our hypothetical Bayesian equilibrium is summarized in Table 19.3.

We have already shown that, given Maria's strategy and beliefs as described in Table 19.3, if Joe has high costs, he cannot do better than using the high-cost strategy. We also need to show that if Joe has low costs, he cannot do better than using the low-cost strategy. By charging a price lower than $8.14 in the first period, he will earn lower profits in that period and the same profits in the second period, so the proposed low-cost strategy is better than any strategy in which he charges a price lower than $8.14 in the first period. If Joe charges a price above $8.14, he invites entry, so he might as well charge the short-run, profit-maximizing price. This will earn him $3,025 in the first time period. Of course, Maria enters and the second-period price of a pizza is $9.33. This earns Joe second-period profits of $1,877.78. The total for Joe over both periods is $4,902.78. By charging $8.14 in the first period, Joe earns a profit in that period of $2,468.04. Maria will not enter, allowing Joe to earn $3,025 in the second period. The total is $5,493.04. If Joe has low costs, his best response to Maria's strategy is to charge exactly $8.14 for his pizzas. He cannot make himself unilaterally better off by charging a price other than $8.14 in the first period.

We turn now to Maria. It is easy to check whether her beliefs on the equilibrium path are consistent with Bayes' theorem since Joe only charges one of two prices in equilibrium. Given Joe's strategy, a belief that any price greater than $8.14 implies that Joe will definitely have high costs and a belief that any price

Table 19.3 **A Proposed Perfect Bayesian Equilibrium**

Joe's strategy

		Pre-entry decision	Post-Entry-Decision Maria *enters*	Maria *stays out*
Joe's type	*high cost*	($11.50, 450)	($10.00, 300)	($11.50, 450)
	low cost	($8.14, 786)	($9.33, 433)	($10.50, 550)

(price, output)

Maria's Strategy

		Joe's Pre-Entry Price $P_J > \$8.14$	$P_J \leq \$8.14$
Joe's Type (revealed to Maria after she enters)	*high cost*	(*enter*, $10.00, 300)	(*stay out*, NA. NA)
	low cost	(*enter*, $9.33, 233)	(*stay out*, NA, NA)

(entry decision, price, output)

Maria's beliefs

		Joe's Pre-Entry Price $P_J > \$8.14$	$P_J \leq \$8.14$
Joe's Type	*high cost*	1	0
	low cost	0	1

(updated conditonal probability of Joe's type)

less than or equal to $8.14 implies that Joe definitely has low costs is exactly in line with how Joe will behave. Maria's beliefs about Joe's behavior are consistent with our proposed equilibrium behavior concerning Joe. Is her proposed strategy concerning entry rational? When the preentry price is less than or equal to $8.14, Maria's expected profits are −$55.56 if she enters and zero otherwise (evaluated using her updated beliefs). She should not enter. When the preentry price is greater than $8.14, Maria's expected profits are $300 if she enters and zero otherwise. She should enter. Therefore, the proposed entry decision for Maria in Table 19.3 is rational.

Finally, we need to consider Maria's beliefs off of the equilibrium path. In this case, Bayes' theorem imposes no constraints on Maria's beliefs, so our proposed beliefs do not violate any of the conditions for a perfect Bayesian equilibrium. What is important is that Maria assign a high probability to Joe having high costs whenever he charges a price between $8.14 and $11.50.

19.3.4 FINDING A POOLING EQUILIBRIUM

Assuming that either player uses only pure strategies, we now need to consider the possibility that the game has a pooling equilibrium. Recall that a pooling equilibrium implies that the informed player's moves reveal nothing about what type of player he is. In this case, it means Joe must choose the same first-period price when his costs are high as when his costs are low. Only then will Joe's prices in the first period not reveal anything about his costs.

Oddly enough, if a pooling equilibrium exists, then entry must be deterred. To see why this is necessary, suppose that entry were *not* deterred. Under a pooling equilibrium, no information is conveyed to Maria by the price Joe chooses. Therefore, if she believes prior to Joe's price/output decision that there is a 90% chance his costs are low, then she must maintain the same belief after his price/output decision. Maria's costs, recall, are common knowledge. So if Maria will enter in the second period, Joe is aware of this. Since entry is not deterred, Joe can do no better than to charge the short-run, profit-maximizing price in the first period. But this price depends on Joe's costs; the profit-maximizing price is $11.50 when his costs are high and $10.50 when they are low. Charging different prices on the basis of different costs is inconsistent with the assumption of a pooling equilibrium. The contradiction shows that in any pooling equilibrium, Maria is deterred from entering.

This means that in order for an equilibrium pooling price to exist, Maria must make negative expected profits from entering the Oberlin pizza market. Since her expected profits if she enters will be $0.9 \cdot (-\$55.56) + 0.1 \cdot (\$300) = -\$20$, this condition is satisfied here.

We have not yet established that a pooling equilibrium exists for our example. All we have shown is that a pooling equilibrium must be one in which Maria does not enter and the condition necessary to ensure this is satisfied. We must still identify under what conditions a pooling price is a rational choice for Joe.

For Maria's post–period one beliefs to be consistent with a pooling equilibrium, whatever price/output combination she observes in period one must not alter her prior beliefs. In order to determine whether a pooling price is optimal from Joe's perspective, we need to compare his expected profits when he charges a pooling price with his expected profits when he doesn't. This means we need to specify Maria's off-the-equilibrium-path beliefs. Suppose she believes that any price above the pooling price (whatever that is) means that Joe has high costs with probability 1 and any price below the pooling price means that Joe has low costs with probability 1.

Two reasonable first-period pooling prices Joe might consider are the short-run, profit-maximizing prices when his costs are high and low. Suppose he charges a pooling price of $11.50 regardless of his costs. Does this satisfy the requirements of a perfect Bayesian equilibrium? If Joe has high costs, this price will maximize his profits in the first period, deter entry, and allow him to maximize his profits in the second period. Clearly, no other price will be preferable. If he has low costs, however, by charging the low-cost, profit-maximizing price of $10.50 in the first period, he can make Maria believe that he has low costs and she will not enter. This allows Joe to charge $10.50 in the second period as well. In short, if Joe has low costs, and Maria has beliefs as we have hypothesized, it would not be rational for Joe to choose a pooling price of $11.50.

Table 19.4   ***A Perfect Bayesian Pooling Equilibrium***

Joe's strategy

		Pre-entry decision	Post-Entry Decision Maria *enters*	Maria *stays out*
Joe's type	high cost	($10.50, 550)	($10.00, 300)	($11.50, 450)
	low cost	($10.50, 550)	($9.33, 433)	($10.50, 550)

(price, output)

Maria's Strategy

		Joe's Pre-Entry Price $P_J > \$8.14$	$P_J \le \$8.14$
Joe's Type (revealed to Maria after she enters)	high cost	(enter, $10.00, 300)	(stay out, NA. NA)
	low cost	(enter, $9.33, 233)	(stay out, NA, NA)

(entry decision, price, output)

Maria's beliefs

		Joe's Pre-Entry Price $P_J > \$8.14$	$P_J = \$8.14$	$P_J \le \$8.14$
Joe's type	high cost	1	0.1	0
	low cost	0	0.9	1

(updated conditonal probability of Joe's type)

Alternatively, consider the low-cost, first-period, profit-maximizing price of $10.50. If Joe has low costs, then by charging this price, he will deter entry and be able to charge the same price next period. No other price is better. If Joe has high costs, though, will he do better by charging a higher price than $10.50 in the first period. The problem is that the higher price, given Maria's beliefs, will induce entry. Since any price above $10.50 will cause Maria to enter, the best price above $10.50 is the short-run, profit-maximizing price of $11.50. We have seen that charging a price of $11.50 in the first period induces entry and results in profits to Joe of $2,025 + $900 = $2,925. By charging the pooling price of $10.50, Joe will only earn $1,925 in the first period, but because he has deterred entry, he will earn $2,025 in the second period. By charging the pooling price of $10.50, his combined profits over the two periods exceed $2,925, implying that even if Joe's costs are high, he can do no better than charging the pooling price in the first period.

The pooling equilibrium is summarized in Table 19.4.

Table 19.5 *Equilibrium Prices Under Various Competitive Situations*

			Period One	Period Two
Symmetric information		Joe has high costs	$11.50	$10.00
		Joe has low costs	$10.50	$10.50
Asymmetric information	Separating equilibrium	Joe has high costs	$11.50	$10.00
		Joe has low costs	$8.14	$10.50
Asymmetric information	Pooling equilibrium	Joe has high costs	$10.50	$11.50
		Joe has low costs	$10.50	$10.50

19.4   Some Welfare Implications

A summary of the equilibrium prices under all the settings we have discussed is detailed in Table 19.5.

If Maria could directly observe Joe's costs prior to making her entry decision, then her optimal decision rule would be simple: If Joe has low costs, do not enter; if Joe has high costs, enter. Therefore, with complete information, the market price in the first period would be $11.50 when Joe has high costs and $10.50 when Joe has low costs. In the second period, the price would be $10.50 when Joe has low costs and $10 otherwise.

If, however, there is asymmetric information, then the outcome depends on the equilibrium selected. As with the case of perfect information, if Joe has high costs, then entry will occur, and prices in the two periods will be $11.50 and $10, respectively. But if Joe has low costs, the price will be $8.14 in the first period when there is asymmetric information and $10.50 when there is perfect information. The lower price/higher output consequence of asymmetric information leads to a welfare gain for consumers. If the equilibrium is a separating one, then the price falls when Joe has high costs, and increases when he has low costs.

19.5   Summary

Strategies in which entry can be deterred by existing firms have been an important part of industrial organization for a long time. Not until recently, however, has an attempt been made to determine the rationality of the stories that have been told. One of the more important stories of strategic entry deterrence has been that of limit pricing. The traditional argument has been that by lowering price and increasing output, an incumbent firm will deter entry by leaving a smaller residual demand than would have been left had the firm chosen a short-run, profit-maximizing price. In certain circumstances, the firm will end up with higher long-run profits by forgoing some of their short-run profits and successfully deterring entry. This argument has always relied on the concept of a residual demand curve.

What we have shown in this chapter is that entering firms would be irrational to think that the incumbent firm will maintain its output at preentry levels once entry has occurred. Indeed, it would be irrational for incumbent firms to do so. Limit pricing, if it is to exist as a rational strategy, must be founded on credible behavior. Residual demand curves, unfortunately, typically assume irrational behavior.

We have established a model, founded on rational behavior, in which price/output can be used as a strategic variable to deter entry. In this model, price (through the choice of output) may credibly signal cost information from the incumbent firm to an entering firm. The entrant's ignorance about the incumbent's costs can actually result in an improvement in consumer welfare.

19.6 Further Reading

The original work on limit pricing by Bain is contained in his article, ''A Note on Pricing in Monopoly and Oligopoly,'' *American Economic Review* 39 (1949), pp. 448–64, which he then extended in *Barriers to New Competition* (Cambridge, MA: Harvard University Press, 1956). In 1958, Franco Modigliani added some rigor to Bain's ideas in his article, ''New Developments on the Oligopoly Front,'' *Journal of Political Economy* 66 (1958), pp. 215–32, as did Paolo Sylos-Labini in *Oligopoly and Technical Progress* (Cambridge, MA: Harvard University Press, 1962). Nearly all modern industrial organization texts have a segment on limit pricing that condenses the work cited above. Examples include Dennis Carlton and Jeffrey Perloff, *Modern Industrial Organization* is 2nd Edition, (Glenview: Scott Foresman & Co., 1994) and *The Theory of Industrial Organization* (Cambridge: MIT Press, 1988) by Jean Tirole.

The game-theoretic work on limit pricing is extensive and much of it is highly mathematical. Important extensions of the traditional limit pricing model has come from Michael Spence, ''Entry, Capacity, Investment, and Oligopolistic Pricing,'' *Bell Journal of Economics* 8, 2 (Autumn 1977), pp. 534–44 and Avinash Dixit, ''The Role of Investment in Entry Deterrence,'' *Economic Journal* 90 (March 1980), pp. 95–106. The particular model presented in this chapter owes its existence to Paul Milgrom and John Roberts, ''Limit Pricing and Entry Under Incomplete Information: An Equilibrium Analysis,'' *Econometrica* 50 (1982), pp. 443–60 and follows the presentation by Jean Tirole in *The Theory of Industrial Organization* (pp. 367–74). A related article is by David Kreps and Robert Wilson, ''Reputation and Imperfect Information,'' *Journal of Economic Theory* 27 (1982), pp. 253–79.

19.7   Discussion Questions

1. Suppose you were in charge of the Antitrust Division of the U.S. Department of Justice and you believe that limit pricing is anticompetitive. How might you go about proving that a firm had engaged in this practice?

2. In what ways other than charging a price below the "monopoly price" could a monopolist make it credible that entry of competitors will not be profitable?

3. In light of the analysis of this chapter, should monopolists be required to make their costs and profits public? How might a monopolist defeat such a legal requirement?

19.8   New Terms

entrant   limit pricing strategy
incumbent   pooling equilibria
limit price   separating equilibria

19.9   Exercises

EXERCISE 19.1

Suppose a monopolist faces a demand of the form:

$$P = 10 - 0.004 \cdot Q.$$

This firm has a total cost function of

$$TC = 3{,}000 + 0.1 \cdot Q.$$

(a) If the incumbent firm produces at the short-run, profit-maximizing output level, what is the residual demand curve facing the entrant?

(b) If it is common knowledge that the incumbent will continue to produce at the output level calculated in (a) if the entrant enters and has the same cost function as the incumbent, will the entrant enter the industry?

(c) Contrast the short-run, profit-maximizing output level and the market price with the limit output level and price, assuming the entrant has the same cost function as the incumbent.

(d) If there are only two periods (preentry and postentry), the discount rate equals zero, and there is perfect information, what output level will the monopolist select for both periods in the traditional limit pricing model?

EXERCISE 19.2

This is a continuation of Exercise 19.1. Suppose the incumbent monopolist cannot precommit to its postentry output level prior to entry, and if the entrant enters the market, the two firms select their postentry output levels simultaneously. That is, they engage in Cournot competition. What is the equilibrium of this postentry subgame. What is the subgame perfect equilibrium of the two-stage game, assuming perfect information and a zero discount rate?

EXERCISE 19.3

This is a continuation of Exercise 19.2. Suppose the incumbent's costs are not known to the entrant. Instead, there is a 50% probability that the incumbent's costs equal $3,000 + 0.1 \cdot Q$ ("high costs") and there is a 50% probability that the incumbent's costs equal $2,000 + 0.1 \cdot Q$ ("low costs"). It is common knowledge that the entrant's costs equal $3,000 + 0.1 \cdot Q$. The monopolist cannot precommit to its postentry output level prior to entry and the entrant is risk neutral. If the entrant enters, the two firms engage in Cournot competition.

(a) Draw the game tree for this game with private information.

(b) Suppose, on the basis of the incumbent's preentry output, that the entrant believes the probability that the incumbent's costs are low is π. If the entrant enters, what will be the equilibrium of the Cournot game? For what values of π will the entrant not enter?

EXERCISE 19.4

Determine a Bayesian equilibrium for the game described in Exercise 19.3. Check that the entrant's beliefs about the incumbent's costs are consistent with the incumbent's strategy and Bayes' theorem.

CHAPTER 20

Cartel Enforcement

20.1   Introduction

A cartel consists of a group of suppliers who have made an explicit agreement to limit competition among themselves for their mutual benefit. A cartel is similar to a monopoly—indeed, the goal of a cartel is to act as if it were a monopoly—with one important difference. A monopoly consists of a single decision maker, whereas a cartel consists of a voluntary association of decision makers, each of which is aware that its profits depend on the behavior of all the other suppliers in the industry. Because of this, management of a cartel involves much more than simply selecting the profit-maximizing level of output and price. Cartel management also includes the allocation of production among the members, the allocation of cartel profits among the members, and the policing of the cartel agreement.

These three aspects of a cartel's operation are not independent of each other. For example, the allocation of profits must take into account the incentives this may provide for members to cheat on the agreement or even to leave the cartel. Similarly, the allocation of production quotas is constrained by the degree to which such allocations will either be adhered to voluntarily or can be policed at low cost.

Complicating the cartel's problem is the fact that in most countries, collusive agreements are considered criminal conspiracies. Where this is the case, domestic cartels cannot enforce their agreements through the courts and must hide their

424

activities to avoid prosecution. Although collusive agreements among governments, such as between the countries in the Organization of Petroleum Exporting Countries (OPEC) cartel, are legal, such agreements are not legally enforceable. As a result, whether they are domestic or international in scope, cartel agreements must almost always be *self-enforcing* and forward-looking and cannot involve incredible threats. Game theoretically, this means the allocation of output and profits among the members of the cartel must constitute a perfect Bayesian equilibrium of the noncooperative game being played.

Between October 15, 1973 and November 1, 1974, OPEC succeeded in raising the average price of Persian Gulf crude oil from $2.05/barrel to $10.35/barrel, or over 500%. Although probably the most successful cartel to date, OPEC is simply the latest in a long series of international cartels. In this century alone, cartels (that we know of) have been formed in the production and marketing of natural rubber, tin, mercury, aluminum, tea, sugar, copper, platinum, potash, diamonds, and coffee.

In a study by Paul Eckbo of 51 cartel agreements involving 18 internationally traded commodities, only 19 were able to raise prices by more than 100%. These "efficient" cartels did not last very long. Although the formal agreements remained in place for many years, these cartels were not able to control prices for more than five years. According to Eckbo, cartels lasted more than four years when concentration of production was high, the demand for the commodity was inelastic, the cartel's market share was high, the cartel members had a cost advantage over nonmembers, and governments did not get involved in the cartel's operation. Cartels have also been most successful where they have had tight control over the distribution of the commodity. For example, the iodine cartel lasted over 50 years by having all iodine sales conducted out of a single cartel office in London.

In this chapter, we will present a game-theoretic model of cartel enforcement proposed by Robert Porter and Ed Green that can account for the instability of cartels. Their model suggests that the source of the problem is cartel members' limited ability to monitor each other. But before we examine their game, let us review what we have already learned about cartels when the members can perfectly monitor each other.

20.2   Cartel Enforcement with Perfect Monitoring

In Chapter 9 we analyzed a repeated Cournot game between two jean manufacturers, Rip and Torn Jeans. This type of game—in which the players move simultaneously each period, the payoff matrix never changes, both players can observe each other's previous moves, and future payoffs are discounted—is often called a **repeated Prisoner's Dilemma with discounting.** One of the perfect Nash equilibria of this game results in both players always producing the Cournot equilibrium output each period. We will refer to this as the **competitive equilibrium.**

As you saw in Chapter 9, repeated Prisoner's Dilemmas often have other equilibria as well. We will call any noncooperative equilibrium in which the players earn higher (discounted) profits than they do in the competitive equilibrium a **self-enforcing cartel agreement.** Such cartel agreements exist as long as both players have a sufficiently low discount rate, the short-term benefits of defection from the collusive output level are sufficiently low, and the cartel profits are sufficiently higher than the Cournot equilibrium profits.

When the cartel contains more than two members, enforcement becomes a problem. Now some subset of the cartel membership must take responsibility for enforcement. That is, cartel members who do not follow through on punishing the defector must themselves be punished; and members who fail to punish those who do not punish the defector must be punished; and so on. Although rigorous analysis becomes much more complicated, our earlier results on repeated Prisoner's Dilemmas with two players can be extended to models in which there are many players. In particular, the "Folk theorem" can be extended.

20.3   Cartel Enforcement with Imperfect Monitoring

Colombia and Brazil currently produce about 40% of the world's raw coffee beans.[1] Suppose they decide to organize a coffee cartel, the Coffee Alliance to Foster Exports (CAFE). Let P_t denote the market-clearing world price of coffee beans in period t (in dollars per kilogram), let $D(P_t)$ denote the quantity of coffee beans demanded worldwide during period t, let $S_C(P_t)$ denote the quantity of coffee supplied by CAFE, and let $S_N(P_t)$ denote the quantity of coffee beans supplied by all noncartel members. All quantities are in millions of kilograms. P_t is defined by the requirement that supply equals demand or

$$D(P_t) = S_C(P_t) + S_N(P_t). \tag{20.1}$$

Equation [20.1] implicitly defines the market price P_t as a function of cartel output. Alternatively, we could rewrite Eq. [20.1] as

$$S_C(P_t) = D(P_t) - S_N(P_t). \tag{20.2}$$

But if the supply of CAFE coffee equals the demand for their coffee, it must be true that

$$D_C(P_t) = D(P_t) - S_N(P_t), \tag{20.3}$$

where $D_C(P_t)$ is the *demand facing CAFE.* Equation [20.3] says that the output the cartel can sell depends on the residual demand for coffee, that is, the difference between the amount of coffee demanded and the amount supplied by other

---

[1]The other 60% is produced primarily by the Central American countries, Kenya and Indonesia.

producers. As the price falls, we would expect world demand for coffee to rise (the demand for coffee is downward sloping) and non-CAFE supply to fall (the supply of non-CAFE coffee is upward sloping). Therefore, the residual demand curve for CAFE coffee is downward sloping. Furthermore, the elasticity of the residual demand will increase as the elasticity of world demand increases and as the elasticity of supply from other producers increases.

Since we would expect both demand and noncartel supply to vary randomly over time, the relationship between P_t and $D_C(P_t)$ is not deterministic, but random. That is, P_t is a function of both the cartel's output and an unobservable random variable θ_t that represents shifts in the residual demand for the cartel's coffee. θ_t is a positive random variable with a mean of 1. Specifically, we will assume here that the residual demand for CAFE's coffee, Q_t, measured in millions of kilograms, equals $10 - \left(\dfrac{P_t}{\theta_t}\right)$. This implies that

$$P_t = (10 - Q_t) \cdot \theta_t. \tag{20.4}$$

So, for example, in order for CAFE to sell 8 million kilograms in some period, the market price that period will have to be, on average, $2 per kilogram.

Equation [20.4] implies that neither Colombia nor Brazil can exactly determine the other's current output from the knowledge of its own level of production and its observation of the current world price for coffee beans. For example, if Colombia's output in any time period were low and yet there were a low market price, this could mean: (1) Brazil's output is high, (2) world demand is low, (3) the combined supply of all other world coffee producers is high, or (4) some combination of these.

20.3.1 THE GAME TREE

The game tree for this repeated Cournot game with uncertainty and imperfect information is shown in Figure 20.1. In the first period, Colombia and Brazil simultaneously select their output for that year. We will denote the output levels chosen in year t by Q_t^C and Q_t^B. In Figure 20.1 we have simplified their choices to choosing "high" or "low" output levels. Their combined output $Q_t^C + Q_t^B$ equals Q_t.

After the two countries select their first-period output, Nature determines θ_t, and, thereby, the world price of coffee, P_t, according to Eq. [20.4]. Figure 20.1 presents a simplified schematic of our game, in which Nature's choice of residual demand and each cartel member's choice of its output results in either a "low" or "high" price of coffee. Notice that the random fluctuations in the demand for the cartel's coffee are large enough that the market price can be either high or low whatever the output chosen by the two countries. As a result, the market price does not reveal the cartel members' production levels.

Initially, both countries observe the market price, but since they do not directly observe θ_t, they cannot directly determine the other country's output. They

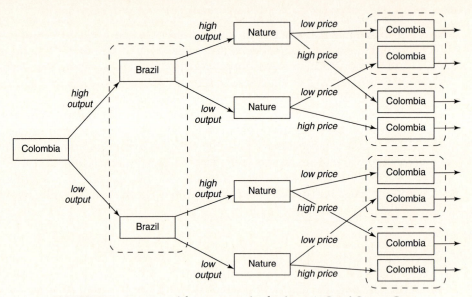

FIGURE 20.1 A portion of the game tree for the dynamic Cartel Output Game.

then simultaneously choose their output level for year two. Figure 20.1 shows four of Colombia's information sets. The first information set consists of a single decision node: that corresponding to Colombia's output decision in year one. In year two, Colombia could be at one of eight decision nodes. These eight nodes are partitioned into four information sets. One information set consists of the two decision nodes that follow a low coffee price and high output by Colombia; a second set consists of the two decision nodes that follow a low coffee price and high output by Colombia; and so on. Only one of Brazil's information sets is displayed in Figure 20.1. This set contains Brazil's two decision nodes for year one, representing the fact that when Brazil moves, it is ignorant of Colombia's output decision.

20.3.2 STRATEGIES

A strategy for Colombia consists of: (1) an output level for year one, Q_1^C, and (2) an output level for year two that depends on the world price observed in year one, $Q_2^C(P_1)$, (3) an output level for year three as a function of the world price in years one and two, $Q_3^C(P_1, P_2)$, and so forth. The possible strategies for Brazil are analogous to those for Colombia. In general, these strategies could be very complex. In this application, we will focus on **trigger price strategies.** In a trigger price strategy, a firm makes inferences (perhaps incorrect) about rival firms from the observation of market price. If market price remains above some critical value—the trigger value—then the firm will infer no cheating on the collusive agreement and will maintain a cooperative output level. If market price falls below the trigger, then some punishment must be imposed on the cheater. In our two-player game, the cheater's identity is known, of course. But as soon as the number of players is three or more, the cheaters cannot be determined. Trigger price strategies depend on four parameters, P^R, T, Q^{comp}, and Q^{coop}, where P^R is the trigger price, T is the number of time periods the punishment will last, Q^{coop} is the cooperative output and Q^{comp} is the competitive output. The trigger price strategy works as follows:

Each year is designated as either *cooperative* or *competitive* depending on the history of the game up to that point. In a competitive year, a member of CAFE produces an output level Q^{comp} and in a cooperative year, it produces an output level Q^{coop}, where $Q^{coop} < Q^{comp}$. The first year is always a cooperative year. After that, if year t was cooperative and the world price, P_t, was above the *trigger price, P^R,* then year $t + 1$ is also cooperative. If year t was cooperative, but the world price, P_t, fell below the trigger price, P^R, then the next $T - 1$ years are competitive and year $t + T$ is again cooperative. The trigger price strategy will be denoted by the four-tuple: (P^R, T, Q^{comp}, Q^{coop}).

The trigger price strategy we have described is a less extreme version of the grim strategy first discussed in the study of repeated games in Chapter 9. Both strategies call for the player to cooperate initially and to continue to cooperate as long as there is evidence that the other member of the cartel is cooperating. With the trigger price strategy, the evidence that the other player is cheating consists of a "suspiciously low" market price, P_t. When such evidence is observed, the strategy requires the player to "punish" the other player by producing at the higher Cournot level. Unlike the grim strategy, this punishment is of limited duration. After a fixed period of time has elapsed, the player begins cooperating again.

A great many pairs of trigger price strategies can form Bayesian Nash equilibria of this cartel game. A smaller, but still large, number of pairs of trigger price strategies that are Bayesian Nash equilibria are also perfect Bayesian equilibria. But some of these equilibria result in higher cartel profits than others. In the next three sections, we will show how to find the "optimal" trigger price agreement.

20.3.3 PAYOFFS

Because Nature's moves are unpredictable, any pair of strategies for Colombia and Brazil will result in a random sequence of prices and profits for both countries. We will assume that both countries are risk neutral and seek to maximize the expected present value of the stream of profits they will earn now and in the future. We will assume that both countries discount a dollar in profits t years in the future by 0.9^t. That is, one dollar one year from now is worth $0.90 today, one dollar two years from now is worth $0.81 today, and so forth. The interval of time between successive output decisions is assumed to be a year.

We will also assume that the cost of growing coffee is the same in Colombia as it is in Brazil. There are no fixed costs and the variable cost is constant at $1 per kilogram. It follows that if Colombia produces Q_t^C million kilograms of coffee, and Brazil produces Q_t^B million kilograms of coffee during any given year, then Colombia's expected profit that year, Π_C, will equal (in millions of dollars)

$$\Pi_C(Q^B, Q^C) = (9 - Q^B - Q^C) \cdot Q^C \qquad [20.5]$$

and Brazil's expected profit that year, Π_B, will equal (in millions of dollars)

$$\Pi_B(Q^B, Q^C) = (9 - Q^B - Q^C) \cdot Q^B. \qquad [20.6]$$

In order to find a trigger price strategy equilibrium we first need to know the Nash equilibrium of the simple, one-shot, Cournot stage game in which Colombia's and Brazil's payoff functions are given by Eq. [20.5] and Eq. [20.6]. You can confirm that the unique Cournot-Nash equilibrium (assuming that both countries can only employ pure strategies) is that both Colombia and Brazil produce 3 million kilograms per year and earn \$9 million in profits per year. For future reference, we will denote this unique Cournot equilibrium output level by S^*.

20.3.4 SOME EQUILIBRIA

As is the case when both players' previous moves are common knowledge, one equilibrium of this game is for both countries to adopt the "stubbornly competitive" strategy of producing S^* every year regardless of the price history. To see that this pair of strategies constitutes a perfect Bayesian equilibrium, note that the past is informative only to the extent that it affects a player's beliefs about what the opponent will do in the future. If one player believes the other is never going to cooperate, then the past is completely uninformative. Furthermore, if the other player is stubbornly competitive, then there is no future benefit from giving up any expected profits today. Hence, the best response to a stubbornly competitive opponent is to be stubbornly noncooperative yourself. This equilibrium amounts to not forming a cartel. We will refer to this as a *competitive equilibrium*.

Fortunately, our game has many more interesting "cartel-like" equilibria. In particular, this game has an entire family of perfect Bayesian equilibria in which both countries adopt a common trigger price strategy of the form (P^R, T, S^*, Q^*). That is, during competitive periods, both countries set their output level at S^*, the one-shot Cournot equilibrium of 3 million kilograms, and during cooperative periods, both countries set their output level at Q^*, where $Q^* < S^*$. We will refer to such an equilibrium as a *self-enforcing trigger price cartel agreement*, or **cartel agreement** for short.

Before we establish that nontrivial cartel agreements exist, we will examine how a cartel operating under such an agreement would behave. The agreement is designed to discourage both firms from cheating and producing more than the cooperative output level Q^* during cooperative periods. *When all cartel members are following the cartel agreement,* they can deduce that a fall in the market price below the trigger price, P^R, must be due to a fall in residual demand. It is never due to cheating by one of the cartel members. Nevertheless, when such a price drop occurs, all cartel members *must follow through and simultaneously increase their output to the Cournot level for* T−1 *periods.* Otherwise, everyone will have an incentive to cheat on the agreement during the cooperative periods. The agreement will result in the periodic outbreak of "price wars" that are caused by an unexpected fall in demand, *not* by cheating by one of the members of the cartel. Such behavior is consistent with the historical record we presented earlier.

Now we will show that nontrivial trigger price cartel agreements exist and provide a numerical example of what they look like. In the process, we will present some mathematical techniques for finding the equilibria of this type of dynamic game. We will proceed in two steps. First, we will show that if one of the two cartel members, say Brazil, adopts the trigger price strategy $(P^R, T, S^*, \tilde{Q}^B)$, then an optimal response of the other member, Colombia, is to adopt the trigger price strategy $(P^R, T, S^*, Q_{TP}^C(\tilde{Q}^B))$, where $Q_{TP}^C(\tilde{Q}^B)$ is simply a best response function for Colombia. That is, Colombia will use the same trigger price and period of competition as does Brazil. As a result, one of the countries cooperates when and only when the other does. For this reason, we will hereafter refer to it as the *trigger price best response function.* Not surprisingly, two players with symmetric profit functions will have the same trigger price best response function.

Suppose Brazil adopts the trigger price strategy $(P^R, T, S^*, \tilde{Q}^B)$ and this is common knowledge. In the first year after the agreement comes into force, Colombia knows Brazil will cooperate and produce $\tilde{Q}^B$ units of coffee. If Colombia produces $Q_{Cournot}(\tilde{Q}^B)$, the Cournot one-period best response to $\tilde{Q}^B$, then it will have maximized its expected profits in the first year. But this output level ignores the future. By producing the Cournot output in the first year after the agreement has come into force, Colombia has increased the likelihood that the market price will be low enough to trigger retaliation by Brazil. If Brazil retaliates (and Colombia may get lucky and avoid this if demand unexpectedly jumps), then it will produce $S^* > \tilde{Q}^B$ in period two. As a result, Colombia will end up with lower profits next period than if Brazil had continued to cooperate and produced $\tilde{Q}^B$. Colombia is faced with a trade-off: Either it can exploit Brazil's cooperation in the first year, produce a lot of coffee, and risk retaliation, or it can increase the likelihood of getting Brazil's cooperation in the future by producing relatively little coffee. There is an output level between 0 and $Q_{Cournot}$ that maximizes the expected present value of the stream of profits Colombia will earn over its entire (infinite!) lifetime. This output level we denoted earlier as $Q_{TP}^C(\tilde{Q}^B)$.

After the first year, Colombia's optimal output during any year depends on whether Brazil is cooperating or not. If in year t Brazil is not cooperating, then nothing Colombia does *that year* will affect Brazil's future pattern of cooperation. Remember, we are assuming that Brazil employs a trigger price strategy and the length of Brazil's periods of noncooperation are fixed at $T − 1$ years and its output during this period of competition is stubbornly fixed at S^*. As a result, Colombia's best course of action is to maximize its expected current profits and produce S^* units of output. That is, the best response to Brazil's production of the Cournot (one-shot) equilibrium output is to produce the Cournot output as well.

If year t is a "cooperative" year, then the following year, the two players play essentially the same game they played in the first year. But this means that Colombia's optimal output is $Q^C_{TP}(\tilde{Q}^B)$, since this was its optimal output in year one and essentially nothing has changed. The conclusion is that Colombia's best response to Brazil's strategy is to produce $Q^C_{TP}(\tilde{Q}^B)$ in cooperative years, produce S^* in competitive years, and cooperate if and only if Brazil cooperates. This means Colombia's optimal strategy is the trigger price strategy $(P^R, T, S^*, Q^C_{TP}(\tilde{Q}^B))$, as we claimed.

20.3.5 CALCULATING THE TRIGGER PRICE BEST RESPONSE FUNCTION

Now we can derive the best response function $Q^C_{TP}(\tilde{Q}^B)$. Let $V_C(\tilde{Q}^B, \tilde{Q}^C)$ denote the *expected* present value of Colombia's profit stream when it adopts the trigger price strategy $(P^R, T, S^*, \tilde{Q}^C)$ and Brazil adopts the trigger price strategy $(P^R, T, S^*, \tilde{Q}^B)$. As we will explain below, $V_C(\tilde{Q}^B, \tilde{Q}^C)$ satisfies the recursive equation

$$V_C(\tilde{Q}^B, \tilde{Q}^C) = \Pi_C(\tilde{Q}^B, \tilde{Q}^C) + \Pr\{P_1 > P^R\} \cdot 0.9 \cdot V_C(\tilde{Q}^B, \tilde{Q}^C)$$
$$+ \Pr\{P_1 \le P^R\} \cdot \big(0.9 \cdot \Pi_C(S^*, S^*) + \ldots + 0.9^{T-1} \cdot \Pi_C(S^*, S^*)$$
$$+ 0.9^T \cdot V_C(\tilde{Q}^B, \tilde{Q}^C)\big) \qquad [20.7]$$

where $P_1 = (10 - \tilde{Q}^B - \tilde{Q}^C) \cdot \theta_t$ is the market price in year one, $\Pr\{A\}$ is the probability that the event A occurs, and $\Pi_C(\tilde{Q}^B, \tilde{Q}^C)$ is Colombia's expected profit in year one and is given by Eq. [20.5].

Before we algebraically simplify our expression for $V_C(\tilde{Q}^B, \tilde{Q}^C)$, let's see how it was derived. Since both countries begin by cooperating with each other, Colombia's expected profit in the first year is given by the first term in Eq. [20.7], $\Pi_C(\tilde{Q}^B, \tilde{Q}^C)$. After the first year, one of two things can occur: Brazil and Colombia can continue to cooperate or they can begin a "price war."

The first possibility will occur if and only if P_1 stays above the trigger price P^R. If this should occur and the two countries continue to cooperate in year two, then essentially the game "begins all over again" in year two. By this we mean that the continuation of the game presents the players with the same strategies and payoffs as they had in the first year. This means the expected present value in year one of Colombia's profit stream beginning in year two—conditional on the two countries not starting a price war—equals $0.9 \cdot V_C(\tilde{Q}^B, \tilde{Q}^C)$. The present value must be discounted by 0.9 since it does not begin until year two. Multiplying this by the probability that a price war is avoided yields the second term on the right-hand side of Eq. [20.7].

The second possibility is that P_1 falls below the trigger price and the two firms fight a price war for the next $T - 1$ years, reverting to cooperation in year $T + 1$. As was the case above, the continuation of the game in year $T + 1$ is identical to the game in year one. As a result, the expected present value in year one of the profit stream that begins at year $T + 1$—conditional on both countries cooperating—equals $0.9^T \cdot V_C(\tilde{Q}^B, \tilde{Q}^C)$. The expected present value of the entire profit stream must be discounted by 0.9^T since the profits are delayed by the intervening price war. In the intervening $T - 1$ years the firm's expected profits each year are $\Pi_C(S^*, S^*)$. So the expected present value in year 1 of this stream equals $0.9 \cdot \Pi_C(S^*, S^*) + \ldots + 0.9^{T-1} \cdot \Pi_C(S^*, S^*)$. Adding this to the present value of the game that resumes after the price war ends in year $T + 1$ and multiplying this sum by the probability that a price war begins in year two yields the third and final term in Eq. [20.7].

With some algebraic manipulation, Eq. [20.7] can be rewritten

$$V_C(\tilde{Q}^B, \tilde{Q}^C) = \frac{\Pi_C(S^*, S^*)}{0.1} + \frac{\Pi_C(\tilde{Q}^B, \tilde{Q}^C) - \Pi_C(S^*, S^*)}{0.1 + F\left(\dfrac{P^R}{10 - \tilde{Q}^B - \tilde{Q}^C}\right) \cdot (0.9 - 0.9^T)} \qquad [20.8]$$

where F is the distribution of θ_t. Earlier we found that $\Pi_C(S^*, S^*)$ equals \$9 million per year and $\Pi_C(\tilde{Q}^B, \tilde{Q}^C) = (9 - \tilde{Q}^B - \tilde{Q}^C) \cdot \tilde{Q}^C$. In what follows, we will assume that the random variable θ_t has the cumulative distribution function

$$F(x) = \frac{2}{1 + e^{-(\ln 3) \cdot x^{15}}} - 1. \qquad [20.9]$$

The cumulative distribution function, you may recall, measures the probability that a random variable, θ_t, takes on a value less than x. Associated with the cumulative distribution function is a probability density function. The area under the density function between two numbers, say x_1 and x_2, measures the probability of a random variable, θ_t, falling between x_1 and x_2. This cumulative distribution function, defined in Eq. [20.9], has a bell-shaped density function, a median and mean of 1, and a standard deviation of 0.071.[2] A graph of the density is given in Figure 20.2.

Substituting our expressions for $\Pi_C(\tilde{Q}^B, \tilde{Q}^C)$ and $\Pi_C(S^*, S^*)$ into Eq. [20.8] results in

$$V_C(\tilde{Q}^B, \tilde{Q}^C) = 90 + \frac{(9 - \tilde{Q}^C - \tilde{Q}^B) \cdot \tilde{Q}^C - 9}{0.1 + F\left(\dfrac{P^R}{10 - \tilde{Q}^B - \tilde{Q}^C}\right) \cdot (0.9 - 0.9^T)}. \qquad [20.10]$$

Colombia's optimal cooperative output, $Q_{TP}^C(\tilde{Q}^B)$, is the output level that maximizes $V_C(\tilde{Q}_B, \tilde{Q}_C)$ holding $\tilde{Q}^B$ fixed. In Figure 20.3 we have plotted six of Colombia's "isopayoff" curves for the case where $P^R = \$3.62/\text{kg}$ and $T = 3$ years. An isopayoff curve consists of the cooperative output combinations that result in the same expected discounted profits for Colombia. The graph of the trigger price

---

[2]This distribution function was chosen over a more familiar one, such as the log-normal distribution, because it is easier to work with analytically and numerically.

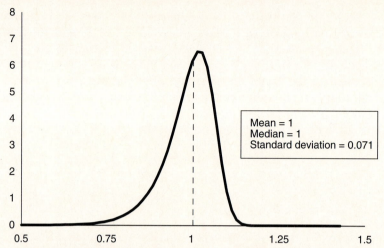

FIGURE 20.2 The probability density function associated with the cumulative distribution function defined in Eq. [20.9].

best response function, $Q_{TP}^C(\tilde{Q}^B)$, consists of those points on each isopayoff curve at which the tangent line to the curve is perfectly horizontal. Because the expected payoff functions are complicated functions, the best response functions do not have simple algebraic expressions. Their graphs must be approximated numerically. Note that unlike many of our previous best response functions, $Q_{TP}^C(\tilde{Q}^B)$ is not monotonic, but rather has a Z-shaped graph.

It now follows that the pair of trigger price strategies $(P^R, T, S^*, \tilde{Q}^C)$ and $(P^R, T, S^*, \tilde{Q}^B)$ form a perfect Bayesian equilibrium for this game if and only if $\tilde{Q}^C = Q_{TP}^C(\tilde{Q}^B)$ and $\tilde{Q}^B = Q_{TP}^B(\tilde{Q}^C)$. This implies that $Q_{TP}^C = Q_{TP}^B$. Graphically, this

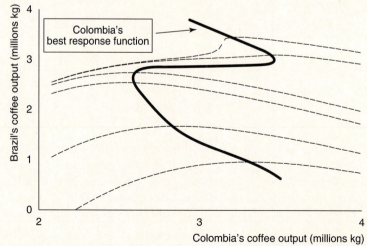

FIGURE 20.3 Several isopayoff curves for Colombia and its associated cooperative best response function.

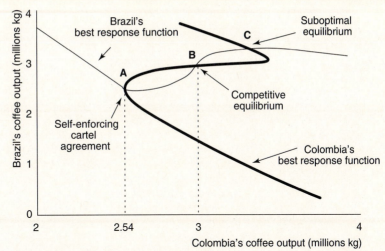

FIGURE 20.4 Brazil's and Colombia's trigger price best response functions.

means the two firm's best response functions intersect along a 45 degree line from the origin. One intersection point is (S^*, S^*), which represents the competitive equilibrium, which we already know to be a (trivial) trigger price equilibrium for this game.[3]

Figure 20.4 plots both $Q_{TP}^C(\tilde{Q}^B)$, Colombia's trigger price best response function, and $Q_{TP}^B(\tilde{Q}^C)$, Brazil's trigger price best response function.

There are three intersection points, each of which corresponds to a perfect Bayesian equilibrium in trigger price strategies. Point B corresponds to the competitive equilibrium in which both countries always produce 3 million kg. Point A corresponds to a nontrivial self-enforcing cartel agreement in which the countries produce 2.54 million kg of coffee during cooperative periods and 3 million kg during competitive periods. Point C corresponds to a third perfect Bayesian equilibrium in which the two countries are actually stuck producing *more than* the Cournot output of 3 million kg during the cooperative periods. Perversely, this results in both countries earning lower profits on average during the cooperative periods than during the competitive ones.

Having now identified all the possible self-enforcing cartel agreements into which Brazil and Colombia could enter, the second step is to find the Pareto optimal one.[4] This is the agreement we would expect the two countries to select. We will now show how to find this optimum numerically.

---

[3]It can be shown with more sophisticated mathematical techniques that Q_C^*, Q_B^* is an intersection point of R_{TB} and R_{TB}^{-1} if and only if $Q_C^* = Q_B^* = Q^* = R_{TP}(Q^*)$. That is, any cartel agreement requires that the two countries adopt the same strategy. This is a consequence of our assumption that the market demand function is linear and that the two countries have identical costs. If R_{TP} has two fixed points, say Q_1^* and Q_2^*, with $Q_1^* < Q_2^*$, then it can be shown that the equilibrium associated with Q_1^* will be strictly preferred by both countries to the equilibrium associated with Q_2^*.

[4]Be careful; we are currently defining Pareto optimality in terms of these two players, not in a societal sense.

GAME THEORY IN ACTION: Cartel Enforcement in Real Life

The model of cartel behavior we have examined in this chapter shows not only that "price wars" are consistent with collusion, but also that price wars may be *required* to enforce the optimal collusive agreement. But this is all theoretical. Do real cartels behave this way? Not surprisingly, few cartels leave around detailed records of their collusion with which to compare to the theory. Fortunately, one nineteenth-century American cartel did: the Joint Executive Committee (JEC). The JEC was a railroad cartel that was formed in 1879 to set train freight prices between Chicago and the East Coast. It operated openly until 1887 when the Interstate Commerce Commission was created by Congress to regulate the railroad industry. During the seven years that the JEC operated, freight rates on this rail corridor were generally stable at $7–8 a ton, but there were three price wars of about 10 weeks duration in 1881, 1884, and 1885. Although this is exactly what we would expect to observe if the cartel members were using trigger-price strategies in a repeated Cournot game, we must be careful about jumping to the conclusion that these firms were playing our game.

First, the railroads in the JEC were probably not Cournot competitors. They are probably better modeled as Bertrand competitors who could offer secret price cuts, implying that their true transaction prices were unobservable. On the other hand, their freight traffic was common knowledge because one of the principal functions of the JEC was to report total grain shipments of each member every week. Fortunately, if we model the cartel members as playing a repeated Bertrand game with observable output but unobservable prices, the resulting game has a subgame perfect equilibrium involving trigger strategies. Several events could serve as a signal of cheating, such as high aggregate demand or a pattern of high market share for one firm and low shares for the rest. On the basis of a careful reading of the records a number of economists have concluded that the members of the JEC played a repeated Bertrand game and used a trigger-price-like strategy based on market share (Robert Porter, "A study in cartel stability: the Joint Executive Committee, 1880–1886, *The Bell Journal of Economics,* 18 [1983], pp. 301–14, and Glenn Ellison, "Theories of cartel stability and the Joint Executive Committee," *The RAND Journal of Economics,* 25 [1994], pp. 37–57).

A repeated Bertrand model of the JEC makes two other predictions: (1) price wars should occur precisely when random shifts in demand would resemble one of the demand or market share signals we mentioned above; and (2) firms should not cheat on the agreement and offer secret price cuts. These predictions have proven much harder to tease from the short series of data available. Robert Porter was not able to find statistically significant evidence of trigger strategy behavior, and Ellison found weak evidence of some secret price cutting, although he did not believe it was too large to invalidate the model's general validity.

20.3.6 THE OPTIMAL CARTEL AGREEMENT

For every possible trigger price, P^R, and penalty, T, there exists an optimal self-enforcing trigger price cartel agreement in which both countries agree to produce 3 million kg during competitive periods and to produce some amount $\tilde{Q}_{TP}$ during cooperative periods. The cooperative output $\tilde{Q}_{TP}$ is a function of P^R and T. For example, as shown above, when P^R equals \$3.62/kg and T equals 3 years,

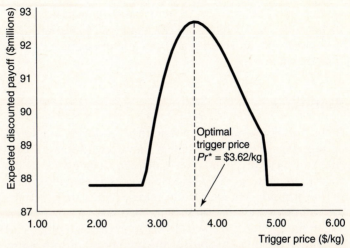

FIGURE 20.5 Holding T at 3 years, the expected present value of Colombia's profits are plotted against P^R. The maximum occurs at $P^{R*} = \$3.62/\text{kg}$.

$\tilde{Q}_{TP}(P^R, T) = 2.54$. For some trigger prices and penalties, the best agreement is simply to behave like myopic Cournot competitors and not collude. That is, for these trigger prices and penalties, $\tilde{Q}_{TP}(P^R, T) = S^* = 3$. This is the case, for example, if the trigger price is \$2.00/kg and the price war lasts three years.

Using numerical methods, it is possible to determine that the optimal trigger price, P^{R*}, equals \$3.62/kg and the optimal penalty, T^*, equals 3 years. We can create a new function that relates Colombia's expected payoffs to different trigger prices and competitive time periods, assuming that the countries optimally choose their cooperative outputs and competitive outputs for any P^R and T. Parts of this function are drawn in Figures 20.5 and 20.6. In Figure 20.5, the parameter T has been set to 3 years and then Colombia's present value of its payoff stream has

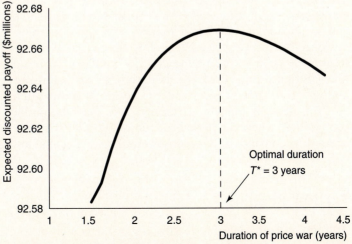

FIGURE 20.6 Holding P^R at \$3.62/kg, the expected present value of Colombia's profits are plotted against T. The maximum occurs at $T^* = 3$ years.

been plotted against P^R. A maximum is reached at $P^{R*} = \$3.62$. Similarly, in Figure 20.6, P^R has been set equal to $\$3.62/\text{kg}$, and the present value of Colombia's payoff stream has been plotted against T. A maximum is reached at $T^* = 3$ years.

20.4 Summary

It has been known for some time that producers would like to limit competition among themselves. The problem they face in doing this is that the incentives to cheat on such agreements is usually very strong and such agreements, even when they are not outright illegal, are almost never legally enforceable. As a result, any group of producers who try to form a cartel are constrained to agreements that are self-enforcing: that is, it is in each member's own self-interest not to cheat. When the producers can costlessly monitor each other's activities, this constraint is not that onerous. As long as the members are sufficiently forward-looking, the cartel can get its members to collude so effectively as to mimic a pure monopoly.

Once monitoring is costly, however, this is no longer the case. Nevertheless, under a wide range of circumstances, cheating can be deterred even though it cannot be directly detected. We have demonstrated this with an example in which the cartel members can only observe the world market price. Cheating by cartel members can only be detected through its effects on the market price. Since prices can change for other reasons—such as fluctuations in demand and in the supply of noncartel members—there is some probability that a decline in the market price will occur even though no cheating took place. Nevertheless, unless the cartel periodically responds to such price movements as if they were caused by cheating, all members will have an incentive to cheat. The resulting "price wars" are the price of maintaining the cartel.

We showed that a trigger price strategy could result in a self-enforcing pricing agreement. Such a strategy works as follows: As long as the market price stays above some fixed level, called the trigger price, all members act "cooperatively" and produce a relatively small quantity of the good, earning relatively high profits. But once the market price falls below the trigger price, then all members revert to competition and produce the Cournot equilibrium output, earning the relatively low Cournot profit. However, they do not do this forever (as would be dictated by the "grim strategy"). Instead, the period of competition is limited.

The result is that the cartel oscillates between periods of cooperation and competition, where the periods of competition are triggered by unexpected drops in residual demand. In its broadest outlines, such behavior seems to be consistent with what we observe in the real world.

20.5 Further Reading

Any recent treatment of industrial organization will devote a significant number of pages to the problem of cartels. See, for example, D. Carlton and J. Perloff, *Modern Industrial Organization* (Glenview, Ill: Scott Foresman & Co., 1990), pp. 208–57. A somewhat dated, but still useful, survey article was written by G. Hay and D. Kelley, "An Empirical Survey of Price-Fixing Conspiracies," *Journal of Law and Economics* 17 (1974), pp. 13–38. Also helpful on oligopolistic behavior is George Stigler's "A Theory of Oligopoly," *Journal of Political Economy* 72 (1964), pp. 55–59.

The model used in this chapter was patterned after Robert Porter's article "Optimal Cartel Trigger Price Strategies," *Journal of Economic Theory* 29 (April, 1983), pp. 313–38. There are, not surprisingly, a large number of recent theoretical studies designed to predict cartel behavior. Among the better known are those by Green and Porter, "Non-cooperative Collusion Under Imperfect Price Information," *Econometrica* 52 (1984), pp. 87–100, and S. Salop, "Practices That (Credibly) Facilitate Oligopoly Coordination," in Joseph E. Stiglitz and G. Frank Mathewson, eds., *New Developments in the Analysis of Market Structure* (Cambridge, MA: MIT Press, 1986, Chap. 9), pp. 265–90.

20.6   Discussion Questions

1. Suppose you worked for the Justice department's antitrust division. And suppose you suspected that a group of firms were colluding using trigger price strategies. How might you go about proving this was the case?

2. It would appear that Brazil and Colombia could prevent debilitating price wars if they could only monitor each other's coffee sales. Since each country could give the other the right to monitor its sales, what might it mean if neither one chooses to do so?

20.7   New Terms

cartel agreement

competitive equilibrium

repeated Prisoner's Dilemma with
  discounting

self-enforcing cartel agreement

trigger price strategies

20.8   Exercises

All the exercises below assume the cartel model presented in Section 20.3.1–3.

EXERCISE 20.1

Suppose Colombia and Brazil can tell whether or not the other is selling any coffee, but they cannot determine the amount sold. Determine whether the following can be a self-enforcing cartel agreement: Brazil sells only in odd-numbered years and Colombia sells only in even-numbered years as long as both honor the agreement; if either country reneges, they both revert to the grim strategy.

EXERCISE 20.2

Suppose that Colombia and Brazil compete against each other for exactly 50 periods, and this is common knowledge. Does a perfect Bayesian equilibrium still exist in which the two countries adopt, at least initially, trigger price strategies? Explain why or why not.

EXERCISE 20.3

Suppose Colombia observes θ_t, the random demand shift parameter for period t, before it chooses its output in period $t + 1$, but Brazil does not observe it. All the other assumptions of the cartel model of Section 20.3 are unchanged, and all these facts are common knowledge. Is it still a perfect Bayesian equilibrium for Colombia and Brazil to adopt the trigger price strategies calculated in Section 20.3.5? Explain why or why not.

EXERCISE 20.4

Another family of strategies for the cartel enforcement game are *harsh trigger price* (HTP) strategies. This family of strategies is parameterized by two numbers: a trigger price, P^R, and a cooperative output level, Q^O. These strategies are similar to the standard trigger price strategy discussed in Section 20.3.4. They are defined as follows: The country initially produces the cooperative output level Q^O and continues to do so as long as the market price stays above the trigger price. When the price drops below the trigger price, however, instead of producing 3 million kilograms of coffee for many periods, the firm produces the *cutthroat* output level of 5 million kilograms for only one period. The firm then returns to producing the cooperative output level Q^O and continues to produce at that level as long as the market price stays above the trigger price. Since the market price is determined by Eq. [20.4], whenever *both* firms increase their output to the cutthroat level the market price of coffee falls zero, whatever the value of θ_t. Show that an HTP strategy is *not* a best response by one country to the adoption of an HTP by the other.

EXERCISE 20.5

This is a continuation of Exercise 20.4. Modify the harsh trigger price strategy as follows: If the price falls below the trigger price *and* the following period the market price does *not* fall to zero, then the firm never cooperates with the other again and instead produces the Cournot equilibrium level of 3 million kilograms forever after. However, if the market price does fall to zero for one period, then the firm returns to the cooperative output level Q^O and continues producing at that level as long as the market prices stay above the trigger price. Explain how this modification helps the strategy become perfect Bayesian.

EXERCISE 20.6

This is a continuation of Exercise 20.5. Modify the HTP (defined in Exercise 20.4) as proposed in Exercise 20.5. Let $V_t(Q^O_B, Q^O_C)$ denote the expected present value of country i's profit stream when Brazil adopts the HTP strategy (Q^O_B, P^R) and Colombia adopts the HTP strategy (Q^O_C, P^R). Using Eq. [20.7] as a guide, find a recursive expression for $V_t(Q^O_B, Q^O_C)$. This expression will involve the probability that the market price drops below the trigger price when both firms are cooperative. $P\{(10 - (Q^O_C + Q^O_B) \cdot \theta_t < P^R\}$, the one-period expected profit functions $\Pi_C(Q^B_t, Q^C_t) = (9 - Q^B_t - Q^C_t) \cdot Q^C_t$ and $\Pi_B(Q^B_t, Q^C_t) = (9 - Q^B_t - Q^C_t) \cdot Q^B_t$, and the discount rate δ.

Index

Definitions will be found on page numbers in **boldface.**
Bibliographic citations are given on page numbers in *italics*.